LANDSCAPING IN NEW JERSEY

An Environmental Approach to Landscaping in the Garden State

Published By
Michael G. Hawkins Lawn And Garden Service
Brick, NJ 08724

Library of Congress Catalog Card Number: 97-93300

Printed in the United States of America on recycled ♻ paper.

Book design by Michael G. and Lois Ann Hawkins
Cover design by Michael G. and Lois Ann Hawkins
Cover photograph by Derek Fell

Managing Editor: Lois Ann Hawkins
Select illustrations by Helene A. Nelson

Includes index
First Edition: April 1997

ISBN 0-9655972-0-2

Published by:
Michael G. Hawkins Lawn And Garden Service
Brick, NJ 08724

Printed by:
Princeton Academic Press, Inc.
3175 Princeton Pike
Lawrenceville, NJ 08648

Contents

This book is dedicated to God,

my wonderful wife and friend, Lois Ann,

my three daughters Helene, Jessica and Loretta,

my three stepdaughters Rebecca, Gabrielle and Rachel,

and my devoted, caring parents, Mary & George.

Thank you for your patience, understanding,

love and support.

Introduction

Landscaping can be defined as the art or work of arranging trees, shrubs, lawns, etc. in an area of ground to make it more attractive and purposeful. I believe it is the relationship between you and your surrounding environment. While working in our landscapes, we can gain an understanding of our environment which helps us plan, organize and maintain the area in which we live.

There are no clear set formulas or designs in a landscape. You may want to start from scratch or redesign your present landscape to arrive at your final solution. People have always wanted to beautify their personal surroundings. Even without experience, you can improve your own yard. With just a few imaginative ideas and careful planning, almost any place can be transformed into beauty.

I was born and grew up in New Jersey. At an early age I started gardening with my parents. My daily chores included helping them cut the lawn, apply fertilizer, plant and prune shrubs, design beds, and maintain and harvest a vegetable garden. I guess you could say the "landscaping bug" bit me early.

In the mid seventies I worked for a large retirement village as an outside grounds maintenance supervisor and gained more experience in landscaping. I then decided to start my own landscaping business and have been doing the same for the last twenty years, as well as attending courses through Rutgers Cooperative Extension for the State of New Jersey Department of Environmental Protection.

"*Landscaping In New Jersey*" is devoted to landscape basics in the Garden state. It discusses the why's and where's, time charts, seed, soil conditions, shrubs, trees and ground covers all pertaining to the state of New Jersey. Pesticides are toxic substances dispersed throughout the environment that kill living organisms. They are affecting the health of wildlife and people and are contaminating the surface and groundwaters of our state. My goal is to educate people about our environment and what we can do to help it survive, starting with our own back yards, by using less or no pesticides. I hope you read and enjoy this book with as much interest and enthusiasm as I have had in writing it.

Chapter 1

Our Environment

Throughout history, humans have manipulated natural resources to produce the food, fiber, and materials they needed to sustain growing human populations. Such harnessing and use of natural resources to meet the needs throughout the development of human civilization have resulted in sometimes beneficial, but often detrimental alterations in natural resource systems throughout the world. Wastes from industries were disposed of in a random manner, and gravel, sand, and minerals were extracted with no environmental consideration. There was little integration of effort, activity, or management of natural resource systems. To maintain the advantage offered by their abundance of high quality freshwater, citizens must be extremely careful with the wastes they generate, the way they use their land, and particularly careful about the quality of water they discharge after it is used for domestic, industrial, or agricultural purposes. Since its inception, agriculture has been tightly linked with natural resources. In many cultures, agriculture is practiced as an extractive industry and soils continue to be degraded throughout the world. Such conversion of land to agriculture purposes alters the entire ecosystem, and the resulting impact on soil structure and fertility, quality and quantity of both surface and groundwater diminishes both present and future productivity.

The history of natural resources reveals the complexity of the interactions between social forces and the environment as well as the interactions among environmental impacts themselves. Various social forces have determined the distribution of land use between natural resource exploitation, agriculture, industry, residence, and recreation. These uses have affected the land through soil erosion, changing wildlife habitats, rates of harvesting or over-harvesting of wildlife and natural resources, and pollution. These changes have interacted in complex ways with streams, groundwater and lakes. During the 1960s, interest in natural resource conservation began to evolve into a more general interest in health of the natural environment. Conservation institutions were in place and functioning, but pollution of the ground, air, and water remained. Public concern intensified and in many instances took the form of a critique of the human relationship to nature as a whole. This shift was symbolized by the first *Earth Day* in 1970. The 1970s saw several advances in the protection of lakes and streams. Pollution control laws, public funding for air and water treatment programs, and active pollution control agencies were established by the early 1970s. High levels of pesticides and other industrial chemicals were found in fresh water fish as a result of many years of unregulated use. The effects of persistent pesticides on other wildlife, notably birds, became evident. Mercury was found in fish due to industrial discharges. Restrictions or the elimination of the use of certain pesticides resulted. Concern grew with groundwater and drinking water. The *Safe Drinking Water Act* and legislation controlling solid waste management was enacted in the seventies. In 1982, a *Groundwater Quality Division* was created.

An instructive set of environmental interactions revolves around the use of salt in removing ice and snow from roads. Salt is a big contributor to several environmental problems. The tons of salt used on a mile of road does not stay on the road. Salt spray has been shown to cause damage to plants over 1,500 feet from the roadside. The white pine has been shown to be particularly susceptible to salt damage, as are fruit trees. The slow but continual buildup of sodium and chloride in our lakes, streams and groundwater is causing other problems for plants and wildlife. Sodium has been shown to aggravate numerous medical problems in humans, such as high blood pressure. Groundwater contamination of wells which supply drinking water has been a growing problem. Additionally, salt acts as a salt lick by enticing deer and other wildlife onto the roads, increasing their likelihood of being hit by vehicles.

Further improvement in air and water quality occurred by 1990, as indicated by increasing populations of fish-eating birds. Applied pollution control technology has removed a large percentage of undesirable wastes from discharges. Pollution prevention, conservation or input management is obviously the most efficient way to reduce pollutant discharges to our waters and air at this time. Modern agriculture achieves high productivity by concentrating available nutrients. Protecting the environment requires that the nutrients be contained in the upper soil layers (away from groundwater) and held within field and farm boundaries. But even when great care is taken, the crop seldom takes up more than half of the applied nutrients which causes off-season leaching into groundwater. Another major area in nutrient flow is the opportunity in agriculture to accept nutrients from "clean" sources such as yard wastes or composting. What about pest control? Longterm control requires managing the genetic evolution of the pests to prevent development of resistance to whatever control measure is used. Integrated Pest Management through use of biocontrols is an essential part of reducing pesticides in the environment.

The plants that grew on the land, or that now grow on the land, largely reflect the status and potential of renewable natural resources. Plant community composition, its growth rate and stage of succession greatly influence environmental quality and animal populations. Well established terrestrial plant communities modify air and water quality, prevent erosion and rapid runoff, retain and recycle nutrients, enhance groundwater recharge, and stabilize stream flows as well as furnish food and shelter for animals. The quality of water resources is closely integrated with land use. The ecosystem concept provides a framework or model for understanding natural resources. The ecosystem is a basic unit of nature and can be defined as "any organizational unit which includes living organisms and non-living substances interacting to produce an exchange of energy and materials between the living and non-living parts." This exchange of matter and energy is organized by information-based systems which can be found in both nature and human society. An ecosystem can then be visualized as a network of components within established boundaries.

The words "environment" and "ecology" have been increasingly in the news for several years. Man has suddenly begun to fear that his resources - air, water, soil - are running out or becoming unfit for use. As a result, pesticide practices are being closely examined, as they are often blamed for environmental abuse. Man needs a place to live with clean water and air, food which is not harmful, and an environment which will not threaten his health and safety. Most people find pleasure in the out-of-doors and enjoyment in observing wildlife. Most want to preserve our environment.

Water is one of our greatest resources. Its unusual properties and abundance make it necessary for all life. Polluted water can fill many of our needs but not the most basic ones. Man and wildlife need **clean** water for drinking and bathing. Most fish and other marine life can survive only slight changes in their water environment. Farmers must not use contaminated water for their livestock and irrigation practices to prevent plant or animal poisoning or illegal residues. **Clean** water is essential. *Soil* has become more important as the need for food increases. In order to feed the numbers of people, fertile and healthy soil is a must. Poor soil practices and misuse cause poor yield and second class crops, especially if root vegetables or forage crops are being planted. Overdoses of pesticides which remain for long periods in the soil may limit planting to only a few crops which will not be harmed by the chemicals. *Air* must be available for any plant or animal to live. It is the source of oxygen for breathing and receives the carbon dioxide waste. Air has the ability to move particles a long way before letting them go. Most of the time this ability aids the farmer. It causes rain, for example. Unfortunately for homeowners, this same ability is the cause of drift. Pesticides carried by the air may be harmful to man and wildlife's health and safety. Pesticides in the air are not controllable and may settle into waterways, wooded areas or barnyards. Drift must be avoided.

Honeybees and other pollinators are necessary for good farming and food production. In many cases where there is no pollination there is no crop. Unfortunately bees are very sensitive to many insecticides. Whenever possible do not spray any pesticide when these or other helpful insects are likely to be in the area. All *wildlife*, fish, birds, and mammals are assets to man. Land which is used only as farmland does not have to be a wildlife refuge. However, care should be taken to protect surrounding wooded areas and waterways when applying any pesticide. Fishing and hunting are very popular sports. If pesticides are carelessly used, these sports can disappear. Pesticide-kills of mammals, birds, and fish in large numbers, have already cut down on fishing and hunting activities in some areas. High levels of pesticides in some of these animals have made their meat unfit for man to eat.

Pesticides In The Environment

Pesticides are a help to the environment when they are used carefully and wisely. For years they have been used to control pests which could be harmful to man. Rats carrying plague or mosquitoes carrying malaria are good examples. These control programs today are necessary, especially in crowded cities and countries with large numbers of people. However, pesticides can harm the environment, too. Any pesticide which is off target is a pollutant and can be dangerous. All of the benefits of pesticides can be canceled through misuse or carelessness.

With the help of pesticides more food per acre can be produced. Diseases, insects and other plant pests can be greatly reduced. There can be higher yields and better crop quality. Less land must be tilled to feed the people. More land is free for wildlife and recreational purposes. Good farm land may become unfit for crops, though. Overdoses of pesticides which remain for a long time in the soil can ruin the land. The crop may absorb the pesticides from the soil and be over the set tolerance at harvest. Or the pesticide may kill all or most plant life and make the land useless for farm or recreational use. *Livestock* are also protected from harmful and annoying pests. Otherwise the penned animals could not escape from constant irritation. The quantity and quality of livestock products - milk, meat, etc. - is improved when the pests are controlled. Pesticide drift onto forage and pasture land or into drinking water can injure livestock. The animals may be poisoned by eating contaminated forage and grasses. Once eaten, these pesticides can also lead to illegal residues in the meat and byproducts of the animals. They may be unfit for humans to eat.

Pesticides can be used to preserve outdoor activities in our parks and camping areas. Fly and mosquito control programs give relief from the annoying pests. Without control programs, outdoor activity is extremely limited for most people. However, drift and overdoses can destroy wildlife, cause trees to lose leaves and ruin recreation areas. Runoff, spills or drift into streams can cause fish kills and make the water unfit for swimming, fishing, or even boating. Drift and overdose can injure or kill birds and mammals. Parks and camping areas with leafless trees, dying plants, and no wildlife are not acceptable as recreation areas. Pesticides aid in controlling insects or diseases that get into an area for the first time. Often these pests have few natural enemies in the new environment. Without a good pesticide program, they can rapidly overrun an area. Gypsy moth and Japanese beetles are good examples of runaway pests. Careless use of wide range pesticides can destroy natural enemies (such as predators and parasites) in an area. Runaway insect or pest populations can result. Pesticides misused in this way may actually help the pests! Honeybees and other useful insects are often injured when pesticides are used carelessly.

Pesticides can be harmless to wildlife when used carefully and on target. Sometimes chemicals can aid wildlife by controlling runaway or annoying pests which could harm the animals. Pesticides can also be poisonous to wildlife. Some chemicals are highly dangerous to wildlife but others are fairly harmless. The toxicity of every chemical to every animal is not known. A pesticide that is only slightly toxic to one living thing may be very toxic to another. A pesticide that is relatively harmless to birds may be highly poisonous to fish or mammals. Wildlife are also important because of their place in the food chain. Food chain is a way of describing how all animals depend on each other. Each animal has a place in the chain depending on the type of food it eats. Animals which eat only plant materials are at

the bottom of the chain. Animals which eat these plant-eaters are on the next level. The animals which eat meat are at the top of the chain. In this complex food chain, each animal has an important place. The loss of any animal disrupts the whole chain.

Pesticides are often used on plants to protect them from pests. Insecticides and fungicides are often used on ornamentals and forest trees to control runaway pests or other serious insects or diseases. These chemicals aid in keeping forests, parks, and lawns green and enjoyable. However, pesticides can injure plants. The injury can range from slight burning or browning of the leaves to death of the whole plant. This injury is called phytotoxicity. Phytotoxicity accidents can result from carelessness or from use of a pesticide which is highly hazardous to plants and trees. Hazard may depend on: type of pesticide, movement, dosage and persistence. Some pesticides remain on the target area for a long time. These pesticides could injure or kill plants which are planted there at a later date. Persistent pesticides can be very useful for long-term insect, disease or weed control. But follow label instructions carefully if future crops or other plants and trees will be

planted in the area. The label will state whether phytotoxicity will be a problem and what plants can be injured. Follow the label instructions carefully and cautiously if you wish to avoid injuring desirable plants. Pesticide application has become more complex in the past few years. The number of different kinds of pesticides available for use has increased greatly. Effects on wildlife and the environment are now known to be important considerations. New highly poisonous pesticides require special equipment and safety measures. If you have decided to hire someone to apply any pesticides on your property, make sure he or she is registered with the New Jersey Department of Environmental Protection as a "Commercial Certified Pesticide Applicator". As our environment is ever changing, pesticide applicators need to know more about safety and proper use than ever before. To help protect the general public, the environment and the applicator, new requirements are always being set. Applicators must show they know how to use pesticides properly before becoming certified.

Start With Your Own Yard

The environment begins with your yard. What you do in and with your yard can end up outside your yard, in your neighbor's yard, in the storm drain or stream, and eventually in the ocean. If you multiply what you do in your yard by the number of people on the block, in your town, in your county, or in your state, the yard starts to look like everybody's business. The environment really does begin with your yard. **Do your part, your surroundings are worth protecting.**

A clean, well-maintained yard looks good. Those who pass by may comment on how beautiful your yard looks, how the neighborhood seems like a great place to live, and how the property values are enhanced by appearances. Those around you are proud to have you as neighbors. The plants in your yard and your neighbors yard, in the woods down the street, in the public park next door, all give off oxygen to help us breathe. They keep the air fresh and clean. Also, plants help to cool the environment by providing shade. Ground covers and other plants hold your soil in place. The soil doesn't wash away, doesn't flow into your neighbor's yard, doesn't clog storm drains and streams, and doesn't carry along pesticides that pollute the water. Your yard can be home to many birds, butterflies, and animals that are interesting to observe and can help to control pests.

Learn about your soil. Not all soils are created equal. Soils have characteristics that make them different and affect their suitability for various uses. Knowledge of soil types and their features can help you solve current problems and avoid future ones. *Texture* - Soil particles vary from coarse to fine, and are classified as sand, silt, or clay. The percentage in each soil determines its texture. Soil texture influences other soil properties such as how readily water moves through the soil and its ability to hold moisture for plant growth. *Slope* - This is the inclination or steepness of the land's surface. Land disturbance that is planned with the slope of the land in mind can prevent erosion and reduce costs. *Depth to water table* - How high the water table rises and how long it stays there, will affect what can be done on the soil. A high water table soil can lead to wet basements, cause septic systems to fail, and restrict landscape plant selection. *Depth to bedrock* - The depth from the soil surface to bedrock influences a soil's potential uses by restricting or increasing the cost of construction. What can we do? You can learn more about the potential for different uses on your property in a soil survey report. A soil survey is an inventory of the soils of a particular region. It includes soil maps showing the location of the dominant soils and the descriptions and interpretations of the soils.

Learn about erosion and sediment control. Soil erosion is the process by which rainfall and moving surface water dislodge and carry soil particles, organic matter, and plant nutrients with them. Erosion around a home not only causes damage to your property and nearby roads, but also affects water quality in ponds, lakes, or streams. Muddy water flowing in your driveway, ditch, or onto the road following a rain indicates that erosion is occurring. Sedimentation is the depositing of soil from muddy water. The eroded soil stops someplace as sediment. It fills ditches, streams, lakes, and shipping channels at considerable cost to taxpayers. The best way to reduce sedimentation is to control erosion. Erosion is best controlled with vegetative cover, but can also be controlled by applying stone, straw, and fabric filters to trap soil particles. In larger flows, water is held in temporary storage basins until most of the soil settles out of the water.

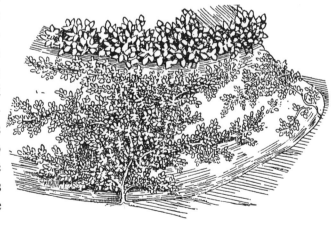

There are several things we can do to help stop erosion. Keep the soil covered. Bare soil is the primary cause of erosion. Plant grass or other vegetation to protect the soil from the impact of raindrops and to hold the soil in place. Mulch bare areas with

straw, grass clippings, stones, wood chips, and other protective cover. Vegetated and mulched areas increase soil infiltration, reducing erosive runoff water. Control concentrated flow. Watch the flow of runoff water during storms. Areas of concentrated flow on slopes should be protected by keeping the channel in grass on gentle slopes and lining the channel with stones or pavement on steeper slopes. Building terraces across the slope will help to divert water away from slopes. Use splash blocks at gutter outlets. Select plants that grow well in the local area and are suitable for the climate conditions in your yard, such as shaded or sunny areas and wet or dry soil. Plant ground covers in shaded areas where grass is difficult to establish and maintain.

Learn how to control stormwater. You have a direct link from your property to nearby lakes and streams. The path of water running off sidewalks and driveways goes through street gutters and storm sewers into a nearby stream, lake, or wetland. The muddy water runoff joins with other runoff and at times results in damaging floods further downstream. By-products of our everyday life, such as motor oil, antifreeze, road salt, soil, pet waste, fertilizers, and pesticides can get into water and affect its quality. Keeping stormwater runoff clean reduces the pollutants that enter public water supply. How can we help? We can sweep fertilizer, soil, and lawn clippings off driveways and walks back onto the lawn. Dispose of any pet wastes by burying them. Keep all gutters and stormwater inlets clear of trash, lawn clippings, and leaves. Contact your municipality for proper disposal instructions for hazardous materials such as pesticides, auto fluids, and household cleaners. Plant trees, shrubs, and ground cover to help rainwater soak into the ground. Limit the amount of paved surfaces on your property. Instead use porous pavements, such as bricks, interlocking blocks, gravel, or porous asphalt. Building roofs, concrete, and blacktop have total runoff. If concrete or blacktop are used, grade it so runoff flows to the lawn. Gravel filter strips and trenches may also be used along a driveway to increase infiltration, but will increase groundwater contamination if oil, salt, antifreeze, and other materials are left on the driveway.

Learn how to care for your lawn. Maintaining a green lawn requires care and time. Concern for the environment has led many people to turn to more environmentally safe lawn-care practices. Using organic fertilizers can help reduce the amount of nitrogen, phosphorus, and potassium reaching local streams. Organic fertilizers contain the same basic plant nutrients as chemicals, but they take longer to dissolve and will stay in the soil longer. Test the soil for alkalinity or acidity (pH). Lawns like a balanced pH for growth. Lime the lawn if it is too acidic. One application lasts for several years. Use environmentally safe and nonchemical ways to control pests. Only one percent of insects are bad for lawns and gardens; the rest are beneficial. Pesticides, however, kill them all. Use plants that need little fertilizer or pest control, such as ferns, myrtle, pachysandra, liliturf, forsythia, and barberry. Consider growing clover in the lawn. It is hardy, stands up to wear, and produces nitrogen needed by other lawn grasses. Clover, however, attracts bees. Mow the lawn no shorter than 2 inches in height. Remember, root growth equals the height of the grass. Mowing close decreases root growth. Good maintenance is essential to a growing lawn. Leave the clippings on the lawn because they are rich in nitrogen. Water once a week, if needed. Grass requires about an inch of moisture a week. Use drought tolerant grasses. Fertilize in October or November to promote root growth and early spring growth. Do not fertilize in the summer or when the ground is frozen.

Learn about gardening. Gardens enhance the environment and the quality of your life by providing beauty, fresh vegetables, and recreation. By following safe environmental practices, you can grow fresh, healthy food while satisfying yourself with a rewarding summer hobby. Plant your garden where the

soil is deep and well-drained and where it is sunny and level. Conserve water and reduce soil erosion by planting rows across the slope.   Plant 3 to 5 rows of vegetables close together to reduce wasted space and weeds. Consider raised beds when using this method. Conserve water. Overwatering washes away soil, nutrients, and pesticides. Remember, too much water will seep into groundwater or flow into other water supplies. Water early in the morning to reduce evaporation. Watering in the hot sun may stress some plants. Add mulch around plants to conserve moisture, control weeds, and increase organic matter. Mulch can be straw, compost, newspaper, bark, wood chips etc. Grass clippings may be used if they are free of pesticides and herbicides. Use plants that naturally repel insects from vegetables and flowers. Some of the more common plants of this type are marigolds, garlic, onion, nasturtium, geranium, and turnips. Avoid overuse of fertilizers and pesticides. Consider using a drip irrigation system for landscaping, vegetable gardens, flower beds and fruit trees. Drip irrigation uses significantly less water than conventional sprinkler irrigation methods.

Learn to help wildlife and they will help you in return. Songbirds and other wildlife add much to the joy of urban, suburban and country living. Birds help reduce the insects that attack your flowers, gardens, lawns, and shrubs. Shrubs, trees, vines, and other plants offer a natural way to attract birds and wildlife to your homesite. Wildlife likes diversity. Edges, the borders between open grass and trees and shrubs, are the favorite habitat for wildlife. Flowering shrubs, grasses, and other plants provide berries and seeds for the birds. Taller and dense growth offers protection to birds and small animals against predators. Plant a rich intermingling of species, size, and shape of plants. Develop a plan for your yard. Wildlife need three things - food, water, and shelter. Along with your personal ideas, consider soil, slope, drainage, exposure, and climate. Added benefits occur where plantings provide beauty, shade, soil stabilization. and runoff control. A few flowering shrubs that attract birds and wildlife include; American Cranberry bush, Bittersweet, Cherry, Crabapple, Firethorn, Flowering Dogwood, Hawthorn, Holly and Redcedar.

Here are some things you can do on *small lots, patios, and balconies*. Use small areas to provide needed food, water, and shelter for a variety of birds and animals. Provide water in a birdbath. Frequently refill and clean. Use a bird feeder during winter and early spring when food is scarce. Corn, sunflowers, and other grains also attract rabbits, squirrels, and other small wildlife. Plant small shrubs and trees near buildings as they are good shelter for birds and wildlife.

Groundwater

What it is, how does it get there, and where does it go? The land surface was traditionally considered to be sufficient to protect the quality of underlying groundwater. It is now recognized that natural soil processes that change contaminants into harmless substances are often overwhelmed by waste products from human activities. Groundwater protection programs require an understanding of the groundwater resource. The purpose of this section is to help the reader become more knowledgeable about groundwater and the terminology commonly used to describe it. A pictorial approach is used to enable the reader to quickly grasp basic groundwater terms and concepts. It should help you make decisions on how to protect and manage your groundwater resource which can affect your entire community.

Where does groundwater come from? Groundwater begins with rain and snowmelt that seeps or in-filtrates into the ground. The amount of water that seeps into the ground varies widely from place to place according to the type of land surface that is present. In porous surface material that water readily seeps through, such as sand or gravel, **40 to 50 percent** of the rain and snowmelt may seep into the ground. Seepage into less porous surface material may range from **5 to 20 percent**. The remainder of the rain and snowmelt runs off the land surface into streams or returns to the atmosphere by evaporation. Seepage into the ground is also strongly influenced by the season of the year. Evaporation is greater during the warm months, including evaporation through plant leaves, known as transpiration. During the cold months, the ground may be frozen, hindering water seepage, and evaporation is less.

The Saturated Zone

Rain and snowmelt that seeps into the ground continues downward under the force of gravity until it reaches a depth where water fills all of the openings (pores) in the soil or rock. This is called the **saturated zone**. The saturated zone typically included numerous water-filled crevices where water can penetrate. The top of the saturated zone is called the **water table**. The water table rises and falls according to the season of the year and the amount of rain and snowmelt that occurs. It is typically higher in early Spring and lower in late Summer. Heavy rainfall or drought conditions may cause changes in the typical pattern, however.

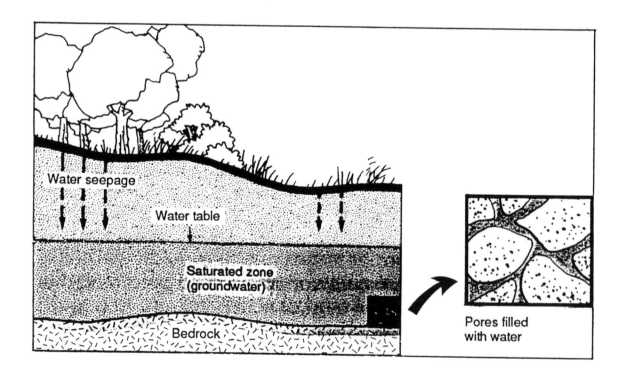

The Unsaturated Zone

A zone is usually present between the water table and the land surface where the openings, or pores, in the soil are only partially filled with water. This is the **unsaturated zone**. Water seeps downward through it to the water table below. Plant roots can capture the moisture passing through this zone, but it cannot provide water for wells.

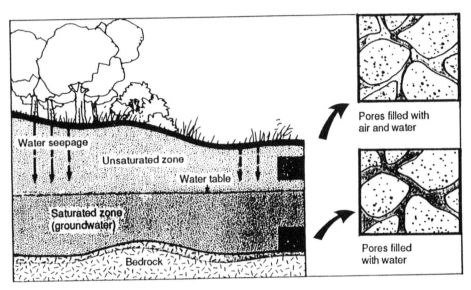

Permeability

Permeability is a measure of how fast water will flow through connected openings in soil or rock. **Impermeability** refers to soil or rock that does not allow water to pass through it. The **specific yield** is the actual amount of water that will drain out of saturated soil or rock by gravity flow. It does not drain out completely because some water forms a film that clings to soil and rock. Permeability is critical for water supply purposes. If water contained in soil or rock will not drain out, it is not available to water wells.

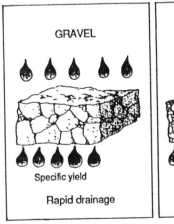

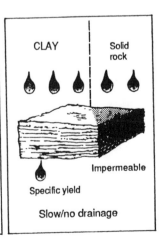

Groundwater
Discharge Points

Groundwater enters the ground in recharge areas and leaves the ground at **discharge points**. Discharge is continuous, as long as sufficient water is present above the discharge point. Discharge points typically occur as seepage into wet-lands, lakes and streams. Springs are visible discharge points at the land surface. If the water table is close to the land surface during the growing season, large amounts of groundwater may be withdrawn by plant transpiration.

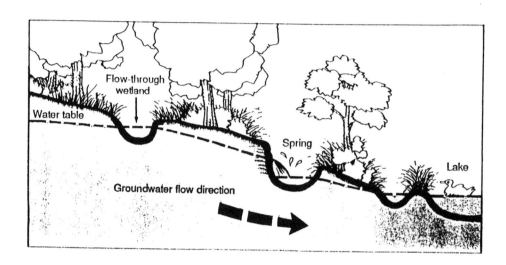

Gaining Streams

Streams that receive groundwater discharges are **gaining streams**. The level of water in the stream is at the water table level for the adjacent aquifer. This is also true for lakes and wetlands that receive groundwater discharges. More than half of the total flow of some streams during dry periods may be from groundwater discharge.

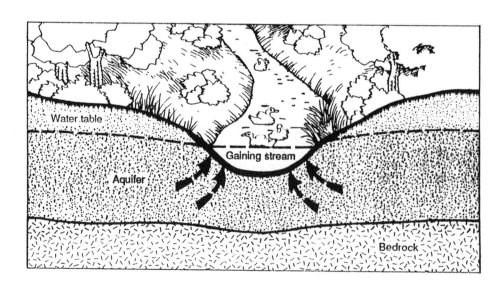

Groundwater Flow Rates

Groundwater moves very slowly from recharge areas to discharge points. **Flow rates** in aquifers are typically measured in feet per day. Flow rates are much faster where large rock openings or crevices exist and in loose soil, such as coarse gravel. It may take years, decades, or even centuries for groundwater to move long distances through some aquifers. However, groundwater may take only a few days or weeks to move for a short distance through loose soil. Groundwater typically moves in parallel paths with little mixing, due to the slow movement, which does not create sufficient turbulence to cause mixing to occur. This becomes an important factor in the location and movement of contaminants that enter the groundwater.

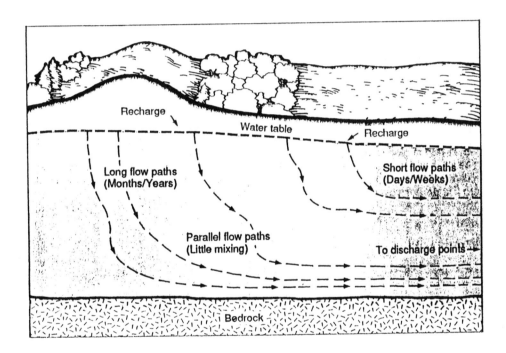

Groundwater Contamination

I will now try to help you gain a better understanding of potential sources, causes and prevention of groundwater contamination. Principal contaminants from each source are identified. Evidence that contamination is occurring is noted, followed by common contamination causes and means of prevention. It should be understood that these brief notations are in no way a substitute for specific investigations of possible contamination sources and means of contamination prevention or remedial action. Proper land use management is the key to groundwater quality protection. Land use activities that result in contaminated groundwater can often be traced to lack of understanding of the potential for contamination, carelessness or negligence. Lack of understanding of the contamination potential may be a result of insufficient information. The following information should help you make more effective decisions concerning groundwater contamination. Again, I have used a pictorial approach to help you understand the basic concepts.

Septic Systems

Contamination Evidence:
- Wastewater shows above ground.
- Detection of excessive bacteria, chemicals in well water tests.

Causes:
- Poor installation and/or maintenance.
- Disposal of household chemicals, such as paint thinners, into the system.
- Overloading the system with a garbage disposal unit.
- Use of septic tank cleaning additives.

Prevention:
- Proper installation.
- Inspection and cleaning every 2-4 years, annually if garbage disposal unit is used.
- Do not dispose of household chemicals into the system.
- Ban hazardous cleaning additives for septic systems.

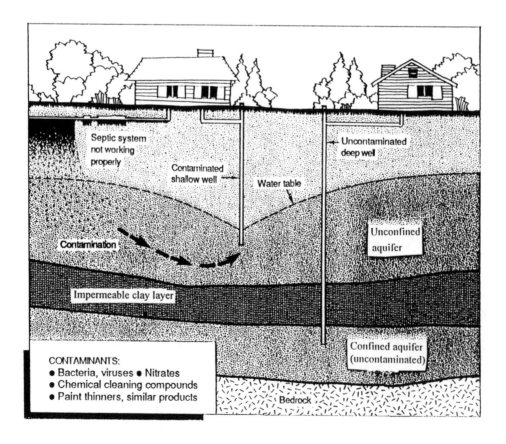

House and Garden Chemicals and Fertilizer

Contamination Evidence:

- Detection of chemicals in well water tests.
- High nitrate level in well water tests.

Causes:

- Improper use and storage.
- Improper disposal in backyard, ditches, low ground, septic systems, overgrown areas.
- Overfertilization and/or ill-timed application.

Prevention:

- Proper use, education and encourage use of less hazardous products.
- Provide local disposal facilities for unused chemicals and chemical containers.
- Careful adjustment of fertilizer application to plant needs and timing.

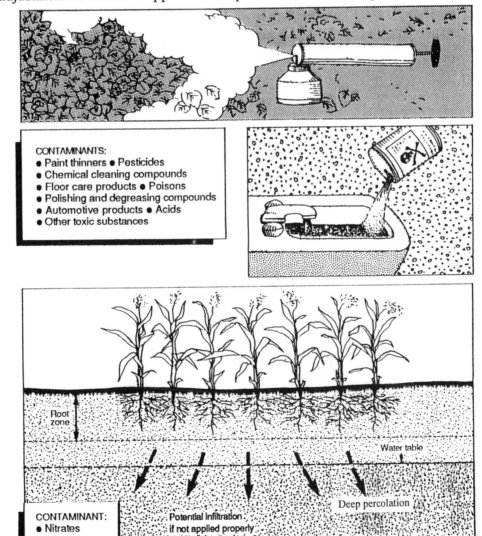

CONTAMINANTS:
- Paint thinners ● Pesticides
- Chemical cleaning compounds
- Floor care products ● Poisons
- Polishing and degreasing compounds
- Automotive products ● Acids
- Other toxic substances

Root zone

Water table

Deep percolation

CONTAMINANT:
- Nitrates

Potential infiltration
if not applied properly

Pesticides

Contamination Evidence:
- Detection of pesticides in well water tests.
- Ill effects on animals drinking water from nearby wells, springs or surface water.
- Ill effects on plants watered with nearby well water.
- Ill effects on aquatic life.

Causes:
- Excessive or ill-timed application.
- Improper storage.
- Leaching through the soil.
- Improper disposal of excess pesticides and rinsewater.

Prevention:
- Follow use instructions.
- Compliance with pesticide certification requirements.
- Reduce pesticide use in recharge areas for water wells.
- Encourage alternative pest control methods.
- Public information/education.

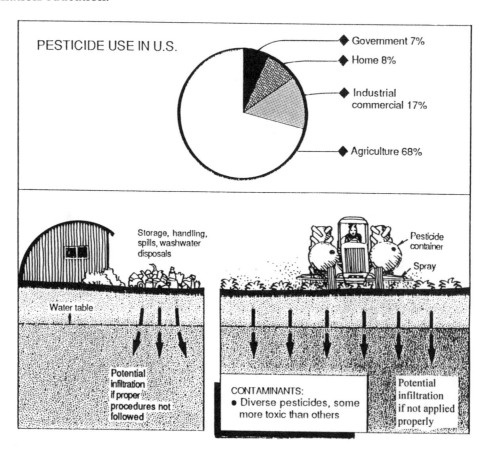

Atmospheric Pollutants

Contamination Evidence:
● Detection of elevated levels of sulfates, nitrates, heavy metals, asbestos, hydrocarbons, other chemical compounds in well water tests.

Causes:
● Emissions from motor vehicles, power plants, industries.

Prevention:
● Federal and state emission controls.

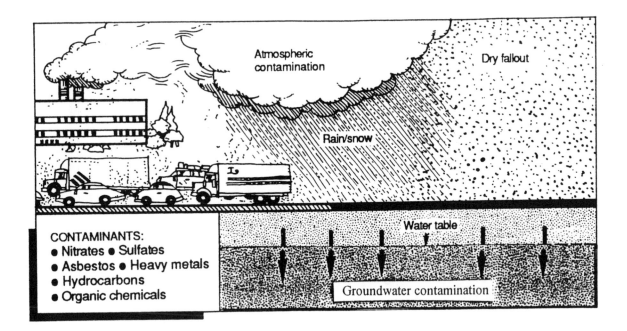

Xeriscape

Xeriscape is a complicated word for an easy way to garden. It is a method of landscaping using plants called xerophytes. A xerophyte is "a plant structurally adapted to growing under very dry or desert conditions, often having greatly reduced leaf surfaces for avoiding water loss, thick, fleshy parts for water storage, and hairs, spines, or thorns." Since one of the main concerns about our environment is, lack of available water, xeriscaping seems to be an approach in the right direction. It is gardening that is established on limited water usage. Done properly, it can save you both work and money.

Xeriscaping was developed, in the past, in areas that suffered severe drought. However, during hot summers, many towns in New Jersey limit the amount of water we can put on our landscapes due to water shortages. Since its principles can be applied to almost any landscape, it is suitable for anyone who wants to or must save water and have a low maintenance garden. The principles of xeriscaping are basically the same as for everything else in landscaping: a good plan and design, soil tests and improvements, if necessary, proper plant selection for each particular situation, a limited size lawn, mulch, enough water, good maintenance practices and lots of love and care.

One of the most important steps in xeriscaping is to have a good ***plan***. Without it, all the money, time and effort may be wasted. Your goal is to group together plants that have the same water requirements. This way, when its time to water, you won't take a chance of overwatering drought tolerant plants that are growing with thirsty plants. Walk around the entire property, with pad and pencil, and locate certain areas you feel would benefit from xeriscaping. It could be a sunny, hot space or densely shaded area where nothing seems to grow. You may want to cut down on your lawn size, which helps save water, and create a low maintenance flower or shrub bed. Use turf alternatives which include ground covers, mulch, decorative stone, sculptures, container plants, decks, patios, raised beds or terraces. Don't get me wrong here! We are not trying to cut down on our oxygen supply (through grass and plants) but are substituting low maintenance, water thrifty plants in return. On these patios and decks we can grow a variety of plants that need less water. The plan will also help you balance beauty with water conservation and work within your budget. Sketch out beds and other areas according to water requirements. Label these areas very low water, low water, and medium water, using whatever terms you like. Try to keep the medium water areas small as they will require more irrigation, what we are trying to avoid.

All the planning, money and work will be worth nothing if the ***soil*** is inadequate. Proper soil conditions are fundamental to good water penetration to the root zone and storage. A plant's good or bad health depends on the quality of soil it grows in. A strong plant that gets adequate nutrients from soil resists diseases and insects and uses less water. The soil must be rich in nutrients and have the ability to hold moisture without becoming soaked. It should have enough humus to make it water retentive but must also be well-draining so roots won't rot. Take soil tests in the areas you want to xeriscape, have them analyzed, advise your local nursery or agricultural agent what you are planning, and ask for their recommendations for soil amendments if any are needed. Remember, chemicals can reduce the activities of good soil organisms, so try and reduce their use. When planting, try to dig the holes deeper than normal. This will encourage the plant roots to grow deeper and become more drought resistant.

Make a list of drought-resistant *plants* or so called low-water-use plants. Again, check the catalogs you get in the mail. Some of them carry these type of plants for our area, and they come with guarantees of satisfaction. Also check with your local nursery to see what they have to offer. I have included a list of plants which should help you get started. Try to pick plants that will live mainly on nature's rain, needing only a little more water from us during the driest periods. However, you do want the areas to look nice with color and blooms, so don't select a group of weedy looking plants just because they don't require much water. There are many annuals and perennials out there that are beautiful and colorful and suitable for xeriscaping. Be careful with exotic plants that come from different areas in our country and even different countries. Some may do very well but others die the very first year. Choose plants that are hardy and are known to succeed in our area, and you should have very little disappointment. These plants have adapted to our climate, soil conditions and rainfall. The use of ornamental grasses is becoming very popular in xeriscaping since they require little maintenance and moisture. You want the area to have beauty and durability combined with water conservation.

Grass is a good supplier of oxygen but it also consumes large amounts of water and fertilizer. If you want to cut back on water usage, then you should reduce the size of your lawn. Some people may want to "just stop watering the entire lawn and we'll save money." This is the wrong approach for our environment. There is nothing worse in a gardener's eyes than a lawn infested with weeds or one that has died. Good lawns are beneficial to our environment, they always have been and always will be. So for purposes of xeriscaping, lets just reduce the size and replace these areas with other less water consuming plants, possibly low-water ground covers. Whether starting a new lawn or just reseeding into an old lawn, choose seeds that are known to be drought resistant. Once they are established, this will cut down on water consumption. Some possible areas to eliminate grass may be: on slopes, where you are scalping the lawn or there is soil erosion, in small or tight areas where you can hardly fit the mower, alongside foundations where you can develop flower or shrub beds or areas where there is dense shade and you have been trying unsuccessfully to grow grass. Improving the soil and deep waterings will encourage deep root growth to pull your grass through droughts. Don't overfertilize since large quantities of nitrogen has adverse effects such as shallow rooting and poor water absorption.

Covering the soil with an inch or two of *mulch* will help the soil avoid drying and compaction. Both of these conditions are stressful to plants. Mulching reduces drastic changes in soil temperature, helps keeps plant roots from freezing, and keeps weeds down. During hot, dry periods mulch keeps the soil cool, absorbs and holds moisture, and reduces evaporation. Mulching may be one of the singularly best things you can do for any landscape. Since mulch holds moisture and reduces evaporation, you'll be doing less watering.

A *water-conserving* irrigation system should be incorporated into your landscape. Of course, this depends on how many and what size areas are to be watered. Make sure you group plants in the very beginning with similar requirements and water them only when they need it. Water during the morning to avoid mid-afternoon evaporation, which is the hottest part of the day. If you have a drip watering system, you can water any time of the day since the water is placed at the base of the root system and not on the foliage. The slow, regular delivery of water directly to the plant root system keeps the zone moist, encouraging deeper growth. Deep root growth helps plants survive during droughts. Fertilizing the plants is also much easier with a drip system. Just drop some food tablets into the filter screen, and you're ready to go. Water lawns separately with water-efficient sprinklers. Some above the ground

portable ones have timers, and different settings for sprays and distances. If you have an underground sprinkler for the lawn, then times and zones can be set any way you wish.

Good maintenance practices include deep watering, periodic weeding, replacing mulch when it has decomposed and keeping a check on insects and disease. As with all plants, take special care of them the first year to give them a good start. Frequent, deep waterings may be necessary until they are established. Mulch does decompose so a new layer may have to be added every spring. Don't let weeds take over. Once every few weeks pull the large ones out with as much root as possible and uproot the small ones with a gardening fork. Keep a check on insects and disease, but remember, not all insects are bad. Just a few of them. Use an insecticide only if absolutely necessary to avoid damage and loss.

Plants for a Xeriscape Garden

Name	Type	Comments
Love-lies-bleeding	Annual	Red, yellow, grows tall, sun, tolerates dry soil, can be used as a hedge.
Pimpernel	Annual	Blue, purple, red, sun, good for edging.
Rock purslane	Annual	Purple, pink, red, white, sun, tolerates dry soil.
Cockscomb	Annual	Orange, pink, red, yellow, sun to part shade, tolerates hot, dry sites
Bachelor's-button	Annual	Blue, pink, purple, white, sun to part shade, tolerates poor dry soil, easy to grow.
Cosmos	Annual	Orange, pink, white, yellow, grows tall, sun to part shade, tolerates heat and drought, very pretty flowers.
Treasure flower	Annual	Yellow, low height, sun, good for window box, drought tolerant.
Phlox	Annual	Pink, purple, red, white, sun, easy to grow, drought resistant and tolerates poor soil.
Black-eyed Susan	Annual	Orange, yellow, grows tall, sun to part shade, tolerates heat and drought.
Mexican sunflower	Annual	Orange, yellow, grows tall, sun, vigorous and tolerates heat, can be used as a hedge.
Nasturtium	Annual	Orange, pink, red, white, yellow, sun to part shade, fragrant flowers, tolerates drought and poor soils.
Globe thistle	Perennial	Blue, sun, tolerates dry soil, attracts bees.
Iris	Perennial	Many colors, easy to grow, drought tolerant.
Mallow	Perennial	Blue, pink, purple, white, coarse and weedy, sun, hardy, low maintenance.
Coneflower	Perennial	Yellow with balck center, sun, strong and disease resistant.
Sage	Perennial	Blue, purple, sun, easy to grow, tolerates dry soil.
Speedwell	Perennial	Blue, pink, white, sun to part shade, long-lived and trouble free.
Fern-leaf yarrow	Perennial	Yellow, sun, aromatic foliage.
Sea Pink	Perennial	Pink, red, white, sun, grows best in sandy soil, tolerates salt.
Lavender	Perennial	Purple, white, sun to part shade, fragrant flowers.

Trees are usually self sufficient and can live on whatever rainfall mother nature provides. However, the following trees require a little less water than others and will do very nicely in a Xeriscape landscape: Norway maple, Black pine, Hawthorn, Locust and Juniper. Once your Xeriscape garden becomes established, it should be a hardy, attractive and self-sufficient ecosystem you will be proud of for many years.

Landscaping for Water Conservation

Let's take Xeriscaping one step further into complete landscaping for water conservation. The purpose here is to help you plan for your home unique and pleasing landscapes that will use less water. By using the correct combination of design, plants, mulches, and watering techniques, you will be able to create landscapes that not only environmentally suit your locale, but also conserve water. In rapidly growing communities, summertime water shortages are no longer uncommon, and restricted water use, particularly outdoors, is increasingly familiar. New Jersey's most easily exploited water supplies have already been developed. Understandably, concerns about the environment and rising labor and capital costs have delayed additional development. For all these reasons, water conservation appears ever more important, and our use of water to irrigate landscaping becomes an appropriate subject for examination.

Experts agree that properly designed and managed landscaping can save large amounts of water. By wisely using water outdoors, we can reduce peak water demand, prevent drops in water pressure that endanger a community's fire-fighting ability, eliminate watering restrictions, and save energy needed to pump water into storage areas around town. Nature can be a very effective guide. Studying how plants react to droughts in the wild teaches us valuable lessons about which plants and combinations of plants will be both aesthetic and practical in landscaping. In New Jersey, abandoned farm fields, the seashore, the Pine Barrens, and, surprisingly, flood plains are some of the environments where we can observe drought-tolerant plants.

Once farmland is abandoned, an ecological process called *old field succession* begins. Years of erosion and heavy cropping often leaves these fields without nutrients to feed plants and without organic matter to retain water. Invading plants have to be tough, durable, and drought tolerant to survive. Old field succession begins first with annual weeds and perennial grasses. An early woody colonizer is the Red Cedar. Because it is so common in New Jersey, many people find it unattractive. As an individual specimen plant the Red Cedar may lack excitement, but as a background plant it can provide an excellent setting for such flowering small trees as naturalized Oriental Crabapples, and native Dogwoods. The display of summer field flowers such as Queen Anne's Lace, blue chicory, and Brown-eyed Susan, as well as the brilliant red and orange fall colors of sumacs and sassafras, is enhanced by the soft green foliage of Red Cedars. In the winter cold this evergreen often turns purple. In time such valued shade trees as Pin Oak, Green Ash, Hackberry, and Red Maple will begin to invade the old fields, and the Red Cedars will begin to be shaded out of the picture.

The sands of the Pine Barrens and the beach provide the ultimate test for drought tolerance in plants, yet many beautiful ornamentals can be found growing in these two sites. Pitch Pines grow in such profusion that, like the Red Cedar, often go unappreciated by the public. Individual specimens, however,

can be very picturesque. The Pine Barrens have several beautiful, drought-tolerant ground covers, such as Bearberry, Wintergreen, and Lowbush Blueberry, which should not be disturbed. Hudsonia, or Beach Heather, creates a gray-green carpet on the sand dunes, but will not survive transplanting. Virginia Creeper forms a vigorous, five-leafleted dune cover along with its three-leaflet, toxic companion, Poison Ivy. Turf grass is conspicuously absent from the Pine Barrens and the beach. Because constant supplies of both water and fertilizer are necessary to keep grass green in excessively sandy soils, homeowners should be encouraged to find alternatives to turf.

Excellent examples of drought-tolerant native shrubs include Bayberry, which can be found growing in profusion among the sand dunes at the beach as well as in old fields further inland, shrubby Gray Dogwood, and the thicket-forming sumacs -- Smooth, Winged, and Staghorn. Native small trees also brighten sandy soil areas: Gray Birch, for example, is prized for its multiple white trunks. The Shad-blow has year-round interest: clouds of white flowers in spring, edible fruits in summer, orange color in fall, and striped gray trunks throughout the year. Both species require spraying to prevent severe insect foliar damage.

The last of the drought-tolerant natural areas is the flood plain. Plants grow on river banks obviously must tolerate wet sites to survive spring flooding, but the river bank in the summer is often as dry and hard as concrete. Of the shade trees native to flood plains, Green Ash, Red Maple, Hackberry, and pin Oak have the most to offer the homeowner.

The Lawn and Water Conservation

When drought occurs, the lawn quickly and obviously becomes stressed. Indeed, of all outdoor consumers of water, the lawn is the main one. Reducing the size of the lawn and using common sense to establish, maintain, and manage it will reduce the quantity of water needed. In most suburban neighborhoods the lawn is the most prominent vegetation. This observation should come as no surprise. The aesthetics of an emerald green carpet, the physical benefits of erosion control and heat absorption, and a ground cover that will endure both passive and active recreation are benefits that only the lawn can provide. The question many homeowners should ask is, "Do I have too much grass?" The answer is yes if the homeowner is trying to grow grass under the following situations:

● Are you trying to grow grass under the dense shade of shallow-rooted trees such as Norway Maple, European Beech, or Horsechestnut?
● Are you trying to grow grass where maintenance is nearly impossible, such as on steep slopes, among rocky areas, or in that narrow space between the walkway and the house?
● Are you trying to grow grass where active play tramples out all vegetation?
● Are you growing grass just because you can't think of anything else to do with your property?

Examine the following two plans of a typical back yard. In the "before" plan (figure 1), nearly all the ground surface is grass. The homeowner must cut around the lower branches of the evergreens and the base of the fence. Grass won't grow under the shade tree. In figure 2, the "after" plan, the lawn is confined to an easy-to-mow panel that "disappears" around the rear of the shade tree; although the lawn is

smaller than in figure 1, it gives the impression of being larger than it really is.   The shade tree with its shallow roots is no longer competing with the lawn. An organic mulch (wood chips, bark or cedar), alone or in combination with an alternative ground cover such as English Ivy, is a more successful and water-saving solution. Drought tolerant ornamental trees create a view from the deck or patio, and their trunks are protected from the lawn mower by a bed of mulch or ground cover. The fence can be used as a growing surface for vines. A vegetable or flower garden and storage shed have been added. With mulches and possibly trickle irrigation, the vegetable garden can provide a practical productive alternative to turf. Once the lawn has been reduced to manageable proportions, it can be given the care and management it needs.

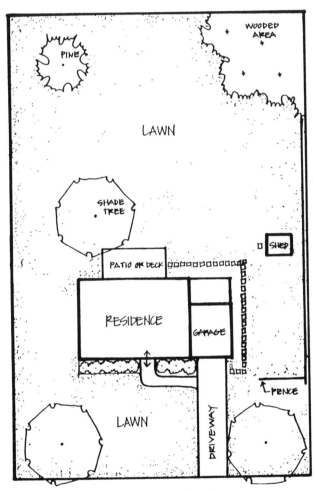

Figure 1. The "before" plan: a conventional landscape.

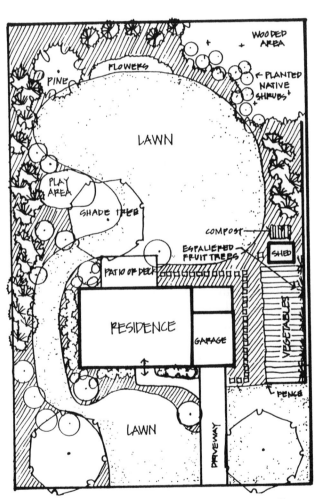

Figure 2. The "after" plan: a landscape planned to reduce lawn area.

Turf Tips

Seed selection - Blue grass mixes are fine for full-sun, rich, moist, and well-drained soil situations, but if your soil type and sun exposure are less than optimum, another type of turf may be more suitable and require less water. The improved perennial ryes, in mixtures with blue grass, have been proven to resist people and drought. Similar results in full sun have been achieved by lawns of tall fescue. In the shade, under low-fertilizer situations, the fine fescues are still the most successful of the grasses.

Fertilizer and lime - Do not overfeed your lawn. Fertilizing two times per year is adequate for a healthy lawn. For a "lean lawn" it is possible to get away with only one feeding, which should be applied in mid to late November. If the lawn is too lush, it will require more water and be susceptible to fungus attack. Lime is even more important than fertilizer; in the acid soils of the East Coast, several of the essential nutrients become unavailable to lawn grasses. Adding lime to raise the soil pH to between 6.5 and 7.0 not only makes these nutrients available, but also makes a lawn more drought-resistant. Depending on the soil pH, one liming every three years should be sufficient.

Mowing - Mowing height is also an important consideration during droughts. Lawns cut shorter than 2 inches are more prone to browning out. I cut all of my lawns between 2 1/2 to 3 inches in height during the summer. Remember, the higher the grass, the less chance of weed invasion.

Watering - Water the lawn only when and where it needs it. When a blue grass lawn needs water it will take on a wilted blue appearance. Become aware of stress areas within the lawn, and water them first: areas in competition with shade and shallow tree roots, compacted soils, and southwest embankments. Watering should be done in the cool of the morning or when the lawn is in shade, if possible. On a windy, bright, sunny day as much as 40 percent of sprinkler-applied water is lost to evaporation. Sprinklers should be set to water the lawn and landscape, not the street, driveway, or sidewalks. In addition, frequent waterings keeps moisture near the surface, promoting the growth of shallow roots, which makes the plants less drought-tolerant. The typical summer thunderstorm may provide 3/4 of an inch of water. No watering should be necessary for a minimum of 4 days, so turn off those automatic timers that control your underground sprinkler system. Remember that millions of acres of crops depend entirely on natural rainfall. Watering is necessary only when rainfall does not occur for an extended period.

Alternatives to Turf - Aesthetic options to the lawn provide visual variety to the landscape, are often easier to maintain, and require less water than lawn grasses. Categories include organic mulches and living alternative ground covers. The creation of a bed that separates the lawn from the shrub border provides a sense of order and harmony in the landscape. A clean, flowing line can reduce maintenance problems. Mowing around tree trunks, shrubs, and clumps of herbaceous perennials is a time-consuming nuisance that often becomes a damaging or fatal experience for the plant. Lime lines should be "drawn" first. Once a satisfactory line is created, a sharp spade can be used to create a permanent bedline. A long hose can be substituted for the lime and may be easier to manipulate. Grass and weeds should then be removed from the bed side of the cut. But the ground cannot remain uncovered. Bare soil is an open invitation to weeds. The homeowner can choose to cover the ground with organic mulches, a living ground cover, or some combination of these alternatives.

Mulching to Save Water

Mulches used during a dry season reduce the amount of water evaporating from the soil, thereby allowing considerable water saving. They also prevent intrusion of water-using weeds and can enhance the aesthetics of a landscape design. The depth of mulch to apply will depend upon the type of material used, 2 to 3 inches being a good guide. In addition, mulches maintain a more uniform soil temperature, which can improve plant growth.

A good organic mulch has the following qualities: it should retain moisture, retard weed growth, create an attractive neutral surface, improve the soil as it decays, and be inexpensive to acquire and maintain. Peat moss, a popular mulch among homeowners, fails nearly all these criteria. Peat, as it dries, actually draws water from the soil, and the following year it provides an ideal seed bed for weeds. It can blow away, float away, and catch fire. Furthermore, peat moss is expensive. Peat moss should be used as a soil conditioner, not a mulch. Wood chips, cedar, or bark mulches are better. Wood chips usually come in two types: winter chips and summer chips. Summer chips are considered to be less desirable because they often contain large quantities of leaf pieces. As the leaves decay, plants mulched with these chips may experience temporary nitrogen deficiencies (their leaves may turn yellow). Scattering a handful of high nitrogen lawn fertilizer in the mulched bed should solve the problem. Shredded bark mulch products are also successful organic mulches. Because they mat together they are less likely to float away than chips. My favorite is shredded cedar mulch. It has a nice clean odor and is excellent in keeping weeds down. It also mats together very well, especially on slopes. Bark nuggets are acceptable, but are expensive, have a tendency to float away, and are not too successful in keeping weeds down.

Drought-Tolerant Plants

Large Shade Trees

Because **shade trees** require 25 to 30 years to mature, homeowners should plant them before any other vegetation. A shade tree located to intercept the hot afternoon southwest sun will provide cooling in the summer and permit solar collection in the winter. The following trees are a few of the most dought tolerant:

Red Maple - This tree grows 40 to 60 feet tall and likes full sun. Fall colors are often red to scarlet and the bark is smooth. Red Maples grow well in both wet and dry sites.

White Ash - Grows 50 to 70 feet tall and likes full sun. Good shade tree chosen mainly for its fall color.

Green Ash - Grows 40 to 60 feet high and likes full sun. Its leaves drop early in fall and grows well in both wet and dry sites.

White Oak - Grows 50 to 70 feet tall and likes full sun. A very rugged, durable tree giving excellent shade during summer. They are long-lived but often slow growing and sometimes don't survive transplanting.

Red Oak - The state tree of New Jersey. Grows 50 to 70 feet in height and likes full sun. It has large acorns and is the primary tree of oak woods. Gives lots of shade and has a moderate to fast growth rate.

Pin Oak - This tree grows 50 to 70 feet tall and likes full sun. Grows well in both wet and dry sites. The low-hanging branches provide screening in the right place in the landscape but cause head room problems for vehicles and people.

Small Trees

Small trees range in height from 15 to 40 feet. Many are understory trees growing at the edge of the woods. They provide a transition planting between natural and more refined areas of property. A good smaller tree has many seasons of beauty, which may include flower display, foliage effects, fall color, and bark or habit interest. In the residential landscape small trees may serve to accent the entrance or filter a view from windows or a patio. If left densely branched, they serve as effective summer plantings for privacy.

Amur Maple - Grows 15 to 20 feet in height and likes full sun. Nice leaf color in the fall, provides good amount of shade for smaller tree and is very cold-hardy.

Gray Birch - Grows 20 to 25 feet high and likes full sun. Multitrunked clumps of three or more are white with black triangles. Attractive tree and grows well in dry or wet sites.

Common Witchhazel - Grows 15 to 20 feet high and likes full sun or shade. A native tree that has yellow flowers and is the last tree to flower in late fall. Some plants actually flower after leaf drop.

Crabapple - Grows 20 to 50 feet in height and likes full sun. These trees are prized for their flower display. In addition to flowers, the ideal crabapple should have small showy red fruit and good resistance to several diseases.

Japanese Tree Lilac - Grows 20 to 30 feet high and likes full sun. Creamy, white clusters of flowers are borne in late June. The cherrylike bark provides winter interest and it is drought tolerant.

Blackhaw Viburnum - Grows 15 to 20 feet high and likes partial shade to full sun. Depending upon pruning, this plant may be a large shrub or a small tree. Fall color is red and long-lasting however, the decaying leaves emit a strange odor.

Evergreens

Evergreens hold their leaves throughout the dormant season. Evergreens may be classed as *narrowleaf*, bearing needles or scales, or **broadleaf**, having a leaf blade and midvein. More important from a landscaping perspective, evergreens may be *significant conifers*, needle evergreens, that grow to heights of 40 feet or more. The remaining evergreens may be broadleafs, scale, or needle conifers, but they are all more shrublike in habit. The following drought-tolerant significant conifers improve our environment by absorbing and filtering out air pollutants and road dust. An addition, they retard winter runoff, screen out unsightly views, and serve as wind breaks. Significant conifers planted in the wrong place, however, become growing obstacles in the landscape.

White Fir - Is tough and drought and urban tolerant.

Atlas Cedar - This true cedar is especially well-adapted to hot dry sites. When locating Atlas Cedar in the landscape, remember that this tree can grow to 150 feet tall and 75 feet wide.

Spruces - They have a formal, classic Christmas tree shape, and look best when young. All spruces (Norway, Colorado, Blue Colorado) are shade-intolerant, which means they will lose branches and die in shade.

White Pine - When young, this pine is a very full plant providing a good screening but in old age it becomes a picturesque flat-topped silhouette on the skyline. If pruned correctly, White Pines can be pruned into a hedge. It is subject to winter breakage and sensitive to wet sites, the seashore and road salt.

Japanese Black Pine - Overall exotic, S-shaped growth habit with sharp needles. This evergreen is seashore-tolerant.

Red Cedar - Grows 15 to 20 feet tall and likes full sun. Grows in abandoned fields, highway embankments and sand dunes. This species is a common sight in New Jersey.

Drought-tolerant Shrubs

Most of the traditional, spring-blooming flowering shrubs are drought-tolerant. Forsythia, Lilac, Spirea, and Weigelia will grow in any well-drained site, provided they receive full sun. Native drought-tolerant deciduous shrubs have already been sited earlier. To extend the blooming season, drought-tolerant, summer-blooming shrubs should be included in the landscape. One flowering shrub that is not drought-tolerant, Doublefile Viburnum, can be a very useful indicator plant, for it wilts badly under drought stress. When this plant begins to wilt, it is time to water.

American Holly - Grows 15 to 20 feet in height and likes part shade to full sun. The spiny leaves and red fruits attract birds, and the plant grows well in sandy soil.

Wintergreen Barberry - This plant has spiny leaves and sharp thorns, making it difficult to place in the landscape. However, summer dark evergreen leaves turn purple in the winter, and yellow flowers are attractive in the spring. This plant is quite drought-tolerant.

Mugo Pine - Commonly used for landscaping. This plant is grown from seed in nurseries.

Dense Yew - One of the best spreading types and can be pruned to form a border when several are planted together. All yews are drought-tolerant but require well drained soils for survival.

Low Water Use Landscaping

Low Water Use Landscaping is a concept that every person owning or working with landscapes in New Jersey should consider seriously. Perhaps you would like to see your high summer water bills reduced. Residents in some areas also are concerned because their water reservoirs are being depleted. Others may simply be looking for a way to escape the more tedious aspects of landscape maintenance. Low Water Use Landscaping (LWUL) can offer significant help for each of these needs. The goal of LWUL is to be as efficient as possible with the use of water for irrigation, consistent with our personal preferences for the type of landscape we desire. This is not an appeal for paving over our yards or for becoming cactus gardeners. Lush, beautiful, functional, and water-wise landscapes can be attained by adopting the following LWUL principles:

1. Water only when and where needed.
2. Improve soil for optimum water holding capacity and drainage.
3. Use low-water demanding plants.
4. Apply mulches.

To see why these principles will work together to minimize water use in your landscape, let's take a look at what can happen when we turn on our irrigation system. You will then see what contributes to watering efficiency and where wasting water can occur. The diagram shows that irrigation water can be wasted in several ways.

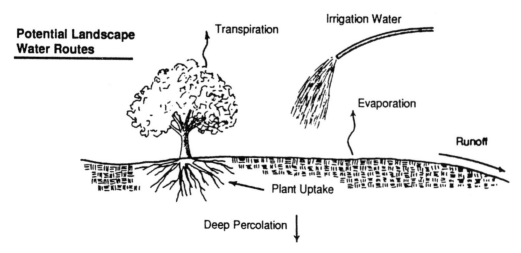

A portion will be lost into the air because of evaporation. On a hot, windy day as much as 40 percent of the water from a poorly designed overhead sprinkler can evaporate before it touches the ground. Evaporation from the soil surface also occurs, reducing water available to plants. Runoff is another common problem. This occurs typically when the soil cannot absorb the water as quickly as it is being applied. Clay soils, for example, cannot take up water at rates higher than about one-half inch per hour, for sandy soils two inches per hour is the limit. Runoff should be avoided not only for the water wasted, but also because topsoil is carried away. Another type of runoff which is all too common is when sprinklers overshoot the planted area and water falls on sidewalks, driveways, or even the street.

A third obvious pathway to water waste is when water goes down beyond the root zone. This is called deep percolation. While deep percolation from rainfall is how our water aquifers are replenished, this is not an efficient use of irrigation. Fourth, we need to look at water in the root zone. Even here water may not be used efficiently. Excess moisture damages plant roots because of a lack of oxygen and this, then contributes to plant root diseases. And, of course, watering weeds only makes our maintenance chores more difficult. Finally, if plants in the landscape are not adapted to site conditions, too much water may be spent ensuring that they survive. Combining these problem areas with our LWUL principles shows how beneficial this approach can be. In fact, water savings of over 50 percent have been attained by following LWUL principles.

Problem	Solution(s)
Evaporation	Use mulches. Minimize overhead spraying.
Runoff	Apply water at proper rate. Irrigate only desired areas.
Deep Percolation	Improve soils for water retention. Apply water at proper rate.
Weeds	Direct water only to desirable plants. Use mulches.
Soggy Soil	Improve soil for good drainage. Do not overwater.
High Water-Demanding Plants	Substitute locally adapted plants.

Drip Watering

Fifteen years ago, you would not have had much success finding a good watering system for low water use landscapes. Consumers were largely limited to the basic oscillating sprinklers attached to the end of a garden hose. These threw a fine mist up in the air and wet whatever was in its range, landscape plants, sidewalks and weeds each getting their share. Luckily, landscape irrigation products have improved vastly in recent years. You can find different systems which are efficient in delivering water to your plants. Used properly, the modern systems can save as much as 50 percent of the water used by less efficient methods.

The most important advance has been the development of drip irrigation. Drip provides a controlled flow of water right where you want it, to the root system of your plant. Wasted water due to runoff, overspraying, and evaporation is greatly reduced or eliminated. An added bonus is that weeds away from the drip line do not get watered. Modern drip systems will pay for themselves very quickly in the

cost of water you save. And systems are available which are easily installed by a homeowner. Although drip irrigation has not proven completely reliable for lawns as yet, there are water efficient sprinklers available as well.

What is drip watering? The concept of drip watering is simple: The slow, regular delivery of water directly to the root zone of your plants, keeping the root zone moist but never saturated. Your plants receive the ideal amount of water at the ideal rate. Your plants thus retain their proper air and water balance and avoid the stress and shock of the "drench and dry out" cycle associated with conventional watering methods. This results in optimum growth and healthy plants. Success with a drip watering system is dependent on two basic goals that are not simple to attain: provide uniform flow from each individual dripper regardless of water temperature or supply pressure, and insure drippers remain clog-free.

Slow, even watering directly to the root zone will:

Save water - up to 70% less water than conventional sprinklers.

Reduce plant stress: resulting in early production, up to 49% faster growth, healthier and more beautiful plants and up to 84% greater yields.

Reduce weed growth - you only water the plants, not the weeds.

Reduce water evaporation - by as much as 70%.

Prevent water run-off and soil erosion.

Saves money - a lower overall installation cost than underground sprinklers because you do-it-yourself, easily.

Saves time - less hand watering and garden maintenance.

Saves energy - the lower operating pressure equals reduced energy requirements.

Versatile & durable - use on flat terrain and hill sides. Hose can be buried or left above ground, year-round, in all climates.

Fertilize automatically - filter and fertilizer applicator supplies plant food through the drip system right to the plants root zone, reducing fertilizer cost.

Xeriscape compatibility - the conservation of water through creative landscaping, especially in drought sensitive areas.

Below is an illustration of a **Drip Watering System** that can be used just about anywhere: square foot garden, container garden, row vegetable garden and widely spaced landscape plantings.

Drip Line System

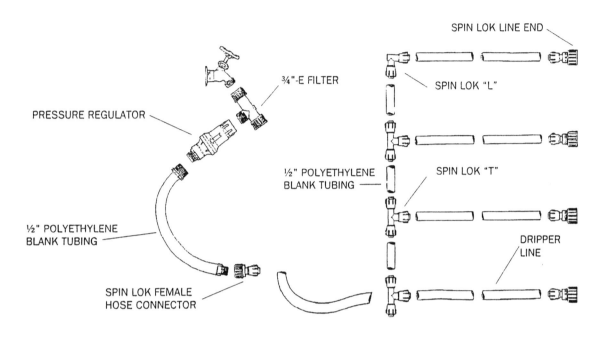

Drip watering can be used for all your landscape needs. Divide your plants into gropups (zones) with similar watering requirements. Plants in full sun should be watered separately from plants in the shade. Seasonal plantings like vegetable gardens should be watered separately from permanent plantings like landscape shrubs. Plants that require frequent, shallow watering such as annual flowers should be grouped separately from plants that prefer infrequent, deep watering like trees. Container plants with confined root systems should be grouped separately from plants in the ground. If possible, plan to have a separate drip watering circuit for each different group. A "circuit" is an arrangement of hose, tubing and watering devices connected to a water source by a single valve. You may want to make a rough sketch of your yard that will assist you in making the groupings.

Exact duration and frequency of watering depends on temperature, wind conditions, soil type and plant variety. For example, more mature plants have deeper roots and therefore require a longer duration watering cycle. Because the water is applied much more slowly with a low-volume system, the watering times will be much longer than you are used to. But if you grouped your plants properly when you planned your system, you should have no trouble arriving at the proper watering schedule through experimentation. Remember that drip systems water the root zone not the ground surface. You may operate dripper circuits in the day or evening since the water is placed at the base of each plant, not on the foliage. Fertilizing your plants is easy with a drip watering system. Simply insert food tablets into the filter screen and you're ready to go. However, when feeding container grown plants for short periods of

time, it is advisable to continue to water beyond the normal watering time in order to flush out all residual plant food remaining in the drippers.   Maintenance is relatively easy too. Once or twice a year remove the end closure and flush each circuit until the water runs clear. In addition, clean the filter screens and check for leaks. If any damage has occurred to the hose or tubing, simply cut out the damaged section and replace it using a compression coupling.

Drippers rated at one-gallon per hour (1 GPH) are best for most installations with medium soil. If your soil is heavy and takes longer to absorb water, you may wish to use 1/2 GPH drippers instead of the standard 1 GPH. Use of these will, of course, require up to double the normal watering time. If your soil is light and absorbs water quickly, you may wish to use 2 GPH drippers. Reduced watering times, but more frequent watering, would then be required. If you are having difficulty getting sufficient spread of the water between adjacent drippers, you may wish to change the drippers to a higher flow rate than might be correct for your soil. This will produce more lateral movement of the water before absorption by the soil begins. Don't forget to adjust your watering times accordingly! A drip watering system delivers water where you want it - directly to the plant root system resulting in healthy plants. It saves money, reduces weeds, reduces water evaporation, helps prevent soil erosion, saves energy, is versatile and conserves water through creative landscaping.

Design Fundamentals

When designing an irrigation system for your low water landscape, there are some basic considerations to keep in mind. Knowing these fundamentals will allow you to work with a supplier or landscaper in deciding exactly what your landscape calls for.

First, each area of your landscape with different watering needs should be provided with a separate system. For example, if you have an area of low water demanding plants, a small section of shrubs and flowers requiring more water, and a lawn, you will need three systems that could be separately controlled. Otherwise, you would run the risk of overwatering one area or underwatering another. Second, be aware of the variety of irrigation system components tailored to different situations. Drip emitters are called for to water trees, shrubs and other areas where plants are not densely packed together. If your plants are irregularly spaced, you can purchase emitters that plug into a delivery line wherever you need them. For large plants you put in several emitters; small plants would require only one. In areas with plants in a regular pattern, such as in a vegetable garden, lines are available with emitters installed at set intervals. On hillsides or for very long delivery lines, look for pressure compensating emitters. Also note that emitters come in different flow rates; 1/2 gallon per hour emitters are best for heavy clay soils while 1 or 2 gph emitters would be for lighter soils.

In some circumstances, emitters may not be the most satisfactory means of watering. For ground covers or dense flower beds you might find it easier to use a soaker hose, which is perforated with minute holes so that water oozes out along its entire length. And, as mentioned above, drip systems have not been perfected for lawns as yet. Instead, consider the new "low-volume" sprinklers. These produce relatively large droplets of water which helps to reduce evaporation.

It is important to stress that no matter how potentially efficient an irrigation system might be, in actual use it is only as good as the person using it. Water waste can occur with any system if it is not monitored well. Knowing **when** to water is very important. The best way to do this is to check your soil moisture periodically. Soil moisture sensors, such as tensiometers, can give a very accurate reading of soil moisture, and some can even be tied into a timer controlling your system. Being sensitive to the condition of your plants can also be a gauge for when to water. Turf grass, for example, takes on a dull green color when water is needed. Another indication it's time for watering is when footprints have remained in the grass the following day.

To encourage drought tolerance in your plants, gradually adapt them to infrequent but deep watering. Even for low-water demanding varieties, it takes about two growing seasons for new plants to develop their roots sufficiently to be able to withstand extended dry periods. After this establishment period, you can begin lengthening the time between waterings. By the following summer, your drought tolerant plants should be capable of surviving at least two weeks without rain or irrigation.

Low Water Demanding Plants

Choosing appropriate plants for your low water use landscape will be the most interesting and challenging step. The challenge will come in actually making your selections from the many possibilities. Whether you prefer a formal landscape or a naturalized look, there are plants available which will do well when others will be stressed from lack of water. As you can see from the list below, there are unthirsty plants of every variety, from flowering annuals to stately evergreens. Note in particular that LWUL fits perfectly with the growing popularity of landscaping with native plants. And a good number of herbs are drought tolerant as well.

Plant Adaptations to Low Water Conditions

Adaptation	Examples
1. Ability to store water	Cactus, Hens-and-Chicks
2. Deep root systems	Oaks, Tall Fescue Turf, Black Pine
3. Summer dormancy	Bluegrass Turf, Narcissus, Tulips
4. Reduced leaf size	Junipers, Thyme, Santolina
5. Thickened or waxy leaves	American Holly, Inkberry
6. Hairy leaves	Dusty Miller, Artemesia

By understanding how such plants are adapted to periods of water scarcity, you will be able to recognize many low water demanding plants when visiting your local nursery. The ability to store water and deep root systems are obvious means for a plant to survive drought conditions. The other adaptations listed bear some explanation.

Summer dormancy might more properly be described as "drought avoiding" rather than "drought tolerant". Plants which show this adaptation take advantage of seasonally abundant rains for growth. During the summer when rainfall is less likely, growth is greatly reduced to the point where some plants go dormant. Bluegrass lawns will survive if allowed to go dormant in the summer even though they turn brown. Once rains return, the grass again will turn green. Many people, though, are unwilling to live with a brown lawn. Be aware that turf can be maintained with a lot less water than you might expect. Just one inch of water per week, including rainfall, will be ample. Replacing bluegrass with a drought tolerant turf such as tall fescue will allow even less frequent watering. To conserve water further, you might consider reducing the size of your lawn to only that area where it serves a functional purpose, such as a play area for children. Strips of grass between the street and your sidewalk or areas under heavy shade trees are places that are really inappropriate for turf. Ground covers are a good replacement for turf and many, once established, require little or no irrigation.

Adaptations 4, 5 and 6 listed above are different modifications to leaves which aid in reducing the amount of water that a plant gives off through the process of transpiration. Reduced leaf size accomplishes this because there is less surface area for transpiration to occur. A protective waxy or thickened covering on the leaf helps to protect it from the drying effects of sun and wind. Similarly, fine hairs reduce transpiration by cutting down on exposure. These tiny hairs give a number of drought tolerant plants an easily recognized silver-gray color. While the list gives you a good variety to choose from, do not feel limited to these plants. There are several others mentioned in this book and your garden center or mail order supplier should have some to consider.

Non Drought Tolerant Plants

Realize also that there is a place in a low water use landscape for plants which are not considered drought tolerant. By improving the soil for retaining moisture, using mulches and drip irrigation, you can call upon a much wider variety of plants. Even some of the thirstier plants can be accommodated.

The key to including these is to restrict them to a special area where you can really enjoy them, such as near your front door. Areas with northern or eastern exposures will be better for moisture retention than southern or western exposures. Scattering such plants around a low water landscape will be self-defeating because it would be practically impossible to provide them with the water they need and, at the same time, avoid overwatering your better adapted plants.

Steps To Success

Low water demanding plants will be most successful if a few common sense rules are followed. **First,** the standard considerations of climate, the amount of sun, and soil pH requirements apply to low water plants as with all plants. **Second,** it is important to realize that drought tolerance will not be found in the plants fresh from a garden center. It will take about two seasons of relatively frequent watering for these plants to become established. After this time, gradually lengthen the time between waterings and water more deeply. This will encourage the growth of deep roots. **Lastly,** during times of drought, do not apply large amounts of fertilizer. Fertilization will bring on growth, but your plants will have a difficult time sustaining such new demands. In general, light fertilizing in the fall or spring will be adequate to keep your plants healthy.

If you already have a landscape that is not predominately made up of low water demanding plants, it may be expensive to replant all at once. Instead, plan a conversion in a series of steps to take place over several years. In this way, you will be able to spread the cost out.

Energy Conservation Around The Home

Can your landscape design help cut fuel costs? You bet it can. Planting trees and shrubs around your home will help to reduce your heating and cooling costs. How much it reduces costs depends on your choice of plants and where you locate them. Trees and shrubs also reduce noise and air pollution, and make your home more attractive and more valuable. Therefore, money spent on landscaping your home is a good investment.

An unprotected home loses much more heat on a cold windy day than on an equally cold still day. Well-located trees and shrubs can intercept the wind and cut your heat loss. Up to one-third of the heat loss from a building may escape through the walls and roof by conduction. Wind increases the convective air currents along outside walls and the roof, thus increasing the heat loss. Infiltration or air leakage can account for as much as one-third of heating losses in some buildings. Cold outside air flows in through cracks around windows and doors, and even through

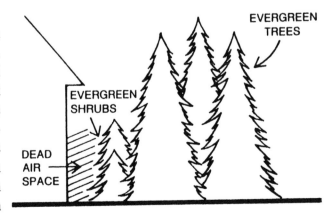

the pores in walls. This produces drafts that may cause you to over compensate by raising the thermostat to unreasonable levels just to maintain comfort. Both windbreaks and foundation plantings can cut down this penetrating power of the wind. Windbreaks of two to five rows of trees and shrubs generally provide good protection. Evergreen trees provide the best protection.

Studies of windbreaks show that windbreaks can reduce winter fuel consumption by 10 to 30 percent. One study in Nebraska compared the fuel requirements of identical test houses which maintained a constant inside temperature of 70° F. The house protected by a windbreak used 23 percent less fuel. In one month, an exposed electrically heated house in South Dakota used 443 kilowatt-hours to maintain an inside temperature of 70° F. An identical house sheltered by a windbreak used only 270 kilowatt-hours. The difference in average energy requirements for the whole winter was 34 percent. The amount of money saved by a windbreak around a home will vary depending on the climate of the area, location of the home, and what the house is built of. A well-weatherized house with adequate ventilation, caulking, and weather-stripping won't benefit from windbreaks nearly as much as a poorly weatherized house. In addition to reducing the force of the wind, windbreaks also can reduce the wind chill impact on people outside the house. Windbreaks can be located to control snow, too. This reduces the energy required to remove the snow from around homes, other buildings, and roads. Make sure windbreaks are located so as to have the desired effect on drifting snow.

The height and density of trees determine the amount of protection they will provide. Windbreaks of two to five rows of trees and shrubs generally provide good protection. Evergreen trees provide the best protection, although low, branching deciduous trees can significantly reduce windspeed. Even a single row of evergreen trees will give some protection. Windbreaks will reduce wind velocity significantly for a distance of about 10 times the height of the trees. Thus, a windbreak 30 feet high protects an area extending as far as 300 feet downwind. Some protection is provided for as far as 20 times the height of the trees. Maximum protection is provided within a distance five times the height of the trees. For onsite assistance in locating and designing windbreaks, and selecting appropriate trees and shrubs, contact your local nursery, tree specialist, landscaper or extension office.

Trees and shrubs planted close to buildings reduce wind currents that otherwise would chill the outside surfaces. These foundation plantings even create a "dead air" space which slows the escape of heat from a building. These plantings also help reduce air infiltration losses around the foundation of the house. Again, evergreen trees and shrubs are thicker and are more effective than deciduous plants. To be most effective, the evergreens should be planted close together to form a tight barrier against air movement. In summer, the same dead air space helps insulate your home from hot outside air, thus reducing the

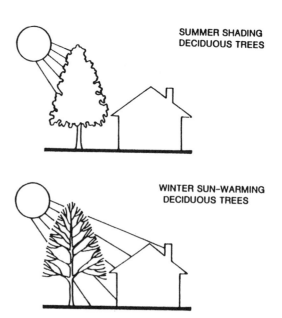

SUMMER SHADING
DECIDUOUS TREES

WINTER SUN-WARMING
DECIDUOUS TREES

need for air conditioning. Trees and shrubs control solar radiation by shading people and buildings from the direct rays of the sun. During winter, deciduous trees and shrubs shed their leaves and let the sun's rays help warm the house. This might be an important consideration if you are planting for summer shade on the southern exposure of your house.

Maples and other trees with full crowns are best for summer shading. Their high branches permit greater visibility and do not block the flow of cooling summer breezes. Evergreens have a cone-shaped crown which provides less summer shade on walls and roofs. Their branches often extend to the ground, blocking visibility and flow of cooling breezes. If planted in the wrong location, they may shield your house from the sun's warmth in the winter. Trees provide maximum shade when planted in groups beside your house. However, a roof need not be totally shaded to achieve excellent results. A study in Alabama showed that air conditioning costs could be reduces effectively as long as a roof averaged 20 percent or more shade for the entire day. Another study showed that an 8° F difference between shaded and unshaded wall surfaces was equivalent to a 30 percent increase in insulating value for the shaded wall. Temperature differences larger than 8° F between shaded and unshaded building surfaces are common.

Deciduous vines that cling to trellises along the wall can afford protection on the south and west sides of your house. But remember that vines which cling directly to the walls may cause some structural deterioration. By providing direct shade on the walls, vines keep surface temperatures down and reduce convection-caused heat gain. Some additional cooling comes from the evaporation of moisture from the leaves. Evergreen vines such as English Ivy should not be used on walls facing south since the vines block the winter sun's warming rays. Vines may help to insulate walls on the northern and western sides by curbing winter winds.

Keep in mind the following things when designing or renovating your landscape. They will help you conserve energy.

● Plant large trees on the south to west sides of the house, and recreation areas to give summer shade.

● Plant evergreen shrubs close to the house to create a dead space for insulation against winter winds and reduction of summer air conditioning costs.

● Plant staggered rows (two or more if space permits) of tall evergreens to block winds and control snow drifts.

● Plant deciduous vines (preferably on trellises) along the wall on the south and west sides of the house to provide summer shade and winter insulation.

TYPICAL FOUNDATION PLANTING

NO SCALE

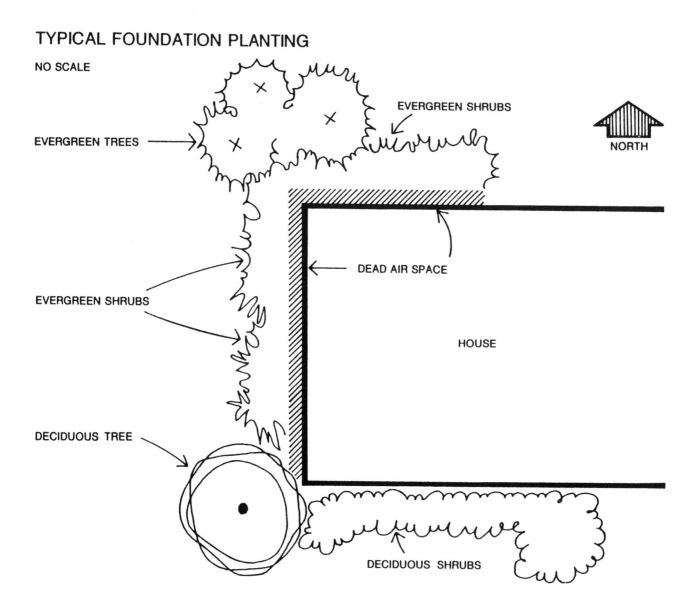

EVERGREEN TREES

EVERGREEN SHRUBS

EVERGREEN SHRUBS

DECIDUOUS TREE

DEAD AIR SPACE

HOUSE

NORTH

DECIDUOUS SHRUBS

Integrated Pest Management (IPM)

Insect, disease, and weed problems are nothing new to landscapers, gardeners and homeowners, and neither are the problems that often accompany the pesticides used to control them. Diminishing effectiveness, increasing cost, and safety considerations are all legitimate concerns surrounding pesticide use. In response, many commercial horticulture professionals have turned to an alternative pest control strategy called **Integrated Pest Management**. Integrated pest management (IPM) is a concept that has gained popularity and acceptance in the landscape industry. It has been around for several years and is a wise approach for landscapers, gardeners and homeowners to take in regard to pest problems in their landscapes. What is IPM? IPM is the use of natural and safe methods to control landscape insects and disease. It is an "environment friendly" alternative to the indiscriminate spraying of chemical pesticides to treat lawns, trees and shrubs. It incorporates all suitable control techniques to keep pest damage below an established threshold level. IPM stresses the management of quality landscape plants, as opposed to chemical annihilation of pests. It is the most efficient and economical method of pest control in the lawn and landscape. IPM focuses on the long term suppression or prevention of pest problems with minimal impact on the environment, non-target organisms, and human health. The use of IPM strategies should result in effective pest control with minimal impact on the environment and on people.

The word "integrated" means that numerous techniques or approaches are used to manage a pest or plant problem. It is important to realize that no landscape can be kept totally free of insect, disease, and weed problems for extended periods of time. These plant pests frequently cause much concern among home gardeners because the injury they cause often negates many hours of hard work. Home gardeners and farmers have traditionally relied on pesticides to control plant pests. However, chemicals are often applied after a problem has developed. Many gardeners would prefer a program which enables them to prevent pest problems from developing at all. In addition, the rising costs of pesticides and concerns about safety of the applicator and the environment have led to the development of an alternative pest control strategy (IPM). The goal of an IPM program is not to eradicate all pests, but to tolerate pests at a level below which they can cause injury. While an IPM program often uses pesticides, the emphasis is put on keeping pest populations down through the use of other pest control strategies so that pesticides are rarely needed, and serious pest problems are prevented. An IPM-trained landscaper controls plant pests by regularly monitoring a landscape and applying scientific knowledge about plants, weather, pests and the environment. It takes extra training and education to be able to diagnose landscape problems and their cause in order to make improved pest control decisions. On-the-spot decision making requires knowledge of the pest life cycle and habits, its interaction with its plant host, natural enemies and competitors, and knowledge of alternative methods of preventing and managing pest populations. Home owners and gardeners can also learn ways to control landscape insects, weeds and disease without pesticides.

Many people think of "pest management" as control using pesticides. Frequently spraying broad spectrum pesticides around the home and yard to suppress insects and fungi used to be a common practice. It usually succeeded in eliminating key pests, but it also created other problems. Broad spectrum insecticides are toxic to earthworms and beneficial insects such as insect predators and parasites that help keep pest populations under control. These beneficial insects provide stability to the complex communities of insects living in soil, turf, trees and shrubs around your home. An insecticide spray

usually suppresses all insects temporarily and causes a delayed outbreak of aphids and mites some 2 to 6 weeks after spraying. Therefore, once you start using insecticides, you may find it necessary to spray again to control outbreaks of aphids or mites. Repeated use of some insecticides may result in outbreaks of scale insects and other insect pests. We now know that proper insect management means **preserving beneficial insects**.

In general, if turf, trees and shrubs are properly selected, planted, watered and fertilized, they can be grown without using pesticides. Natural enemies of the pest such as predators and parasites may be used in an IPM program. Numerous cultural methods have been found which help control some pests that include fall planting, rotation of crops and the use of plants and seeds that are resistant to disease and insects. Often cultural methods, natural enemies, and careful use of selective pesticides are used for a successful integrated control program.

What does IPM actually do? IPM sharply reduces pesticide use. This helps alleviate a threat to wildlife and water quality. This is especially important here in New Jersey, the most densely populated and urbanized state. Since IPM controls plant eating insects such as aphids with little or no pesticides, beneficial insects are protected. This promotes healthier plants without endangering the safety of children and pets. IPM offers homeowners the most advanced plant care techniques available. Studies prove emphasis on natural pest controls reduces pesticide use by 40 to 88 percent. IPM offers an environmentally sound program and a healthier landscape.

The two main components of IPM are scouting for pests and utilizing a variety of pest population control methods. These include mechanical, biological, cultural and chemical tools, use of resistant varieties and prevention. Listed are brief descriptions of IPM methods:

1. **Prevention** - The home owner or landscaper can plant grasses, trees and shrubs that are resistant to insect infestation and disease. Monitoring plants every two weeks during the growing season can identify pests before they cause significant damage.
2. **Physical controls** - Pests can often be easily removed from flowers and shrubs. For example, aphids and mites can be removed with a strong jet of water. Bagworms can be hand picked off of plants.
3. **Horticultural controls** - Manipulating the growing conditions of plants (nutrients, pH) keeps them healthy. Healthy plants are much less vulnerable to insects and disease. Proper pruning and mulching is also used to control harmful pests.
4. **Biological controls** - IPM employs nature's own methods for controlling landscape insects and disease. Beneficial insects such as lady beetles and spiders can be used to destroy harmful pests such as aphids and mites. A nonpathogenic fungus can be used to protect plants from disease.
5. **Chemicals** - The prudent use of pesticides can be part of an IPM program although chemicals are normally used as a last resort. Environmentally safe pesticides such as horticultural oil or insecticidal soap can be used to treat specific insects and diseases.

What about the cost? An IPM program usually costs the same as traditional landscaping approaches which rely heavily upon pesticides. In some cases, the cost is even less because of the reduction in pesticide use. It will also make lawns, trees and shrubs healthier and healthy plants are more resistant to insects and disease. IPM requires training in all phases of turfgrass, trees, shrubs, flowers, soil, pest management and cultural practices. It usually involves intensive field monitoring, good record keeping

and consideration of different pest control strategies. Together, these components form the basis for the decision-making process that will determine the success of the IPM program. The goal is simple: to keep pest populations or damage at a tolerable level. This level is called the **pest response threshold level** (PRTL) and is determined by the number of pests or the amount of pest damage that can be sustained before unacceptable reduction in quality occurs. PRTL levels vary from site to site and are based on the use of the area and the user's needs or expectations. Two examples are as follows. In the case of a home lawn, the primary reasons for well landscaped property are soil stabilization, energy conservation and aesthetic value. The level of pest damage that can be tolerated depends on the value that is decided on by the owner. For a golf course aesthetic value is important, but playability is the primary concern. If the surface of a putting green is disrupted by disease injury or weeds, this may interfere with the roll of the ball, thus affecting the outcome of the match. In this case, the PRTL for golf putting greens is extremely low. However, the threshold levels for fairways and roughs are usually much higher since a smooth, blemish-free surface is not as important.

Monitoring or scouting is the process of finding the suspected pest, identifying it, and determining whether the pest is present in great enough numbers to justify control. Traditional pest control programs have been based on the calendar. Sprays were applied at certain times of the year, regardless of whether the pest was actually present. In an IPM program, regular plant inspections (about every 2 weeks) are an essential way to keep track of changes in pest problems. In addition to plant inspections, insects are monitored through the use of insect traps, especially **pheromone traps**. These pheromones are similar to attractants emitted by the female to attract the male. Traps can indicate when an insect is first present in an area, and how its population is changing. Based on monitoring, pest control decisions can be made according to what pests are known to be present, not on what is thought to be present. Regular monitoring can prevent pest problems because potentially serious infestations can be discovered while they are still minor. In addition, when plants are inspected on a regular basis it is possible to keep track of biological control agents such as lady beetles.

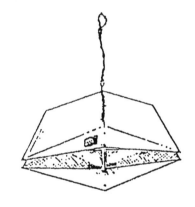

It is monitoring which makes an IPM program different from a "see and spray" program. It requires knowledge of plant culture, plant identification, damage symptoms, key pests and their life cycles, aesthetic injury levels, and pests managed by various control tactics. In addition to plant monitoring, environmental monitoring is essential because it enables the landscaper to stay on top of environmental conditions which favor a particular disease, weed or insect.

It is important to find the insects or other pests actually responsible for the damage observed. Indirect evidence may or may not indicate the presence of a pest. An example: holes in leaves may be caused by late frost damage, not by chewing insects. Do not assume guilt through association with the damage. Once found, the suspect pest must be **identified**. In some situations, an insect that is present in great numbers may not be the cause of damage. Identification is also important because some kinds of pests are more damaging than others. Once you know what kind of pest is present, you can better judge whether the potential damage justifies control measures. Knowing the identity of a pest also enables you

to learn about its biology and use other IPM tools to control it. Identifying pests may be a difficult task for the beginner, but along with the pictures and descriptions in this book, there are many good reference books that provide photographs and drawings of pests. As you become more familiar with diseases, insects, and weeds identification becomes easier.

Record keeping is an essential part of monitoring but for purposes of discussion, I'll treat it separately. Good records are kept to keep track of:

- When and where pests may attack.
- Early pest activity.
- Pest levels related to the plants' condition.
- Beneficial organisms and competitors.
- Results of control tactics.

A formal record keeping system that is consistently used while monitoring is essential to a successful IPM program. Records are critical to be able to evaluate the effectiveness of the program and to predict future pest activity. In many cases, IPM specialists use landscape maps on sites, identifying each plant and its location. Monitoring notes are recorded on it directly during each site visit. Others use check-off monitoring charts, which highlights the presence and level of pests seen as well as weather, etc. Accurate records of pest problems at a particular site can be a valuable aid. Record keeping can help in determining the best location and timing for a pesticide application, if it is necessary. A good record keeping system should include the date, name of pest, weather conditions, where the pest occurred, the amount of damage it caused, control measures used and the results.

Once a pest problem is noticed, the IPM manager goes through a decision-making process to determine how to respond. Does the problem need control immediately because damage is evident? Could the problem potentially cause damage later? Are any beneficial organisms present? Is this the proper time to control the pest? Once the decision is made to control the problem, a combination of controls (cultural, biological, host plant resistance, pesticides) to manage the pest is decided upon. The least toxic control spray should be prioritized, and treatments that will least affect beneficial organisms present, such as horticultural oil, insecticidal soap, and Bt. The least proficient choice is a broad-spectrum, residual pesticide.

Cultural Control

Many pest problems in the landscape are the result of plant stress from either poor soil conditions, poor plant quality, or improper plant location (wrong amount of sun, soil moisture, etc.). When plant growth conditions are less than ideal, the plant is put under increased stress that can make it more susceptible to insect and disease problems. Regular soil tests can provide a great deal of useful information about plant growing conditions which the homeowner can use to prevent pest problems.

Physical Control

Many pest problems can be prevented with physical means. A weekly washing from the hose will remove common pests such as aphids, while other insect or disease-infected plant parts can be removed by pruning. Barriers such as burlap tree bands can be effective. Insects such as gypsy moth caterpillars and elm leaf beetles will hind under the bands during the day, where they can be destroyed. In addition, physical barriers such as mulch can be used to reduce weed levels around landscape plants. Mulch has the additional benefit of increasing soil moisture retention. Watering plants at the right time of day can help reduce diseases. Mowing the lawn at the right height can help the grass develop deeper, stronger roots, thereby making it healthier. When plants are healthier, they build up resistance against insects, disease and stress. Try to use resistant plant varieties. Some are naturally resistant and others have been bred to be resistant to insects and diseases. Use of these plants can have a positive impact in the reduction of pest problems.

Biological Control

This is the use of other living organisms to control a pest. Naturally occurring predators, parasites and diseases are usually very effective in reducing pest populations. Two of the most common are the lady beetle and the preying mantis. When we increase the numbers of these natural enemies, we are practicing biological control. There are many others which are commonly present, but are so small that

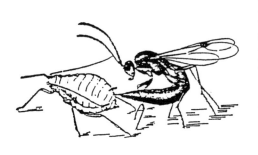

they are seldom seen. To bring more beneficial insects into your landscape you must increase favorable conditions for the natural enemy so that it can become more numerous. One way is to allow fallen leaves and other debris to accumulate around the bases of shrubs (not too deep of course) to provide overwintering sites for lady beetles and other predatory insects. Avoid using broad-spectrum pesticides as much as possible. Predatory insects will only come to your site if other insects are available. If you've destroyed all insects in the area, you're setting yourself up for a future invasion, and when it comes, you'll have no alternative but to use more chemicals. Without food, beneficial predators will move on to some other location. When the use of pesticides is limited, natural predators and parasites are encouraged to be around. The New Jersey Department of Agriculture operates a laboratory in which many of these beneficial organisms are raised for release throughout the state.

Pesticide Control

As mentioned earlier, pesticides are part of an IPM program, but they are used differently than in a conventional pest control program. The plant monitoring which is part of an IPM program enables the gardener to pinpoint just those areas of the property where a problem is serious enough to warrant pesticide control. Spot sprays can represent a great savings in the amount of pesticide applied to a property

when compared with a conventional program in which all plants would be sprayed. In terms of preventing the spread of many existing pest problems, one approach in the home landscape is the use of a dormant oil or an insecticidal soap. These compounds are safe for the applicator and the environment, and are effective against a wide range of insects. In many cases, they represent a viable alternative to more toxic materials.

Pesticides are commonly used for economical control of the pest population. Properly timed applications frequently provide adequate control so that additional applications are not necessary. Spray only targeted plants or areas to preserve natural enemies as much as possible. By using pesticides and other pest management tools carefully, you can enjoy reasonable freedom from pests without endangering yourself, your family or your pets. The blanket spraying of pesticides to control landscape insects, weeds and diseases is becoming less acceptable, particularly in the Northeast. IPM techniques ensure healthy lawns, gardens and landscapes. Using less pesticides means less harm to people, wildlife, forests, streams and our total environment.

Landscape Friends

What do birds, bugs, butterflies and worms all have in common? They're all welcome visitors to our landscape. Birds are one of the most overlooked means of natural insect control. Birds capture many thousands of insects everyday to eat themselves and feed their young. Although they do eat berries and seed, they usually seek out insects first. A chickadee can eat from 100 to 300 insects a day and brings more to its young, and a brown thrasher can devour up to 500 insects a day. A house wren can kill over 600 insects a day while feeding its young. Besides these three there are many other birds that are "beneficial": doves, bluebirds, sparrows, purple martins, titmice and woodpeckers, just to mention a few.

Managing your bird population can help control insects. It's very simple! The more birds you can attract to your landscape, the less insect pests you will have. How do I attract more birds to my property? All birds have basic needs: food, water, shelter and nesting areas. When you plant a variety of shrubs, trees, flowers, ground covers and vegetables, you are creating a "diverse" landscape. Certain plants need more sun and others don't, just as certain plants need more water, and others require less. Some perennials grow small and don't flower, while others grow very tall and have beautiful blooms. The same diversity should be promoted with "bird gardening". Try to attract as many different species as you can. Certain birds eat certain insects as noted below:

Chickadee - aphid, potato beetle, leaf miner.
Robin - potato beetle, cutworm, leaf miner, white grub.
Purple finch - aphid, potato beetle, flea beetle, leafhopper, leaf miner.
Sparrow - cutworm, leafhopper, root maggot.
Starling - Japanese beetle, slug, white grub.
Purple martin - mosquitoes.

Not all birds live on insects. Some thrive on berries and seeds, such as the Mourning dove and Meadowlark. Birds have different shapes and colors, chirps and songs, and are a complete delight to

have in any landscape. One of the easiest ways to attract birds is to create what is called a "friendly" environment. Plant fruit trees and shrubs that have berries, flowers with edible seeds like sunflowers, and grasses, which seed during the year. All of these are attractive to birds. Birds will stay in an area as long as there is enough food. During the spring and summer months, cut down on birdfeeders with seed. We want them to eat the insects pests. An occasional light feeding once every few weeks will keep them in the area, but we don't want them just living on seed we provide. Let's not defeat the purpose of our "bird" garden.

Stock the feeders during the colder months to attract the birds during the off-season and keep them around. Bird feeding season usually extends from October through April. Water is absolutely necessary for birds to survive, so put up a couple of birdbaths. They like to bathe and drink and having birdbaths around will help increase their visits. The bath should be out of reach of cats and other prey. Some people say it should be completely out in the open so birds can see any possible enemies. Lois, how-

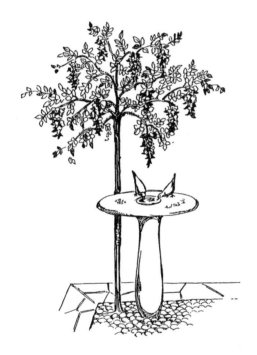

ever, put ours in a small compact area that has a fence on one side, the bath is actually nestled under a small lilac bush, with an oak tree on the other side. The birds love it. One bird feeder is 10 feet away near a holly tree and the other is in the center of our back yard, so we can watch and enjoy them while they are feeding. Our surrounding neighbors have three cats. The cats sometimes lay under the feeders (hoping) which seems to keep the squirrels away. All things considered, there seems to be peaceful co-existence.

Sometimes, birdbaths sold in stores can be too fancy or too expensive. Try buying a good size clay pot and saucer, turn the pot upside down, fill the saucer with water and place it on the base of the pot. This is an easy birdbath and the birds like it. The only problem is, it may be too close to the ground and predators may start hanging around. Give it a try, if you don't have any cats in the area. Always keep the birdbath full of clean water, especially during warm weather. Birds love to drink and cool off on a hot summer day. Create a habitat similar to those found in the woods, and you'll attract birds. Trees, brushy coves and spreading vines are all conducive to birds nesting places. When it comes to birdhouses, birds are very particular about size, entry holes and the location. Buy a few different size houses, place them in secretive places, and I'm sure you will attract some feathered friends.

A well-planned landscape having a variety of trees, flowers, shrubs, houses and birdbaths should attract and keep birds happy throughout the year. Tall oaks, beeches and pines have excellent pirches. Shrubs that bear fruit provide good landing spots and provide food as well. Also plant sunflowers, as the seeds are one of birds favorite foods. Don't create a habitat that is too neat. Birds like areas that resemble wildness.

Trees That Birds Like
Oak, Beech, Maple, Crabapple, Dogwood, Mountain Ash, Holly

Shrubs That Birds Like
Firethorn, Bayberry, Forsythia, Evergreens,
Blueberry, English Ivy ground cover, Rosa Rugosa, Wisteria

Flowers That Birds Like
Sunflower, Rudbeckia, Celosia, Black-eyed Susans,
Calendula, Zinnia, California Poppy, Forget-me-not

Butterflies

One of the best ways to enjoy your garden, on a warm summer day, is to have beautiful butterflies fluttering here and there. Butterflies are blessed with striking colors and markings, and they bring added life into any landscape. Inviting the decorative insects into your garden enhances the beauty of shrubs and flowers. Butterflies are, however, very fussy insects, so your success in attracting them will depend on what you plant. Welcoming them is an easy task if you share your garden by growing the colorful flowers they prefer. Growing flowers to feed them is a practical ecological benefit every gardener can provide. Flowers are needed for nectar during the growing season. Butterflies are pollinators that visit many kinds of flowers during the year. Witnessing the excitement and activity as they flit from flower to flower in a kaleidoscope of color is an experience no gardener should be without. Plant as many as room permits to help attract and sustain these living treasures.

They all start as an egg which becomes the larval stage, a caterpillar. During their caterpillar stage, they are a source of food for birds and during their adult stage, a source of pleasure for the gardener. Don't worry about the caterpillars eating too much of your plants, birds will keep them under control. It's all in the balance of nature. After eating, caterpillars pupate in a *chrysalis* and then transform into beautiful butterflies. Depending on the type, the life span ranges from several weeks to eight to nine months.

Choose a site on your lot that gets plenty of sun and is protected from the wind. Butterflies also need water, so place a small birdbath (you can substitute a small bowl or shallow pan) directly in the garden. Keep the bath filled with fresh water or they might not use it. Butterflies also like to bask in the sun. A few, well placed large rocks will give them a place to land. Cut down on the use of insecticides, as the same chemicals that eliminate unwanted pests will also kill butterflies. They like the hot weather, this is why you'll see more of them during the summer months. Butterflies take shelter at night in weeds,

trees, shrubs and flowers, so the more plants you have around, the more they'll stay in your area. During the day they like hot open spaces fluttering from flower to flower. Butterflies like to lay their eggs in "weedy", natural spots, so let a small area, maybe near woods, get weedy.

Butterflies like flowers of all colors, those that have fragrance, and those that don't. They do, however, seem to like small flowers arranged in clusters, such as the sedum. Their tongues may not be long enough to drink the nectar from the base of large or very long flowers. Keep this in mind when choosing flowers or flowering shrubs for your butterfly garden. Try mass planting of a specific type and watch as butterflies go from one patch to another. Below is a partial list of plants that attract butterflies. Check with your local nursery, I'm sure there are several others available. Be sure to plant spring, summer and fall flowering ones in mass plantings, this way butterflies will stay around the entire growing season. Butterflies love sun, need water, and like certain plants. If you remember these few things, butterflies should visit your landscape frequently.

Trees That Butterflies Like
Flowering Dogwood, Sassafrass, Oak

Shrubs That Butterflies Like
Spiraea, Blueberry, Rhododendron, Butterfly Bush,
Trumpet Vine, Lilac, Hydrangea, Honeysuckle (vine)

Flowers That Butterflies Like
Alyssum, Candytuft, Forget-me-not, Grape Hyacinth, Lavender,
Marigolds, Sweet William, Asters, Rudbeckia, Lobelia,
Coreopsis, Joe Pye Weed, Sunflowers, Scarlet Sage, Cosmos,
Cone Flowers, Yarrow, Zinnias, Daylilies, Phlox, Pincushion

Friendly Bugs

As gardeners we are always pestered by insects. We are tempted to eradicate any insect in and out of sight. Some bite and others sting, and let's face it, they're just plain ugly. What's even worse, they have lunch in our flowers and plants. Chemicals will kill them all, but do we want to? Of the more than 86,000 species of insects in North America, 76,000 are considered harmless or beneficial to our environment. Pesticides indiscriminately kill beneficial insects as well as pests. It is important to realize that not all insects are pests. A landscape and its surroundings have many insects that are "beneficial" since they eat harmful insects. A gardener must learn to identify all garden insects to determine whether they are friends or foes. There are many books available that provide illustrations of common insects.

Insects represent approximately 80 percent of all animal species. Even greater than their abundance is their potential to reproduce. A single pair of houseflies could produce an estimated 400 million tons of flies during the course of a summer if all their offspring survived. Why then are we not knee-deep in insects? A number of factors keep populations in check. Environmental factors such as weather and the availability of food are important. Beneficial insects, mites and pathogens that are natural enemies of

insects also play a major role in their control. All insects have natural enemies that attack one or more of their life stages. Insects may become pests when natural enemies fail to regulate them. This often happens when an insect is introduced into a region where its natural enemies don't exist, when cultural practices favor an insect over its natural enemies, or when pesticides destroy natural enemies.

When humans introduce or manage natural enemies to suppress insect populations, it is termed biological control (bio = living) or biocontrol. In practicing biological control, a number of important principles should be kept in mind.

1. The success of biological control agents in maintaining the "balance of nature" relies on suppressing, rather than eliminating, the pest. Because natural enemies depend on the pest for development, a certain population level of the pest is necessary to sustain them. This level may need to be high, low or intermediate. Keeping pest populations at an acceptable level may be achieved by combining the actions of natural enemies with other means of control. This is called Integrated Pest Management (IPM).

2. In contrast to fast-acting pesticide applications, control of pests by natural enemies may take time. Natural enemies must search out pests to consume or lay eggs in them. Time may also be required for the development of a natural enemy before the pest is affected. Once established, natural enemies can offer relatively permanent controls that are self-regulating (needing no human intervention), provided environmental factors or pesticides do not create an unfavorable habitat.

3. Biological control is often more effective in some years than in others. Success will depend on environmental conditions such as weather and management practices.

Lady beetles and spiders are two well known groups of insect predators. Predators are usually larger than the insects they attack and they consume more than one prey during their development. They are most effective against insects that live in groups such as aphids, scale insects and mealybugs. Adult predators often deposit eggs near a prey population where, after hatching, the larvae search out and consume them. In general, predators are less likely than parasitoids to provide total biological control of an insect pest for two reasons: they are less selective for a single pest and they usually don't reproduce as rapidly as the pest. The use of broad-spectrum pesticides, in many cases, can make things worse. Besides killing all insects, including the "good" ones, insects can build up a tolerance to chemicals after repeated applications. If only a few of the targeted pests survive an application, this pest can produce resistant offspring. In this case, we often increase the pest population that we're trying to eliminate. There are also pests in the landscape that we never knew existed, because the natural predators kept them in check. But when we kill the "good guys", the secondary pests come out in full force with nothing left to control them. Now we have an entirely new pest problem.

How do we attract more beneficial insects to our property? Simple! Develop an environment they want to be in. Plant the plants they like. Besides eating the "bad guys" many adult predators eat the nectar found in flowers and flowering shrubs and trees. Be diversified by planting perennial and annual flowers, several kinds of flowering shrubs and trees and flowering vines. Planting the right flower varieties to encourage and foster these natural enemies minimizes damage to your landscape by controlling pests such as aphids, whiteflies and corn ear worms. This method of natural control both promotes biodiversity in the landscape and cuts down on the need to use other, toxic control methods. Certain bugs

have their preferences, so the more the merrier. Some useful flowers that attract beneficial insects are: White Lace, Coriander, Summer Yarrow, Sensation Cosmos, Alyssum and Sunflowers. Many bugs feed only at night. Add some mulch and stones giving them a place to hide during the day or they may turn out to be some other predators lunch. If you build a welcoming habitat, they're sure to arrive. Beneficial insects need a chance to restore the balance of nature. Let's give them a try!

There are other ways to beat the enemy. Besides bringing in beneficial insects, plant flowers, shrubs and trees that are known to be insect resistant. Grow a diversity of plants. Many insects are attracted to specific plants, so either avoid them or try to camouflage them. Certain herbs and flowers are natural insect repellents. Use them as "companion" plantings among the others. Some plants possess the natural ability to repel certain types of pests. Companion planting is the practice of strategically placing insect-repelling plants next to plants that will benefit from their natural properties. Companion plants can hide others with strong odors, leaf patterns or colors. They can act as a trap crop to entice a pest away from its neighbor. Companion plants also attract beneficial insects and predators to the landscape. These pollinators and predators are an excellent means of pest control.

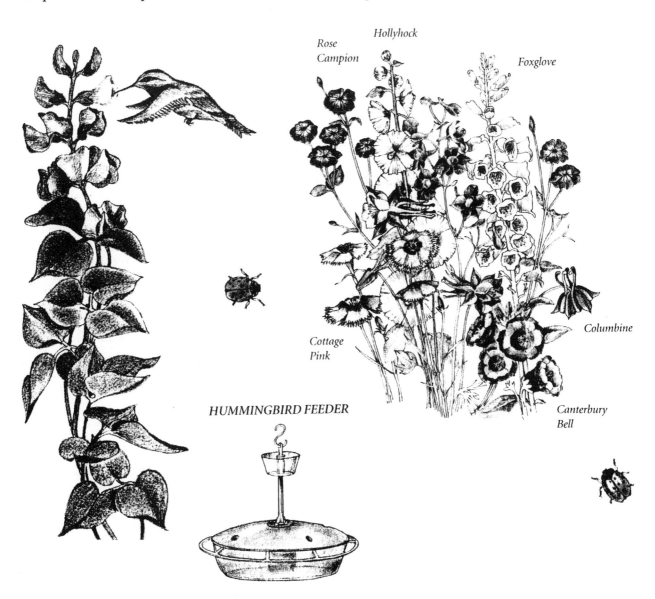

Hollyhock

Rose Campion

Foxglove

Columbine

Cottage Pink

HUMMINGBIRD FEEDER

Canterbury Bell

Pest Deterrent Plants

Plant	Pest
Allium	Many insects
Artemisia	Carrot fly, black flea beetle and others
Aster	Most insects
Basil	Flies, mosquitoes, use as trap plant for aphids
Calendula	Most insects
Catnip	Flea beetle
Chive	Aphids
Chrysanthemum	Most insects
Daffodil	Rodents
Dill	Attracts predatory wasps; repels aphids, spider mites
Eggplant	Potato beetle
Flax	Potato bug
Garlic	Cabbage looper, Japanese beetle, aphids, snails, root maggots
Geranium	Most insects including leafhopper
Grape hyacinth	Rodents
Henbit	Most insects
Lavender	Many pests because of aroma
Marigold	Many insects including nematode, squash bug
Mint	Ant, flea beetle, white cabbage moth, rodents, aphids
Nasturtium	Aphid, squash bug, cucumber beetle, woolly aphids, whitefly
Onion	Most insects
Petunia	Leafhopper
Radish	Cucumber beetle, squash bug
Rosemary	Bean beetle, cabbage looper, cabbage moth, attracts bees
Sage	Cabbage moth, cabbage looper, odor confuses many pests
Sunflower	Attracts predators such as birds, predatory wasps, lace wings
Thyme	Cabbage worm, aphids
Wormwood	Carrot fly, black flea beetle
Yarrow	Attracts predators such as ladybirds, predatory wasps

Plant a few of them around plants you know will be bothered by pests. Thyme, basil, mints, rosemary are all herbs that repel aphids, flies and caterpillars. Garlic is not only good for your heart, it is one of the best companion plants around. Mix them in with other flowers, shrubs and vegetables as a good line of defense. When the growing season is over, you can help reduce the pest population for next year by removing dead plants and cleaning up any debris where the pests may overwinter.

The "Good Guys"

Lady Beetles - Lady beetles (1/8" - 1/4") are common insects. Many species are found worldwide. They are generally brightly colored beetles in various shades of red, orange, brown or black, often with spots. The larvae are elongate (1/4" - 1/2"), somewhat flattened, and are usually covered with brightly colored spots or bands. Both larvae and adults are predators, feeding mainly on soft-bodied insects like aphids, scale insects, mealybugs and whiteflies, and on the eggs of many pests.

Ground Beetles - Ground beetles (1/8" - 1 1/2") have dark, shiny and somewhat flattened bodies, sometimes with iridescent blue or green coloring. Most larvae and adults are primarily predaceous (living on others). Adults and larvae generally live on or beneath the soil or in plant litter, though some climb trees. They are active mostly at night.

Lacewings - Adults (1/4" - 1") of both green and brown lacewings are fragile-looking insects with conspicuous wings containing many net like veins. The larvae are usually brown, flattened and elongate, and have an "alligator like" appearance. Green lacewings are very common and found in many habitats, though they prefer somewhat open areas. Brown lacewings are found in wooded areas. The larvae and adults of both families are predaceous, and can be extremely important in the control of aphids. Larvae are sometimes referred to as "aphid lions."

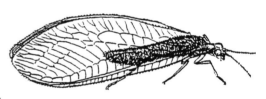

Praying Mantis - Praying Mantis (2" - 4") are slow-moving, green or brown insects with an elongate body and long, thickened and spiny front legs. They have highly movable triangular heads that are fairly distinctive. Mantids eat a variety of insects (including beneficial ones) that move within range. They can be found on vegetation where they sit motionless while waiting for prey.

Spiders (non-insect) - All spiders are predaceous. They usually kill their prey by injecting venom. The garden spider uses its web to capture insects.

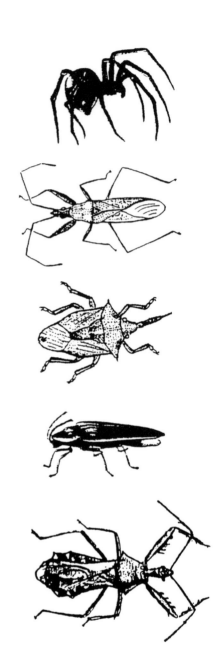

Damsel Bug - Damsel bugs (1/8" - 3/8") are usually most active during the summer which helps lower the buildup of aphids in the fall. They eat eggs and immature stages of many kinds of insects, including thrips and leafhoppers.

Soldier Bug - Adults (about 1/2") are light brown and flattened, with a spine on each side of the thorax. They attack more than 100 different insect pests and will climb into trees to get their prey. Adults overwinter in protected areas and then emerge in spring. It loves young gypsy moth caterpillars.

Fireflies - Lightning Bugs (up to 3/4") are soft-bodied and brown or black in color. The male makes most of the "lightning" action at night to signal females. The larvae feed on many insect pests including snails and cutworms.

Assassin Bug - Adults (1/2") are brown or black with large eyes in a narrow head. Their front legs are armed with spines used for grabbing prey. They love aphids, Japanese beetles, leafhoppers and unfortunately, bees and butterflies.

Parasitoids

The majority of insect parasitoids are tiny-to-moderate sized wasps that cannot sting humans. Some flies and a few beetles are also included in this group. Parasitoids are usually smaller than their hosts, they lay eggs on or inside the host, and their development kills the host. In contrast to predators, parasitoids need only a single host to complete their development. Adult parasitoids are often better searchers than predators, and are frequently host-specific, attacking only one or a few closely related pests. Host specificity, searching ability and a high reproductive rate make many parasitoids effective control agents because they can respond rapidly to increases in host populations. Parasitoids may attack any life stage, but most attack either eggs or larvae.

Ichneumon Wasps - Ichneumons (1/8" - 1 1/2") are common wasps and may be the largest family of insects. Most species have slender bodies and a long ovipositor (stinger), but they are harmless to humans. Many are brightly patterned with yellow, brown and black. Many ichneumons attack the larvae of moths and butterflies. Some are important enemies of sawflies and other insects. Typically, they lay an egg in their host. After hatching, the ichneumon larva eats its host as it develops.

Braconid Wasps - Braconids (1/16 - 1/2") are inconspicuous brown or black wasps, usually smaller than ichneumons. They are often seen on flowers, particularly those in the carrot family. Most species are beneficial, but some attack other natural enemies such as lady beetles. Adults attack the larvae of moths, butterflies, beetles, flies and aphids, laying one or several eggs in or on the host. The silken cocoons of small braconid larvae can often be seen on the outside of the body of hosts such as caterpillars.

Parasitic Flies - Most parasitic flies (1/4" - 3/4") resemble houseflies, though they may be larger, stouter and covered with bristles. Others appear more bee - or wasp like and are densely hairy. Adults often make a characteristically loud buzzing noise in flight. Parasitic flies are found in many different habitats and they attack a wide variety of insects. The larvae of moths, butterflies, beetles and sawflies are most commonly attacked.

Pathogens

There are three primary types of disease-causing microorganisms or "pathogens" that affect insects: bacteria, fungi and viruses. Pathogens have had only limited success in biological control programs, because they are not usually present at levels high enough to control pest populations. On the other hand, pathogens are the least visible biocontrol agents and may be much more important than they appear. Insects infected by pathogens usually show a change in coloration and appetite, are slower moving, and may appear stunted, shriveled or swollen. Diseased individuals sometimes have very characteristic behaviors, such as clinging to the very top of a plant before dying. Most bacteria and viruses must be eaten by an insect for it to become infected, whereas fungi can enter through the body wall.

The development of microbial insecticides such as *Bacillus thuringiensis* (Bt) has allowed some pathogens to be mass-produced and applied much like chemical pesticides. Unlike other biological controls, microbial insecticides provide only temporary control and may need to be reapplied. They are

usually selective and therefore safe for humans, other animals and beneficial organisms. Insect-eating nematodes are often grouped withpathogens. These nematodes are tiny, thread like worms that feed and reproduce within certain insects. Infested insects usually die within 24 hours. Because they require a moist environment, insect-eating nematodes are most effective against insects living in soil, such as lawn grubs and fleas.

Viruses - Insects infected by viruses (mostly caterpillars) become pale and appear to "melt" as their fragile bodies disintegrate and the contents turn to liquid.

Bacteria - Insects infected by bacteria don't loose their body structure but become dark and "rubbery" before ending up dried and shriveled. They may discharge fluids from the mouth.

Fungi - Insects infected by fungi usually keep their shape and color, but become hard and "mummy like". They often appear "fuzzy" from the fungal growth.

How Is Biological Control Accomplished?

There are three basic ways to make use of insect natural enemies.

1.   Natural enemies already present may be conserved or increased in effectiveness by appropriately managing their environment (IPM). Whenever possible, monitor to determine levels of pests, their damage, and beneficial insects. Food for adult parasitoids can be provided by leaving or planting nectar and pollen-producing plants throughout the landscape. Keep observing to determine if pest levels are severe and warrant control. If an insecticide is needed, use one that targets the pest and is the least harmful to natural enemies. Even fungicides can be harmful to biocontrol by killing fungi that are biocontrol agents. microbial insecticides, where effective, are especially useful by not killing natural enemies.

2. Government agencies may import beneficials from other countries to provide controls for insects that have no established natural enemies. An example is the alfalfa weevil. The alfalfa weevil was a serious pest but has been effectively controlled by three wasp parasitoids released in the late 1960s, and is no longer a significant pest.

3. Beneficial insects may be made more effective through direct manipulation that changes the kind or increases the numbers through periodic or large-scale releases. Some natural enemies are available for home gardeners through commercial suppliers. Successful control requires knowing the appropriate natural enemy for a particular pest, proper timing for release and, possibly, some behaviors of the pest and the natural enemy.

Beneficial Species	Eats	Insect Pest
Damsel Bug		Aphids, leaf hoppers, mites
Lady Beetle		Aphids, rootworms, weevils
Parasitic Wasp		Aphids, gypsy moths, cutworms
Lacewing		Aphids, white flies
Assassin Bug		Leaf hoppers, mites, potato beetle
Spiders		Flies, fleas, treehoppers
Frogs/Toads		Snails, slugs, flying insects
Praying Mantis		Many insects (including beneficial)
Birds/Bats		Grubs, caterpillars, mosquitos
Soldier Bug		Many insects, including gypsy moth
Fireflies		Many pests, snails and cutworms

The "Bad Guys"

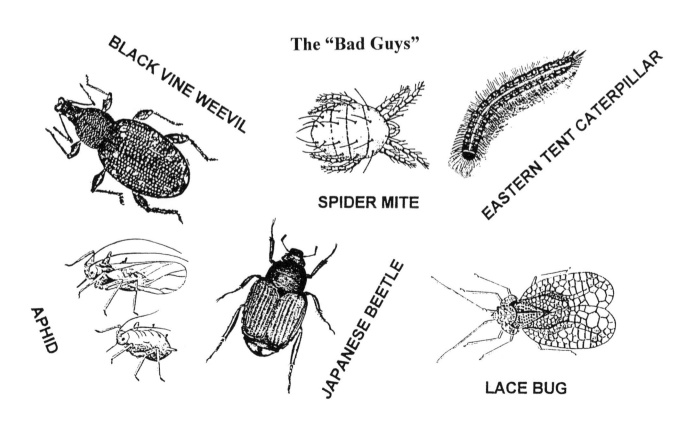

BLACK VINE WEEVIL

SPIDER MITE

EASTERN TENT CATERPILLAR

APHID

JAPANESE BEETLE

LACE BUG

The Lowly Earthworm

Talk about friends, this guy's a real buddy and deserves our utmost respect. Historians believe the fertility of the Nile river was due to the abundance of the wonderful earthworm. They may be right. Worms are one of the earth's oldest inhabitants. There are literally thousands of species of earthworms in the world, with the nightcrawler being the largest in New Jersey. They have no eyes, lungs, feet or ears. Worms use their longitudinal muscles to extend the front part of its body into the soil ahead, and pulls its back part up behind it. They breathe when air present between soil particles diffuses through their skins. When these air pockets are filled with water (rainwater or heavy irrigation) the worm is forced to the surface. This is why you see so many worms crossing roads or driveways after a heavy rain. The earthworm is valued all around the world, and with good reason. Although they eat dirt, are slimy (not really) and ugly, the earthworm is one of our most beneficial friends in the environment. When worms dig, they loosen the soil, mix it and aerate it. As they move, they actually eat some of the soil. and their fecal deposits, called castings, enrich the soil. Worms, therefore, have an important role in soil ecology. They live in the upper layers of soil and compost but, during the winter, they dig deeper to avoid the frost and do the same on very hot days to avoid dehydration. However, they come to the surface at night, when its cooler, to feed and release their castings. In loose soil, earthworms are capable of moving quickly. When they burrow, they eat large quantities of dirt that contain nutrients and cast out the remains on the surface. Earthworms are hermaphrodites, having both male and female sex organs. Cross-fertilization takes place and the eggs are buried in the earth in capsules, which protect the young until they hatch as fully developed worms.

An old gardeners tale is "turn over a spadeful of soil, and if you see worms squiggling, you know the soil is healthy." And if you don't see any worms, there may be something preventing them from being there. A soil test may be necessary. When earthworms are present in the soil, plants are usually healthier. They are truly nature's recycler as they eat organic matter in soil, decaying leaves and compost. Their castings are rich in soil nutrients and bacteria which improve soil fertility. When they burrow, their channels allow nutrients, air and moisture to penetrate more deeply in the soil. This movement also helps lessen thatch problems (sounds like nature's own aeration machine). How do we get more of these friendly guys into our landscape? The easiest way is to increase the organic matter. Worms are attracted to compost and decaying piles of leaves and grass clippings. You can go out and buy a large quantity of worms and release them in several areas of your yard. Some may stay and others may leave, depending on the fertility of your soil. You can also encourage worms to come by limiting cultivation. The more the soil is dug, raked and tilled, the less earthworms will want to be there. Cutting down on pesticides will also help, as many of these products also kill worms. Worms like cool, moist places so adding mulch will be a plus. They don't like bare ground or dry earth. Mulch also insulates the ground which helps prevent worms from freezing. Be kind to our earthworm friends, for they are kind to us.

> ## Earthworm Facts
>
> In 24 hours, an earthworm can eat it's own weight in soil.
> American night crawlers grow up to 10 inches.
> Australian night crawlers may grow longer than 2 feet.
> Cleopatra claimed the earthworm contributed to Egypt's fertility and therefore declared it to be sacred.
> An acre of good soil in the U.S. has about 50,000 worms.
> Britain estimates theirs to be around 3 million per acre.

Home Gardening and Landscaping

One of the most positive actions a homeowner can take to reduce exposure to pesticides is to cultivate a natural home garden, which can include shrubs, flowers and vegetables. Over the past ten years, enthusiasm for home gardening has grown enormously. There are many simple ways you can reduce or eliminate the need for pesticide use in your garden. The most effective approach to successfully controlling garden pests is to employ a combination of techniques.

● **Healthy Soil** - Any discussion of successful gardening and landscaping must begin with the importance of rich, fertile soil. Healthy soil is better able to yield healthy plants and healthy plants are better able to resist insects and disease. Each season should begin with raking the soil and mixing in organic matter such as compost to add essential nutrients. In the case of vegetables, it is advisable to turn over the soil while mixing in the compost.

● **Beneficial Insects** - It is important to recognize that not all insects in a landscape or garden are "pests." Their surroundings contain many insects that are actually beneficial because they feed on insects that are harmful. Therefore, a gardener must learn to identify insects and determine whether they are harmful or beneficial.

● **Companion Planting** - Some plants possess the natural ability to repel certain insects and diseases. Companion planting is the practice of strategically placing insect-disease-repelling plants next to ones that will benefit from their natural properties. For example, planting garlic among vegetables helps fend off Japanese beetles and aphids. Marigolds interplanted with cucumbers discourage cucumber beetles.

● **Diversified Planting** - A common practice among home gardeners is to plant a single species all in one area or in a straight row. This encourages pest infestation because it facilitates easy travel of an insect or disease from one host plant to another. By intermingling different types of plants and by not planting all together or in a straight row, an insect is forced to search for a new host plant thus exposing itself to predators. This approach corresponds well with companion planting.

● **Trap Plants** - Some insects, if given a choice, will feed on one type of plant over another. For example: maggots prefer radishes over corn and tomato worms prefer dill over tomatoes. Therefore, certain plants can be strategically placed so that they lure harmful insects away from the plants you wish to protect. These are commonly referred to as "trap plants." Once the trap plant has become infested, the target insect can be picked off and dropped in soapy water or the entire plant can be pulled up and disposed of.

● **Barriers and Traps** - Barriers and traps are types of mechanical controls that can be employed to capture or impede pests. A collar made of thick paper or cardboard which is placed around the stem of a plant and pressed into the soil an inch or so deep will prevent cutworms and other burrowing insects from getting into the soil around your plants. An effective technique for trapping non-flying insects is to bury tin cans in several parts of your yard so that the lip of the can is flush with the soil surface. Some bugs will fall in the can and be unable to get out. The can should be emptied often. A board or thick

piece of paper painted yellow and coated with a sticky substance such as tanglefoot will attract and intercept aphids and other small flying insects.

● **Mulch** - Mulching is the spreading of organic matter around plants. It is one of the most effective methods for combating weeds. Mulch also helps soil retain moisture and stay cool. Mulch should be added when plants are four to six inches high.

Research has proven that healthy plants can withstand many pest problems. Stressed and unhealthy plants, on the other hand, are more susceptible to pest problems. Many problems in the landscape are secondary problems resulting from plant defenses being low because of: poor soil, poor plant quality, improper planting, improper pruning and improper maintenance practices. For many, many years landscape pests have been controlled by using chemicals. Today, however, people have a choice. Safer and more effective means of pest controls are constantly being researched, tried and in many cases accepted. Products that are safe for the environment, wildlife and people are now being sold in stores and nurseries. People can now try different methods to see which works best in their landscape. The best approach to a sound, healthy landscape includes purchasing resistant plants, good planting and maintenance practices and environmentally safer pest control. Following are some of the more common, safer, accepted methods of pest control for insects and diseases.

Insects

Remember, many insects in our landscape are friendly and, in fact, help us keep the unwanted ones under control. Therefore, we do not want to kill all insects, just the ones doing damage. Once you have identified the damaging pest, there are several methods of control that can be used.

Sticky Traps - These traps attract insects by color and hold them using a sticky material. Place the traps in strategic spots around your property before insects emerge. Monitor the traps to make sure beneficial insects are not being trapped too. They are successful in catching large numbers of aphids and whiteflies.

Pheromone Traps - They release an odor based on the sex hormones of certain insects. The insects are lured onto a sticky tape or into a bag. Place the trap near the plants you are protecting. These type of traps are also a good method of monitoring the specific pest to check changes in populations and plant health.

Hand picking - An old, safe and effective method of insect control especially with larger insects. It's an easy, immediate way of reducing a pest population. Wear gloves to avoid any reactions to the insects or plants. If any eggs are visible, remove and destroy them too.

Water - Many insects can be taken down with a spray of water. Make sure you hit the undersides of branches and leaves where many insects and their eggs dwell. Spray early in the morning, allowing the plants to dry before midday. Using this method several days in a row may disrupt the insects' breeding cycle.

Safer and Effective Pest Controls
(A reduced or insignificant effect upon humans, wildlife and the environment)

Insecticidal Soap - A product formulated to kill certain pest insects, while not hurting the beneficial ones. This soap breaks down within two weeks, does not harm the environment and is safe around wildlife and people. Many people use their own soap remedies, but a commercial one is recommended for optimum performance. It is easy to use and effective against many pests. Insecticidal soap is a contact product, so it must touch the pest to work.

Horticultural Spray - There are two grades sold, a heavy dormant oil and a light oil. The heavy dormant oil is used on deciduous shrubs and trees during the winter to smother eggs and overwintering adults hidden in the bark and foliage. The light oil is an effective insect control because it can be sprayed on foliage without harm, even in summer. Both oils smother the pests and their eggs. Directions must be followed precisely to avoid plant damage. Both oils are low in toxicity and are not harmful to beneficial insects if used properly.

Bt (*Bacillus Thuringiensis*) - This is a parasitic bacteria that is used mainly against caterpillars, but can control other insects. Different formulations must be used for different pests to be effective. It is easy to use and sold in many nurseries. However, when using Bt, the application timing is very important. To be effective, it must be eaten by the pest, and it breaks down rapidly. Therefore, it is critical to make sure you have identified the pest accurately and find out when the most active period is so you can spray at this time.

Milky Spore Disease (*Bacillus Popilliae*) - A disease of insects that can be used to control pest populations. It is most effective against white grubs, especially Japanese beetle grubs. It acts more slowly than chemical pesticides but remains active in the soil for years.

Botanical Poisons - Although they are natural, these are actual poisons that have been extracted from certain plants. They do kill many insects, including the beneficial ones. Some are so toxic, they are not recommended for vegetable gardens. These should be used only if all else fails, and should be handled very carefully. Two popular products are **Neem** and **Pyrethrum**.

Diseases

Healthy Soil - The environment below the ground is crucial to a plant's health. Take a soil test to determine the pH level and if any major nutrients are lacking. Keep the proper pH level and drainage for the specific plants you have. Make sure they get the correct amount of water, sunlight and fertilizer. This will build the plants' defenses against disease attacks.

Resistant Plants - As mentioned before, prevention is the best method in your defense. Purchase plant varieties that have been bred specifically to be resistant or tolerant to diseases. Resistant plants have the ability to repel specific diseases and tolerant plants will survive even if infected.

Spacing - Disease thrives in areas that are damp and have poor air circulation. The more air circulation, the faster plants will dry from watering. If plants are too close, disease will spread rapidly. Proper spacing allows light and air to reach the plants.

Prevention - Don't wait for something to go wrong. Prevention is a lot cheaper and better than pumping on the chemicals after you have a problem. Monitor your entire landscape at least once every week, and during the summer, maybe twice. Take your journal with you and make notes. Most fungal diseases occur slowly, so if they're caught while in the first stages of development, control will be easier. Inspect your plants for any appearance changes. With experience, you'll learn the difference between insect and disease damage and be able to determine exactly what disease has infected the plants.

Plant Wounds - Shrubs and trees receive wounds from animals, nature and man. If a wound is not treated immediately, the plant becomes vulnerable to insect pests and disease. Broken branches and bark injuries may be treated by wrapping the branch or replacing the bark, adding moist peat moss, and then wrapping the wound with tree tape. Check the injury within two to three weeks.

Fungal Disease - Treatment always depends on the type of disease present. Sometimes, removing the infected leaves or branches is all that is needed. Other situations demand the use of organic fungicides as a control strategy. These are safe to the environment but still should be handled with care. Some of the more popular organic fungicides are: antitranspirants, baking soda, fixed-copper compounds, fungicidal soap, lime sulfur and sulfur. In some cases they are as good or even better than chemical fungicides. Bring a sample of the diseased plant to your local nursery and ask for their recommendations.

Mulch - Fungal spores are generally spread in two ways: in the wind and rain or irrigation bouncing the spores from the soil onto plants. By spreading a mulch around your shrubs and flowers you are creating a barrier against splashing water.

Pruning - Proper pruning of plants is crucial in the fight against disease. Thinning out shrubs allows light to go in and increases air circulation. Immediately remove any diseased leaves or branches, rake up and throw away to prevent spreading of the disease. Also, keep all pruning tools clean and disinfect them with a bleach solution made up of four parts water and one part bleach. Disinfecting pruning tools also helps prevent the spread of bacterial plant diseases.

Cleanup - Always remove and dispose of any infected plant materials. In the fall, give your yard a thorough cleanup. This will help reduce overwintering areas for spores. Clean again in the spring to get any areas you missed. Never compost any infected plant materials.

Our environment depends on us and what we can do to help. It depends on how we waste or conserve water, how we plant and what plants we plant for each particular situation. We must cut down on the use of chemicals and pesticides, work with our environment through Integrated Pest Management, and plan our landscape to better help ourselves and our community. We should learn to plant in specific areas with specific shrubs for energy efficiency, take soil tests every several years, and invite environmentally friendly insects and creatures into our landscape. Read and learn about Bio Friendly landscaping with people, animals and pets and the environment kept in mind. Our attitude must change.

Attracting Bats

Here are a few reasons why homeowners should attract bats to their yards. A single bat eats between 3,000 to 7,000 flying insects in one night. Talk about a voracious appetite! They usually feed at night when mosquitos are very active. Bats do not like to fly into people's hair, are not interested in people and are very shy. They usually will not attack people or other animals, but will bite you if handled. Bats are one of the very best natural means of insect control. If you buy a bat house, place it away from your house in a southwestern exposure to maximise heat from the sun. Paint the house a dark color (black or dark brown) to absorb more heat. The bat house entrance should be 15 feet off the ground.

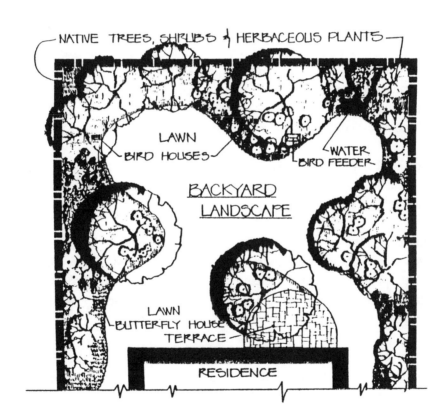

Guidelines for You to Attract Wildlife

Chapter 2

Getting to Know Your Landscape

The Tour

Now it's time to walk outside, with pencil and pad, to find out what you and your family needs from your yard. This will give you a realistic view of what you have to work with. It would be a good idea to take pictures of the landscape. You can refer to them later so you won't have to keep going outside to check on things you may have forgotten to write down. Starting from the front of the house, walk out to the road and give your entire front yard a good, long look. Make an entire page a list of pros and cons, the things you like and the things you dislike about the exterior. On a second page, draw a picture of the house, sidewalks, driveway and fences if any. On a third page, list shrubs, flowers and trees and their names if you know them, and their locations. While you look around, decide if you want minimal barriers between you and your neighbors or if you want privacy reserving most of your yard for personal enjoyment. Ask yourself the following questions. How does the lawn look? Is it well groomed and lush or is it barren and have a lot of weeds? If so, what are the reasons. Is there too much shade, too much sun, not enough water readily available or too many trees whose roots absorb most of the water and nutrition? How does the walk look? Does it need repairing or possibly should have narrow flower beds on both sides for color? Are any shrubs or trees dead and should they be removed or replaced? Make notes about everything.

Now start walking around the rest of the yard evaluating and making notes about any special requirements just as you did in the front. Most family activities are performed in the back yard. Carry a 50 ft. tape measure with you for any measurements needed. Take a look around and decide how much space will be reserved for appearance and which areas will be used for recreation. Would you and your family like: an outdoor cooking facility, a deck or patio, a swimming pool, vegetable garden or perhaps all of the above? Draw the areas and approximate dimensions on page two. What activities do you and your family like? Horseshoes, badminton or perhaps a children's play area. Make notes and sketches to be analyzed later. Do you need areas for work or storage, clothes lines, garbage cans or a shed for tools, equipment or fertilizer? Don't forget a flower bed to help beautify the back yard. Most important of all, allow an area for relaxation in a shady or quiet spot or perhaps a hammock under your favorite trees. After all, with all of this hard work you'll need a place to read, nap or just relax.

A successful landscape design depends on how you modify, enhance and protect your property's good points. A successful, functional landscape depends on how well you understand your land's characteristics. It should look good twelve months of the year, not just a few. Knowing where the sun or shade is at different times of the day helps you plan where to put certain plants and which areas are good for activities. Level areas of land have less wind protection so trees, large shrubs or structures may be needed to help control the climate.

One last thing, identify all of the existing plants and note if they add or detract from the landscape. Some plants are an asset and others are a liability. Mark down all locations of utilities (sewer, telephone, electric, air conditioner), all faucets and meters and where you may want new bibs. Take a final walk around your property, take more notes and make a final inventory of all present plants. Again, write down all the good things about your property. Make specific notes about anything unpleasant and what should be done about it. You may have missed some things on your first tour.

The Plan

Any landscape can be transformed into the garden of your dreams with careful planning, lots of love and hard work. How much money is spent depends on how you would like it to eventually look. The average suburban home has room for gardening flowers, fruit, vegetables and of course a lawn. With careful planning its possible to make space for most outdoor activities, add property value and provide beauty for the family to enjoy.

A good garden design must account for everyone who lives in the home. If you involve people while drawing up the plans and respect their opinions, you may get help during the actual construction. If you have small children, many areas may have to be childproofed for safety. By following a few low maintenance practices, any landscape can be turned into a beautiful attraction. By reading books, talking to neighbors, family and friends and visiting your local nursery, you will find there are hundreds of annuals, bulbs, trees and shrubs that need little attention and will bring beautiful color into any landscape. In this chapter, I will be sharing with you some of the principles of landscape design which will help you complete a basic plan.

Whether you are designing a new landscape or renovating an old one, an opportunity arises to be creative. One of the first steps in developing a plan is to make a recording of all the conditions of the land. Before you can have a clear view of what your landscape needs, you should get to know all of it's characteristics. The size of your house, size of the property, the amount of sun and shade and type of soil are all factors which can help you decide what you can or cannot do. Also, the design should be for all of the people who live there, and be useful and beautiful. One of the key items in making a landscape successful is to accentuate it's positive points. A limited budget should not influence you from making a good landscape plan. Most of the development and planting can be done by the owner and family and can be done in phases budgeted over several years. A comfortable and beautiful landscape becomes an expression of your personality.

Once you have logged all the good and bad features and listed and located all the main plants, you are ready to go inside to make your comprehensive plan. The dinning room table can be used for many things such as eating, family discussions, games, arts and crafts and of course drawing your landscape plan. Any corrections can be made on paper with an eraser rather than extensive time and dollars if you had to correct mistakes you actually made in your yard. Before we start the actual plan we must take some more notes. Another vantage point for planning is from inside the house. Take a look outside from windows on all sides of the house. We all spend a lot of time in our homes and taking a moment to

look outside at a beautiful flower garden or attractive serene lawn can refresh our spirits during a busy day. Make notes about what you like and don't like about the view from each window and what you would like to see.

Now that you have toured your property from inside and out, made lists of everything, it's time to put all of this thinking and sketching into a plan. A landscape plan can mean anything from a rough sketch to a full blown architectural drawing done to scale. First you must choose which type of landscape you want, formal or informal. A formal landscape is one that is symmetrical and has almost perfect balance to it. Fountains, sculptures, sheared perfect hedges, balanced shrubs or trees on both sides of a structure and centered entryways are all signs of a formal landscape. Informal landscapes often include curves, random plantings, lower maintenance areas and irregular terrain. Whichever style you choose basic landscaping has four principles: balance, proportion, unity and variety.

Balance

To use color or shape to create equal appearance on both sides of an object. It may mean creating an identical image on both sides in a formal design or a more subtle balance such as a group of small shrubs on the left and a larger shrub on the right in an informal design.

Proportion

When choosing shrubs and trees try to keep the sizes and shapes in scale with one another. Be especially careful with trees as they may become overwhelming when they mature.

Unity

In a unified landscape, no one element stands out among the rest. All plants and structures work together as one piece rather than scattered all about. Design a uniformed background first, such as a lawn or flower garden, and use this background as a neutral element around which you'll plant your units to give variety, balance and proportion.

Variety

Ah yes, the spice of life! It also applies in landscaping. Don't be monotonous. Select plants in a variety of shapes, sizes, colors and textures. Annuals, perennials, wildflowers, bulbs, flowering trees and shrubs all create beautiful settings. Just make sure you pick the ones that are compatible with your soil and light conditions.

Using these guidelines should help you decide which landscape will be serviceable and enjoyable for many years to come. Buy several sheets of large white posterboard from your local stationery store, have a good ruler and some different colored pencils (preferably brown, red, green, yellow and orange) for sketching lawn areas, flower beds, shrubs and trees. Make a basic drawing of your property showing all the boundaries, building, walkways, trees, driveway and any features you feel won't change. This is the site plan. Draw this as if you were in an airplane looking down. Mark places where hose bibs are and where you may want to put more. Note any trees and shrubs you want to remove, add new shrubs and trees, vegetable gardens, fences, mulch, rock gardens etc. and mark them in their respective areas. On the analysis sheet, record conditions for all the good and bad elements that affect the entire lot, such as shade and sun areas, low level areas (possible drainage problems), slopes and poor spots in the lawn surface. Combine all of your previous notes from the tours and last two drawings onto one sheet as your final plan. Mark everything as accurate as possible, label all structures, areas and plants. Make this final plan neat and understandable. If you find it is too complicated or cluttered, you may want to have it made by a landscaping architect. An effective landscape design is not as easy as it looks.

This is a good time to develop a maintenance program. Time and money will be saved with a preventative program rather than spent on unforeseeable repairs. As your landscape changes and matures, so do you and your family. Proper planning for the future should help your landscape and family adapt together gracefully. The fun of designing is to be able to find spaces for the activities important to you. The entire plan comes down to three major items: make a list of all elements that will not change, draw a plan of the present landscape as many of these resources will go into your final plan, make any changes and decide how much space is needed for family activities.

Here are a few things to keep in mind before you start to do the actual work.

- There is enough water and outlets available.
- There is enough sun or shade for certain plants in specific areas.
- You account for any pet usage.
- You foresee how the landscape will look in 5 - 10 years.
- You provide for any heavy footwork to certain areas.
- You provide for lighting and security.
- You checked the plan for balance, proportion, unity and variety.

Soil Conditions

All landscapers and gardeners must first learn about their surroundings. This includes getting to know your particular environment and soil. As you become familiar with these two important conditions, they will guide you in planting the right grass seed, trees, shrubs, flowers, ground covers and vegetables. No matter what location or size, all landscapes have certain basic requirements for plants to survive. As all plants are different, all variables are different too. If you are serious about landscaping or gardening, in this book they will be used interchangeably, then you must learn about soil.

Soil is made up of silt, sand, clay and organic matter. The organics are actually decayed plant material collected near the soil's surface. Minerals are the remains of rocks exposed to the environments elements for hundreds of years. Ideal soil is fertile, high in organic matter and well drained. Pick up a handful of your soil and squeeze it. If it stays in a tight sticky mass it is probably high in clay content. If it crumbles loose and doesn't hold any shape it has a high sand content and won't hold moisture. The proper texture of soil will mold in your hand but crumble when squeezed tightly. Soil plays an important role in all plants growth as it feeds and waters their roots.

Clay soils are hard to work with because they stay wet and are heavy. Sandy soils are light and easy to work with but water and nutrients pass through too quickly. The texture of the soil influences the type of plants you can use in your landscape. Soil drainage is very important as plant roots need air and water. If the soil holds too much water and does not drain your plants will suffer. The best way to check your soil's fertility and pH is to do a soil test. You can either buy a soil test kit and do it yourself, have a professional landscaper do the test or collect several samples, in separate jars, of various locations on your property and bring them to your agricultural agency. This way you can find out the nutrient level of the soil. When you find out the results, you can make changes if necessary. Your county agricultural agency will be able to make recommendations to help you bring your soil nutrients to acceptable levels.

How to Take a Soil Sample

Begin sampling by making a vertical cut to a depth of 6 to 8 inches with a spade or trowel.

Make a second cut at a 45° angle to the first, removing the wedge-shaped section and setting it aside.

Make another vertical cut 1/2 inch from the first cut and as deep.

Place this slice in a clean container, mix the soil and remove any plant material and stones. Take soil from different locations and put in separate containers.

To measure soil fertility accurately, however, you must prepare samples from more than one spot within the area of concern. Separate samples will allow proper recommendations for each site. On the average, most plants thrive when the soil pH is between 6 to 7. If you find the pH is lower, the soil is too acid and lime should be added to help neutralize it. A soil test is the only way of indicating lime requirements and also gives information necessary for adjusting the proportions of nitrogen, phosphorus and potash. The test can indicate how much fertilizer is needed or when enough has already been applied. Too much fertilizer can cause more damage than not enough. Proper organic matter levels are necessary in maintaining a good physical condition of the soil. Whatever landscaping you intend to do, proper preparation is important for good growth.

Learning About Soil

A balanced fertilization program is one of the most important cultural practices for improving the health and appearance of landscape trees, ornamentals and lawns. Insect, disease and physical stress may be the symptoms of bigger problems beneath the soil. Many landscape areas have poor soil that cannot maintain good, healthy growth. Such problems can be pH related, macro or micronutrient deficiencies, low organic matter or the result of toxins in the soil. The list is growing longer as we learn more about the nutrient requirements of a healthy plant.

In the forest, the recycling of nutrients occurs naturally when leaves and other organic materials decompose. Problems occur on landscapes where the natural cycle is disrupted. Most trees and shrubs in a landscape have to compete for nutrients with grasses and other ground covers. Without new organic matter being introduced, the soil is soon depleted. With a balanced fertilizer program, one can only improve the health and appearance of these plants, but also reduce the amount of damage caused by pests and physical stress. This will save time, money and the environment by reducing pesticide usage, tree and shrub removal and replacement. A comprehensive tree, shrub and grass fertilization program should include both a spring and fall application program. It is recommended that a lower nitrogen analysis, higher phosphorous and potassium is used during the fall. This helps the plants prepare for winter stress and improves root and carbohydrate reserves for the winter.

Social practices have disrupted or stressed natures natural cycle, either in environmentally sensitive areas or where social demands (the best lawn on the block) have created an imbalance. We must go beyond the typical N-P-K fertilizers by supplying carbon rich organic materials in a constructive and usable form for soil, plant and microorganisms. Sandy soil is difficult to maintain because of a lack of organic matter and the inability of the sand to hold nutrients long enough for plant uptake. Clay soil will often lead to nutrient and compaction problems because of a lack of organic matter. Fertilizer will not correct this problem and will often lead to the buildup of salts. However, high concentrates of organic matter and natural wetting agents can penetrate the encrusted soil and begin restoration. Established trees and ornamentals in urban settings are often deprived of renewable organic matter during the course of grooming. Transplants need additional care to establish good root development and aid in the uptake of usable nutrients, sugars for metabolism of enzymes and the storage of carbohydrates. In newly excavated areas where topsoil has not been properly added into the area, conditions often lead to future compaction problems, lack of microbial activity and result in plant stress and death.

Carbon is the basic chemical element of all living things and a requirement for all plant and animal life. In the soil, it must exist in the proper ratio with nitrogen to optimize soil functions and promote fertility. If there is too much carbon in the soil as organic matter, soil bacteria will tie up the nitrogen and try to break it down, and the plants growing in that soil will exhibit poor growth and color. If nitrogen is too high, the soil microbes will be overactive, depleting what carbon does exist and causing lush growth and poor soil conditions over time. Although we don't usually speak in terms of fertilizing with **carbon**, that's exactly what we do when we apply natural organic matter along with other plant food nutrients. Nitrogen may be the plant's primary concern, but if we look at a fertilizer from the soil's point of view, carbon is the vital ingredient. The relationship between these two is technically known as **The Carbon:Nitrogen** (or C:N) **Ratio,** and agronomists strive for the right balance to achieve optimum growing conditions. Too much carbon can reduce available nitrogen for the plant, while too much nitrogen can deplete soil carbon.

Soil is a complex, living environment. It is full of microscopic bacteria, fungi and other organisms as well as the earthworms that are the visible representatives of bioactivity. **Humate** is a natural organic ore that is derived over centuries from plant origin and bacterial action. Humate has the natural ability to make all plant and soil processes happen more efficiently. Humate enriches the organic content of the fertilizer and the soil. It builds "**Humus**", the organic part of the soil, which is composed of living and once living things. Humus provides water holding capacity, increases fertilizer utilization and improves bacterial action. It also forms the physical structure of the soil and helps to maintain soil temperature.

Humate contributes to a desirable balance of all available trace elements, which are found in humate, seaweed extract, and in the soil itself. These trace elements include manganese, boron, molybdenum, zinc and copper. Like seaweed extract, humate has the ability to chelate (make available to plants) controlled quantities of nutrients which are normally inert and unavailable to plants. Seaweed extract is a source of micronutrients such as iron, copper and zinc. It also contains natural chelating compounds that change other micronutrients found in the soil and fertilizer into a useable form so that the plant roots can absorb them easily.

Organic matter is like a battery of stored energy that was organically derived from the sun through photosynthesis. Soil microbes use up this energy to perform their decomposition activities, so you need to periodically recharge the soil with new supplies of organic matter. Sustained by organic matter, the organisms can continue to do their jobs of maintaining soil moisture, holding nutrients and minerals within the root zone, aerating the soil, and processing fertilizer nutrients into highly available forms. Without new supplies of organic matter (carbon), the soil organisms will eventually die of starvation. When carbon is used up, decomposition will stop. Nitrogen speeds the rate of decomposition, so if carbon is low, and inorganic nitrogen is applied, this imbalanced ratio leads to higher rates of serious problems such as: thatch, disease and pest infestations, soil compaction, low moisture holding capacity and wasteful leaching of nitrogen. Unfortunately, too often the response to these problems is chemical applications that provide only a short-term fix. A soil-based strategy is a more efficient, long-term approach. Yes, nitrogen is nitrogen, but applying inorganic nitrogen without the carbon will eventually cause more problems than benefits. Application of organic based materials provides both nitrogen and carbon for the most sensible and efficient fertilizer approach.

There are many types of slow-release fertilizers on the market today. And while all organic fertilizers are naturally slow-release, all slow-release fertilizers are not organic. Other types range from synthetic nitrogen that is chemically designed to break down slowly to quick-release forms of nitrogen that are merely coated with a hard shell. If the slow release of nitrogen is a requirement of your fertilizer application, a true high carbon organic product adds the dimension of providing energy and food for the soil along with a slow-release nutrient source. Synthetic sources of slow-release nitrogen only provide the single dimension of a slow-release nutrient.

By adding organic matter back into soils that have been depleted, even the most difficult soil conditions can be improved. Humus matter and cellulose fiber help break up soil compaction and recondition soils by improving soil aeration. Natural wetting agents improve water absorption and retention. Several companies, listed in the back, have responded to our environmental problems by making products that help us manage our soil's organic matter. These products may be liquid fertilizers, organic matters that rejuvenate the soil structure, soil amendments that add beneficial soil microorganisms, root and plant growth stimulants, plant growth supplements, thatch management products and slow release fertilizer/soil builders.

There is a very simple gardening **Golden Rule**: the better the condition of your soil, the better garden you will have. Providing an optimum environment for plant growth should be the first objective of any landscape project. Healthy and vigorous plants are the best defense against attack or invasion by various pests. A healthy landscape is likely to recuperate readily from modest insect or disease attacks without the use of pesticides. Reaching for more fertilizer and more pesticides is not the best answer. Consider adding an organic matter, such as compost, to either a sandy soil or a heavier clay soil. This improves water and nutrient retention in a sandy soil, and improves drainage and aeration characteristics in a heavier clay soil. Thoroughly mixing the organic matter into the soil will improve and enlarge the root-zone system. An extensive root system occupying larger soil volumes provides the plant greater capability to withstand adverse environmental conditions and plant stresses.

Compost - or is it Black Gold??

Compost is decomposed plant material mixed with soil. Some gardeners may consider compost a form of fertilizer, but its most important function is to increase the organic matter content of vegetable or flower soil. Adding compost to the garden soil improves the soil structure by making it more granular. Building up organic matter in a soil increases both its water-holding capacity and its productive ability. Plants growing in such soil can better withstand drought conditions. Vegetables, flowers, lawns, and small fruits all grow best in soils that have a high organic content. Although good yields are possible by adding to the soil only mineral fertilizers, or only organic materials, best results can be obtained by using both. Garden crops receive the benefits of humus from the organic matter, and higher mineral nutrients from the commercial fertilizer. The humus helps hold needed nutrients in the soil so plants can utilize them readily. Perhaps the best way to dispose of yard and garden wastes is by composting, either on a large scale by municipalities or by individuals in backyards. Composting is an easy, inexpensive procedure yielding valuable humus that can be returned to garden soil, or used as mulch around landscape plantings.

Materials For Making A Compost Pile

For decomposition of the plant material in a compost pile to occur, nitrogen, water, oxygen, and soil must be present. The microorganisms in the soil decompose the plant material, which is mostly carbon, by the process of oxidation. As the microbes utilize the carbon, two-thirds of it is converted into carbon dioxide that is released into the atmosphere, while one-third passes into microbe cells, and thus stays within the pile. Loss of carbon from a compost pile is evidenced both by the generated heat and the reduction of the pile's weight and volume as decomposition proceeds.

Nitrogen (also found in raw organic materials) is used by the microbes for protein synthesis. In the composting process, the ratio of carbon (C) to nitrogen (N) in the plant materials is important. Adequate nitrogen must be available for the microbes so they can rapidly increase their numbers, and thus speed the decomposition process. Soil commonly contains a carbon-to-nitrogen (C:N) ratio of 10 to 1. When there is insufficient nitrogen, the microbe population cannot grow, and decomposition slows. When there is too much nitrogen, the excess is lost by runoff or by leaching. Since most individual materials available for composting do not fit an ideal ratio, a variety of materials should be mixed when adding to the compost pile. Fresh lawn clippings (not treated with pesticides), weeds and alfalfa possess high levels of nitrogen (low C:N). Leaves, shredded paper, hedge clippings, cornstalks, crushed corncobs, and sawdust are all good sources of carbon for a compost pile (high C:N). Food scraps from the kitchen, such as banana peels and apple cores, may attract flies, so they should be covered up with other plant materials, such as leaves or grass clippings. Animal fats, bones and other household garbage are inappropriate in the compost pile as they do not compost easily, and may attract dogs and other animals. Neither should diseased plant material (leaves, branches) be put in the compost.

Making The Compost Pile

There are many different ways a compost pile can be constructed. A 30-foot section of snow fence makes a nice, economical enclosure for a compost pile 10 feet long and 5 feet wide. Three-bin turning units made of concrete or treated lumber make turning compost easy, and produce a usable product in a relatively short time (see following instructions). A pit 2 1/2 feet deep is another type of compost-holding unit. It is easy to conceal, and will keep plant material moist for rapid decomposition.

Modern technology has also come up with several other types of mobile composters, two of them being a rotating composter and a rolling composter. A rotating composter is composed of a rotating drum (with holes in it), a handle for turning and a door opening for depositing the materials. New debris

is added to and mixed, by a turn of the handle, with material that has begun to decompose. A rolling composter is even easier to operate. It is shaped like a sphere, has holes for breathing, and a lid opening to deposit the materials. The pile is turned simply by rolling the sphere. When the compost is ready, just roll it to the desired location and dump it out. Either of these composters can be purchased from several mail order companies and can cost between $80 to $300.

Locate the compost pile in an out-of-the-way area that can be screened from view, yet is accessible to water. Flowering vines or tall annuals grown around the compost bin will easily conceal it. A partial shade location is desirable. Full sun may cause excessive drying. Full shade will retard such drying out, but will lower pile temperatures, resulting in a slower spring and fall decomposition. There are no special procedures in preparing compost. With a little experience, each person will develop or adapt measures that meet his/her needs. Best results can be obtained by "stockpiling" materials until there is enough to build a pile that is at least 3 feet by 3 feet square, and 3 feet high, but no larger than 5 feet by 5 feet square, and 5 feet high. A mixture of various yard wastes will promote rapid and uniform decomposition. Since smaller particles decompose more rapidly, it is advantageous to chop or shred hedge prunings, cornstalks, and other coarse materials before adding them to the compost pile.

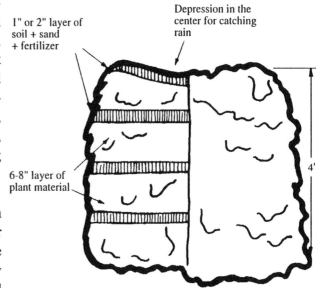

1" or 2" layer of soil + sand + fertilizer

Depression in the center for catching rain

6-8" layer of plant material

4'

Cross section of a compost pile

Build the pile up in layers. Start with a 6 to 8 inch layer of plant material topped with a 1 to 2 inch layer of garden loam. A topdressing of fertilizer should be added to each layer to provide the nitrogen needed by the microbes. A 10-6-4 or 12-12-12 fertilizer should do the trick. Continue these layers until the pile is 3 to 5 feet high. Because of the remarkable ability of soil and humus to absorb odors, no unpleasant odor will come from a compost pile that is well-aerated and contains within it layers of soil. An important exception is: a large quantity of fresh lawn clippings in the pile will pack together and prevent good air movement through the pile. The resulting lack of oxygen will allow development of offensive odors, as well as slowing down decomposition. For efficient and uniform composting, lawn clippings should be mixed with other organic materials. Adding lime to the compost pile is often recommended because some compost becomes acid. However, I believe agricultural lime should be added only if a soil test shows the finished product to be acid.

A moisture content of 40 to 60 percent promotes multiplication of beneficial microbes in the compost pile. To supply this moisture, each layer of plant debris, soil, and fertilizer should be soaked with water, though too much will cause the leaching out of the soluble fertilizer salts. The composting material should feel like a damp sponge. A drop or two of water should drip out when tightly squeezed. The pile should be supplied with moisture during the entire composting process to ensure rapid and complete decomposition. Heat is generated during the composting process, the pile often reaching 150° to 170° F, temperatures high enough for the destruction of some weed seeds and plant diseases. If the pile is not

kept moist enough, the materials may get **too** hot. The resulting product will have a **burned appearance**, be light in weight and have no value as compost. To ensure uniform, rapid decomposition, the pile must be turned regularly to provide the needed aeration (oxygen). The more frequently the pile is turned, the more rapidly the heat will build. The pile should be turned by bringing the inside material to the outside.

Hastening Decomposition

The decomposition rate depends upon several factors: type of materials used, size of particles, and amounts of moisture and oxygen present. Some techniques that can be used to speed decomposition of the plant material by the microbes are:

- Chop or shred the materials to be composted.
- Add a high-nitrogen, complete analysis fertilizer to the pile.
- Turn the compost once a week during the season, adding some water each time.
- Incorporate barnyard manure into the pile.

Each technique will hasten decomposition, but best results can be obtained by using all. A well-managed compost pile containing shredded material that is turned and watered regularly will be ready in about 2 to 4 months. When finished, the compost will be dark brown and have an earthy odor. You will not be able to distinguish individual organic components that went into the pile. A pile or bin containing unshredded materials and left unattended may take a year or longer to decompose. Piles prepared in late fall will not be decomposed by spring. Lawn clippings that have been treated with herbicides should not be collected and put into the compost, until three or four mowings after the herbicide was applied.

Leaf Composting

Many homeowners have an excessive quantity of leaves in the fall. One alternative for dealing with leaves is backyard composting. This process involves primarily the microbial decomposition of organic matter. Leaves may be composted by piling them in a heap. Locate the pile where drainage is adequate and there is no standing water. The leaf pile should be at least 4 feet in diameter and 3 feet in height. If it is too small, it is difficult to maintain adequate temperatures for rapid decomposition. If the pile is too large, the interior will not obtain the oxygen needed for adequate, odor-free decomposition. If there is sufficient space and material, two or three piles will provide greater flexibility. One pile can contain compost for immediate use, the second is actively composting, and the third receives newly fallen leaves. If there is space for only one pile, new material may be added gradually to the top while removing the decomposed product from the bottom. Composting may be done in a loose pile. However, for the most efficient use of space, it can be contained in a bin or other enclosure. The sides of this bin should be loose enough to permit air movement. One side should be open, or easily opened, for turning the pile and for removing the finished compost.

Many instruction sheets advocate constructing the pile in layers that may include grass clippings, fertilizer, limestone, manure, soil, and leaves. With leaf composting, the pile can be constructed of leaves only. Unless leaves are collected in a very wet condition, add water while placing them in a pile. Without moisture, the microorganisms will not function. Moisten to the point where it is possible to squeeze droplets of water from a hand-held mass of leaves. Dead leaves lack adequate nitrogen for rapid decomposition. Therefore, a high-nitrogen fertilizer added to the pile may speed up decomposition. However, since leaves fall only for about 2 months a year, there are 10 months for decomposition before space is needed for the next batch. So, while it is generally unnecessary to add fertilizer, for more rapid decomposition and a product with a higher nutritive content, about 1/2 cup of 10% nitrogen fertilizer per 20 gallon can of hand-compacted leaves could be added. Fresh manure could be substituted, but it may cause odor problems.

Ordinarily it is unnecessary to add ground limestone because the pile seldom becomes too acidic. If fertilizer has been added, an equivalent quantity of limestone will counteract any acidity. Little or no limestone should be added if the compost is to be used on acid-loving plants. Some guides on leaf composting recommend adding layers of soil periodically to the piles to supply the microorganisms needed for decomposition. I have not found this practice to be necessary, because leaves, themselves, contain a multitude of microorganisms. Avoid packing the materials too tightly. Too much compaction will limit movement of air through the pile. Shredding the leaves generally speeds up composting. The composting pile must be kept moist, but not soggy, for proper decomposition. The pile should be periodically turned or mixed. The main objectives of turning are to shift materials from the outer parts of the pile closer to the center for better decomposition, and to incorporate oxygen. During warm weather, turn the pile once a month. In cool weather frequent turning is not recommended because it allows too much heat to escape. Piles should be turned immediately if ammonia or other offensive odors are detected. If space is available, turning may be accomplished by shifting the entire pile to an adjacent area or bin.

Within a few weeks after starting, the pile should be hot in the center. Heating generally indicates that the pile is decomposing properly. Failure to heat may be caused by too little or too much water, improper aeration, packing too tightly, or a pile that is too small. As leaves decompose, they should shrink to less than one-half of their original volume. During dry weather it may be necessary to add more water. The moisture content of the interior of the pile should be observed while turning. Finished compost should be dark and crumbly with much of the original appearance no longer visible. It should have an earthy odor. Normally, leaf compost will be ready in 6-9 months. Before using compost, "screening" may be necessary to remove the larger partially decomposed materials. These materials will sometimes be present in composting piles because not all items decompose at the same rate. The undecomposed organic matter clumps may be broken up and added to another active compost pile for additional decomposition.

The major horticultural use for leaf compost is to improve the organic content of soil. Most New Jersey soils need an increase of 1/2 to 1% in organic content, particularly to improve moisture-holding capacity and tillage, making the soils easier to cultivate. Sandy soils, such as loamy sands and sands, and soils with a very high clay content are improved the most by an increase in organic matter content. Leaf compost is not normally a fertilizer, because it is too low in nutrients. Compost serves primarily as an organic amendment and as a soil conditioner. Soil mulch is another valuable use for leaf compost.

Drought damage to plants is reduced because of an increased water-holding capacity of the soils. The added organic matter provides a food source for desirable soil micro-organisms. Leaf compost can also be used as an organic mulch on the surface of soil in place of peatmoss, straw, etc. It can help make more water available for plant growth and decrease water evaporation losses from the soil. Leaf compost keeps the soil cooler in hot weather and warmer in cold weather, controls weeds, makes the soil easier to cultivate, and increases biological activity of earthworms and other soil organisms. It may also be used in potting soil. However, no more than 25 to 30% of the potting soil should be leaf compost as it frequently continues to decompose. Following are instructions for construction of a stationary 3-bin compost turning unit. It can be be made into a 2-bin or 4-bin unit depending on your preferences.

Construction of Stationary 3-Bin Compost Turning Unit

Materials:

(4) 12' treated 2 x 4s
(4) 10' treated 2 x 4s
(1) 12' or (2) 6' 2 x 6s
(9) 6' cedar 1 x 6s
(22') of 36" wide 1/4" hardware cloth
(12) 1/2" X 4" carriage bolts
(3 lbs) 16d galvanized nails
    or (3 ls) 3" galvanized deck screws
(1/2 lb) 8d galvanized casement nails
    or (1/2 lb) 2" galvanized deck screws
(250) poultry wire staples
    or power stapler with 1" staples

Tools:

hand saw or circular power saw
drill with 1/2" and 1/8" bits
screwdriver
hammer
tin snips
tape measure
pencil
3/4" socket or open-ended wrench
carpenter's square
safety glasses
ear protection

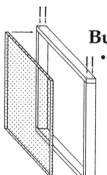

Build Dividers:

• Cut each 12' 2x4 into (2) 36" pieces and (2) 33" pieces.
• Screw or nail (2) 36" pieces and (2) 33" pieces into a 36" square.
• Repeat for other 3 dividers.
• Cut (4) 36" long sections of hardware cloth.

• Bend back edges 1-1/2".
• Stretch hardware cloth inside each frame.
• Check for squareness and staple screen every 4" around the edges.

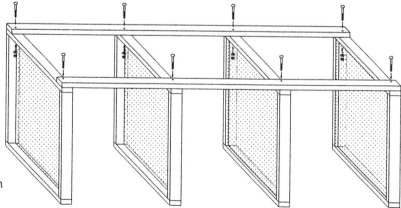

Assemble Frame, part 1:

• Cut the (4) 10' 2x4s to 111-1/2" lengths.
• Position (2) 111-1/2" 2x4s on top of the dividers.
• Drill 1/2" holes 1" from inside edge of 111-1/2" 2x4s, 1-3/4" and 37-3/4" from both ends, through centerline of dividers.
• Secure with carriage bolts, washers, and nuts, but do not tighten.

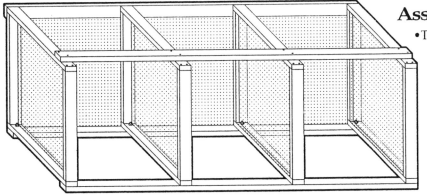

Assemble Frame, part 2:

- Turn unit and use the same process to install the top back 111-1/2" 2x4.
- Install the top front 111 1/2" 2x4 so that the front edge is 2 1/2" back from the front edge of dividers.
- Using a carpenter's square or measuring between opposite corners (equal diagonals mean the box is square), make sure bin is square and tighten all bolts securely.
- Fasten a 9' long piece of hardware cloth securely to back of frame with staples every 4".

Install Runners for Cedar Slats:

- Cut (4) 36" long pieces of 2x6s for front slat runners.
- Rip cut (2) of these to 4-1/2" wide and nail or screw securely to front of outside dividers, flush with top and outside edges (save remainder of rip cuts for use as back slat runners.)
- Center the remaining full-width boards on the front of the inside dividers, flush with top edge and fasten with nails or screws.
- Cut (1) 36" long piece of 2x6 for back slat runners, and rip into (4) 1" pieces.
- Attach back slat runners on sides of dividers parallel to front runners leaving a 1" gap for slats.
- Cut all 1x6 cedar into slats 32" long.

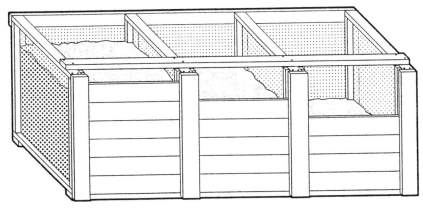

Shade, Algae & Moss

There are many areas of shade around our homes in which we have trouble growing a variety of plants. There are different types of shade. Day-long shade is usually along the north side of a house or near a wall. Half-shade are areas that usually have full sun half of the day and shade during the rest. Finally we have light-shade which is usually around trees. Most plants need some amount of light. While planning your landscape make sure you take into account shaded areas as this will determine what plants or grass seed you can buy. A shady landscape has always been challenging but there are many local plants that will grow happily. In shade there is a lot of competition with trees for nutrients, light and water, so it may take awhile to see the effects of your labor. The right plants can co-exist with trees in the shade if you follow the right management practices. Shaded areas stay wet longer so you must water carefully. Allow the area to dry completely before the next watering. Water shaded areas deeply as tree roots will absorb most of the water. When the summer is extremely hot, shade may be an asset to the landscape. One of the most common indications of too much shade is a green moss growing in the lawn.

At times, lawns become infested with two weedy type plants that are different from all the others. Algae and moss can disrupt the aesthetic appearance and functional value of a lawn, even though they seldom compete with the turf or crowd it out. Both are more inclined to occupy space where, for one reason or another, lawngrasses fail to grow well. Often wet soggy soils are conducive to occupancy by both of these weeds. Other environmental conditions are also responsible for the presence of these undesirable threadlike plants.

Algae are single-celled plants that form a dense green to blackish-green crust on wet soil surfaces. This crust reduces air and water movement into the soil and prevents lawngrasses from spreading readily back into infested areas. As turf thins out from any cause, and light reaches down to the soil surface, algae may start to develop. **Mosses** are small, primitive, branched plants that produce a thick, green growth over either wet or dry soil surfaces. They have shallow roots and are easily raked out of infested areas. Soil compaction, inadequate amounts of fertilizer nutrients in the soil, acid soil conditions, lack of adequate light for turfgrasses, poor surface soil drainage, poor internal soil drainage, and too much or too little irrigation can all cause areas to be weakened and these two weedy plants develop. Moss and algae do not kill grass; they simply fill in the open spaces as the grass dies out. Some of the conditions associated with moss and algae, and their correction, are as follows:

Excessive shade: In general, moss and algae are more tolerant of shade than are higher forms of plant life, and this in part accounts for their ability to invade lawns and replace grass in shady spots. Although moss can be found in full sun, if your moss is confined to shady spots, planting shade-tolerant grasses may help. In truly heavy shade, you might consider thinning or removing some trees, or planting a shade-tolerant ground cover such as pachysandra or myrtle.

Soil compaction: This is often the culprit because grass roots have difficulty penetrating compacted soil. Deep compaction of heavy soils may require complete reconstruction of the lawn. However, soil aeration can be improved by annual use of a core aerator. You can rent them or hire a lawn service. Get the aerator which actually removes cores of soil and deposits them on the surface.

Low pH: Acid soil is sometimes but not always a factor. Take a soil test or have one done by your local Cooperative Extension office. Most lawn grasses grow best at a pH between 6.0 and 6.5. If your soil is acid, the grass will thin out and allow moss to move in.

Low soil fertility: The soil test will also test for major soil nutrients. Our soil is often low in potassium, which is necessary for good root systems. The application of nitrogen at proper times can also encourage grasses to grow well.

Improper watering: Most lawn grasses need 1 to 1-1/2 inches total water per week. If there is no rain, apply 1/2 inch every four days.

Where algae and moss have become a problem, rake them out, correct conditions that caused the weakened turf, and then reseed with recommended lawn grasses. Because mechanical removal is so easy and effective, chemicals are seldom necessary. However, if large areas are becoming infested, you can buy products which will kill moss and algae. A product called DeMoss is available in a formulation for lawns, as well as in a formulation for general use. However, the moss and algae may return if the underlying conditions are not corrected. When using chemicals, **read all labels and follow directions precisely**. Certain plant species are sensitive to applications of DeMoss. Avoid spraying uninfested grass or adjacent vegetation. Also, treated surfaces may become temporarily slippery, so traffic should be restricted until the sprays have dried.

Landscape Fabric

Tired off the war on weeds? Try using landscape fabrics to protect your investment. In the past, black plastic was used by almost everyone to keep weeds down. However, black plastic keeps water and air away from the plant roots, unless you poke thousands of holes in it. Then what happens? It breaks apart too easily. Landscape fabric to the rescue! Landscape fabric blocks weeds and, at the same time,

allows water, air and natural nutrients to find their way to your plants' and shrubs' roots. Plastic won't let water, air and fertilizer pass through the surface except at stem openings. This can make the soil moldy and plants lose vital stimulation for growth.

Landscape fabrics keep sunlight from penetrating the ground, so weeds can't grow. It gives the necessary sun blockage so that weeds cannot make food for their own use (photosynthesis). The fabric lasts for years to make your landscape look professionally manicured with minimal effort. They resist tearing, puncturing and rotting, and installation couldn't be any easier. Landscape fabric can be used anywhere to prevent weeds from growing. Use it under decks, near poolsides, behind retaining walls, as well as under patios and sidewalks. It can also be an effective way to prevent soil erosion and protect drains from clogging. Landscape fabric is a cost-effective way to control unwanted weeds and grasses.

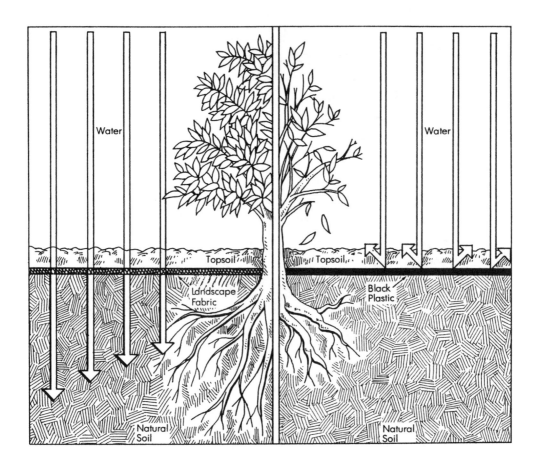

The basic procedure for installing landscape fabric is to:

1. Clear the proposed area of all weeds and grasses.
2. Unroll the fabric over the plant bed area.
3. If placed over existing plants, cut an "X" over each plant, slip plants through the opening and push the fabric under the plant base.
4. Fold any excess fabric under.
5. Cover with a minimum of two inches of mulch. Certain mulches break down and should be replenished periodically. Landscape fabric may deteriorate after prolonged exposure to direct sunlight.

Fabrics do have their drawbacks, though. Shrub and tree root surfacing and rooting into the fabric can occur depending on the species in question and the fabric used. In some situations vole problems in the site can increase due to favorable habitats formed by the landscape fabric. I would never use fabric when planting a flower garden. Can you imagine cutting or poking hundreds of small holes to plant your flower seeds or small plants? It would be more practical to plant more flowers to choke out any weeds. Landscape fabrics are usually easy to cut with a pair of scissors, won't unravel and should last for several years. If you want to create a weed free landscape around shrubs and trees, without the use of pesticides or spending hours pulling weeds, installing landscape fabric is a practical alternative.

Tools Of The Trade

Working in your landscape can be a difficult chore if you don't have the right tools for the job. If you are a long time gardener, you probably have many tools collected over the years, but if you're a beginner, you may have only a few. You'll find that as you're interest in gardening increases, your tool collection will also increase. Gardening tools can be considered anything that makes cultivation easier. Many years ago, people had a variety of hand tools that were used for small and large jobs. There were some large machines available, but they had to be pushed and pulled and by the end of the day, people were exhausted. Gardeners today have a choice of thousands of tools and aids to make life easier in the landscape. From small hand tools to large machines, many of them are power driven and take half the time to complete the task. In many cases, old standbys have just been improved.

A beautiful landscape is the result of dedicated hard work. And this hard work can be transformed into beauty and pleasure if the right tools are used. Every landscaper and gardener will agree that **you must use the right tools for the right job.** If you feel comfortable doing the work, you will get more pleasure from doing it. Listed are tool tips, gardening tools and functions.

Tips

- Purchase tools that fit the size of your yard, garden, and hands.
- Purchase quality tools. Some will last for years while others may not make it to the end of the season.
- Try to buy lightweight tools. They come in everything now from shovels to pruners to hammers and rakes. Make it easier on yourself.
- Some companies sell ergonomic tools that make pulling and pushing easier. They may cost more but they are really worth it.
- Have some fun. Buy tools with wild colors that brighten the day. They also won't get lost so easily.
- Keep your tools in excellent condition for your safety. Replace anything that is broken beyond repair. Clean them on a regular basis and disinfect those that come in contact with any diseased plants.
- Store tools in an easily accessible place. Some carts hold many hand tools.

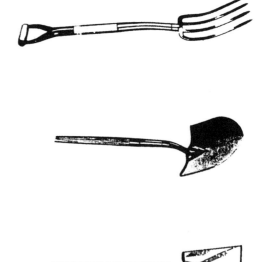

Spading Fork - Four sharp tines attached to a three to four foot handle with a D-grip. Used to turn over garden soil and compost. Excellent for dividing perennials with dense roots.

Round shovel - Curved, pointed blade attached to a long handle. One of the gardeners most used tools. They come in different sizes and shapes. Used to dig and move just about anything (mulch, soil, gravel, stone, sand, cement, plants etc.) to anyplace. Excellent for digging holes.

Spade - Very similar to a shovel but has an almost flat blade. Used for digging, turning and cutting through soil and sod. Also can be used for edging garden beds, short walkways and dividing perennials.

Trowel - Small, hand metal shovel (scoop) with a plastic or wood handle. In most cases, the blade is slightly curved making it easier to push into the ground. Used for planting, moving and mixing soil, transplanting and working with containers or small plants. Inexpensive ones bend, buy a sturdy one.

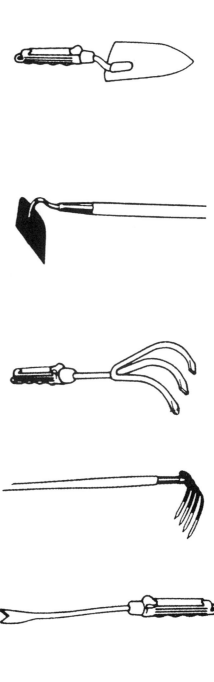

Hoe - A rectangular blade approximately 6 inches wide attached to a long handle. One of the most useful garden tools. It is used for moving and cultivating soil, making garden beds, breaking up soil clumps, cutting small weeds below the surface. Excellent for making rows in a vegetable garden.

Hand Cultivator - Commonly has three prongs attached to a short handle. It is used for tilling small areas, removing weeds, breaking up the top layer of soil for seed preparation or aeration. Excellent tool when working with containers and raised beds, or adding amendments to soil.

Long Cultivator - Usually four or five curved tines attached to a long handle. Excellent for breaking up soil and weeds and mixing soil amendments. One of the most important garden tools.

Hand Weeder - A metal shaft, with a sharp cutting edge, 12 to 16 inches long attached to a plastic or wood handle. Used to cut and lift up deep-rooted weeds. Good when not too many weeds are present.

Garden Rake - A row of steel tines, a few inches long attached to a long handle. Excellent tool for breaking up soil clumps, leveling soil, and removing debris. Also used for spreading gravel, mulch and mixing soil amendments.

Lawn Rake - Has flat, flexible steel, plastic or bamboo tines attached to a long handle. It is used to sweep up clippings, leaves and other debris without harming the grass.

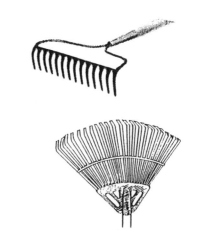

Hedge Shears - Large scissorlike blades attached to long straight handles. Used to trim hedges, shrubs and cut small branches up to 1/2 inch thick. Good for shaping.

Lopping Shears - This cutter has two, arms length handles with a curved bypass cutting head or anvil cutting head. The long handles give good leverage but do not twist the blades as they may become bent. Excellent for cutting branches up to two inches thick.

Hand Pruning Shears - This has a hand sized handle, a pivot point and one or two cutting blades. It is a multipurpose cutter used for pruning small branches or stems and hard, dead branches up to 3/4 inch thick.

Bow Saw - This saw has a metal frame shaped like a bow with a large toothed blade connecting the ends. It is mainly used to cut wood 2 inches or more in diameter and can cut as deep as the bow frame. Bow saws cut faster than most handsaws but keep pressure on the blade while cutting or the cut may start angling off rather than go straight through.

Pole Saw - A long pruning saw attached to a pole that can reach up to 20 feet into trees. Some have a combination saw and lopper on the same end. The lopper can be used to cut smaller branches and is operated by pulling a long cord handle. Do not climb ladders to cut branches. If they are out of reach of a pole saw while you are standing on the ground, its time to call in a professional tree service.

Pruning Saw - These are the most common gardener's saws. There are different shapes and sizes but most have curved blades, with very sharp triangular teeth, to draw down into the wood. Used for cutting any kind of branch from 1 inch to 12 inches in diameter. Some types come in a folding model to be put into your pocket or special made holster.

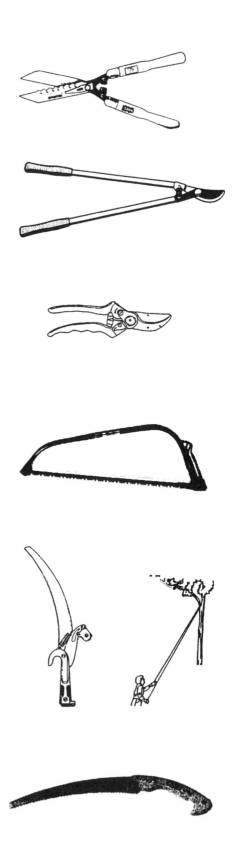

Pruning Knife - This usually is about 4 to 6 inches long and has a curved blade that folds into a curved handle. It is a valuable tool that is used for cutting any small shoots or branches.

Hatchet - A hammer-sized, wedge-shaped cutting and driving tool attached to a wood or metal handle. Good for cutting sharp edges on wood poles and for driving stakes into the ground. The same cutting head on a longer handle is usually referred to as an axe.

Grass Shears - Hand held grass trimmer with scissor-like blades. Used to trim grass and weeds around poles, trees, mailboxes and other structures. Ok to use on small landscapes with little trimming. Wear gloves or you may get blisters. If you have an average size piece of property, I would suggest buying a battery operated hand trimmer.

Power Hedge Shears - Two sets of blades with many moving, sharp, pointed teeth and can be either electric or gas powered. To me, this is a necessary tool used to trim and shape all kinds of hedges, vines and even small trees. Heavy duty models will cut branches up to 1/2 inch thick.

Gardening Gloves - These are a must. It's good to have several pairs around for different chores. Rubber or vinyl gloves are a necessity when working with chemicals or pesticides. If you have roses, buy the kind that have sleeves up to the elbow for added protection.

Pressure Sprayer - Metal or plastic tank that has a wand and adjustable spraying nozzle. They can hold from 1 to 3 gallons of material, either water, liquid plant food, or pesticides and with the wand, you can reach into tight areas.

Spray Nozzle - Usually made of plastic or metal and are attached to the end of a hose. They come in different types such as the twist, trigger, fan, or pistol. I prefer a brass, twist type as you can change the settings from a fine mist to a hard spray in a matter of seconds, and the pattern can be left on.

Hose-end Sprayer - These small tanks, made of glass or plastic, attach to the end of a hose. They are used to apply liquid fertilizers or pesticides. The nozzle spray is usually adjustable and controls the dilution ratio of water and the concentrate.

Watering Can - Every gardener needs one. Made from metal or plastic, they come in a large variety of shapes and sizes. The spout usually has a round head with many small holes. Many uses - a necessity.

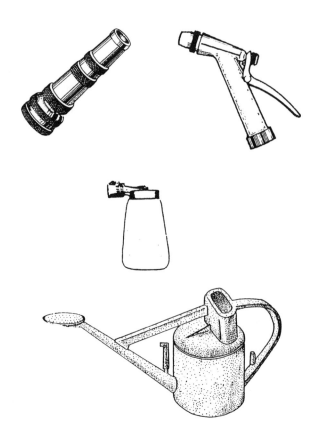

These are the basic tools of gardening. However, there are a few other essentials you need: wheelbarrow, watering hose and a small plastic or metal bucket.

Gardening should be done in the daylight to avoid accidents. Wear good shoes, gloves, breathable, protective clothing, a hat and use sunscreen. Wear ear protectors and safety glasses when operating power tools. If you have back problems, back support belts are available. Purchase quality tools, use the right tool for the job, keep cutters sharp, and keep them clean and in good working condition. When sharpening edges, always sharpen the beveled side of the blade. Metal tools will rust, so make sure they're always dried off and wiped down with a rag and a little oil for protection. Over the years, proper tools will become comfortable to work with and help make your gardening more effective. Start off with the basic tools first and match them to the size of your landscape. As your interest in landscaping grows, so will your tool inventory. Tools are a gardener's best friends, they are truly our "helping hands". Choose and use them wisely for a *close encounter of the gardening kind*.

Lightscaping

An easy and economical way to make your yard and home beautiful and safe is to use outdoor lights to highlight the landscape. Low voltage lighting transforms dark walkways into safe passageways or a clump of shrubs and trees into eye-pleasing shapes and shadows. There are several advantages of an outdoor lighting system: safety, security, beauty, economy, and portability. The lights use a principle of

"low voltage" design so they're completely safe for use around pets and children. Because they use low wattage bulbs, they are economical to operate. A set of six to ten lights actually uses less electricity than a 100 watt bulb.

A complete system consists of a transformer, a low-voltage cable and a lamp fixture. It can be installed in a couple of hours with a screwdriver and shovel. The transformer reduces 120 volts (house) to a safe 12 volts. Lighting kits are all portable. If you're not happy after you installed them, simply move the lights to another location. The transformer plugs into a standard house outlet and they range in size from a small unit, which powers several lights, to a large model that powers up to thirty lights. Some transformers are available with added security devices such as a timer that turns the lights on and off, and a photo control that switch the lights on at night and off at dawn. Other options are: photo controllers with timers and motion sensors. There are several different outdoor lighting fixtures available to achieve different effects. Following are some of the most popular styles and their special uses and effects:

Tier Light - One appealing aspect of using tier lights is the way they can be modified, by adding or removing tiers, giving different looks and effects. Using only the top tier, maximum light output is achieved. If you want a more traditional look, add one or two tiers for a more subtle effect. Placed in strategic spots, these lights are great for lining walkways, driveways, and erasing intruder-hiding shadows. Guests and family will appreciate the light cast downward as the glare is shaded from the eyes.

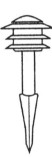

Bollard Light - This light is cylindrical in shape and diffuses light to create a soft, beautiful glow. It is excellent for accenting pool areas, flower and shrub beds, and walkways. With the lens shield on, a 180° lighting can be provided in any direction. With it off, you get a 360° lighting for full surrounding coverage.

Mushroom Light - With this style, the light is directed downward. Mushroom lights are used to highlight paths, ground covers, low growing shrubs, and give an interesting appearance while the large top conceals the light source. Several styles and different sized shades are available. The effect against snow is particularly pleasing. The change in shade size or height alters the intensity of the circle of light.

Globe Light - This light provides subtle illumination that covers a large area without any annoying glare. Globe lights can come in a frosted globe or shaded globe, which gives a downward lighting effect. Still another features a white globe in a black frame. Globe lights should be used around ponds, activity areas, swimming pools, decks, and patios.

Well Light - Designed to be buried as it casts light upwards creating a variety of special effects. Uplighting is a technique that creates very dramatic effects around your home. Well lights can be buried in flower and shrub bed areas or under an ornamental tree you wish to highlight. They are easy to install and colored lenses are available for special touches. Try them on each side of your entrance doors for added security.

Floodlight - One of the most popular and can be used in a variety of ways. Floodlights can provide hundreds of illumination effects, spraying light in the yard to make objects, plants and areas come alive at night. They can be aimed along a fence, wall or deck, or used as backlights behind trees, shrubs, and flowers along foundations. Floodlights can be mounted just about anywhere: ground level or attached to walls, trees, posts etc. There is a variety of colored lenses available for extra effects. With an optional motion sensor, floodlights will frighten any intruder in the yard. For maximum illumination and security, floodlights are the way to go.

Surface/deck Light - The popularity of wooden entertainment decks and pool decks has made outdoor lighting companies respond with new products developed especially for these places. Deck lights not only provide a decorative touch in daylight, but extend the deck use well into the night. Deck lights come in two basic styles: the edge/surface light and the deck light. Edge lights can be installed on any flat surface, wall or in the ground. They are used to illuminate steps and walks either near your front door or rear deck. Deck lights come in different shapes (square, rectangular) and are used for hard to light areas such as under steps or deck railings. Light is directed outward in a controlled pattern for good brightness, without glare. Wires are easily concealed under boards. One style, a diamond shape, casts light in several directions. Most are available in pine, cedar or redwood and can be stained to match any deck.

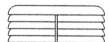

In most cases, complete deck light sets are available for any of the above lights. Companies offer special brackets for installing most existing sets on decks, railings or steps. Accessories are available at major home centers and hardware stores.

Designing And Planning Your Outdoor Lights

To design the lighting system, first take a look at your landscape in the daytime. List the most attractive features, shrubs nestled in a corner, an unusual tree or a small pond to reflect the lights. These are areas to be highlighted. At the same time, note areas that are usually very dark and need illumination for security reasons. Consider steps, paths, and obstacles that people may trip over. List outdoor activities your family may enjoy at night. These are areas you may want to light. Make sure you locate the fixtures where they won't interfere with walking, playing, lawn mowing or trimming or cause unpleasant glare into neighbor's windows. Most of all, make sure they are located where its easy to service them. Write and sketch everything down on large, white artists paperboard. Place all fixtures, draw all wires, add color lenses if desired and mark all dark areas and walkways.

Many different lighting effects can be achieved using low voltage lights. Consider the following effects before purchasing a system. Then incorporate these effects into particular areas of your yard.

Uplighting - Accomplished using well lights or floodlights to highlight objects, such as trees and shrubs, from the ground.

Downlighting - Achieved using floodlights on walls, fences or in trees to illuminate objects or large areas from above.

Shadowing - Using floodlights or well lights near ground level. The lights are aimed up through a tree or large shrub to cast its shadow onto a surface.

Silhouetting - Placing a light behind a tree, plant or object to silhouette it against a vertical surface.

Spotlighting - Achieved by aiming a floodlight at specific objects and surfaces.

Background lighting - Used to illuminate statues, walls, trees or other tall objects. This can create dramatic effects when combined with other techniques.

Low voltage outdoor lights are very easy to work with. The cable can be laid under flowers, around shrubs, placed near foundations or buried under ground cover plants or mulch. Before burying any cable, make sure all the lights work and you are pleased with your arrangement. Experiment with different lighting arrangements. An interesting yard becomes eye-catching through the creative use of outdoor lights. Check the appearance from your neighbors yard and across the street. If need be, cut shrubbery back or relocate for a better effect. A good quality light set should last for many years with very little maintenance. The lights should be cleaned occasionally to remove dirt, spider webs, leaves and other debris that accumulates. With a little proper planning, your landscape can brighten up even on the darkest of nights.

Gardener's Journal

Now is a good time to start a gardener's journal as you and your landscape will reap the benefits. It will help you record the successes and failures, and the reasons why. Records can save you time, money and mistakes. Note when and where bulbs are planted so the following year you won't dig up present ones when planting new ones. When you visit your local nursery, bring your journal and write the names of plants you like. Make special notes if they thrive in shade or sun. Check to see which are more disease and insect tolerant. As the season progresses, note drainage problems, insect or disease damage. This way next year you'll remember to spray them. A journal list helps you know what has to be done at other times of the year. There are many garden journals available. Good record keeping can be a gardener's best friend. Here are just a few things you can put in to get started:

- Landscaping goals.
- Catalogue source names and phone numbers.
- Magazine and newspaper articles on gardening.
- Bloom height and times of flowers.
- Different professional designs that you like. Change to suit your needs.
- Budgets and expenses.
- Planting and pruning times.
- Numbers and types of plants it takes to fill special areas such as a flower bed.
- Pictures of your landscape.
- Individual plant records.
- Records of companion planting.
- Soil test records.
- List all disease and pest problems and what steps you took to remedy them.
- Amendments you added to the soil.
- Weather conditions in certain areas (wind, rain, sun, shade).
- Note all successes and failures and their locations.
- Things you forgot to do.
- List any sprays and fertilizers you have used and their effectiveness.
- Make a general maintenance program listing things to do by month.
- Changes you would like to make the following year.

Notes

Chapter 3

Lawn Care

Ablade of grass, using the sun's rays as it's main source of energy, synthesizes carbon dioxide, water and minerals to promote green growth. It removes pollutants from the air acting as a filter and gives off oxygen in return. Most of the grasses in your lawn came from Europe. Early colonists brought them here to feed their livestock. Those cultivars that were able to survive frequent cutting and grazing became our present turfgrasses. After World War II, many improvements were made. State Universities became interested and developed their own turfgrass varieties which now are available to us. Many new varieties of seed are being developed every year. Some have good tolerance to drought, insects, diseases and heat. Using two to three different types in a blend proves successful as each one has it's own strengths and weaknesses. Turfgrass research has discovered a fungus carried by seed that lives in the plant called endophyte. This fungus has the ability to repel many surface insects. Introducing these new types of grass into your lawn helps make it healthier and reduce the use of insecticides.

It is most important to realize that in any landscape the house is the dominating factor and the surrounding grounds furnish the setting that compliments the house. The green, restful expanse of a well kept lawn is one of the most important elements of landscaping. A beautiful lawn provides a setting in the overall picture. It should have a smooth turf and give an impression of freedom and openness. Like all other living things, grass must achieve harmony with its environment. Green grass filters dust and pollen from the air we breath and replenishes the oxygen supply, cools down surrounding areas, purifies water and absorbs noise pollution. It also makes an ideal carpet for work or play. Healthy dense lawns resist disease, insects and drought and can even crowd out crabgrass and other weeds.

A lawn is any area of land covered with one or more types of turfgrasses. There are generally six grass plants growing in every square inch and almost one million plants in every 1000 square feet. This means that in the average American lawn of 10,000 square feet there are between eight to ten million plants. Some grass types grow well in heat, others in cool climates. Some are thick bladed and others are very fine. But all types are capable of forming luxurious green lawns that we have all come to admire. A clear understanding of how grass grows will help you create a healthy and beautiful lawn. Stems and leaves all grow out from the crown area of the plant which is located near the ground surface. As grass grows at its base and not from its tips, you can mow tips off without harming the plant itself. Blades form at joints near the sheaths and become mature parts of the plant. When the grass is cut new blades emerge. Tiny root hairs grow in search of nutrition and water. When the grass grows higher, more and more roots develop. On the other hand, short cut grass have smaller roots and need more nutrients and water to survive. There must be a balance and if that balance is broken, the lawn will suffer.

Contrary to popular belief, grass roots do not absorb food from the soil. A grass plant manufactures it's own food through a method called photosynthesis. The sun's energy helps leaves turn carbon dioxide into sugars (plant food). The sugars are then broken down into protein and fats. Grass roots take in water and raw materials which cause photosynthesis and bring in nutrients to make food. Grasses are very successful in adapting to their environment. The grass family has several thousand species and varieties.

The ones I will be discussing are considered lawngrasses having the following pre-requisites: compatibility with other grasses, beauty, disease resistance, persistence, adaptability to changing mowing conditions and a wide range of soil adaptability.

Seed

No two lawns anywhere are the same. There are so many variables - climate, soil, different varieties of grass and the maintenance they receive. Kentucky bluegrass is one of the most desirable turfgrasses for New Jersey lawns. Selecting a turfgrass variety adapted to the environmental conditions in your area is the first step in the establishment of a durable and beautiful lawn. Although all personal preferences differ, most homeowners want their lawns to be dark green. High quality turfgrass seed is one of the best investments a homeowner could make. The purchase of certified seed guarantees the seed was grown and tested under specific conditions for germination, variety and purity. Also certified seed guarantees freedom from most weeds and unwanted fillers.

By now you should have evaluated your landscape's conditions so far as shade, sun, trees, low areas that hold moisture etc. In New Jersey the three most common turfgrass mixtures are: Kentucky bluegrass plus a fine fescue, Kentucky bluegrass plus a perennial ryegrass and a combination of all three. Such mixtures are good for areas that have both sun and shade. Bluegrass grows well in sun and fescues do well in shady areas. Bluegrass has a vigorous underground rhizome system (spreads by underground stems) and has rapid recovery from heavy traffic. Buy seed that has a bluegrass content of at least 30 to 50 percent by weight. Fescues, particularly a creeping red fescue, are desirable companions with bluegrass as they are more shade and drought tolerant. Red fescue is also a rhizome system grass and preferred over chewings fescue, as chewings is a bunchgrass (grows in clumps). Kentucky bluegrass and creeping red fescue is a good mixture for the average lawn that has areas exposed to full sun, partial shade and varying soil and moisture conditions. For these reasons it is generally recommended to have a grass seed mixture rather than planting the entire lawn with only one variety. A single type may not be well adapted to all of your conditions. All grass species vary in their range of adaptation.

Consider the following when deciding which is the best for your lawn:

- Your quality standard.
- How you will use the lawn.
- The amount of shade and sun.
- Quantity of trees.
- Amount of maintenance required.

Homeowners have different ideas about what a quality lawn is. It could be a beautiful dark green lawn that is the envy of the neighbors, but is probably the most expensive and time consuming to maintain. Or, it may be a tall fescue lawn being lighter in color and coarse in texture but less expensive in maintenance. The average lawn is probably between both extremes. Following are the main turfgrass varieties in New Jersey.

Kentucky Bluegrass

One of the most versatile and recuperative turfgrasses having a dark green color with a medium texture. As it spreads by rhizomes it will form a tightly knit sod. It tolerates partial shade and lower mowing in high traffic areas. The soil should be well-drained and fertile as there are high water requirements in the growing season. During warm, dry spells Kentucky bluegrass will go dormant to escape drought but will recover when a good amount of water is applied. It is susceptible to several diseases but there are improved varieties which are more resistant than common types. Common types have a broad genetic base which helps them adapt to many environmental conditions.

Perennial Ryegrass

This is considered a bunch-type grass used in mixtures because it germinates quickly. It has a dark green color and is medium to coarse in texture. Ryegrass is not tolerant to temperature extremes either hot or cold, one of the reasons it is used mainly in a mixture. Blended with bluegrass improved varieties, it provides high durability in heavily used areas. It grows well in many soils, even damp ones, and is tolerant to shade.

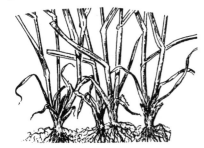

Fine Fescue

This is a general name for a group of fescue species. They have very fine leaf blades. In shady areas, chewings or creeping red fescues are used as they are compatible with Kentucky bluegrass and are better than most cool season types. They germinate and establish very quickly, form a very fine-textured turf and are medium to dark green in color. In dry weather they might loose some color but their drought tolerance is high making it a good blend to use.

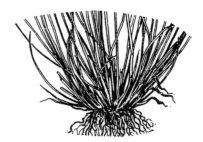

Tall Fescue

This grass forms a deep root system adaptable to wet and clay soils. It is drought tolerant and adapts well to shady areas. Tall fescues are very coarse and have a medium to dark green color. Thatch, disease or insects are rarely a problem with tall fescues. As it is a fast growing grass, more frequent mowings are necessary.

All of the above are good grasses for our area, blend well together and are well known for their widespread usefulness. The type of seed you use depends greatly on the soil condition. Many new varieties of seed are being developed every year. Some have very good tolerance to drought, insects, disease and heat. Using at least three different types in a blend should prove successful as each one has it's own strengths and weaknesses. To establish a healthy, permanent lawn selecting the proper seed is essential. A lawn that has a single grass type gives you uniform growth and color but it's weakness is that if it were to develop a condition to which the grass is susceptible (disease, insects), you may loose the entire lawn.

Purchasing Seed

After you have decided which grass or blend is best for you, go out and purchase a "high quality seed". Some of the seeds available in stores are inexpensive, low quality blends. Your dollar investment for purchasing a high quality seed is small compared to your time and amount of work needed to establish a lawn. Most seed is sold in attractive convenient packages but the average buyer is not familiar with the seed and relies on the package's appearance for quality and choice. People also have a tendency to shop for the lowest price, which is usually not the best in quality. Understanding what is in a box of seed will help you in selecting the right seed which, in the long run, is the best investment for your property.

By law, all seed packages are required to list an analysis which contains the important information about the seed. An example of a seed label or analysis is shown below. The seed listing must show the different types of grass by weight, the germination percentage and purity, the weed seed content and date tested. Purity and germination are the principle factors. Purity is just what it means, the percentage of pure seed of a certain species present in that particular lot of seed. For example, 35% of the mix shows Merion Kentucky bluegrass. This means that 35% of the package contains living seeds of that specific grass. Germination is the percentage of live seed that will germinate (begin to develop) under laboratory conditions. For example, if the seed shows 35% Merion Kentucky bluegrass with a germination percentage of 85%, this means 85% of the 35% Merion should germinate. Seed looses it's ability to live within time, so the date of germination testing is very important.

Blue Seed Co.	Lot No: 123
Brick, NJ	Test Date 1-2-95
60 % Bluegrass	85 % germination
30 % Perenn Rye	80 % germination
◎	
Other Ingredients:	
2.50 % Crop	
7.00 % Inert	
0.50 % Weed Seed	

When the analysis shows less than 100%, the remaining percentage is composed of crop seeds, weed seeds and inert matter. Crop seed content are normally plants that are grown for profit. They may include difficult weeds to eradicate such as orchardgrass, Timothy or bromegrass. These plants can become quite a serious problem in a home lawn because of their coarse weedy appearance. Only purchase seed that contains absolutely no crop seed. Weed seed refers to those undesirable plants not normally grown for lawns such as wild onion and chickweed. The lower the percentage of weed seeds, the better off your lawn will be. Noxious weeds are those defined as "problem weeds" such as quackgrass. These weeds are considered difficult to control with chemicals. Purchase seed without any noxious weeds. Inert matter refers to the weight of material that will not

grow (anything that is not a seed) such as soil, bulking agents, chopped corn cob stems or sand added to meet weight requirements. Don't blame the seed on a lawn's failure. A good seed germinates and grows reasonably well but it's survival depends on the environment and maintenance. Avoiding those undesirable seeds and fillers can help eliminate problems in the future. A top quality seed will have .00% crop seeds and less than .10% weed seeds. Selecting the right grass type, purchasing a high quality seed and a sound maintenance program are all important in having a healthy, beautiful lawn. Developing a good lawn is a long-time proposition that can ensure future pleasure and satisfaction.

Installing A New Lawn With Seed

Why do so many people have trouble getting their grass to grow? If you can't get the seed to germinate, you won't have a lawn. Following proper procedures and planting a top quality seed are the keys to a successful lawn. Let's start with site preparation. It all begins with your soil. Soil provides grass with nutrients and water, and also acts as an anchor for the roots. Grass grows in the same soil year after year. Changing the soil texture under growing grass is hard to do and very expensive. Therefore, the effort you put into soil preparation now will be reflected in years to come. We previously discussed soil in Chapter 2, but let's go over some important points again.

Soil is classified by the proportion of silt, clay and sand that it contains. In size of individual soil particles, clay is the smallest, silt is a little larger and sand being the largest. All lawns need air, moisture and mineral nutrients for proper growth. In a clay soil, the particles hold so closely together that they have a tendency to hold water and don't have much room for air. Water penetrates very slowly to the grass roots and the lawn could possibly die. Sandy soil, on the other hand, has too much room for air, but valuable nutrients and water can become lost quickly. The most satisfactory surface soil for lawns would be in between a clay soil and a sandy loam soil. This dark colored soil, better known as top soil, contains silt, clay and sand. It has sufficient room for air to circulate and retains water and nutrients.

Installing a new lawn usually means either developing an unlandscaped yard or replacing an existing poor one. The best time of the year to build a lawn is in the fall between September 1 and October 15. Fall planting is preferred to spring and summer because warm days and cool nights are ideal for seed germination and growth. Also there is less weed competition than in spring or summer. Preparing the seedbed is one of the most strenuous and time consuming steps in establishing your lawn. First, take a walk around the property and remove any debris (branches, covered wood, cement). Man-made materials may create chemical reactions in the soil and rotting wood can promote mushrooms and attract termites and other insects. Fertilizer and lime are very important at this time. Take a soil test. This will give you recommendations so far as needed lime and other nutrient requirements. It is the only way of indicating lime requirements and it will give information necessary for adjusting the proportions of nitrogen, phosphorus and potash. Soil tests can tell you how much fertilizer is needed or when enough has already been applied. Too much fertilizer can cause more damage than not enough.

Using a broadcast type spreader, apply fertilizer, lime and any other recommended amendments. Rent a rototiller and work the soil to a depth of at least four inches. It is better not to till a wet soil as it

may clog. The deeper you can cultivate the soil before seeding, the deeper the plants will establish their roots. This will allow the plants to reach down for moisture during dry spells and anchor their roots deeper for strength during freezing weather.

With a rake, or professional grading equipment if you can find it, remove all rough debris including large stones. Rake the entire area to what is called a finish-grade while establishing a gentle slope away from the house. This will help keep surface water away from foundation walls. Improper grading increases mowing time and can cause drainage problems which encourage weeds. Using a rope and level will help determine the amount of slope. A good grade is approximately a one to two foot drop away from the foundation per every one hundred feet. Walk around, fill in any low spots and level any hills. If you feel you will have any major drainage problems that you can't fix now, consult a professional landscape or drainage contractor. Be careful with trees. They are quite sensitive to the amount of soil that is above their roots. After all the preparatory work is completed, use a large water roller (can be rented) lengthwise on the lawn. When done, lightly rake the surface to fill in any depressions caused by the roller. Now roll in the opposite direction and fill in any depressions again. You are now ready for seeding.

A starter fertilizer should now be applied. The starter fertilizer should be high in phosphorus to encourage strong root development. A high phosphorus fertilizer is usually also high in nitrogen which helps the grass green up quickly. After the final seedbed has been prepared, it is critical to incorporate the seed into the soil at the proper depth. Divide the total seed quantity in half. Use a broadcast spreader and seed the entire lot in one direction. When completed, apply the remaining seed at right angles to the first (opposite direction). Then lightly rake the seed into the soil so it is covered no more than 1/4 inch. In sloping areas, where erosion is a concern, it may be necessary to apply a covering of straw mulch. Most garden centers have this mulch or have access to it. Please make sure the kind you buy is "weed seed" free.

Within time, as the seed germinates and grows, the mulch will disappear. You can give the entire area a light covering of straw mulch as it hastens germination by keeping the soil moist, and helps prevent birds from eating the seeds. It should be put down at a depth of approximately 1/4 inch thick. However, it is not necessary to do so.

Watering is critical, at this time, as the top layer of the soil must be kept moist for seeds to germinate. Water the entire area heavily the first time and then at least once daily until the lawn is established. Not enough water may keep the roots near the surface, resulting in a grass that will be unable to withstand periods of draught. As soon as the grass is 3 to 4 inches in height it can be mowed. Keep the mower setting between 2 1/2 to 3 inches for the rest of the year.

Ten Steps To A New Lawn With Seed

1. Acquire a soil test.
2. Rough grade and remove all debris.
3. Apply lime if needed and basic fertilizer.
4. Apply any soil amendments suggested by the soil test.
5. Till the soil to a depth of at least 4 inches.
6. Finish grading with rake and add top soil to lower areas.
7. Apply a starter fertilizer and rake into top one inch of soil.
8. Sow high quality seed and rake to cover with at least 1/4 inch of soil.
9. Lightly roll entire area in two directions.
10. Straw mulch necessary areas to help prevent erosion.

Installing A New Lawn With Sod

Sod may be described as "the surface layer of soil filled with grass roots." In layman's terms it is an "instant lawn". Sod has been sold in sections or strips for many years, as far back as one can remember. New homes, that need instant lawns to help encourage their sale, are generally sodded. Busy homeowners who are dissatisfied with their present lawns buy sod to have their lawns quickly re-established. Using sod is one of the fastest and simplest ways to put in a lawn. Usually it is developed in a specially prepared open field and harvested after growing through at least one winter. It is then stripped with special machines that cut it into rolls covering approximately 10 square feet of soil. People can buy sod from a "sod farm" and have it delivered to their doorsteps if they have large areas to be covered. Or, they can purchase small quantities from their local nurseries for smaller repairs.

Sod can be laid at almost any time of the year as long as the ground is not frozen. However, if the sod is put down during hot summer months, more frequent watering will be required for it to establish. Early winter sodding is not a good idea as sod may dry out and die if the roots aren't established before the winter freeze. The best time to lay sod is spring or fall. Besides being used on entire lawns, sod is perfect where erosion is a problem on areas where it is difficult to get seed to grow. A good high quality sod contains permanent grasses such as Kentucky bluegrass or bluegrass cultivar blends. Since commercial sod usually does not contain shade tolerant red fescues, using a red fescue mixture in shady areas may be necessary. It all depends on your particular situation.

Establishing a lawn using sod can help control erosion, keeps weeds to a minimum and provides a usable surface much faster than seed. Of course turfgrass success with sod depends on the selection of seed variety, proper soil preparation, proper installation and good maintenance practices. Preparation of the soil is just as important for a sodded lawn as it is for a seeded one. Sod can be a functional lawn within three weeks versus six weeks or more for a seeded lawn. It doesn't take a great deal of care to establish, as long as you keep it moist until the roots grow together securely with the soil.

When buying sod select a high quality healthy grass. Sod that has grown in a local sod farm usually survives better since it is accustomed to a similar environment as yours. When you purchase sod make sure that:

- It is damp but not too wet.
- It is definitely not dry.
- It has cleanly cut edges that will fit together nicely.
- There are no yellowing areas; must be uniformly green.
- It is dense with a uniform clean cut.
- It contains no visible weeds or diseases.
- It does not fall apart easily.

Don't buy cheap sod as it may contain thatch, disease or weeds. The best sod will likely have new varieties of seed that are disease and insect tolerant. Do not order the sod until the ground is totally prepared. Sod must be laid within twenty four hours of when it is delivered. Grass plants produce heat which cannot be released when sod is rolled up too long and this heat can kill it. The grass may start to turn yellow and the roots may dry out. If you intend to lay the sod in a day or two, unroll it as soon as it is delivered, lay it out grass upwards in a shady area and keep it watered.

Site Preparation

Preparation of the soil is critical before laying sod. Initially, sod grows almost anywhere and in almost any soil. However, it won't survive very long if the soil is not rich enough to provide healthy lawn growth. The sod's growth depends on the type and quality of the soil. Soil preparation is essentially the same as for seeding a lawn. When ordering the sod make sure you have agreed on a delivery date so you can have the site completely prepared.

Installation

Just before laying the sod, put down a starter fertilizer high in phosphorus for root growth. Make sure the soil is damp but avoid overwatering. When laying sod, it is usually better to establish a straight line by using stakes and a long string as a guide. Lay your first row along a sidewalk or driveway. Unroll the strip, check the alignment and pat it down to make sure it lies evenly. Lay the second strip end to end with the first but do not overlap the ends. Be careful not to stretch the sod in any direction as it may shrink later leaving gaps. Finish the first row laying all the strips end to end. Place a board or piece of plywood on the first sodded

strip. Kneel on the board to lay the rest of the sod and keep moving the board forward as the job progresses. This will help push the roots of the sod into underlying soil. Start the second row alongside the

first but stagger the strips so that ends in one row never line up with adjacent rows. Create a brick-wall pattern. The end should line up midpoint of the first row of sod. This helps make the lawn even. Continue this procedure throughout the entire lawn, using stakes and string to make straight lines. When you come to an odd sized area, like a curved corner or end, cut the strip to fit using a sharp knife or spade. If you have any sloped areas, lay the first strip along the bottom and work upwards. This will help prevent the sod from sagging down the slope. Lay the strips horizontally across the slope. If it is very steep, use short stakes to pin the strips to the ground. Use at least three stakes per strip, one at each end and one in the middle. Leave the stakes in until the roots are established in the soil. Do not waste any sod. At the end of rows, cut off any large excess pieces and use them to start new rows. After the job is completed, roll the entire area with a water roller (can be rented) to help make good contact between the roots and soil. Roll the area from different directions, eliminating any air spaces between the sod and soil. The roller should weigh between 60 to 80 pounds. If it is too heavy the sod may slide. If the temperature is above 80° F lightly water the sod before rolling. Fill a bucket with top soil. Check the entire area for cracks and exposed areas and spread the top soil into these areas.

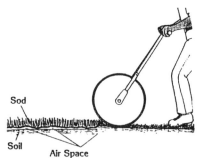

Sod lawns require the same care as seed lawns. Bluegrass responds to more intensive management than ryegrass or fescue. Water the sod daily for at least two weeks and during hot weather it may even need watering twice a day. Sod roots in the soil in about 10 to 14 days. After this time watering should be deeper and less frequent to encourage a deeper root system. However, do not overwater sod as it will not root properly if kept saturated. You can start mowing when the grass starts to grow. A height of 2 - 2 1/2" during cool weather and 2 1/2 - 3" during hot weather is recommended. Never cut off more than 30-40% of the leaf blade. After the sod has rooted, follow a fertilization program suggested for established lawns. Usually three fertilizations per year are recommended for high quality turf, one in spring, a second in early September and a final application in late October.

Hydroseed

A third method for establishing a new lawn is hydroseed or hydromulch. This is a process where seed, a wood cellulose fiber, fertilizer and water are mixed together and then power sprayed through a large hose. This is a high pressure application available only through a professional service. With this method, seed is sown, fertilized, watered and mulched all in one easy application. All materials are evenly distributed and the fibrous material in the spray keeps the seed moist, just like a topdressing. Hydroseeding can also be used on an existing poor lawn. First, the existing weeds must be killed with a herbicide, and then the lawn mowed very low at approximately 1 1/2 inches. Use a dethatching machine to remove all loose materials and then hydroseed. So far as expense, hydroseeding costs more than seeding but less than installing sod. It is a good method to use when there is a large area to cover or when there are slopes. This type of lawn requires regular watering to insure adequate moisture for successful germination and proper growth of seedlings. The wood cellulose fiber helps retain moisture and prevent birds from eating the new seeds. One drawback of hydroseeding is that it is not a do-it-yourself method for establishing a lawn.

Benefits Of Hydroseeding

- The seed germinates faster.
- Less chance of soil erosion.
- A uniform distribution of fertilizer, seed and mulch.
- Difficult, irregular areas are easier to seed.
- Walkways and driveways are easy to clean up with just water.
- The mulch eventually turns to humus and becomes part of the soil.

Basic Lawn Care

A thriving well kept lawn is the basic element of an attractive landscape. Healthy green turf provides the setting for your house and surrounding landscape. It is an asset to any residence. Besides its aesthetic contributions, healthy turf reduces dirt, dust and pollution surrounding the home and supplies oxygen for us to breathe. A beautiful lawn pleases the eye and wears well. It is relatively easy to maintain, survives winters and if properly cared for, lasts many years. Maintaining high quality turfgrass requires a combination of proper maintenance and sound pest management. A good maintenance program helps to reduce pest problems but it will not completely eliminate them.

Good lawns don't just happen. They are the result of careful planning, proper installation and good maintenance practices. Some people enjoy lawn chores, giving them satisfaction, exercise and relaxation but others feel they are an unpleasant duty. Lawn care does involve a considerable amount of time and work. Growing grass is not too difficult in New Jersey since our cool, moist climate is conducive to growth. But do to our sandy soil condition, special attention must be given to watering, liming, fertilizing and pest control. There are many lawns that have deteriorated because simple maintenance practices were not followed. It may get frustrating at times when it seems as though our efforts are not being rewarded, but even the best of lawns have problems that need fixing. All homeowners should be concerned with the appearance of their lawns. Beautiful landscapes increase property value and improve the surrounding environment. Please remember that we will be dealing with basic, practical methods to help you grow and maintain a healthy attractive lawn.

Fertilizer

Fertilizer is a natural or synthetic chemical used to enrich soil to promote plant growth. Plants do not require added chemical compounds to live because they are able to synthesize whatever compounds they need. However, land may become exhausted of one or more specific nutrients, and it is then necessary to add these nutrients to the soil in the form of fertilizers. Fertilizers supplement the essential nutrients that are not supplied in adequate amounts by the environment. We can think of fertilizing as soil building and not plant feeding. Fertilizer improves the structure of soil and provides nutrients. It makes grass plants strong so they can withstand weeds, drought and heavy traffic. Balanced fertilization helps a lawn in many ways. It stimulates growth making the turf thicker which crowds out weeds and makes the

grass hardier to respond to insects and disease. Grass should get all of its nutrition from the soil. But many residential properties are in such bad condition that the soil is incapable of sustaining the turf. Therefore, we must provide nutrition to our grass with fertilizer. The best all around meal for lawns is the application of a slow-release granular fertilizer in the spring and fall. How much effort and time you want to give your lawn determines the kind and cost of the fertilizer you buy. There are three basic kinds of fertilizer: organic, slow release and soluble synthetic. Most people probably use the soluble synthetic type as this is the one mostly sold in stores or nurseries.

Organic

Natural fertilizers come from plant and animal sources. They include dehydrated manures, fish products, bone meal and granite dust. When applied, these materials break down slowly in the soil and provide long-term, steady nutrition. They encourage and help build better soil structure. It's only drawbacks are that it is very slow acting and does not have much of a "punch" to it. Natural blends usually contain additional bacteria that helps the soil come "back to life" quicker. Even though they are slow to break down, the gradual lasting change is more beneficial for the lawn. Watering after an application helps to speed things up. Sometimes they are more expensive than chemical fertilizers and are not as available.

Slow Release

These fertilizers contain water insoluble nitrogen. They have a tendency to give the grass a quick shot of green. The nitrogen is slowly released into the plant, so if properly applied there is little risk of the grass burning. They can make a poor lawn look better much faster than organic fertilizers and usually cost less. Most chemical fertilizers can burn the grass if not watered soon after application because of their high salt content. Chemical fertilizers may also kill soil minerals that are responsible for soil formation and nutrient production. An over chemically treated lawn, in time, may not get natural nutrition from the soil and become dependent on chemicals alone.

A few characteristics are:

- Dependent on environmental conditions for release such as water, temperature and type of soil.
- Slow to leach out.
- Applied less often at higher rates.
- More expensive than water soluble.
- Very seldom burns lawns unless abused.

Soluble Synthetic Fertilizer

These products are less expensive and are what we call "predictable" in that you know what the results are before they are applied. You can purchase them with additions to help control crabgrass, weeds and insects. However, you must read the labels carefully as many of these types must be applied at certain times of the year to be effective.

A few characteristics are:

- May have to apply more often at lower rates.
- Danger of fertilizer burn if product is overlapped.
- May quickly leach out (wash down) into soil.
- If applied when the lawn is wet, it may have to be watered in to avoid burning.

Now that we are familiar with the basic type of fertilizers, let's find out what's in the bag. Grass needs approximately 16 elements for healthy growth. Turfgrass suffers from various nutritional deficiencies. Each year there are thousands of research areas devoted to turf nutrition by universities. Soil analysis and climate play an important role in growing healthy turf. With the knowledge of certain essentials, fertilizers and turf nutrition can become understandable. Below are the major, secondary and minor nutrients (elements). Each one has its role in the growth of turf. Since soils cannot provide all of them in sufficient quantities, fertilizers are necessary.

PRIMARY NUTRIENTS: Nitrogen, Phosphorus, Potassium

SECONDARY NUTRIENTS: Calcium, Magnesium, Sulfur

MINOR NUTRIENTS: Iron, Manganese, Chlorine, Boron, Copper, Zinc, Molybdenum

Of these, nitrogen, phosphorus and potassium are used in the greatest amounts. Most commercial fertilizers generally provide these three primary nutrients.

Nitrogen (N)

Of the three major nutrients, nitrogen is considered to be the most important and is the element that makes the most difference in the growth and color of grass. An efficient fertilizer should be able to supply enough nitrogen for immediate greenup and then ration the remainder over a prolonged time period, usually at least a couple of months. During this period, grass should maintain its color and vigor and grow at a reasonable rate. Nitrogen is a plant stimulator. It feeds the grass, helps sustain soil life which produces vigorous growth and greener color. All nitrogen fertilizers convert to nitrate which leaches (passes through) from the soil easily. Too much at any one specific time contributes to burning, disease, pollution and unnecessary mowing of long grass. Amounts are shown on the bags in pounds per 1000 square feet of grass area. Most experts agree that about 3 to 4 pounds per year are required for a

lawn to be healthy. Failure to add nitrogen to your turf, even for one season, could cause the grass to become invaded with weeds and thin out. Commercial fertilizers come with a wide variety of nitrogen contents that range from 5 to 50 percent.

Phosphorus (P)

Grass requires less phosphorus than nitrogen. Once it is in contact with the soil it becomes tied up (stays put). This nutrient encourages strong grass root growth and helps resist disease. It stays near the surface, is not readily lost by leaching and can accumulate year after year. Phosphates are gradually released to plants over an extended period of time. For newly seeded lawns, large quantities are needed to promote root development. Soil cannot be productive if it doesn't have good structure.

Potassium (K)

Usually called potash, it assists in the production and passage of food in the plant, improves tissue and builds resistance to disease and protects the plant from the elements. Grass requires almost as much of this nutrient as it does nitrogen. Healthy lawns need a continuous level of potash through periodic fertilization as some is lost by leaching when the soil is watered. Although water washes away much of the potassium in the soil, there are sufficient amounts left to make high supplements unnecessary. Potassium is found in all plant life and helps in the production of protein.

The secondary nutrients help the primary nutrients from getting locked up in the soil. Calcium neutralizes salt and helps grass toughen up. Magnesium helps builds roots and darkens the color. Sulfur releases nitrogen into the soil and controls the soil's pH level. The minor nutrients are needed for grass to grow, but many soils have a good supply of these nutrients and most commercial fertilizers contain them, so it is not necessary to purchase or apply them individually.

The Label

All chemical companies recommend that you apply fertilizer at a specific number of pounds per 1000 square feet. Fertilizer bags have numbers on the front such as 15-5-10. These numbers represent the percentages of nitrogen, phosphorus and potassium in that order. For example, the numbers 15-5-10 on a 25 pound bag means that 15% of the weight of the ingredients is nitrogen, 5% is phosphorus and 10% is potash. When calculated out, this equals 3.75 pounds of nitrogen, 1.25 pounds of phosphorus, 2.50 pounds of potash and the balance of the bag (17.5 pounds) is some type of filler or fiber. This sounds like a lot of inert extra material, and it is, but here's why. Nitrogen in its pure form is a gas and cannot be bagged. Phosphorus and potassium are solid materials but dangerous in the presence of moisture. Each of the nutrients must be in a different form before they can be handled and useful to plants. There are many different forms of N, P, K and not all forms do a good job in providing nutrients to grass. This is why certain inert products, which neutralize some of the acidifying effects of the chemicals, are put into the bags. All fertilizer bags have recommended settings right on the package for many different

types of spreaders. If your spreader is calibrated correctly, there is very little chance of mistake. The ideal fertilizer should completely fill the nutritional requirement of the plant. Unfortunately, to be a "complete" fertilizer all it has to do is list the three major nutrients on the bag, N, P and K.

Combinations of fertilizer and pesticides have become popular and widely used. Some combinations contain herbicides for weed and crabgrass control and others include fungicides or insecticides. The advantages of these type products are: time, labor and equipment are saved as you can do two or more jobs at once. In addition, the cost of the material is usually less than the ingredients purchased separately, less of the material is handled and less storage area is needed. There are disadvantages to these combinations the main one being in the ability to apply the product at the proper time. The best time to control weeds or insects may not necessarily be the best time to fertilize. However, many weeds and insects are also busy during spring and fall, so an application of a combination fertilizer usually will give satisfactory results.

When To Fertilize

In the spring grass uses stored winter food, cool weather and rains to grow. Spring is when grass plants send out their shoots to form stolons, tillers and rhizomes. **Heavy** spring fertilization should be avoided as this promotes excessive shoot growth. This only increases additional mowing of tall grass. Because turfgrasses are subjected to summer mowing, family activities, weeds and disease, they require at least one fertilization in the springtime. In general, the best time to fertilize is before a period of active growth. For cool season grasses in New Jersey, this means spring and fall. During the hot summer, these type of grasses usually try to go dormant as a natural protection from heat and drought. Fertilize at the beginning of these periods so the lawn will get the full benefit of nutrients during its entire growing period. During late spring and early summer there is a rapid growth of grass. This means more mowing will be necessary. Why try to get the grass to grow more quickly and is it worth the extra cost to fertilize and cut the lawn just to have it look greener? One fertilization in early spring, another in early fall and a final application in late fall is all that is necessary, not four times or more as some people do. I fertilize my own lawn twice, spring and late fall, that's it. My lawn's happy and I'm happy.

During the summer, cool season grasses slow down in growth. It is not recommended to fertilize during these months as you will be trying to force them to grow. Weeds may grab the nutrients first and there is a good chance of fertilizer burn in dry or hot conditions. Fertilizing lawns in July and August is not recommended because of drought and heat related stress. If water is available and you do irrigate the entire season, fertilization requirements will be higher due to nitrogen loss from leaching. High nitrogen fertilizers should not be applied beneath the drip line of shrubs from July through mid September. This application may induce late season growth which could stop "hardening-off" exposing the shrubs to possible winter damage.

Because of shorter days and cooler nights, fall fertilization is desirable. It greatly increases the grass density and promotes tiller and rhizome spreading. Grass utilizes the feeding this time of year as it has used up some of its stored food while coming out of summer dormancy. As grass makes most of its roots in the fall, fertilizing then will encourage deep, strong roots. Deep roots are the main key to a

healthy lawn and they will help reduce watering requirements the following year. Fall feedings provide nutrients the turf needs for winter storage. The grass will draw on this reserve during the spring for growth and the summer for heat and drought stress. Even though the blades growth has slowed down approaching winter, roots are still growing.

Advantages Of Fall Fertilization

- Feeds grass after coming out of summer stress and dormancy.
- Encourages deep, strong roots to fight disease, stress, insects, heat and drought and reduce the water requirements for the following year.
- Provides the nutrients needed for grass to replenish its stored energy.
- You will have a greener lawn earlier the following spring.

Fertilizer manufacturers formulate the different mixtures to fit the habits of people as well as those needs of plants. Depending on the fertility of the soil, grass will loose its dark green color within 4 to 10 weeks after application. This is why many gardeners use too much fertilizer on their lawns. They must have that dark green look almost the entire season. The average lawn will stay "healthy" with two feedings per year. There are many factors that influence the rate at which grass consumes nutrients. I have tried to set up some guidelines to help you decide what kind of fertilizer to buy and when to apply it.

Methods Of Fertilization

The three most common methods of applying fertilizer are: shoulder carried broadcast, push type broadcast and liquid hose sprayer.

Shoulder Broadcast

The shoulder held broadcast method is fairly accurate. This inexpensive piece of equipment straps onto your shoulder and spins out fertilizer as you turn a hand crank while walking. The trick here is to make sure you walk in straight parallel lines and turn the crank at an even rate. This equipment can throw the fertilizer in a swath that can reach 8 feet or more depending on how fast you are walking and cranking. It is excellent for small to average size lawns.

Liquid Spray

This method uses an inexpensive bottle sprayer that is connected to your watering hose. Mix the fertilizer in the bottle according to directions, attach it to your garden hose, turn on the water and you're ready to go. Walk in a straight line and spray the liquid back and forth in front as you go down the line at a relatively slow pace. This method can be quite accurate but there is a

tendency to over cover areas especially if your concentration is interrupted. In this case, certain areas may become greener and grow more than others. And if you have a combination fertilizer and weed control mixture in the bottle, too much weed killer in one area may injure the grass.

Push Broadcast

In my opinion, the best and most accurate method of applying fertilizer, seed, lime or weed killers. It may be more expensive, $40 - $60 for a good one, but with proper handling and cleaning it will last for years. There is little chance of underlapping or overlapping if you walk in a straight line, watch the fertilizer throw out and keep an eye on the wheel marks. With a broadcast spreader, the fertilizer is metered through a single opening and is spun out evenly on both sides up to 12 feet. This is similar to the shoulder type method but the container holds more and you can keep an eye on wheel marks for accuracy. The average lawn can be done in less than 10 minutes.

No matter which method you use, make sure your equipment is properly calibrated (proper measuring marks). Problems can occur from too little or too much fertilizer. Uneven distribution can result in different shaded patch lawns. It is very easy to say a lawn should receive about 1 pound of fertilizer per 1000 square feet but this is hard to measure. Each brand has different particle sizes and weights and the flowability is not always the same. This is why each piece of equipment must be individually calibrated per the manufacturers specifications.

Fertilizer normally comes in two forms: granular or liquid. Liquid fertilizer has become very popular during the last twenty years and is a very good method of application. It can give almost immediate results but does not last as long as granular and must be repeated more frequently. They are also more expensive and may not supply an adequate amount of nitrogen each time applied. Granular fertilizer is easier to apply, less expensive and can be purchased in a time slow-release form. However, it should not be put down during hot summer months. Also, it should be watered immediately to make sure there will not be any burning and to help the nitrogen start breaking down in the soil. Every time you water, the pellets release small amounts of nutrients into the soil. Fertilizer burn is greatly reduced and turf receives nutrients over a longer period of time.

Water

Our life and entire environment depends on water. It helps move food and waste materials in the bodies of all living things. Water helps grow plants for food and produces power for use in homes, schools and industry. Every living thing is made of water and depends on it to live. Water that soaks into the soil is taken into plants through their roots. The most essential part of nurturing all of your landscape is to make sure it has enough water to grow and survive. Proper watering practices play a major role in turf's ability to tolerate stress and pest problems. The questions are when, how much and how often do you water your lawn? Lawns need to get the right amount of water at the right time. Improper watering may lead to many different lawn problems. Frequent light waterings cause more

harm than not watering at all. This doesn't encourage roots to grow deeper so they can reach water during periods of draught. Turf that suffers from lack of water will go dormant, which allows weeds to take over. If the lawn does go dormant, leave it that way as fluctuation between active growth and dormancy can be worse. Dormancy is a natural occurrence to preserve the roots and crowns of the plant.

The average lawn in New Jersey needs at least 1-1 1/2 inches of water every week during the growing season. Some of this water may be supplied by nature. Buy a gauge and keep track of how much water does come from rainfall. If nature provides the needed rain, do not water any more. Excess water can make grass susceptible to weeds and fungi. One inch of water wets the soil approximately 4-6 inches deep. Another way of measuring is to place empty cans in the area to be sprinkled. Check the cans every 1/2 hour until the inch is reached and then move the sprinkler to another area. How much water your lawn needs is determined by several factors. There is no set rule. It depends on your type of seed, soil, sprinklers, time, expense and the appearance you want.

Soil Type

Sandy soils do not hold water very well and need more frequent watering. Any water applied beyond the holding capacity of the soil moves below the root zone. Overwatering sandy soil can carry nutrients and nitrate-nitrogen below the root zone where there is potential for groundwater contamination. Sandy soils can store only a few inches in the root zone area. If rain doesn't come within ten days during warm weather, you may see draught symptoms. With this type of soil, one inch or two 1/2 inch waterings per week is usually enough. If you have deep loose top soil, watering once or twice should be enough and maybe three times if there is a dry spell. Clay soils usually have slower infiltration rates. They hold water much better than sandy soils and sometimes are too wet for proper grass growth. Soil enriched with organic matter soaks up and holds water, and the more the soil is able to store water, the longer grass can go without rain or your watering.

Grass Type

The type of grass has a definite bearing on the amount of water required. Some grasses require abundant watering while others can survive with little. Blue grass requires more water than fine fescues. In many cases fine fescues can go for long periods without moisture and recover quickly when water becomes available. Tall fescues have deeper roots that reach down for sub-surface moisture. More recently developed lawn grasses generally provide a deeper rooting turf thereby reducing water requirements preventing the waste of irrigation watering.

Rainfall

In New Jersey we usually get sufficient rainfall in the spring and fall. It is the warm to hot summer months we have to worry about. It takes less water to improve lawn quality in spring or fall because of

the cooler temperatures than it will in summer. But if nature does not help, be ready to intervene with your hose.

Watering may be done almost any time of the day from early morning (the best) to three P.M. Many believe evening sprinkling can save water due to reduced evaporation. However, disease thrives during warm, humid nights so it is better to put the grass to bed as dry as possible. If watered after 3 P.M., the grass may not have sufficient time to dry out by night. Others feel it is not good to water in the sun because of greater evaporation losses and the moisture will not reach the root zone. Watering in the sun, in my opinion, is beneficial to grass as it cools the turf on contact. Newly seeded or sodded spring lawns need regular and deep watering all summer as the roots are not yet developed deep enough to search out whatever water is available and will be more able to adequately survive the next summer. Many people think grass roots grow only three to six inches into the soil. This is not true! There are many long hair-like roots that grow far below the surface roots. In good deep soil, roots may go down as far as twenty four inches depending on the type of grass, it's age and how often and deep the soil is watered.

In spring, the ground is fairly well saturated. As weather warms up plants become more active and start using up soil moisture. Food that was stored in its roots during the winter is being released. Add some nitrogen and spring rains and you will see incredible growth that occurs only in spring. Most lawns look very lush during this time of year. Additional watering is not needed now. As spring ends the soil begins to dry out. When summer begins the top inch of soil is now drying out. As summer progresses, soil dries from the top downward to possibly 2 to 3 inches. This is where the depth of the roots become important. Shallow roots wilt quickly and may even die during the summer but deep rooted turf will stay healthy. Most summers mean hot weather and not much rain. Even after a heavy summer rain soil dries out quickly. Cool season grasses, even healthy ones, may go dormant. You can tell the soil is getting dry when you walk on the grass and you leave footprints. It doesn't have the strength to spring back. This is the first stage, a loss of resilience. In the next stage, grass looses its fresh green color and takes on a dull, almost blue tint. Finally, the blade tops start turning brown and may even die. This is another reason for having a deep rooted lawn. Even though grass tops die, the water stored in the root system keeps grass crowns alive for a while longer.

If the grass does go dormant it is better to leave it this way rather than trying to revive it, as fluctuations between active growth and dormancy can be damaging. Dormancy is nature's way of protecting the crowns and roots of the grass. This may also happen when rainfall is reduced and town watering restrictions are enforced. As the summer dry spell comes, condition your lawn gradually by increasing watering intervals and reducing the quantity. When draught conditions appear, about 1/2 inch of water every week should keep grass crowns alive.

When fall arrives, grasses will green up again. Improper watering leads to several lawn problems: disease, shallow roots, insect and weed infestation. Water is lost by the soil usually in two ways: evaporation and transpiration. Evaporation occurs when the heat of the summer sun removes the moisture from the soil by drying. Transpiration is the loss of water through the plant surfaces and accounts for the major portion of water loss. The average water loss in our area is approximately 1 inch of water every week. During mid summer and if there is a dry wind blowing, the weekly loss may increase to 2 inches. Irrigation schedules should be managed to replenish the moisture that is lost by evaporation and use by

the plant. During certain periods of little or no rainfall, community water restrictions may force you to water your property less or not at all. You can reduce the water without loosing the lawn. Although opinions and estimates vary, the average lawn that has gone dormant may need 1 1/2 inches of water every two weeks during a drought period to prevent the turf from dying. During these periods, try not to play or walk on the lawn. It may not recover from any damage as quickly as healthy grass. Once the drought is over, dormant lawns that have received some water usually take about three weeks to fully recover and when natural rainfall and cooler temperatures return in the fall, regular irrigation practices can be resumed.

Watering Guide

- Water weekly and deeply, penetrating the soil 3-4 inches to encourage root growth.
- Water in the early morning to avoid disease and other lawn problems.
- Overwatering doesn't allow air to circulate near the roots and encourages fungus.
- Clay soils hold water, therefore water less.
- Sandy soils do not hold water well, therefore water more.
- Let the grass and weather determine your watering schedule.

As each soil particle has its fill of water, the additional water is free to move down to the next particle. How deep water penetrates also depends on the amount of moisture present in the soil when the water is applied. In a lawn, grass roots absorb the water around the soil particles. In dry soil, 1 inch of water penetrates approximately:

Sand - 12 inches,   Loam - 5-10 inches,   Clay - 3-5 inches

Disadvantages Of Light Watering

- Shallow rooting and possible drying of root system.
- Encouragement of shallow rooted weeds, example: crabgrass.
- Environment conducive to disease and insects.
- Compaction - packed down soil that prohibits roots from getting water and food.
- More water use and greater water loss which can become expensive.

Methods Of Watering

Many lawns suffer severely from lack of water especially during frequent dry periods during the summer. Watering with the garden hose is time consuming and not very effective. Hoses are sufficient for watering small areas of shrubs, flower gardens or vegetable gardens but not lawns of any considerable size. Effective watering can be accomplished by using any of several sprinklers available today.

Portable sprinklers are an inexpensive way of watering your lawn. They are especially helpful if you have an average to small size lawn, 10,000 square feet or smaller. No matter which kind you choose, make sure the water is evenly distributed over the entire lawn or you may end up with damp areas or hot spots. Pick one that will give uniform coverage with minimal waste. Each type of sprinkler has its own water delivery pattern. There are three commonly used varieties of portable sprinklers: whirling, impulse, and oscillating. When you choose one make sure it will efficiently cover the area in which it will be used.

Whirling

This is a classic among portable sprinklers. It has propelling jets at the end of one long arm and makes a circular spray pattern in the air. Most of the water falls at a distance between 4 - 10 feet. The distribution can be uneven if no overlapping system is used. However, the efficiency increases when areas are overlapped and this sprinkler is quite useful.

Oscillating

This sprinkler has a long arched perforated pipe that sweeps back and forth and delivers water in a rectangular or square pattern, adjustable to any size. It is excellent for use in overlapping patterns to give full coverage without wetting driveways, walks or homes. Sometimes the high spray of water is subject to drift in winds. It is quite useful on average size lawns.

Impulse

Definitely my favorite!! An internal jet rotates the sprinkler and delivers pulses of water in any part to a full circle. Sometimes called a "machine gun" type, rapid jets of water are shot out and when the pattern is completed, it swings back to the beginning to start over. The pattern is excellent and when you match up two patterns side by side, coverage is near excellent.

Underground Sprinkler

This type has many advantages over any portable sprinkler and should seriously be considered if you have a large lawn (over 10,000 square feet). One major advantage is it doesn't ever have to be moved. They are great but not everyone can afford them. For a 10,000 square foot lawn it may cost $2000 to $4000 or more to have a system installed professionally. If you do the work yourself, it may cost $800 to $1200 and be prepared to spend at least one week after work or two to four whole days to install it. However, it can be installed in stages. If you can't afford to put in the whole system at once, you can do

it one section at a time. Automatic sprinkler systems usually use timer activated fixed or pop-up heads. These heads are attached to underground piping. The system can be controlled automatically or manually using a clock timer and are an excellent way of even water distribution on large lawns. Ninety percent of underground systems today are made of plastic. The advantages to the homeowners are: less cost, speed of installation, can be tested above ground first and minimum disturbance of existing grass or garden. When purchasing a system, you should deal with an established nursery or professional installer. The final product depends on how well the project was planned and quality of workmanship.

If you intend to have an underground system, have it professionally installed assuring it will perform properly. Remember, each area of lawn has its own particular soil, shade and sun conditions and therefore its own watering needs. Automatic systems can over or underwater the landscape and there may be runoff or drainage problems. Advantages of an underground system are:

- Can water the landscape while you are not home.
- Can be shut off when it rains.
- Can be set to water for any length of time.
- Can be set to run at any time of the day without you being there.
- You determine what and how many days you want to water.
- Can water different zones without watering others.

If you are installing a new lawn, now is the time to consider an underground system since it is harder to do after the lawn is established. It must be designed for complete coverage so that the spray from each head lands on the adjoining heads.

Watering Tips

- Overwatering can cause problems for all plants.
- As summer approaches, reduce water to help plants adjust to drier conditions.
- Don't sprinkle lawns, soak them to encourage root growth. Deep roots need less water.
- Never water at night, morning is the best time.
- If grass goes dormant, leave it that way; water deeply once in a while to keep it alive.
- Shallow watering results in shallow roots deep watering results in deep roots.
- Let the weather and grass conditions determine your watering schedule.
- Choose a sprinkler that fits the conditions of your landscape.
- Sandy soils need more water and rich loam soils need less.
- Each section of your landscape is different and has its own watering requirements.
- Good soil requires less watering which helps cut down expenses.
- Less water in spring stimulates roots to go deeper for moisture preparing them for summer heat.
- A newly seeded lawn needs constant moisture to help it germinate.
- Less frequent but deep watering is better for the entire landscape.
- Shaded areas require less water.

If you have developed a strong, healthy turf, your watering time and expense will be reduced significantly. Plants have changing requirements and the amount of water they receive depends on your own specific conditions. There is no set rule. Without enough water plants become weak and are easy prey for disease and insects. Whenever the grass is watered, do it regularly and thoroughly. Newly seeded lawns should be watered throughout the summer to help establish the roots. Water is rapidly becoming a scarce commodity, so good watering practices are becoming a necessity. During dry seasons many communities impose watering restrictions. If this happens, you can help it survive until cool, wetter, fall weather arrives by doing the following:

- Stop fertilizing; this forces the grass to grow which increases its need for more water.
- Help reduce stress by raising the height of the lawnmower; let the grass grow higher and mow less often.
- Eliminate weeds which compete with grass for water.
- Take special care of areas under trees as they also compete with grass for moisture.

Mowing

Grasscutting is one of the most important parts of any good lawn maintenance program and is also one of the least understood. Proper mowing gives grass an attractive, uniform appearance. It influences turf density, general health and provides a degree of weed control. How grass is mowed and how often, can affect a lawn's health and appearance. Regular mowing at the proper height keeps grass growing vigorously, but scalping turf weakens grass inviting weed and insect invasion. Improper mowing can cause more lawn problems than any other maintenance practice. Many lawns are cut with dull blades, not often enough or too much and too short. Lawns should not only be cut, they should be pruned neatly, just as you would cut and shape a hedge. Frequent cutting promotes stronger lateral plant growth. A poor lawn can look better if properly mowed and poor mowing can ruin the quality of a good lawn. Just as different grasses require different upkeep, each person has different requirements of their power equipment. By choosing the right type of mower, your grasscutting chores will be faster and much easier.

Cool season grasses have two seasons of growth, spring and fall. These cycles are related to changes in temperature and day length. In early spring, leaf growth is rapid and mowing may be necessary every 5 to 6 days depending on rain and fertilizer applications. As the season progresses into summer, the temperature increases, soil moisture becomes less available and the rate of growth reduces to the point where mowing is necessary only once every 10 to 14 days. When fall arrives, the day length decreases, temperatures get cooler and plant growth increases. Growth is not as rapid as in the spring, and is a tillering type as plants enlarge and many new leaves are produced from the main plant. Grasscutting may increase again to once every week. As grass blades must produce enough food for the entire plant, much leaf blade is necessary. If these blades are frequently cut off too low, food production is reduced to the extent that the grass plant is literally starved. Continued close cutting reduces the depth of root growth and underground stems called rhizomes. The overall effect of close and frequent mowing is thin turf and the inability to withstand heat, disease, weed competition and drought.

Cutting Height

Cutting height has a great influence on root growth. Each species of grass has it's own tolerance to mowing height. In New Jersey, the most common grasses are bluegrass, ryegrass and fescue. These grasses can tolerate a cutting height of 2 inches very well. There are new dwarf varieties of ryegrass and bluegrass that can even tolerate closer cuttings. A general rule is never to cut off more than one third of the total leaf surface. The cutting height of your lawn depends on the season. In early spring the grass depends on food stored in its roots to start growing. The first cut should be relatively short, around 2 inches. This removes some of the dead grass tips, allows more sunlight to reach new blades and stimulates the turf. After two or three cuts, the mower height should be raised to about 2 1/2 inches and left that way until summer arrives. Mowing at this height encourages grass to thicken by growing new tillers from the main plant and new stolons and rhizomes.

Mowing at a height of 2 to 3 inches screens out light to the soil adding natural weed control. This prevents establishment of weeds such as crabgrass, that require light to germinate. A higher cut also encourages a deeper root system allowing them to get moisture and nutrients from the soil. Grass can now develop greater stress tolerance. During the summer, healthy grass may naturally go dormant (stop growing). The cutting height should be raised to 3 inches and left there all summer. This provides a cooler soil surface, lessens evaporation of the soil moisture and inhibits weed establishment. Improper mowing height is often a primary reason for poor lawns. Mowing too low produces shallow rooted turf susceptible to weeds and disease. Mowing too high may result in unwanted thatch accumulation (if the grass is not bagged) and a ragged appearance as some grass blades fall over and others stand up straight. Allowing grass to grow too high also produces a stemmy plant rather than close growing, dense turf. Mowing should continue as long as the grass continues to grow.

Try to avoid midday mowing when temperatures reach 85 degrees or more and the turf is dry. It is better to mow early in the morning or late in the afternoon. During late summer and fall keep the cutting height around 2 1/2 inches and try to extend the mowing intervals allowing grass to store up its food reserves for winter. Cutting the grass into the beginning of November and removing leaves and clippings will help reduce damage from lawn diseases, such as snow mold, during late winter or early spring. Do not mow wet grass. Unless there is an absolute emergency, let grass dry and mowing will be faster and easier, and the lawn will look nicer. Wet clippings are discharged from the mower in small heavy piles that must be removed because of grass yellowing and suffocation. It is wise to alternate the cutting pattern. Change your starting point so your not always following the same wheel marks. Within time, this can compact the soil. Make one mowing in a clockwise direction, the next one in a diagonal pattern and the next in a counter clockwise direction. This helps prevent a striped look and assures a sharp, even cut. Be very careful around trees when mowing. If they get bumped, and are not taken care of immediately, the bark may die. Since the nourishment trees require rise through the bark, the tree may die if the bark is removed from around its base.

If no more than one third of the leaf blade is removed, the grass clippings can be left on most lawns. They are short enough to disappear into the turf and decompose, returning nutrients back into the soil. Since refuse disposal costs have dramatically increased, and some landfills no longer accept grass clippings, many individuals and governmental agencies are seeking alternatives for disposal of clippings.

During the maximum grass growing period, the municipal refuse load in some New Jersey suburban communities may contain nearly one-third grass clippings. Collected clippings become anaerobic (living, active) rather quickly because of their high demand for oxygen. After becoming anaerobic they emit very unpleasant odors. Therefore, grass clippings (in quantity) are difficult to handle and process. From my own experience with handling and disposal of grass clippings and discussions with other lawn care professionals, we suggest considering the following methods to reduce landfilling:

Return To Lawn - It is desirable to leave grass clippings uncollected on the lawn so they are recycled, contributing to soil organic matter and supplying part of the fertilizer needs of the lawn. Adopt a mowing schedule to keep clippings short enough to filter through growing grass and not remain as a mat on top of the lawn. Never allow the grass to double its height between mowings. Research and experience indicate that only 1/4 to 1/3 of the grass length should be removed during mowing. This approach not only eliminates collection and disposal problems, but also contributes to improvement of the lawn.

Garden Mulch - Grass clippings can be used as a garden mulch. Clippings should be dried in the sun for a day prior to being used. They can be spread on garden soil to check weed growth, reduce soil spattering, and moderate soil temperatures. As a precaution, do not use grass clippings from herbicide treated lawns until after three grass cuttings have been made.

Composting - Grass clippings can be composted, particularly when incorporated into a leaf compost pile. However, grass has a high nitrogen content, a much higher demand for oxygen than leaves, and a tendency to mat, thereby greatly reducing the passage of oxygen. Composting piles containing grass clippings thus readily become anaerobic. This, in turn, can produce strong, unpleasant odors. These odors are particularly noticeable when the pile is disturbed. Because of these problems, grass clippings should not be composted alone, but rather mixed with composting leaves. The partially decayed leaves which have a low demand for oxygen, will serve as a bulking agent permitting more oxygen to reach the grass. Grass, which is high in nitrogen, will provide a more rapid decomposition of the leaves. The clippings will also contribute to a better end product than that obtained from composting leaves alone. The resulting compost can be used as a soil amendment, as a mulch for gardens, flower or shrub beds, or as a potting medium.

There are many kinds of lawnmowers, in all different shapes and sizes, you may choose from: small walk behinds, reel, rotary, gas, electric, manual, riding, large rotary, recycling, hover and solar. I will be discussing the most commonly used mowers for homeowners with small lawns to very large lawns. Two of the most popular types are the rotary and the reel. Check the type that best fits your needs and then buy the best quality you can afford. Make sure you buy equipment that is large enough for the job (this goes for all gardening tools).

Before you purchase a lawnmower you consider the following:

- **Maneuverability** - must be light enough to push but heavy enough to get the job done and be able to move around different objects without problems. How much lawn do I have to cut? Do I need a small or large mower?
- **Height Adjustment** - must be easy to adjust with levers. Some mowers have nuts and bolts to change the height of cut. You don't need this extra work.
- **Pull Start Or Electric** - depends totally on your preference and physical condition. It may take several pulls to start the engine or one or two button pushes for the electric but the electric is more expensive.
- **Grass Catcher** - make sure it is easy to put on, take off and empty the catcher.
- **Side Or Rear Bag** - with a rear bag you can trim close to objects on both sides of the mower.
- **Gas Or Electric** - gas mowers must be refilled with fuel and are louder. Electric mowers are quieter but you must carry around an extension cord and are recommended for small lawns only.
- **Quality** - I strongly suggest buying a quality mower from a reputable dealer. Nothing beats a good warranty and most dealers stock replacement parts for immediate service.

Walk-Behind

These mowers usually come in sizes between 19 to 22 inches in width and are good for small lawns under 10,000 square feet. Most are side or rear discharge and come with bagging attachments for disposal of lawn clippings. Rear bag machines are more desirable as the bagging attachment mounts in the rear, giving closer trimming capabilities on both sides. Side discharge bags mount on the side which restricts the ability to trim on that side. Also the side bags get in the way of trees, shrubs etc. Most walk-behinds are rotary types except for reel mowers which will be discussed next. A rotary machine has a horizontally moving high speed blade that cuts on impact. Impact cutting has a risk of fraying the grass, so make sure the blade is always sharp. They are easy to handle and can withstand rough use. You can buy either a hand push or self-propelled model with an electric or recoil pull start. The hand push are fine for small lawns as long as they are not too heavy. Self-propelled are more expensive but make the mowing job easier. Gasoline engines are quite loud (I recommend wearing ear protection) and fuel must be added throughout the season. These are the most popular on average to larger lawns (5000 to 10,000 square feet).

Electric mowers are very quiet and do not have to be refueled, but do use the household electricity which can become expensive depending on time usage and size of the lawn. Also, it is inconvenient to carry and move around a long electric cord and you risk the chance of cutting the cord if there are a lot of objects to cut around. They do not have the power of gas machines and are usually recommended for small lawns only. Gas mowers have the power to cut high grass and weeds and chop leaves into mulch in the fall.

Reel Type

Once very popular, the reel mower is now second behind the rotary. They are preferred on very fine lawns because their scissors cut action produces a nice, clean cut and can be adjusted quite low. The reel mower has difficulty cutting high grass or weeds and will not trim close to trees, fences or walls. Grass is cut by the mower blades pushing the grass blades against the mower bed knife. If the blades and knife are kept in proper alignment, sharpening is not required as often as rotary mowers. This minor advantage is offset in that adjustments and sharpening should be done by a professional service shop. Push type are available for the very small lawn but the self-propelled models are recommended for most lawns. If you maintain the mower adjustments properly and sharpen the blades every spring, it should last for many years. The power driven reel is not very efficient when it comes to high weeds and grass or chopping up debris and leaves. It is a lawn mower and should be used for this purpose only.

Mulching Or Recycling

These mowers have become very popular in the last few years. They are rotary mowers designed to cut the grass blades several times so they fall back into the turf, rather than being bagged or left on top of the grass. Since the clippings are much smaller they decompose quicker. The distinctive design of these mowers creates a vacuum in the housing which suspends the clippings so they can be cut several times. Mulching mowers are also good for chopping leaves into useable mulch during the fall. All of this chopped and recut material enriches the soil and improves the grass.

Mulching kits are also available for regular rotary mowers and usually cost around $20 to $30, but are not as effective as dedicated mulchers. There are drawbacks with mulching mowers. They do not work well when grass is too long or wet. However, things are always being improved. If you are interested in purchasing a mulching mower, check with a reputable dealer about improvements that have been made in these areas.

Large Mowers

The three most common ones are: rear engine riding, lawn tractor and walk-behind. These mowers are best suited for lawns over 10,000 square feet, however, because of easy maneuverability, some homeowners do buy and use them efficiently on almost any size lawn. They come in all different shapes and sizes and cutting widths range from 26 to 72 inches or more. All of them are gas powered and most are available with an electric start engine. Horsepower ranges between 5 to 20 HP.

Rear Engine Rider

This mower has very good visibility as the engine sits behind the operator and the steering is in the front. It is primarily a grasscutter and may come with a bagging attachment but usually does not accept other garden equipment except for maybe a small pull along trailor. All operator's controlls are easily accessible from the drivers seat. The turning radius is very good, so if you have a large lawn with many obstacles or turns, this is a good choice. More storage room is needed but the grasscutting job of a larger lawn becomes a lot easier.

Lawn Tractor

A lawn tractor is different than a rear engine rider in two ways. First, the engine is situated in front of the operator which gives more stability to the tractor. Second, it has the capability of accepting more accessories such as small carts, trailers, drag blades or aerate spikers. Garden tractors are even larger, with more horsepower, larger cutting widths and are designed to accept almost any accessory for lawn or garden needs including: pull equipment, snow removal blades, plows and cultivators. Most tractors have the capabilities of becoming grass mulchers with added manufacturers equipment.

Walk-behind

This type of mower is very popular with landscape professionals, and definitely my favorite lawn-mower. Cutting widths usually range from 36 to 72 inches and horsepower from 8 to 20 HP. With this mower, everything is in front of the operator and it works on the same principle as a self-propelled small hand mower with more control features. All are rotary cutting, usually having 3 or more cutting blades, are gas powered and most can be purchased with an electric start. They are very dependable, easily maneuverable and give a nice clean cut. Prices are fairly expensive, ranging from $1000 to over $4000 depending on the size, cutting width, horsepower and manufacturer. I have been using this type mower for the last fifteen years and am completely satisfied. Although used mainly on larger lawns, a small 36 - 40 inch cut walkmower is perfect for lawns 5000 square feet and larger. Almost all come equipped with bagging attachment capabilities.

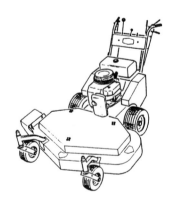

Operating Mowers Safely

Proper safety techniques are essential while operating any lawn mower. Reading the manufacturer's manual and following it's suggestions will not only give you safety tips, it's maintenance suggestions will help you lengthen your mowers life and keep it in good working order. Every year thousands of

people go to medical emergency rooms with lawn mower injuries, which could have been prevented if safety measures were followed. What could be dangerous about mowing grass? A mower is designed to cut grass and that involves heavy, very sharp knives that can cut and throw objects in addition to grass. Carelessness is often the cause of accidents and is one of the easiest problems to overcome. Attention to detail and a clear knowledge of the danger points will allow safe operation of mowers. Being in a hurry is the second biggest cause of accidents. The pressure to improve efficiency by getting more done is a real work place hazard. The following are tips for mower safety developed by experts in the field.

● Read the owners manual and respect the manufacturers advice. Most have made great efforts to make their equipment safe. Allow their recommended safety practices to save you from injury.

● Dress properly. Forget shorts, tennis shoes, sandals and flip-flops; they invite disaster. Wear long pants, heavy shoes and eye protection. A dust mask can be useful if it has been dry weather. Use hearing protection devices or wear a set of ear plugs.

● Fill the tank prior to mowing when the engine is cold. Remember that gasoline can explode or burn outside of the engine too. Don't fill tanks in a closed space. Do it outside where fumes can't collect and explode. And, of course, **NO SMOKING** while filling. Check for gas leaks and fix them.

● Check the area to be mowed. There may be loose objects that can be thrown by the blade. Hidden objects may stop the mower abruptly and cause injury. Most mowers have shields to prevent objects being thrown to the rear or side but they may very well go out the chute to injure a person standing nearby. Keep others from within 100 feet of mower operation.

● Don't reach under the deck to clear the mower. Evidence says that a lot of people will do it and forget that danger is waiting under that deck, even when the engine is off. Blades are sharp and may even start the engine if pushed fast enough. And don't reach into the exit chute; you may reach in far enough to hit the blade and the blade will win. If you must clean under the deck or change the blades, wear heavy gloves, use blocks to hold blades and disconnect the spark plug wire or other electrical connections.

● NO RIDERS! Horror stories start with those having to do with passengers falling off moving machinery and being injured by wheels and blades. Even small riding mowers can run over children. It is difficult to say no to a pleading child but you will be doing them a favor by being firm. If your machine has a ROPS(roll over protection structure) installed, don't remove it.

● Watch that slope. With a walk behind mower, mow across the slope. With a riding mower, mow up and down to avoid tipping. The mower can still tip over if the slope is too steep. As an alternative, plant a ground cover or flowers there that do not require mowing.

Reel mowers may not be as hazardous as those with rotary blades but many of the above safety tips apply too. Keep your hands out from between the reel (blade) and the bed. Above all, remember the heavy, fast moving sharp blades on the mower and treat them and the rest of the machinery with respect.

Trimming And Edging

Besides grasscutting, two other maintenance practices, trimming and edging, give your landscaped yard a professional, manicured appearance. Trimming refers to cutting the remaining grass in hard to reach areas that was not reachable by your mower. A number of specific tools are available to make these chores easier. Hand shears, or long handled grass shears (allows you to stand up while cutting) are very useful for trimming small lawns. If you have a large lawn or many areas to be trimmed, I suggest buying either an electric or gas powered string trimmer. As in the case of mowers, carrying around an electric cord can become annoying but the electric trimmer is fairly quiet. Although it is louder, if there is a lot of trimming to be done, a gas powered trimmer is the way to go. A string trimmer cuts with a whirling nylon filament line that rotates at the end of a long metal shaft. The cutting swaths (amount that can be cut in one sweep) range from 6 - 12 inches or more depending on the machine. Besides normal trimming, it can be used to cut patches of high weeds or grass. Some models can even edge walks and curbs with the right attachment. Edging refers to trimming the lawns edges vertically which gives the landscape a professionally finished look. If you have a small amount of edging to do, such as a short sidewalk, then a longhandled manual star shaped rotary edger is sufficient. If you have a larger lawn, and want to edge some garden beds, flower beds, the sidewalk and driveway then you may want to purchase an electric or gas powered edger.

It is important to use power equipment very carefully around trees, plants, wood fencing, outdoor lighting, bed edging, foundations and most important, people and pets, as severe damage can occur. Wear the proper clothing (goggles, long pants, hats, shoes, gloves) for the specific job when operating any kind of power equipment. Mowing, trimming and edging are all critical parts of a good lawn maintenance program.

Aeration

Occasionally, even carefully maintained lawns for no apparent reason loose their vigorous, healthy appearance. Turf cannot live without nutrients, air and water. Every time you walk on the turf or use a heavy mower you are causing pressure on the soil, thereby compacting it. Areas become compacted by heavy traffic, improper watering, mowing the grass constantly in the same pattern and water runoff during heavy rains.   Compaction drives out the air in soil. This layer seldom goes deeper than 4 inches but can hinder root development. Check the soil in several areas every spring by pushing a wooden matchstick into it with your thumb. If it goes in easily, the soil is not compacted. If it's hard to push in or just goes in 1/2 inch, it's time to aerate.

Compacted soil does not let grass roots grow and an entire lawn may die because of it. Compaction destroys the tiny air pockets in soil structure causing poor drainage. This results in shallow root systems and possible buildup of thatch, as grass roots grow near the surface rather than growing downward. If your soil is compacted, this may lead to other lawn problems such as disease or weed infestation. If a thick layer of thatch develops above the soil line, fertilizer and water won't penetrate the soil. Lawns

that have thatch problems or continuously compacted soil may require two areations per year, spring and fall. Average lawns that are moderately maintained should be aerated at least once every two to three years.   Aeration can be just as important to a lawn's survival as any routine maintenance.

What is aeration? Aeration is the process of pushing holes into or removing plugs from the soil to reduce compaction and encourage deeper grass roots. It is soil cultivation of turf without disturbing the grass plants. Theoretically, the punching of holes also loosens the thatch layer which helps in its decomposition. Aeration allows water, fertilizer and air to reach the roots of grass which promotes more and deeper root growth. Breaking through thatch with an aerator is easier than using a dethatcher and raking or vacuuming the lawn, with almost the same results.

There are several ways you can aerate your soil. One of the easiest is to wear aeration sandals while cutting the lawn or doing any landscape work in the yard. These sandals are available from some garden centers and many mail order garden catalogues. The spikes are usually around 1 1/2 inches long and put thin holes in the soil, but do not remove plugs. For small areas, there is a turf plugger with two hollow pipes that you can step on to remove plugs. Another less effective method, but can be used on larger lawns, is a spiker pulled behind a riding mower. This creates narrow holes, like slices, in the soil but does not remove plugs. These slices may be useful for thinning thatch but are not a means of relieving soil compaction. The spikes seldom penetrate the soil very deeply but the indentations provide a suitable spot for new seed to settle and germinate. Another machine not to be overlooked is called a slit slicer. The blades can be triangular or round and when the machine moves it slices small slits in the soil. In my opinion, and some experts will disagree, this is not a very good method of aeration but, like the spiker, enables seed to get a little below the surface helping it to germinate.

Finally, there is a machine called a power core aerator. This is the machine to use. It is gas powered and can be rented from most rent-all stores. These machines have many hollow tines, usually 5 to 6 inches in length and 1/2 to 3/4 inch in width, and are considered to be the best and only true aerifiers.

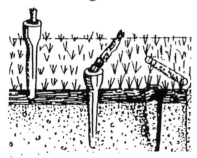

They actually pull out 3 to 4 inch or larger plugs (depending on the depth setting) from the soil leaving open holes that reach into the root zone. These holes will allow water, air and nutrients to travel to the roots and improve turfgrass health. The plugs of earth are removed and deposited on the lawn surface.

Weather conditions, watering and regular lawn activity will help these plugs decompose creating a top dressing. If you don't want to wait a few days for decomposition to occur, the plugs can be chopped up with your lawnmower and turned into a dressing. Some people rake up the plugs to use for their gardens etc., but I would not do this. Raking may cause some of the plugs to fill the holes again, defeating the original purpose for aerating. We want these holes to stay open for as long as possible, allowing roots to grow throughout. The core aerator is power driven and can be a bit touchy to handle for the inexperienced

operator, so please make sure to go as slow as possible or have a landscape professional do the job. This machine really does *pull you* around, so you must pay strict attention at all times.

The best time to aerate is during periods of cool weather, usually spring or fall, when the grass is actively growing. This will help the grass recover rapidly. Aerating during the summer is not wise, as the grass plants are coping with heat and less moisture and don't need the added stress. The ground should be moist to allow the aerator tines to penetrate the turf several inches and remove the plugs. Grass rooting will improve as the holes fill with new actively growing roots. If it hasn't rained recently, water the lawn to at least a one inch depth and then aerate. Make sure you run the machine back and forth and crisscross the entire area for better coverage. Check the plugs and if they are hard and dry and less than 2 inches long, give the lawn another light watering. Make sure you wait until the water has soaked in and try again. If the soil plugs are clay, in this case I would rake them up as gently as possible and throw them away. On slopes, aerification is particularly helpful as the holes provide small reservoirs for holding fertilizer, seed and water. Be extra careful when running the machine on slopes. Immediately after aeration is an excellent time to fertilize and overseed the entire lawn.

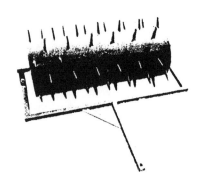

Lack of air space may cause poor soil drainage. Roots have trouble traveling through compacted soil resulting in shallow root systems. When oxygen enters the holes, the decline in soil health is reversed. Soil microorganisms are stimulated, which helps bring the soil back to life. Grass roots grow more vigorously as soil penetration is easier. Aeration, at least every third year, is one of the most beneficial maintenance practices you can do for any lawn.

Lime

Most New Jersey soils are acid by nature and within time, become more acid. Turf grasses don't grow well in highly acid soils. Acid conditions can be caused by the leaching out of calcium and magnesium from the soil, the overuse of organic materials such as peat moss or compost and yearly high applications of nitrogen in fertilizer. Acid soils are called "sour" and alkaline soils are "sweet". Soil reaction is measured by the quantity of hydrogen (H) in the soil which measures in numerical units between 1 and 14. A unit of 7 is considered neutral, therefore soils with a pH of less than 7 are considered acid and those with a pH higher than 7 are considered alkaline. Acid soil is an indication that magnesium and calcium are low and it needs replenishing. High acidity also may cause other nutrients to be unavailable to plants. Lawn grasses grow best in a soil that is only slightly sour. Therefore, an alkaline substance is needed to remove the acidity and make the soil neutral. This substance is called lime.

Ground limestone is a compound of calcium or magnesium and calcium that is capable of counteracting acidic harmful effects on grass. There are three major kinds of lime: burnt lime, hydrated lime and

ground limestone (calcium carbonate). We will only talk about ground limestone since over 90% of all lime used in the United States is this type. Calcium carbonate is the cheapest and most abundant type of lime. Dolomitic limestone contains almost equal parts of calcium carbonate and magnesium. Purchase a soil test kit or bring a couple of samples to your local agricultural agency for testing. A soil test will tell you what your soil pH is and also other important soil information. Sandy soils usually require more frequent liming in lesser amounts than clay soils that require less applications but in larger amounts. Pulverized (ground) limestone is readily available and inexpensive. In this form it is harmless and incapable of burning your skin or plant life unless grossly misused. However, ground limestone is difficult to pass through spreaders because of caking and is very dusty. A proper hat, glasses and mask should be worn to avoid absorption of the dust. Granular lime is better for home use. It has a fine texture and the dust particles are almost all removed. It costs a little more but has these advantages:

- Goes through a spreader easier. Is dustless and will not drift into areas where it is not wanted.
- Will not get all over clothes and be brought into the house.
- Much easier to clean up after application.

Limestone dissolves slowly by contact with soil acids. This will allow it to stay longer in the soil. It moves through the soil at about 1 inch per year. Depending on weather conditions, 50 to 75 pounds of limestone per 1000 square feet will last approximately three years, so it's a good policy to lime your lawn about every third to fourth year. Limestone conditions the soil and will help loosen clay types.

Lime performs several very important functions:

- Corrects soil acidity. Furnishes important plant nutrients - calcium and magnesium.
- Reduces the solubility and toxicity of certain elements in the soil such as aluminum, manganese and iron. This toxicity could reduce plant growth under acid conditions.
- It promotes availability of major plant nutrients. Calcium acts as a regulator and aids in bringing about the desirable range of availability of many plant nutrients.
- It increases bacterial activity and hence induces favorable soil structure and relationships.

The amount of lime to be applied varies on your lawn's particular requirements. Soil tests and advice are readily available from your local extension office which will help determine the exact amount to be applied. A good rule of thumb is to lime your lawn once every three years if necessary, but not more. Too much lime is as damaging as none at all. Liming is a very important addition to any good lawn maintenance program. It is not a cure-all to lawn problems, but by correcting soil acidity, lime creates favorable conditions in the soil for healthy lawn grasses. You may lime at any time of the year, except for midsummer, but to maintain maximum efficiency, the best time is in the fall. The winter snow and rain, combined with freezing and thawing of the soil, aid in the penetration of lime into the soil. Try not to apply when the soil is too wet as it is difficult to get an even distribution. Lime must be spread evenly as it doesn't move horizontally. Attractive lawns are the result of hard work and a carefully planned maintenance program which should apply not only to the grass, but to the soil itself. This should include regular soil tests and the addition of lime into the program.

10 steps to a healthy and attractive lawn:

1. Start off the year with a good spring cleanup, removing all unwanted debris. Make the first cut relatively low to remove dead grass tips, allow sunlight to reach new blades and stimulate the turf.

2. Take a soil test and add soil amendments and lime as needed.

3. Choose the right seed that is adaptable to your specific area and conditions.   In New Jersey, this means Kentucky bluegrass, perennial ryegrass and fescue types.

4. Fill in bare spots with a good seed mixture and top soil before weeds take over.

5. If you have had serious trouble in the past with crabgrass or other grassy weeds, apply a pre-emergent to help prevent their germination.

6. Aerate the lawn. This reduces soil compaction, allows water, air and nutrients to reach the roots encouraging a deeper root system and helps break through any thatch layer.

7. Add the right fertilizer to help build better soil structure. The slow release type are more beneficial as they extend the benefits over a longer period of time.

8. Develop good mowing practices. Mowing can make or break a lawn.

9. Let the grass and weather determine your watering schedule. When you water, water deeply penetrating the soil at least 3-4 inches. Light waterings encourage shallow root systems.

10. Control weeds and other lawn problems culturally, if possible. Use pesticides as a last resort.

Maintaining a quality turf involves more than fertilization, watering and mowing. It demands proper cultural practice, occasional dethatching, aeration, soil tests, lime, and knowing when to perform these practices. The main concern is to create deep rooted turf that will flourish. A healthy lawn is the best defense against heat, drought, weeds, insects and disease. Most lawn grasses like to grow high but are prevented by our constant mowing. This removes the long blades that would photosynthesize sunlight and nutrients that the plant needs for food. It is our job to replace the nourishment with water, air and fertilizer. A lush, green lawn sets off trees, flowers and shrubs more than anything else in a landscape. If the lawn looks bad, the rest of the landscape suffers.

Notes

Chapter 4

Lawn Problems

In this chapter, I will be discussing lawn problems and how to deal with them. Weeds, insects, fungus and rodent pests are problems that even the best of lawns can get. Maintaining a high quality lawn requires good pest management with proper maintenance practices. In landscaping, the word pest refers to any unwanted conditions in your environment such as: plant diseases, weeds, insects, rodents, fungi, etc.

Pesticides

Pesticides are chemicals used to control pests. Some pesticides only have to touch the pest to kill and others must actually be swallowed. Following are descriptions of various types of pesticides commonly used:

Insecticides are chemicals used to control all types of insects. They kill by touch or swallowing. Some kill by both methods. Others, called systemics, may be injected, fed or absorbed into the host animal or plant that is to be protected and when the insect feeds on the host, it eats the chemical and dies.

Fungicides are chemicals used to control fungi that cause molds and plant diseases. They all work by contact with the fungus. Some fungicides are systemic, that is the roots absorb the chemical, move throughout the plant system and kill the fungi. Others are protectants, and before the disease starts, are designed to prevent the plant from getting any disease. This type is very useful when a particular disease has been attacking the plant year after year. Finally, eradicants kill the disease after it appears on the plant.

Herbicides are chemicals used to control any unwanted plants anywhere: lawns, flower beds, gardens, gravel areas, woods, etc. Herbicides can be selective or nonselective. Selective kill certain plants while not affecting others. They control many broad-leaved plants but do not damage desired grasses. Nonselective are toxic to all plant life. These are used where no plant life is wanted such as under fences, in driveways, industrial areas or parking lots. Some nonselective herbicides are soil sterilants that eliminate all vegetation and delay the invasion of new vegetation for several months. They are mainly used along railroad tracks, parking lots and roadsides. Herbicide application timing is very important. You can make preplanting treatments, preemergence treatments or postemergence treatments. Manufacturers put directions on the labels for the best time to apply herbicides to get the best results.

Preplanting herbicides are usually made before the crop planting. Examples are when planting a vegetable garden, flower beds, shrubs beds or a new lawn. These chemicals may be incorporated right into the soil or even spread on top, depending on the directions. Preemergence herbicides are applied

after the crop is planted but before weeds appear. An example is applying a crabgrass preemergent to prevent germinating crabgrass seeds after the lawn seed crop has been planted and is growing. Postemergence chemicals are applied after the crop or weeds appear and must be very selective. They have to control the unwanted weeds but cannot harm the crop.

Miticides are used to control ticks and mites, usually by contact to be effective. These animals are so small that great care must be taken to cover the entire area in which they live.

Rodenticide chemicals are used to control rats, mice and other rodents. Most of these chemicals are stomach poisons and usually come in the form of baits. Caution must be used when applying rodenticides because of the hazard to wildlife and domestic animals.

Some pesticides such as a "broad spectrum insecticide" applied over the entire lawn may kill all insects. Not only will the targeted pest die, but beneficial insects that feed on pests, such as spiders, ants and ladybugs may die too. Pesticides have their place in our environment but there are many undesirable side effects. We should use them only as a last resort, only after other more natural methods have failed or when a specific pest has become so overwhelming that the natural defense system of the landscape is being threatened. Before buying pesticides please make sure you have tried other methods, some of them being discussed a little later in this chapter.

Identify

Lawns are damaged by different pests in different ways. There are many commercial combination fertilizers that contain insecticides, fungicides and herbicides. If certain lawn problems cannot be controlled through general maintenance, they must be properly identified and then treated. We must choose the right pesticide to control the right pest. We can do this by first identifying the pest. Sometimes one pest is blamed for damage that is actually caused by a different one, or even by weather conditions. If you have taken a soil test and visibly checked for insects or fungi and still cannot identify the pest, call in a professional landscaper or bring several samples to you local nursery or extension office for assistance. After the pest has been identified, you must find out the time and best stage to control it. The stage at which pests can be best controlled is not the same for all.

Consider Alternatives

Not all diseases or insects are necessarily pests. They may just be resting on plants or may be eating other unwanted insects. Sometimes damage may be very little or too late in the season to warrant a chemical control. We must learn to determine if any control is really necessary. There are other ways to control pests without using pesticides. Cultivation and hand pulling weeds, using natural enemies of pests such as predators, using plants that repel pests, buying grass seed that is disease resistant and proper maintenance practices especially watering and mowing are all alternatives to pesticide usage. We must consider alternatives and possibilities. Sometimes chemicals give immediate results but to help our environment, wouldn't it be worth it to wait a little longer and get almost the same results.

Choose The Right Pesticide

Once a pest has been identified, and you have determined that chemical control is absolutely necessary, you must choose the right pesticide for the job. The pesticide must:

- Not injure turfgrasses and be effective against the target pest.
- Have a label giving directions on use.
- Not be harmful to beneficial fungi, insects or other plants it may touch.
- Not move from the treated area to harm other plants or animals.
- Be the proper formulation to be used in the equipment the applicator owns.

Always consider the impact a pesticide may have on the environment. To choose the best control, you must identify the pest, find out when it is best controlled and what chemicals will control it. Try not to apply them more often than is absolutely necessary and make sure you have first eliminated any possible cultural or biological method before you apply a poison.

Handling And Applying

Pesticides are manufactured to control pests mostly by poisoning them. There are many pesticides that are also poisonous to humans, and may even kill them. Others are fairly safe but can irritate the nose, mouth, skin or eyes. You should always wear proper clothing when handling these chemicals. The extent of protective clothing depends on the toxicity of the pesticide. Pesticides can enter your body in either of three ways: oral, dermal or inhalation. If the small particles enter through your skin or lungs, you may not even know you are poisoned.

Oral - Pesticides may accidentally enter through the mouth while smoking or eating before washing the hands or if improperly stored in food containers and not labeled.

Dermal - Pesticides enter the skin by not wearing the proper clothing. Wearing pesticide soaked clothing or letting the chemicals fall on the skin while spraying or mixing is dangerous. Certain areas of the skin are more susceptible than others. Be extremely careful with the eyes, wrists, armpits, groin and feet and make sure you cover and take care of any abrasions as they allow pesticides to enter more quickly.

Inhalation - Pesticides in the form of fumes, spray or dust can be inhaled. Take particular care while mixing any chemicals or reading directions with an open container. If using any pesticides indoors, be sure to use a respirator available at some hardware stores, garden centers or mail order catalogues.

People can be poisoned no matter how the chemical enters the body. Avoid spills or splashing when mixing. Read all labels and wear the proper clothing - shoes, long pants, long sleeve shirt, gloves, hat, goggles and if necessary, a mask or respirator and any other clothing the manufacturer recommends. Rubber gloves are excellent when mixing and applying pesticides and cleaning equipment. Wash all chemicals off your skin immediately and wash the clothes separately from your other laundry. Always

mix chemicals below your eye level and with your back to the wind to avoid splashing or wind spraying. If you spill any pesticides, wash yourself immediately with soap and water. Keep a container of anti-bacterial liquid soap in the work area.

If a spill occurs, contain it and clean it up immediately with an absorbent material like cat litter or sawdust. Mix only the amount of chemical you need to treat the desired area. Try to avoid making excessive amounts and then have leftovers - a pesticide is a hazardous waste and difficult to discard. Make sure you check the equipment operation and calibration before you fill it with the chemical. Improper calibration can lead to excessive residues on turf and plants which may harm animals, humans or the environment. Make several maintenance checks throughout the year and repair any problems as soon as discovered.

When applying pesticides, there are several safety precautions to be followed. Don't be careless. You are responsible not only for yourself but other people, pets, wildlife and the environment. Make a copy and keep them in your work area or shed.

Clean up spills

Wash yourself and laundry

Spray only target
avoid any drifts

Safe Handling And Use Of Pesticides

- Read and understand all labels especially emergency medical procedures and antidotes. Keep a small safety kit near your equipment.

- Do not apply any (dry or liquid) pesticides at temperatures above 90 ° F.

- Plan ahead - have plenty of soap and water available for cleanup and emergencies.

- Check the label for proper clothing to wear.

- Apply chemicals during the right weather conditions. No excessive heat or wind.

- Use the safest, most effective pesticide.

- Move pesticide containers carefully. Carelessness can result in spills.

- Never put groceries or pet supplies near pesticides. Never allow children or pets near pesticides.

- Store pesticides where they are protected from direct sunlight, water and temperature extremes.

- Do not work in any kind of drift spray, as chemicals can be absorbed.

- If chemicals have spilt on your gloves, don't wipe them on your clothes. They may soak through to your skin.

- Never smoke, eat or drink while handling pesticides.

- Keep all children and pets out of the area to be sprayed and remove any toys or pet supplies.

- Never blow out clogged nozzles or hoses with your mouth.

- Make sure there are no leaks in tanks or spreaders.

- Constantly check your equipment. If it needs repair do so before finishing the job. Make every effort to avoid drifting from the target area.

Safety does not end with the completion of a job. The equipment still must be cleaned and stored properly. Wash the outside of the equipment and rinse the inside at least three times. Follow the label directions for cleanup - they are put there for your safety. If there are any empty pesticide containers perforate both ends so they may never be used again. Wash your body thoroughly with soap and water. If your clothes were exposed to chemicals, wash them separately from other laundry. Store pesticides where they will be protected from the elements. The facility should be dry and well ventilated. Do not store fertilizer, feed, seed, food or pet supplies with the pesticides. Store the chemicals in their original containers only. Separate them from each other by type to avoid contamination. Keep the facility locked to prevent any children or pets from entering and post a sign "Pesticides Inside". Explain to family members that pesticides are dangerous and can be killers.

Reentry time is the time you may go back into the treated areas. Usually labels state this time but on the safe side, do not reenter until the area has completely dried if a liquid was sprayed or 48 hours after a granular was applied. Always protect yourself, other people and the environment by using safe procedures when working with any kind of chemicals. Safety precautions are for everyone's good. Municipalities are becoming more aware of problems concerning the disposal of excess pesticides and empty pesticide containers. Most labels advise you of the proper methods of disposal but local communities are becoming more strict in their requirements, so it would be smart to contact them.

Weeds

For centuries, weeds have been a challenging problem for gardeners and homeowners. Many years ago, weeds were controlled with plows, hoes and other garden equipment by cultivation or tilling. In the 1900's there was a major breakthrough in weed control when the first herbicides were developed. These relatively inexpensive chemicals have revolutionized weed control methods. A weed is defined as "any unwanted plant" in a given area of land. Weeds can grow anywhere: lawns, gardens, roadsides, athletic fields, woods etc. Just about anywhere there is vegetation, weeds grow. My discussion about weeds and their control will be limited to those growing in lawns, gardens and surrounding areas. Most soils contain millions of weed seeds. Some weed plants can create over 10,000 seeds. Purslane, a common lawn weed, produces in one season, more than 2 million seeds. Eventually, all lawns are subject to and attacked by crabgrass or other weeds. The goals of every homeowner and gardener should be to keep weeds within an acceptable level that is not unsightly. There is nothing wrong with having a few weeds scattered in your lawn, garden or shrub beds. This is normal and acceptable.

Weed seeds are naturally in soil but are also spread in several ways: they travel in the air and can attach themselves to animals, humans and lawn equipment. Once they are deposited in the soil, they sprout and grow, competing with grass, flowers, vegetables and shrubs. Some seeds wait dormant in the soil for years, germinating whenever they get sunlight and moisture. Weeds grow more easily in an area

that is poorly maintained. Having a weed free lawn is one of the main concerns of many homeowners. People first think of chemical control instead of correcting watering procedures, changing poor mowing habits or liming and improving soil fertility. Some weeds are inevitable even in the best of lawns. Weeds can be divided into 4 classes: annual grasses, annual broad-leaved weeds, perennial broad-leaved weeds and perennial grasses and grasslike weeds.

Annual Grasses - Annual grasses germinate, grow and produce seeds in one season. They resemble desirable turfgrasses in their growth habits, but differ in texture and color. Examples of annual grasses are crabgrass, foxtail, goosegrass and annual bluegrass.

Annual Broad-leaved Weeds - Annual broad-leaved weeds also germinate, grow and produce seeds in one season. In most cases, however, they do not resemble desirable turfgrasses in form, color or texture. In general, the leaf width is much broader than that of turfgrasses. Examples of annual broad-leaved weeds are black medic, henbit, prostrate spurge and knotweed.

Perennial Broad-leaved Weeds - Perennial broad-leaved weeds persist for more than one growing season. They do not resemble turfgrasses in leaf shape or texture, but usually have wide or broad leaves instead. Dandelions, wild violets, plantain and clover are examples of perennial broad-leaved weeds.

Perennial Grasses And Grasslike Weeds - Perennial grasses persist for more than one growing season because of their perennial root systems. They may resemble some desirable turfgrasses, yet can usually be distinguished from them when found together in a turf stand. Examples of perennial grasses and grasslike weeds are smooth bromegrass, yellow nutsedge, wild garlic and quackgrass.

There are three methods used to control turf weeds: **cultural** practices, **mechanical** and **chemical**. Proper management using all three methods discourages weeds and encourages healthy grass.

Cultural

One of the most important ways to control weeds in the lawn is to have a healthy, dense turf. Even trained weed specialists rely on good cultural practices as a line of defense against weeds and use herbicides as a last resort. Herbicides are considered valuable tools as additions to cultural practices but are not to be used as substitutes for them. If misused, they can cause serious harm to people and the environment. It is hard for weeds to establish themselves in a high quality lawn. A shaded soil surface discourages weed germination. Weeds are often the result of improper maintenance practices. They are sometimes caused by improper mowing, frequent light waterings and improper fertilization. Certain conditions also permit weeds to invade such as compacted soil, infertile or sour soil, thatch buildup, insects, turf disease or maybe as simple as growing the wrong type of grass in the wrong area.

Mowing - Mowing the grass at the proper height helps shade and cool the soil which protects the root system from draught and high temperatures. This reduction of stress on the root system helps the turf grow more vigorously and increases its ability to avoid weed invasion. The higher the turf is cut, the deeper the root system grows. If the turf is cut short, roots will be closer to the soil surface. If the roots

are too close to the surface, they will be exposed to drought and high heat stress. Proper mowing practices can be an effective weed control method.

Water - Proper watering can help turf live through periods of excessive heat and drought. Water must be applied deeply but not often. Frequent light sprinklings encourage shallow root growth. The soil should be soaked to a depth of 3-4 inches encouraging a deep, broad root system helping the turf resist weeds.

Seed - Using a high quality seed that is weed free is another step in weed control. When you buy seed, check the label for guaranteed "weed free". This was discussed in more detail in chapter 3. Purchase seed with the least possible percentage of weed and crop seeds. Also, check on new varieties that have been developed as "resistant" to drought, disease and insects. Planting these varieties is easier than battling with pests.

Nutrition - Providing proper amounts of nutrients helps keep turfgrasses growing and develop a good root system that spreads. Spreading roots develop new grass blades reducing bare spots in the fight against weeds. Slow release forms of fertilizer release nitrogen over an extended period of time. Many manufacturers now produce mixtures containing slow and quick release together. The thinking here is that the quick release part stimulates the initial growing and the slow release part is available later in the season.

Mechanical

Still an effective means of weed control, manually hand pulling or digging is efficient in small areas, when only a few weeds are present or if you have extremely sensitive plants. There are quite a few mechanical weed control devices available today that are good for small areas such as: weed slicers, weed rooters, hotbed weeders, dandelion diggers, asparagus knives and others. These tools are helpful in removing weeds through digging, cutting, slicing, pulling etc. Lots of energy is used, good for the heart, but in most cases the roots are cut and not completely removed allowing them to grow back. These tools are good for temporary removal and appearance.

Chemical

Sometimes cultural and mechanical weed control are not enough. Perennial weeds with deep root systems cannot be controlled unless the entire system is removed or destroyed. After other methods have failed, chemical control may be required. The right selection and application of herbicides will effectively control a wide variety of weeds with a low risk of turf or ornamental plant injury. Herbicides vary in their persistence in plants and the environment. Nonpersistant herbicides quickly control weeds and then the chemical decomposes within a couple of weeks. Persistent herbicides remain active in soil for 3 months or more, which give the advantage of extended weed control.

Herbicides come in various formulations: liquid, pellets, powders and granules. Granular forms are the most popular and widely used by homeowners to eliminate broad-leaved weeds. Most herbicides selectively kill certain weeds. The first step in good weed control is to properly identify the weed. If you cannot identify the weed, check in a weed identification book at your local garden center or bring a sample to the nearest extension office. If you pick a herbicide that is not matched to the weed, the result will be poor weed control.

Annual weeds complete their life cycle within one year. They must reseed in order to reproduce and don't tolerate good mowing practices. The problem they cause is usually temporary, and not worth the trouble to treat, unless we're talking about a grassy weed like crabgrass. Biennial weeds live for two years but usually do not cause a major problem in turf. Perennial weeds live more than two years and keep coming back year after year unless controlled. Those perennials that creep along the top of the soil are difficult to control because of their extensive root systems. They respond favorably to lime and fertilizer. Even shorter grasscutting will not harm them but may injure the grass. This group of creeping weeds is not so easily controlled by chemicals. They can establish in even the best well-kept lawns. Herbicides strong enough to kill them may injure turfgrass as well.

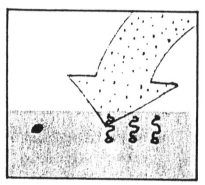

pre-emergence

Broadleaf weeds are either annual or perennial and perhaps the easiest weeds to kill. Chemical control is extremely effective. Just within the last decade, a preemergence broadleaf herbicide called ISOXABEN was developed. This is a broad-spectrum herbicide that controls over 30 broadleaf weeds as they germinate, with little or no risk of leaching in groundwater. For those weeds that escape this herbicide, we have postemergence chemicals that should do the trick. However, this type of herbicide moves readily in the soil and may reach groundwater. Low use rates reduce the risk of high levels of groundwater contamination. Fall is usually the best time to control broadleaf weeds because they are actively growing and storing food in their roots for winter survival and spring startup. Also injury to non-target ornamental plants from drift is reduced because they are hardening off for the winter. Non-target injury is more likely to occur in the spring when all plants are starting their new growth. If there are a lot of weeds in the spring, this is an acceptable time for control as they are beginning their active growth. The herbicide kills the foliage but may not travel to the roots.

Annual grassy weeds reproduce each summer and fall by casting their seeds into the soil. The seeds then stay in the soil over winter and germinate in the spring. Keeping grass cut as high as possible helps shade out the seedlings even if they germinate. If the lawn is not infested, hand pulling or digging works as long as you get the roots. However, chemical control in the form of a preemergence is the most effective. These chemicals work on the germinating seeds only and will not kill already existing weeds. Preemergence herbicides are usually put on the lawn in early spring before the weed seeds germinate. A good guide for crabgrass control is to apply the preemergence when the forsythias are blooming. Do not apply them too early though, as the concentrate may become too low to adequately control germinating seeds. The same chemical should control other annual weeds such as goosegrass, foxtail and annual

bluegrass. As the seedlings germinate, they come in contact with the herbicide and are killed. If you have desirable new seedlings emerging or plan to seed the lawn in the spring, a herbicide called Siduron will provide control of annual grass weeds but not harm the development of new seedlings. You can even put this chemical down the same day you are seeding without any problems. If you failed to apply

a preemergence or put it down too late and you have crabgrass or other grassy weeds growing, there still is help. A postemergence product in the methanearsonate family (DSMA) can be used (usually it takes 2 applications 14 days apart) and gives very good control.

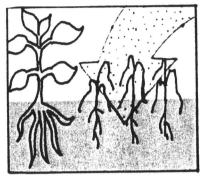

post-emergence

When applying a herbicide, do not place it within 1 foot of any flowers or shrubs as any broad-leaved plant is susceptible to herbicides. They should not be allowed to contact any part of a desirable plant including the roots. When applied to soil too close to the plant, the herbicide may be washed into the root zone by your own watering or a heavy rain. Before putting down a herbicide, I suggest you mow the lawn and water it well. After applying the chemical, you won't be able to cut it for several days and if you used a granular form, you won't be able to water it either. Watering ahead of application encourages weed growth, making them more responsive to the poison and help the granules stick to the leaves of the target plant. Herbicides are effective anytime the plants are actively growing but are most effective in the fall. When weeds are controlled in the fall, and reseeding is done, turfgrasses have a chance to fill in the spots before crabgrass emerges in the spring.

Most herbicides can be applied with a broadcast spreader, spray bottle attached to a hose or a small pump tank sprayer, depending on the size of the area to be treated and chemical formulation. Different mixtures of herbicides are readily available to homeowners. Mixtures usually contain two or more active ingredients which broaden the range of weeds controlled. Another advantage of a mixture is the reduced rate of each herbicide which increases safety to desirable grasses and plants. Avoid application when the wind may cause drift to other ornamentals. If the herbicide accidentally contacts desirable plants, wash it off immediately.

A Few Common Weeds

Buckhorn plantain - A well-rooted perennial producing hard to mow seedheads in the summer. It spreads by seeds and the roots regenerate.

Chickweed - Moves aggressively into thinned areas. Creeping perennial that spreads by seeds.

Crabgrass - An annual that grows rapidly during hot, dry weather. Grows from seeds produced in previous years. If allowed to spread, it can smother the lawn.

Dandelion - A perennial with jagged leaves and a deep root. Yellow flowers turn into puffballs containing seeds. The wind-borne seeds are produces in spring.

Foxtail - An annual that grows during the summer and produces seeds for the following spring.

Ground Ivy - A perennial, low creeping weed that can be hard to kill. Responds to fertilizer and lime, and spreads fast.

Nutsedge - Perennial that spreads by seeds and runners. Seedheads develop during summer.

Oxalis - Perennial that produces a very large amount of seeds every year.

Quack grass - A perennial that has narrow leaves growing on tall stems. Spreads by seeds and runners.

Sorrel - A perennial that forms a shallow rosette stage during the first year. Can be easily controlled by hand pulling or a light dose of herbicide.

Spurge - An annual that grows vigorously during the summer. Spreads by seeds and can be easily habd pulled.

Insects

A landscape is generally a complex and competitive environment. There are more than 700,000 insect species that have been identified and a little over 10,000 of these are considered harmful pests. Only a few of these species are actually responsible for injury to turf. However, this small amount can do quite extensive damage and an unusual quantity of these insects present in the lawn may be a warning. Some are so small, they are hardly noticeable. Others, such as fleas and ticks, are very troublesome to pets and people but don't harm the grass. Sometimes damage is not immediately noticed and reaches an advanced stage before it is recognized. When this occurs, the turf may be damaged beyond repair. Proper identification becomes very important to help determine the correct treatment.

Identifying the insect pest is the first and most crucial step in proper management. Having someone familiar in diagnosing insect problems help you is a good way to learn, but if this is not possible, there should be several books available at your local garden center or library that will help with identification. You must become familiar with the adult and larval stages of the most common insects in your area. Understanding their life cycles helps to diagnose the problem. You should know what time of year to look for certain insect pests and what damage they can inflict on turfgrass.

Let me first identify some of the most common turf damaging insects in our area. They are divided into two categories: surface insects and sub-surface insects.

Surface	**Sub-surface**
Armyworms	Billbug Grubs
Cutworms	White Grubs
Chinchbugs	Nematodes
Sod Webworms	

Surface insects destroy the grass by either extracting the plant juices or chewing the blades. They often live in debris or thatch above the soil level and do most of their damage at night. Sub-surface insects destroy grass by eating the roots causing the entire turf to die. Surface insects hide in the grass, burrowing into small debris or thatch, making them hard to find. One way to find out if they are present and to help make an identification is to cut both ends out of a coffee can and push it into the ground. Put a small amount of liquid detergent into water, mix it and pour this into the can. The detergent irritates the insects skin and forces it to come out of the turf and float to the top. This may take 5 to 10 minutes to occur. Here are some indications that surface insects are active and descriptions to help identify the pest.

- In the evening, small moths are seen flying in zigzag patterns across the lawn.
- A large amount of birds are pecking holes in the grass looking for insects.
- The turf appears to be dying along walks, patios, curbs and driveways.
- Grass blades are chewed off almost at soil level.

Armyworm - ranges from 3/4 to 1 1/2 inches long and has a plump segmented body. It varies from a greenish-gray to brown color with a yellow-white stripe running down its back which ends in a "V" on the head. Eggs are laid in low growing plants such as grass, flowers and shrubs. As soon as the larvae hatch, which is usually within 10 days, they immediately start eating. Damage often happens in late summer or fall and the lawn turns brown with circular ragged patches. Armyworms usually move in large groups devastating most of the vegetation in their path.

Cutworm - ranges from 1 to 2 inches in length, has three pairs of legs and additional prolegs on the abdomen. It is black, brown or greenish-gray with lighter stripes along the side. The larvae hide at the soil surface during the day and feed at night chewing along the edge of grass blades. They are solitary feeders, not like the armyworms who mass together. In late spring, adult moths lays eggs on weeds and grass blades. The eggs hatch within ten days and the larvae eat grass until fully grown. Damage occurs during the warmer months with patches of closely cut grass. When the larvae mature, they dig in the soil, pupate and change to moths.

Chinchbug - when mature, is approximately 1/6 of an inch long. Females deposit eggs in soil debris, grass blades or weeds. The eggs hatch within 10 days as reddish nymphs with a white band on their backs. Chinchbugs insert a slender beak into grass plants, inject a toxin and extract plant juices. If not stopped at once, they will spread rapidly until large areas of turf are destroyed. Chinchbug activity usually starts when temperatures average in the middle to high 70's. Symptoms usually appear first along sidewalks or driveways where heat is radiated. In open sunny areas, the grass starts to brown in irregular patches. As chinchbugs grow older they have black bodies and develop white wings.

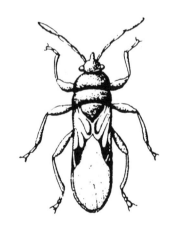

Sod Webworm - is a worm-like insect, light brown in color ranging from 1/2 to 3/4 inch in length. It has stiff hairs sticking out from dark circular blotches throughout the segmented body. Adult moths are visible spring through summer. Female moths fly over grass in a zigzag pattern and drop their eggs into the turf. The eggs hatch within ten days and the larvae immediately start chewing the blades, often cutting them in half or severing the plant at the crown. The areas have a yellowish-brown irregular appearance that is quite similar to damage caused by drought. Sod webworms stay hidden during the day and spin silk like tunnels in thatch areas.

Sub-surface insects usually live through a four stage cycle: egg, larvae, pupa and adult. The majority of these insects do their damage in the larvae stage but some do damage in both, the larvae and adult stages. In the larvae stage, plant roots are devoured thereby killing the entire grass plant. Detection of sub-surface insects is not as easy as finding those that live above. You must actually dig and probe into the soil to find them. Here are some indicators of sub-surface insect activity and descriptions to help identify the pest.

- Entire sections of turf can be pealed back like a piece of carpet.
- Upon inspection, the grass roots are chewed off just below the surface.
- Birds, moles, skunks and other small animals are digging in turf searching for food.
- The turf has an overall thinning appearance.

Billbug Grub - The adult billbug grub comes out of hibernation during the first warm days of early spring. It is a clay colored beetle with a long snout measuring from 1/5 to 3/4 inch in length. The adult beetle feeds on grass and lays its eggs onto the grass blades or the soil. Within 15 days, the eggs hatch into legless, white grubs, 1/2 to 3/4 inch in length, with an orange-brown head and a dark, humped back. It does its damage by chewing the grass near the crown and devours roots below ground level, causing patches of yellow or dead grass.

White Grub - is one life cycle phase of the May, June, Japanese or European Chafer beetle. It ranges from 1 to 1 1/2 inches in length, has a brown head, six legs and a smooth and shiny segmented body. These grubs damage the lawn by chewing and devouring grass roots. Damage often occurs between summer and fall, especially during dry, hot spells. The turf can be rolled back like a carpet, exposing the feeding grubs. During the winter, they burrow deep into the soil to hibernate. When the soil warms up in spring, they come out of hibernation and start eating grass roots again. In mid-summer, grubs pupate into adult beetles and emerge from the soil. They stay above ground for a few weeks, feeding on flowers (especially roses) and other foliage. Then they burrow into the soil, lay eggs and a new life cycle starts.

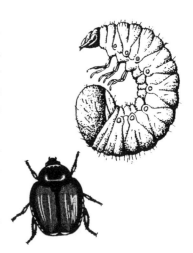

Nematodes - are very small plant parasites visible only through a microscope. They can live off animals, plants and man and can cause a number of diseases. They are eel-shaped, legless and have smooth unsegmented bodies that are covered with a transparent skin. Nematodes shed their skin as they pass through their successive larval stages. Plant nematodes have a hollow spear used to puncture plant cells. Their eggs hatch into the first of four larval stages. After the final stage, nematodes develop into male or female. Each life cycle may last three to four weeks. Most nematodes spend a part of their lives feeding on roots in soil. Soil moisture, temperature and structure all affect their survival. They move very slowly but can be transported

by lawn equipment, running, flooding water, shoes or tools. Most of the turf's injury is caused by a secretion injected into the plants when the nematode penetrates the roots with the stylet. The feeding process allows plant tissue to break down, causing galls and distorted foliage. This decreases a plant's ability to accept nutrients and water from the soil. The turf shows signs of nutrient deficiency and the damage gives an ideal beginning for diseases to enter. Nematodes are always surrounded by bacteria and other viruses. Control can be attained using soil sterilants which emit gasses effective against nematodes. Other chemicals, called Nematocides, are effective and can be applied to certain grasses tolerant to these chemicals.

Serious damage can usually be prevented with regular inspections and prompt action when a problem is recognized. You should look for discolored or growth stunted areas and by detecting symptoms early, you can prevent the buildup of pests. Some insects feed only during the day and others at night. Some are destructive at certain times in their lifecycles and at only particular times of the year. Good insect control is determined on proper identification and knowledge of it's behavior. Different insects thrive in moist, warm conditions, others in hot, dry conditions. Soil type and quality and the amount of sunlight or shade have influence in insect establishment. Insects usually do most of their damage during warm periods, summer and early fall, as the turf has been weakened by draught and excessive heat. The damage is compounded because this is the time of year when insect populations are the highest. Insects that feed underground are harder to control than those that feed above. It is hard for the insecticide to make contact, as it must penetrate any thatch and move through the soil to be effective. Short term pesticides loose some of their potency before the target pest is reached. If your lawn has a thick layer of thatch, it should be removed or aerated first before the chemical is applied.

Before any control can be made, the pest must be identified. Certain symptoms in lawns such as browning or yellowing of grass blades or patches that appear to be withering, may be caused by diseases, poor soil conditions or improper fertilization or watering, rather than insects. It is important to check all possible causes before any pesticides are applied. After a problem has been correctly identified, consider an assortment of management strategies. You can prevent most turf insect problems by using good cultural practices. Home lawns receiving regular irrigation rarely have insect problems. With adequate water and fertilizer, grass plants quickly overcome insect injury. An evenly scattered 10 percent loss of grass plants due to billbug injury will be easily filled in by actively growing, well maintained grass plants. However, a poorly managed lawn may experience an overall thinning effect due to a scattered 10 percent plant loss.

As with all lawn problems, certain cultural treatments should be tried first. Selecting the right resistant grass and maintaining it properly is a main line of defense. Thatch accumulation is a great place for insects to live and breed, so if you have any over 1/2 inch thick, remove it by dethatching. Keep in mind all of the beneficial insects that live in a healthy lawn. Ants and spiders will eat a large percentage of the eggs and larvae of many pest insects. Parasite wasps destroy insects eggs when they lay their own eggs in the same area, to hatch and kill the pest. Ladybugs are an excellent control of aphids and soldier bugs eat all above ground insects. Many beneficial insects live in garden, flower and shrub beds and move out into lawn areas in pursuit of food. This is a good reason to have a well balanced, diverse landscape. The main weapon to maintain a healthy landscape is to keep its natural defense in balance.

Nematodes are a large class of soil-dwelling organisms. Some are destructive plant parasites, while others, **beneficial nematodes**, prey on pupae and larvae of harmful insects. Beneficial nematodes are one of the most popular methods of biological insect control. They are natural enemies of soil insects. These microscopic insect predators already exist in the soil. They actively search for pre-adult insects. After invading the larvae or pupae, the nematodes release bacteria that kills the insect host within 24 hours. They feed on the insects body, reproduce, and seek out more pre-adults. When all larvae and pupae have been killed, the nematodes starve to death and biodegrade. Beneficial nematodes are an ideal biopesticide (living organisms that kill pests). Highly effective and economical, they work over a long period of time and provide important environmental advantages over insecticides. They do not have any negative impact on groundwater, soil, livestock, crops, pets or people. They live in the soil for just a few months, until they run out of prey. Because of this, nematodes never become a permanent part of an ecosystem.

Milky spore disease is a biological control product that when sprayed on the turf, enters the soil and sickens grubs. The bacteria multiplies over a few years eventually wiping out most grubs in the lawn. As it lingers in the soil. it comes alive when grubs move into the area and attacks. Check with your garden center or extension office for locations to purchase Milky Spore Disease.

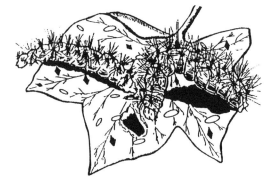

Sod webworms can be controlled with insecticidal soap sprays or *Bt* (bacillus thuringiensis) a bacteria that preys on caterpillars. Insecticidal soap is a contact pesticide that must touch the pest to kill it. It is usually mixed with water and sprayed on the lawn. This irritates insects at the soil surface and forces them to move upwards onto grass blades to dry off. They are now vulnerable to predators, especially birds. Also the soap may actually kill soft bodied insects. *Bt* is a natural bacterial that kills most leaf-eating caterpillars but is harmless to beneficial insects, pets, wildlife, plants or man. It comes in a dry powder form. It is produced from a very small rod-shaped bacterium and is the safest on the market. Caterpillars feed on the leaves containing the *Bt* spores and toxic crystals. The spores and crystals enter the stomach and the crystals begin to dissolve. Within 24 - 48 hours the stomach wall is broken down, the spores begin to invade the body, and the caterpillar stops feeding. At this point, the weakened caterpillar is likely to be attacked by certain parasites. During the next 48 - 96 hours, the spores completely invade the body and germinate, causing an infection that kills the caterpillar. The new bacteria which grow from the germination of spores within the caterpillar are unable to form additional spores or toxic crystals. When the dead caterpillar falls to the ground and decays, the *Bt* bacteria also decay. Therefore, there is no insecticide build-up in the environment.

Occasionally, even well managed lawns become infested with annual grubs, webworms or other insect pests to an extent that damage becomes obvious. When turfgrass insect injury is severe, even if the grass is being maintained at the highest level practical for the situation, consider using an insecticide. Minimum impact starts with proper cultural practices that reduce the need for insecticide

applications. Other ways to reduce impact are to reduce the amount of pesticide applied by treating only heavily infested areas, and to use the lowest effective rate. Perhaps the greatest potential for reducing pesticide impact is to use biocontrol products, microbial pesticides, short-residual products and low-toxicity products wherever possible.

Since most of the insects that attack the grass blades eat at night, the best time to spray a contact insecticide is early evening. This way the insecticide will kill the insects by direct contact or will rub on them as they move around in the turf. If you are applying a granular type, you can put it down at anytime of the day, except when it is hot. Excessive heat plus the chemical can damage the lawn. For above ground infestation, the turf should be watered well at least one day before treatment. The insecticide should be put down as soon as the grass is dry and then not watered in for 48 hours, unless the label indicates to do so. If the targets are underground pests, follow the same procedure as above but water the lawn immediately after application to carry the chemical into the soil where the insects are. For maximum efficiency, read all labels and follow instructions.

Broad-spectrum insecticides kill most insects, pests and beneficial ones. There are several insecticides that will kill just about any insect around. These have the advantage of instant control. They should only be used when a pest infestation is so severe that other measures have failed to control it. Many insect species have built up a resistance to insecticide treatments. Insecticides come in several forms: liquid concentrates to be mixed with water, wettable powders for dissolving in water, dry granular which is ready to use and several dust formulations. The same spreaders and sprayers used for other lawn treatments can be used for insecticides. Whenever you apply an insecticide, it should be spread beyond the visibly affected area as insects are constantly moving and extending their territory and damage. If the affected area is severe, sometimes repeated treatments are necessary for complete control. Only apply an insecticide when and where there is a severe problem.

Lawn Disease

Lawn grasses respond to the care or neglect they receive from people and nature. We must constantly watch for symptoms of pest attacks so we can correct the trouble before it gets worse. Every lawn is subject to any one of many fungus diseases. Each disease has it's own favorite moisture and temperature liking. Turfgrass disease occurs any time of the year. Some diseases can happen in the middle of winter under a blanket of snow and others grow during hot, humid conditions of summer. Diseases can occur when there is a lack of water and the lawn is under drought stress and others happen when the soil is saturated with water. Most diseases are a result of high nitrogen fertilizers, improper mowing, poor maintenance procedures or extreme weather conditions.

Turf diseases are caused by parasites called fungi. Fungi live in soil and thatch formed by decaying roots, leaves and debris. They actually lack the ability to make their own food but can obtain it from other plants, called hosts. During this process is when they cause the actual disease. Most lawn diseases are more severe on lawns that receive repeat amounts of high nitrogen fertilizer. Soils that hold a lot of water, or are lacking in potassium, can produce disease-like symptoms. The reproductive spores of fungi are everywhere in soil and grasses. Usually, for a disease to appear, there must be a susceptible

lawngrass and an environment fitting to the specific fungus. A few diseases need warm weather and some need cool weather, but most of them require humidity. One of the best ways to prevent or control a disease is to find out the cause, know the symptom and how the disease survives and spreads. Fungi spread through reproductive structures called spores, and are easily carried by water, lawn equipment, shoes, wind, etc. There are a large number of diseases but only a few can cause severe damage.

It is important to try and identify the disease as soon as possible since once a disease is established, other fungi usually join in the destruction. When this happens, identification of the original causing organism becomes almost impossible. Disease prevention is more desirable than fighting it after damage has started. Lawn disease control begins with an accurate diagnosis based on your knowledge of your own grass and its susceptibilities. Listed are the most common lawn diseases found in New Jersey.

Brown Patch

Brown patch spreads in a circular pattern, starting from a central point and can cover an area from a couple of inches to several feet. Leaves turn a purplish-green color, collapse and then turn brown. The dead leaves usually stay upright but after a couple of days, the diseased grass appears crushed. One characteristic of brown patch is a gray-black mycelium appearing near the perimeter called the "smoke-ring". This is mostly seen in the morning, when grass is wet from dew and disappears when the grass dries in the sun. Brown patch occurs during periods of high temperatures and humidity. It can strike very suddenly and severe damage can occur overnight. It usually attacks only the stems and blades. High temperatures, 75 to 95 ° F, high humidity, excessive moisture and thatch all create perfect conditions. To control brown patch reduce high nitrogen fertilization, reduce shade, remove thatch, aerate the lawn, water deeply only when necessary and raise the cutting height on your mower. If you have a severe condition which seems to be spreading, apply a recommended fungicide.

Leaf Spot

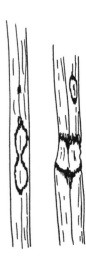

In New Jersey, bluegrass is one of the most popular and useful grasses and leaf spot is one of the most destructive turfgrass diseases around. Leaf spot first appears as rust-colored in the turf. Inspecting the grass stem reveals small leaf-spots or "lesions" outlined in purplish-black. As time passes, the lesions get larger and merge, with increased activity. If not controlled, the advanced stage continues into the crown and then the root system, causing the blade to die, a condition that is known as "fade out". Leaf spot is active during spring, summer and fall when moist conditions are present. Other symptoms of leaf spot include yellow grass blades and turf infected with large chlorotic (green-yellow) patches. People often mistake this condition as an iron deficiency or lack of nitrogen. This disease is also known as "melting out". Many times it first appears in the shade. To control leaf spot, aerate the lawn to improve drainage, reduce fertilization and raise the mowing height.

Dollar Spot

Dollar spot appears as yellow-green or bleached blotches of grass about the size of a silver dollar. As the disease progresses, the spots turn tan and grass blades have straw-colored lesions in the shape of an "hour glass". During morning hours, when moisture is present, a cobweb may appear over the area. Dollar spot is active in spring and summer when weather conditions are moist and warm, and if not controlled, can go right into fall. This disease is very damaging when the lawn is suffering from stress, such as lack of inadequate moisture. Dollar spot can grow into larger dead areas that form depressions in the turf. It is very common in areas with a lot of precipitation in the air (fog), and on lawns that are nitrogen deficient. To control dollar spot, reduce thatch, water deeply only when necessary, reduce the amount of shade and increase applications of nitrogen fertilizer.

Fairy Ring

Fairy rings are circles formed by bands of grass that are darker and faster growing than on either side of the band. The band can range from 3 to 15 inches in width and extend over 40 feet. Usually mushrooms are present in the infected area. This disease is caused by fungi growing in decayed matter, such as rotting wood or branches located below the soil surface. The large amount of mycelium present, traps gases and air and prevents water penetration. The infected area receives an excessive amount of nitrogen, causing a dark green growth in the fairy ring. This excessive amount of nitrogen and toxins cause the area to eventually die. It is hard to control fairy ring with a fungicide. Aerate the lawn to improve water penetration. If fairy ring becomes too severe, you may have to replace the entire lawn.

Fusarium Blight (Summer Patch)

This disease shows a "frog eye" ring of infected grass with what appears to be healthy grass in the center. Fusarium usually occurs in spring when warm, humid weather arrives. The early stage shows orange lesions on the grass blade. When temperatures are in the 70's, infested areas die. Brown rings appear in the turf with some green growth inside the ring giving the area a "frog eye" appearance. If not controlled, large areas of turf can be completely destroyed. Fusarium can remain active throughout the summer until cool weather arrives. It goes dormant during winter months and reappears in the exact same area the following year. To control fusarium blight, reduce thatch, aerate the lawn and cut back on fertilization.

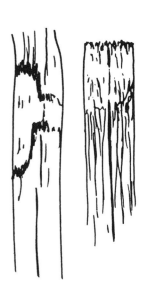

Powdery Mildew

Powdery mildew first appears as a white powdery covering on the top of grass blades. It is found in moist, shaded areas suffering from poor air circulation. It grows quickly until it covers an entire plant with white powder. If not controlled, powdery mildew will continue a suffocating activity until the blades turn yellow and die. Thinning of turf becomes severe in infected areas. This disease encourages an overall weakness in turf that can bring about other problems. When it becomes severe, it looks as if lime was spread over the infected areas. To control powdery mildew, avoid high nitrogen fertilizers, eliminate shade and prune trees and shrubs for more air circulation.

Rust

Rust commonly appears during the months of July and August. The early stage shows lesions looking like yellow-orange marks on grass blades. As the disease gets worse, the lesions increase until the leaf surface breaks open and spores form small orange sacks. If not controlled, the leaves will then yellow progressing downwards from the tip. The diseased area will appear to have a rusty look. The dust is composed of many spores and will attach itself to shoes and clothes while walking through the turf. The spores may also be spread by maintenance equipment and wind and if they land on grass with enough moisture, a new infection may be started. To control rust, fertilize and then water frequently for a few days to force growth. This pushes the rust on the blades upwards so you can cut them off with a mower, bag the clippings and throw them away.

Stripe Smut

Stripe smut is an unusual disease as it is most active when temperatures are in the 50 to 60° range, unlike many that thrive in the heat. It first appears as yellow-green streaks on the grass blades, that eventually turn gray. The plants stop normal growth and become stunted. When stripe smut progresses, the gray streaks open and release black soot-like spores that spread along the blade veins, eventually causing the blade to split into ribbons. When the disease becomes severe, grass blades curl from the top down, turn a light brown and eventually die. To help prevent infection, reduce fertilization and watering, remove thatch and aerate the lawn.

Pythium

Pithium is one of the fastest, most destructive of turfgrass diseases. It usually happens in warm climates but can occur anywhere under the right conditions. Under prolonged periods of wet, humid weather, when temperatures are between 85 to 95° F, pythium is very damaging. Entire lawns can be completely destroyed within 24 hours. Pythium starts as small spots up to 3 to 4 inches in diameter, with a white, cottony growth covering diseased areas. As the disease progresses, grass blades turn dark and greasy and patches run together causing streaks. These streaks follow natural water drainage, allowing pythium to spread easily and cover long distances where slopes are involved. To help control pythium, reduce watering and aerate the lawn to improve drainage.

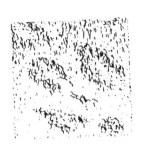

Red Thread

This disease attacks almost all common turf grasses in the United States, however it is generally in cooler regions. Red thread becomes active when temperatures range between 65 to 75° F especially when there is a lot of moisture present in the air. It appears as irregular patches of off-colored turf, varying from several inches to several feet in diameter. A pinkish-red mycelium rises from the grass blade sheaths and binds injured blades together. As red thread progresses, the leaves become twisted and brown, eventually drying out and turning to tan patches of dead turf. To control red thread, check your soil pH and add lime if necessary. Make sure the grass has an adequate supply of nitrogen.

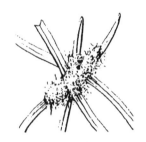

Slime Mold

Slime mold generally occurs in moist, warm spring weather but can appear after heavy rains or irrigation during summer and fall. It first resembles yellow or white slimy masses growing over the grass.When these irregular patches dry, they form gray, white or black powder structures that are easily swept from grass blades with a broom. Slime mold is not a parasite but an organism that feeds on decaying material in the soil, otherwise known as thatch. When the atmosphere is extremely humid, the disease covers surrounding grass blades with spore masses. A natural thinning of turf occurs if the suffocating effect becomes severe.

Snow Mold

Snow mold usually occurs from late fall through spring, when there is an excessive amount of melting snow or moisture and temperatures range from 35 to 45° F. Damage can be severe when snow covers the turf for long periods. Gray snow mold has tan to grayish-white "halos" ranging in size from a couple of inches to several feet in diameter. The "halos" may extend across each other forming large irregular patterns. The grass becomes matted closely to the ground and often dies. Pink snow mold patches are generally smaller but can cover very large areas and have a bright pink mycelium. This disease causes similar damage to gray snow mold. To help control snow mold, remove any thatch, aerate to improve lawn drainage and water deeply only when needed. If the problem has existed in the past, reduce high nitrogen fertilizer in the fall.

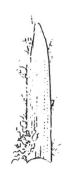

Now that we are familiar with some of the characteristics and symptoms of the most common lawn diseases in New Jersey, let's talk about various means of control. Most plant diseases can be held in check with good cultural practices. Science has made great strides in developing plants and grass that are resistant to one or more major diseases. This biological control is much more desirable and sometimes more reliable than chemical methods of control.

The term "management" is used in preference to "control", because control implies finality and often leads to people drawing the wrong conclusions. When people think in terms of control, they are often under the misconception that the treatment they are applying will eradicate the disease and that it will disappear and not return. Most diseases appear year after year, however, and sometimes several times during the year. Strategies need to be developed to manage these diseases on a continuing basis. These strategies should include an integrated approach that incorporates any cultural or biological means of managing the disease and applications of fungicides only when necessary. Turfgrass disease management begins with selecting the correct species or cultivars. The improved types of Kentucky bluegrass are the best cultivars for high maintenance lawns. They have resistance to most major diseases. Resistance to stripe smut can be obtained by planting a blend of three or more of these improved Kentucky bluegrass cultivars.

Good cultural practices that encourage biological management are important in maintaining a healthy lawn. These include core aerating, fertilizing, liming and irrigating for the improved Kentucky bluegrass cultivars used on home lawns. Aerating should be done at least once every two years, with the soil from the core plugs reincorporated to help modify any thatch. Have a soil test done before initiating a maintenance program, to determine the levels of nitrogen, phosphorus and potassium in the soil. Deep watering several times a week will be effective in maintaining high populations of beneficial microorganisms that will help manage the soil. Remember, prevention through a good maintenance program is one of the best lines of defense against lawn disease.

Listed are just a few ways to help prevent lawn disease:

- Plant a mixture of grasses instead of just one variety. Diseases can be quite selective and if one is affected, the others in the mixture will survive and prevent complete destruction.
- Do not overwater. Water deeply in the morning only when needed, especially during the hot summer, and never water at night. Warm, humid nights are excellent conditions for many diseases to take hold.
- Prune out dense shade areas to help air flow.
- Remove excess thatch and aerate to reduce soil compaction and allow air, moisture and nutrients to reach grass roots.
- During the fall cleanup, remove any diseased plants or shrubs from bed areas, to get a good start in the spring.
- Disinfect any of your tools that have been used to remove any diseased plants, to prevent spreading.
- Review your maintenance program. Effective programs that are used to control insects and weeds also reduce losses from lawn diseases.

Most diseases are the result of weather conditions and poor maintenance practices. You may think you have a lawn disease, but it may actually be the result of pet damage, nutritional imbalance, wear and tear, stress from sudden environmental changes or insect damage. It is difficult for inexperienced people to properly diagnose a lawn disease and in many cases, once a disease is visible, it is too late for treatment. Healthy lawns can take care of minor attacks from most diseases. If a disease does take hold and cultural practices have been tried without success, you may have to resort to chemical control.

There are several fungicides commonly used to help prevent and control lawn diseases. All fungicides work by contact with the fungi. Some are systemic, meaning that the target plant is fed or injected with the chemical which then moves throughout the plants system killing the fungi. Contact fungicides work on the outside of the plant and should be applied before the disease starts. Both systemic and contact fungicides come in various forms: powders that are mixed with water to be sprayed, liquids that are sprayed and granules that are applied with fertilizer spreaders. Granules are easier to apply and more accurate than the spray type, which prolongs their effectiveness. Special quart jar attachments are available for use with a garden hose and provide a decent distribution of liquid fungicides, but when a wettable powder is used, the jar must be shaken constantly to insure good suspension of the chemical. Use an attachment that delivers a coarse spray and a large volume of water. The fungicide mixture in a quart jar will cover about 500 square feet of lawn when applied with a garden hose attachment according to recommendations. A sprinkling can may be used on very small lawns, garden flower areas or shrub beds.

If you have had serious disease problems in the past, a good maintenance practice would be to include at least one fungicide application in your program for two years. One application in late spring may prevent a year's worth of trouble. All directions should be followed carefully and the spreading should be done so as to give complete and uniform coverage. You can achieve this by spreading one half of the application in one direction and the second at right angles to the first. Except for systemics, which should last up to 30 days, a single treatment may not be enough if there is severe damage. Read directions, but normally a second application can be made within two weeks, which will help control the disease more and protect any new foliage against an attack. Some fungicide formulations contain a

spreader sticker to attain good coverage and adherence to the foliage. When using a granular on the lawn, apply it early in the morning or evening. Often it is damp at those times and this will result in better adherence. Fungicides are relatively safe when used according to the directions, but are poisonous and should be handled carefully. Avoid ingestion and contact and wash thoroughly when the job is completed. Although lawn diseases can become serious problems, they are usually controlled by environmental conditions.

Thatch

Thatch has become a serious problem in today's lawns. It is a misconception that "leaving clippings on the lawn creates thatch". Agronomists and turf specialists at universities agree that "grass clippings don't cause thatch". According to Bill Pound, extension turf specialist at Ohio State University, "finely chopped clippings contribute virtually nothing to the thatch layer". Coleman Ward, professor and extension turf specialist at Auburn University, agrees. "Any organic matter finely-cut clippings might add to the thatch layer is made up of highly digestible components." Ward says, "Small clippings can be easily digested by soil micro-organisms, and therefore don't cause a problem. Thatch is made up of components such as cellulose, hemicellulose and lignin that are difficult for soil microbes to break down."

What is thatch and what causes it? According to D. Hatch, extension agent of Oregon State University, "thatch is a layer of partly decomposed organic material - including living and dead stems, roots, and shoots - that develops between the green zone of the grass and the soil surface. It accumulates when grass produces organic matter faster than conditions permit organic matter decomposition". A moderate layer, 1/2 inch thick, benefits your lawn. It helps reduce soil compaction, provides a cushion effect for increased wear tolerance, serves as a buffer to heat and drought extremes, and prevents some annual weeds from germinating. Thatch improves grass resiliency and helps to insulate the soil against air temperature extremes. Direct low and high temperature kill of many grasses occurs more on thatchy lawns. As thatch depth increases, the proportion of roots in the thatch layer also increases. Difficulties may develop with excessive thatch because grass

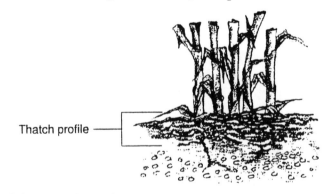

Thatch profile —

plants rhizomes and roots grow within the thatch layer and not deep in the soil (shallow rooting). Fewer roots reach the soil and the turf becomes less drought tolerant. The overall quality of the turf starts to decline when thatch builds up. It becomes unresponsive to irrigation, fertilizer, pesticides and can easily be damaged by stress.

So, how do you know if your lawn has too much thatch? Cut out several small pieces of turf, from different areas, about 2 inches wide by 2 inches deep with a trowel or knife. Inspect the plugs starting from the the bottom up. You should have a layer of soil with roots, an area of thatch and then grass.

Measure the thatch layer. If it is more than 1/2 inch thick, you may have a thatch problem. If it is over 1 inch thick, you should do something about it immediately, as long as it is not during summer.

If the thatch dries out, it may become hydrophobic (water repellent) and localized dry spots often show up throughout the lawn during summer. Other potential problems with excess thatch include increased disease and insect activity. An increase in diseases such as fusarium blight, pythium blight and leafspot is associated with an increase in thatch. Thatch also creates an ideal habitat for overwintering of billbugs and sod webworms. Sod webworms have difficulty surviving in bare soil, therefore thatch is important for increased populations. All of the above are just some of the reasons why landowners should try to prevent excessive thatch from forming. Thatch problems seem to be more evident when production of an excellent turf is emphasized. The level of practiced management has a definite impact on the rate of thatch accumulation. A few factors that encourage a build-up of thatch are: higher mowing (from 3-4 inches), vigorous turfgrass cultivars (bluegrass), heavy applications of fertilizer (particularly high nitrogen), excessive soil acidity and poor soil drainage. Excessive fertilizer produces vegetative material faster than plant material can decompose. However, grass clippings do not contribute to thatch. Clippings are 80 - 90 percent water, and whatever remains is digested by soil microbes.

Thatch control is an integrated approach that involves understanding what thatch is, biological prevention control and if necessary, mechanical removal. Let's get a little deeper into what causes thatch to form. Research shows that certain vigorous grass cultivars and excessively high mowing increase the amount of thatch. Excessive, frequent watering may reduce the decomposition rate by excluding air and cooling the thatch layer. Soils that are very acid, cold or wet, and soils composed of sand or heavy clay seem to have appreciable thatch accumulation. Turf that has been treated frequently with pesticides to eliminate problems caused by disease and insects may have heavier thatch. This is why some of the nicest lawns in your neighborhood have thatch related problems. Water and fertilizer should be applied enough to maintain good growth but not so much as to produce excessive, unnecessary growth. Waterlogged conditions can restrain thatch breakdown by microorganisms.

Bacteria and other soil microorganisms help decompose thatch. But, let's talk about earthworms for a minute. Research shows that earthworm activity plays an important role in reducing thatch. Thatch is not usually a problem when earthworms are present, as they mix soil into the thatch layer and improve soil aeration. Earthworms process large quantities of organic debris and soil which makes it easier for decomposing fungi and bacteria to break down thatch. Earthworms can digest thatch, create channels for soil aeration and drainage and reintroduce microorganisms back into the thatch layer. Maintaining a soil pH between 6 to 7 encourages earthworm activity. So, any management practice that may harm earthworms, such as the excessive use of any pesticides (especially broad-spectrum insecticides), should be avoided as decreases in the earthworm population will increase the amount of thatch.

Cultural Practices To Help Reduce Thatch

By avoiding the practices just discussed, you may achieve a better balance between the decomposition and production or organic matter. Choose the proper grass seed, as turfgrasses vary in the rate of developing thatch. Improved cultivars of Kentucky bluegrass and Red Fescue may develop a thatch

while under high maintenance programs, whereas tall fescue and perennial ryegrass seldom have thatch accumulation. Crowns, stems and roots have a relatively high lignin content. Lignin is an organic compound that is highly resistant to microbial breakdown. Vigorous species and cultivars with high lignin content accumulate thatch more readily than those with lower lignin content.

Thatch prevention is managed by the proper use of pesticides and fertilizers and implementing cultural practices. Mowing the grass regularly at heights between 2 to 3 inches can help slow thatch buildup. Only remove the clippings when the grass is wet or extra long. An irrigation program that permits some drying and warming of the soil between saturated periods will promote decomposition, as will lime applications to correct excessive acidity. Retain populations of beneficial organisms in your lawn by using pesticides carefully and only when absolutely necessary.

Mechanical Methods For Removing Thatch

Mechanical removal of thatch is common and desirable if the layer inhibits water movement into the grass zone. Remove thatch in the spring or fall so the turf will have about three weeks to recover before excessively hot or cold weather occurs. You can remove thatch with a vertical mower, a power rake, a rotary mower with a spring attachment or a hand rake. Power machines are more effective and easier to use, but can be quite touchy - so be very careful. Deep raking with a self-cleaning hand rake is satisfactory for small areas, but it is hard work. Power machines can be rented at most tool rental companies. With a power rake or vertical mower, thatch is cut or torn out by blades or bars rotating in a vertical plane. In contrast to the flat blades of rotary mowers, these blades or bars stand on edge. If you are using one of these machines, the following procedure is suggested:

● Set blades 1/8 inch above the ground when the machine is on a level, hard surface.

● Make one pass over the lawn and remove debris.

● Make a second, third, or fourth pass removing debris after each pass.

● Stop as soon as chunks of turf begin to tear up.

● Mow the dethatched lawn one or two settings below normal mowing height and remove clippings.

● Fertilize and irrigate to stimulate grass growth for quick recovery.

Springs made to attach to the blade of rotary mowers can do a satisfactory job. One or two trips over the lawn annually will keep thatch manageable. Recently, some manufacturers have come out with a "dethatching blade" that comes equipped with steel prongs that physically tear the thatch layer during a mowing operation. You must be very careful using this type of blade as a considerable amount of material is pulled to the surface, including desirable turfgrass.

The last power machine I will discuss is a core aerator. Core aeration is not looked upon as a method of thatch removal, rather it is an effective means of preventing thatch from developing. Anyone who has a high maintenance lawn program should consider core aerating at least every two years. The machines hollow tines remove plugs of thatch and soil from the lawn and deposit them on the surface. These plugs then decompose back into the thatch layer after rain, irrigation, lawn mowing or regular wear and tear. This soil addition increases microbial activity, thereby reducing thatch. One core aeration will do wonders for any lawn. When using any of these machines, a small amount of grass will also come up, but if the lawn is relatively healthy, this amount is unavoidable and acceptable. There are times, even if proper cultural practices have been used, when fertilizer supplements and pest control are necessary.

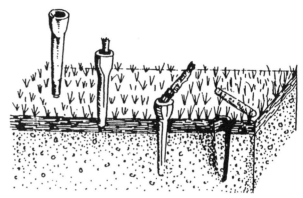

Core Aerification is the removal of soil cores.

Even though clippings have been returned to the soil, they may not produce enough nitrogen. Insects and fungi sometimes reach damaging levels even in the best of lawns and applying the proper chemical control is a better choice than loosing large areas of turf. Poorly maintained lawns that have been neglected for years may require applications of various pesticides, fertilizer, lime and seed to help recovery before cultural practices can be implemented.

Shade

Light is critical to any kind of plant's growth. Maintaining a healthy turf under good conditions is not an easy task, but growing grass under adverse conditions, such as shade, can be both challenging and frustrating. To help you determine the problem and be able to suggest methods of action to help either correct the problem or find suitable shade growing plants, I must first define shade. Shade can be light, medium or heavy. Full sun is of course 100% of daily available sunlight, which is very good for turf development.

Light Shade is between 75% to 100% of daily available sunlight that reaches a particular area. Any sunlight would usually be in the early morning or late afternoon. North sides of buildings, fences or walls produce this as well as single tall trees with a heavy canopy of leaves that cast a complete midday shadow. In most cases, this amount of sunlight does not present a problem for turf development.

Medium Shade is between 25% to 75% of daily available sunlight that reaches a particular area. This can be an open area that has no direct sunlight due to clustered tall trees with a heavy canopy of leaves high off the ground or overhanging branches of trees adding shade to the north sides of buildings, walls or fences. You should be able to maintain a satisfactory lawn under these conditions but it becomes difficult as the light diminishes towards 25%.

Heavy Shade is less than 25% of daily available sunlight that reaches a particular area. Heavy shade includes areas where light is obscured by a thick stand of trees with branches quite close to the ground, areas under stairways or decks on the north side of a house or north facing other places which get only a small amount of reflected light. It is very hard to grow a lawn in this amount of light, so a more shade tolerant ground cover would be more practical. Typical problems associated with shade are:

● Reduced sunlight.

● Reduced air circulation and higher humidity.

● Prolonged wetness after irrigation or rain.

● Moss and algae growth.

● Lawn disease problems.

● Grass and trees compete for water and nutrients.

● Reduced grass tillering and shallow grass root system.

Several factors must be considered when trying to grow turfgrass in shady conditions: the type of turfgrass, maintenance practices, any modifications that must be made to help make conditions more favorable and any alternatives such as planting shrubs or groundcovers. Grass may be difficult to grow under trees that are shallow-rooted or cast heavy shade. But by removing some lower branches, you can improve air circulation and light conditions. Lower branches should be removed to a height of 10 feet or more allowing early morning and late afternoon light to enter. Also thinning (selective removal of branches) the entire tree lets more light penetrate. It also helps to increase the amount of fertilizer, lime and water in these particular areas. If removing some of the lower branches didn't help, it may be necessary to remove some of the trees or plant a groundcover.

Choosing the proper shade tolerant grass species is the most important decision you will have to make. Fine leafed fescues are the preferred seed for dry shaded areas. Pennlawn, Ruby, Banner and Jamestown are just a few varieties of red fescue that grow well in shade. Two varieties of Kentucky bluegrass that are shade tolerant are Glade and Warren. Fescues, which are the dominate shade grass seed mixes, are not very tolerant to high levels of nitrogen. Fertilizer application of once or twice a year should be sufficient, normally in April and September. Have the soil tested every year and maintain the pH at 7. Apply lime if the pH is lower. Fescues grow well in cool, dry shade but are not recommended for poorly drained soils. Perennial ryegrass may also be considered as it performs well in shade, however, it gives a good cover in the beginning but may thin out by the end of the year. The area should be reseeded spring and fall for perennial ryegrass to be used successfully.

One of the most obvious characteristics of shade is the reduction of sunlight. This means turf root growth is: reduced, grows closer to the soil surface and is subject to disease, drought and stress. Grass

develops improperly, exhibiting thinner, longer blades than those grown in sunlight. Another characteristic of shade is the reduction of air circulation, a very important factor in good turf development. Restricted wind causes increased humidity above the turf. This results in weakened turf, with delicate grass blades which are more susceptible to activity injury and disease. If dense shrubs are present that impede air circulation, they also should be thinned out or removed and planted somewhere else. Tree and turf root competition is a third factor that must be considered. Research shows that many tree roots grow 3 to 6 inches below the soil surface which happens to be the same area where turfgrass roots grow. This places the roots of these two popular plants directly in competition for nutrients and water. There is also some evidence that certain trees release toxic chemical substances which restrain growth or in some cases, actually kill turfgrass. This destruction is called **allelopathy**. Raising the cutting height encourages a more extensive root system helping the grass compete with tree roots for nutrients and water.

Grass loss in a shaded environment could also be due to disease. Diseases such as leaf spot, powdery mildew and dollar spot are all common in shaded areas. If disease is the cause, aeration, removal of thatch if it is heavy, and the removal of the diseased clippings usually reduces the areas susceptibility. Pesticides, especially broadleaf weed killers, should be used sparingly in shaded areas. Crabgrass control is not necessary in shaded areas since it needs high light intensity to grow. If any weeds are present, spot treating them should be sufficient. If moss has become a problem, rake the moss area to a depth of at least 1/4 inch and remove it. Re-establish the area with top soil and a shade tolerant seed. Fine fescue, either a chewings or creeping red, should be the dominate turfgrass in a shade environment. A dense turf should help reduce any moss problems. Do not use broadleaf herbicides on the new grass and keep tree leaves raked up as necessary.

Proper water maintenance is very important in shady areas. Light, frequent sprinklings should be avoided as this encourages shallow rooting. Heavy watering keeps the soil wet longer which is especially important during long, hot dry spells. Water deeply but infrequently. Tree leaves deflect rain yielding an uneven soil moisture pattern. Tree roots usually compete with the grass for available moisture. Turfgrasses in shade usually need at least one inch of water per week, wetting

the soil to at least a 4 inch depth. Try to keep all activities away from the grass until it is fully established and then limit it the first year. An alternative to planting grass in shade is using ground covers that are more tolerant to shade. A few ground covers available are English Ivy, Pachysandra or Myrtle. A complete listing of ground covers is found in Chapter 6. If you have less than 25% available sunlight, ground covers are the way to go. This will help you avoid the frustration of replanting grass every year only to see it die during the summer.

Turfgrasses grow better in sun although some species grow satisfactorily in the shade. The greater the reduction in daily available sunlight, the more difficult it is to grow and maintain a respectable lawn in a shaded area. Alternatives such as decks or patios can satisfy many practical and aesthetical situations. For areas that have heavy traffic, try wood chips, cedar mulch or a variety of other mulches. Separate the mulch from any well growing grasses using edging or landscape ties. Flowers or shrubs that are shade tolerant can be added for color. The final solution depends on each individual site and condition, the amount of time and dollars you are willing to spend on installation and maintenance, and what you as an owner would like to have in your overall landscape design. Grass can coexist with shrubs and trees as long as certain management procedures are followed. With proper selection, these areas require little maintenance and can be beautiful.

Moles and Voles

The moles found in New Jersey are insect eating mammals, not rodents as commonly believed. They have a naked, pointed, snout extending nearly 1/2 inch in front of the mouth opening, very small eyes and no external ears. The forefeet are large and broad with the toes webbed to the base of the claws. The hind feet are small and narrow with slender, sharp claws. Average adult size is about 7 inches long with a 1 to 1 1/2 inch bare tail. The fur is short, dense, and velvety.

Moles feed mainly on insects, grubs, and worms they find in the soil, but also eat some roots, tubers, bulbs, seed, and seed pods. Their burrowing often dislodges plants, and plants may become damaged by

exposing roots to drying. Although not considered serious pests, they can cause havoc in small garden plots and their tunnels are an annoyance in lawns.

Moles live in the seclusion of underground burrows, rarely coming to the surface, even then often by accident. Moles are generally loners, active all year, and eat from 70 to 100 percent of their weight each day, at frequent intervals. A mole makes a home burrow in high, dry spots but hunts in soil that is shaded, cool, loose, moist, and populated by worms, grubs and other insects. Most of a mole's runway system is made of

shallow burrows, ranging over its hunting grounds, and may be used once or several times at irregular intervals. Mole tunnels are readily used by other animals, including voles and deer mice which move through the runways, helping themselves to grains, seed and tubers, for which the mole is blamed. Moles dig rapidly using their powerful feet and claws to push the earth behind them. Large mounds appear overnight and prolonged activity leads to long raised tunnels.

There are several methods used to control moles. The most effective method is a trap. Several different traps are available at hardware stores or nurseries, and include the scissor-jawed, harpoon, and the choker. When a mole's sensitive snout encounters a strange object in its burrow, the mole is likely to plug or seal that portion and dig around or under the object. For this reason, set mole traps straddling or encircling a runway, or suspend a trap above the runway, according to directions. To determine which runways are active, stamp down short sections of surface runways and inspect daily for any raised sections, then restamp. Repeat several times to determine if runways are used daily.

Selection of a frequently used runway is important to the success of your control efforts. Set traps at least 18 inches from a mound in active runways. Although traps are generally expensive, several traps will result in a higher degree of success. Traps can be used year-round because moles are active all year. Carefully follow all instructions with the trap for best results, and be very careful. Don't let any pets or children near traps as they can be dangerous. The scissor-jawed trap is set so that the jaws straddle the runway. The choker loop trap is set so the loop encircles the mole's runway. The harpoon trap is set directly over the runway so that its supporting stakes straddle the runway and its spikes will go into the runway when tripped. I feel the harpoon is the most efficient of the three traps.

The presence of moles in the lawn is usually an indication that you have a grub worm problem. If the problem is severe, and the lawn is being destroyed by both grubs and moles, it may be time to apply an insecticide. Insecticides used to reduce the grub population may leave the lawn unattractive as a food source to moles, thus indirectly reducing the mole population.

If you do not want to kill the mole, capture it alive and transport it to another location. Here are three methods for capturing moles alive. Moles are active in early morning or evening. Approach very quietly when the earth is being heaved up, strike a spade into the ridge behind the mole and throw it out on the surface. Occasionally a mole can be driven to the surface by forcing a stream of water with a hose into an open burrow for several minutes.

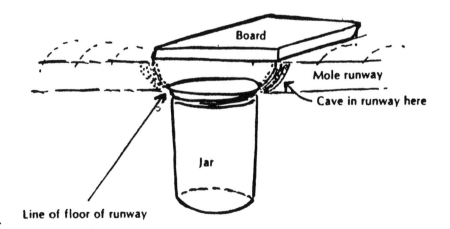

Finally, bury a 3 lb. coffee can or a wide-mouth quart glass jar in the path of the mole and cover the top of the borrow with a board. This pitfall trap method is effective when used in an active runway. Make sure you cave in the runway just in front of the jar on both sides. When the mole is caught, transport to another area such as the woods.

Repellents such as mothballs, poisonous baits and various fumigants are generally ineffective in reducing the mole population. However, moles favor the taste of Wrigley's Juicy Fruit gum. When they swallow the gum, it sticks to their digestive system and eventually kills them. Place wads of this gum in active runways so the moles can locate them easily. Moles may avoid the gum if they detect the scent of humans, so do not wad gum with bare hands. Many other "home remedies" you may hear of are not only ineffective, but may be dangerous to use, especially in vegetable gardens. Items such as broken bottles, ground glass, broken razor blades, wads of fiberglass, bleaches, household lye, and thorny rose branches are of no proven benefit.

Voles

Voles reach a length of 5 to 7 inches at maturity. Their dense fur is grayish to brownish, and the underparts are generally gray, sometimes mixed with yellow or buff. A vole's life span is short, ranging from 2 to 16 months. Breeding occurs primarily in spring and summer, and they may produce from one to five litters per year, each litter averaging three to six young. Females mature in 35 to 40 days. Voles do not hibernate, so they are active day and night throughout the entire year. They construct a complex tunnel system, with surface runways and numerous burrow entrances. A single tunnel system may contain several adults and young. Voles eat a wide variety of crops and plants, with a preference for grasses. In late summer and fall, voles store seeds, tubers, bulbs, and rhizomes in their tunnels. Voles also cause damage by the extensive tunnel systems that they build, resulting in root destruction and soil washouts.

There are several ways to control voles. Eliminate weeds, ground cover, and crop litter in and around the garden, lawn, and other cultivated areas. This reduces the availability of food and cover for voles, thus decreasing the capacity of these areas to support them. Lawn and turf areas must be mowed regularly, especially if a garden is nearby. A weed-free or vegetation-free strip is an excellent buffer around areas to be protected. The wider the buffer strip, the less likely voles will cross it into the garden area. Frequent tillage in the garden removes cover, destroys existing runways or tunnels, and will eliminate a high percentage of the existing population.

Several effective baits have been developed for vole control, usually labeled for noncrop areas. Rates and method of application vary. Wire or metal barriers, at least 12 inches high,

with a mesh size of 1/4 inch or less will exclude voles from a garden area. Bury the bottom edge 6 to 10 inches to prevent voles from digging beneath the barrier. Mouse traps can be effective in reducing the vole population. Place the trap perpendicular to the runway with the trigger end in the runway. Apple slices or a peanut butter-oatmeal mixture make good baits. In general, fumigants are not effective due to the complexity and shallowness of the tunnel systems. Repellents and frightening agents have not proven effective, either. However, some rabbit, deer and field mice repellents are labeled for voles.

A section of roofing shingle placed over the burrow opening and baited with an apple slice will attract voles. A trap can also be placed under this shingle, because voles are readily attracted to shingles or pieces of plywood placed on the ground. Shingles should be bent to form an A-shaped roof. Plywood or flat material should have small blocks under the corner to allow for a crawl space. These items can also serve as bait sites. Leave in place a few days before baiting to allow the animals to become accustomed to them.

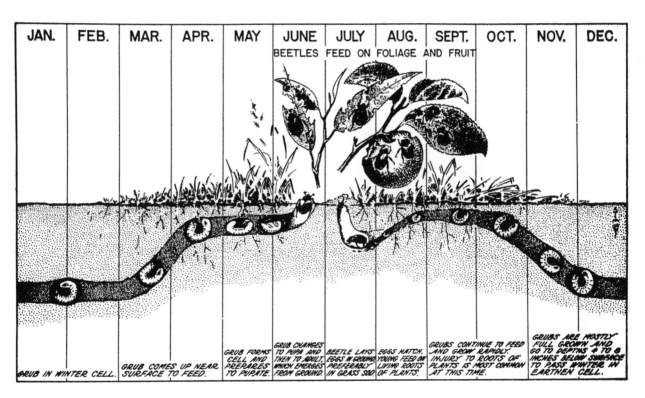

Seasonal life cycle of the Japanese beetle

Chapter 5

Shrubs and Trees

Shrubs, beds, mulch, and trees all help your landscape look more beautiful, be more serviceable and increase property value. Well chosen shrubs, mulch, and trees can help enhance the appearance of a house, wall or fence, window, driveway or barren spot. Any area can benefit from careful planning, correct choices and imaginative ideas. Shrubs are very adaptable and considered by many professional gardeners, the backbone of low maintenance gardening. Once shrubs are well established, there is very little maintenance except for general pruning. Throughout the growing season, shrubs can give beautiful displays of flowers from such plants like hydrangeas, forsythias, lilacs, weigelas, azaleas and rhododendrons. From late fall through winter, shrubs such as the red burning bush and red berries of holly and pyrocanthia add much needed color to a landscape. Choosing landscape plants sometimes can be a confusing and difficult process. I think this is because there are so many ornamental plants to choose from. Hopefully, I will be able to give you enough information to help you choose the right plant for your property.

Shrubs have many functions in a landscape. They add background and structure, serve as soil stabilizers, wind and noise barriers and furnish shelter to wildlife. They are easy to grow, are fairly pest resistant and in most cases, very durable. Shrubs should be present in every landscape as they yield year round color, whether it be all green or beautiful flowers, and they come in many shapes, sizes, colors and textures. Landscape plants need specific environments for best growth. When choosing a hardy plant, three things should be considered. Will the plant grow in your area? Will the plant grow in the kind of soil you have? Will the plant need sun or shade? The answer to question one is easy - all plants mentioned in this book will grow in New Jersey. Question two is about soil. Many landscape plants need specific soil conditions for healthy growth. Most shrubs and trees grow best in well drained, moist soils. It will be very important for you to know what soil conditions exist on your site and how well the soil drains. Poorly drained and soggy soils are not ideal for most landscape plants. With careful plant selection, however, even these sites can be nicely landscaped.

The third question refers to sun or shade, which I'll call light requirements. Ornamental plants need light to grow, but some plants require full sun all day, while others tolerate some shade. Still others may require a shady area of filtered light to grow best. It is important for you to know the light condition of different areas of your landscape so you can choose plants that will grow well in that light condition. It is frustrating to choose the wrong plant and watch it scorch because the sun was too bright and hot or become weak and spindly because the shade was too heavy.

Ornamental plants grow to many sizes. You may choose from ground cover plants as small as 6 inches, shrubs of many sizes, and large trees to over 85 feet tall. It is very important to know what size plant you want for the landscape. So when you decide on plants you want, think about how big the plant will be when it is fully grown. Some trees grow quickly and become large in just a few years, while others grow more slowly and take many years to reach maturity.

Physical and Ornamental Traits

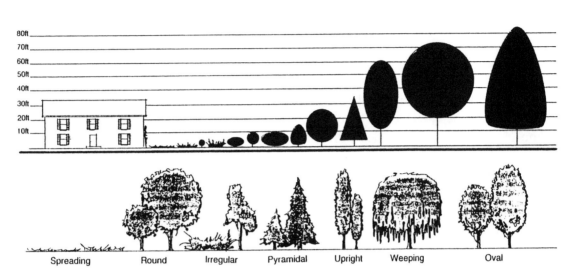

Shape - Plants also grow to many shapes. Some plants may grow tall and thin, while some may be short and rounded, and still others are very low and spreading. Many words are used to describe plant shapes and forms. The drawings above will help show the various forms of landscape plants.

Color - When we imagine plant color, most people think green. This is a natural response because most plants are green. But there are many shades of green, such as the bright yellow-green of a privet shrub, the gray-green of junipers, and the dark blue-green of the hollies. And many plants have other colors. The leaf color of many trees and shrubs will change with the season of the year. This adds interest and offers a pleasant color change to the landscape. Many plants have colorful flowers or berries. So when considering plant color, be sure to think about flower color along with the foliage color.

Plant Types and Their Usage

Broadleaf Evergreens Add Distinction

Broadleaf evergreens are ornamental plants with comparatively broad or wide leaves that remain green throughout the year. Some of the most attractive plants for landscape beautification are found among the broadleaf evergreens. Many of these plants can and should be used in New Jersey landscapes. Rhododendrons, including azaleas, are the most spectacular of this group of plants. Their magnificient floral displays in late May and early June are a sight to behold, and their rich, broad evergreen leaves add interest to the landscape throughout the year. Holly is a must for gardeners of distinction. The blue holly cultivars produce bright red berries for the fall and Christmas season. It must be remembered, however, that only the female holly plants produce fruit. Male plants must also be grown for pollination and fruit production to occur. The dark bluish-green, spiny leaves of the blue holly produce interesting patterns in form and texture. The smaller leaved Japanese holly is excellent for foundation and

low hedge plantings. Its bright, shiny evergreen foliage is most pleasing to the eye, particularly when the leaves glisten in the sunlight following a rain. The evergreen euonymus is available both as a ground cover and a shrub and has leaves in many sizes with considerable variation in marginal variegation (two and three-tone leaf color). The boxwood is a good choice for formal clipped or informal evergreen hedges and foundation plantings. In most cases, boxwood looks better when it is allowed to grow un-clipped in a natural fashion.

Broadleaf evergreens can serve the landscape in many ways. They can be used in shrub borders and foundation plantings, and the larger plants make excellent specimen plants. As ground covers, broadleaf evergreens offer one of the most extensive uses. Periwinkle has been an old standby for years, as has Japanese spurge (Pachysandra). The hardy selected cultivars of English ivy can also be used if they are not subjected to south and west exposures that are completely open. These ground covers can be grown in sun or deep shade as long as they do not have to compete with a competitive root system, such as that of a Norway maple. Broadleaf evergreens tend to look their very best when used in naturalistic plant-ings with a few deciduous shrubs and trees for contrast.

To grow healthy broadleaf evergreens in New Jersey, the gardener must select the right site and then practice a few simple cultural techniques. Because these plants are evergreen and their leaves are broad, the site should afford the plants good protection from the sun and wind. This is particularly important during the winter, when exposure to the wind and warm rays of the sun would cause the leaf temperature to rise and moisture to be lost. Excessive moisture loss from the leaves (desiccation), will result in death of leaves, stems or the entire plant. Many broadleaf evergreens can withstand the cold temperature of most winters provided they acclimatize slowly during the fall. They are most commonly injured by rapid changes in temperature. A good site for the tender members of the broadleaf evergreens is in the north shadow area of a building, fence or planting of large, narrowleaf evergreens, such as pine, hem-lock, spruce and fir. Soil for most of the broadleaf evergreens should be of the organic type. Avoid heavy and poorly drained clay soils. Although the plants like moist soil, they do not tolerate having their roots too wet. Therefore, the site should be well drained.

Deciduous Ornamentals Change With The Seasons

Deciduous ornamentals are plants that drop all their leaves at the end of the growing season and re-main leafless during the cold winter period. Their spring or summer flowers, combined with foliage changing from delicate green in spring through dark greens in summer to brilliant fall tones, make many of them garden favorites. Deciduous ornamentals include such plants as honeysuckle, forsythia, burning bush, dogwood and maple.

Narrowleaf Evergreens Provide Bold Character

Narrowleaf evergreens are ornamental conifers with comparatively long, slender leaves (needle-shaped) that remain green throughout the year. They include firs, junipers, spruces, pines, yews, cedars and hemlocks. Not only do they shelter the home and reduce the effect of wind chill factors, but they

also eliminate summer traffic noise, provide summer cooling and provide screening in all seasons. Narrowleaf evergreens can be employed in city plantings, particularly where there are broad turf areas (8 feet or more) in center panels of boulevards, and in raised planters where they can mingle with deciduous shrubs and trees, providing a strong foliage color contrast. Many narrowleaf evergreen cultivars are available to fit your landscape needs. Check with your local garden center for the best selections. These improved cultivars may have improved foliage colors, narrow tops, weeping growth habits or dwarf growth habits that may be desirable in your landscape.

How A Healthy Plant Grows

Now that you have a basic understanding of plants physical and ornamental traits, their shapes, colors and sizes, and plant types and usage's, I'll talk a little about how plants grow.

How Do Roots Grow And What Are Root Functions?

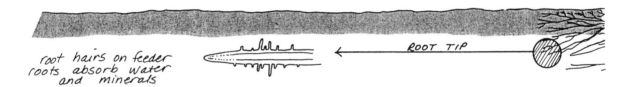

root hairs on feeder roots absorb water and minerals

ROOT TIP

Roots are opportunistic - they do not grow in any particular direction. Root growth flourishes in soils that supply adequate oxygen, water, nutrients, support and warmth. Roots will not grow in soil that lacks adequate oxygen or is hard and compacted. A healthy root system is essential for optimum top growth. Tree roots are distributed under and out from the plant canopy. They can extend a distance of 4 to 7 times the projected area of the canopy. The root zone is irregularly shaped and can have a diameter 1 to 2 times the height of the tree. The fine, non-woody roots grow upward toward the soil surface. These small roots branch and their many root tips form the primary water and nutrient absorptive tissue of the tree or shrub. Fine feeder roots absorb water and nutrients that are essential to food production by the leaves. The return of the food to the roots is essential for continued root development. The large, woody roots anchor the plant and conduct water and nutrients from the fine feeder roots to the stem. The conductive tissue of roots and stems is similar in form and function.

How Do Stems Grow And What Are Stem Functions?

cambium- increases stem girth

xylem- transports water and minerals upward

phloem- transports food manufactured by leaves

Plant stems increase in length and thickness by laying down successive layers of cells much as bricks are laid in building a wall. Woody stem growth is the result of cell division in a thin layer of cells called the cambium. The cambium is just under the protective bark layer and becomes active in the spring in response to warm weather. Xylem cells are produced to the inside of the cambium and phloem cells to the outside. The phloem and bark do not accumulate and are sloughed off as the stem increases in diameter. Most of the tissue in a woody stem is accumulated xylem. Stem length increases as active cells produce new cells at the stem tips. The new cells differentiate into xylem, cambium and phloem. A branch attached to the trunk about 5 feet from the ground increases in thickness and adds length but remains at that height. Stems provide the framework to physically support the leaf canopy and serve as a transport system that connects roots with the leaves. They also provide storage for food manufactured by the leaves. The multi-branching framework, progressing from large limbs to small twigs, exposes the largest possible leaf area to sunlight. The xylem transports water and nutrients up the stem. Sugars manufactured by the leaves are distributed to all growing parts of the plant in the phloem. Stems store surplus food for continued growth during the season and over winter to support spring growth.

How Do Leaves Grow And What Are Leaf Functions?

The bud scales that protect the leaves during the winter open in the spring so leaves can expand. The cells of the young leaf are produced by meristems, which increase the thickness and width of the leaf blade. Leaf structure and orientation depend on the amount of light striking the leaf blade. The primary function of the leaf is to manufacture the sugars that all other parts of the plant require. The chloroplasts manufacture sugar and give the leaves their green color. A network of veins supplies the chloroplasts with water and nutrients and provides a route for movement of the manufactured sugars to other parts of the plant. Pores, called stomates, regulate the flow of air into, and water vapor out of, the leaf. As water evaporates from leaf tissue, cooling the leaf, additional water is pulled up through the plant by tension on water in the xylem. A waxy coating, called cuticle, protects the epidermal layer - the outermost layer of cells - and helps prevent excessive moisture loss.

How Do Flowers Grow And What Are Flower Functions?

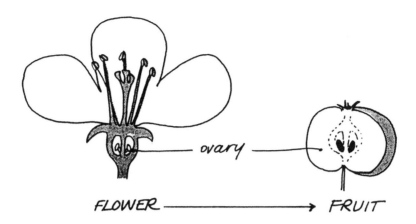

Woody perennials grown from seed go through a juvenile stage of growth, possibly as long as 8 to 10 years, during which they do not form flower buds. In mature plants, flower buds can form on mature wood in late summer to bloom the following spring, or on the current season's growth to bloom later in the summer. The basic purpose of a flower is reproduction. Most plants have complete flowers that have both male and female parts and so are capable of producing fruits. With those that don't, both male and female plants must be grown in close proximity to ensure fruit production.

Water Movement In Trees And Shrubs

Plants evaporate a large amount of water through their leaves. As the water evaporates, it pulls water into the leaves through the stems and roots. The lost water is replaced by the roots' absorbing additional water from the soil. Water movement in woody plants occurs in a thin layer of xylem cells under the bark of stems and trunks. Water movement can be disrupted by injury to the active xylem when the bark is removed or damaged by insects or disease. Such a disruption can occur in the roots, on the trunk or in the branches. On a hot summer day, a mature silver maple can loose up to 58 gallons of water per hour. Without this water movement, trees and shrubs could not move nutrients to the leaves or carry on other vital physiological processes. An adequate supply of water is essential to manage plant health. The plant must also be able to distribute the water to all living parts. Many plant problems are related to disruption in the flow of water into or within the plant.

Balanced Plant Growth

Proper plant growth depends on all plant parts functioning in balance with each other. Injury to the roots will lead to a corresponding amount of injury to the leaves. Repeated injury to the leaves can lead to reduction in root growth. The plant structure is divided into approximately the following proportions: 5 % fine feeder roots, 15 % larger or transport roots, 60 % trunk or main stem, 15 % branches and twigs and 5 % leaves.

Fitting Into The Landscape

Careful landscape planning can increase your family's enjoyment of your property and add significantly to the value of your home. Far too often homeowners begin landscaping without a plan. They plant a few shade trees here and there and evergreen shrubs around the house's foundation. This haphazard approach rarely looks good, often does not fit in with the family's activities and can cost as much as a well planned landscape. Most important, an unorganized planting can increase the time and money needed to maintain the plantings. Review Chapter 2, **The Plan**, and make sure you consider your landscape an outdoor extension of your home. Look for ways to increase privacy in certain areas of your landscape. Once you have identified the major features of the yard, you are ready to put your ideas on paper by making a plan.

To place ornamentals properly, you need some sort of plan. A scale drawing provides a birds-eye view of your property and should accurately locate the major features of the landscape. Measure as accurately as possible using graph paper. Once you have a scale drawing analyze the environmental features of your property. This can be done most easily by laying a clean sheet of paper over your plan and tracing onto it. Look at the way the sun moves across your property. Mark very shady areas where shade-tolerant plants can be used. If the sun shines on the house too much during the summer, mark spots to plant deciduous trees. These trees will shade the house in summer but allow the sun to shine on the house in winter when they drop their leaves. Do you need to protect the house from winter winds? Mark the direction of the prevailing winter wind. Keep in mind a windbreak must be at least 1 1/2 times its height away from the object to be protected. Make a note of areas where snow drifts onto walks and driveways. A planting of shrubs may be able to act as a living snow fence.

What are the soils like? Many times poor subsoil is left on the surface of the site after construction. Such soil is not very good for growing plants. Have the soil tested to determine its pH and possible amendment needs. Areas where water collects need to be marked so that plants intolerant of poor drainage will not be planted there. If possible, correct drainage problems before planting. Mark good views to be saved and poor views to be blocked out. Note sources of noise that may be muffled with a planting of dense trees or shrubs. Are there areas where unwanted traffic is killing the lawn or compacting the soil? Perhaps a planting of low shrubs or a ground cover can direct traffic to walks.

Identify Use Areas

Landscapes can be divided into areas according to their use. The *public area* is the part of your property that will be seen by passers-by and guests. This area is usually where cars are parked and guests enter the property. Trees should frame the house and a pleasing foundation planting should be developed. Walks should not be obstructed by spreading or low branched trees or shrubs. Plantings should not interfere with outdoor lighting and should not obscure the house and number. The foundation planting has several objectives. It needs to accent the space next to the main entrance but not contain several elements that compete for attention. The planting should help attain a visual balance by complementing the architectural style of the house. Avoid a congested and overgrown look by using plants

that are in proper scale with the house. The use of low maintenance plants will cut down on the amount of work necessary to keep the planting looking good.

The main entrance can be accented by using plants with interesting and eye-catching color, shape or foliage texture in the planting space next to the main entrance. The same eye-catching plants, used elsewhere in the landscape, will draw attention away from the main entrance. Plants can be used to give more "weight" to the lighter side of the house. The plants used in the foundation planting need to be in scale with the house. One-story homes with long, low roof lines look best with dwarf evergreens or other small plants. Two-story homes can accommodate larger plants. The foundation plants should be one-third to one-half the height from the ground to the bottom of the roof. An example of plants in the proper scale with a house are shown in both figures below.

A continuous planting of shrubs is better than single plants scattered along the foundation of the house.

The plants used in foundation plantings should be in scale with the house, one third to one half the height from the ground to the bottom of the roof.

A continuous planting provides a more unifying effect than individual plants scattered along the foundation. The use of pest-resistant plants will reduce the amount of maintenance required. Using dwarf or slow growing shrubs reduce the amount of pruning needed. The *private area* provides privacy, pleasant views and small garden spaces. These can be achieved through the use of screens, hedges or fences. Medium or large shrubs are needed for screens or hedges. If a hedge is to be installed, the plants must be tolerant or shearing. Screens are usually not sheared. The private area often includes an open lawn or play area. The ornamental plants surrounding this area must be selected with care. Most lawn grasses will not grow in dense shade. Planting large shade trees where they will eventually shade the

lawn completely will make growing grass difficult to impossible. The same is true of vegetable gardens. These need to be located in areas where they will be exposed to full sun. The *service area* may include such necessary objects as trash cans, air conditioners and clotheslines that need to be screened from view. This can be done with shrub plantings. Plantings should not obstruct access to the service area. Do not use plants with attention-getting characteristics in or near the service area.

Develop A Planting Plan

Once the plan is complete, it is time to select the plants. Select plants for the characteristics you need to meet the goals of your plan. Ornamental characteristics should be secondary to function. Make sure plants selected fit the environmental conditions you have identified as existing on the site. Trees should not interfere with overhead or underground utilities, and all plants should be planted where they'll have adequate space to develop. When designing the foundation planting, be sure to consider the overhang of the house. Plants growing under the overhang may not get the benefit of every rain and hence are often growing in excessively dry soil. On the other hand, avoid planting directly in front of a downspout, as during rainy weather, the plants may suffer root injury from soggy soil. Use plants with thorns judiciously. They make excellent barrier plants but are unpleasant to prune. Plants with fruits can be ornamental, but place

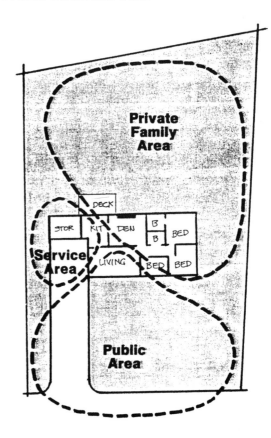

them carefully so they won't drop fruits onto walks, patios, driveways or into swimming pools. A continuous bed planting of shrubs will be easier to establish and maintain than plants scattered about the lawn. The shrub bed can be mulched for weed control and plants can be more easily fertilized. Consider the seasonal effect of the planting. A row of shrubs along walks or the driveway may cause snow to drift and increase snow removal problems. Such plantings may be injured when snow is shoveled or blown onto them.

Consider All Features In Picking Shrubs

You should consider all features in choosing shrubs. To do this takes as much creative effort as painting a landscape picture. When you select shrubbery, consider all ornamental characteristics, such as flowers, fruit, color and texture of foliage, and winter effect on the plants. You can achieve plantings that are pleasingly varied and interesting in all seasons of the year. Shrubs may be used as foundation plantings, screening and area dividers at the same time. Try to recognize a shrub's limitations as well as its possibilities, and use it in your garden design wisely and artistically. Note the shade tolerance and soil moisture conditions listed in the plant selection guide. A shrub may grow in adverse conditions, but

it will seldom thrive. A common, inexpensive shrub, flourishing in ideal conditions of soil and light, can contribute more, ornamentally, than a rare expensive one that, though beautiful in its natural habitat, may struggle for existence in your landscape. If, however, you want a plant for which ideal conditions are not available, a young one will more easily adapt to the situation. The older the plant, the greater the shock in moving it and the more attention it will require. You can avoid becoming a slave to your garden if you use few plants that require special care.

Purchasing Trees

Many individuals throughout New Jersey have begun to recognize the many values trees bring to urban and rural communities. Trees remove carbon dioxide and other pollutants from the air, help control erosion, block winter winds, reduce heating and cooling costs, add value to homes and businesses, and generally create a positive community image. If our community and private trees are to be healthy and long-lived, careful attention must be given to their selection, planting, and management. Every tree planted will require care over the decades of its life span. Plans for future, ongoing maintenance must be a part of every tree-planting program.

Trees play a major, but often silent, role in our lives. Trees along our streets, in our parks and public areas, natural areas, and in private yards, provide a wide range of benefits. Used properly, they improve the air we breathe, beautify the environment, provide wildlife habitat, reduce energy consumption during summer and winter, enhance our self-image, and generally make New Jersey communities a more pleasant place to work and live. Before any planting operation is initiated, consideration must be given to the planting site. Trees chosen for a project must fit their intended site spatially, be compatible with the given environmental conditions, and not pose unusual maintenance problems. Good trees generally grow slowly, so they should be the first plants to be placed on the property. Trees are the basis of good design, and so their location has more influence than that of any other plant. Trees provide shade during the summer, protection from winter winds, protection from the noise of nearby street traffic, screening from the outside and elimination of undesirable vistas, and they add a sense of security and comfort. Trees can be used to modify heat and cold, as well as to compliment and develop natural beauty.

When trees are used near architectural structures, they can bridge the gap between the buildings and the ground on which they stand. Trees also can divert attention, hide unwanted views, balance sloping ground, and provide accent and a center of interest. Probably no other natural feature can provide such a changing array of interest throughout the whole year. The lush, tender green of the early spring blends into the development of leaves and foliage to a rich, harmonizing mass of green. In the spring, flowers of certain trees have an inspiring quality and are followed by the fruit and seed production. These multiple forms of growth are truly miracles of nature. As trees mature, other qualities become evident. The differences in branching systems become more pronounced. Texture and color in bark give year-round interest. Autumn color makes worthwhile a whole year of waiting to see their glowing hues. During extended winter periods, trees stand dramatically silhouetted against sky, earth and buildings.

Trees grow slowly, so you might consider purchasing a tree that is already partly grown. Most large-growing trees should be planted at least 30 feet from the house, depending on the shape. Narrow upright

or pyramidal trees can be placed much closer, while those with pronounced spreading branches may need even greater distance. Small trees should be at least 15 to 20 feet apart or more, depending upon their shape. Important questions to be answered before planting begins are:

- What is the ultimate size and shape of the tree? Will it still fit the site in 20 or 30 years after increasing in height and width? Will the tree grow into power and communication lines? Will small trees with low-growing branches create problems for vehicular and pedestrian traffic?

- What maintenance will the tree require? Will the tree produce messy fruits and seeds? Will the pruning needs of the tree and fall leaf drop create an unusual amount of landscape waste? Does the tree have serious insect and/or disease problems? Will the tree become a favorite roosting spot for birds? Will trees crack sidewalks and other paved areas?

- Will the tree thrive in the site's climate and soil conditions? Will the tree tolerate alkaline soils (pH above 7.0), sun or shade, and wet or droughty conditions?

- Will tree species that tolerate deicing salt be used near driveways or roadways? Will trees interfere with snow removal?

- Has attention been given to creating diversity in the landscape?

- Do tree selection criteria emphasize longevity, desirable ornamental characteristics, and site appropriateness instead of fast growth rate and price?

- Will tree planting take place in the vicinity of gas, water or cable conduits? If you are unsure, call your local utility company for more information.

Appropriate rootball sizes necessary for full recovery of the tree after transplanting.

Trunk caliper (inches)	Minimum rootball diameter (inches)
½	12
¾	14
1	16
1½	20
2	24
2½	28
3	32
3½	38
4	42
4½	48
5	54

Trees ordered from a local nursery or retailer should be inspected before they are planted. Any trees differing in size, age, species, or condition from what was ordered should be rejected and sent back for refund or replacement. Reputable nurseries adhere to landscape plant specifications set forth in the *American Standard for Nursery Stock*. The following checklist will help you evaluate trees upon their arrival. *Size*--Trees should have the dimensions specified in your order (trunk caliper, height, container or rootball size, degree of branching, etc.). *Form*--Trees should be typical of their species or cultivar. Numerous broken branches are a sign of mishandling. Shade trees should have a straight trunk with a well-defined central leader and equally spaced branches forming a symmetrical crown. Trees with multiple leaders and narrow branch angles with included bark (bark between the branch and the trunk that

turns inward), and trees pruned improperly (flush cuts) should be rejected. *Vigor*--Stems should show signs of adequate growth either in the current year or previous year. Buds, bark, branches, and leaves should not be shriveled, desiccated, discolored, or show signs of insects or disease. *Trunk appearance*--Discolored, sunken, or swollen areas in the trunk are warning signs to tree buyers. Bark cuts and scrapes also are undesirable. Finally, trees with visible wood borer (insect) galleries in the trunk, and those showing signs of sunscald or cracking should be rejected. *Roots*--Rootball size for balled and burlapped trees is based on trunk caliper and must follow guidelines set forth by the American Association of Nurserymen. The ball of earth should not be excessively wet or dry and should be securely held together by burlap and stout twine, and for larger trees, a wire basket. The trunk should be centered in the rootball and should not move independent of the rootball. Trees purchased as "container-grown" should be well-rooted and established in the container in which they are sold. Roots of bare-root trees should arrive in moist burlap and packing, and they should be damp and flexible.

The best time to plant trees is in early spring well before bud break. Bare-root trees can be planted as soon as soils become workable in early spring but should be installed before buds swell and new growth begins. Besides early spring, container-grown and balled and burlapped trees may be planted later in spring, in early summer, or early fall. Plantings made in mid-summer (July and early August), late fall, and winter (November to early March) are more prone to failure. As trees await installation, they must be protected from mechanical injury, drying out, and overheating. The best protection is to plant trees as soon as possible after they are delivered. Bare-root trees are especially susceptible to harmful drying of the roots. They should be held in a cool, sheltered location with the roots covered with moist straw, hay, or damp burlap. Similarly, soil balls and containers are best held in a cool, shady area and kept moist until they are planted. Planting holes should accommodate the plant's root system comfortably. The completed hole should be at least twice the width of the root mass. In heavy clay or poorly drained, compacted soils, the hole should be two to three times the width of the roots.

Planting Method For Well-drained Soil   Planting Method For Poorly Drained Soil

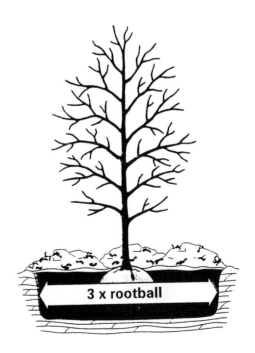

The depth of the hole should allow the top of the root system to sit level or slightly higher than the surrounding ground. Do not dig deeper than necessary because the tree needs firm support below to keep it from settling. Planting too deep will make it difficult for roots to receive oxygen and can result in tree death. Soil removed from the planting hole should be used as backfill. Adding organic matter to the backfill has not been proven beneficial to tree establishment. However, in heavy clay or rocky soils, it may be necessary to add some organic amendments to the backfill soil.

Planting Trees

Bare-root Trees

The very first thing to do is prune any damaged root tips with a clean, sharp pair of pruning shears. Then, build a firm, cone-shaped mound of soil in the middle of the planting hole. Spread the roots evenly over the mound and adjust the tree's depth to correspond with its original depth in the nursery. Add backfill in layers over the roots until the hole is three-fourths full. Water or gently tamp to settle the backfill and remove air pockets. Visually inspect the tree and straighten if it settles to one side. Complete backfilling of the hole until the backfill matches the surrounding grade. With your fingers, make a small trench around the circumference of the hole and water again slowly, allowing the water to build up and then drain several times.

Bare-root Tree

Balled And Burlapped Trees

You should always handle trees by the soil ball. After you have moved the tree next to the planting hole, remove any wire basket if the integrity of the soil ball will not be changed. Gently lift and lower or roll the soil ball into the hole. Backfill layers of soil around the ball until three-fourths of the hole is full. Lightly tamp the backfill with the shovel handle or hands to eliminate air pockets. Then remove all twine from around the tree trunk to eliminate the possibility of girdling. If you didn't remove the wire basket because the ball would have broken up, remove, by cutting, the top one-third of it now. Cut away the burlap from the top one-third of the soil ball allowing water to freely penetrate to the roots. Complete backfilling and water thoroughly using the same procedure as mentioned before.

Container-grown Trees

Always handle trees by the container or root mass. After the tree is next to the hole, gently remove the plastic, metal, or fiber container and inspect for circling roots. Make four or five vertical cuts along the side of the root mass with a sharp knife to sever circling roots and help trees get established. Lower the tree into the hole making sure the top of the root mass is at or slightly higher than the surrounding grade. Face the tree in the desired direction and adjust so that it is vertically plumb. Follow the same procedures for backfilling and watering as described for balled and burlapped trees.

Mulching the ground around newly installed trees will help conserve moisture, reduce turfgrass and weed competition, and eliminate potential damage from lawn mowers and trimming equipment. Mulches such as wood chips, ground bark, pine needles, compost or cedar mulch should be applied over the developing root system to a depth of two inches. Grass clippings should not be used because they compress and mat together, restricting water and oxygen movement. *Fertilization* at the time of planting is generally not recommended. Research has shown that fertilization is ineffective until the tree has partially re-established its root system. *Pruning* at planting time should be limited to alleviating problems and ensuring good branch structure. Do not thin a tree to compensate for root loss! Rather, prune to remove broken, crossing, crowded, or rubbing branches and any dead or diseased tissue. Remove basal sprouts, encourage a central leader, and eliminate narrow crotches with included bark. Pruning paints or sealers do not necessarily prevent decay or promote rapid pruning would closure and are not recommended. Leave lower branches on trees to stimulate root and trunk diameter growth. In general, two-thirds of the tree height should be left as crown (branches and leaves).   Whenever removing branches back to the trunk, always cut just outside of the branch bark ridge thereby preventing injury to the branch collar. Careful pruning will promote rapid wound closure and inhibit spread of decay in the trunk.

Pruning A Deciduous Tree After Planting

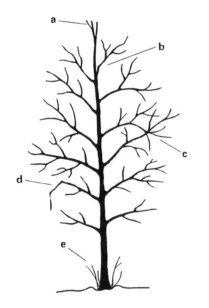

(a) remove a competing terminal,
(b) eliminate narrow (weak) crotches,
(c) eliminate crossing or rubbing branches,
(d) remove broken, damaged, or diseased
    branches,
(e) remove basal sprouts

Staking or guying large trees, bare-root trees, or those having high wind resistance, such as evergreens, especially on exposed sites, is an important ingredient to successful tree planting. Stakes for support should be attached to the tree low on the trunk with flexible web belting or any strong, soft, wide strips of material to prevent girdling injury. The purpose of staking or guying is to prevent movement of the lower trunk and root system. Movement of the top is desirable and will strengthen the tree. *Watering* is the single most important task for new tree owners, but watering timetables are almost impossible to give. As a general rule, 1 inch every 7 to 10 days should be adequate during the first growing season. However, the amount of water to be delivered depends on the amount of rainfall received, moisture-holding capacity of the soil, and drainage characteristics of the

site. Newly planted trees should be inspected at least once a week to determine if watering is necessary, and more often during hot, dry weather. Remember, trees can be killed by overwatering.

Trunk protection may be needed for smooth, thin-barked species (ash, crabapple, maple) to prevent sunscald injury. Standard paper tree wrap should be applied from the bottom up so that it overlaps like shingles. Wrap up to the first major branch and secure with a plastic expandable tape. Tree wrap should be used from early November to early April during the four to five year establishment period. Rabbits and mice can also damage the trunks of small trees during the winter. Protect trunks with wire mesh, hardware cloth, or other products specifically designed for this purpose.

Tree Wrap For Trunk Protection

Insect and disease pests often attack trees already under stress or weakened. Keeping trees healthy will reduce insect and disease problems. Regularly examine trees for unusual or suspicious spots, lesions, growths, or any other irregularity on the bark, branches, or foliage. If you think you've found a pest, identify it before applying a pesticide. Not all pests require control measures, some cannot be treated practically, and/or the time period for effective control may have passed. Sometimes simply pruning diseased branches from the tree or removing insects by hand will control the pest problem. If you are uncertain about your diagnosis, consult a local nursery, landscaper, tree specialist or extension office.

For easy clarification, let's divide trees into two main groups, deciduous and evergreen. *Deciduous* trees are those whose leaves die during the winter. They are often considered the principal plant growth in most of the country. *Evergreen* trees are those that hold their leaves during the winter, and thus keeping their green foliage throughout the year. They may have slender needles, such as , Pines, Cedars and Firs, or broad blades (broadleaf evergreens) like the American Holly or Gum. Following is information on several of the most common trees grown in New Jersey. All of these are strong trees, and with the proper attention should give you many years of service and pleasure.

Beech - This is a round-headed, spreading tree that is one of the most popular garden plants. They have graceful architecture, smooth bark and finely cut leaves. Some have weeping branches bearing foliage to the ground. Others that are erect, can be used as hedges if properly trained and pruned. An American beech has smooth, silvery bark that is elegant all year. Beeches prefer full sun and lots of room to grow. Considered a large tree - grows 50 feet or more.

Elm - One of the most beautiful trees in North America. The most typical form is a divided trunk with two or more ascending stems with upward-sweeping branches. This architecture gives it the appearance of a wineglass. Elms are widely used as a street tree in many communities. They should be planted far from others of its kind to avoid the spread of diseases, especially, Dutch elm disease. This particular disease nearly killed all American elm trees in the United States. Considered a large tree - grows 50 feet or more.

Oak - There are many varieties of this large, majestic tree. They are valuable as ornamental landscape trees or as community street trees. Oaks have brilliant color in the fall ranging from scarlet to purple. They are large, stately trees that grow best in wide-open landscapes. Oak trees offer favorable conditions for small wildlife such as, birds and squirrels. An oak has rough, grayish-brown bark and deeply cut leaves. Oaks have a tendency to hang onto many of their leaves for a good part of the winter, which can be an annoyance for those people who like to have their landscapes completely cleaned up in the fall. One variety of oak, the Scrub oak, grows well near the seaside and dry, rocky areas. Considered a large tree - grows 50 feet or more.

Maple - This is a wonderful shade tree, especially for large lawns or open landscapes. It has a light gray bark, and with its many branches, stands out in winter, especially in the snow. They grow fast, are long-lived, hardy and can grow well in most types of soil. One popular maple, the Scarlet Maple, is beautiful in all seasons and all landscapes. Be careful not to plant it too close to roads or driveways as many of the roots grow within the top two inches of soil. Also, they are susceptible to de-icing salts and may actually die. It may be very hard to grow grass under most maples, even using a shady seed, as the maple roots battle fiercely with grass roots for water and nutrients. A hardy ground cover would have more of a chance surviving. Considered a large tree - grows 50 feet or more.

Poplar - This is a tall, slender tree that grows in columnar form. It is very fast growing and has light leaves that rustle in a breeze. It is valuable in landscaping when several are planted in a line as a windbreak. It is not recommended to plant a popular too close to foundations, driveways, sidewalks or streets as the roots can clog drains, and damage pavement and concrete. A medium tree - grows up to 50 feet.

Bradford Pear - This is one of the best ornamental trees around. It is resistant to many tree blights and pests. The leaves are glossy and deep green, and in the spring the tree has an abundance of beautiful white flowers. The Bradford pear is used by many communities as a street tree since it is tolerant to pollution, poor soils and has beautiful blooms. This is a relatively hard tree to thin out when it gets larger and should be done by a professional tree expert. Considered a medium tree - grows up to 50 feet.

Birch - A valuable plant used in "naturalistic" landscapes as it is multistemmed and gives a clustering effect. It has white bark and fine, dark green foliage. The Birch grows well in almost any soil, and can be used anywhere in the landscape, even rock gardens. However, it will not thrive if planted near larger plants that are competing for water and nutrients. Considered a medium tree - grows up to 50 feet.

Flowering Dogwood - In my opinion, the best ornamental tree available for home landscapes. There are pink and white dogwoods and, in the spring, both have beautiful flowers. In the summer, the foliage is very dark green turning to purple-red in the fall. Birds love the red berries and during the winter, this is a very attractive tree. Dogwoods grow best in well-drained, moist soil and partial shade. Considered a medium tree - grows up to 40 feet.

Magnolia - There are several species of this beautiful, slow-growing tree. The saucer magnolia has blossoms that grow up to 8 inches across and are shaped like cups. The magnolia usually blooms in early April and show quite an overwhelming display. However, once the flowers drop, the area becomes quite messy with all of the brown flower petals. It is best to plant magnolias in the early spring in deep, moist soil in a sunny area. Considered a medium tree - grows up to 30 feet.

Flowering Crabapple - Many, many different varieties allow you to choose size, branching form and blossom shade. There are varieties that are resistant to several diseases, so check with your local nursery. The crabapple grows in a well-drained, moist soil with plenty of sun. The many blooms of crabapples are a wonder to see, and the small red fruits are attractive to birds. Considered a medium tree - grows up to 50 feet.

Flowering Cherry - Absolutely beautiful ornamental trees that have an elegant appearance. Cherries will grow in just about any type of soil, as well as it is well-drained and needs lots of sun for full flowering. They flower in the spring, but the blooms are short lived, only about 2 weeks. The bark is a beautiful dark mahogany-red and looks wonderful in snow. Considered a medium tree - grows up to 40 feet.

Linden - The Linden is a tight, well organized tree perfect for a home landscape. It has small heart-shaped leaves, is pollution tolerant and is very popular in communities as a street tree. This is a very pretty shade tree in a lawn or near a patio. It flowers in early summer with sweetly scented blossoms that are attractive to bees. It is happy in any well-drained, moist soil with plenty of sun. Considered a large tree - grows 50 feet or more.

This list should give you a head start on deciding what trees will look and grow best in your landscape. If you are still undecided or can't find anything here you like, look for a book in your public library on trees and check with your local nursery.

Evergreens keep their leaves all year long. The leaves are shed and replaced very gradually, so the plant always has foliage. Evergreens are usually classified as narrow-leaved (conifers) or broad-leaved. Conifers are plants that bear cones and needles. Narrow-leaved evergreens are extremely important in landscaping because of their color, form and use. They can be used as foundation plantings, borders and windbreaks. Their size ranges from very small to very large and form from low spreading to tall pyramidal. Evergreens come in many different colors such as, various shades of dark greens, bluegreens, purple or silver hues. Some conifers cannot handle pollution well, so they are not suited for community street plantings, but are excellent when used in home landscapes. Most of them have great endurance and can be planted in a variety of soils. Conifers are among the most important plant groups for the landscape. They provide year-round interest and their cold hardiness and general resistance to pests and diseases make them permanent, undemanding, low-maintenance garden investments. Just about all they need for perfect health is a well-drained location, ample water, and occasional fertilizer. Mulching is beneficial. Almost all, especially the golden-leaved varieties, thrive in full sun. Spruce trees are an excellent windbreak because of their long taproot, they are hard to blow over. A few of the larger conifers, such as Hemlock and White Pine are especially useful as hedges, windbreaks or screens to block out unwanted scenery or service areas. Properly selected and planted conifers help shelter a house from winter winds which in turn, reduce the heating cost. From ground cover to vertical accent, there is a Conifer for every garden need.

Many of the broad-leaved evergreens are low-growing, shrub-like plants such as Rhododendron, Azalea, Euonymus, small Holly, Privet and Barberry. These plants can also be used as foundation plantings for protection, or low windbreaks when planted as a hedge. They also can add beauty to borders and flower beds. If you are having trouble growing grass in certain areas, low-growing evergreens can be used as ground covers. Certain bushes have berries that attract birds and others have foliage that

turns scarlet in the fall. Evergreens are low-maintenance plants. As long as they have water, food and are pruned occasionally, they will continue to beautify your landscape 12 months of the year, for many years to come.

Trees greatly enhance both our rural and urban environments because of their scenic, recreational, and comforting qualities. As a result, significant time, effort, and money are spent on planting and maintaining trees in the landscaping around homes, businesses, public buildings, streets, and parks. Although insect and disease problems are often unpredictable or unavoidable, many major tree injuries in the landscape are **caused by people**. It is important to be aware of these injuries, how to prevent them, and of methods for keeping trees healthy. The following are some of the more common injuries and suggestions for avoiding them.

Care of Trees

Trees can be injured if improperly handled during planting or if planted at the wrong depth. Symptoms due to improper planting may occur soon after planting or not until several years afterward. Correct handling, planting and care techniques help to ensure survival of newly planted trees.

- Depending on tree species, plant in the early spring or fall.
- Prepare the planting hole properly so that roots are not cramped.
- Prevent roots from drying out before planting.
- Remove plastic (always) and burlap wrapping on balled trees whenever possible. Alternatively, after placing the tree in the planting hole, burlap should be loosened from around the trunk and/or cut away and removed from the top part of the ball, with the remainder left in place.
- Plant the tree at the same depth that it was growing in the nursery.
- Water immediately after planting (and periodically) for two seasons to maintain a moist, but not waterlogged, soil. Ideally, trees need about one inch of water every seven to ten days.
- Support the tree with rubber-protected (or similar soft material) guy wires attached to two sturdy stakes or poles. Remove support wires once tree roots have established (usually within 2 years).
- Mulch soil at the base of the tree to maintain soil moisture, control weeds, and minimize mower damage. Maintain mulching to a maximum depth of 2 to 3 inches.
- Do not fertilize when planting. Wait until about one year after planting.

Proper Pruning Method

Pruning every two to three years helps to improve tree vigor and maintains an attractive, natural shape. Pruning is also done to remove dead or diseased branches, and to remove branches near utility lines and buildings. Properly pruned trees can rapidly form callous tissue to compartmentalize injured tissues. Improper pruning, however, creates excessive wounding that reduces vigor and predisposes the tree to attack by diseases and insects.

Pruning can be done at any time of the year, but pruning some trees in the spring results in excessive sap flow or "bleeding" that is considered unattractive. Check with your local extension office, nursery or tree expert for the best pruning time for the species in question. Prune living branches as close as possible to the trunk or connecting branch, without cutting the branch collar. Make a smooth cut. Remove broken tops and branches as soon as possible after storm damage or other injury. Prune diseased branches anytime during the year, but do so only during dry weather. To prevent disease spread, cut 6 to 8 inches below the affected tissue with surface sterilized pruning tools. To sterilize tools, dip them in denatured (70%) alcohol or 10% bleach between cuts. Thoroughly wash and dry tools after use.

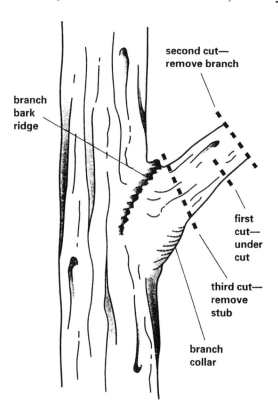

Treating Wounds

Properly cleaned and shaped wounds help prevent tree decay. Treat wounds by removing dead and torn bark tissue, then scribe and round the edges of the wound with a sharp knife. Although wound dressings have no proven healing value, commercial asphalt-based preparations   specifically for tree wounds or orange shellac can be applied to wounds as a cosmetic treatment.

Flooding

Tree roots need oxygen to survive. In soils that remain wet for long periods, roots can suffocate and die. Trees with sustained root injury exhibit a progressive decline, early fall coloration, premature leaf drop, small leaf size, twig and branch dieback, and sucker formation on the trunk and large branches. Excessively wet soil conditions can also favor the activity of fungi that attack roots and cause disease. Changes in normal drainage patterns due to grade alteration may cause flooding and kill trees.

● Avoid changes in drainage patterns that cause water to back up over roots for extended periods.
● Whereas some trees tolerate wet locations, low areas where drainage is poor and flooding may occur are inadequate sites for most species of trees.
● Species that thrive in wet locations may not survive if changes in drainage patterns divert water away.

Lawn And Garden Equipment And Chemicals

Use equipment carefully to prevent serious injury to tree trunks, branches, and roots.

- To prevent injuring trees accidentally with lawn mowers or weed-eaters, grass should be kept away from tree trunks.
- Mulches can be used for a "mower buffer."
- Choose all pesticides wisely. Use all chemicals only in the precise manner described on the label.
- Certain herbicides (weed killers) can kill trees.
- Many herbicides that are safe for grasses are *not* safe to use around trees.
- Recently transplanted trees are especially susceptible to herbicide injury.
- Avoid excessive use of commercial fertilizer-herbicide mixtures near trees.
- Overdoses of fertilizer can kill trees.

De-icing Salt

De-icing compounds used on highways, driveways, and sidewalks in winter contain sodium chloride and/or calcium chloride. These chemicals are toxic to trees. Trees are injured when salt is absorbed by their foliage and roots.

- Avoid or minimize the use of salt around trees.
- Use sand, sawdust, or other insoluble abrasives on icy surfaces.
- Place trees and shrubs that are sensitive to salt as far as possible from problem areas.
- Select planting sites that are not subject to salt-contaminated waters, and place shallow diversion ditches between roadways and plantings.
- When vegetation must be placed near roadways, utilize salt-tolerant plants.

Trees can be considered a permanent foundation of all landscapes. They are usually bought for three reasons: shade, protection and appearance. Small and large trees provide shade in varying amounts. When tall trees provide shade on a house during the summer, the air conditioning bill will be reduced. The trees must be fairly close to the house, though, to give significant results. Planting deciduous trees, that loose their leaves every winter, allow the warm rays of the sun to add heat to your house when it needs it most. A small tree producing shade on a patio will cool the patio and give you an area to relax in during the hot summer. Certain trees are excellent in screening the yard and giving protection from dust and noise pollution as well as unsightly areas. They can form a barrier to hide anything unpleasant. We all like beautiful trees and there are many that will enhance the appearance of the landscape. However, limit your selection to the few that accomplish your main goals.

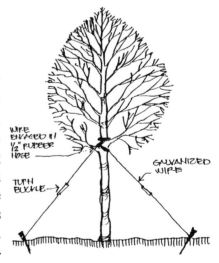

Purchasing Small Ornamentals

Now that you know more about plant requirements and how they grow, let's go, with pencil and pad or your gardening journal, to pick out some shrubs and trees for your landscape. I would suggest going to the nursery on a weekday rather than a weekend, as it will be less crowded and you may get more personal attention. Try to speak to the owner, as he or she should be the one most knowledgeable in helping you pick the best plants for your needs. Show the owner your plans, drawings and requirements, where you would like certain shrubs or trees planted and see if he agrees. Check and see if they have examples of the plants you want and see what else they have to offer. If you can't find a specific plant, I'm sure they will be able to order it for you within a reasonable amount of time.

A visit to your local garden center or retail nursery can be an exciting experience. You will see many kinds of ornamental plants packaged in several ways. Some may be in plastic containers of various sizes. Others may have their roots and a ball of soil wrapped with burlap and covered with moist bark. These are called "balled-and-burlapped" or "B-and-B" plants. Still others may be packaged with their roots in boxes or paper. Regardless of how the plants are displayed and packaged, you should always look for good quality plants. What should you look for when buying plants? First, you should consider choosing species that are not problem prone. Look for good foliage color and strong branches. Avoid plants that are root-bound in containers. Root-bound plants have roots that have become too large for that container. You can see the roots growing out of the drainage hole of the container (see figure 1). Be sure bare roots have been adequately protected from moisture loss and bud break has not yet occurred (see figure 2). The soil ball of B-and-B plants should remain firm, rounded and intact when handled. Fairly new burlap cloth should hold the root ball. Avoid plants with root balls that are too soft, saggy, pancake shaped or too small (see figure 3).

When buying a plant in a pot, check that it is not "rootbound." Roots extending through the drain hole is the bottom are an indication of this problem.

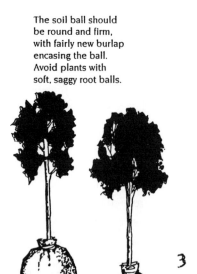

The soil ball should be round and firm, with fairly new burlap encasing the ball. Avoid plants with soft, saggy root balls.

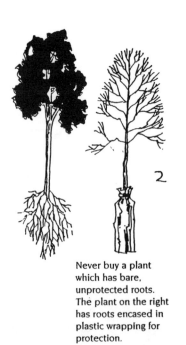

Never buy a plant which has bare, unprotected roots. The plant on the right has roots encased in plastic wrapping for protection.

Planting Methods

You should prepare your soil area for planting before buying the plants. If you buy plants before you have had a chance to do this, be ready to protect the plants until planting time. Most important is to protect the plants from drying. Place the plants in a partially shaded area protected from drying winds. Most nursery plants can dry out rapidly. Look at them each day and water them as needed. If it will be more than three or four days before you can install these plants, you need to provide additional protection for the roots. Cluster the plants close together and mulch the roots with compost, bark mulch or peatmoss. This will help keep the plants moist until planting. Many gardeners and horticulturists have their own ways to plant shrubs, just as I do. However, there are certain basics I'm sure almost all would agree on and that is what will be covered here. Shrubs and trees are the backbone of your landscape. They must be planted carefully and properly ensuring they will get a good start. Trees, shrubs and ground covers are all planted the same way, with just a few things different because of type or size. The method of planting depends on how the item is sold, usually balled and burlapped, bare rooted, in a flat or in a container.

Balled and Burlapped (B&B)

These plants have a ball of their original dirt surrounding the roots and wrapped in a biodegradable material called burlap. The soil ball should be round and firm, with fairly new burlap encasing the ball. Avoid plants with soft, saggy root balls. When you are ready to plant, dig a hole twice as wide as the ball and about three inches deeper than the height of the ball. Mix a small amount of top soil and peat

moss together and put three inches of the mixture into the bottom of the hole. This will allow the downward roots to get a good healthy start. Set the plant down in the hole with the burlap still on, and make sure the root ball is about one 1 inch above the surrounding surface. We are allowing for a certain amount of the plant to sink after being watered several times. Turn the plant around several times, place the best side forward and make sure it is straight. Return enough of the soil you previously removed, to hold the plant stable, cut the string holding the ball, spread open and fold down the burlap away from the base. Prune off any broken roots.

Gently fill the hole half way with water and let it drain. Add more soil, tamp it firm, water again, and let it drain. Fill the hole, tamp again and, depending on the size of the shrub or tree, drive a stake, possibly two, beneath the hole but don't damage the root ball. Tie the plant securely so it won't lean, create a saucer watering basin around the plant and soak the soil well. Wait one day, water well again, let the soil dry and mulch with shredded bark to retain moisture.

Now that the planting is complete, remove any damaged limbs with a sharp pruner. During the hot summer, water deeply and only when needed. While late fall is approaching winter, keep all of your shrubs and trees well watered but hold off fertilizing them until next spring. Where there are excessive windy spots, it may be a good idea to provide winter protection.

Containers

A shrub or tree purchased in a container is planted approximately the same way as B&B except there is no burlap involved. Remove the plant from the container and loosen any roots that encircle the ball but make sure not to break the ball. Follow the same procedure as with B&B.

Bare-root

Dig a hole large enough to accommodate all of the roots easily. Mix some top soil and peat moss together and form a mound in the center bottom of the hole. Place the plant into the hole and spread the roots over the mound. Remove any broken roots with your pruner. The old soil line mark should be present on the base. Put the plant into the hole so the mark is even with the surrounding surface level. Add more soil, tamp it down and water gently. Finish filling the hole, but leave the very top loose until growth starts. Make a saucer watering basin and soak deeply but gently. Within two weeks, a light layer of mulch may be added. Wait until the plant matures a little and then add more mulch. Keep watered deeply but only when needed.

Never buy a plant which has bare, unprotected roots. The plant on the right has roots encased in plastic wrapping for protection.

Flats

Plants sold in flats are usually perennial flowers, annual flowers, vegetables and ground covers. Carefully separate the plants from the flats and one another. If they can't be gently pulled apart, you can cut them with a sharp knife. The spacing of each plant is important, so ask where you made the purchase, how far apart they should be planted. This will, of course, depend on how large the plant grows and how much you want in a given area.

When To Plant

There are so many different kinds of plants and trees with so many different suggestions on when to plant them, it would be hard to list them all. In my opinion, most plants can be planted in early spring and early fall, depending on weather conditions, plant availability and whether or not you take extra special care of them until they mature. I will, however, give you some well accepted guidelines on when to plant certain varieties.

So far as shrubs and trees, September and October are prime times to plant. The increased precipitation, cool nights and warm days are excellent for root growth. Planting at the right time of the year can make a big difference so far as how much transplant shock they receive and how well they will survive. B&B and containers should be planted in the fall. This gives them a long time of warm soil and cool nights which promotes strong root growth before the soil temperature gets cold in winter. Bare-rooted plants are handled differently. They loose most of their water absorbing capabilities during transplanting and new roots readily won't develop until spring. So the best time to plant bare-rooted shrubs and trees is very early spring, just before buds break.

Since there so many different kinds of evergreens used in landscaping, I feel I should mention a little about them now. Evergreens come in all different shapes, sizes and colors and are extremely useful and very versatile. They are classified as either broad-leaved or narrow-leaved. Narrow-leaved are those that have thin needle-like foliage such as pine and hemlock and range in color from yellow-green to blue-green. Broad-leaved are those that have wide leaves like rhododendrons, azaleas and hollies and may have beautiful flowers or berries. They come in many sizes from large trees and shrubs, to medium size shrubs and low groundcovers that range from 40 feet high to 1 foot high. Evergreens provide shade, relief from winds and can give beautiful flowers most of the year. Some favorites are; Norway spruce having large pinecones can reach a height of 100 feet, Colorado blue spruce shaped like a pyramid, having green to bluish foliage, and of course, yews, hollies, rhododendrons and azaleas. Most evergreens should be planted in August and September after new growth has hardened off. Certain evergreens, like firs and hemlocks, prefer late spring planting.

Plant Problems

Diagnosing plant problems can be a difficult task. In this section, I will try to help you identify ornamental plant problems. Proper plant selection and care are the first steps in preventing plant problems. To diagnose plant problems, you need to know how a healthy plant grows. Refer to the early part of this chapter. The symptoms of a plant disorder appear when one of the normal plant processes or functions is disrupted. You can use the symptoms to narrow down the possible causes of the problem. Problems can occur on roots, stems or leaves, but symptoms may or may not be seen on other parts of the plant. Trees and shrubs in the urban environment are frequently stressed by draught or flooding because root growth is restricted by roads, sidewalks and walls. Urban sites often subject roots to changes in the water table, poor drainage and competition for water when the roots of many landscape plants grow together. Many factors increase plant stress. Protect plants by preventing their exposure to these abuses.

Healthy plant + stress = Decline begins

Weakened plant + stress = Decline and dieback

Declining plant + stress = Disease and insects attack

Stresses Affecting The Susceptibility Of Plants To Disease

- Improperly applied herbicides.
- Winter Injury.
- Soil too dry or too wet.
- Overmulching.
- Repeated lawnmower injury.
- Pavement built near tree.
- Girdling from wires.
- Soil compaction.
- Road or walkway deicing salt runoff.
- Planted too close to building.
- Branches broken during storms.

Long-lived trees and shrubs can be exposed to stresses that cause them to begin a decline in shoot growth and leaf size. Additional stresses cause weakened plants to show dieback of branches in the uppermost part of the canopy. Finally, a combination of stress and pathogens cause a plant disease and increase the dieback. For example, trees and shrubs weakened by draught are more susceptible than healthy, vigorous plants, to attack by canker-causing fungi and defoliating fungi. A weakened plant stores less food and so carries less into spring to support new growth. Of course, there are pathogens and insects that can attack a very healthy tree or shrub if the genetics of the plant make it susceptible to stresses.

Diagnosing Plant Problems

Plant problems can be grouped into four major categories: cultural, environmental, diseases and insects. In many cases, a combination of these problems leads to a plant disorder. **Cultural problems** arise from the care of plants in a landscape setting. Such practices as watering, fertilizing, site selection and preparation, use of chemicals and mulching may lead to plant problems if done improperly. **Environmental factors** that cause plant problems include drought, excessive rain, hail, lightning, high or low temperatures, and environmental pollutants. Unlike cultural problems, these problems are usually beyond the control of individuals. **Diseases** are brought about by infectious agents - bacteria, fungi, nematodes and viruses. Common diseases include leaf spot, vascular wilts, cankers and root rots. **Insects** may cause plant problems by chewing plant parts or sucking plant juices. As you attempt to diagnose plant problems, it's important to recognize that one factor alone is rarely the cause of a plant problem. For instance, plants suffering from draught stress or fertilizer deficiencies are often more vulnerable to attack by diseases and insects. Mechanical damage to plants enhances the chance of disease.

Cultural Problems

Landscape plants need specific environments for best growth. I have already discussed the three questions to consider when choosing a plant, earlier in this chapter. Besides the ones listed above, other cultural problems exist such as plant quality, plant handling and improper plant management practices.

Plant Quality And Handling

Regardless of how plants are displayed and packaged at your local garden center or retail nursery, you should always look for good quality plants. When a recently transplanted shrub or tree fails to grow and the cause cannot be associated with drought, excessive moisture or insufficient roots, the plant may have been injured before planting. It may have dehydrated while in storage or in transit, or it may have been subjected to excessively high temperatures. Recently transplanted plants may not have root systems large enough to support their shoot growth. Therefore, you should prune transplanted shrubs and trees to help reduce water loss during the establishment period. When pruning, do not head back the ends of the branch tips: rather, thin out undesirable stems and help maintain the tree or shrub's natural form. Sometimes trees are dug with inadequate root systems. Do not accept such plants for planting. Industry standards have been established to assist in determining proper root ball diameter. Did the plant die after you planted it? You will increase your chances of success when you follow the previously mentioned planting instructions. Be sure to protect the roots before planting, set the plant at the proper depth, use a good planting soil, firm the soil around the roots, keep the ground moist and mulch around the plant.

Improper Plant Management Practices

Proper planting and care maximizes growth of landscape plants and keeps them healthy. Improper cultural practices or lack of care can retard growth or weaken the plant's ability to withstand adverse environmental conditions or pest attacks. Improper cultural practices can even enhance disease development. Watering plants lightly through overhead sprinkling in the evening or at night, for example, can create wet foliage conditions that favor leaf diseases. Allowing plants to get too dry may predispose them to cankers. Blue spruce, for example, usually does not show wilting or other symptoms of drought stress, but drought conditions will increase the possibility of infection by Cytospora canker.

Pruning At The Wrong Time

The least desirable time to prune is immediately after the new growth has developed in the spring. At that time, much of the food stored in the roots and stems has been used to develop new growth, and the new foliage should replace this food before you prune and remove the foliage. Otherwise, considerable dwarfing, dieback and decline of the plant may occur. It is advisable to limit late fall pruning, which stimulates new growth on some plants. This growth may not have sufficient time to harden off before

cold weather arrives and so may be damaged or killed by low temperatures. Late pruning also removes valuable food reserves. Prune when twigs, branches and limbs are dry and when the weather forecast calls for dry weather for a week. This is most important in fall and spring, when diseases are active and easily transmitted to vulnerable plants. Whenever possible, avoid pruning the tender spring flush of growth to avoid tearing new bark tissue and opening wound sites for disease organisms to enter. Spring flowering trees and shrubs should be pruned shortly after flowering to avoid removing flower buds, which form in late summer on mature wood and overwinter. Prune plants that bloom after the end of June in late winter before new growth starts. These plants develop their flower buds during the spring growth period.

Bleeding of pruning wounds can be heavy on certain trees, such as birch, dogwood, sugar maple and elm. Minimize bleeding of susceptible trees by making small cuts - less than 3 inches in diameter - and pruning in summer. Bleeding is very likely if severe pruning is done just before growth begins in the spring. Bleeding doesn't harm the tree, but if it's heavy and persistent, it may injure the bark below the pruning cut and cause slow callusing of the lower wound.

Incorrect Pruning

Topping (heading back) is, unfortunately, the most common method of reducing tree size. It is more rapid than thinning, but the results are, in most cases, much less desirable. Regrowth is vigorous and upright from the branch stubs. The new branches form a compact head and broomlike terminals, and they may be weakly attached to older branches. Thinning-out pruning can be used to reduce the height and spread of a tree. Cut branches to lower laterals. Some limbs may be removed completely. A thinned tree retains its natural shape and is less subject to problems than a headed or topped tree.

Excess Fertilizer

Too much fertilizer can stimulate vegetative growth to the detriment of flower and fruit production. Excess fertilizer is especially damaging during dry weather. As the soil water decreases by evaporation and plant use for transpiration, fertilizer salts can become more concentrated in the soil around the roots. Plants exposed to these conditions will dehydrate. How quickly dehydration occurs will depend on the concentration of fertilizer salts. Always follow instructions when using fertilizer on plants, and water ornamental plantings during dry weather. If you apply too much fertilizer, you may be able to leach it out of the root zone by applying liberal quantities of water to the soil.

Lack Of Water

All plants require some water, and most plants require large quantities if they are to grow normally. Though most plants receive adequate moisture from rainfall or irrigation, plants sometimes become dehydrated, particularly after transplanting or when growing in containers or in adverse sites in a landscape, such as under building overhangs. After transplanting, water plants periodically the first growing

season and possibly the second. Water plants in containers and adverse sites regularly to assure adequate water for growth. Be sure to remove burlap - especially plastic burlap, which is commonly used to wrap root balls - from the sides of the root ball and lay it in the bottom of the planting hole at planting time. Attempts to remove the burlap completely may destroy the root ball and damage the root system. Drought-stressed plants are unable to take up nutrients for proper growth.

Excess Water

Too much water around the roots of most plants used in the landscape can cause them to decline and ultimately die. Plants with waterlogged roots often contract root rotting diseases. Plants require oxygen in the soil for good growth and development. Often plants are placed in shallow depressions hollowed out of heavy clay soil. Under these conditions, little or no drainage is possible even if you place rocks or gravel in the bottom of the planting holes.

Girdling

Plants may decline in vigor because of girdling by a wire or nylon rope encircling the stem, girdling roots or vines, or damage by people. Non-deteriorating ropes used to secure the ball of soil during transplanting and wires that supported newly planted trees should be removed when they're no longer needed. At planting, be sure to distribute the roots properly in the planting hole. For plants that were produced in containers, this means making sure that no encircling roots are left to girdle the stem as the plant grows. Many homeowner activities can also girdle valuable plants. The use of lawn mowers has increased the incidence of "lawnmower blight", or physical injury to plant trunks and stems.

Overmulching

The roots of plants need oxygen at all times. Overmulching kills the roots of shallow-rooted plants by suffocation. Symptoms of too much mulch include chlorotic foliage (yellow leaves with green veins), abnormally small leaves, poor growth and dieback of older branches. Disease organisms that thrive under conditions of low oxygen can become active and attack the roots. Sometimes the old root system will be rotted as the plant tries to send out new roots into the mulch layer.

Insecticide/Fungicide Injury

Applying the wrong chemical or improperly applying a pesticide can injure plants. The most common form of pesticide injury is leaf burn, particularly on the margins or tips of the leaves. The propellant in aerosol sprays or the emulsifying agent in emulsifiable concentrates can be responsible for injury to some plants. Dormant oils applied at the wrong time of the year or to sensitive species can also injure plants. Sulfur applied during hot weather may burn the foliage.

Herbicide Injury

If the new growth of plants is malformed and the leaves cupped and chlorotic (yellow or white), it is possible and highly probable that a weed killer has been applied nearby. Some weed and feed lawn fertilizers contain weed killers that should not be applied above the root zone of valuable trees and shrubs. Spray applications of weed killers should be made only on calm days because certain formulations may drift onto valuable plants and cause various malformations of growth. Non-selective herbicides should be used with caution because they may wash into areas where they could kill valuable plants. Spray equipment used to apply weed killers should not be used for other lawn and garden chemicals. The improper use of weed killers damages or kills many plants each year. *Read the pesticide label.!*

Environmental Problems

Shrubs and trees may also suffer from many problems brought on by the environment, such as nutritional deficiencies, soil type, weather related and natural occurring plant processes. Let's cover a few of these very important problems.

Nutritional Deficiencies

Deficiencies of nitrogen, phosphorus and potassium can be corrected by fertilizing. The primary symptom of nitrogen deficiency is an overall yellowing of the leaves, beginning with the oldest leaves. As the older leaves are depleted of nitrogen, they may drop. Small, dark green leaves with a blue to purple tinge can be an indication of a phosphorus deficiency. The symptoms occur first on the older leaves, and the lower leaves may turn yellow. In a potassium deficiency, the margins of older leaves become chlorotic, then scorched. The leaf margins may also curl downward. The older foliage drops prematurely, giving the plant a sparse look.

Soil pH determines the availability of the nutrients in the soil solution. Some plants, such as rhododendron or azalea, have difficulty absorbing iron unless the soil pH is between 4.5 and 5.5. Pin oak and holly will show iron deficiency symptoms at a pH above 7.5. Correcting a high soil pH over the entire area of a tree's root zone may not be worth the effort but maintaining a low pH for a number of shrubs is more feasible. You can lower the pH by applying sulfur and you can raise the pH, if desired, by adding lime. Iron deficiency in landscape plants that require an acid soil will cause young leaves to turn yellow while the main veins remain green. In advanced stages, brown spots occur between the leaf veins. Plants commonly affected by iron deficiency are pin oak, azalea, blueberry, rhododendron and holly. To treat plants, spray them with iron chelates. These are available from most nurseries and garden centers and provide a suitable solution for small plants.

Spraying large trees is not practical. Use trunk implants of soluble iron sources on trees. The plastic capsules are inserted into holes drilled in the trunks. As the tree grows, they cover the capsules. The disadvantage of this method is the necessity of drilling the holes in the tree trunk to make the implants. Trees vary in their ability to tolerate repeated wounding. Drilling a series of holes in the trunk every two

to three years may become a more serious problem than the deficiency. Keep trees with implants well watered and fertilized so they heal as quickly as possible. Adding fertilizer that contains iron to a soil that is not sufficiently acid may not help. The plant roots may not absorb the additional iron until the soil is made more acid.

Soil Type And Moisture

The soil type can lead to problems with some ornamental plants. Some plants are intolerant of particular soil types. For instance, most cherries do not grow well in poorly drained clay. As discussed earlier, some plants require acidic soils and will display nutrient deficiency symptoms on soils to which they are not adapted. Plants growing poorly because of soil intolerances can not easily be helped. Select replacement plants better adapted to the soil at the planting site.

Soil moisture problems are usually related to soil drainage. Poor drainage can be the result of the soil type or the grade. Excessively drained soil fails to retain moisture. Plants must tolerate dry conditions or be given additional water. Clay soil drains poorly. That is, once clay soils are saturated, they retain moisture longer than other soil types. Plant roots growing in clay can be injured by excessive soil moisture during wet weather or by excessive irrigation. Soil modification in the planting hole will not have long-term benefits. Water from the surrounding area will more easily enter modified soil, flooding the root system. Improving clay soils is difficult, but can be done by aeration. Sandy soils drain very well but retain little moisture for plant growth. Adding organic matter will improve the water-holding capacity of sand for a while, but the organic matter will decompose over time and the soil will again hold less moisture. As with clay, it may be easier in the long run to select plants that will adapt to the growing conditions on the site rather than try to change them.

Drainage problems can be related to the grade or slope of the site. Both dry and wet situations can occur. Plants on the top of a berm or slope may suffer from dryness. Water will soak into the soil at increasingly slower rates as the surface layer becomes saturated. If water is applied faster than the soil will absorb it, the excess runs off the hill and does not benefit the plant. Wet spots occur in low areas where water collects from surrounding higher ground. A similar situation occurs when a tree or shrub has a planting well around it. If the surrounding lawn is watered too often, the water may run into the planting well and drown the plant. Wet areas can occur where downspouts from the building empty. Often this is near the base of a plant, which is injured by the excessive amounts of water. Plants growing in mulched beds or planted in slight depressions will be most seriously affected. Such injury usually occurs only during prolonged wet weather or when the combination of irrigation and rain is too much for the plant. Dry areas often occur near buildings, particularly under overhangs. Plants in these areas are often sheltered from the rain and so experience very dry soil.

Weather Related Problems

Weather conditions have a lot to do with how your landscape plants grow, whether they succeed or fail. Listed are some of the main problems that have to do with your landscaping and the weather.

Lightning

Lightning strikes can cause various symptoms. They usually loosen some bark, which hangs on the tree in strips. The amount of bark loosened will depend on the severity of the strike. Sometimes only a narrow strip is loosened; other times a large portion of the circumference of the trunk is affected. A tree struck by lightning may show no symptoms until it dies mysteriously days or years later. The lightning bolt may pass through the trunk and seriously damage the roots. Remove loose bark and broken branches as soon as possible after the strike. The tree may show no other effects or it may die suddenly within a short time. All you can do is to reduce other stresses, such as dryness and pests.

Snow & Hail

Wet snow that accumulates on tree and shrub branches can bend them over. Some may break and must be removed. Bending damages the bark and cambium tissue, leading to cankers or death of the stem the following growing season. Shrubs that would collapse under heavy snow loads can be protected or supported. To protect small shrubs, place crates or wooden frames over them in the fall. The crate or the slats on the frame will support some of the snow load. Taller shrubs can be wrapped with cord. Tie the cord to the base of a stem and then wind it around the shrub. The tied bundle of stems will help support one another. Hail can damage the bark on young branches and shred the leaves. Branches with heavily damaged bark may die. Prune away these dead branches.

Wind

Wind injury is usually obvious and not difficult to diagnose. Plant branches or the trunk can be broken by the wind, trees can be uprooted and forked trees can be split. Cut back the stubs of broken branches to just outside the shoulder ring. Split trees can be put back together with a combination of threaded steel rods and cables, but the results may not justify the expense. A large uprooted tree should be removed, but you may be able to save smaller trees. You need to replant the exposed roots as soon as possible. Sometimes the roots are not exposed but the root zone if lifted up when the tree's roots are pulled upward. In either case, brace the tree for support and then water to settle the soil back around the roots. Some dieback may occur. The extent will depend on the amount of root injury the tree suffered.

Cold Injury & Frost Cracks

Cold injury should not be confused with browning of evergreen foliage. The winter injury described here is the death of entire stems of either evergreen or deciduous trees or shrubs. Plants affected by this type of injury often try to leaf out or even flower in the spring. Soon after the first hot weather occurs, however, they wilt and die. Often very little of the plant will try to leaf out. After the new shoots die, shrubs may send up new, more vigorous shoots from the base. These can be used to renew the plant. Trees will also try to grow, then die, but there may be no regrowth.

A frost crack is a long, deep narrow crack running up and down the trunk of a tree. The crack is usually on the south or southwest side of the trunk but can occur on any side. Young trees or older trees with smooth bark are most susceptible. The crack occurs when the sun warms the trunk in winter, causing tissues to expand. When clouds or buildings block the sun or at sunset, the temperature of the trunk drops abruptly to that of the surrounding air and the trunk contracts. The outer part of the trunk cools and contracts faster than the inner tissues. This difference in contraction rates causes the outer trunk to crack from the inside to the outside. Prevent frost cracks by wrapping young trees with paper tree wrap. The wrap should start at ground level and go all the way up to the first main branches. Once a crack occurs, nothing can be done. Fertilizing a low vigor tree may speed up growth and close the crack more quickly. Frost cracks can allow rots or canker diseases to get established in the trunk.

Winterburn

Evergreen foliage is killed during late winter. The sun thaws the foliage, which then refreezes rapidly when the sun is blocked or at sunset and the foliage temperature rapidly drops. Thawed foliage may loose water that can't be replaced by roots in frozen soil, so the plant dries out. The symptoms are browned foliage in the spring, especially on the south or southwest side of a planting or plant. Prevent the problem by shading susceptible plants. Use burlap screens, discarded Christmas trees or any other simple shade source. Because injury usually occurs in late winter, you need not apply the protection until after Christmas.

Frost & Ice

The blackened, limp tissues of frosted annual plants are a common sight in fall and occasionally in spring. Such injury on landscape plants may be less obvious and go unnoticed until later. Spring frosts are more of a problem than autumn frosts because landscape plants will usually have developed some cold tolerance by early autumn. Frosted flowers and new growth will be limp and turn brown. The browned and dead new growth of evergreens can remain on the plant until well into the summer. When noticed then, the frosted growth raises concerns about diseases when, in fact, the injury occurred many weeks before.

Ice causes two types of injury to branches and trunks. The weight of the ice causes trunks and branches to break. If the limbs do not break, the conductive tissues inside the stem may be injured, resulting in dieback of the plant in the summer. Plants that are regularly bent over by ice can be supported. Smaller plants can be supported with a bicycle tire inner tube looped loosely around the stems, but larger plants require cables. The supports need to be flexible - rigid supports may cause breakage at the point of support. Such breakage commonly occurs when wooden props or stepladders are placed under ice-laden branches. Do not try to remove the ice. It normally melts in a short time. Ice-covered branches are heavy, so trying to remove ice is likely to cause additional damage.

Leaf Scorch Caused By High Temperatures

Hot, dry summer weather can cause leaf scorch. The leaf tissue on the edges and between the main leaf veins die. Eventually the entire leaf may be dead except for a narrow band of live, green tissue along the veins. The tree may be affected uniformly or on only one side or just on a few branches. Plants growing near roads or in other situations with much reflected heat and light are most likely to be scorched. Scorch can also be a symptom of insect and disease problems that interrupt the flow of water from the roots. Root diseases can reduce root efficiency so that less water reaches the leaves, which then scorch. If you can diagnose and stop the problem, you may be able to stop the scorching. Scorching related to high temperatures may be due to lack of moisture or an inadequate root system. If dry soil is the cause, watering may stop the scorching. If the plant just does not have enough roots, it may scorch during very hot, windy weather even though soil moisture is adequate. Little can be done in this case. Allowing the soil to dry excessively before watering can kill the roots. Then when the plant is watered, the reduced root system cannot supply enough water to the leaves.

Chemical Related Problems

Salt

Salt spray can cause brown foliage on evergreens or "witches broom" (a cluster of twigs that forms on a branch) on deciduous plants. Prolonged exposure to salt spray can lead to dieback. Salt spray can drift to plants from nearby roads as the tires of passing cars kick up a salty spray. The water evaporates, leaving a salt residue. Short plants can be protected from the spray with tar-backed burlap screens. It is very hard to protect larger plants. Road salt can also be a problem when salty runoff accumulates salt in the root zones of plants growing near the road. Salt can injure landscape plants when salt used on porches and sidewalks is shoveled or swept onto nearby shrubs, where it accumulates on the foliage or in the root zones. Most chemical deicers will have the same injurious effects, though calcium chloride is not as harmful as sodium chloride. Fertilizer is sometimes used, but it, too, can build up to toxic levels. Sand and ashes are not toxic but have the disadvantage of being easily tracked into the house. A third source of salt can be softened water running into septic systems. Evergreens will display browned foliage that forms a rough spiral as it moves up the tree. Trees may grow well for a number of years and then show symptoms when their roots finally reach the source of the salt. Tree species vary in their susceptibility to salt injury. A susceptible species such as white pine should not be planted near roadsides where salt will be applied.

Animal Related

The most common type of injury caused by pets is urine burn on shrubs or in the grass. The urine of dogs can cause browned or blackened areas on the lower parts of plants and burn spots in grass. Cats confined to a small area can cause plants to decline because of the excess salt that builds up where they urinate. Repeated applications of repellents may be used to discourage stray animals. Occasionally

other types of injury occur. Girdling can be a problem if dog chains are tied around a tree trunk. As the animal pulls the chain around the trunk, the chain wears the bark and girdles the tree. Horses, goats and sheep will sometimes eat the bark from trees. Cats may use young tree trunks to sharpen their claws. Girdled plants very often die. Rabbits and mice will eat the bark of trees and shrubs during the winter. When the feeding encircles the stem, it dies. Girdled stems may try to leaf out in the spring but will die shortly after. Girdled evergreen stems will turn brown. You can use repellents or cylinders of hardware cloth or sheet metal to protect the trunks and stems of trees and shrubs. The repellent or rodent guard needs to extend above the usual snow line so the animal cannot stand on the snow and feed above the protected area. Squirrels will clip off branches and gnaw the bark of trees. Squirrels clip the branches for use in nest building but drop many to the ground.

Naturally Occurring Plant Processes

Some characteristics of plants are often wrongly diagnosed as diseases or other serious plant problems. These naturally occurring processes should be distinguished from plant problems.

Fall Needle Drop Of Evergreens

Narrow-leaved evergreens often turn yellowish in late summer or early autumn. This is usually the normal shedding of the oldest leaves. A rather sudden yellowing affects the oldest set of needles on all the branches. The yellowing is uniform from the top to the bottom of the tree. The needles at the tips of the branches stay green. On a windy day, the yellowed needles blow off the tree and litter the ground. This is a normal process, so nothing needs to be done. If the yellowing is not uniform, if it occurs earlier in the season or if the needles at the tips of the branches turn brown, the cause may be something other than natural fall needle drop.

Bark Shedding

Tree bark falls off as the tree grows. Some trees tend to shed bark in large patches or strips. The amount of bark shed can vary from year to year. Sycamore and silver maple trees tend to be most noticeable when shedding bark. Sycamore sheds bark in patches. When the bark drops off, the stem is bright green and then develops normal bark coloration. Silver maple sheds bark in strips, and the newly exposed bark is orange on healthy branches. Bark shedding can be a sign of disease or some other problem. If the bark drops off and exposes bare wood, the shedding is a symptom of some type of problem. If the bark drops off and exposes new bark but not bare wood, the shedding is probably normal. Normal shedding can occur quite suddenly.

Spring Leaf Drop

Some broad-leaved evergreens, such as holly, drop their oldest set of leaves in the spring as new growth begins. A sudden yellowing of the oldest leaves occurs uniformly from top to bottom. The leaves at the branch tips remain green and healthy. Once the yellowed leaves drop off, no further yellowing and leaf drop occur.

Girdling Roots

A tree is girdled when something is wrapped tightly around the trunk, choking off the flow of water and nutrients. Some trees, particularly maples, can girdle themselves with roots that grow around the trunk. As the trunk and root increase in size, the trunk is girdled. An early symptom is a reduction in leaf size on the branches supplied by roots below the girdling root. These branches will develop fall color earlier than the rest of the tree. Eventually the branches die. If the tree has more than one girdling root, the entire tree may show symptoms.

A girdling root will affect the appearance of the tree trunk. Most trunks flare out or get wider where they enter the ground. A girdling root will prevent the flare. In some cases, the trunk will actually get narrower. A long, sunken area may occur in the trunk where the portion affected by the girdling root did not grow as well as the surrounding trunk. When you suspect a girdling root, carefully remove the soil down to where the roots connect to the tree (generally 12 to 18 inches down). Inspect the trunk for girdling roots. You can remove girdling roots, but the results may not always be desirable. Girdling roots are functioning roots, so removing them may kill branches not now affected. The presence of many girdling roots aggravates the problem. After removing girdling roots, fertilize the tree and water during dry weather.

Failure To Flower

Plants fail to flower for various reasons. One of the more common reasons is plant immaturity. Trees, in particular, must reach a certain age before they begin to flower. If the plant is old enough, the growing conditions may be too poor to allow flowering. Plants that require full sun, for instance, may grow but fail to flower in the shade. Cold winter temperatures may kill the flower buds. This often happens to forsythia, flowering dogwood and peach. Nothing can be done to prevent this type of injury. Plants that are not fully hardy in New Jersey will be most susceptible to cold injury. Improper pruning may cause failure to flower. Some plants bloom only on last year's wood. Cutting the plants back severely removes all the flowering wood. This happens most often on climbing roses. Florist's hydrangeas carry flower buds at the branch tips through the winter. These are often pruned off in the spring. Overfertilizing with nitrogen can sometimes cause plants to grow only leaves and stems. Such plants will be quite large but without flowers.

Failure To Fruit

A plant may fail to fruit because of all the reasons listed for failure to flower. If there are no flowers, there can be no fruits. A plant may have flower but fail to have fruits. One of the most common explanations is lack of proper pollination. Some plants cannot pollinate themselves. They require a plant of the same species but of a different variety for cross-pollination. Two trees of the same variety will not pollinate each other. They must be different varieties.

Lack of pollination can occur if cold, rainy weather occurs when a plant is in full bloom. Such weather will keep bees from working, thus reducing or preventing pollination and fruit-set. A frost while a plant is in flower will kill the flowers and prevent fruit-set. Some species are dioecious. This means all the flowers on a plant are either male or female. Both a male and a female plant must be present and cross-pollination must occur for the female to produce fruit. Examples of dioecious plants are holly, bittersweet and yew.

Disease Problems

What is a plant disease? A disease is a disturbance of normal plant growth. It may be caused by a living pathogen, such as a fungus, or by non-living factors, such as frost or excess salt. Symptoms of disease include death of leaves, twigs, large branches or roots. You may notice a gradual yearly decline and progressive dieback of the tree or shrub. The gradual reduction of growth and vigor of a landscape plant in poor health is usually due to a complex of living pathogens that attack a plant weakened by environmental stresses, such as summer drought periods, soil compaction or road salt. Living plant pathogens are fungi, bacteria, viruses and nematodes. Fungi are microscopic molds that grow like threads of a spider web. Pathogenic fungi get food by growing inside living plant tissues. They reproduce by producing millions of dust-sized seedlike spores. Some spores are blown about like pollen, while others are splashed from plant to plant by rain and irrigation.

Bacteria grow as colonies of single microscopic cells. Usually they are splashed by rains and carried by mists onto wet plant surfaces, where they swim into the breathing holes of the leaves. Once inside the leaves they can parasitize the plant, killing flower buds and leaves. Often bacteria will progressively move down a shoot, killing the twig and stopping at a larger branch. Fungal spores and bacteria can cause new infections when weather conditions are favorable for plant disease and when plants are susceptible. Usually, favorable disease conditions are several days of warm, wet weather, particularly in early spring when succulent new buds, flowers, leaves and shoots are rapidly growing. A few days of wet leaf surfaces allow fungal spores to swell and germinate, and the delicate fungal threads to penetrate into the moist environment inside the plant. Wet leaf surfaces also allow bacteria to swim through stomates (air holes) to the interior of the leaves. Once inside the plant, the fungus and the bacteria are safe from dry weather.

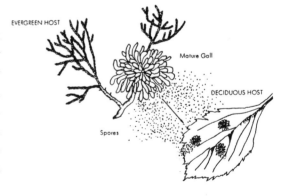

Viruses slow the growth of the plant but otherwise cause only mild symptoms, such as patterns of light and dark greens on a leaf. Landscape plants showing virus symptoms usually acquired the virus from the original propagation material. The leaf symptoms, often called mosaic or mottling, appear when the climate, usually cool weather in spring, favors symptom expression. Nematodes are small worms, less than 1/16th of an inch, that live in the soil. Plant parasitic nematodes feed on roots, much as aphids feed on leaves, and thus weaken the plants.

Urban Environmental Stresses

Some landscape plant problems may look like diseases but are actually caused by adverse environmental factors in the urban setting. These are decline, leaf tatter and leaf scorch. Decline is the most prevalent problem of ornamental plants in the urban environment, particularly in plants alongside roads and sidewalks. Following are a few diseases that are commonly found in New Jersey. For further information and diagnosis, contact your local nursery, extension office or tree specialist.

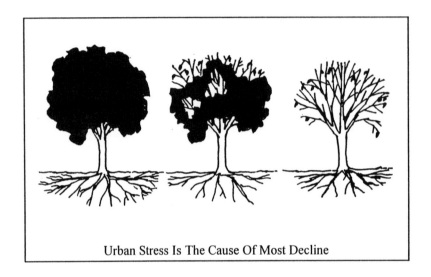

Urban Stress Is The Cause Of Most Decline

Symptom - Landscape trees and shrubs with decline show thin foliage and dead branches in the crown adjacent to apparently healthy branches. Branch dieback begins in the top of the canopy in deciduous trees and on the lower branches in narror-leaved evergreens. On deciduous plants, the leaves change color and drop earlier in autumn, and the spring flush of growth occurs later than in healthy trees of the same species.

Cause - All the factors discussed previously under "urban plant stress" contribute to decline. Pathogens are frequently involved, but urban environmental stress is of primary importance.

Control - Revitalize the root system of the declining plants in the following way. Bore holes in the lawn in the fibrous root zone under and just beyond the drip line of the plant canopy. The holes should be 18 to 24 inches deep and 2 to 4 inches wide. Space the holes in rings around solitary plants, or space them evenly between plants growing in beds. Space the holes 1 foot apart. Then, fill the holes with sand, coarse bark or sphagnum peat moss. This will improve the aeration and permeability of the soil and help to restructure the soil. Most important of all, water trees and shrubs during dry periods of spring and summer. Fertilizer can be added to the holes in future years, if needed.

Foliar Diseases

Leaf diseases are divided into descriptive groups by symptoms, such as leaf tatter, scorch, powdery mildew, leaf spot, gall, scab and anthracnose.

Leaf Tatter

Tatter

Symptom - Leaves have jagged, open spaces between their main veins.

Cause - When spring leaf buds are expanding, a sudden frost can kill the whole bud or the tip of the bud. Injured leaves may suddenly turn brown or black a day or two after the frost. When an expanded bud is injured by frost, leaves that emerge have a torn or tattered appearance because portions of the leaf tissue are dead.

Control - There are no practical means of preventing frost damage.

Leaf Scorch

Symptom - Leaf scorch is the yellowing and death of the margin of a leaf. Sometimes tissue between veins is also killed.

Scorch

Cause - Leaf scorch is caused by the inability of the plant roots to bring up enough water to the leaves during dry, hot weather, particularly on windy days following several rainy days. Scorch often is followed by premature leaf drop. Needles of pines, firs or spruces show scorch as a brown discoloration of the leaf tips. Scorch on conifer needles may be the result of hot, dry weather, or high winds in dry, cold weather when soil moisture is locked up in ice. The real problem is usually the soil, either it is too dry because of drought, or roots have rotted from overly wet periods preceding the drought. Recently transplanted trees are very susceptible because they have not yet established an extensive root system.

Control - For preventing spring and summer leaf scorch, revitalize the root system as described under "General decline and dieback."

Fungal And Bacterial Leaf Diseases

Leaf spot, leaf blotch, leaf blister and shot hole are symptoms of leaf diseases. Shot hole occurs when dead leaf tissue falls out, leaving a hole. A number of leaf diseases that occasionally damage ornamental plants are caused by fungi and bacteria. Many species of fungi cause leaf diseases. Leaf diseases cause leaves to fall prematurely, leaving trees and shrubs without the green factories that produce

food for them. Repeated defoliation of trees and shrubs makes them progressively weaker. Most deciduous plants can withstand several defoliations without serious damage, but broad-leaved evergreens usually do not recover from a defoliation. Most fungi and bacteria that cause leaf diseases require a wet leaf surface for an extended time, usually about 24 hours. The wet leaf surface allows the fungal spores to swell, germinate and penetrate the plant, and the bacteria to swim to a natural opening in the leaf surface, such as a stomate. Leaf-infecting diseases are more severe if the fungus or bacterium is present at budbreak, when the leaves are tender and new. If the weather is dry during budbreak, infection occurs later in wet weather after leaves are expanded. Late infections seldom harm the plant.

Bacterial Leaf Spots

Symptoms - Bacterial leaf spots may appear similar to fungal leaf spots, so it may be difficult to distinguish the two. Leaf spots caused by bacteria are often initially light green and look water-soaked. Later, these leaf spots usually turn brown or black and may have definite margins.

Bacterial spot

Cause - Many species of bacteria may cause bacteria leaf spots of landscape plants. These bacteria are often splashed from the soil onto wet foliage where they enter a leaf through its breathing holes (stomates) or wounds. Thereafter they spread from leaf to leaf when plants are watered or during rainy periods. Bacterial leaf spot of English Ivy is a good example of a common bacterial leaf spot.

Control - Avoid using high nitrogen fertilizers on susceptible plants. Only fungicides containing copper may be effective against bacterial blights and bacterial disease, but copper may burn the foliage of some cultivars.

Scab

Symptoms - Scab is similar to a large leaf spot, but the affected area looks dull, is usually dark olive green and has indefinite margins. The fruit symptoms are usually sunken, corky, dark olive areas.

Cause - Scab is a fungal disease that attacks many species, including crabapple, apple, quince and pear. The disease in some years can completely cover leaves of susceptible cultivars. Such severe infections, referred to as "sheet scab," will defoliate an entire tree. The loss of infected leaves weakens the tree. Scab can defoliate a tree or shrub several times in one season. The scab fungus forms two types of spores. The first type is blown about in the wind and causes the first infections in the spring. These infections form

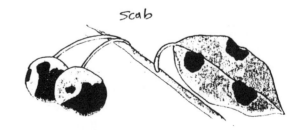

Scab

a second type of spore that is spread by rain splash and infects only the same plant or nearby plants of the same species. The more rainy the season is, the more the disease spreads throughout adjacent plants. If you can prevent the first type of spore from infecting the plant in early to midspring, the plant will escape further infections that season. The first type of spore is formed on fallen leaves of the previous year.

Control - Rake and discard all fallen leaves before spring. If your plant has a history of serious scab infections, apply a fungicide when swollen flower buds show a half inch of green tissue. Follow with applications, as needed, to protect the plant throughout the blooming period, whenever dew or rain threatens to wet leaves for a 6 hour period. Replace highly susceptible cultivars with resistant cultivars.

Leaf Curl And Leaf Gall

Symptoms - Leaf curl and leaf gall are the more serious of the leaf blister diseases. Leaves become puffy and the tissue is thickened, puckered and brittle. The puckering distorts the shape of the leaf, causing it to curl. Often the puckered areas are different colors than the green leaf tissues.

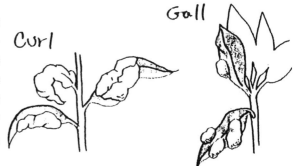

Cause - One genus of fungus, Taphrina, causes most of the blistering diseases on numerous trees and shrubs. This fungus invisibly remains on the bare branches after leaves have fallen and multiplies there in early spring. Rains splash the fungus onto emerging leaves. The disease is most severe when leaf emergence and elongation occur during rainy weather. The disease is most common on non-bearing, flowering cultivars of peach, cherry and plum.

Control - Apply a single dormant spray before budbreak to the bare branches and trunk. More extensive fungicide spray programs can be used to control leaf curl, but the homeowner might best consider replacing the plant if the disease renders the plant unsightly despite a dormant spray.

Anthracnose

Symptoms - The leaf symptoms of anthracnose are dead areas of the leaf that develop along main veins, often in a V-shape from the margin of the leaf. If infection occurs before and during budbreak, anthracnose can cause buds and young expanding leaves to turn brown and die.

Cause - Several trees, including sycamore, maple, white oak, ash and dogwood, are very susceptible to anthracnose. When the disease becomes severe, it deforms the plant, making each one an unsightly addition to a landscape. Susceptible plants are distorted by the death

of shoots and buds, which causes the plants to grow asymmetrically. Affected branches may look crooked and angular. Often clusters of shoots, "witches brooms", grow from one area of a branch. When the fungus grows through the bud or down the leaf petiole into the wood, it kills the branch. In the wood, the fungus grows as a canker. Each year's new buds, shoots and leaves may become infected by spores produced on the cankered wood in early spring. The disease is most severe when springs are cool (average temperatures less than 60° F) and wet.

Control - The most effective control is to replant using resistant trees as substitutes. For anthracnose, most oaks are less severely affected than white oak. Otherwise, revitalize the root system as described under "General decline and dieback."

Powdery Mildew

Symptoms - Powdery mildews are caused by over 1,600 species of fungi. The fungi often survive the winter tucked away in the scales of the buds. Therefore, the first infection of the mildew often are seen on the tips of new shoots. Mildews may also form a minute ball about the size of a grain of pepper, filled with microscopic spores. In midsummer, these special air-blown spores often infect healthy plants.

Control - Plant susceptible species in locations that receive direct sun all day, and space plants for good air circulation. Several fungicides are registered for controlling this disease on specific woody ornamentals. Follow all label directions and warnings.

Needlecasts

The spores of needlecast diseases of conifers infect needles when the humidity is high and the leaves are wet. The most severe infections usually occur on the bottom half of the tree and on the shaded northern side. The disease is most severe at these sites because water tends to remain on the foliage for long periods, and this moisture favors spore germination. Dense foliage dries slowly and the disease spreads from branch to branch. Tree-to-tree spread is increased by close spacing of trees that allows rain to splash spores from diseased to healthy trees.

Control - Most fungal diseases of conifers can be partially controlled by the following cultural practices. Avoid planting in low areas, depressions or shady areas where soil moisture, humidity and dew tend to remain high for prolonged periods. Plant so that air can circulate freely around the trees and avoid dense plantings (too close to each other). Control weeds and tall grasses so that weed growth does not favor the buildup of humidity and moisture around the lower branches. Controlling weeds by using herbicides or mowing may also eliminate goldenrod, which is the source of pine needle rust spores. Avoid any drought

Needlecast

sites that stress trees and maintain tree vigor by watering during the periodic droughts of summer. Early spring fertilization can help a diseased tree recuperate. Buy only clean and healthy nursery stock to reduce the chance of bringing disease to your landscape. Remember that most needlecasts are spread by rain splash, so distance your plantings. Of course, always avoid planting young trees near older, diseased plantings and try to prune shrubs or trees only in dry weather.

Rust Diseases

Rusts are caused by a complex group of fungi. The fungi produce spores in pustules that break through the plant epidermis. The spores are generally reddish brown, orange-red to orange, and dry and dusty. Many plants, from grasses to pine trees, get rust diseases. A common experience is to walk through tall grass infected with rust and emerge with shoes coated in orange-red spores. The rust diseases produce several different spores, each spore capable of infecting a different plant. The cedar-apple rusts are a good example. Spores formed in galls on cedar infect apple leaves, causing leaf spots. Spores formed on apple leaves infect only the cedar needles, causing galls. Rusts generally infect healthy, vigorous plants in preference to weak plants.

Cedar-apple Rust

This disease is actually a complex of three diseases caused by three rust fungi: apple rust, hawthorn rust and quince rust. All three diseases can infect most varieties of eastern red cedar and many cultivars of juniper, apple and crabapple. In addition to these plants, the hawthorn and quince rusts can infect mountain ash and pear. Quince rust can also infect cotoneaster and dwarf Japanese quince.

Symptoms And Cause - The symptoms on the deciduous hosts are familiar to most growers and landscapers. The leaves have yellow spots on the upper surface. In late summer, brownish clusters of threads or cylindrical tubes appear beneath the yellow leaf spots, or on fruits and twigs. The spores formed in the threads or tubes infect the leaves and twigs of junipers during wet, warm weather in late summer and early fall. Galls and swellings on the junipers appear about seven months later and form gelatinous masses of spores after about 18 months. The rust diseases are very conspicuous on red cedar and junipers during spring, when the galls are covered with the orange-brown, gelatinous masses. Rust spores formed on the gelatinous masses can not infect other junipers. They infect the twigs, fruits or leaves of deciduous hosts during wet, rainy weather in early spring. The symptoms of quince rust on red cedar and juniper include perennial, elongated swellings on the branches, which may crack and form cankers. In damp, spring weather, cushion-shaped, orange gelatinous blisters burst through the bark of the swellings. Quince rust disease damages the ornamental value of susceptible cedars and junipers, killing young branches and weakening plants when cankers occur on the main trunk.

The symptoms of the apple rust and hawthorn rust on red cedar and juniper include brown, spherical galls on the branches. Apple rust galls are often over 2 inches in diameter; those of hawthorn rust are seldom over 1/2 inch in diameter. They form about 18 months after infection occurs and may remain on the juniper branches for years. Apple rust galls produce spores for only one year, though the hawthorn

rust galls will produce spores for several years. The apple rust galls have circular markings on the surface that make them resemble the surface of a golf ball. From the centers of the circular markings protrude cylindrical, orange-brown, gelatinous horns, masses of spores, in wet spring weather. The hawthorn rust gall on junipers do not have the circular pattern on the surface, and the orange-brown gelatinous horns are tongue-shaped rather than cylindrical.

Control - If practical, destroy nearby junipers or prune off galls in late fall or early spring before crabapples bloom. Avoid planting susceptible deciduous hosts nearby red cedars. Plant resistant hawthorn varieties and cultivars.

Pine Needle Rust

Pine needle rust is a common disease in the northern states, but it seldom causes serious damage. The needle rust kills older needles on seedlings and younger trees up to the sapling stage.

Symptoms - In spring, infected trees will show browning of the lower needles on the trees. With the onset of spring, orange droplets appear on foliage, and by late May and June, orange blisters become evident.

Cause - The blisters, which may resemble pine needle scale, are masses of spores that cannot infect other pines. Instead, the spores infect the leaves of asters and goldenrod in early summer. By late summer, orange spores have formed on the undersides of the lower leaves. In cool, wet weather in late summer and into fall, a second set of orange spores on the undersides of aster and goldenrod leaves are carried by winds to pine needles, where they cause new infections.

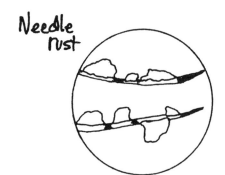

Control - Attempts should be made to eradicate asters and goldenrod in the immediate vicinity of the planting site. Controlling other weeds will also help increase drying of the lower foliage following rain or dew. Keeping foliage dry is very effective in inhibiting infection by the spore. No recommendations for chemical control have been developed and no chemicals are currently used for control of pine needle rust as of this publication. However, as more and more chemicals are being developed every day, it would be wise to check with your local nursery or agricultural agent to get the latest information.

White Pine Blister Rust

White pine blister rust is a serious problem in many areas in northern states. The severity of the disease is related to the weather conditions. Cool, wet weather with surrounding temperatures averaging below 67° F from July to September favor infection of pine by the rust fungus.

Symptoms - The fungus infects needles and young stems through their stomates. The fungus grows into the wood, causing cankers (areas of dead bark). The bark becomes discolored and turns yellowish at the canker margins. Cankers will kill a tree if they grow into the trunk. If branches contain cankers about 4 inches from the trunk, the tree may die. Pruning out limbs with cankers more than 4 inches from the trunk will protect the tree. Cankers are most easily seen in the spring when orange-yellow pustules protrude from the bark of the cankers. In late spring and early summer, these areas will form blisters containing a sticky, yellow-orange fluid that later turns dark and hard.

Cause - The pustules and blisters on the pines are part of the spore formation cycle of the rust fungus. Spores produced on the pine, however, can infect only plants in the genus *Ribes*, which includes gooseberries and currants. *Ribes* infected with white pine blister rust form orange and brown spores on the undersides of their leaves. The brown spores form in hairlike projections under the leaves in late summer and early fall. From these projections arise the spores that infect the pines.

Blister rust

Control - Homeowners can avoid loss by planting species, such as red pine, that are not susceptible. Certainly, eastern white pine should not be planted in areas of high disease incidence. In areas of low disease incidence, look for evidence of rust on all currants and white pines within at least 400 feet of the planting site and proceed with planting. If rust is evident, plant a species not susceptible to the blister rust.

Oak Wilt

Symptoms - Wilt, defoliation and the premature drop of leaves help distinguish this vascular wilt from other causes of wilting.

Cause - Oak wilt is caused by a fungus carried by sap-feeding beetles and certain other insects that visit wounds in bark. Infected red oaks may die within a few weeks, but white oaks may linger on for two to three years of decline. The disease can spread down a row of oaks as diseased roots infect healthy roots of nearby trees. Roots of trees belonging to one species can graft with one another, and this facilitates disease spread.

Control - Infected trees should be removed and wood, including stumps, should be debarked and split. Otherwise, the wood will bloom with the fungus beneath the bark and insects will seek the spores and carry them to healthy trees. Closely planted trees should be treated to remove the chance of root grafting. This is best done by passing a root cutting blade 2 feet deep at the midpoint between the trees. This severs root connections between trees.

Dutch Elm Disease

Dutch elm disease is a vascular wilt that killed nearly all American elm trees in the United States, except where susceptible trees were isolated far from others of their kind. American elms as street trees exist today only in municipalities that have a monitoring and control program. The Siberian and Chinese elms and the hybrid elms are resistant to the disease.

Symptoms - Wilting, yellowing foliage and leaf drop first occur on one or a few branches. Then the entire tree may wilt and die in a few months to a few years.

Dutch elm disease

Cause - Bark beetles that feed in the branch crotches of elm trees and burrow tunnels and lay eggs in dying or dead elm wood carry the fungus that causes the vascular wilt disease. Beetles generally are attracted to stressed trees rather than healthy trees. Controlling the beetles may help control the disease. Quickly destroying dead elm wood and dying trees and keeping healthy trees vigorous helps to limit the spread of the disease.

Control -Contact your professional landscaper, local nursery or agricultural agent immediately to confirm diagnosis. Prune out infected branches immediately. When pruning, cut well below the area showing symptoms, at least 6 feet below the brown vascular discoloration on the wilted branch. The pathogen usually is a distance beyond the symptoms. Systemic insecticides and fungicides have not been proven fully effective. Closely planted trees should be treated to remove the chance of root grafting. Follow the same procedure as mentioned in Oak wilt, using a root cutting blade between trees.

Galls

Symptoms

Crown gall is a tumorous growth of tissue up to several inches or more in diameter. It is generally found at the soil line or on roots and usually has a rough surface. Crown galls differ from natural burls. Burls are hard and woody like the trunk wood, whereas the crown galls are more like rotting wood.

Cause - Crown gall is a disease caused by bacteria. The crown gall bacteria live in the soil and enter the plant at the site of a wound, perhaps from a shovel or lawn mower. Once inside the plant, the bacteria stimulate gall formation. Infected plants often grow very slowly and continue to decline in vigor year after year.

Control - Avoid wounding plants when transplanting, cultivating or mowing. Dig up and destroy infected plants, removing the surrounding soil carefully and disposing of it away from other plants. Replant with resistant plants. All types of narrow-leaved evergreens are immune to crown gall.

Crown gall

Insect Problems

Insects cause many kinds of plant disorders and associated symptoms. The purpose of this section is to describe general types of insect damage to help you diagnose plant problems caused by insects and distinguish insect damage from disease and environmental damage. Symptoms of destructive insects are usually observed before the insects themselves are found. In many cases, suspected insect injury can be confirmed by locating the insect. In some cases, however, damage is not observed until after the insects have completed the damaging part of their life cycle and have left the plant. Some of these common insect-derived plant symptoms may be confused with plant diseases. If your plant exhibits one or more of these general symptoms, you may want to read both the insect and plant disease sections of this book. A careful comparison of all possible causes of these general plant symptoms is necessary to make a correct diagnosis of the plant problem. The most common types of plant symptoms caused by insects are briefly discussed and illustrated.

Branch Dieback

Branch dieback

Wood-boring insects such as the bronze birch borer may cause significant damage to plant vascular tissue that results in a dieback of the infested limbs or branches. Branches damaged by other causes and weakened trees in general may be particularly susceptible to insect borers. Branch dieback may also be caused by diseases, environmental factors, cultural factors, insects, or a combination of two or more of these factors. Another type of branch dieback is twig dieback caused by twig girdlers or twig pruners. Twig dieback may be caused by beetle larvae boring inside twigs or by the feeding of adult beetles that completely girdles the twigs. This type of damage occurs most frequently to oaks, maples, hickory and flowering fruit trees.

Chewed Or Skeletonized Leaves

Some insects, such as leaf beetles and some sawflies, chew the plant tissue off one side of the leaf while leaving the opposite leaf cuticle and the veins intact. The damaged leaf then looks like a lacy skeleton of a leaf. Most caterpillars and adult beetles chew through the entire leaf. The damage may appear as tiny or large holes in the leaf, or as irregularly shaped leaves with jagged edges. If plant leaves

are still growing when the insect feeds, the damage may later appear to have smooth edges around the feeding holes. Only insects cause these types of damage.

Gall or swelling

Cankers And Swellings

Many beetle larvae and caterpillars bore into tree trunks, shrub bases or limbs, causing them to swell. When you cut these spindle-shaped galls open, insect tunnels and frass should be visible. Insect borers often attack trees that are weakened or damaged by other causes. In some cases, borers and plant pathogens are associated with the same canker.

Stems And Leaf Galls

Stem and leaf galls

Several large groups of insects have many gall-forming species. These include the gall wasps, aphids and sawflies. Some families of gall-forming insects are so diverse that an insect species exists for almost every common tree species. Stem and leaf galls may also be caused by plant pathogens. Leaf galls, however, are usually caused by an insect or mite. If you open fresh leaf galls with a knife, you can usually find a small aphid or other insect larvae.

Leaf Curling Or Rolling

Leaf curl

The saliva of some sucking insects, especially aphids, may cause plant leaves to fold, curl or pucker. These insect symptoms can be confused with some plant diseases that cause similar symptoms. You can diagnose the damage as insect damage if you find the aphids themselves inside the curled leaves. Some caterpillars, called leafrollers, use silk threads to hold leaves in a curled or rolled shape. These leafroller caterpillars may also be found inside the rolled leaves.

Common Groups Of Insects
That Damage Landscape Plants

Although thousands of insect species have been identified as pests of landscape plants, most of them can be grouped into 26 categories of sucking, leaf-chewing, case-making, gall-forming, root-feeding, stem-boring and scale insects. Knowing what kind of insect is responsible for plant damage is critical to successful control of insect problems because various insects are more susceptible to some insecticides than others. Classifying insect pests into the following categories is adequate for effective control of 95 percent of the insect problems likely to occur on landscape plants.

Sucking Insects - Aphids, Lace bugs, Leafhoppers, Mealybugs, Plant bugs, Spittlebugs, Thrips.

Leaf-chewing Insects - Caterpillars, Leaf beetles, Sawflies, Scarab beetles, Weevils.

Shoot, stem and trunk borers - Bark beetles, Clear-wing moths, Flat/round-headed wood borers.

Root-feeding Insects - White grubs, Weevil grubs.

Tent and Case-making Insects - Bagworms, Tent caterpillars, Webworms.

Gall-forming Insects - Gall midges, Gall mites, Gall wasps, Spider mites.

Aphids

Aphids are soft-bodied, slow moving insects that reproduce rapidly. Many aphids prefer to feed on young, succulent growth. Some feed in sheltered locations, such as inside leaves that they have caused to curl or become distorted. Aphids attack trees and shrubs of all kinds but do not usually seriously in-jure them. New plant growth may become distorted or stunted before predators and parasites decimate the aphid population. The greatest damage may be from the sticky, sugary aphid excrement called honeydew.   Honeydew may fall on automobiles or furniture below infested trees. Sometimes a black fungus called sooty mold will grow on the honeydew deposited on foliage below aphid colonies. Aphids are present on most plants, generally at non-injurious levels. The honeydew excreted by aphids may be useful for identifying aphid populations. Natural con-

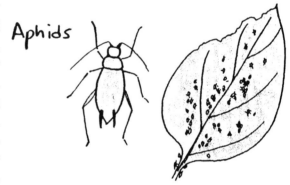

trols, including natural enemies such as ladybugs, lacewings and parasitic wasps, usually bring aphid populations under control shortly after they become noticeable. Before applying any insecticide treat-ments, search the aphid colonies for these natural enemies. High numbers of these beneficial insects usually indicate that aphid problems are being controlled without your intervention.

Lace bugs

Lace bugs (so called because of their broad, lacelike forewings) are usually whitish and 5 to 6 mm long. They are flat and oval to rectangular, with the head hidden beneath a thin, flat hood. The nymphs are black and often covered with spines. Many species feed on the undersides of leaves. Upper surfaces of infested leaves turn yellow or brown between leaf veins, while the undersides become speckled with black, shiny excrement and cast skins of immature bugs.

Leafhoppers

This is a large family of plant feeding insects. Adults range in size from 3 to 15 mm and come in an endless variety of colors. Feeding damage may appear as white stippling or browning of the foliage, or curling and withering of leaves. The immature leafhoppers are usually greenish yellow and rapidly scoot sideways along the undersides of leaves when disturbed. Adult leafhoppers fly when disturbed, appearing like tiny, green moths as they dart towards a different branch.

Leafhopper and injury

Mealybugs

Mealybugs can be recognized by the flaky covering of gray, white or pink wax over their entire bodies. They are soft-bodied, 4 to 12 mm long, and they move slowly. All mobile life stages appear similar except for their size. Mealybugs can be found feeding on stems, shoots or leaves of susceptible plants. They have many natural enemies that usually keep populations under control.

Mealybugs

Plant Bugs

Adult plant bugs are 2 to 7 mm long, and green, yellow or bronze, occasionally with black stripes. They feed on the foliage, young shoots or fruits of a large variety of plants. Plant bugs inject a small amount of saliva into plant tissues when they feed, causing new growth to become distorted or leaves to develop necrotic (dead) patches or leaf spots. Immature bugs are shaped like adults but have shorted wing pads instead of full-length wings.

Spittlebugs

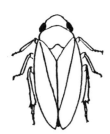

Spittlebug gets its name from the frothy mass of spittle that larvae produce and hide in for protection. Larvae removed from the frothy mass are usually greenish, soft-bodied, leafhopperlike and under 10 mm long. Spittlebugs suck plant sap but are rarely numerous enough to cause plant damage. The adults are stout-bodied, leafhopperlike, dull colored and rarely over 12 mm in length. Spittlebugs are commonly found on junipers and pine trees and are quite unattractive. However, they inflict little damage on mature plants. The best "control" of spittlebugs on ornamentals is to tolerate the situation until it passes, a matter of a few weeks. If action is required, forcefully hosing the plants is usually sufficient, if repeated two to three times.

Thrips

Thrips and injury

Thrips are small, 1 to 4 mm in length, cigar-shaped insects. Adults have narrow, fringed wings not usually visible without a hand lens. They are particularly common on flowers, flower buds and dense leaf buds. Feeding damage to unfolded leaves may cause the leaves to be distorted when they develop and unfold. To diagnose heavy infestations of thrips, look for dark, shining drops of excrement and the small, cigar-shaped adults.

Caterpillars

Because the great majority of feeding by a caterpillar is done during the latest larval stages, defoliation may appear to occur very suddenly. Often problems are not detected until feeding is nearly over and treatments are no longer benefitial. To detect potential problems early, watch for the small larvae and the early phases of leaf or needle feeding. In some situations, the pelleted excrement (frass) of the young caterpillars on the ground may tip you off to an infestation developing within a tree. For most caterpillars in shade trees and ornamentals, *Sevin* is a standard insecticide for control. Also, B.t. (Bacillus thuringiensis), a microbial insecticide that is exceptionally safe to use, is effective against most caterpillars if you apply it so that the insects ingest it. Apply insecticides against caterpillars that make protective structures (fall webworms, leafrollers, etc.) shortly after the eggs hatch. Treatments made later may fail to reach the insects.

Caterpillar

Leaf Beetles

This is one of the largest plant feeding families of beetles, with more than 2,000 species found in North America. Adult beetles are often brightly colored or metallic and 3 to 12 mm long. Leaf beetle larvae are soft-bodied and pigmented and usually feed on plant leaves along with the adults. Feeding

Leaf beetle and injury

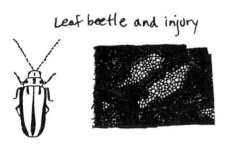

damage by the more important landscape plant pests appears as patches of skeletonized leaf tissue where the beetles have eaten away all the plant tissue except the upper leaf epidermis. Several species of leaf beetles can feed on trees and shrubs. Extensive feeding damage is usually preceded by small holes cut into leaves by the adult beetles or small areas of skeletonized feeding injuries made by adults or young larvae. By watching trees for these indications, you can anticipate the need to make an insecticide treatment before serious damage has occurred.

Sawflies

Sawflies superficially resemble caterpillars but are taxonomically very different. Sawflies are the larval stages of a group of wasps. Unlike caterpillars, which have only two to four pairs of prolegs, sawflies have prolegs on every abdominal segment. It's important to distinguish sawflies from caterpillars because sawflies are not susceptible to B.t., a widely used microbial insecticide for caterpillars. Adult sawflies are small, 8 to 25 mm, dark, flylike wasps. Most larvae are either leaf-chewing and caterpillarlike, or moggotlike leaf miners that cause leaf blisters or leaf blotches.

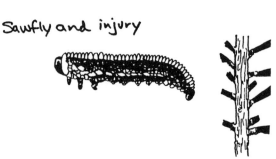

Sawfly and injury

Scarab beetles

Scarab beetles have hard, stout bodies. The last three to seven segments of the antennae are leaflike and capable of opening or closing. Familiar members of this family include the May or June beetles, Japanese beetles and rose chafers. The larvae or grubs develop in the soil. They are thick, C-shaped white grubs with well developed thoracic legs. Mature adults and larvae range in size from 4 to 30 mm.

Scarab beetle

Weevils

More than 2,500 species of weevils have been identified from North America. Weevil adults are characterized by a broad, beak-like snout. Most weevils are 4 to 10 mm long, slow-moving and dark-colored. Adult feeding damage often appears as a crescent-shaped notch cut out of the leaf edge. Many weevil larvae (root weevils) feed on plant roots in the soil. Larvae are white, legless, C-shaped grubs. Weevil grubs can be distinguished from scarab grubs by their lack of legs. Some weevil larvae, such as white pine weevil and root collar weevil, develop under the bark of shoots or trunks.

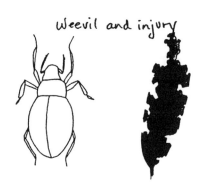

Weevil and injury

Bark beetles

Adults are small, 2 to 4 mm in length, hard beetles, brown to black, with a down-curved head barely visible from above. The larvae borrow under the bark of weakened trees in distinctly patterned galleries. These beetles can cause the premature death of weakened trees. They also spread fungal diseases, such as the Dutch elm disease. They are gregarious insects, preferring to attack trees already

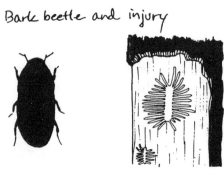

Bark beetle and injury

infested with bark beetles. They may also attack dead or cut wood. Bark beetles successfully breed in trees that are severely stressed or dying. Newly transplanted trees may be particularly susceptible to attack by these insects. Proper cultural practices to promote tree vigor are often the most important means of controlling most bark beetle problems. Often, these techniques are sufficient for control. A few bark beetles are capable of killing healthy trees, either through coordinated mass attacks or through introduction of fungus diseases into healthy trees (elm bark beetles). Sanitation and insecticide applications are of great importance in managing these pest situations.

Clear-wing moths

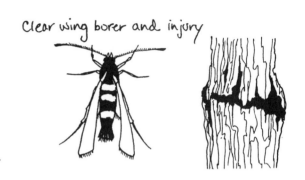

Clear wing borer and injury

Adults of this family are known as clear-wing moths because the wings lack scales. Adult clear-wings mimic wasps in color and hovering behavior. The larvae are white, legless worms that resemble round-headed wood borers. Clear-wing borers, however, do not have enlarged, rounded heads. The larvae bore into roots, stalks, branches and trunks of many species of trees and shrubs.

Flat-headed wood borers

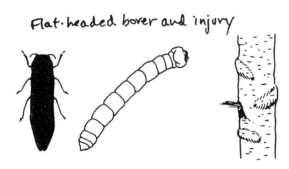

Flat-headed borer and injury

The flat-headed wood borers include several destructive pests of forest and shade trees. The adults are 5 to 15 mm long, somewhat flattened and have a beautiful metallic shine. The larvae are all wood borers that tunnel under the bark of trees. The first thoracic segment is strongly flattened, giving the larvae the name flat-headed wood borers. The larvae are white and legless. The most familiar member of this group is the bronze birch borer.

Round-headed wood borers

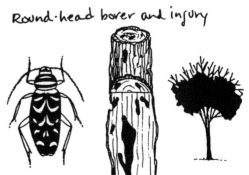

Round-head borer and injury

The adults of this family are called long-horned beetles because of their extremely long antennae. Some species have long legs as well. The common locust borer and several related species are chestnut brown with bright yellow stripes and mimic a wasp. The larvae are white, segmented worms with slightly enlarged, round heads. They lack visible legs. Larvae bore under the bark of trees into the wood. Some species are very destructive.

White grubs & Weevil grubs

The two most important groups of insects that feed on landscape plant roots in the soil are weevil larvae and scarab beetle larvae. These immature soil insects are often referred to as "white grubs." Weevil grubs vary in size from 1/16 inch to 3/8 inch long, while the larger scarab grubs may reach a length of 1 1/2 inches.

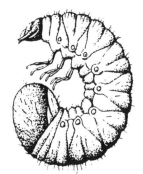

Weevil grubs can be distinguished from scarab grubs by the weevil grubs' lack of legs. Larvae of the black vine weevil are frequent pests of landscape plants. Scarab grubs, such as June beetle larvae, occasionally attack trees and shrub roots. Scarab grubs become a serious problem when trees or shrubs are planted into an area previously maintained as sod. The starving grubs then feed on the tree or shrub roots, causing serious damage.

Bagworms

Bagworms are large caterpillars that build cases out of leaf material. These cases are usually tubular or cylindrical and may be soft or hard. The bagworm can seriously damage cedars, junipers, arborvitae, willows, oaks and maples. Sometimes individual branches or entire plants are completely defoliated. New bags usually start to appear in June, especially in areas where older, large bags are present. Each bag may contain up to 1000 eggs. Control may be accomplished by either hand picking and destroying the bags or spraying *Bt (Bacillus thuringiensis)* in heavily infested areas. Adults are dull-colored moths.

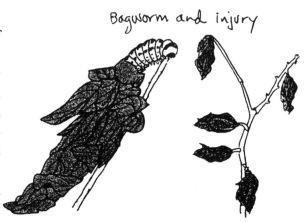

Bagworm and injury

Tent caterpillars

Adult moths are light brown, about 1 inch in length and have two white stripes across each wing. Damage is done during the larvae stage, which can reach a length over two inches. In early spring, at

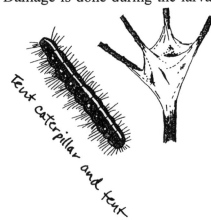

Tent caterpillar and tent

budbreak, look for silken webs in tree forks or trails traveling along main branches. They prefer flowering fruit trees such as cherry and apple, but when infestations are high, they will attack birch, willow, plum, oak and maple. Control by pruning out the egg masses and destroying the webs. The use of insecticides in spring is effective but the silken "nests" should be penetrated. Most tent caterpillars and webworms feed at night and return to their tents before morning.

Webworms

The adult moths are between 3/4 inch to 1 inch long, have folded wings that are usually all white or white with black spots. Damage is done in the larvae stage which are approximately one inch long when mature. Some are yellowish white with black heads and others are brown with red heads. Both have black tubercles running down their backs that are covered with long gray hairs. These insects attack many different types of trees but prefer elm, mulberry, poplar, oak, willow, apple and many other fruit trees. These caterpillars construct "webs" in the branches and only feed inside the web which gets larger as they grow. The webworm appears twice a year, usually in May and again August through October. To control, prune out the webs as they appear but for larger infestations *Bt* can be sprayed. See picture for tent caterpillars.

Spider mites

Spider mites are about the size of the smallest object you can see with your eyes (0.1 to 0.5 mm). Despite their small size, these mites can cause significant plant injury. Spider mite damage usually appears as a light speckling on leaves, followed by a general bronze discoloration. Heavy infestations can bronze an entire tree. The easiest way to diagnose spider mites is to tap an infested branch over a white piece of paper. Dislodged mites will appear as tiny specks moving on the paper. Spider mite populations develop rapidly under hot, dry conditions, and plants under stress are particularly susceptible to injury. Spider mite problems can also be induced through the use of certain insecticides which destroy natural enemies of the spider mites.

Proper watering and fertilizing plants is a primary means of limiting spider mite injury. Forceful hosing of the plant foliage can be particularly useful because it can crush and dislodge many of the mites. When heavy mite populations occur, it may be difficult to get control with any pesticide. Soap sprays can be used to suppress mites on plants that are not injured by the soaps. Spray a small part of the plant, then check it in four to five days to test plant sensitivity to soaps. Such a treatment is best applied in early summer before mite populations get too large.

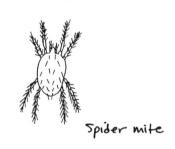

Spider mite

Insect Control For Landscape Plants

Insect pests in the urban environment are naturally kept under control by predators, parasites and pathogens. These natural enemies regulate populations of plant feeding insects. Without them, populations of pest insects would rapidly increase and defoliate their host plants. All landscapers and homeowners should take advantage of insect enemies by enhancing their activity whenever possible. Sometimes natural enemies do not provide acceptable control of landscape insects. In these situations, it may be necessary to apply an insecticide to suppress insect pest populations and prevent plant injury. Insect injury to landscape plants can be prevented or reduced by proper cultural practices, plant selection and application of environmentally sound pesticides, such as horticultural sprays and microbial insecticides.

Relying on insecticides alone is not wise as insecticides are frequently more toxic to natural enemies than they are to plant feeding insects. Insecticide applications may cause outbreaks of mites and certain insects that could result in increased plant damage. Other reasons for minimizing insecticide use include potential plant injury, toxicity to mammals and contamination of groundwater.

Causes Of Insect Outbreaks And Plant Injury

Trees and shrubs are often planted in unfavorable environments that makes them susceptible to insect damage. For example, the pine needle scale is seldom destructive in the forest, where it is found in low population densities, but in nursery and landscape situations, the same insect often reaches outbreak proportions and can ruin the aesthetic value of the plants and even kill them. The unnatural conditions in the man-made environment induce unusually high and destructive insect populations. Despite quarantine regulations, many foreign insect species have been accidentally introduced into the United States. Away from their natural environment, many of these become pests. The black vine weevil, the gypsy moth and the mimosa webworm are examples of introduced species that have become serious problems to ornamental plants. In this country, these insects became pests when they found an abundant food supply, a favorable climate and few or no effective natural enemies.

Many ornamental trees and shrubs are chosen for their beauty and planted without proper consideration of their suitability for a particular site. Some trees and shrubs planted in New Jersey are native to more southern climates and become severely stressed because of winter injury. Winter injury can make these plants susceptible to attack by insects. Most of the commonly used shade trees are native species from the forest that have been moved into the city. These trees, while visibly healthy, are often in a low state of vigor because of exposure to full sunlight and moisture stress. Insect pests of native species always abound in neighboring woodlots, but there they are usually only secondary problems. In weakened shade trees, the same insects may build up to damaging levels. Drought stress or nutrient stress may also weaken trees and shrubs and make them more susceptible to insect attack. Birch trees adequately watered and fertilized are less likely than stressed trees to be attacked by the bronze birch borer. Proper watering and fertilizing of Euonymus and Taxus plants allow them to compensate for root pruning by root weevils, while stressed shrubs may be seriously injured by the same amount of root pruning. Sudden outbreaks of aphids, spider mites and scale insects may occur when pesticides wipe out their natural enemies. Ladybugs, lacewings, parasitic wasps and other natural enemies devour or parasitize aphids, scales and mites, keeping populations under control.

Some insects are more tolerant of insecticides than their natural enemies are. Applications of insecticides may stimulate a rapid outbreak or a delayed resurgence of mites and aphids, depending on the relative toxicity of the pesticide applied. Outbreaks of scale insects, leaf miners and other insects protected inside galls or under waxy secretions are frequently associated with pesticide application because the pests are physically protected from insecticides but their natural enemies are not. Natural enemies of all plant feeding insects are adversely affected by pesticides. Aphids, scale insects and mites have been used as examples because they reproduce rapidly and have obvious outbreaks associated with pesticides.

You can maintain healthy trees and shrubs and prevent insect problems in many ways. The first step in a sound landscape management program is proper identification of the pest problem. Insects found on a sick-looking tree may have nothing to do with the problem. At the same time, it may be difficult to find some serious insect pests, such as borers and root weevils. When insects are suspected of damaging the leaves, stems or roots of a plant, they should be properly identified by a reliable source. Most insects can be preserved in rubbing alcohol and carried in a small bottle to your local garden center or extension office in your county. Once you know the proper identity of the insect, you can get more information on the life cycle and biology. In Chapter 1, I discussed natural, microbial and conventional methods of insect control for grass, shrubs and trees. Following are two charts listing "pest resistant" shrubs and trees that will grow well in New Jersey.

Pest Resistant Shrubs

Key:
Height - maximum height
D/E - D = deciduous, E = evergreen
Flower - Time of flowering
Light - 1 = shade, 2 = 50% shade/50% sun, 3 = 25% shade/75% sun, 4 = full sun

Shrub	Height	D/E	Flower	Light
Abelia	6 ft	D	July - September	2-4
Arrowwood Virburnum	10 ft	D	May	3-4
Barberry	5 ft	E		3-4
Bayberry	9 ft	D		2-3
Beautybush	10 ft	D	May	3-4
Belle Honeysuckle	10 ft	D	May	3-4
Boxleaf Honeysuckle	5 ft	D	May	2-3
Butterfly bush	10 ft	D	July	4
Dense Japanese Yew	4 ft	E		1-4
Doublefile Virburnum	10 ft	D	May	3-4
Enkianthus	10 ft	D	May	3
Forsythia	10 ft	D	April	3-4
Fragrant Winterhazel	15 ft	D	April	3
Gray Dogwood	15 ft	D	May	1
Hick's Japanese Yew	10 ft	E		1-4
Inkberry	8 ft	E		2
Linden Virburnum	10 ft	D	May	3-4
Mockorange	12 ft	D	May	3
Red Chokeberry	8 ft	D	May	2-4
Spicebush	12 ft	D	Sept	2-3
Spreading English Yew	3 ft	E		1-4
Weigela	9 ft	D	May	4
Winterberry holly	10 ft	D		2-4
Witchhazel	10-30 ft	D	Nov - Feb	2-4

Pest Resistant Trees

Key:
Height - maximum height
D/E - D = deciduous, E = evergreen
Flower - Time of flowering
Light - 1 = shade, 2 = 50% shade/50% sun, 3 = 25% shade/75% sun, 4 = full sun

Tree	Height	D/E	Flower	Light
American Beech	70 ft	D		3-4
Amur Corktree	45 ft	D		4
Amur Maple	20 ft	D		3
Baldcypress	70 ft	E		4
Black Gum	50 ft	D		2-4
Bur Oak	80 ft	D		4
Dove Tree	40 ft	D	May	2
European Beech	60 ft	D		3-4
Franklinia	30 ft	D	August	3-4
Ginkgo	80 ft	D		4
Hickory	60 ft	D		4
Hornbeam	60 ft	D		3
Ironwood	30 ft	D		3-4
Japanese Umbrellapine	30 ft	E		3-4
Kousa Dogwood	30 ft	D	June	3
Lebanon Cedar	60 ft	E		4
Red Oak	75 ft	D		4
Sassafras	60 ft	D		3
Sourwood	30 ft	D	June	2
Star Magnolia	20 ft	D	April	2-3
Sweetbay Magnolia	20 ft	D	May	2-3
Trident Maple	25 ft	D		4
Tulip Poplar	90 ft	D	May	4
White Fringetree	20 ft	D	May	4
White Oak	80 ft	D		4
Yellowwood	50 ft	D		4

Pruning Times And Methods

Now that I have discussed landscape design, how to choose plants, the diseases and insects that attack them, and some controls, one more important issue must be addressed -- proper pruning times and methods. To many people the act of pruning is a chore that has to be done but are not sure why they have to, how and when. Cutting tools should be kept sharp, clean and oiled to avoid rust, prolong life and help performance. Sharp pruning tools make nice clean cuts and won't tear any bark. Use common sense when pruning, don't take any chances. Watch how you are standing or kneeling, wear heavy gloves (preferably leather) and always keep your hands and feet away from the cutting area.

Entire books have been written on "correct pruning times and methods", but here I'll cover only the basics. Pruning is a way of influencing size, quality, changing shape, inducing vigorous growth or maintaining the attractiveness of plants. Pruning does occur naturally, when branches have served their purpose, they die and fall to the ground. This, however, does not keep plants as attractive as we want them to be, so we resort to our own method of pruning with tools. But before we prune our shrubs and trees, we must have some knowledge of how they behave, what effect removing parts will have on the plant, how much to remove and when. Let's concern ourselves primarily with shrubs. Trees should be left alone to grow as they want naturally. The only times I prune a tree, are if lower branches have died, a branch is growing to close to another object and it might interfere with the object, or the tree needs to be seriously thinned out for either air circulation, to let sunlight in, or to bear more blossoms or fruit. In the latter case, I leave this to the tree professionals, who know exactly what they are doing.

In most cases, shrubs consist of several trunks or stems growing from a base. As plants mature, they renew themselves through canes that develop from the base. Canes can vary in length depending on the species of the plant. Some species, like forsythia, can develop canes 6 to 8 feet long in one season. As canes mature, they branch and become trunks. As these trunks grow and bear more foliage, the top usually becomes so dense that light and air is blocked from the plant's base. New shoots starting from the base may die. This is natural (nature's way) pruning, but it creates legginess in the shrub which can become detrimental to it's health. As the trunks age, this may result in weaker annual growth and fewer and smaller flowers produced. Whenever we prune a plant we can expect some type of reaction in the plant. With deciduous plants, pruning in the dormant season, usually late winter to very early spring, results in vigorous growth the following season. Winter food is stored in the root system and removing part of the top reduces the amount of buds. When spring arrives and growth starts, the stored food is distributed to these fewer buds which results in greater vegetative growth, flowers or fruit. When branches are cut back all around a shrub, the buds that are immediately below the cut are usually the ones that start growing first. This results in several more shoots that will grow in the same area that was once occupied by one. This pruning is very useful when a dense hedge is required, but not good for individual shrubs. They must be pruned more carefully to allow more sun and air circulation in to avoid killing new growth at the base. When you cut a branch back to a bud, *make the cut just above a bud that is growing in the direction you want the branch to grow.*

When is the best time to prune? In most cases it is late winter or early spring, the dormant period. This is just before the leaves and flowers start to appear. Early pruning helps scars to heal quickly. One of the first things to do is remove any broken branches, dead wood or spindly branches (suckers). This

is really all you need to do for the plants health. Aesthetically, this may be enough or you may want to modify the shrub for various reasons. Pruning shrubs every year keeps them healthy and attractive. Pruning broken branches or dead wood can be done at almost any time of the year, but full pruning is usually based on the flowering habit of the plant. Deciduous plants can be divided into two groups as to flowering time: spring bloomers and summer bloomers. Any shrubs that bloom in the spring, which is usually up to the middle of June, go into the winter dormant stage with buds already formed on wood that was produced during the growing season. Those shrubs that flower in the summer, produce their blooms on wood of the current season's growth. Some shrubs need complete pruning every year and others may only require corrective thinning. Remember, unnecessary pruning can result in the loss of its natural form, flowers or fruit. There should always be a reason to prune a plant.

A primary reason for pruning is to encourage new growth at the base. This requires the removal of any old canes, which opens up the center for light and air circulation, to encourage new canes. A good rule of thumb, to which most professionals agree, is that any spring-flowering shrubs should be pruned after they have bloomed and summer-flowering shrubs should be pruned during the dormant season. Removing branch tips up to 10 inches long helps control the size and shape of the shrub and increases the amount of blooms next year. This type of pruning is sometimes called "heading back". Heavy pruning, cutting more than 15 inches back, removes many of the spindly branches and stimulates the main branches to produce fewer but larger blooms. If you want to keep shrubs symmetrical, prune off any shoots that grow past the natural form when they appear. It is not advisable to cut any live branches towards the end of the growing season, as any frost may damage new growth that may appear. Suggested pruning times are as follows:

Plant	Pruning Time
1. spring blooming shrubs	late spring, as soon as the blooms fade
2. summer blooming shrubs	late winter, very early spring
3. fruit trees	late winter, very early spring
4. birch, maple, poplar trees	fall

The right cut is very important when pruning. One of the simplest methods is called pinching. By using your thumb and index finger, pinch off the spent blossoms of flowering shrubs. This encourages new growth in shrubs such as azaleas and rhododendrons. On pines and spruces you can snap off the entire new growth to help the plant grow fuller. If you want to remove an entire stem, cut it at ground level. When cutting shoots, place the pruner directly against the main stem and cut upwards to avoid making a ragged cut or tearing the bark. Pruning is easier for you and healthier for the plant when the branches are young and pliable. It takes less effort and any wounds left by the pruners will quickly heal. There is also less

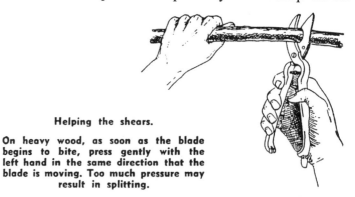

Helping the shears.

On heavy wood, as soon as the blade begins to bite, press gently with the left hand in the same direction that the blade is moving. Too much pressure may result in splitting.

chance for insect invasion or disease and less plant scarring. Thinning a tree or shrub involves eliminating branches or stems flush with the base of the plant. This lets more light into the center and improves air circulation. In my opinion, heavy thinning should be left to tree specialists. If branches are cut off at the base, new shoots won't grow back since there were no buds left below the cut.

When branches are pruned back, the plant starts new growth from the bud just below where the cut was made. Check the branch you want to cut, decide which way you want the new branch to grow, find a bud facing in that direction and make a cut just above that bud. Make a clean cut at a slight upwards angle so the bark won't tear or damage. Cutting back to a live bud helps prevent the spread of disease or infection.

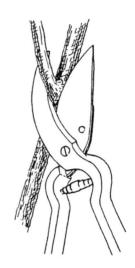

Note that blade of shears is next to main branch. Always cut from the side to remove a branch at a bad crotch.

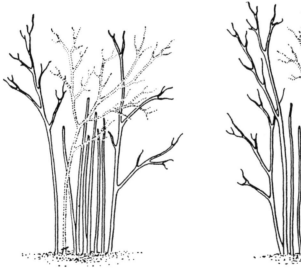

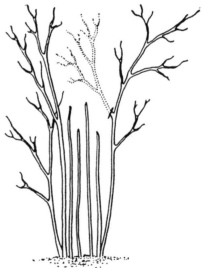

Left: In pruning shrubs, always remove an old cane that curves over the center of the plant, casting shade. Right: After main thinning of old canes, top thinning may be practiced by removing a branch that shades the inner part of the shrub.

Prune For Health

- Remove any diseased or insect infested branches.
- Remove any dead wood and damaged or broken branches.
- Cut any suckers right at ground level.
- Remove any awkward branches that ruin the shape or appearance.
- Use proper tools and make sure all blades are sharp.

Every plant is an individual with its own character of growth habits. Even plants of the same species may grow and react differently because of location, age and environmental situations. A good gardener must study and learn about his or her plants and their reactions to different stimuli. Pruning should not be considered a burdensome task. Shrubs and trees are usually chosen because we like their shape and growth rate. This is why we should keep a natural style when taking pruners in hand. Pruning is an important maintenance practice that can be used to keep your landscape healthy and attractive. Simply allow the tree or shrub to take it's natural course in size and shape, and prune only out of necessity. Shrubs and trees are essential to provide the permanent "backbone" of the garden. Perhaps most important of all is leaf color and texture, gorgeous and astonishing in its range and beauty, that all garden designers ultimately work with. Experienced gardeners know that "woody" plants also offer an amazing variety of seasonally-changing ornamental features, from showy blooms to spectacular fall foliage and winter fruits, that present opportunities for the orchestration of changing effect every bit as dramatic as that of herbaceous perennials. Because shrubs and trees represent life-long, and sometimes substantial, investments, it is important to start with the best varieties available - preferably those that offer not only just the right structure and foliage, but more than one season of showy interest, as well.

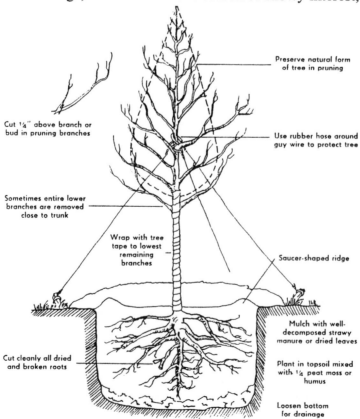

Root Pruning An Evergreen

Root pruning an evergreen.

Same treatment for deciduous shrubs if whole top is to be removed for renovation.
1st Step—Mark circle at spread of branches.
2nd Step—Tie up lower branches with soft rope completely around plant.
3rd Step—Mark circle two-thirds distance from trunk to mark at spread of branches.
4th Step—Sharpen spade.
5th Step—Thrust spade vertically into ground to full depth, cutting off roots.
6th Step—Untie branches.

Chapter 6

Flowers and Ground Covers

An Understanding Of Our Floriculture Industry

Floriculture includes the production and marketing of blooming potted plants, foliage potted plants, garden bedding plants, and cut flowers and foliages. Unlike other agricultural commodities, floriculture encompasses thousands of different plant species, and has the greatest number of unique cultivars. The floriculture and nursery industries are the fastest growing sector of agriculture. Demand for bedding and landscape plants will likely be one of the strongest demand areas for the next several years. Landscape contractors, homeowners, institutions and others needing to maintain the appearance of their property are the primary buyers. Demand for herbaceous perennials and flowering bulb plants is excellent. Consumers are seeking larger and higher quality plants, multicolored varieties, and plants with rich, vivid colors. Demand is improving due to consumer environmental concerns, better products and new varieties of plants. Potential for growth is strongest with field production of perennial cut flowers.

The U.S. market is considered one of largely untapped potential when compared to buying habits of other Western nations. Each household may spend about $200.00 on floral products this year. Cut flowers and bedding plants represent nearly two-thirds of purchases. U.S flower growers first felt the effect of international trade when Dutch flowers entered our marketplace in the early 1970s, followed soon after by Columbia. This trade threatened domestic cut flower production and historically altered the U.S. cut flower industry. As of 1992, Columbia accounted for 80% of all flowers imported into the U.S.; the Netherlands 10%; and the balance from many other nations. Of total nursery and greenhouse crops imported to the U.S., cut flowers represent 70% of this import trade. Additionally, Columbian-grown flowers hold nearly an 80% share of the entire U.S. cut flower market. The value of cut flower imports more than doubled from 1981 to 1985. In 1990 it was estimated to be an industry worth more than $313 million.

With the globalization of the floriculture marketplace imminent for both plants and flowers, the U.S. flower growers are in need of an organized national marketing effort. This need for an integrated and encompassing promotional program for U.S.-grown floral products is stronger than ever before. We need improved communication among growers, wholesalers and retailers. Information on consumer attitudes and values which influence floral purchasing habits is also lacking. More consumer focus, rather than production focus, is necessary to increase per capita floral consumption. Regional market information is needed to expand markets within each state. Production technology has advanced at a much greater rate than marketing activities. Efficiency of transport, rapid communication, mass market, and convenience store floral retailing and the use of toll-free numbers to sell flowers have altered the ways in which the industry does business. Consumers demand better quality products, encouraging more direct buying and selling. Particularly influencing distribution of plant material is the increasing volume of

plant sales at supermarkets. Growers also recognize the need to provide care and handling information to supermarket floral department staff to maintain quality products. Small retail florist businesses, once the backbone of the industry, are repositioning their market strategies to compete with the mass market floral retailers.

Flowers are a simple celebration of life's beauty, and there is a deep satisfaction in sharing these pleasures of the eye and heart. Growing flowers adds color, form and fragrance to the landscape. A flower garden can be large or small: a long elaborate border, a simple front yard bed or a collection of window boxes and patio containers. All have their own special ambiance. Creating beautiful gardens with easy to plant and easy to grow annual and perennial flowers are one of the most rewarding aspects of landscaping. Enhancing your home value has never been easier. Without costing a fortune, your home can have a look of elegance that landscape architects would charge hundreds of dollars to create. This chapter covers all different kinds of flowers, ground covers and vines, and different ways to arrange them so they can be used in your landscape. They are often grown in combination, are readily available at garden centers and are relatively easy to care for. These are the plants that beginning gardeners feel the most comfortable with when trying to landscape their yards. You will find down-to-earth, easy-to-understand helpful advise in selecting the right plants for the right locations.

Annual flowers are those plants that germinate, flower(bloom), set seed and die in one growing season. A few examples are: Marigold, Pansy, Petunia, Salvia, Verbena, Alyssum, Morning Glory and Phlox. There is an enormous universe of annual ornamentals that play valuable and beautiful roles in landscaping. They are short lived but compensate by devoting every moment to flowering. With the right choice in annuals, it is possible to create colorful designs that blend color from spring through fall. You have to spend more time in preparation and choosing the right plants, but the possibilities are limitless and the rewards are substancial. Perennial flowers are those plants that come back every year from the original roots and bloom right through the summer and fall. They are quite adaptible to a wide range of climatic conditions and soil, however, they grow best where there is at least a 4 hours of sunlight available. A few examples are: Forget-me-not, Cardinal Flower, Columbine, Sweet William, Baby's Breath and Bleeding Heart. Flowers add color and fragrance to any landscape. They can be small or large and can be in any location. A few areas where annuals and perennials can be used are: entranceways, paths or walkways, around poles, mailboxes, lampposts, any corner of your yard, around trees, along foundations, in shady areas, sunny areas and any type of container and window box available. Every part of your yard represents a different challenge. Flowers can be grown in long elaborate borders or small front yard beds and all have their own special atmosphere.

Flowers bring color and beauty to any home, inside and out. Everyone enjoys having flowers around and get an even greater pleasure growing them around their own home. To plant and enjoy an outstanding flower garden, you must coordinate the plants with their surroundings. Careful planning will bring great satisfaction. Combining various plants and colors is artistic and challenging. To be successful, plants must work well together. One of the first items to be considered is the location you want planted and to determine the type of flowers. Next, make a list of flowers that are suitable for various conditions of climate - shade, sun and soil. When the list is complete, a diagram should be drawn to show the actual planting based on time of bloom, color and height. Flower gardens cannot be planned until the location has been determined and the location limits the type and quantity of flowers that will be planted.

Planning A Flower Garden

When planning the flower garden, location so far as sun, partial shade or shade is very important. Before starting, review your landscape as every flower garden is part of a larger environment. There are flowers adapted for any location, good and poor soil, shade, sun, dry conditions and moist conditions. First pick several areas you want to plant and the types of flowers that will grow in those areas. Now you are ready to begin the actual planning. Many factors must be considered for the garden to be successful and effective. To do this properly, you should develop your plan on paper before the actual planting. So, get your colored markers or crayons out and buy a couple of sheets of large white posterboard. Also, collect all of those seed catalogues you receive in the mail. Most of them have complete details on most of the flowers they offer and many color pictures. Color schemes, height and time of bloom must all be considered when developing your garden. Make several lists of flowers according to light requirements, sun, partial shade and shade. Then make a subheading under each category and arrange the plants according to height. Below is an example of a 5ft. X 10ft. plot.

                              10ft.

	Rear of Garden	
5ft.	High	12in. or more
	Medium	6in. to 12in.
	Low	1in. to 6in.
	Front of Garden	

Using your colored markers, locate color groups according to the scheme you want. This plan is valuable as it presents a color picture of the garden before money is spent or labor is used to create something you may not be happy with. From the prepared flower list, make selections of plants for color, keeping in mind the height of the plants. Once you know where and what type of garden you want to plant, determine its shape and size and record the actual measurements on the posterboard. An alternative to hand coloring the flowers on your plan, is to look through the catalogues, find flowers you like, cut them out with names and paste them on the plan in the desired locations. Don't forget to add the bloom times. When completed, the overall picture may be more pleasing and give you a better view of what your garden will really look like. Make sure you call the company and ask for another catalogue to keep on hand. Make a final determination of which plants you want and how many will be required to fill in the area allotted to each variety. Add all data required such as: names, colors, blooming periods, quantities, heights, light conditions and where you intend to buy the plants.

If you are ordering from catalogues, make sure you check shipment times (some flowers are shipped at different times of the year than others) and approximate delivery dates. If you are buying from your local nursery, you can wait until the bed is prepared before buying the plants. If the garden is to be

straight lines, an example being the rear against a fence or wall, and the front being straight, then it's easy to put four stakes(one in each corner) and tie a string between each stake. Inside the stakes is your working area. If the front line is going to be irregular, however, it is wise to use a garden hose or thick rope and lay it from one end of the back edge, bring out to the front, make your design, and connect it with the opposite end of the garden's back edge. If the garden is to be irregular all around, then just use the hose and make whatever pattern you like. Inside the hose is your working area. If the bed is to be completely circular, locate the center and drive a stake into the ground. If it will be 10 ft. in diameter, tie a 5 ft. string to the center stake and attach a loose pointed stake to the end of the string. Trace a complete circle, lightly digging the loose stake into the ground, and drive in stakes in the circle line approximately 2 ft. apart to form the outer edge. After completing a few small beds you will become an expert in bed designing.

Preparing the soil for your flower garden is important for it to be successful. Healthy plants can only survive in good soil. One of the best soils is a readily crumbled, rich dark-colored loam soil, but not all of us have this type. Many of us have to deal with sandy, gravel or clay type soils, which means amendments must be added to improve its fertility. For good plant growth, sand or clay has very little value. However, different plants have different root systems and nutrient requirements. Some need a very high humus content, others low, and some need higher nitrogen plant foods than others. Fortunately, most of the annual and perennial flowers that survive in New Jersey are adaptable to most kinds of soil, with a little help from us.

First we must make the soil friable, that is, easy to work with and no clumps. This helps in proper soil organism activity and aeration. Humus, peat moss, bagged top soil, Michigan Peat and shredded leaves are all good additions with soil benefits. These organic matters help make a sandy soil more compact (moisture retaining) and a clay soil more open (less compact) for better drainage. If you have a compost pile that has aged for at least 1 to 2 years, such good humus material is ideal for flower gardens. Test your soil in the fall to determine the pH and the nutrients required. Lime is a great soil corrective. It brings the soil to the right condition for best plant growth. Lime helps soil bacteria become more active and aids soil particle decomposition. Fertilizer is used to enrich soil to promote plant growth. Some plants react favorably to almost any kind of fertilizer and others have more satisfactory results with only certain kinds. Don't wait till spring, if you are having a professional laboratory conduct the test, as it may take a few weeks to obtain the results because soil testing labs are busiest at that time.

Prepare the soil by loosening up the top 4 inches, add a good humus material and mix in thoroughly. The flower bed should have an application of humus every spring before planting. If you have the time, prepare the beds in the fall before spring planting so the soil can settle. If not, you can prepare them in the spring as long as you allow sufficient time for the soil to settle before you plant, at least two weeks and after a good, soaking rain. As mentioned before, use a garden hose or thick rope to establish the outline of each bed or border. They can be moved easily and are especially useful when laying out curved or circular beds. Work the soil to a depth of 4 to 6 inches, or at least deep enough to provide adequate space for the plants' root systems. Incorporate organic matter, such as peat moss, compost or Michigan peat at this time. You can use hand tools or power tillers. If the bed site has poorly drained soil, select species that are tolerable, raise the bed to improve drainage or choose a better site.

*Preparation Of Beds Is Important Because
It Will Be A Long-term Planting*

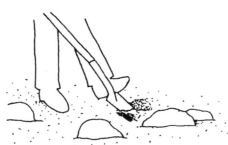

Work soil to
8 to 10 inches

For rock gardens,
work the soil a
few inches.

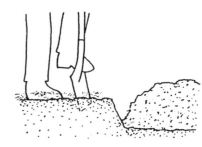

Organic matter can
be incorporated while
working the soil.

You must eliminate all weeds during this initial soil preparation period before plants are added or seeds are sown. Untold difficulties arise when perennial weeds, such as quackgrass, grow through a carefully planted bed. Because of the diversity among perennials, it is risky to chemically treat weeds in close proximity to valuable plantings. It may be possible, however, to treat individual weeds with a herbicide recommended for use on perennials. You may need to apply fertilizer when you prepare the beds. Follow the recommendations of the soil test report. If you didn't test the soil, apply a complete fertilizer, such as 5-10-5, at a rate of 2 pounds (4 rounded cups) per 100 square feet. Work the fertilizer into the soil as you prepare the bed. The ideal soil pH is slightly acidic (6.0 to 6.8). If the pH is too low or too high, adjust it at the same time you apply fertilizer. To raise the pH (make it more alkaline), add ground limestone as recommended by the soil test report. To lower the pH (make it more acidic), add sulfur, ferrous sulfate (iron sulfate) or aluminum sulfate.

Adding generous amounts of organic matter will also help to lower soil pH and keep it at the desired level. Normally, pH needs to be adjusted only once, but it is desirable to test the soil the following year to be sure the pH is at the recommended level. If not, topdress the soil with limestone or aluminum sulfate. To increase soil moisture retention, spread a 2 inch layer of mulch over the surface of newly prepared beds. Use bark chips, pine needles, compost or shredded mulch. This will also help suppress weeds and increase plant hardiness. Apply only a thin layer of mulch to heavier clay soils because these soils do not drain as rapidly and may stay wet too long. You may need to add organic mulch each year as it decomposes.

Now that you have framed out the garden and prepared the soil, its time to start planting. In most cases, you will probably purchase your annuals and perennials in what are called "flats." Depending on the size of each plant, you may get 18 to 48 or more individual plants to each flat. Each plant has its own little root ball or square that can be popped out of the containers quite easily. I recommend watering the entire flat of plants before removing them. This will ensure an even distribution of water and make them easier to remove from their individual containers. It will also allow you time to make changes in your design after planting a few. Dig a hole with a trowel that is twice as wide and about 1/2 inch deeper than the root square and place the plant in the hole in a straight position. Fill in the hole and press down the soil firmly around the plant. If you intend to spread mulch around the flowers, it may be easier to put the mulch down first and then plant, digging the holes right through the mulch. As long as the root ball has some soil around it you won't have any problem. This will help you avoid trampling on and smothering all of the flowers, if you decided to add mulch after they were planted. To make smaller plants more visible, plant them in clusters in the same colors. When flowers are planted in masses, here some red, there some yellow and over here some white, do not plant them as individuals but groups of a certain kind and color. Remember, the total effect is the objective, not individual plants. If planting flowers in areas where there are no backgrounds, such as along walks or driveways, they should be planted in groups for a more striking effect. Planning a flower garden means you should first find out as much as you can about the plants you intend to use. Send away for catalogues having to do with flowers and gardening. At the end of this book is a listing of free catalogues for home and garden.

As the growing season passes, cultivation plays an important role in gardening. The soil around each plant should be stirred slightly from 1/2 to 1 inch in depth to help the plant breath and kill weeds. This should be done at least once every month as weed control can be best accomplished when they are young and small. Depending on the size of the area, garden hoes, forks, cultivators, hand weeders, and weasels can all be used to cut off or uproot weeds to kill them. This frees the plant from weed competition for light, moisture and food. Adding mulch will also keep weeds to a minimum, conserve soil moisture and protect the roots from excessive heat or cold.

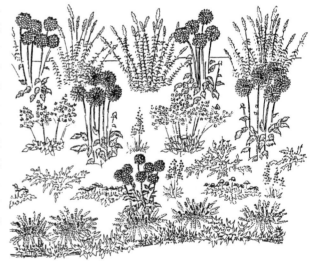

Perennials

Perennials have long been popular with gardeners and homeowners throughout the world because they are relatively easy to grow and offer diversity of color, form and bloom sequence. The 19th century British plant experts William Robinson and Gertrude Jekyll played prominent roles in popularizing the perennial border and developing guidelines for its design. They grouped border perennials together and tiered them with the tallest plants (such as delphiniums) in the back and lower growing plants in the front to separate the border from the lawn. The border was set against the backdrop of a hedge, usually yew or boxwood, or a wall. Careful selection and placement combined harmonious color schemes and

contrasting forms to provide interest and a sequence of continuous bloom. Perennial borders in this form, however, presented certain disadvantages. They required a great deal of space and attention and could be viewed from only one side. The background hedge competed for light and slowed air circulation, encouraging the back row to lean forward unless staked. These faults inspired the island bed concept at Bressingham Gardens in Norfolk, England, in the 1950s. When planted in relatively narrow islands, the flowers could be viewed from all directions and shading by hedges or walls was eliminated. Taller specimens were placed in the middle of the bed, their height usually no more than half the width of the bed.

> *Versatile, long-lived, and available in nearly infinite variety, perennials are America's fastest growing group of plants in popularity!*

Today, limited space often makes it impossible or undesirable to devote an area entirely to growing only one type of plant, such as perennials. The trend is toward mixed borders or beds that include trees, shrubs, perennials, bulbs and annuals. This allows you to select plants that go well together to create year-round color and interest. There is also a movement toward less formal, low-maintenance gardens. Perennials may be planted directly in lawns or in ground covers, such as periwinkle or English ivy - a practice known as "naturalizing." Perennials having a low spreading habit may also be used instead of more traditional ground covers. Dried flowers and leaves are left on the plants for winter interest and for use in dried arrangements. More ornamental grasses are used, as well as massings of one or a limited number of other perennials. By combining many species, you can create a spectacular display.

The versatility of perennials is truly amazing. Some low varieties spread to cover the ground and some reach into heights well above our heads to provide screening and background. Forms range from spiky verticals to blocky masses to nearly transparent, rounded clouds. Textures range from fine, dense leaves to foliage that is huge and tropical-appearing. And there are perennials for every kind of growing situation: dry soils and wet, hot exposed slopes and cool shady woodlands, northern climates with harsh and cold winters, and southern climates with mild and warm winters. And the color! From dramatic effects to the subtle, you can find flowers of every hue imaginable, bloom seasons in every month of the year, fall and winter seedheads, and evergreens and deciduous foliage in a symphony of greens, yellows, reds, purples, blues, whites and black. Add to this versatility a long-lived and relatively care-free life, as well as rapid effect, often maturing the second season after planting, and you end up with a truly exciting group of plants for garden and landscape worth a lifetime of exploration.

Rudbeckia (Coneflower)

The term "perennials" commonly means "hardy herbaceous ornamental plants." Hardy perennials are, with some exceptions, non-woody plants having roots that live through the winter while the tops die back to the ground. This distinction separates hardy plants from tender perennials and annuals, which flower, set seed and die in the autumn frosts. Some perennials will last almost indefinitely. Others tend to be short-lived and many last only a few years. Peony, daylily and iris are extremely long-lived, while columbine, and shasta

daisy tend to be short-lived, flowering for two or three years. When selecting plants, remember that "perennial" doesn't necessarily mean "perpetual." The maintenance required for perennials also varies with the species. For example, chrysanthemum and delphinium need attention each year, whereas hosta and peony generally require little care after they are established. A relatively low-maintenance garden is possible, but it requires careful selection of plants well suited to the climate and planted in an appropriate location.

Columbine

Perennials are usually sold under their botanical names (genus, species, cultivar) by the more reputable nurseries. This is because common names can be confusing: one plant may have three different common names, or one common name may refer to three different plants. It helps to know both the botanical and common names. However, every plant has only one unique botanical name. Occasionally, these names are changed by plant scientists to better describe the plant. When that happens, the old name becomes a synonym for the new. Most modern reference books on perennials refer to the plants by botanical name, so learning to use these specific names can help you find information more quickly and accurately.

Example:

Common name: Garden mum
Botanical name: *Dendranthema grandiflora*
Synonym: *Chrysanthemum X morifolium*
Cultivars:
'MinnGopher'
'Snowsota'
'Mellow Moon'

Caring for perennials can be a type of creative expression. Perennials offer a wide variety of forms, colors, textures and sizes. In many cases, they are long lived, compared with annuals, and can require relatively low maintenance. They also provide a vigorous new stock for transplanting and trading with neighbors and friends. Perennials are versatile. From the thousands of species and varieties available, you can select perennials that will thrive in any type of site, from wet to dry, fertile to infertile, sun to deep shade. They often provide the solution for problem areas, such as steep slopes, hillsides and rocky areas. Notable examples of perennials that will thrive in these special conditions are listed in the following chart.

Perennials for Moist to Wet Sites	Perennials for Shady Sites	Perennials for Hot Dry Sites	Perennials with Fragrance
Aster	Astilbe	Achillea	Artemisia
Astilbe	Brunnera	Anthemis	Convallaria
Euphorbia	Convallaria	Armeria	Dianthus
Heliopsis	Dicentra	Artemisia	Echinacea
Hibiscus	Geranium	Asclepias	Hemerocallis
Hosta	Hemerocallis	Aurinia	Hosta
Iris	Heuchera	Coreopsis	Lavandula
Lobelia	Hosta	Dianthus	Monarda
Mertensia	Iris	Echinops	Paeonia
Monarda	Mertensia	Euphorbia	Phlox
Oenothera	Myosotis	Gypsophila	Salvia
Physostegia	Polygonatum	Hemerocallis	Thalictrum
Primula	Primula	Lavandula	Thymus
Rudbeckia	Thalictrum	Liatris	Viola
Salvia	Trollius	Oenothera	
Saponaria	Viola	Penstemon	
Tradescantia		Rudbeckia	
Trollius		Salvia	
		Saponaria	
		Sedum	
		Veronica	

Perennials for Cut Flowers		Low Maintenance Perennials	Perennials for Naturalizing
Achillea	Penstemon	Achillea	Achillea
Anemone	Phlox	Asclepias	Ajuga
Anthemis	Physostegia	Brunnera	Aquilegia
Artemisia	Rudbeckia	Calamagrostis	Asclepias
Aster	Salvia	Dicentra	Baptisia
Astilbe	Sedum	Echinacea	Convallaria
Convallaria	Trollius	Echinops	Coreopsis
Coreopsis	Veronica	Heliopsis	Dicentra
Delphinium	Viola	Hemerocallis	Echinacea
Dianthus		Hosta	Heliopsis
Echinacea		Iris	Hemerocallis
Echinops		Liatris	Hosta
Gypsophila		Limonium	Liatris
Helianthus		Paeonia	Lobelia
Heliopsis		Papaver	Monarda
Hemerocallis		Platycodon	Phlox
Heuchera		Sedum	Physostegia
Hosta			Rudbeckia
Iris			Tradescantia
Liatris			Veronica
Lupinus			Viola

Five Steps In Designing A Perennial Garden

Designing a perennial flower garden and seeing it develop before your eyes is rewarding. It takes time, knowledge and experience to prepare a good plan. The planning stage is too often overlooked by the impatient gardener, and this results in a haphazard collection of plant materials. The eye needs a sense of order. Too many variations in sizes, shapes, colors and textures create confusion. Remember that the most spectacular gardens all begin with a carefully thought-out design that has strong lines and structure.

Determine The Points Of Viewing

Place beds or borders where they can be readily seen and admired. Try to locate them in areas of high visibility, such as the front yard, near windows, the porch or patio, while keeping in mind other factors such as soil type, drainage, pH and light. Also consider that certain trees, such as black walnut and butternut, produce a chemical in their roots that is toxic to many plants, including peonies. Locate susceptible plants a minimum distance of 60 feet from such trees. Perennials with shallow root systems are less likely to be affected. Some trees, such as red maples, have a shallow root system and will compete with perennials for moisture.

Existing Yard

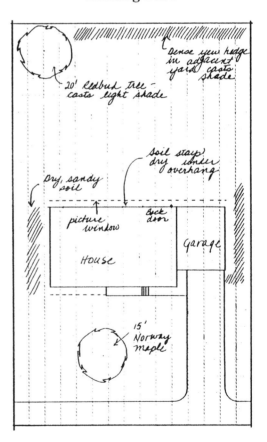

Consider Existing Conditions

Carefully record the location of existing plants that you want to keep and other permanent or temporary fixtures, such as a compost pile, posts, trash barrels, septic tanks, sheds, swings etc. Indicate any low or high points and shaded areas of the property. Determine the soil type(s) such as clay, sand or loam, whether it is acid or neutral and well drained or poorly drained.

Decide On Style - Either Informal Or Formal

An informal style follows the natural terrain by using curved, flowing lines. It creates balance without being symmetrical and highlights existing and future plant specimens. A formal style uses straight, geometric lines to determine the shape of the bed. It often relies on symmetry, matching one side of the garden with the other. The rectangular shape can be repeated in other architectural elements, such as the

house, pool, lawn or patio. Most decisions on style are a matter of personal preference. Here are a few points to consider. If your property has no outstanding natural features and is relatively flat, you may use either style. If your yard is irregularly shaped with slopes, hills, rocks or mature trees, the informal style is preferred. Consider the style of the house and select the style of garden that complements it best.

<table>
<tr><td>**Formal Design**</td><td>**Informal Design**</td></tr>
</table>

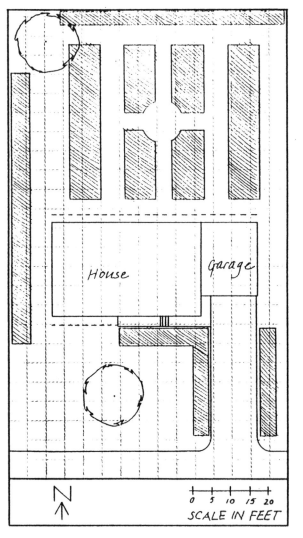

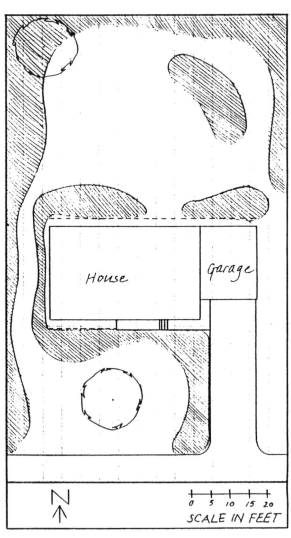

Choose Type Of Display

Three types of displays are commonly used for perennial gardens - the border, the island bed and the naturalized area. A border is a cultivated area that bounds an expanse such as a lawn, walkway, driveway or wall. If it is flush against a wall or hedge, the border should not be any wider than 4 to 6 feet for ease of maintenance. For a wider border, plan a narrow path between the wall and the garden for access. The path will be hidden from view and will improve air circulation behind the tallest plants, which should reduce disease problems. For a pleasing relationship between the depth of the border and the size of the yard, do not allow it to exceed one-quarter of the total width of your yard. An island bed is a cultivated area surrounded by an open expanse, such as a lawn. It is accessible from all sides, which makes it easier to maintain. It admits more sunlight and encourages better air circulation. This type of display can break up large, open areas. You do not need to segregate perennials in the garden. Many can be naturalized along a stream, in lowlands or in dry meadows so that they look as if they are part of the natural landscape. Some can be naturalized in lawns or ground covers, and a number can be used as groundcovers themselves. You can use many wildflowers and ferns in such locations.

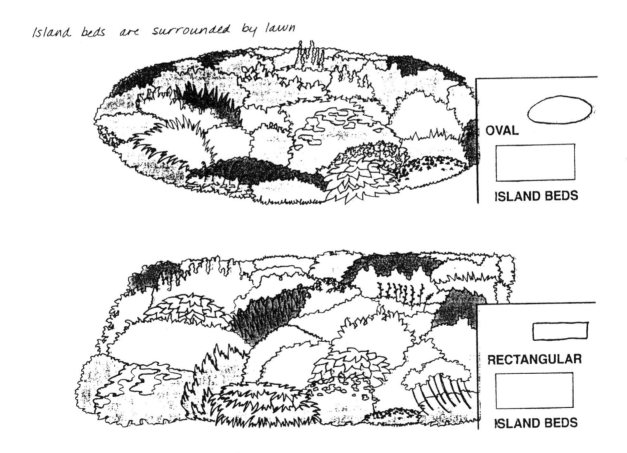

Island beds are surrounded by lawn

OVAL
ISLAND BEDS

RECTANGULAR
ISLAND BEDS

Select Plants

When selecting plants, make a list of your favorites. Consider the space limitations of the site: would smaller, compact plants be appropriate? Should taller plants with spreading habits be included? Match the soil type, light levels and site climate with the requirements of preferred plants. Carefully consider individual plant characteristics, as well as the overall character of the garden.

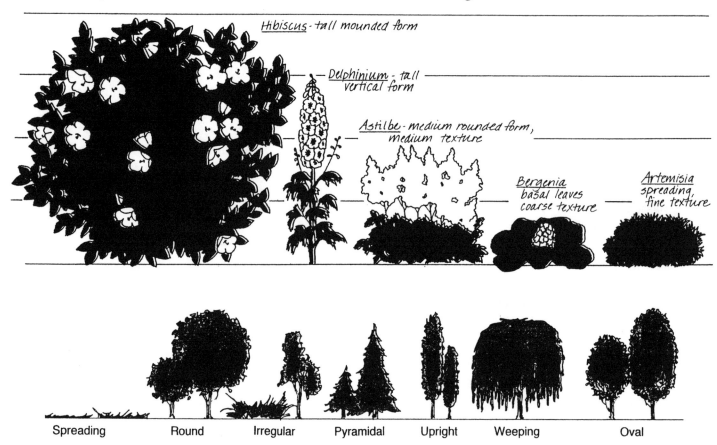

Each perennial has a general shape or form. Basic forms are vertical or columnar, such as delphinium; mounded, such as astilbe; and horizontal or prostrate, such as creeping phlox. Most perennials fall in between these three forms. Use a variety of forms to create the most pleasing effect. Perennials vary in height from the tiny woolly thyme about 1/2 inch tall to the lofty rose mallow up to 8 feet tall. The standard method of arranging heights is "stair-stepping." Shorter plants are placed in front, medium height plants in the middle and taller plants in the back. Break up this progression a bit to keep the garden interesting and more natural. Be careful not to completely hide smaller plants behind taller specimens. A newly planted bed can look rather bare if plants are spaced at recommended distances for mature specimens. To avoid this bareness, space plants closer together and transplant a few out of the bed as they become crowded. This will also help control weeds. Or use annual plants in bare areas until the perennials grow into their allotted space. You also can cover bare areas with a 2 inch layer of mulch. The plants will fill in the bare spaces as the garden matures over a few years.

Texture refers to the overall appearance of a leafy plant, not to the feel of it. Perennials are commonly grouped as coarse, medium or fine textured. Create spatial illusions by using different textures. Plants with coarse textures appear closer than they really are, while those with fine textures recede into the distance. Examples are: coarse texture - bergenia, hollyhock; medium texture - astilbe, iris, rudbeckia; fine texture - baby's breath, lavender.

Color

Perennials are noted for their usually short-lived but remarkable flower color. Thus, an understanding of color and the relationship of colors is important. This will allow you to select and arrange species and cultivars to create pleasing and harmonious displays. Warm, vibrant colors, such as red, orange, and yellow, tend to stand out in the landscape. They can also make a distance seem shorter. For these reasons, use warm colors as accents or for long distance viewing. Use them carefully, however, because they are quite intense and can overpower the rest of your garden. Cool, peaceful colors, such as blue, green and purple, tend to recede into the landscape. They are especially effective for close viewing and in masses. Many homeowners and gardeners use various color schemes.

A *monochromatic* (using one color) scheme includes different flowers that have various tints and shades of a single color, such as blue. Another popular color is white. Several famous gardens are fashioned around an all-white theme, such as the white garden at Sissinghurst Castle in Kent, England. Choosing a particular color can be especially effective in complementing the color of your house. An *analogous* (using several colors) scheme uses two or more hues that are adjacent or neighboring on the color wheel, such as red, red-violet and violet. Another possible scheme is orange, yellow-orange and yellow. A *complementary* scheme uses colors opposite each other on the color wheel, such as yellow and violet, red and green, or orange and blue. White-flowered and silver-leaved plants may be used to blend areas where colors meet.

A *semi-chromatic* color scheme divides the color wheel in half and uses any three adjoining colors, such as blue, violet and red; or red, orange and yellow. This approach is very popular today. A *polychromatic* scheme includes any and every combination of colors. This type of design yields a great variety of colors and can be very festive. It is important to note, however, that even gardens of this type with seemingly haphazard arrangements achieve their success only through careful planning. Listed is a color guide of some of the more popular perennials.

Blue to Purple	Pink to Red	Yellow to Orange	White	Gray to Blue	Variegated
Ajuga	Achillea	Achillea	Arabis	Achillea	Aegopodium
Aquilegia	millefolium	Anthemis	albida	Artemisia	Ajuga
Aster	Anemone	tinctoria	Aruncus	Cerastium	Heuchera
Brunnera	Armeria	Asclepias	Aster	Dianthus	Hosta
Campanula	Aster	tuberosa	Astilbe	Echinops	Lamiastrum
Centaurea	Astilbe	Aurinia	Cerastium	Festuca	Lamium
montana	Centranthus	saxatilis	Dendranthema	cinerea	Miscanthus
Delphinium	Dendranthema	Coreopsis	Dianthus	Gypsophila	Polygonatum
Erigeron	Dianthus	Dendranthema	Dicentra	Lavandula	Pulmonaria
Hosta	Dicentra	Euphorbia	Dictamnus	Sedum	Sedum
Iris	Echinacea	Gaillardia	Echinacea	Thymus	Thymus
Lavandula	Eupatorium	Geum	Galium		
Liatris	Geranium	Helenium	Goniolimon		
Linum	Hemerocallis	Helianthus	Gypsophila		
perenne	Heuchera	Heliopsis	Hosta		
Mertensia	Iris	Hemerocallis	Iberis		
Nepeta	Lobelia	Iris	Iris		
Phlox	cardinalis	Ligularia	Leucanthemum		
Platycodon	Lychnis	Lysimachia	Paeonia		
Salvia	Paeonia	punctata	Phlox		
Tradescantia	Phlox	Oenothera	Veronica		
Veronica	Physostegia	Papaver	Yucca		
Viola	Saponaria	orientale			
		Rudbeckia			
		Sedum			
		Trollius			

Perennials vary considerably in when and how long they flower. A bloom chart, such as the one in this chapter, will help you coordinate flowering periods to prolong a colorful display or to concentrate color during a particular time. If you own a summer home, for example, you might want to plant an August-flowering perennial bed. If you live in your home year round, you might want to plan a garden for spring, summer and fall color. Although perennials can provide continuous bloom throughout the growing season, there are usually three or four peak periods when the display is at its best. The following drawing will give you some idea of a continuous blooming display.

This bed is designed to provide continuous bloom throughout the growing season.

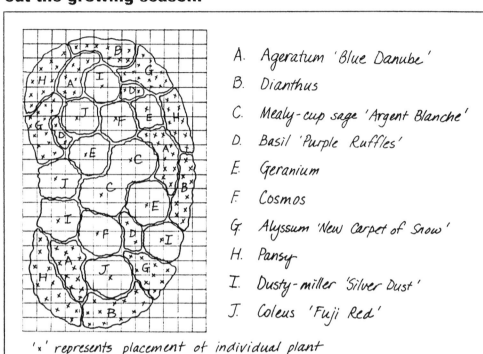

A. *Ageratum 'Blue Danube'*

B. *Dianthus*

C. *Mealy-cup sage 'Argent Blanche'*

D. *Basil 'Purple Ruffles'*

E. *Geranium*

F. *Cosmos*

G. *Alyssum 'New Carpet of Snow'*

H. *Pansy*

I. *Dusty-miller 'Silver Dust'*

J. *Coleus 'Fuji Red'*

'x' represents placement of individual plant

Remember also that perennials are grown for other attributes than flowers. Colorful or interesting foliage and fruit, unique forms and fragrance also provide interest. In a garden timed for continuous blooming, expect to see a fair amount of green foliage with intermittent flowers, rather than a solid mass of color.

Choosing Perennials

Perennials are available in many forms: as seeds, as dormant bare-root plants, in seedling packs like annuals, in 4 and 6 inch pots and in 1 gallon containers. Larger plants represent a considerably larger investment than their smaller counterparts. However, they will produce a full look sooner and you may see each plant's foliage and possibly flowers before you purchase it. Although more wildflowers and ferns are becoming available, you usually have to obtain the more unusual ones from specialized nurseries. Many nurseries now offer perennials as first-year seedlings in plastic "cell packs." These plants might take an extra year to establish, but the cost per plant is considerably less.

Mail-order businesses generally wait to ship dormant plants until the weather is suitable for planting. However, many of these companies operate in southern states and plants sometimes arrive when snow is still on the ground in the north. In such cases, store dormant plants in a cool, dark location where the

temperature stays above freezing, and keep the packing material slightly moist. If the holding temperature is not below 50°F, watch the plants closely because they may yellow and deteriorate if they are kept longer than one to two weeks. Wrap the plants loosely in plastic and keep in a refrigerator if you have room. If not carefully protected from desiccation, the plants will deteriorate very quickly. Another way to handle newly purchased bare-root plants is to pot them in containers and grow them in a protected area, a coldframe or similar structure until you can safely plant them in their permanent location. Or plant bare-root plants directly in the ground, if it's workable. A light, sandy well drained soil is desirable. Cover plants with slitted row covers (available from several catalogues) or similar plant protectors until the danger of frost has passed. Be sure the protectors are ventilated, or remove them on sunny or warm days. Then move plants to their permanent location. If they are very small, it might be better to allow them to grow for a year before transplanting.

Many perennials are relatively trouble-free and grow best in a loose, moderately fertile loam with adequate moisture. The best time to plant most perennials is in the spring so the plants can establish a good root system before winter. This will also reduce the possibility of heaving, a common problem with poorly established perennials in northern climates. You can also plant new divisions in late summer, but be sure the roots have at least a month to develop before cold weather sets in. A few perennials are at their best when planted in August: bearded iris, Oriental poppy, peony and many woodland wildflowers. Potted perennials can be planted any time during the growing season.

Growing Perennials From Seed

Many perennials can easily be grown from seeds, such as columbine, delphinium and rudbeckia. Use small pots or trays containing cell packs to start seeds. An important key to successful seed starting is having the right containers. Wooden flats, egg cartons or plastic "six packs" are okay, but newly developed **Kord Fiber flats** have become popular with seed companies. They are stiff-sided, lightweight and portable, and they hold the right volume of soil mix. Kord flats keep germinating seeds evenly moist and produce strong, vigorous seedlings to plant out in the garden. These biodegradable flats are made from recycled pressed pulp and are sturdy enough to last several seasons. If you have decided to plant heat loving vegetables and flowers indoors first, here is a way to do it easily. A well crafted, U.L. approved **electric propagation mat** sets up an ideal temperature controlled environment. Just plug it in and set seed containers on top. Its thermostat automatically maintains necessary warm temperatures day and night. This is the ideal aid for raising strong vegetables and

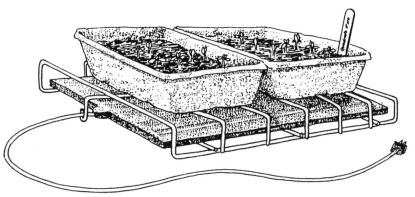

many flower seeds. If you are a serious gardener, and start seeds early indoors every year, a table top **grow light** is one of the best investments you can make. Seedlings will thrive in this constant light bath and mature into stocky, healthy transplants that succeed in the garden. The above three items are available from **Shepherd's Garden** Seeds.

A standard, well drained growing medium works well for most perennials. Seed packets should include essential information, such as when to sow, how deeply, germination temperature and other information. Sow seeds at the recommended rate and time (spring, summer or fall) in a sterile medium, either scattered (broadcast) or in rows, and cover them with the recommended amount of growing material which is usually about two to three times the diameter of the seed.

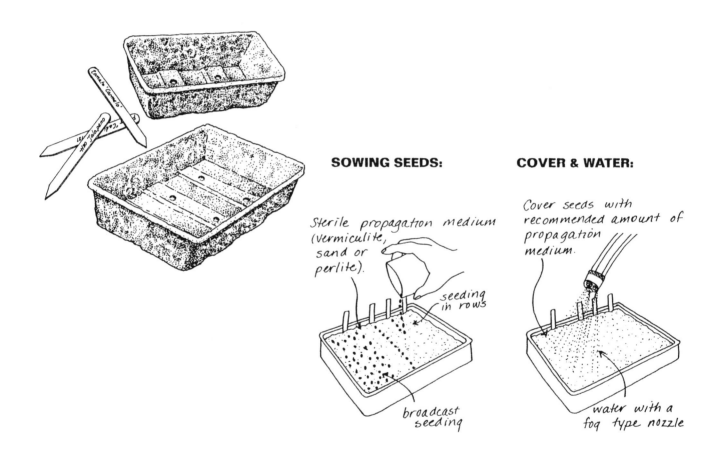

SOWING SEEDS:

Sterile propagation medium (vermiculite, sand or perlite).

seeding in rows

broadcast seeding

COVER & WATER:

Cover seeds with recommended amount of propagation medium.

water with a fog type nozzle

Label the containers and water very carefully to avoid washing away the seeds. Place the containers in a warm location where the soil temperature is at least 70°F. Cover with plastic to keep the medium moist. As soon as most of the seeds have germinated, remove the plastic and move the containers to a cooler location (60 to 65°F) in bright light to harden seedlings. You can also start seeds in outdoor seedbeds either in an open or a protected area., such as a coldframe. The seedbed should have porous, well drained soil that you have prepared thoroughly, leveled, tamped with the back of a rake and leveled again before seeding. After preparing the bed, sow the seeds and cover, following directions on the seed packet. Moisten the seedbed with a fog-type nozzle and be careful not to wash away the seeds.

Fertilize the plants as soon as the leaves expand, using a complete fertilizer such as 20-10-20 at the recommended rate and frequency listed on the product label. If the frequency is listed at once a month, you should probably fertilize more frequently at reduced rates, e.g., twice a month at one half the monthly rate. Make sure you use a sterile growing medium and watch for diseases and insects. Transplant seedlings to larger containers (4 to 5 inches) as soon as root systems have developed. Overwinter seedlings of most species in a protected location, such as a coldframe, until final transplanting the following spring.

Transplanting Young Plants

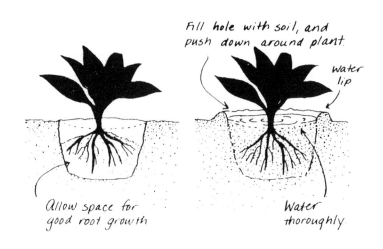

The best time to transplant young plants, whether grown from seeds or cuttings, is in early spring after the soil has thawed but the plants are still dormant. This is usually 4 to 6 weeks before the average date of the last freezing temperature in the spring. Use stakes to mark where the plants will go before you set them out. Be sure to allow enough space. Dig holes in prepared beds using a trowel or spading fork. Make the holes large enough so that roots have plenty of room and plant at a depth to accommodate each root system. Firm the soil around the roots so there are no empty spaces between roots and soil and water thoroughly.

How do you store any leftover seeds? Most seed packs come with high germination rates, and most varieties will keep easily for the next growing season. The worst enemies of successful seed storage are humidity and heat. Never leave leftover seed packets outside in the garden or in an unheated outdoor garden shed or garage because high humidity and dampness will ruin them. A sealed mason jar or freezer-weight ziplock bag is an ideal storage container. Keep seeds dry and in your coolest room or, better still, in a refrigerator. Plan to use them the next season.

Maintenance

Water your perennial garden when the soil becomes dry. This will vary with soil type. Watch new beds for signs of wilting. Young, newly planted perennials will need more frequent watering than mature, established plants. Water thoroughly and try not to splash water on the foliage. Use a trowel to check the soil for moisture - soil should be moist 3 to 4 inches deep. It is better to water thoroughly and less frequently than to apply many superficial waterings. Apply a 2 inch layer of mulch over the bed or border at least every other spring, tapering it off gradually near each plant. You may apply a layer of winter mulch 2 inches deep to help prevent winter injury, especially heaving. A winter mulch can help unreliably hardy plants survive the winter.

You may have to stake tall plants as they grow. Stake each stem individually instead of trying to tie them all together. Tie the plant to the stake with plastic strips or wire covered with a plastic coating. Make a double loop of the wire with one loop around the plant and the other around the stake. This keeps the stem from rubbing against the stake. For tall, arching plants, make or purchase circular rings and attach them to the stakes to support plants and to maintain their natural form. A three-legged support called a peony hoop is less obstructive than poles in the garden. Tomato cages can be used in the same way.

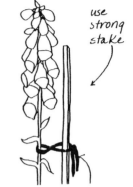

use strong stake

Apply fertilizer as growth begins in the spring. Because many soils have adequate phosphorus and potassium but are deficient in nitrogen, use a complete fertilizer every 3 to 4 years and supplement it with nitrogen-based fertilizer other years. However, most perennials are not heavy feeders. Organic matter added at the time of planting can provide sufficient nutrients all year and eliminate the need for fertilizer. If plants are not vigorous and foliage is light green or yellowish, applying a nitrogen-based fertilizer would be beneficial.

Cultivate perennials as frequently as needed to control weeds. Most weeds can be killed by using an action hoe or a similar tool. Work the top half-inch of the soil. If you cultivate much deeper, you can injure plant roots. Frequent, shallow cultivation is better than occasional, deep cultivation. Try not to walk in the beds while weeding. Soil can be easily compacted, which limits root growth. "Dead-head' - that is, remove old flower heads - after blooming unless the fruits are ornamental. This prolongs the flowering period of many perennials, especially dianthus, coreopsis and shasta daisy. A few species will bloom a second time if the stems are cut back after flowering. Examples are delphinium, false indigo and globe thistle. The flowers won't be as numerous on the regrowth, but cutting back does result in a longer, although not continuous, flowering period.

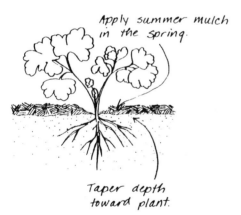

Apply summer mulch in the spring.

Taper depth toward plant.

Propagation Methods

Many vigorous perennials crowd themselves and require dividing every few years. Also, the most aggressive types can escape and choke out other plants around them. Dividing is often done in the spring while they are still dormant. This avoids subjecting the newly divided plants to harsh winter temperatures and reduces the chances of heaving. The method of dividing varies among types of perennials. In general, vigorous new shoots from the outside of a clump are preferred for replanting, but you can use all shoots, if desired.

To make digging easier, water the bed well a few days beforehand if the soil is dry. Before dividing, prune the plants by half if stems are still present. Dig out the entire clump. Divide the healthy living portions into smaller clumps by working them apart with your fingers or making small cuts with a sharp

knife. Divide large, dense clumps using two spading forks back-to-back. In general, replace one or two healthy divisions in the original hole and plant the others elsewhere. Some species have large taproots and should not be divided or moved unnecessarily. Examples are baby's-breath, balloon flower and lupine. There are several other ways to propagate perennials. You can propagate chrysanthemums by stem and root cuttings; iris by rhizome pieces; anemone and perennial phlox by root cuttings; and peonies and bleeding-heart by taking roots with one or more "eyes." Consult other gardeners, your local nursery and catalogs or books for more details on specific methods.

Propagation By Stem Cuttings: Garden Mum

For stem cuttings, such as of chrysanthemum, cut off actively growing shoot tips and remove the lower leaves. Application of low strength rooting hormone will generally enhance rooting. Place in a well-drained propagation medium and keep well watered.

Propagation By Rhizome Division: Bearded Iris

Lift a clump of plants with a spading fork. Cut off and discard old rhizomes from the current season's growth. Replant healthy rhizomes at the same depth they had been growing.

Propagation By Root Cuttings: Garden Phlox

  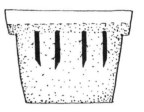

Cut off young roots close to the crown and return the parent plant to the garden. Distinguish top of cutting from bottom by the angle of the cut. Remove any fibrous lateral roots and treat with fungicide powder. Plant with the bottom end down in a well-drained propagation medium. Water just enough to keep soil from drying out.

Propagation By Crown Division: Bleeding Heart

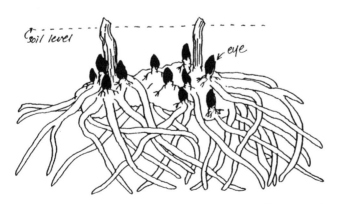 

Dig roots and crown with a spading fork in the fall. Lift carefully so as not to break roots, and knock off excess soil. Cut crown into sections, each having one or more eyes (more eyes will give a bigger plant next year). Cover with plastic to prevent desiccation and replant as soon as possible at the same depth they had been growing.

Controlling Diseases And Pests

Although most perennials have few major disease or insect problems, several pests can attack them. These pests vary in type and severity from area to area and year to year. You can control most of them effectively if you follow these general recommendations:

- Buy plants that are free of diseases and insects.
- Buy disease-resistant species when available.
- Keep your garden free of weeds, fallen leaves, and diseased or insect-infested plants.
- Remove seriously diseased or insect infested plants as soon as you notice them.
- Apply fungicides and insecticides only as needed.

If a serious problem develops, three types of pesticides are used on perennials: fungicides for diseases, insecticides for insects and miticides for spider mites. These are usually applied as dusts or sprays. Many come ready to use.

Diseases

Of the many diseases that attack perennials, aster yellows, botrytis blight, powdery mildew and rust are the most serious. *Aster yellows* causes the yellowing of leaf tips and flowers, also stunting of the plant and abnormal growth. Leafhopper insects carry this disease from plant to plant. Asters, mums and some others can get aster yellows. The only cure is to remove the infected plants and control leafhoppers. *Botrytis blight* is a gray fungus mold that attacks leaves, stems and flowers. Most flower petals are susceptible, especially peony flowers in wet weather and shasta daisy in late summer during times of heavy dew. *Leaf blotch* can be caused by other fungi as well. Brown spots are a common problem on peony, iris and mum. *Root rots* (fungus bacteria) can be serious problems for perennials in moist soil. The best solution is to improve soil drainage, especially over winter, or move the plant to a more suitable location. *Powdery mildew* is a fungus that covers leaves with a whitish substance. Avoid overcrowding and planting in wet or shady locations. It often occurs on phlox and delphinium. *Rust* causes reddish brown spotting on leaves, stems and flower parts. It is common on hollyhocks.

Insects

The most common insects that attack perennials are aphids, beetles, caterpillars, leafhoppers, spider mites, and thrips. *Aphids* are small sucking insects that are concentrated at the tips of young shoots, on stems and on the undersides of leaves. *Beetles* feed on leaves, stems and flowers. *Caterpillars* usually feed on leaves. *Leafhoppers* are small, leaping insects that feed on many kinds of plants by sucking sap. *Spider mites* are very tiny pests that feed on leaves and stems. Look for fine webs to indicate their presence. They are usually located on the undersides of leaves. Mites thrive in hot, dry weather. They are very difficult to see without a magnifying glass (look for movement). Shaking the leaves over a white paper is another way of determining their presence. *Thrips* are very small insects, sometimes with wings, that suck sap. Leaves may be finely mottled. Thrips will attack growing points and flowers.

Guide To Perennial Chart

Names - Each perennial has a single, specific botanical name that includes a genus, which is capitalized, followed by a species, which is written in lowercase letters. Perennials may have one or several different common names that differ from one region to another. Frequently, the genus is used as a common name, such as delphinium, hosta or iris. When many species within a single genus are being discussed, the abbreviation "ssp." follows the genus.

Colors - These include currently available flower colors. New cultivars are released every year that will add to this list. Many seed and nursery catalogs indicate the latest selections available. For plants grown primarily for foliage, the selection and care guide lists foliage color.

Height - The height of perennials varies considerably from species to species, and from one particular environment to the next. Also, many dwarf cultivars are available. Plants will often be taller in shade or in rich soil. The guide gives the common range for plants in flower. Foliage height may be much less.

Spread - It is necessary to allow sufficient room for perennials to develop properly. Spread tell you the mature spacing recommended between the center of one plant and the center of the next. For a complete look sooner, plant closer together and remove extra plants before crowding occurs.

Bloom Period - The time and duration of flowering for a given perennial is important to consider when designing a garden. Actual dates of bloom can vary up to 3 weeks from year to year, depending on the weather. The dates given are approximate and can vary by a couple of weeks. For plants grown for foliage this is the period of significant ornamental value.

Light - Most perennials prefer full sun to light shade. Some tolerate different light levels, and a few require either full sun or deep shade. The guide indicates the optimum light level or range of light levels for each plant. Three light levels are used: sun, part shade and shade.

Special Notes - This category includes miscellaneous care instructions, suggestions for use and special features, as well as undesirable characteristics. Plants that self-seed may be propagated by transplanting seedlings.

There is no group of plants more versatile and attractive than perennials. The wide range of colors, forms, foliage, bloom times and environmental requirements is such that almost any desired effect can be accomplished. Whether it's a formal or informal border, or a mass planting near a fence or woods, perennials can help you complete your landscape. I have collected for you a varied list of favorite perennials that will all live in New Jersey. Keep in mind that they are "hardy" perennials that will overwinter in our area. As you review the list, try to have a color flower catalog nearby so you can see what they look like. Check off the ones you like best, and then some. The more plants you have, the more surprises and satisfaction you will receive.

Botanical name Common name (s)	Color	Flowering height (feet)	Mature spread and form (inches)	Bloom period	Light	Special notes
Achillea Coronation gold yarrow Fern-leaf yarrow	Yellow	2-4	36; mound	Mid June-October	Sun	Dead-head to prolong flowering. Aromatic foliage. Excellent dried flower.
Achillea hybrids Common yarrow	Pink, white red yellow	1 1/2 - 3	24; spreading mound	Late June-September	Sun	Can be invasive. Dead-head to prolong flowering.
Aconitum spp. Monkshood, Aconite Wolfsbane	Blue yellow	3-5	12-24; mound	August-October	Sun to part shade	All parts of the plant are poisonous. Grows well in moist soil. Needs cool nights.
Adenophora Ladybells	Blue	2-3	Spreading	July-August	Sun to part shade	Durable plant with deep blue flowers. May become invasive.
Ajuga spp. Bugleweed Carpet bugle	Blue purple white	1/2 - 1	9-24; spreading	April-June	Any	Some have variegated or purple foliage. Can be invasive. Commonly used as a ground cover.
Alcea Hollyhock	Orange pink red white yellow	6	Spreading	June-September	Sun	Beautiful, desirable plant. Plant in clumps. Prefer well-drained, neutral to slightly sweet soil.
Anemone X hybrida Windflower Japanese anemone	Pink white	2-4	18-24; mound	August-October	Sun to part shade	Will not grow well in areas with dry summers or wet winters. Protect from wind, use mulch.
Alchemilla Lady's Mantle	Yellow	1 1/2	Spreading	June-August	Sun to part shade	Blends well with other colors. Very hardy and pest resistant.
Anthemis tinctoria Golden Marguerite Yellow chamomile	Yellow white	2	18-24; mound	June-September	Sun	Prune back in late summer. Foliage is fragrant. Dead-head to prolong.
Aquilegia spp. Columbine	All colors	1-3	12; mound	May-July	Sun to part shade	Is short lived but self seeds. Dead-head to prolong flowering. Grows best in moist soils.
Armeria maritima Thrift Sea pink	Pink red white	1/2 - 1	6-12; spreading	May-June	Sun	Grows best in sandy soil. Clumps tend to rot in moist or heavy soils. Tolerates salt.

Botanical name Common name (s)	Color	Flowering height (feet)	Mature spread and form (inches)	Bloom period	Light	Special notes
Artemisia ludoviciana Silver king Silver queen	Silver foliage	2-4	24; mound	May-October	Sun	Excellent dried flower.
Artemisia schmidtiana Silver mound Wormwood	Silver foliage	1-2	18; mound	May-October	Sun	Grown only for its foliage, which is also fragrant. Soil must be well-drained. Do not fertilize.
Aruncus dioicus Goat's-beard	White	5	36-60; mound	June-July	Part shade to shade	Prefers moist soil
Asclepias tuberosa Butterfly weed	Orange	2-3	12; mound	June-August	Sun	Tolerates poor, sandy, dry soil. Attracts butterflies.
Aster Aster	Blue pink purple	2-4	12 spreading	June-October	Sun	Hardy, grow in any soil. Need lots of water.
Astilbe False spirea	Pink red white	2-4	12-24; mound	June-August	Shade	Grows best in deep, fertile soil high in organic matter. Protect from wind.
Aubrieta deltoidea Purple rock cress	Purple	1/2	18-24; spreading	April-June	Sun to part shade	Ground cover. Trim back halfway after flowering. Prefers well drained soil.
Baptisia Wild Indigo	Blue	3-4	24-48; mound	May-June	Sun to part shade	Intense blue flowers. Plants are extremely long-lived in well-drained soil.
Boltonia Boltonia	Pink white	3-5	12-24; upright	August-October	Sun	Looks good with ornamental grasses. Low-maintenance plant with attractive leaves.
Brunnera Siberian forget-me-not	Blue	1 - 1 1/2	12-18; spreading	April-June	Part shade to shade	Can be invasive. Tolerates dry soil and tree roots.
Calamagrostis Feather reed grass	Gold heads	4-6	36; vertical	June-frost	Sun to part shade	Non-spreading ornamental grass. Very showy.
Calamintha Calamint	Purple	1-2	12; spreading	August-October	Sun	Fragrant foliage. Good choice for rock gardens.
Campanula Bluebells	Blue white	1	12; mound	June-August	Sun	Needs good drainage. Good for rock gardens.

Botanical name Common name (s)	Color	Flowering height (feet)	Mature spread and form (inches)	Bloom period	Light	Special notes
Chelone spp. Turtlehead	Pink white	2-3	12-24; mound	August-October	Sun to part shade	Tolerates moist soil.
Chrysanthemum Mum	Many colors	1 - 1 1/2	12-18; spreading	August-October	Sun	Very versatile, showy. Low maintenance.
Convallaria Lily-of-the-valley	White pink	1/2 - 1	6; dense clump	May-June	Part shade to shade	Fragrant flowers. Berries are poisonous. May be invasive.
Coreopsis Tickseed	Yellow pink	1 1/2 - 3	12; mound	June-October	Sun	Dead-head to prolong bloom. Prefers heavy, moist soil.
Crambe Colewort	White	5	48; spreading	June	Sun	Large clusters of flowers. Requires good amount of moisture.
Delphinium Delphinium	Blue laven pink purple white	6	36; upright	June-October	Sun	Large spike of flowers. Require rich soil and protected location.
Dianthus Pink Hardy carnation	Pink red salmon white	1/2 - 1 1/2	12-15; basal	June-August	Sun	Needs fertile, well drained, slightly alkaline soil. Flowers are fragrant.
Dicentra Bleeding-heart	Pink white	2	24; arching stems	May-June	Part shade to shade	Needs rich, moist, well drained soil. Mulching helps.
Digitalis Foxglove	Pink red white yellow	4	6-12; upright	June-July	Sun to part shade	Average to moist rich organic soil. Excellent cut flowers.
Echinacea Purple coneflower	Pink white	3-5	18-24; mound	June-October	Sun to part shade	Needs well drained soil. Fragrant flowers and are excellent for cutting.
Echinops Globe thistle	Blue	3-4	24; mound	July-October	Sun	Tolerates dry soil. Attracts bees.
Epimedium Barrenwort	Pink white yellow red	1/2 - 1	12; spreading	May	Part shade to shade	Good ground cover. Tolerates tree roots.
Eupatorium Joe-pye weed	Purple white pink	4-7	36; upright	August-September	Sun to part shade	Needs moist soil. Fragrant leaves. Butterflies love it.
Euphorbia Spurge	Yellow	1 - 1 1/2	12-18; mound	April-June	Sun	Long-lived. Milky sap may irritate skin.
Galium Sweet woodruff	White	1/2	12; spreading	May-June	Shade	Ground cover. Has fragrant foliage.

Botanical name Common name (s)	Color	Flowering height (feet)	Mature spread and form (inches)	Bloom period	Light	Special notes
Gentiana Gentian	Blue pink white	1/2 - 1	12; spreading	July-October	Sun to part shade	Low growing. Good for front of borders.
Geranium spp. Cranesbill	Blue pink purple red white	1/2 - 1 1/2	12-24; mound	April-August	Sun to part shade	Tolerates alkaline soil. Needs moist but well drained soil.
Grass - Festuca Elijah Blue grass	Blue	1 1/2	10; mound	all year	Sun	Ornamental grass that holds color all year.
Grass - Hakonechloa Aureola	Cream	1	24; arch	all year	Part shade	Ornamental grass that holds color all year.
Gypsophila Baby's breath	Pink white	2-3	24-36; mound	June-frost	Sun	Needs well drained alkaline soil. Excellent cut or dried flower.
Helenium Sneezeweed	Orange yellow	3-5	18; mound	August-October	Sun	Tolerates wet soils. Impervious to pests.
Helianthus Sunflower	Yellow gold	3-5	24; upright	August-October	Sun	May require staking. Good partner for ornamental grasses.
Heliopsis False sunflower	Orange yellow	3-4	24-48; upright	July-October	Sun	Good for the center of an island bed and tolerate dry soils.
Helleborus Christmas rose	Green pink white	1 - 1 1/2	12; mound	March-May	Part shade to shade	Grows best in rich, moist soil. Great for woodland gardens.
Hemerocallis spp. Daylily	Orange pink red yellow	1 1/2 - 4	18-36; upright	June-September	Sun to part shade	Easy to grow and trouble free. Newer cultivars spread less and flower more. Sensational.
Heuchera Coralbells	Pink red white	1-2	12; arching stems	May-August	Part shade to shade	Grows best in moist, well drained soil.
Hibiscus Rose mallow	Pink red white	5-8	24-30; mound	July-August	Sun	Large, shrubby plant. Very large flowers. Tolerant of moisture.
Hosta spp. Plantain lily	Purple white	1-4	30-36; mound	June-September	Part shade to shade	Grows best in moist soil. Grown for variegated foliage.
Iris Bearded iris	Many colors	1/2 - 3 1/2	12-15; upright	May-June	Sun	Cut back to 6 inches in fall. Some cultivars rebloom in fall.
Knautia Knautia	Red	2 1/2 - 3	12; upright	June-September	Sun	Long, wiry stems that blow in wind. Likes well drained soil and dry heat.

Botanical name Common name (s)	Color	Flowering height (feet)	Mature spread and form (inches)	Bloom period	Light	Special notes
Lamiastrum Yellow archangel	Yellow	1/2 - 1 1/2	12-18; spreading	May-June	Any	Ground cover. Can become invasive.
Lamium Dead nettle	Pink white	1/2 - 1	12-18; spreading	May-June	Part shade	Ground cover. Can become invasive.
Lavandula Lavender	Purple white	1-3	18; mound	June-September	Sun to part shade	Trim back in spring. Is resistant to heat and has fragrant flowers.
Lavatera Tree mallow	Pink	6	24-30; mound	June-October	Sun to part shade	Large, shrubby plant. Good combination with ornamental grasses.
Leucanthemum Shasta daisy	White	1-4	12-24; mound	June-September	Sun to part shade	Dead-head to prolong flowering. Do not crowd.
Liatris Blazing-star	Purple white	2-5	12-24; vertical	July-September	Sun to part shade	Excellent for cutting and drying. Looks best planted in groups.
Ligularia spp. Groundsel	Yellow	3-5	36-48; upright	July-August	Part shade	Prefers moist, rich soil and cool temperatures.
Limonium Sea lavender	Purple	2	18-24; basal foliage	July-August	Sun	Salt tolerant. Requires excellent drainage. Excellent dried flower.
Liriope Creeping lilyturf	Purple white	1 - 1 1/2	12; clump	July-August	Sun to part shade	Superb ground cover for dry shade. Will fill out quickly.
Lobelia Indian pink	Red purple	2-4	12-18; vertical	July-September	Part shade	Grows best in moist, acid soil. Mulch in summer.
Lupinus Lupine	All colors	3-4	18-24; upright	May-June	Sun to part shade	Grows best in well drained, moist, acid soils. Sensitive to heat.
Lysimachia Loosestrife	Yellow	2-3	18; mound	June-September	Any	Prefers moist, organic soil. Can become invasive.
Malva Mallow	Blue pink purple white	2-4	24; mound	July-October	Sun	Coarse and weedy but are hardy. Low maintenance.
Mertensia Virginia bluebells	Blue	1/2 - 2	12; mound	April-May	Part shade to shade	Foliage dies down in July.
Monarda Bee balm	Pink red white laven	2 1/2 - 3	12-24; mound	June-August	Sun	Grows best in moist soils. Has fragrant foliage and may become invasive. Attracts hummingbirds.

Botanical name Common name (s)	Color	Flowering height (feet)	Mature spread and form (inches)	Bloom period	Light	Special notes
Oenothera Evening primrose	Yellow	3/4 - 1 1/2	12; spreading	June-September	Sun	Large, open flowers. Are hardy and like well drained soil.
Paeonia Peony	Pink red white	2-3	24-36; mound	May-June	Sun	May require staking. Grows best in deep, fertile soil.
Papaver Oriental poppy	Orange pink red white	1 1/2 - 3	18-24; mound	June	Sun	Best planted in groups. Foliage dies down after flowering.
Penstemon spp. Beard-tongue	Orange pink purple red white	1/2 - 3	12-18; mound	June-August	Sun to part shade	Requires well drained soil and make excellent cut flowers.
Phlox Summer phlox	Blue pink purple red white	2-4	18; vertical	July-September	Sun to part shade	May need staking. Fragrant flowers. Grows best in moist, well drained soil high in organic matter.
Physostegia False dragonhead	Pink white	2-4	24; mound	July-October	Sun tp part shade	May become invasive. Flowers appear on terminal spikes.
Platycodon Balloon flower	Blue pink white	1 1/2 - 4	12-24; upright	July-September	Sun to part shade	May require staking. Prefers acid soil. Absolutely reliable.
Polemonium spp. Jacob's ladder	Blue pink	1 1/2 - 2	9-18; mound	May-August	Any	Prefers moist soil. Dead-head to promote flowering.
Polygonatum spp. Solomon's seal	White	1-4	12-36; arching stems	May-June	Shade	Long-lived and have fragrant leaves. White edges glow in soft light.
Polygonum Smartweed	Pink red	1/2 - 1	12; spreading	May-October	Sun to part shade.	Ground cover. Can be invasive.
Primula Primrose	Many colors	1/2 - 1	6-12; basal foliage	April-June	Varies	Delicate flowers. Prefer moist soil. Good rock garden plant.
Prunella Self-heal	Pink red white	1/2 - 1	12; spreading	June-July	Sun to part shade	Great ground cover for shade. Good for rock gardens and under trees.
Pulmonaria Lungwort	Blue pink	1 - 1 1/2	12-24; spreading	April-June	Part shade to shade	Variegated leaves. Easy to grow and low maintenance.

Botanical name Common name (s)	Color	Flowering height (feet)	Mature spread and form (inches)	Bloom period	Light	Special notes
Rudbeckia Black-eyed Susan Coneflower	Yellow black center	2-3	24; mound	July-September	Sun	One of the best available. Strong and disease resistant.
Salvia Sage	Blue purple white	1-3	12-24; mound	June-September	Sun	Easy to grow and tolerates dry soil.
Sanguisorba Burnet	White Pink	3-5	upright	August-September	Sun to part shade	Dense spikes of flowers. Combine with ornamental grasses.
Saponaria Soapwort	Pink White	1/2 - 1	1; spreading	June-September	Sun	Cut back after flowering. Requires good drainage.
Scabiosa Pincushion	Blue purple white	1 - 1 1/2	12; mound	June-September	Sun	Doesn't like wet soil. Slow growing.
Sedum spp. Stonecrop	Pink red white yellow	1/4 - 1 1/2	6-18; spreading	June-September	Sun	Succulent ground cover that attracts bees. Long-lived.
Sidalcea Checker-mallow	Pink white	3	12-24; mound	June-August	Sun	Dislikes heat and short-lived.
Stokesia Stokes' aster	Blue white	1 - 1 1/2	12-18; mound	July-September	Sun to part shade	Resents wet soil. Good cut flower. Needs good drainage.
Thalictrum Meadow rue	Laven yellow white	3-5	24-36; mound	June-August	Sun to part shade	Long-lived. Prefers moist soil.
Thymus spp. Thyme	Pink white blue	1/4 - 1	12; spreading	June-August	Sun	Ground cover with fragrant foliage. Easy to grow.
Tiarella Foam flower	White	1-2	Clump	May-September	Part shade to shade	Requires a cool, moist area.
Tradescantia Spiderwort	Blu pink purple white	1 1/2 - 3	15-30; mound	June-August	Any	May become invasive. Cut back to ground in fall.
Trollius Globeflower	Yellow orange	2	24-36; mound	June	Sun to part shade	Grows best in rich, moist soil. Beautiful flowers.
Veronica spp. Speedwell	Blue pink purple white	1/2 - 4	12-18; mound or spreading	June-August	Sun to part shade	Tolerates wet soils. Intense blue flowers. Long-lived and trouble free.
Viola spp. Violet	Blue purple red white	1/2 - 1	12; mound	April-June	Part shade to shade	Grows best in moist soil. Flowers are fragrant.

Annuals

Annuals are those garden ornamentals that flower during the first season of growth and then either produce seeds and die or are killed by frost in the fall. Other plants often treated as annuals include biennials (plants normally requiring two years or parts of two years to complete their life cycle) and tender perennials that are unable to withstand winter conditions in the North, although some may withstand light frost. Annuals can provide "instant color" in a landscape and are popular garden flowers. They can put on a splendid show during the summer, are generally easy to grow and inexpensive, and they thrive in a wide range of soil types and climatic conditions.

Annuals can be used alone in a garden in beds or borders, as foundation plantings, in window boxes, in planting tubs, as temporary hedges and screens, and as vines. They can also be used with other herbaceous plants, such as bulbs or perennials, or to fill empty spaces or add color to patios when planted in pots or other containers. Annuals are at their best, however, when planted in large expanses or beds. Depending on location and design, annual flower beds can fill a variety of roles in the garden. Although providing color is their main function, annual flowers have other uses. They can be a continuous source of cut flowers for the house. Flower borders can act as a transition zone or division between two areas of the landscape, such as the patio and lawn. Equally important, annuals are an inexpensive, although temporary, way to landscape. Not only does this allow for endless variety and combinations of colors and shapes, but annuals may also act as fillers before more permanent plants such as perennials, shrubs and trees become established.

Regardless of how annuals are used, they are best in groups of no less than three to five plants. Indeed, annuals are most effective when grown in large groups or varicolored drifts of the same plant, or a variety of plants of the same color. Rarely is a single plant effective because it tends to become lost in the overall landscape. Examples of bright combinations would be a center of red geraniums with a border of blue ageratum, or a center of pink petunias with a border of white sweet alyssum.

Planning An Annual Garden

Proper flower garden planning is very important and considerable thought should be given to it. The garden location will depend on a number of factors: available space, slope, exposure (sunny or shaded), size and shape of the lot, presence of large shade trees, location of adjacent buildings, drainage and soil type. Annuals grow best in full or at least partial sun. Only a few do well in full shade. It is important to plan before digging up a bed. The following ideas should help in choosing an appropriate location.

Unity

The bed should fit into the whole landscape and should not seem out of place. Try these techniques:

- Set the bed into an existing border or foundation planting around the house.
- Continue a line of existing objects, such as walks, walls or fences.
- Reflect the geometric patterns of the house, pavement or existing plantings.
- Use mass planting, putting many plants of a single cultivar together.
- Make the bed large enough so that it does not look like an afterthought.

Variety

Make the bed different from the rest of the yard. Use brightly colored flowers and choose plants of various heights. Plant a bed that juts out slightly from an existing bed. Take care not to make a bed so different that it seems out of place.

Accent

Create focal points in the landscape. Direct the viewer's eye to natural focal points in the yard, such as the front door, a birdbath or a distant view. Consider how the garden will be viewed from windows. Beds planted near focal points such as mailboxes, birdbaths and landscape lights should be broad enough to provide a base and visual balance for the object. Direct the viewer's eye away from poor views. Beds should not be located near garage doors, sheds, compost piles or unattractive neighboring lots.

Softening and Screening

Reduce the impact of unattractive objects or views. Use large flowering plants to hide garbage cans, well covers or compost piles. Large flowering plants, vines or tall flowers such as hollyhocks can soften a blank wall such as the side of a house or garage. Plant low flowers in front of the non-flowering stems of tall flowers and vines. The five steps in designing an annual garden are basically the same as mentioned for designing a perennial garden. However, a wide variety of containers can be used with annuals to make a display, such as tubs, planters, hanging baskets, columns, trees made from several to many hanging containers, jelly jars, free-standing forms of animals and other figures. Some of the smaller containers such as patio pots and tubs are movable so that they can be used in a variety of locations, indoors and outdoors, from patio to porch, balcony or other area. Many kinds of annuals are used as cut flowers in bouquets and floral arrangements. Several are

Marigold

popular for drying, including cockscomb, globe amaranth, honesty, immortelle, statice, strawflowers, summer cypress, unicorn flower and some of the grasses. Most can be dried easily by hanging them upside-down in a dry, airy location out of the sun. Flowers for cutting are often located in a separate garden or location so that they do not detract from other plantings when they are removed. Spacing should be done according to directions, and growing in rows is preferred for easier culture.

Decide if the garden is to be an annual or combination garden. Most gardens are combination gardens containing annuals, bulbs and perennials. Make sure you save space for bulbs and perennials that might be acquired and planted in the fall. You may want to select a few fragrant plants. Two very popular bulbous plants often grown with annuals are tuberous begonias and dwarf dahlias. Other summer-flowering bulbs such as gladioli and caladiums can be combined with annuals as well.

Selecting Annuals

Each annual has a general shape or form. Basic forms are vertical or columnar, such as sunflower, and horizontal or spreading, such as sweet alyssum. Most annuals fall in between these two forms. Use a variety of forms to create the most pleasing effect. Annuals vary in height from about 3 inches tall (alyssum) up to 10 feet tall (sunflower). The standard method of arranging heights is "stair-stepping." Shorter plants are placed in front, medium height plants in the middle and taller plants in the back. Break up this progression a bit to keep the garden interesting and more natural. Be careful not to completely hide smaller plants behind taller specimens. A newly planted bed can look rather bare if plants are spaced at recommended distances for mature specimens. To avoid this bareness, you can cover bare areas with a 2 inch layer of mulch. The plants will quickly fill in the open areas.

Annuals are commonly grouped as coarse, medium or fine texture. Create spatial illusions by using different textures. Plants with coarse textures appear closer than they really are, while those with fine textures recede into the distance. Examples are: coarse texture - hollyhock, sunflower; medium texture - marigold, petunia, wax begonia, zinnia; fine texture - lobelia, sweet alyssum, forget-me-not. Annuals

Sunflower

are noted for their outstanding flower color. An understanding of color and the relationship of colors will allow you to select and arrange species and cultivars to create pleasing and harmonious displays. Warm, vibrant colors, such as red, orange and yellow, tend to stand out in the landscape. They can also make a distance seem shorter. For these reasons, use warm colors as accents or for long-distance viewing. Use them carefully, however, because they are quite intense and can overpower the rest of your garden. Cool, peaceful colors, such as blue, green and purple, tend to recede into the landscape. They are especially effective for close viewing and in masses. I have made a list of annuals that will all live in New Jersey. Pick your favorite ones, and remember, be bold and daring. Annuals only last one year, and if you don't like the way something looks this year, you can try different ones next year. Soil preparation and maintenance are the same as with perennials, so review that section when ready to plant.

Botanical name Common name (s)	Color	Flowering height (inches)	Light	Special notes
Adlumia fungosa Allegheny vine	White pink	Vine to 10 feet	Part shade	Grows best in rich, moist soil. Good screen.
Agapanthus Lily-of-the-Nile	Blue white	18-36	Sun to part shade	Great pot plant. Blooms for at least 2 months.
Ageratum Flossflower	Blue pink white	5-12	Sun	Easy to grow. Good edging plant.
Alonsoa spp. Mask flower	Red orange white	18-36	Sun	Easy to grow. Good cut flower and pot plant.
Amaranthus spp. Love-lies-bleeding	Red yellow	24-72	Sun	Useful as annual hedge. Tolerates dry soil.
Anagallis monelli Pimpernel	Blue purple red	4-18	Sun	Use in rock garden or as edging.
Anchusa capensis summer forget-me-not	Blue white	15-18	Sun to part shade	Good container plant. Requires extra moisture.
Anisodontea African mallow	Pink	24	Sun	Shrub type. Good for large container.
Antirrhinum Snapdragon	Many colors	6-48	Sun to part shade	Excellent cut flower. Cut back for repeat bloom.
Asperula Woodruff	Blue	12	Part shade to shade	Excellent ground cover. Grows best in moist soil.
Begonia Wax begonia	Pink red white	6-12	Sun to part shade	Very reliable. Excellent houseplant.
Brassica oleracea Flowering cabbage	Green pink purple white	12-18	Sun	Is an excellent edger and tolerates frost. Colorful foliage in fall.
Brugmansia Angel's trumpet	Pink white yellow	36-48	Sun to part shade	Enormous, fragrant trumpet-shaped flowers. Can bring them indoors in fall.
Calandrinia spp. Rock purslane	Purple pink red white	6-24	Sun	Tolerates dry soil. Good rock garden plant.
Campanula Canterbury-bells	Blue pink white purple	24-36	Sun	Grown best in moist soil.
Celosia Cockscomb	Orange pink red yellow	6-36	Sun to part shade	Tolerates hot, dry sites. Good dried flowers.
Centaurea Bachelor's-button	Blue pink purple white	15-36	Sun to part shade	Excellent cut or dried flower. Tolerates poor, dry soil. Very easy to grow.

Botanical name Common name (s)	Color	Flowering height (inches)	Light	Special notes
Cleome Spider flower	Pink purple white	36-48	Sun	Can be used as screen. Easy to grow and strongly scented.
Coleus Coleus	Orange pink red white	8-24	Sun to part shade	Has colorful foliage. Excellent houseplant.
Collinsia spp. Blue-eyed Mary	White pink purple blue	18-24	Shade	Easy to grow. Good potting and rock garden plant.
Collomia spp. Collomia	Red pink cream	12-24	Sun	Easy to grow. Good rock garden plant.
Coreopsis Annual coreopsis	Orange pink purple yellow	8-36	Sun to part shade	Self-seeding. Tolerates poor soil.
Cosmos Cosmos	Orange pink white yellow	12-48	Sun to part shade	May require staking. Grows in poor soil. Tolerates heat and drought.
Cymbalaria Kenilworth ivy	Purple white	4-6	Sun to part shade	Tolerates alkaline soil. Excellent in hanging baskets.
Dahlia Bedding dahlia	Many colors	12-24	Sun	Excellent cut flower. Deadhead to promote flowering.
Dianthus Sweet William	Pink red white	6-24	Sun	Excellent edging plant. Prefers alkaline soil.
Diascia Twinspur	Pink orange	9-12	Sun	Good in rock gardens or in pots. Easy to grow.
Dorotheanus Livingstone daisy	Many colors	3-8	Sun	Good ground cover. Grows in poor sandy soil.
Dyssodia Dahlberg daisy	Orange yellow	4-12	Sun	Prefers sandy soil.
Echium lycopsis Viper's bugloss	Blue purple white	12-36	Sun	Good in rocky soils. Attracts bees.
Emilia javanica Flora's paintbrush	Orange yellow	12-24	Sun	Tolerates salt, heat and drought. Good cut flower.
Exacum Persian violet	Blue purple white	8-24	Part shade	Excellent pot plant. Fragrant flowers. Likes moist, well drained soil.
Felicia Blue marguerite	Blue	6-8	Sun	Excellent window box plant. Likes hot conditions.
Fuchsia spp. Fuchsia	Pink purple red white	12-48	Shade	Excellent flowering pot plant. Often used in hanging baskets.

Botanical name Common name (s)	Color	Flowering height (inches)	Light	Special notes
Gazania Treasure flower	Yellow	6-8	Sun	Leaves are covered with fine white hairs. Great for window box. Drought tolerant.
Gerbera Transvaal daisy, gerber daisy	Many colors	15-24	Sun	Excellent cut flower and often used in containers.
Gomphrena Globe amaranth	Orange pink purple white	6-24	Sun	Excellent dried flower.
Gypsophila Baby's-breath	Pink white	12-24	Sun	Excellent cut or dried flower.
Helianthus annuus Sunflower	Red white yellow	15-72	Sun	Tolerates heat and useful as screen.
Helichrysum Strawflower	Orange pink red white	12-36	Sun	Excellent dried flower. Prefers sandy soil.
Heliotropium Heliotrope	Blue purple white	12-72	Sun	Fragrant flowers.
Helipterum spp. Sunray, everlasting	Pink white yellow	24	Sun	Excellent dried flower.
Hypoestes Freckle-face	Pink white	12-24	Sun to part shade	Good pot plant. Pinch frequently to keep bushy.
Iberis Candytuft	Pink purple white	8-15	Sun to part shade	Very easy to grow. Flowers quickly in cool weather.
Impatiens Lady slipper	Many colors	8-24	Sun to shade	Very easy to grow. Prefers rich, light soil.
Impatiens wallerana / hybrids New Guinea	Many colors	8-24	Sun to part shade	Good winter pot plant. Pinch back for bushy plants.
Justicia Brazilian plume	Pink	36-48	Sun to part shade	Superb plant for an urn. Requires good garden soil.
Lantana Yellow sage	Orange pink white yellow	12-48	Sun	Tolerates salt. Good plant for pots. Deadhead to promote flowering.
Lathyrus Sweet pea	Many colors	8-30	Sun	Fragrant flowers. Some varieties climb to 10 feet. Requires support. Excellent cut flower.
Limonium Sea lavender	Blue pink purple	12-24	Sun	Excellent cut and dried flower.
Lobelia Lobelia	Blue pink red white	4-10	Sun to shade	Good for hanging baskets. Excellent for edging.

Botanical name Common name (s)	Color	Flowering height (inches)	Light	Special notes
Lobularia Sweet alyssum	Purple white pink	3-10	Sun	Good groundcover. Quick to bloom.
Malcolmia Virginia stock	Pink purple white	4-8	Sun to shade	Gray foliage with fragrant flowers. Use as edging plant.
Myosotis Forget-me-not	Blue pink white	6-24	Part shade	Grows best in moist soil.
Nemophila Baby-blue-eyes	Blue white	6-12	Sun to part shade	Use as an edging or in a rock garden.
Nierembergia Cupflower	Purple white	6-12	Sun	Good flowering pot plant. Ideal for edging a border.
Nolana Chilean bellflower	Blue	4-12	Sun	Tolerates drought. Good for edging and in hanging baskets.
Osteospermum Osteospermum	White blue	12-18	Sun	Daisy shaped flowers. Beautiful in any garden or container.
Otacanthus Brazilian Snapdragon	Blue	36-48	Sun	Fragrant foliage from spring to frost. Good for large container.
Pennisetum Fountain grass	Pink bronze	24-48	Sun	Graceful form and showy seed heads. Good centerpiece in a container.
Penstemon spp. Beard-tongue	Pink purple white blue	24-36	Sun	Requires ample moisture. Good cut flower and can be used in rock gardens.
Petunia Petunia	Many colors	10-18	Sun to part shade	Easy to grow. Excellent in beds or baskets.
Phlox Annual phlox	Pink purple red white	6-15	Sun	Easy to grow. Drought resistant and tolerates poor, sandy soil. Deadhead to encourage flowering.
Polygonum Knotweed	Pink red	3-4	Sun	Spreads and is useful as a ground cover.
Rudbeckia hirta Black-eyed Susan	Orange yellow	24-36	Sun to part shade	Tolerates heat and drought.
Salvia Scarlet sage	Red pink purple white	10-30	Sun	Very striking flowers. Attracts hummingbirds.
Schizanthus spp. Butterfly flower	Orange pink purple white	10-24	Sun to part shade	Good potting plant.
Senecio Dusty-miller	Silver foliage	8-15	Sun	Silver, woolly leaves. Excellent edging plant.
Tagetes spp. Marigold	Many colors	8-36	Sun	Many forms and heights. Very easy to grow. Foliage odor may repel pests.

Botanical name Common name (s)	Color	Flowering height (inches)	Light	Special notes
Thunbergia Black-eyed Susan vine	Orange white yellow	Vine to 6 feet	Sun to part shade	Good ground cover. Can use in hanging baskets.
Tibouchina Glory bush	Purple	36-48	Sun	Flowers August to frost. Very large blooms that attract butterflies. Superb for container.
Tithonia Mexican sunflower	Orange yellow	24-64	Sun	Very vigorous and tolerates heat. Excellent cut flower. Can be used as an annual hedge.
Torenia Wishbone flower	Blue purple	8-12	Sun to part shade	Excellent potting plant that tolerates heat.
Tropaeolum Nasturtium	Orange pink red white yellow	6-12	Sun to part shade	Flowers may be fragrant. Grows best in poor soil. Tolerates drought.
Tropaeolum Vine Canary-bird vine	Orange red yellow	Vine to 10 feet	Sun to part shade	Makes a good quick screen. Blooms from June to frost. Climbs through trellises, shrubs and hedges.
Ursinia spp. Sphenogyne	Orange yellow	8-24	Sun	Silver foliage with fragrant flowers. Is a good potting plant.
Vaccaria Soapwort	White pink	24-30	Sun	Excellent cut flower.
Venidium Cape daisy	Orange & black	18-24	Sun	Silver foliage.
Verbena Verbena	Blue pink red white	8-16	Sun to part shade	Spreading habit. Good winter pot plant. Fragrant flowers and tolerates heat. Useful in baskets and rock gardens.
Viola spp. Johnny-jump-up, tufted pansy	blue orange purple red yellow	4-12	Sun to part shade	Very colorful. Nice to have in any garden, container or hanging basket.
Xeranthemum Immortelle	Pink red white purple	24-36	Sun	Gray foliage. An excellent dried flower.
Zinnia spp. Youth-and-old-age	Orange pink purple red white	4-48	Sun	Many flower forms and heights. Quick and easy to grow. Excellent cut flower.

Annuals for the Beginner	Annuals for Poor Soil	Annuals for Dry & Hot Conditions	Annuals for Moist & Cool Conditions
Ageratum	Love-lies-bleeding	Cockscomb	Pot marigold
Cockscomb	Cockscomb	Cornflower	Canterbury bells
Spider flower	Cornflower	Spider flower	Pink
Calliopsis	Spider flower	Calliopsis	Globe candytuft
Cosmos	Calliopsis	Cape marigold	Sweet pea
Sweet alyssum	Livingstone daisy	Livingstone daisy	Monkey flower
Petunia	Morning glory	Snow-on-the-mountain	Forget-me-not
Annual Phlox	Sweet alyssum	Baby's breath	Baby blue-eyes
Marigold	Poppies	Statice	Wishbone flower
Nasturtium	Nasturtium	Poppies	Verbena
Zinnia		Annual phlox	
		Scarlet sage	
		Zinnia	

Annuals for Shade or Full Sun	Annuals for Shade	Annuals for Edging	Annuals for Cut Flowers
Wax begonia	Woodruff	Ageratum	Snapdragon
Periwinkle	Wax begonia	Pimpernel	Pot marigold
Sweet alyssum	Job's tears	English daisy	China aster
Forget-me-not	Coleus	Sweet William	Cornflower
Violet	Foxglove	False blue flax	Chrysanthemum
Pansy	Persian violet	Lobelia	Clarkia
	Fuchsia	Sweet alyssum	Calliopsis
	Impatiens	Virginia stock	Cosmos
	Monkey flower	Baby blue-eyes	Stock
	Forget-me-not	Chilean bellflower	Love-in-a-mist
	Primrose	Creeping zinnia	Painted tongue
	Mignonette	Dusty-miller	Pincushions
		Marigold	Marigold
			Verbena
			Pansy
			Zinnia

Annual Vines	Annual Hedges	Annuals for Hanging Baskets	My Favorite Annuals
Balloon vine	Amaranthus	Kenilworth ivy	Cockscomb
Cup-and-saucer vine	Snowcup	Glory flower	Calliopsis
Glory flower	Sweet wormwood	Fuchsia	Petunia
Moonflower	Spider flower	Heliotrope	Marigold
Morning glory	Angel's trumpet	Impatiens	Zinnia
Sweet pea	Sunflower	Morning glory	Begonia
Purple bell vine	Tree mallow	Lobelia	Pansy
Black-eyed Susan vine	Mexican sunflower	Chilean bellflower	Morning glory
Canary-bird vine		Ivy geranium	Impatiens
		Petunia	Lobelia
		Creeping zinnia	Sunflower
		Black-eyed Susan vine	Snapdragon
		Verbena	Cosmos

Vines & Climbers

Climbing plants can be divided into two categories: those that climb on their own and those that need our help to direct themselves upward. The ability of this group is to provide vertical accents, color and beauty in the garden and on a wide range of structures, such as, arbors, trellises, garages, fences, posts, walls and gates. Climbing plants reach up beyond the level of our eyes and elevate the garden to wherever we choose. They greatly increase the apparent size of the small garden, giving it a third dimension. Whenever we want to camouflage an ugly wall or post, there is a climber that will do the trick. Vines soften and bring romance into a garden as they wind through colorful shrubs or flowers, fences or trellises. An area that needs some summer shade is an ideal place for a vine as its foliage help block the sun and its flowers light the area with color. Flowering vines can, with good effect, be grown up trees or intermingled with climbing or shrub-type roses, providing interesting color and color contrasts. Climbing plants are very versatile, convenient and low maintenance.

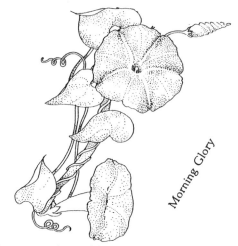

Morning Glory

Vines are of great value but often have been neglected because many gardeners fail to realize their potential. Vines lend themselves admirably to vertical structures found in contemporary gardens. They partially cover and blend the structures with other plantings. Certain vines with coarse foliage or dense habit of growth are useful on fences or arbors. These vines are also used for screening objectionable views, either permanently or temporarily, until other plantings are large enough to achieve the effect desired. They may also be used to give shade and privacy to a porch. They will break the monotony of a long fence or stone wall, and can be trained to form a definite pattern on a blank wall. Properly selected and used, vines can contribute greatly, both to the beauty of your property and to your enjoyment of gardening.   Vines are used in contemporary designs to soften the harsh lines of space dividers or baffles. On steep banks or under shade trees where grass can be grown only with difficulty, or not grown at all, certain vines, such as ivy, make great ground covers. In areas where space is very limited and high shrubs would require too much room, they can be used instead of shrubbery to achieve the effect of a narrow space divider or barrier. Carefully consider the use to which a vine is to be put before making any selection. In some cases, it might be desirable to cover an entire fence with a solid mass of foliage, so you want a vine with dense foliage. To add pattern and interest to a stone wall without entirely covering it, a slower growing type with interesting leaves would be more desirable. A vine with fragrant flowers certainly should be considered for a porch or patio, or near a window that is frequently opened.

Vines are divided into three types according to their method of climbing - whether by tendrils, twining or clinging. The kind of support to be provided will largely determine the type of vine to be selected. The grape is probably the best known of the vines that climb by means of tendrils. These are slim, flexible shoots - or in some cases, leaflike parts that act as tendrils - that quickly wrap themselves around anything with which they come in contact to support the vine for further growth. The twining vines climb by winding their stems around any available support. These two types are suited to climbing on wires, trellises or arbors. They can be grown on flat surfaces only if proper supports are provided

for them. The climbing vines are better adapted to climbing on even, vertical surfaces. These fall into two types. One, such as the Japanese creeper (*Parthenocissus tricuspidata*), climbs by means of tendrils with disk-like adhesive tips that attach themselves firmly to any surface, even glass. The other type, like the English ivy (*Hedera helix*), climbs by means of small aerial rootlets, or holdfasts, at intervals along the stems. These dig themselves into the crevices of any rough-textured surface, such as brick, and cling tightly. When allowed to trail on the ground or climb in the joints of a dry-laid stone wall, they will root and form new plants.

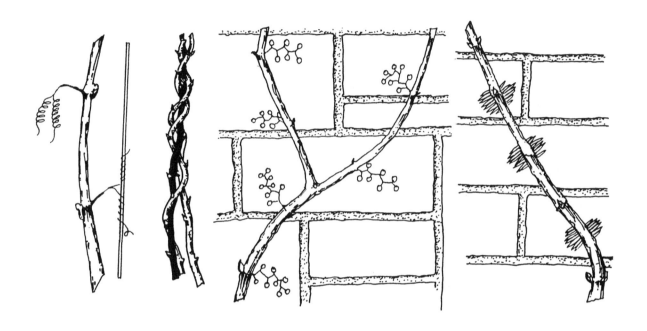

Some vines climb by means of tendrils.

The twining vines climb by wrapping their stems around any available support.

Some vines climb with tendrils having disk-like adhesive tips that stick to even flat surfaces.

Other vines have small aerial rootlets that dig into the crevices of rough-textured surfaces.

Clinging vines are best used on brick or masonry walls. They should never be used on the walls of frame buildings as their method of climbing might damage the wood of the structure. Also, they cling so closely to the wall that dampness is likely to collect under them and rot the wood. If, however, vines seem desirable in certain cases, the trellis on which they are trained should be far enough from the siding to allow air to circulate freely behind the vine. The trellis should be removable so that it may be laid on the ground to permit painting of the siding without damaging the vine. Supports of some kind are essential in growing vines and must be sturdily constructed of durable materials. It is discouraging to see a beautiful, healthy vine ruined after several years growth because the structure on which it is trained has collapsed. A little care and thought in building is well worth the time.

Maintenance

Flowering vines need time and warm weather to grow and twine up before they burst into bloom. You can give them a head start by starting their seeds indoors about 4 to 6 weeks before the last frost date. Then transplant your seedlings into the garden when the weather is warm and temperatures both day and night have risen into the 50s. This way, they'll have enough growing time to bloom beautifully in late summer, when other annual flowers are spent. Otherwise, seeds can be sown directly into prepared ground when the weather is warm and settled. Flowering vines are at their best on a fence, trellis or arbor. Climbing plants are usually less vulnerable to diseases and insect pests than flowers or shrubs. Usually, a heavy spray of the leaves discourages any invading insects. When pruning climbing plants, the right location must be chosen and the right time of year. It would be helpful if you are familiar with the blooming characteristics of the plant. Always prune just above a node (growing point). As when pruning shrubs, cut back to the bud that is pointing in the direction you want the growth to go. To open up a dense plant, cut just above a bud facing outward. To fill in a thin plant cut back just above a bud facing inward. Usually, climbing plants that flower in the spring bloom on the previous year's growth and should be pruned after they have bloomed to allow new growth time to get ready for winter. Those plants that flower in summer or fall bloom on the present year's growth and should be pruned in late fall to early winter when the plant is dormant or the following spring before new growth becomes visible.

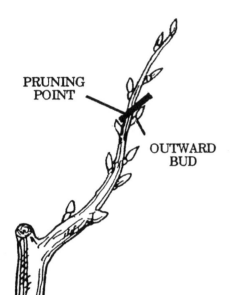

PRUNING POINT

OUTWARD BUD

Certain vines grow and climb so vigorously that dense foliage can slow air circulation and block the sunlight from reaching inner branches. If left untended, these plants may even die leaving you with a big mess to cleanup and discard. These vines should be thinned out. Generally, the best time to thin out any climbing plant is in the summer. If you are expecting a severe upcoming winter, however, thin out in late spring to allow new growth to strengthen before winter arrives. Cut out any unhealthy or dead branches first. Step back and take a look. Sometimes, this is all that is necessary. If it is still crowded, cut off any thin shoots (suckers) at the point of origin and any large ones right at ground level. If a lot of thinning is necessary for the plant to survive, cut back as much as you feel is necessary, but be selective or you may loose everything.

Inspect climbing plants on a regular basis for signs of disease or insect pests. If any branches are diseased, cut back to a healthy part of the branch. The whole branch does not have to be removed. Remove any dead branches or stems as they invite pests and disease. Do not let diseased parts lay on the ground as the disease could spread to the base of the plant. Dispose of them in the garbage. Also disinfect your pruning tools with bleach before pruning another plant. If the roots of your climbing plant are spreading out too far and becoming invasive in other areas, it may be necessary to prune their roots. By severing the outside feeder roots, you curb the growth and may stimulate flowering. Prune the long

shallow roots 5 to 6 feet from the base of the plant using a long garden spade and push straight down. If you want to prune most of the roots to avoid invasion, cut a trench about 6 to 10 inches deep with the same spade in a complete circle or half circle, depending on allowed space, around the plant. The following climbing plants or vines will all grow in New Jersey. Some are annuals and others are perennials, but all will brighten and beautify your landscape.

Actinidia - Arctic Beauty Kiwi - This is a very hardy plant that has uniquely decorated leaves. They start pink, become white in the middle, then green at the base, for a wonderful tricolor effect. This elegant combination lasts from one end of the season to the other. Lighting requirements are full sun to partial shade. The average plant grows 15-20 feet in good garden soil. The handsome leaves have all the appeal of flowers. One of the best vines for covering an arbor.

Aristolochia - Dutchman's Pipe - This is a vigorous vine known for its large heart-shaped leaves. Once established, it completely takes over fences, walls and just about anything, with its twining stems and thick foliage. It is a good shade and privacy plant if trained on a trellis, arbor or high fence. The brownish purple tubular flowers resemble a Dutchman's pipe. This vine grows 20-30 feet in full sun to partial shade in moist soil. If heavy, dense shade is desired, this is the vine for you.

Campsis - Trumpet Creeper - A perfect perennial vine to be used alone on posts, fences or clambering through shrubs and trees or following wire frames in flower beds. Trumpet creepers beautify the landscape with their spectacular blooms and graceful behavior. Easy to grow and virtually maintenance free, they make life a little easier for the gardener. Hummingbirds are attracted to the red trumpet-shaped blooms in summer. They have large leaves and grow rapidly attaching themselves to whatever lies in their path, and need strong support. They are easy to grow in almost any soil in sun or partial shade.

Clematis - Clematis - A perennial that can bloom in spring, summer and fall. The vines grow fast and are easy to train along any support. Just face them in the direction you want them to go. They like rich, well-drained soil and prefer full sun to partial shade. Clematis is a great performer and can have blue, pink, purple, red or white fragrant flowers. The blooms in July and August are absolutely gorgeous. Clematis can be used alone on posts, fences or trellises or allowed to clamber through shrubs, or follow wire frames in flower beds. They enrich any landscape with their graceful behavior and glorious blooms. I would not recommend using a heavy mulch in summer, as this can promote Clematis wilt.

Lonicera - Honeysuckle - A tough, hardy perennial that climbs by twining. The red trumpet-like blossoms are a favorite of hummingbirds in June and July. The flowers are profuse and very fragrant, and the vine can grow up to 20 feet. Can be used on a porch or any other structure. Honeysuckle can become invasive so it needs plenty of training to keep it from spreading everywhere. Aphids like Honeysuckle, so be prepared in spring for a battle. They are easy to grow and virtually maintenance free, except for training. This plant compliments almost any garden.

Ipomoea - Morning-Glory - This is an annual vine that will twine vigorously on any support offered to them. They do best in full sun as they like heat. The brilliant large blossoms open every morning and are particularly attractive to hummingbirds. Certain varieties can grow easily in a large pot with well-drained soil and something to twine around. This is an excellent plant to be used on fences, trellises or posts. The only difficulty may be in starting the seed. When the soil is warm, soak the seeds overnight and plant them the next day. A fast growing member of the morning glory family is the "Moonvine" or Moonflower. In the late afternoon, the flowers start to unfurl and by night they are in full bloom. Your summer evenings will be filled with a delightful fragrance. This plant likes full sun and average soil.

Hydrangea - Climbing Hydrangea - This is a vigorous, perennial vine that has smooth foliage and fragrant white flowers in summer. It is an excellent covering for a wall, fence or rock garden. It can grow on practically any structure and gives a lovely display. Be careful though, as it clings with holdfasts and may weaken mortar. Climbing hydrangea is slow starting but can grow up to 50 feet. It grows best in sun to partial shade and rich, well-drained soil. Hydrangea is attractive in winter because of its bark and arrangement. Lateral branches shoot out up to 3 feet from the support, giving a rich texture.

Wisteria - Wisteria - This plant is very useful in many different settings. The woody vine has lovely and astonishing fragrant flowers that grow in clusters up to 1 foot long. These vines are very strong, so a sturdy structure is required, preferably metal. The vines wind together and form small trunks several inches thick. Plants grow rapidly as long as 25 ft. and can completely smother any structure. The vigorous growth can be controlled by severe pruning, sometimes twice a year. The pruning also encourages flowering. No matter how much you cut, it usually comes back. This is a low maintenance plant, except for the pruning, and has blooms that range from white to purple red to very deep purple.

Bulbs

The term bulb has come to include a wide range of plants that are herbaceous perennials. They require a dormant period, during which there remains a large storage root or stem from which the plant will grow again the following year. Flowering bulbs are an essential component of the well planned garden or landscape, adding interest and bright colors in a way that shrubbery and other herbaceous plants cannot. Here in New Jersey, our climate is well suited to growing many hardy and tender flowering bulbs. Bulbs that are planted outdoors in the fall and flower in spring are called hardy bulbs because they will survive very low temperatures over winter. Hardy bulbs include tulip, daffodil, crocus, hyacinth, lily and many others. Not all "hardy" bulbs can survive deep soil freezing. Tender bulbs such as dahlia and gladiolus must be dug and stored indoors over winter and replanted every year.

Plants included under the term "bulb" include true bulbs such as lily, ornamental onions and tulips; corms such as crocus and gladiolus; and tubers, including tuberous begonias and dahlias. Millions of bulbs are sold in the United States each year, for very good reasons. Bulbs are *easy to grow*. Most bulbs contain a preformed flower bud and all the food required for blooming when purchased. It takes minimal skill to make bulbs bloom, provided a good site is selected. In addition, bulbs are generally maintenance-free and pest free when planted properly and given a bit of fertilizer. Bulbs are *colorful*. A chief attraction of all bulbs is that they provide color. Spring-flowering bulbs provide color from early March,

before many trees and shrubs bloom, through June, when annuals are planted. Summer bulbs help fill out the garden from June through September. Bulbs are *inexpensive*. Most common bulbs are relatively inexpensive. They are considerably cheaper when purchased in quantity, and hardy species can last for many years. Bulbs are *flexible*. Bulbs are relatively small and may be moved, if required, so they are flexible landscape components. Bulbs fit in around existing shrubbery, in wooded areas, in rock gardens and in other niches where they add interest to a landscape. Bulbs are *compatible*. Bulbs are excellent mixers. They combine especially well with spring-flowering perennials. Spring bulbs are often over-planted with annuals to hide their dying foliage. No garden or landscape reaches its full potential without a few of these plants.

Structure of Bulbs

Bulbs are underground food storage organs that contain large amounts of stored carbohydrates. This food source is often used up during the blooming period and is replenished by the bulb's leaves before they turn yellow or are killed by frost in the fall. True bulbs such as tulip and lily are made up of many swollen leaf bases growing close together below the soil surface. Carbohydrates are stored in the leaf scales. Inside is a very small preformed flower called the flower primordium. Barring a very poor environment, the flower primordium will mature and bloom. Bulbs that do not bloom are called "blind."

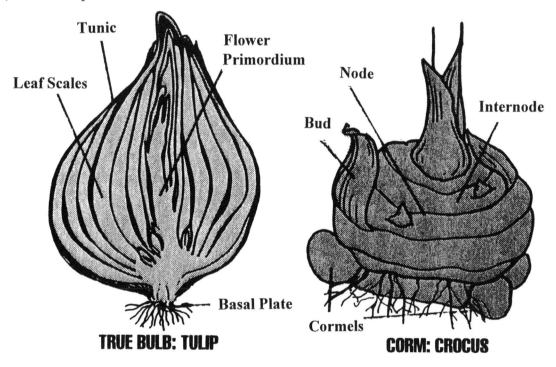

TRUE BULB: TULIP   **CORM: CROCUS**

The flattened base of a true bulb is called the basal plate. It is the area from which all roots originate and should always be planted down. Last year's withered stem may linger on the top side of the bulb. An undamaged bulb is often covered by a thin papery sheath or tunic. Corms, from which crocus and gladiolus grow, are actually swollen stems and have nodes, internodes and lateral buds growing from the nodes. A new corm forms atop the old one each year, and clusters of small corms, called cormels, grow around the base. Flowering stems grow from several buds on top of the corm.

On very flat corms, such as those of anemone, it may be quite difficult to distinguish top from bottom. Look for last year's shriveled stem, and plant it upward. Tubers, such as tuberous begonias and dahlia, are swollen roots that have one to several eyes at one end near the old stem. Unless an eye is present, a tuber cannot grow.

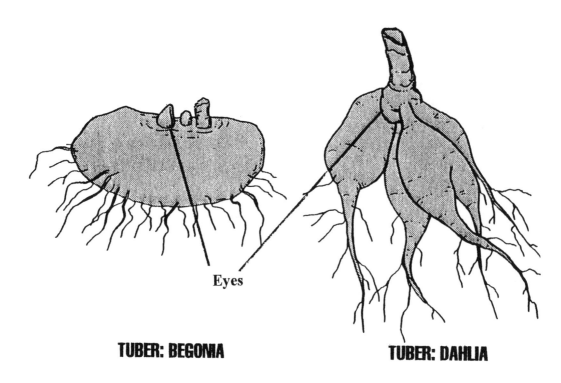

Eyes

TUBER: BEGONIA   **TUBER: DAHLIA**

Buying Bulbs

Bulbs are required by law to be pest and disease free and to undergo routine inspection by the state Departments of Agriculture before being put on the shelf to be sold. Many bulbs are imported from the Netherlands and are inspected by the U.S. Department of Agriculture before shipment.

When buying bulbs, keep the following tips in mind. *Look for large bulbs.* The larger the bulb, the more food is available to nurture developing blossoms. Larger bulbs usually cost more, but they also produce more and larger flowers. Smaller bulbs can be quite satisfactory in your garden, but below a certain size, they may not bloom the year that they are planted, though they should in future years. Bulbs are often graded and sold by circumference. Many hybrid daffodils, however, are graded by weight because a single bulb may actually consist of two or more bulbs united at their base, resulting in a form that cannot be measured by circumference. *Avoid root plate damage.* Look at the bottom side of each bulb. If it's nicked or scarred, do not purchase it because root growth may be poor. Lily bulbs should have a few large, firm roots still attached to the basal plate. *Avoid moldy and shrivelled bulbs.* Mold or decay indicates poor quality or disease. Shrivelling indicates water loss, which is often due to improper storage. Bulbs should be firm and plump. *Avoid soft or sour-smelling bulbs.* Occasionally, a

bulb (tulip especially) may look normal but has lost most of its weight to a fungal disease. Such bulbs will not bloom and should be avoided. *Buy from a reputable source*. Word-of-mouth can lead you to a reliable garden center. Mail order is also a popular route. Several bulb catalogs are listed in the "Mail-Order Sources" section at the end of this book. Gardening neighbors can be a source of bulbs, too. *Buy in quantity*. Often, the more bulbs you buy, the lower the price per bulb will be. Try ordering with a friend or several neighbors to get the discount. Prebagged bulbs are often the best bargain in garden shops, but they may be damaged by improper storage. This is a problem particularly with lilies and dahlias. On the other hand, by buying prebagged bulbs, you avoid bulbs that have accidentally fallen into the wrong box in a bulk, pick-your-own display. *Be wary of sales*. There are good sales and bad sales. An early-season discount is probably a good buy. But a picked-over late season sale may net you only low-quality shrivelled bulbs along with a few saved dollars. As with most seasonal items, the earlier you shop, the better the selection, but you are likely to pay the full price.

Many bulbs are available in several cultivars. Horticultural varieties may differ not only in color, but also in height. flower form, fragrance and time of bloom. Check the commercial descriptions of named varieties to be sure the plants fit your requirements. Some species of bulbs have an unusually large number of cultivars that have the same general origin but differ greatly because of extensive breeding and selection. In these cases, cultivars with similar characteristics are grouped in divisions or classes. Daffodils, dahlias, tuberous begonias and tulips are often described this way. Recognizing the similarities and differences between hybrid varieties can add to the pleasure of growing bulbs. Tulip hybrids are classified into divisions based on time of bloom and type of flower. Daffodils are grouped by the American Daffodil Society on the basis of flower form. In a daffodil flower, the center part, which may be a long tube or a short disk, is called the trumpet or cup. The circle of petals surrounding the cup is the perianth. Like all members of the daisy family, dahlia flowers are inflorescences composed of hundreds of individual flowers. Each petal is really a single ray flower, and the central yellow disk is made up of many disk flowers. The American Dahlia Society recognizes 14 classes of dahlias based on flower form. In addition, growers further divide those classes by flower size, from AA (over 10 inches in diameter) to P (less than 2 inches). The flower forms of the Tuberous Begonia are unusual. Several flower forms can appear on the same plant, but under good conditions, one type should predominate. Separate male and female flowers occur on the same plant as well. Female flowers are small and may produce seeds and male flowers are large and showy.

Bulbs in the Landscape

Before ambition runs away with your pocketbook in the garden center, be sure you have a master plan in mind. Like annuals and perennials, bulbs can be used in the landscape in many ways. The same methods for creating a garden plan, as mentioned before for annuals and perennials, can be used for a bulb garden.

Beds - The most frequent use of bulbs is in flower beds. Plan the bulbs as a permanent feature, although they may be moved, if necessary. Some large bulbs can be striking when planted singly, but most are more attractive and noticeable when planted in groups of six or more. Never plant in straight rows in a display garden.

Containers - Window boxes and patio containers of summer-flowering bulbs are very popular. For example, tuberous begonias, calla lilies and caladiums can be planted in containers in lightly shaded areas. Spring-flowering bulbs are less commonly grown in containers outdoors because they may freeze over winter if the container is left aboveground. Although the bulbs are hardy, they cannot survive if frozen completely. However, if you sink the container in the ground in fall and unearth it in spring, you may avoid freezing the bulbs.

Foundation Plantings - Bulbs easily fit in among shrubs and are commonly used to add color to a shrubbery border along the walls of a house. However, many bulbs do not grow as well where tree and shrub roots compete with them for food and water.

Grassy Plantings - Some homeowners find it delightful to have early-blooming bulbs pop up through the lawn. Although it's not a problem for the grass, this may be impractical because such areas should be left unmowed until bulb foliage begins to yellow, often in mid-June. Leaves must be left on a bulb to make food to build up the bulb for next year's flowers.

Cutting Garden - Here belong all your leftovers from other plantings or old groups you have divided. No design is necessary, and bulbs are planted in rows because this garden is not for visual display but to provide cut flowers for the table and house.

Naturalized Areas & Rock Gardens - To naturalize, toss a handful of bulbs on the ground as if you were sowing grass seed. Then plant them in whatever random pattern they land. No manmade rows or clusters here, bulbs appear in natural "drifts" or "waves." Naturalized plantings are perhaps best suited for wooded areas, side yards and other open, low-traffic locations. The shortest bulbs work well in rock gardens where the effect is due to an interesting grouping rather than a mass of color.

Growing Bulbs

Good hardy bulbs contain all the ingredients to bloom the year after planting and will do so if they are planted in a well drained area and are not damaged by animals. If the area remains puddled or soggy several hours after a normal rain, it is probably poorly drained. In wet soil, bulb roots may stop growing and rot. The site should also receive at least six hours of full or partial sun each day. Less sun will keep the bulb from making adequate food to support next year's bloom. A few bulbs prefer a shady site, such as tuberous begonia and caladium. Deciduous trees do not normally create enough shade in May and June to interfere with food production of spring-flowering bulbs. Bulbs will tolerate most types of soil, although one rich in organic matter is preferred. Improve organic content by adding well composted manure, leaf mold, peat moss or compost; add fertilizer as described in the next section, and work the soil to a depth of 8 to 10 inches before planting.

When setting bulbs out, be careful to plant at the correct depth below the soil surface, measured from the top of the bulb. Generally, the larger the bulb, the deeper it is planted. Hardy bulbs are set deep to survive winter's cold, usually at a depth 2 1/2 times their size, but most tender bulbs are planted close to the soil surface. Consult the planting guide for specific depths.

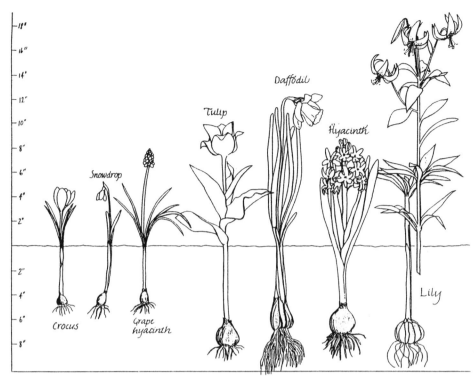

Plant a little deeper in very sandy soil, and a little shallower in heavy soil. A hand trowel is commonly used to spotplace one bulb at a time, but stainless steel tubular bulb planters are also popular. Bulb planters usually have depth measurements etched in the surface to help ensure proper planting depth. This tool comes as a hand planter or on a long handle, an excellent idea for large gardens or for gardeners with back problems. Push the planter into the soil to the proper level. Then scoop the soil out of the hole, using wrist action. Drop the bulb in, basal plate down, and replace the soil. After planting, water to encourage root development.

Most hardy bulbs may be purchased only in autumn, but lilies and some alliums are also available in spring. Some catalogs now offer prechilled bulbs that may be planted in spring and will bloom immediately. All hardy bulbs should be planted as soon as possible after they are obtained. For best results, bulbs should be in the ground by mid-October. Some, such as tulip, may be successfully planted until the soil freezes. There is no harm in planting early, even if some growth occurs. Rarely, a new bulb will produce leaves in fall but not flowers. Existing clumps of bulbs may be moved any time after the leaves have died back and bulbs are fully dormant. Summer-flowering bulbs are available for purchase in late winter through late summer, depending on the plant. Some, like tuberous begonias, are started indoors. No tender bulbs should be planted outdoors until the soil has warmed to 65° F average temperature and danger of frost is past.

Flowering the second or third year after planting is influenced by previous and continuing care. To thrive, bulbs must be able to "fill out", to replace food reserves used in growth and flowering each year. At planting time, mix in a slow-release fertilizer high in phosphates, such as bone meal (1-11-0) or a complete commercial bulb fertilizer such as 5-10-5 at the rate of 2 pounds/100 square feet. Bone meal is recommended at 5 to 6 pounds per 100 square feet or 1 ounce (2 tablespoons) per square foot. New research indicates that nitrogen is much more important to bulbs than previously thought. Although it's not essential, some gardeners like to fertilize hardy bulbs again in spring to give the roots a quick burst

of energy and success for subsequent seasons. Use a complete fertilizer such as 5-10-5 or 12-12-12 at the rate of 2 pounds (4 1/2 cups) per 100 square feet. Rake it in lightly and water. Fertilize tender bulbs, in this manner, twice during the growing season. Next fall, add bone meal, bulb fertilizer or superphosphate again to hardy bulbs and turn it under with a trowel. Be careful not to disturb shallow bulbs.

Proper postbloom care helps ensure good flowering next season by allowing the plant to put its energy into filling bulbs. Developing seeds compete with growing bulbs for food, so cut off the flower stalks as close to the leaves or ground as possible. Do not cut leaves back until they are completely yellow, however. As long as leaves are green, they continue to feed the bulb. Planting and fertilizing are the major chores for fall, but you may also wish to place 2 to 3 inches of mulch above the bulbs to help insulate the soil. Alternate freezing and thawing cycles may cause soil heaving, which disturbs roots and can expose bulbs to killing cold temperatures. Gently rake back heavy mulches such as oak leaves in early spring as shoots begin to emerge. Straw, peat moss, compost and other light mulches may be left in place and will add organic matter to the bed as they decompose.

Parrot Tulip

If you cannot plant bulbs immediately after purchase, hold them in a dry area with good air circulation at temperatures between 60 and 65° F. A basement shelf is a good location. Avoid storing bulbs in a garage or any area near exhaust fumes. Plant hardy bulbs even in late fall, if necessary. Hardy bulbs held over winter and planted in spring will not flower. They need the cold temperatures of winter to induce proper growth. Leftover bulbs can be forced indoors, however. Check stored bulbs monthly for moisture buildup or deterioration. Discard any diseased bulbs or storage material immediately, before others are contaminated. A midwinter fungicide dusting of tender bulbs may be necessary. Never store bulbs in a refrigerator with apples. Apples produce a large amount of ethylene, a natural ripening hormone that is deadly to bulbs. The tiny preformed flower bud within a tulip bulb will abort if exposed to even a very small quantity of ethylene. For the same reason, bulbs should never be dropped or bruised, damaged tissue produces ethylene.

Some bulbs, such as daffodils, snowdrops and grape hyacinths, multiple readily. Others, including tulips and hyacinths, merely replace the old bulb with a new bulb each year. Bulbs are best divided and transplanted when dormant, in late June or July. When dividing tubers, cut them into pieces with a clean, sharp knife, being sure that each section contains at least one bud or eye. Dip exposed sides in a commercial bulb dust or dilute fungicide as a protective measure. Gladiolus corms are fairly easy to propagate by breaking off the small corms (cormels) that are grouped around the base of the main corm. Cormels require about two years to reach blooming size; store in slightly moist medium (40°F) over winter, and soak in water for two days to soften them before planting. Cover with only 1 to 1 1/2 inches of soil. Follow the same procedure for lily bulblets (aerial bulblets) and bulbils (miniature bulbs), but do not store them over winter or soak before planting. Professional propagators or advanced hobbyists may try propagating true bulbs and corms by "scooping," "scoring," or other special techniques. Further information on these methods is available in standard propagation books.

A question often asked is, why didn't my bulbs bloom this spring? There are a few reasons that bulbs do not flower. If the bulbs were planted last fall, dig down to see if they rotted in the soil. If they did, the planting site is poorly drained. If you don't find the bulbs at all or see only withered green leaves on the ground, perhaps a rodent ate them. If leaves appeared with no flowers, question the source and the storage technique. Bulbs purchased at any end-of-year sale may not have been stored properly, and the flower bud may have been dead at the time of purchase. Before buying many bulbs on sale, buy one or two and cut them longitudinally to make sure the flower bud is alive. If it is brown or dried up, the bulb will not flower next spring. This is a fair test of the quality of the remaining bulbs.

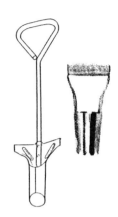

If you stored the bulbs near apples or in a garage, ethylene gas may have caused the flowers to abort. If the bulbs were planted in a previous fall, they may have received insufficient light or the leaves may have been cut back prematurely last year, resulting in insufficient food reserves to support flowering this year. With some bulbs, including tulips and hyacinths, decline may be expected after two to three years or even sooner. These bulbs are best treated as annuals in a display garden.

Bulbs are one of the easiest of all garden plants to grow as long as they have some sun, good drainage and a little fertilizer once in a while. They perform reliably in a wide variety of conditions with little care after planting. They are often one of the most cost effective landscape perennial plants available.

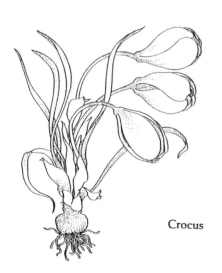

Crocus

Bulbs offer such a wide range of forms and colors, they should have a place in everyone's landscape. They look best in clumps or clusters, and require very little room. Clumps of 30 or more bulbs in an area make a strong visual statement. In the same space that a good size shrub takes, several different types of bulbs can be planted for a display that lasts through the many weeks of spring, summer and fall. Bloom times can vary, even in the same area, because of weather conditions but you can depend on a colorful and long-lasting show with bulbs.

Tiny bulbs of all types are effective when planted at the base of trees where they have a natural protection against winds. Tiny bulbs can also be planted around other larger bulbs to add depth to your plantings as well as a wonderful color accent. To create a naturalizing effect, toss handfuls of bulbs onto the ground in a woodland setting and bury them where they land. As with any flower garden, remember to put taller plants in the rear. Bulbs can create a truly romantic garden that will delight and stir the senses with beauty and fragrance. *Remember your hands* - for every bulb you buy, a hole must be dug.

General Blooming Sequence of Some Common Bulbs

Name	March	April	May	June	July	August	Sept	Oct
Crocus spp.	XXXX	XXXX						
Iris spp.	XXXX	XXXX	XXXX	XXXX	XXXX			
Snowdrop	XXXX	XXXX						
Snowflake spp.	XXXX	XXXX	XXXX					
Winter aconite	XXXX							
Crown imperial		XXXX	XXXX					
Daffodil		XXXX	XXXX					
Glory-of-the-snow		XXXX	XXXX					
Grape hyacinth		XXXX	XXXX					
Greek anemone		XXXX	XXXX					
Hyacinth		XXXX	XXXX					
Tulip spp.		XXXX	XXXX					
Allium spp.			XXXX	XXXX	XXXX	XXXX		
Poppy anemone			XXXX	XXXX				
Star-of-Bethlehem			XXXX					
Wood hyacinth			XXXX	XXXX				
Caladium (foliage)				XXXX	XXXX	XXXX	XXXX	
Lily spp.				XXXX	XXXX	XXXX	XXXX	
Tuberous begonia				XXXX	XXXX	XXXX	XXXX	
Calla lily					XXXX	XXXX		
Canna					XXXX	XXXX	XXXX	
Dahlia					XXXX	XXXX	XXXX	
Gladiolus					XXXX	XXXX	XXXX	
Autumn crocus spp.						XXXX	XXXX	XXXX
Belladonna lily						XXXX	XXXX	
Persian buttercup						XXXX	XXXX	
Resurrection lily						XXXX	XXXX	
Tuberose						XXXX	XXXX	

Ground Covers

Ground covers can be considered any low growing vegetation. They are plants that can serve you in many ways on difficult sites where other plants fail to grow. Some are adapted to steep slopes, dense shade, dryness, poor drainage, salty or acid soils, wind exposure and odd shaped areas. For about every site problem, there is an adapted ground cover that will thrive, cover and protect the problem site, and add variety and harmony to the entire landscape. They may be used to cover bare areas, prevent wind or water erosion of the soil, regulate foot traffic and tie together unrelated features in the landscape. And what about grass? In your landscape, there may be places you want grass plants but, for some reason, it won't grow. Or you may just want less grass to maintain. Perhaps the area may be too wet, dry or shady. Even the best shady grass seed may be having a hard time surviving under a favorite tree. A good alternative would be to use ground covers as lawn substitutes. Ground covers lower landscape maintenance if used where lawn mowing isn't practical. However, you should avoid planting a ground cover just because nothing else seems suitable. This may lead to excessive costs and unsatisfactory results.

In most cases, ground covers are considered low maintenance plants. They take less water, fertilizer, weeding and work than almost any other landscape planting. Ground covers can be used in areas where no other plant can be grown. However, they must be planted carefully paying attention to each one's individual requirements. Ground covers can take a long time to establish. It may take one to three years, depending on the climate, the type and how closely the plants are set. The ground must be deep enough to support plant root growth and water must be available often, to prevent the roots from drying out. Until the plants cover the entire area desired, weeding will have to be done. A light spreading of mulch between the plants will help keep weeds down until the cover spreads together. In general, no matter what type of groundcover you choose, soil preparation, planting and maintenance are basically the same. Once established, a successful ground cover planting chokes out weeds, shades and cools the soil, prevents soil erosion and conserves soil moisture. The appearance of a healthy ground cover can be attractive and lush.

A groundcover can be any plant covering the ground. Grass is a groundcover, just as low-growing shrubs, annual and perennial flowers and vines are. But when people hear the word groundcover, they automatically think of low-growing creepers such as, ivy or pachysandra, usually because groundcovers are used in difficult, dark or shady areas, such as under trees. One of the most common is pachysandra, also called Japanese spurge. This is very tough and hardy and is excellent when used under shade trees or shrubs. It grows to a height of 6 to 12 inches, spreads by underground runners, and stays green throughout the winter. It spreads quickly and can become invasive. Another popular groundcover is *Vinca minor,* also known as periwinkle or myrtle. Some consider this to be the best because it has a long life, is lush, has small flowers and mixes very well with bulbs. It grows to a height of 4 to 6 inches and has glossy, dark leaves that stay green throughout the year. Not too many groundcovers survive under dense maple trees, but this one does. *Hedera*, better known as ivy, is the last of the big three. It is lush green, spreads rapidly, widely used in areas of erosion and climbs or covers just about anything with very little maintenance. It thrives in dense shade and is happy even in poor soil. Ivy with variegated leaves are less hardy and need more light.

Common Ground Covers

Botanical name Common name	Height (inches)	Form	Flowers	Shade Tolerant	Comments
Aegopodium Goutweed	12	Upright		No	Leaves are variegated green and white.
Ajuga Bugleweed	6	Spread	Summer	Yes	Fewer flowers in shade. Showy in small places.
Cerastium Snow-in-Summer	6	Spread	Summer	No	A contrast of silvery foliage and white flowers. Fast spreading.
Convallaria Lily-of-the-Valley	8	Upright	Summer	Yes	Fragrant, white flowers and adaptable to banks and slopes.
Epimedium Barrenwort	12	Upright	Spring	Yes	Green foliage with red variegation. Red or yellow flowers.
Hedera English Ivy	12	Spread		Yes	Many hardy new cultivars. A most popular groundcover.
Hemerocallis Daylily	24	Upright	Summer	No	Orange, pink, red or yellow flowers. Few pest problems.
Hypericum St. Johnswort	12	Spread	Summer	No	Dark green foliage with bright yellow flowers.
Juniperus conferta Blue Pacific	8	Spread		No	Soft, blue-green foliage and low, spreading growth habit.
Lonicera Honeysuckle	24	Spread	Summer	Yes	Vigorous, twining growth habit with fragrant flowers.
Pachysandra Japanese Spurge	8	Upright		Yes	Full sun causes foliage to turn yellow. Use only in shady sites.
Phlox Moss Phlox	4	Spread	Spring	No	Massive white, blue or pink flower display.
Sedum spurium Dragon's Blood	4	Spread	Summer	No	Red flowering creeper. Good for sunny rock garden.
Vinca Periwinkle	6	Spread	Spring Summer	Yes	Light blue flowers and glossy green foliage. Avoid wet sites.

An herbaceous perennial (HP) ground cover is a plant that does not develop persistent woody tissue as a shrub or tree does, but rather has soft or succulent seasonal growth. HP ground covers such as daylily grow new stems, leaves and flowers each year that die down to the ground in the fall, thus escaping winter stress. These are replaced by new growth the next spring from underground buds. They may be more expensive originally than annual plants but in the long run perennials are more economical. HP ground covers can be a substantial part of most landscapes and, if properly cared for, last almost indefinitely. They provide summer flowers; vary in size, texture, form and flower color, and have a wide range of adaptability to various soils, degrees of shade and climates. Once these perennials are established, they multiply rapidly to fill in the ground area. A few varieties of HP's planted in a mass probably produce more color for the investment than many other permanent plantings. The following common ground covers are herbaceous perennials: Goutweed, Bugleweed, Snow-in-Summer, Lili-of-the-Valley, Barrenwort, Daylily, and Dragon's Blood.

The following chart can be used to determine how much land area (in square feet) can be planted with 100 plants at various spacings.

Planting Guide For Ground Covers

Quantity	Spacings (inches)	Coverage
100 plants	4" apart	will cover 11 sq. ft.
100 plants	6" apart	will cover 25 sq. ft.
100 plants	8" apart	will cover 44 sq. ft.
100 plants	10" apart	will cover 70 sq. ft.
100 plants	12" apart	will cover 100 sq. ft.
100 plants	15" apart	will cover 156 sq. ft.
100 plants	18" apart	will cover 225 sq. ft.
100 plants	24" apart	will cover 400 sq. ft.

This chart can be used to determine how many plants you will need for various square footages when the plant material must be installed at spacings listed across the top of the table.

Number of Ground Cover Plants for Given Areas
(spacing in both directions in inches)

Sq. ft. of planting area	6 in.	8 in.	9 in.	12 in.	18 in.	24 in.
100	400	225	178	100	45	25
200	800	450	356	200	90	50
300	1200	675	534	300	135	75
400	1600	900	712	400	180	100
500	2000	1125	890	500	225	125
600	2400	1350	1068	600	270	150
700	2800	1575	1246	700	315	175
800	3200	1800	1425	800	360	200
900	3600	2025	1602	900	405	225
1000	4000	2250	1780	1000	450	250

When you are ready to plant your ground cover, the area must be thoroughly prepared before you set the plants out or they may dry quickly. The soil should be worked at least 6 inches deep. Spread some organic matter, such as peat moss or Michigan peat on the ground and work it into the soil. Use a commercial fertilizer (purchase it at the same place you bought the ground cover) while preparing the soil. Dig and work it into the soil as you did with the organic matter. Make sure you follow the recommendations on the fertilizer container. As soon as you dig one hole, bury a plant so the roots are completely covered. When all the plants are planted, water the entire area thoroughly to give the roots a good start. Then water heavily at least once a week to promote a deep, healthy root system. Approximately 1 inch of water every week should be enough for development.

Although ground covers can be planted almost anytime of the growing season, early spring is the best time. This will allow the plants to become established before hot summer months and the cold winter. When you plant ground covers, space them according to the chart. Remember, closer planting will help cover the area more quickly, but the cost will rise. A well-established ground cover needs very little maintenance. Occasional pruning to keep it in check, fertilizing, weeding and water are usually all that is required. Ground covers may suffer winter injury, just as other plants do. If there is an extremely dry winter, the foliage may get windburned. In severe cases, considerable damage may occur and soil areas become bare. In the spring, these areas are open to weed invasion. Winter damage can be reduced by spraying the plants with an anti-transpirant spray. This will cut down on some moisture loss. These sprays are available at most garden centers. Spraying your plants in fall will help protect them through most of the winter.

Hostas, Ornamental Grasses and Ferns

Shade in the garden is a delight on a warm summer day. Shade can enhance and extend the variety of color and texture of plants in the garden. Gardening in the shade can be exciting and provides a great opportunity for developing a beautiful landscape. Careful selection of plants and proper garden site preparation will do much to bring beauty to your shaded garden. Shade has been described in many ways such as full, half, partial, light, heavy, filtered, open, etc. The degree of shade is a continuum and cannot be put into distinct categories, but these descriptions should help you determine which plants will work in your situation. And remember, each yard has its own unique characteristics. For more information about shade, see chapter 4.

Hosta is becoming America's number one selling perennial. These popular shade perennials remain attractive from their spring emergence until autumn frost. Handsome foliage grows lush in nearly all soil conditions, performing best in slightly acid to neutral soil but tolerating some alkaline conditions especially if organic matter is added. Summer is graced by their lovely lily-like blossoms of white to lavender to deep purple. Some Hosta flowers are fragrant, much like the heavy perfume of an Easter Lily. Choosing a Hosta may be as simple as selecting any large green, blue, or gold plant with round leaves to serve as a garden background or foundation cover on the north side of a building or house. Large variegated plants also serve well as foundation plantings, mass groupings or as single specimen-plants. With many choices of leaf shape and size, only color and variegation remain to tantalize the gardener's intent on planning a new shade garden or revising an existing space.

Hosta are hardy, long-lived perennials fitting a wide range of shade tolerance and climate zones. Each year the clump increases in dimension and therefore in value, rewarding the gardener with many years of their beauty, diversity and durability. **Hostas are a good investment!** Hosta is a good choice for the predominant perennial in the shade garden as it has an endless variety of size, color, texture and shape. It is a creative way to blend with other species. Hosta natural textures, can be used just as easily in rock gardens and Japanese gardens alike.

Green shade of Hosta blend most easily with all other colors of Hosta and companion plants. Often greens can be used to set a dramatic garden "stage" by choosing leaf size, and color to accent a neighboring planting. Using large greens to form a backdrop will show off more colorful varieties of plants, while the practice of placing larger leafed plants in the foreground with small-leafed plants behind gives an illusion of stretching out your garden. *Blues* need darker areas of shade and cool temperatures to hold their deep blue colors. Lighter areas or direct sunlight tends to fade them out to green, a trait that may even be useful to add interest in a garden display. Blues are great accents next to gold colored blossoms or foliage as well as many other bright annuals such as pink impatiens. *Yellow to golden* foliage, like nature's own packaged sunlight, brightens the darker corners of our gardens. Many gold Hosta hold their color best in dappled (filtered) light, but with soft or deep yellow tones, they are a perfect accent against blue flowers, foliage or blue Hosta cousins. They blend nicely with Hosta in the gold-margin variegated types which brings out the bright gold of both Hosta types. Golden-yellow Hostas make a showy background for bright red plantings such as red Impatiens or red-flowered, red-leafed begonias. Gold-tone Hosta planted in brighter light, such as a half-day of sun, make a handsome landscape with red-foliage Coleus.

Hosta with unique variegation patterns are best planted close to the viewer so they can be truly appreciated. Some emerge beautifully marked in the spring but gradually fade into solid green as the season progresses. They become a lovely backdrop for annuals such as Impatiens and Caladiums that come into maturity as the spring markings fade. Unique variegated Hostas are a delight for both confirmed collectors and beginning gardeners who are looking for that "something special" Hosta. Variegated Hosta will show margins of white, cream, soft gold, apple-green or dark green shades which contrast with the leaf center. When using mass plantings, their variegation gives interest through the day as the light and shadows of your garden area changes. Because variegated Hosta range in all sizes from dwarf to handsomely large, there should be a variety just right for every garden! Many varieties are perfect as specimen plants and are sure to become an eye catching conversation piece.

Dwarf Hosta (less than 10 inches high) are becoming increasingly popular in gardens. Due to their diminutive size they can be planted between tree roots or among rocks and crevices where there is little soil. They are also used in Japanese gardens due to the restricted planting space. They look great in ornamental containers, in old tree stumps, or in secret pockets throughout your yard. Many of the dwarf Hosta bind the soil (stoloniferous) making a good ground cover. Small gardens have become popular in recent years for a variety of reasons, the biggest reason being that gardeners and plant collectors run out of room! Dwarf plants allow a gardener to collect many different varieties of plants and still enjoy the specialties of its larger cousins without taking up so much space. Dwarf plants tend to have a more compact growing habit making a great background for the showy blossoms.

There are several Hosta that are desirable for their fragrant flowers. These Hosta work great planted near doors, windows, next to a deck, or along a well traveled path so their lily-like scent can be fully appreciated. They require more sun to bloom well, but are still a joy even in full shade. Several Hosta seem to perform better than others and show less sunburn in 3/4 to full sun. The leaves of these Hosta may still burn in hot, dry summers. The gold shades are generally able to take more sun, some even require more light to develop their gold color. Most Hosta grow well in sun if kept watered. In a sunny landscape, Hosta can thrive when planted behind a screen of ornamental grasses.

Fertilization may help Hosta growth. Heavy fertilization of Hosta is not usually recommended, but an application of a slow-release fertilizer applied just as growth begins in the spring may give more vigorous growth. Foliar feeding can be done with a foliar type fertilizer every few weeks during periods of active growth. However, I would use one-tenth the recommended dosage and avoid the hottest part of the day for application. Fall is the best time for planting Hosta. Cool autumn air prevents the foliage from growing, yet the soil stays warm enough so that roots continue to grow deep. A perennial that is established in the fall will show vigorous growth in spring, resistance to stress, and a likelihood of flowering that first season.

Ornamental grasses are a nice addition to any garden. They inspire feelings of freedom and adventure.

Designing with grasses has become a popular garden idea, especially with gardeners looking for a naturalistic gardening approach. Grasses provide year-round interest to any landscape. More and more, discerning gardeners are discovering that there are no finer plants for accent and architectural effect, or for dried arrangements. In the heat and drought of summers, they prove outstanding, performing well under adverse conditions. Some provide a fine textured composition and the tall ones provide a strong linear effect adding a new dimension to your landscape. They also work well in restoring the natural look on the outskirts of your yard to blend with surrounding fields or extended yards. Forms of grasses range from mounding to the almost bolt upright and size range from small to towering. The contrast in texture ranges from very fine blades to broad blades. The fine textured types are enhanced by being planted near a bold textured plant or other objects with a solid form such as rocks or ponds. The broad range in foliage colors covers several shades of green to deep blue tones, yellow-green, bright red and striking fall bronze. Because grasses change through the season, consider their placement in your design, especially when winter interest is important. Certain grasses contrast well with conifers and evergreens.

Grasses also add interesting texture and color to the winter landscape and are effective both as individual specimens or in groups for a striking effect. The taller types should be cut back in the spring. Early spring brings cool season grasses that add freshness of color, most attractive as a backdrop for

blooming bulbs and spring blooming perennials. During hot summers, these grasses do well when cut back to about six inches in height. Cool fall temperatures will bring out new growth. Warm season grasses stay dormant longer and begin growth later in the year, reaching their peak during the warm summers. Warm season grasses quickly fill in just as the bulbs begin to turn yellow and fade; thus they work well planted with bulbs or among early spring bloomers. Tall grasses can be used as screens or background plants or to create a shady spot for Hosta or other shade lovers. Most grasses prefer full sun, but there are several species that tolerate locations with varying degrees of shade. These species can be used for ground covers, as specimen plants or in groups with Hosta, ferns or other woodland plants. Ornamental grasses are flowing and carefree as they set the stage for other flowering perennials. As autumn approaches and colors change, the flowers and seeds of grasses add joy to any garden landscape. To dry, cut before seed ripens, and hang upside-down in a dark place. Ornamental grass plants are usually sold well-rooted in pots for easy establishment. Let your imagination take you through the plans and possibilities of striking combinations that will color the seasons.

Ferns thrive in the shade! Most varieties of these friendly fronds are easy to grow and need a minimum of care. They have a remarkable range of foliage textures and colors that impart a light, airy, cooling effect in the shady landscape. In general, a loamy soil with plenty of humus will support ferns, especially in areas of deep shade. They need ample moisture during their growing season and a year-round mulch. Traditional landscaping has placed ferns into backgrounds or on the north sides of houses as foundation covers, simply to be ignored if not fully forgotten! Today ferns are placed as accents, specimens, and borders, each adding its own unique texture, form, and grace as breezes puff feather-like movements through the fronds. Many fronds grow with the look of delicate green laces, a perfect contrast to the heavy leaves of a blue Hosta or a compliment to the nodding plume of an airy Solomon's Seal. Large ferns such as the Ostrich Fern, which can grow to heights of four feet or more, do well as background plants. Ostrich Fern, like its namesake, can't fly, but it can be aggressive and is best used in an area where it can be contained or else appreciated for its ground-covering capacity. The umbrella-like form of the Maidenhair Fern allows this lovely variety to be used equally well as an accent plant, mass-planted as a ground cover, or guiding footsteps along a pathway. Wood Ferns of the crested varieties grow in a small lacy form, making them quite useful as a border. With their finely divided frond tips, the crested Wood Ferns invite close-up admiration. Smaller ferns add a delicate touch to shady rock gardens or other accent spots. Berry Bladder Fern tucks into small spaces as does the Japanese Painted Fern. Japanese Painted Ferns are ideal plants used as a ground cover in an area close to the garden path and their colorful variegated fronds hold their own as unique eye-catchers. Ferns are usually sold bare root or in pots.

Container Gardening

Gardens have always been a part of our culture. Throughout the years, the home landscape has had many changes from small square gardens of herbs and flowers to large intricate details of the Victorian era, finally to the garden as an extension of our indoor and outdoor living environment. Urban living, with its many apartments and condominiums, has created another kind of garden style. This style brings an emphasis on use of very limited space. It is called "container gardening" and can be very enjoyable.

As a result of this lifestyle, traditional garden designs are being replaced with small ones having greater visual appeal. The basic goal is to create an attractive, enjoyable space in the limited area available. All it takes is a sunny spot on a deck or patio and you can enjoy floral beauty all summer long. Since these spots normally call for closeup viewing, it is important to select container plants which not only have an extended season of flowering, but also have decorative foliage before, during and after the blooming season. Many gardeners have temperamental houseplants in mind when they think of container gardening. But there are many bulbs, annuals and perennials which will do very well in containers outdoors from late spring until autumn. To serve these small space gardeners, varieties of compact, early to flower, and vigorous, prolific bloomers have become very popular. Many are the result of newer breeding efforts and are easy care flowers that do well even in difficult situations. For small areas, such as patios and terraces, the amount of space is important. It should be divided into two kinds: visual space and usable space. In these situations, outdoor activities are usually limited to relaxation, perhaps a small table and chairs for having coffee, reading a favorite book or taking a nap, so the visual space should reflect these feelings.

Container gardening is very adaptable. Plants can be moved to any location in your garden. They can also be moved from one home to another if need be and outdoors in the summer to indoors during the winter. Doorways, window boxes or small tables in bright corner rooms can now all become garden spots. For some garden lovers, small areas may be their only opportunity for growing plants. But, let's not forget those that have large yards. Container gardening is not limited to those with only small areas to fill. Large yards have some bland or unsightly areas that need some spicing up. Try that old shed, for example. Add a few well placed pots of your favorite flowers around the shed. Place a container on top of that old stump with a drooping type of plant and watch what happens. I love my wife's idea. In our backyard we have an old oak tree that has three main leaders. In the middle a good size crotch has formed. Lois filled the crotch with soil, broke a brick into several large pieces, and jammed the pieces into  a couple of strategic places so the soil would not wash away. Then she planted white and purple impatiens. They are doing remarkably well, have spread and now we have some wonderful color in a normally barren place. I am sure you can come up with some unusual ideas yourself. Give it a try! A little imagination can transform any space into beauty.

A container garden can be formed by using planting screens, small shrubs, annual and perennial flowers, vines, small needle or broad-leaved evergreens, bulbs or ground covers in just about any space available. Most important, it is necessary to select the types of plants that fit both the area available and the mood you are trying to create. In gardens with limited space, try to use special features such as water sounds, small night lighting, and small sculptures that will enhance the visual effect. Small water displays are available at most garden centers, are easy to hook up, virtually maintenance free and create a very pleasant, relaxing atmosphere. Nightlighting has become very inexpensive and is easy to do. Most gardening or home improvement stores have kits that range from four to twenty lights. You have a choice of several different light fixtures, each one achieving a different effect. For small areas, I would recommend directing the light upwards into the plants (underlighting) to emphasize form.

Flowers are not a permanent element in the landscape as they either die completely (annual) or die back to the ground (perennial), so they should be considered only an accessory. Since we are talking about limited space, and probably limited time, as most people do not spend their winters on either their patio or terrace, annuals give the most color. However, to be most effective, they should have a background if at all possible. Try not to plant too many different kinds of flowers or colors. Keep the garden simple. Planting flowers in masses is very effective for small gardens and is quite striking. Keep one thing in mind when you are selecting flowers for your containers: sunlight! Most flowers need at least a half day of sun to put on any kind of a show that is worth while. If the area has a lot of shade, check in other parts of this chapter for shade tolerant flowers and ground covers (impatiens are a good choice). As a last reminder, almost any type of small plant is suitable for containers as long as there is drainage.

There are many kinds of containers available. They may be made of clay, concrete, glass, metal, ceramic, wood and plastic and the choice ranges from glass jars, cans, pots, boxes, baskets, tubs, watering cans, wheelbarrows, window boxes etc. Containers may be portable or permanent. Don't limit yourself to traditional pots, though. Anything that will hold soil and hold up to a lot of watering will be just fine. Choice is usually based on cost, strength, durability and attractiveness. The shape and size of a container must be consistent with the shape and size of the plant. Tall plants grow better and are more attractive in tall containers just as small plants do better in small, wider containers. Make sure they are large enough to accommodate root growth, and that there is a provision for drainage. Many of the containers sold today have drainage holes already in the bottom for excess water removal. Watertight containers allow excess water to build up at the bottom which will injure plant roots due to lack of oxygen and cause root rot. All plants need proper aeration. If you find a container you like but it doesn't have any drainage holes, you must make them yourself. This is quite easy to do using a standard electric drill with a wide bit.

Porous containers, such as clay, may require more frequent watering to maintain the proper plant moisture. This is due to evaporation of water through the container walls. Clay pots can evaporate up to 50% of the water directly through the walls. If using clay pots, I would suggest mixing some peat moss with the soil before planting. Peat moss absorbs water and holds it longer, allowing plants to draw on the moisture when needed. If you have large containers with only one or two plants, adding a layer of mulch on top will help reduce water evaporation and discourage weeds. You can apply water with a sprinkling can or hose, whichever is easier. During the summer, watering your containers should be done at least every three days, if not more.

Small quantities of soil have a tendency to dry out quickly. This is why you should plant in the largest container suitable for the ultimate size of the plant. The more soil the container holds, the slower it will dry out. If not watered often, flowers may start to die and weeds will take over. Container plants are surrounded by air which increases moisture evaporation. They should be watered thoroughly and frequently. However, frequent watering leaches the nutrients, so you must feed them often. Use a commercial water-soluble (mix with water) or time-release (dry granules) fertilizer at least once every month. Never water anything with a hose that has been laying in the hot sun for hours. It may contain water hot enough to damage both plant foliage and the root system.

Planting In Containers

Now we're ready to do some planting. Select a container that suits the size of your plant or plants when they will be full grown. Check the bottom and make sure there are sufficient drainage holes. If not, use a standard electric drill and put several holes in the bottom using a good size bit. Depending on the size of the container, place 1 to 2 inches of small pebbles, crushed sea shells or gravel in the bottom to help drainage and prevent soil leakage. Purchase a good bagged commercial potting soil which contains peat and vermiculite mixture. This mixture helps drainage but also holds moisture long enough so the plant roots can absorb it and nutrients. Bagged soil will also be weed and disease free. I would not recommend using garden soil or your regular property soil, as these soils may have insects or diseases present. Once you have planted, these problems may be hard to control. I would not use last years potting soil either. The many waterings from last year, may have washed out (leached) the nutrients. Words of wisdom - when you are starting with fresh, new plants, start with fresh, new soil.

In very large containers that have more room than needed for root development, you can add some salt hay or packing peanuts to fill in some of the space before adding soil. Add some soil, place your

plants in, add some more soil and then water well. Make sure the top of the root ball is at least 1 to 2 inches and the very top of the soil layer is below the container lip. If you are planting small bare-root plants, make a small mound over the gravel or peanuts, spread the roots over the mound and fill the container to within 1 inch of the lip. A good rule of thumb is to place the largest plant in first and then position the rest before burying them. And the largest doesn't always have to go in the center. Be original, its more fun. Make sure when combining plants, to keep ones with similar needs, water, light etc., together. Anything you can grow in your garden, can grow in a container, depending on size of course.

Hanging wire or wooden baskets are excellent containers. Buying a hanging basket may be beautiful but can also be expensive. Making your own basket can be an adventure, and chances are, will cost a lot less. Baskets usually come in either wire or wood. I prefer wood to wire. Even though the wire basket may last longer, I like the natural look of wood. In either case, your choices for baskets and flowers are almost endless. Wire baskets can either be used alone or placed in another container to steady it. With a wire basket, first line the basket with a 1 inch layer of damp sphagnum moss and then fill the center with soil. You can either poke holes through the sides of the moss and soil and then place the plants through the holes into the mixture or just place the plants on top and add more soil. Wooden baskets are usually a little tighter and may not need moss added. If this is the case you can use just the soil mixture. Watering may be needed more often than pot containers as hanging baskets are more exposed to the elements (sun, drying winds).

A hanging basket can bring instant color and fragrance to your garden, patio, porch, balcony, house or any other area that suits you. It is easy and fun to make, a pleasure to look at and extremely versatile.

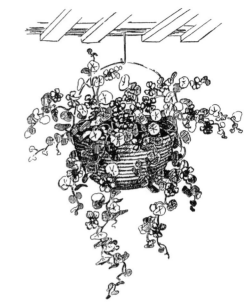

Obviously, hanging baskets can be moved anywhere you want them. This is extremely helpful when it comes to weather conditions. You can make a basket as simple or as fancy as you want. And if the proper plants are chosen in the spring, when the outside season is over, they can be moved inside for you to enjoy. Here are some recommendations for container flowers:

Partial shade - Pansies, snowdrops, primroses, crocus, cockscomb, coreopsis, ivy, persian violet, candytuft, lobelia.

Sun - marigolds, alyssum, lobelia, dahlia, sweet william, twinspur, blue marguerite, treasure flower, cupflower, osteospermum, dusty miller.

Shade - Blue-eyed Mary, fuchsia, impatiens, lobelia, coleus, begonia, caladium.

Hanging baskets - ivy, geranium, snapdragon, petunia, lobelia, impatiens, begonia, fuchsia, lantana.

Window boxes - depending on light intensity, almost any small annual flower and some small vine growing plants.

Let's not forget about small shrubs. Any small shrubs can be grown in containers: small boxwoods, Christmas trees, pine trees, privets, tall spiral junipers, and of course the ever popular rose family. All of these shrubs can be used alone or as a centerpiece with vine type plants such as verbena and ivy gracefully outlining the container. Just make sure the roots have room to grow so they don't become rootbound and die.

Window Boxes

Now we come to one of my favorite containers, window boxes. Growing flowers in window boxes is a simple and flexible method of decorating outdoors. They are an enjoyable way of gardening as they are inexpensive (once the box has been made or purchased) because the desired flowers are annuals. Annuals cost less than other flowers and provide abundant rewards. The proper combination of flowers can give stunning effects that all can enjoy. Window boxes can be put together rather quickly and will last the entire season. They can be enjoyed from inside the house or out. If wind is a problem where the window box will be, pick low growing plants with sturdy stems. Avoid plants with thin stems and leaves like climbing vines. Pick windows that you normally look out every day. And make sure to choose some windows on the front of your home so the neighbors and passers-by can see. Of course, the size of the box depends on the size of the window. Most garden centers sell several types of boxes that

usually come in plastic or wood in all different colors. The boxes normally have drainage holes and come complete with brackets to fit under most windows. When you get the boxes home, line them up and fasten them securely according to instructions, but do not secure them permanently. It is easier to replace the soil each year if you can remove them. Boxes can become quite heavy after the soil and flowers are in, so make sure everything fits just right. If the boxes are made of wood, make sure they are redwood, cedar or any pressure-treated wood. These are rot-resistant and last longer. After the flowers have begun to grow, you may want to move the boxes around to different windows for different looks. If this is the case, buy plastic containers that fit into the boxes before adding the soil. Then plant in the plastic containers, and when you want to switch windows, all you have to do is move the containers and not the entire box.

The Plants

Annuals are the best flowers to use in window boxes. Annuals resist pollution, disease and in most cases, insects. Design your box gardens the same as you would any other garden. Decide the colors you want, the size that will grow best and make sure you plant flowers with the same requirements together. When you purchase annuals in flats, check the underside of the roots for any disease and check the foliage for insects. If the foliage is green, the stems are strong and the plant has many buds, chances are

they're in good shape. Decide on color schemes and types of flowers. Use at least two per box, perhaps three or four depending on the size. If the boxes will be in the shade most of the day than you can plant impatiens, coleus, pansies and lobelia. If they are mostly in the sun you have a much broader spectrum of flowers to choose from including portulaca, geraniums, lobelia, marigolds, salvias and petunias. If the boxes are not in strong winds, then you can add a variety of small climbing vines that mix well with many flowers. If you leave your windows open a lot, try some flowers with fragrance such as verbena, sweet alyssum, rosemary and dianthus. If you are putting a box at the kitchen window, try growing herbs such as dill, sweet basil, anise, thyme, parsley, oregano and sweet marjoram.

Planting

Planting is the same as with any other containers. Make sure there are drainage holes in the boxes and add some pebbles or broken sea shells to the bottom. Purchase a commercial potting soil and fill to about one inch from the top of the box. These specially made soil mixes tend to hold moisture better. Set the plants in the box according to heights (taller ones in the rear, smaller ones in the front) and colors and bury so that the top of the root ball is just below the soil level. Water all plants well and keep watering them at least three times a week, even more during the hot summer. A good rule of thumb, if the soil

is dry, its time to water. When the flowers die, pinch them off (deadhead) to promote more flowers. I would suggest feeding them with a commercial fertilizer at least once every month and keep a check for any noticeable amount of insects. Window box gardening is guaranteed to be fun and rewarding. Create a bit of art, peace of mind and romance at your window's ledge.

Roses

*The universal fascination with roses
has quite a long and distinguished history, reaching back
as far as the reign of Cleopatra.*   Spring Hill Nurseries

Roses are considered by many gardeners to be the *romancers* of the garden. Their welcoming beauty is seen throughout the United States near patios, porches, foundations, along driveways and walkways, in containers and window boxes, and just about anywhere else imaginable. Roses can be grown anywhere as long as you make a reasonable effort. When cut and brought inside, nothing else is more elegant than a display of roses. All around America, roses are honored for their beauty and quality. They are an excellent garden plant and can provide you with perfect, fresh and beautiful cut flowers. Enjoy them in the garden or in bouquets for the home, office or giving them to friends and family. Roses can be used in cooking, cake decorating and are in many vitamins. When you think of a rose, you can think of a flower that has become immortal. Roses, as a group, are among the most versatile and useful of all plants. While the classic Hybrid Teas are without a doubt the world's most popular exhibition flowers for the collector, there are roses for nearly every landscape and garden use. They are some of the toughest, easiest, and most rewarding landscape plants you can grow. Over the past two decades, the liberation of "America's Favorite Flower" from the collector's garden out into the larger landscape has taken on the proportions of a revolution. Of course, the beloved Hybrid Teas and the specialist rose garden are glorious fixtures in American gardening, and here to stay as an important part. The expansion of roses into shrubs for the larger landscape is a benefit to all gardeners.

There are endless varieties of roses: edging roses, tree roses, climbing roses, trailing roses good for slopes, container roses and finally those for the formal rose garden. Many are disease and pest resistant, cold tolerant and their many vibrant colors are a season-long delight. *Floribundas* are considered by many to be the work horses of the flower garden. They can be grown in beds, walkways, containers, on patios or as hedges where privacy is needed. Floribundas are low maintenance, disease resistant, have abundant flowers and grow in a wide range of soils. They are easy to care for and mix well with other flowers. ***English*** roses are

known for soft shades and beautiful fragrances. They look wonderful in mass plantings and have a long blooming season. *Miniature* roses are easy and fun to grow, and can provide color in just about any place. They are very hardy and bloom continuously throughout the season. Use them in planters, hanging baskets, all kinds of pots, beds, borders, just about any place there is sun. Miniature roses can even be used as a ground cover. *Shrub* roses are a smart choice for beginning gardeners as they are hardy, disease resistant and easy to care for. They are an excellent substitute for any shrub that blooms only once a year. Shrub roses adapt to many different types of soil and will give you continuous color all season. *Rugosa* roses are splendid additions to any bed or border. They are noted for their hardiness and ability to live in many adverse conditions, including beach areas where there is a lot of sand and salt. They have strong, thorny canes that make an attractive hedge. *Tree* roses add color and form to any garden bed, especially when mixed with perennials, annuals or shrubs. If left in their containers, they add beauty to any deck, patio or balcony and are portable enough to be moved to any desired location for special effects. Tree roses are easy to grow either planted or in a container, and take up very lit-

tle space. They usually come in sizes ranging from 18 to 36 inches. *Climbers* are very easy to grow and among the most popular rose plants in landscaping. They are versatile adding height or length to any area, depending on the pruning technique. Climbers are excellent plants for garden structures as they create spectacular shows on trellises, arbors, walls and fences. *Hedge* roses are excellent when used for screens or boundaries. They are easy to grow, disease and insect resistant, thrive in summer heat and considered by many gardeners to be the "beautiful" living hedge. Hedge roses blend in with just about any architectural style in the landscape. They can be used to cover up unsightly areas, control foot traffic or ensure privacy. *Hybrid teas* are considered by many to be the ultimate in garden beauty. If someone mentions the word rose, this is the flower most of us think of. They require a minimum of care and are usually disease free. These elegant roses can be grown easily without a "green thumb."

When purchasing roses, make sure you get them from a reputable nursery or mail order company. In most cases, they have been planted in "test gardens" for a year or two and evaluated by experts before being released to the public. They are judged on form, hardiness, disease and insect resistance and foliage, among other things. Today there are many types that thrive in adverse conditions. Roses are a beauty to behold but take a tremendous amount of time, care and love. Be prepared for disease, cold effects, insects, deadheading, extra watering, weeding, mounding and thorn cuts but have an elegant, scented garden that will stir your senses. Today, roses are no longer being isolated by themselves, but are being integrated into entire landscapes. Bicolor roses look perfect when planted with sunflowers, daisies and dahlias. Small mini roses are being planted in pots and containers with other small annuals to create a long blooming display till frost.

Planting

Roses love sun, so the bed or garden should be placed in a sunny location, preferably protected from north winds. The location should receive at least 6 hours of sun a day, but for maximum blooms and an excellent show, 8 hours or more are better. Try to stay away from trees and shrubs because of root competition. To be on the safe side, roses are almost always planted in the spring and are always pruned in the spring. This makes it very easy to remember.

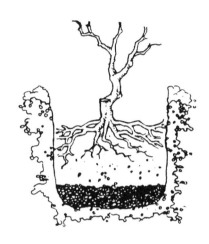

Roses can be planted in the early fall, however, if temperatures reach near 0° F, winter injury or even death may occur. So, why take the chance? Once you have picked the site, its time to prepare the soil. Roses like a slightly acid soil with a pH of 6.0 to 6.5. Again, a soil test of the area would be recommended, as roses can be quite expensive and we don't any to die. If the soil needs to be made more acidic, add some sulfur and if it needs to be made less acidic, add some lime. The soil test should give recommendations. The rose garden should be in an open, sunny location sheltered from north winds. If you are making separate beds, rather than incorporating into a flower garden, make the beds at least 4 feet wide. This makes it easier to maintain and gives a better showing. Soil preparation is crucial to successful roses. It should be rich and well drained to avoid root-rot.

If you have purchased roses from a mail order house, unpack them at once when they arrive, place the roots in water for about an hour, and then plant them. If you can't plant them immediately, they should be heeled in and covered with soil or mulch until ready to plant. Dig a hole at least 18 to 20 inches wide and the same depth. Remove rocks and other unwanted debris. Add a quart of peat moss to a quart of soil and mix well. Pour this mixture into the hole and form a mound at the bottom. Remove any wrapping from the bush and trim any broken or damaged roots back to healthy tissue. It is best to use hand pruners and make clean cuts. Firm the mound and spread the roots around it. Make sure the bud union is slightly above ground and steady the bush. If more soil mixture is needed, gently lift the plant and add some underneath. Fill the hole about two-thirds and firm the soil with your hands. Fill the hole with water and allow it to soak in. Wiggle the plant very slightly to remove any water pockets and fill the hole to the top with the soil mix. At this time, prune the canes back about one third and also remove any weak or dead canes. You should make the cuts (at 45 degree angles) slightly above any strong buds facing outwards which will result in larger blooms. Add some loose soil over the plant creating a 6 inch soil mound to protect it from drying out. Leave the mound there until new growth is about an inch long, then wash it away and add mulch.

Tips For Healthy Roses

Water Deeply
Feed Several Times Each Year
Prune In Early Spring
Deadhead Throughout The Season
Prepare For Winter

Rose Care

Roses should be pruned only in the spring but cut back after they go dormant in the fall. Watch the forsythias. When they are in full bloom, and buds appear on the rose bush, its time to prune roses. Make sure your shears are clean, sharp and disease free and wear a long pair of gloves to protect you from thorn cuts. Remove all dead wood and cut canes back to good wood with an angled cut just above a good outwards facing bud. Be careful not to tear any bark. The idea of pruning is to make the plant healthy. Pruning roses the right way at the right time means healthier plants and larger blooms. Shaping your new, young rose in the very beginning, will help it take the form you want in future years. Thinning out your new and old bushes will improve air circulation, reducing the chance of disease. Remove any branches thinner in diameter than your little pinky finger and any canes that are growing from the center of the plant to let more sun in. Also, remove any sucker canes emerging from the roots of the bush. If borers are a problem in your area, apply a pruning compound (available at local nursery) to all the cuts 1/2 inch or more in diameter. I've heard people use white glue or clear nailpolish as a sealer alternative. Check where you bought the roses from before applying anything, they are the ones who should know.

If you want larger blooms, you must remove most of the buds from a stem. With your fingernail, gently remove any clusters of tiny buds. This is best done early in the season. Once the first blooms fade, deadhead (remove with fingers) them immediately. Find the first leaf that has five leaflets and cut the branch just above this leaf. This helps many kinds of roses bloom again. Certain roses, such as shrub and climbing, bloom only once a year so it's not necessary to remove the spent blossoms. However, to help climbers stay in bloom longer, cut them back as soon as the first blooms are done. Make sure you leave two five-leaflet leaves on each cane, and new stems with a flower will grow. The purpose of pruning is to produce strong roots, canes and an overall healthy plant.

Roses need lots of water. A complete soaking at least once a week will keep them healthy and blooming all season long. If you have a lot of plants in one area, soaker hoses or drip watering are excellent methods of complete and even watering. If your bushes are scattered throughout your landscaping, the sprinkler system or individual sprinkler will be just fine. Overhead watering helps keep the foliage clean and knock off unwanted insects. However, with overhead watering, you should do this early in the morning so the leaves have time to dry. The leaves should be dry before sundown, wet leaves are prone to disease. Check the soil moisture around the roses at least once a week. They need at least one inch of water every week, especially during the hot, dry summer. Adding mulch will help keep moisture in, keep weeds down and cut down on water usage. Water deeply to promote good root growth.

Mound up soil and mulch loosely around stems to help keep them from drying out.

Fertilizer should be applied at least three times a year to ensure strong, healthy plants with maximum blooms. A balanced 5-10-5 commercial fertilizer or any especially prepared rose food is fine. I recommend watering the area first, applying the fertilizer, work it into the soil, and then watering well again. This will help prevent any burning of the plant. Fertilize immediately after pruning in the spring, while the plants are budding, and the final application about two months before the first frost date. Also add some peat, Michigan peat or compost to the soil twice a year and work it in. When adding mulch, stay away from grass clippings as they may mat down and straw which usually contains weed seeds. Also, don't let the mulch actually touch the canes. If you have mulched the area and want to fertilize, move the mulch to the side, fertilize, scratch it into the soil and water, and then replace the mulch.

There are quite a few insects and diseases that will attack roses. Just to mention a few: spider mites, aphids, rose beetles, thrips, Japanese beetles, midges, mildew, black spot and rust. Walking among your roses doing regular inspections is probably the best way to keep insects and diseases to a minimum. Hand picking insects, pruning dead and diseased branches and having a spray or dust program will keep your roses healthy all season. A good preventative maintenance program works quite well if you are diligent about it. Purchase a combination insecticide and fungicide from your garden center and spray all roses when necessary. The combination spray should be a systemic (absorbed through the roots). Personally, I don't care for dusts or powders as they have a tendency to clump on a leaf when applied and wash off quickly during rain. And if their is any wind at all, you end up with some in your face no matter how careful you are.

> *Different colors of roses convey different emotions! Red stands for love and respect, white for purity and innocence, yellow for friendship and dark pink for gratitude.*

Roses need to be prepared for winter or they may die. The mixture of cold temperatures and drying winds may cause dieback. If properly cared for, most damage can be pruned off when spring arrives. All different classes of roses differ in their hardiness, so to be on the safe side, prepare all roses for winter. Stop fertilizing (usually in September) approximately eight weeks before the first frost. Any tender new growth may be killed by the cold and make the plant more susceptible to winter injury. Also keep roses watered until the soil freezes to help avoid winter stress. This preparation for winter cold is called **hardening off.** We don't want them growing when they should be sleeping. After a hard freeze and the roses go dormant, prune the canes back to about 2 to 2 1/2 feet to help the plant from drying out. Remove any diseased or dead branches and discard. Spraying any exposed parts with an antidesiccant (Wiltpruf) for added protection. The easiest and most satisfactory protection you can give is to mound soil up around the canes to prevent any water collecting around the

base, deter rodents and help protect against wind. Do not scrape up soil that is around the plant as this may expose the feeder roots to the cold. Purchase or bring in soil from other parts of your yard for the mounding. Form the mound approximately 12 inches high or less. Do not completely bury the canes. You can purchase plastic-foam cones from your garden center or mail order company to place over the plants. However, I recommend these cones be used only when temperatures are extremely low, around 10° F to below 0° F. If your area has strong winter winds, you may want to surround each plant with a burlap fence. To do this, buy a few lengths of 1" x 2" firring strips, cut them into stakes, place four stakes around each bush and staple the burlap to each stake.

When temperatures are expected to go below 15° F, different things are done for different types of roses. With **climbing roses**, you should remove the canes from their supports and lay the canes on the ground. Cover them with soil or some type of mulch. The entire plant can also be left on the support and wrapped in burlap for protection. **Tree roses** can be wrapped with burlap or brought indoors, depending on the size. Use the same wrapping method as previously mentioned. Tea roses need a little more protection. Use a mixture of soil and mulch such as cedar or pine bark chips. Wrap, as above, using double layers of burlap for wind protection. Make sure you don't allow fallen leaves or spent blooms to buildup around the plants. Rake out all unwanted debris from the garden before mounding or fencing. In the spring, just as new growth starts, remove any protection. Be careful, new growth is very tender and can easily be damaged.

If you plan to use your roses for cutting and displaying, cut the bloom at a 45° angle above a five-leaflet leaf facing outward preferably early in the morning. Make sure you choose blooms that are just starting to open. Try not to cut too much foliage from new roses the first year. Let the shrubs become established for a couple of years. Always look for and treat any kind of insect or fungus problems immediately. All roses love and need water, fertilizer, winter protection and lots of care. A healthy rose will be a blossoming rose.

Tree Rose

How To Winterize A Rose

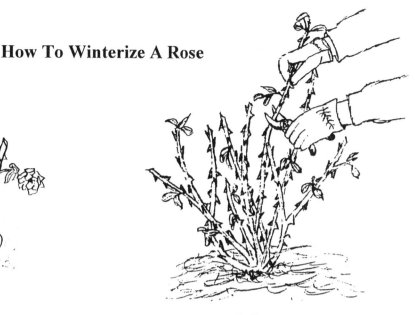

1 Harden Off

To prepare a rose for winter weather, stop fertilizing about 6 weeks before the first frost. Keep it watered until the soil freezes to avoid stress.

2 Prune

Cut back the canes to avoid drying out in wind. Wait till night temperatures are below freezing for a few days and then cut back to about 2 feet. Of course, remove any diseased or broken branches.

3 Mound Soil

After cleaning area of leaves and debris, build a mound of soil or compost over the entire plant to a height of 12 inches. Firm the soil around the canes and spray the exposed canes with an antidesiccant (Wiltpruf). After the mound has frozen, put about 2 inches of mulch over it. This helps prevent periods of freezing and thawing, which can damage the plant.

4 Early Spring

When the threat of frosts are over and buds are starting to swell, pull the mulch away. After the mound has thawed, spread it out around the base of the plant. Be careful not to hurt and new shoots.

Poisonous Plants

There are many poisonous plants that we as gardeners must be careful of. Some are quite toxic to the human body, while others may cause only a slight skin irritation. However, there is one plant we are all aware of as gardeners that is notorious for its irritation - *poison ivy*. Poison ivy (*Toxicodendron radicans*) is found in nearly every part of New Jersey. It is known by several different names, such as three-leaved ivy, poison creeper, climbing sumac and poison oak. Although it can grow as a self-supporting, erect woody shrub, its usual growth habit is a slender vine running along the ground, or growing on shrubs and trees. The vines can grow to several inches in diameter over a period of years.

Poison ivy has three leaflets occurring alternately along the stem. Leaflets are usually smooth, but may be either a dull or glossy green. Leaf margins (edges) can be smooth, toothed, and/or lobed. Leaves on the same vine often have a number of color and leaf margin combinations. It is possible, however, that all leaves on a vine will have the same general character. Because there are no distinguishing characteristics to warn an unsuspecting individual that a vine is poison ivy, the old saying of **"leaflets three, let it be"** should be remembered. The flowers of poison ivy are typically inconspicuous and arise in clusters above the leaves. The berrylike fruit has a smooth waxy appearance and is gray to white in color. After the leaves drop in the fall, the berries are a distinct identifier of the poison ivy plant. As a vine climbs shrubs and trees, it produces numerous "aerial roots" which attach to the tree or shrub. The "aerial roots" give the vine an appearance often described as looking like a "fuzzy rope."

Poison ivy is often found in fence rows, railroad embankments, roadsides, parks, nature preserves, many other wooded areas, and sometimes, your own yard. Always be on the lookout for this plant in these areas regardless of the season. Poison ivy plants produce an oil called *urushiol*, which is usually

capable of causing severe skin irritations the year round. There is always the potential of transferring some of the oil present in the leaves, stems, fruit, roots or flowers of poison ivy to the skin. Although contact with the plant is normally the method of exposure, an individual can also be exposed by handling clothing, tools, objects or animals which have become contaminated with the oil or by smoke from burning the plants. The symptoms associated with poisoning usually appear within 12 to 24 hours, but may appear in a little as 3 or 4 hours or be delayed for several days. The time span is dependent upon an individual's sensitivity, the amount of oil that contacted the skin, and the season.

Spring and summer are the times of greatest potential for problems. Damaged leaves exude the oil, which is easily transferred to skin, clothes and objects. Symptoms are itchiness, skin inflammation, swelling and the formation of blisters. For severe cases of poison ivy, a doctor may prescribe a cortisone skin cream or other medication to help reduce swelling and itching. For less severe cases, over the

counter skin creams with cortisone are also available in most stores. Bathing the contaminated area with a non-oily soap, immediately after contact, may reduce the reaction. In either case, check with your pharmicist or doctor.

Control Measures

Two general methods of control of poison ivy are cultural and chemical. Cultural methods should not be attempted unless the individual is tolerant to poison ivy. Individual sensitivity to poison ivy varies greatly. Natural immunity is originally present in all persons, but is lost after the first contact with the oil. Subsequent contact with the oil will result in skin irritation, although severity of the reaction may vary. Therefore, always take care when attempting to eradicate this plant. Individuals must also be careful when using chemical methods so that desirable plants are not mistakenly killed or injured.

Cultural

Burning is not a recommended method for eradication. Burning produces soot particles which carry the oil into the air. Individuals coming in contact with the smoke may experience severe cases of poisoning. Poison ivy can usually be dug out when the soil is wet and there are only a few plants. However, attempts to remove roots from dry soil are futile. Pieces of root remaining in the soil may sprout and replace the original plants. Plowing is also of little value, since the disturbed root systems will sprout. Repeated cutting of the plant back to the ground surface will eventually starve the root system and the plant will die. However, repeated cutting increases the chances of exposure to the toxic oil.

Herbicides

This is the method I recommend for getting rid of poison ivy. Several herbicides are effective in the control of poison ivy and can be found in pre-mixed or easily used formulations at local home and garden centers. Other chemical products will control this plant, but may not be registered for use around the home and are designated as *Restricted Use Products* (RUP). If these chemicals are required, contact your local county extension office for procedures and recommendations or a landscaper who is a Certified Pesticide Applicator.

Other Poisonous Plants

The effects of poison ivy can be very serious. However, there are many other innocent looking plants that may be harmful to us in one way or another. The seriousness of the effects may be determined by the age and size of the person, medication he or she is taking, the last time a full meal was consumed, the immunity to the contacted plant and other factors. Listed are some of the more common poisonous plants that we may come in contact with. Some may never bother you and others may be the cause of your unexplained rash. Usually, plant poisoning is not lethal, but it can cause mild ill feelings such as nausea, itching or burning sensation, diarrhea, sweating, rapid breathing among others. If you have any of the following plants or are planning to purchase them, I would consider labeling them when planting, especially if children will be around. Young children accidentally ingest many things, including plants and berries.   If you feel a poisoning has occurred, call 911 or your doctor. Identify the plant and take a piece with you wherever you go.

Narcissus

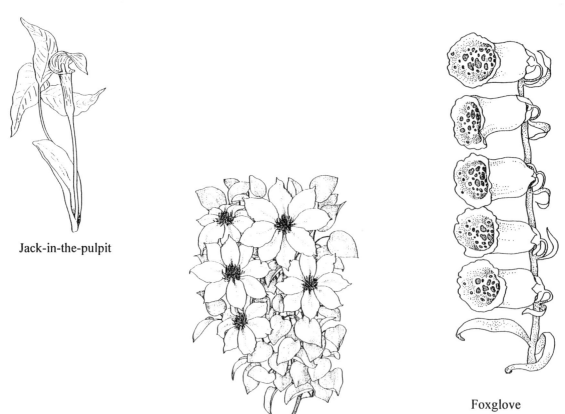

Jack-in-the-pulpit

Clematis

Foxglove

Common Poisonous Plants

Name	Part
Angel's trumpet	Entire plant
Bleeding-heart	Leaves
Clematis	Leaves
Delphinium	Entire plant and seeds
English ivy	Leaves
Foxglove	Leaves
Hemlock	Entire plant
Holly	Berries
Hyacinth	Bulb
Hydrangea	Leaves
Jack-in-the-pulpit	Entire plant
Lantana	Leaves and berries
Lily-of-the-valley	Leaves and flowers
Lobelia	Leaves and stems
Lupines	Leaves and seeds
Monkshood	Entire plant
Moonflower	Seeds
Mountain laurel	Leaves
Narcissus	Entire plant
Philodendron	Leaves and stems
Poison ivy	Entire plant
Privet	Berries and leaves
Sneezeweed	Entire plant
St. John's-wort	Entire plant
Star-of-Bethlehem	Entire plant
Wisteria	Seeds
Yew	Berries

This list is just a few of the many poisonous plants that may affect certain people. All of the above, except for poison ivy, have their place in a well landscaped yard or garden. Always wear gloves when doing any kind of gardening and make sure you wash them in warm, soapy water from time to time.

Chapter 7

By the Sea

Environmental Factors

Landscaping and gardening is different at the shoreline than it is inland. The salt air, wind and sandy soil all create difficult conditions for plants to survive. A major factor, which we cannot control, is the salt bearing wind. Most of the salt falls within 2 to 3 hundred feet of the ocean, creating severe problems for those who live in that specific area. The most damage occurs during winter and spring storms as they travel inland from the ocean. Dry storms (without rain) with strong winds deposit salt on plant leaves, that desiccate leaf tissue leading to dieback of branches and even death. Each of the above problems must be dealt with separately, however, to help ensure successful gardening. Although beach plant life is somewhat restricted, ocean front property owners must learn that using native plants is the best solution. These are the survivors, the ones that have lasted hundreds of years in this particular climate. They have adapted well and have become tolerant to the seashore.

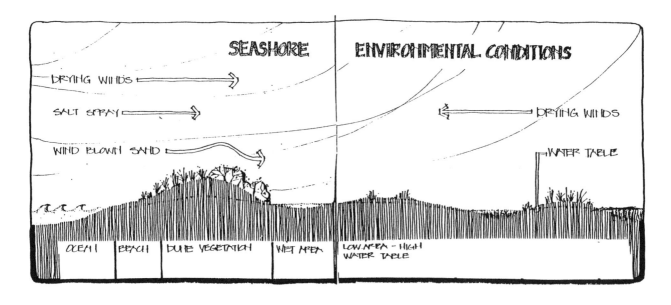

Wind

Before buying trees or shrubs, first learn about your particular area. Wind conditions on the coast vary considerably depending on the time of year. During winter and spring, winds affect all plants dramatically. Because of nearby salt water, trees and shrubs have shallow root systems rarely going deeper than 3 feet. During severe storms, trees may easily be toppled over, damaging both the tree and anything near it. Try to minimize wind resistance by planting trees which naturally will not exceed more than 25 to 30 feet high. New tree plantings should be staked immediately and remain staked for at least two years. The same should be done with larger shrubs.

At the seashore, where neighbors or visitors are always around, privacy is important. However, the proper planting of trees and shrubs will enhance your home. Don't put large plants in front of windows to keep people from looking in. During hot summer days, they will interfere with cool breezes. Protecting the house during the winter is necessary, but cooling it during the summer is too. Plant shade trees where shade is needed the most during summer. Properly located fences, shrubs and trees give privacy and protection without blocking out pleasant views. To protect smaller shrubs and flowers, plant windbreaks where needed. By creating adequate shelter, many of the plants that grow inland will now be able to survive near the beach.

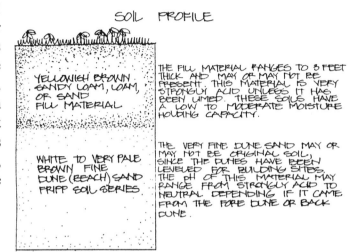

SOIL PROFILE

YELLOWISH BROWN SANDY LOAM, LOAM, OR SAND FILL MATERIAL

THE FILL MATERIAL RANGES TO 3 FEET THICK AND MAY OR MAY NOT BE PRESENT. THIS MATERIAL IS VERY STRONGLY ACID UNLESS IT HAS BEEN LIMED. THESE SOILS HAVE A LOW TO MODERATE MOISTURE HOLDING CAPACITY.

WHITE TO VERY PALE BROWN FINE DUNE (BEACH) SAND FRIPP SOIL SERIES

THE VERY FINE DUNE SAND MAY OR MAY NOT BE ORIGINAL SOIL, SINCE THE DUNES HAVE BEEN LEVELED FOR BUILDING SITES. THE pH OF THIS MATERIAL MAY RANGE FROM STRONGLY ACID TO NEUTRAL DEPENDING IF IT CAME FROM THE FORE DUNE OR BACK DUNE.

Salt

When deciding on what plants to buy, keep in mind that salt spray and salt flood damage can be devastating. Salt spray damage can be lessened by washing plants with fresh water at least once a week. If a flood is expected, saturate plants and soil with fresh water to lessen foliage and root damage. Salt flooding draws moisture out of plant roots. Once the flooding is over, saturate the plants again, to leach the salt through the soil, which lessens the damage. Frequently damaged plants can come back by developing new shoots. To leach salt through the soil, provide good drainage and thorough fresh water saturation. It's easier to prevent salt damage than trying to correct it. Proper fresh water practices help prevent salt buildup. Purchase plants that are salt tolerant.

Sand

The very sandy soil condition at the seashore creates a major problem for plants. This limits the quantity of plants to choose from, so native plants must be considered the mainstay of the seaside landscape. Before wasting time and money on plants that may not survive, you must learn about your individual soil. Have a soil test taken at least once every year. Good soil provides the nutrients that root systems need to be healthy plants. Beach sand has a coarse texture. It has relatively large grains, with large air spaces in between, and loses nutrients and water easily. Sandy soil has only a few of the essential nutrients plants need to survive. Fertilizer will wash quickly down below the root zone where it becomes unavailable to the plant. Heavy fertilizings with water soluble fertilizers quickly leach through the soil and pollute groundwater. Smaller, more frequent fertilizings are recommended to keep a supply of nutrients around the roots, minimizing leaching and loss of nutrients. When fertilizing, do not overwater. Slow release nitrogen remains in the soil longer. Sand, by nature, is also more acidic, and acidic soils sometimes prevent plants from using nutrients. The beach gardener should choose plants that are acid soil tolerant or apply lime at regular intervals to replenish that which has leached away.

In sandy, windswept areas, moisture drains quickly. Plants may suffer from drought conditions. While inland weekly waterings may be sufficient, plantings at the beach may need water every three to four days, depending on the season. Before planting shrubs, trees and flowers, soil preparation is extremely important. Adding abundant amounts of humus to the sand is essential. Your first thought may be to import top soil, however, top soil is much heavier than sandy soil and will quickly pass through the lighter sand. The addition of organic matter (Michigan peat, compost) increases the nutrient and water holding capacity but will be lost in a few years. Adding amendments will help new plantings become established, but should be replenished every year. When planting, mix a good amount of the amendment with sand and put some in the bottom of the hole. Place the plant in, fill the hole with more of the mixture and water well. We want sand in the mixture so plants will acclimate to the natural sandy condition.

Heavy mulching also helps hold moisture and keep soil cooler but should also be replaced yearly. Mulches at the seashore may include compost, pine needles, salt hay, cedar, barks, seaweed and eel grass. When using free mulches found on the beach, wash the salt off before placing around plants. Adding two to three inches of mulch should be sufficient to keep weeds down and minimize watering.

Landscape Techniques

Dune Stabilization

Dunes are considered one of the shore's primary defenses. They act as a buffer against water, wind and salt spray. Shore communities throughout New Jersey encourage dune building. They offer safety to humans and property. Dunes are formed of loose sand where ocean winds blow from one direction. Sand accumulates around an object that has become an obstacle to the ocean wind. The wind causes sand to move and grow in height as well as width. The side of the dune that faces the wind is usually longer and not as steep as the opposite side.

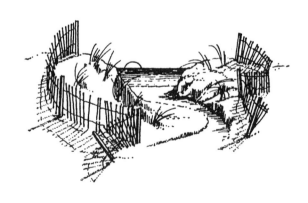

Certain grasses, American beach grass and salt meadow cordgrass, thrive in sand and are wind and salt tolerant. These plants are excellent for establishing dunes. Once they become established, their root systems spread rapidly underground to form a net that helps fight erosion. The more sand they are covered by encourages the roots to penetrate deeper in the dunes. Dune grasses must be protected from foot traffic, however, as they do not tolerate any trampling. Dunes can also be established by strategic placements of snow fences perpendicular to the wind. The formed mounds of sand can then be planted with grasses and fertilized to encourage growth. Most dune grasses can be purchased in existing clumps from local nurseries. These clumps can be divided into smaller clumps containing at least 3 to 4 stems each. When planting, stagger the clumps at least 20 inches apart and 10 inches deep. Make sure you fertilize and water the plants immediately to encourage root growth. Dune building is a long and complex process but the reward is a useful, natural windbreak that should give you years of protection.

Windbreaks

Winds, loaded with salt spray, create a hostile environment for many plants along the Jersey coast. The immediate shore area is composed of several distinct microclimates, as seen below.

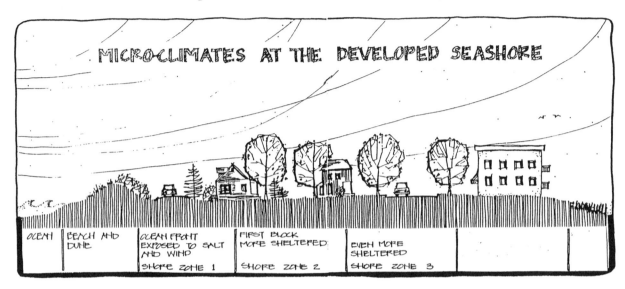

Only a few very hardy plants will survive in zone 1 as they are continuously exposed to the strong winds and salt spray. In zone 2, there are more plants that are tolerable to these conditions, as the severity of the conditions lessens. In zone 3, even more plants are tolerable as they become protected. Windbreaks add protection, not only for people and structures, but also for vegetation. Certain plants that are acclimated to beach sand, such as Japanese black pine, Red cedar, Rugosa rose, Beach plum, Pfitzer juniper, Bayberry and Inkberry all are good windbreaks if planted in strategic areas or as hedges. It is advisable to plant several different species rather than stick with one type of plant. Besides adding variation and different colors, you avoid the possibility of losing all the plants due to insects or disease. Planted in the right areas, mass plantings of small trees and large shrubs will effectively block damaging salt spray and winds. Windbreaks can also reduce air-conditioning costs in summer and heating costs in winter. With proper design and placement strategies, winds can be channeled upward or away from valuable properties. By placing small shrubs and trees at the edge of the windbreak, winds can be channeled upward, preventing weaker or new plantings from being destroyed.

Raised Beds, Containers And Flowers

Using raised planting beds of all shapes and sizes can provide ideal living conditions for small shrubs, flowers and vegetables. You still have to worry about the salt spray, but not so much about soil. The most popular raised beds are made of landscape ties. In most landscape beds, I do not recommend using black plastic, but in this case I do. Form the bed with landscape ties, line it with plastic and slit it here and there for drainage. Fill the bed with top soil, Michigan peat, compost or other soil amendment and complete the planting. The plastic prevents the loss of good soil and nutrients from leaching through the sand. Periodically, the soil should be replaced to remove any salt buildup. Small container

soil should also be replaced with fresh soil mix. Larger beds can be flushed with fresh water to leach the salt into lower soil levels below root zones. Exposure to winds and salt sprays will dry beds and containers faster than in the ground. For these reasons, frequent, heavy watering may be necessary.

When it comes to flowers, none are that tolerant to the heavy winds and salt spray that accompany coastal storms. However, spraying them with fresh water once a week, and before and after a storm will help. Most annuals and perennials that grow inland will survive at the beach if they are planted in protected areas, raised beds or containers. Containers are easy as they are portable and can be moved anywhere, anytime. Raised beds should be placed in protected areas (by fences, near buildings, behind windbreaks), if possible, out of the prevailing winds. Adding mulch to raised beds will help prevent moisture loss from winds. As a general rule, bulbs do very well near beach areas due to the fact that they like sandy soils. Vines can add decoration and privacy to homes on the beach. However, because many beach lots are relatively small, vines may not be a good idea. They have a tendency to crawl and spread, even on your neighbor's property. If you plan to grow vines, perennials are more hardy and salt tolerant than annuals.

Lawn Care

Lawns at the seashore have the same benefits as anywhere else. It absorbs the sun's heat, gives off oxygen, has a cooling effect on the surrounding environment, reduces the severity of the hot sun on sand and makes an ideal carpet for work or play. Grass also helps reduce erosion by water and wind. Contrary to many other plants, grass is fairly tolerant of salt in the soil and air. Where other plants may die because of salt flooding, grass will survive. There are, however, problems accompanied with growing a lawn at the seashore. The main problem is, of course, sandy soil. As previously mentioned, sand has very poor water and nutrient retention. People who move to the shore area are accustomed to overwatering and overfertilizing heavier soils. The same practices at the shore area will leach nitrates and nutrients into the ground water, increasing pollution and robbing grass of necessary nutrients. These practices may also lead to insect and disease problems. Maintaining an attractive, healthy lawn on the shoreline demands special management.

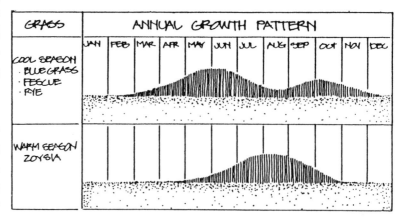

Lawns at the seashore should be watered more often and more lightly than those that are inland with heavier soils. During rainless periods, 1 to 1 1/2 inch of water per week is all that is necessary for inland lawns, but a shore lawn may need the same amount of water every four days. Also it is recommended to fertilize more often but with less amounts each time (lower the control number on your spreader handle). For summer homes, Zoysia grass may be more useful than a bluegrass mixture. Zoysia grows shorter, requires less water and fertilizer, grows well in sandy soil, and needs less mowing. However, it doesn't stay as green as other

grasses and is extremely invasive, especially in neighbors lawns. If your lawn will be subjected to heavy foot traffic, there are some low-maintenance grasses available. Kentucky-31 tall fescue, perennial ryegrass and some red fescue varieties combined with bluegrass, provide a tough, fairly luxuriant, low-maintenance lawn.

Planning Your Landscape

When planning your seashore landscape consider the following: how much time will you have to maintain your plantings, how much effort you are willing to give, how much money you are willing to spend, and will you be spending only weekends here, renting your property to visitors or are you a year-round resident?

If using non-native plants that are not adapted to the area, special maintenance requirements such as replenishing organic materials, fertilization and extra water may be necessary. When using native plants that have adapted to the area, maintenance costs and time will be less. Native plants thrive in the soil conditions and do well without extra water or care. In the plant lists that follow, many native plants are noted. Most of them are woody plants. As mentioned before, most annual and perennial flowers that grow inland will add beautiful color to the seashore if planted and maintained properly. Because of windy conditions, tall flowers should be staked or placed in protected areas. Plants that are listed by zones correspond with the drawing of Micro-Climates. While going over the lists, remember that plants that can be grown in zone 1 will survive in zones 2 and 3, but plants listed in zones 2 and 3 are less likely to do well in zone 1. Some of the plants listed may not be readily available from nurseries or garden centers. You can either order them if so desired or accept recommendations from the nursery. All land in New Jersey is owned by someone, and that permission is necessary before plants can be taken.

Key:
S - sun
SH - shade
D - deciduous
E - evergreen
WS - wet site tolerant

Shore Zone 1

Name	Type	Height	Traits
Eastern red cedar	tree	25-30'	S-E
Japanese black pine	tree	25-30'	S-E
California privet	shrub	15'	S-D
House hydrangea	shrub	3'	S-D
Memorial rose	shrub	2'	S-D
Pfitzer juniper	shrub	5-6'	S-E
Rugosa rose	shrub	4-6'	S-D
Sea buckthorn	shrub	25-30'	S-D
Bayberry	native shrub	4-5'	S-D
Beach plum	native shrub	6-8'	S-D
Inkberry	native shrub	5-6'	S/SH-E-WS
Wax myrtle	native shrub	25'	S/SH-semi E
Boston ivy	ground cover	vine	S-D
Shore juniper	ground cover	1'	S-E
Bearberry	native ground cover	1'	S-E
Sweet clematis	native ground cover	vine	S-D
American beach grass	native grass	2'	S-D
Little bluestem	native grass	3'	S-D
Saltmarsh cordgrass	native grass	1'	S-D

Key:
S - sun
SH - shade
D - deciduous
E - evergreen
WS - wet site tolerant

Shore Zone 2

Name	Type	Height	Traits
Colorado spruce	tall tree	40'	S-E
Ginkgo	tall tree	45'	S-D
Golden weeping willow	tall tree	40'	S-D-WS
Hackberry	tall tree	35'	S-D
London plane	tall tree	50'	S-D
Sycamore maple	tall tree	40'	S-D
Thornless honeylocust	tall tree	40'	S-D
Pitch pine	native tall tree	35'	S-E
Virginia pine	native tall tree	60'	S-E
Japanese flowering cherry	small tree	15'	S-D
Pinus mugo	small tree	25'	S-E
Russian olive	small tree	15'	S-D
Seedless mulberry	small tree	20'	S-D
Silver poplar	small tree	25'	S-D
White poplar	small tree	25'	S-D
American holly	native small tree	20'	S-E
Blackhaw viburnum	native small tree	15-20'	S/SH-D
Service berry	native small tree	20-30'	S/SH-D
American arborvitae	shrub	25-40'	S-E
Autumn olive	shrub	10'	S-D
Birdnest spruce	shrub	3'	S-E
Buckthorn	shrub	15-18'	S-D
Chinese holly	shrub	8'	S-E
Cotoneaster	shrub	1-6'	S/SH-D
European cranberry	shrub	8'	S-D
Euonymous	shrub	4-5'	S-D

Key:
S - sun
SH - shade
D - deciduous
E - evergreen
WS - wet site tolerant

Shore Zone 2

Name	Type	Height	Traits
Honeysuckle	shrub	3-15'	S-D
Japanese holly	shrub	3-15'	S-E
Mugho pine	shrub	4'	S-E
Firethorn	shrub	6'	S-D
Rose	shrub	5-6'	S-D
Spirea	shrub	2-10'	S-D
Wintergreen barberry	shrub	4-6'	S-E
Yew	shrub	3-15'	S-E
Black chokeberry	native shrub	6'	S-D-WS
Brilliant chokeberry	native shrub	6'	S-D-WS
Running serviceberry	native shrub	4'	S-D
Summersweet	native shrub	5-6'	S-D-WS
Winterberry	native shrub	8'	S-D-WS
Beach heather	ground cover	vine	S-D
Beach pea	ground cover	vine	S-D
Deer tongue	ground cover	grass	S-D
Fox grape	ground cover	vine	S-D
Redtop	ground cover	grass	S-D
Switchgrass	ground cover	grass	S-D
Virginia creeper	ground cover	vine	S-D

Key:
S - sun
SH - shade
D - deciduous
E - evergreen
WS - wet site tolerant

Shore Zone 3

Name	Type	Height	Traits
Callery pear	tall tree	25-35'	S-D
Chinese elm	tall tree	30'	S-D
Green ash	tall tree	40'	S-D
Laurel leaf willow	tall tree	40'	S-D
Oak	tall tree	40-60'	S-D
Siberian elm	tall tree	40'	S-D
Tree of Heaven	tall tree	40'	S/SH-D
Atlantic white cedar	native tall tree	40'	S/SH-WS-E
Pitch pine	native tall tree	40'	S-E
Red Maple	native tall tree	40'	S-D-WS
Sassafras	native tall tree	35'	S-D
Sour gum	native tall tree	40'	S-D-WS
Sweet gum	native tall tree	40'	S-D-WS
Virginia pine	native tall tree	30'	S-E
Crabapple	small tree	15-25'	S-D
Washington hawthorn	small tree	20'	S-D
Flowering dogwood	native small tree	20'	S/SH-D
Gray birch	native small tree	20'	S-D
Nannyberry	native small tree	15-20'	S-D
Aucuba	shrub	8-10'	S-E
Butterfly bush	shrub	10-12'	S-D
Cherry laurel	shrub	8-12'	S-E
Common witchhazel	shrub	10-12'	S/SH-D
Glossy abelia	shrub	5'	S-D
Japanese barberry	shrub	6-7'	S-D
Japanese euonymous	shrub	10-12'	S-E

Key:

S - sun
SH - shade
D - deciduous
E - evergreen
WS - wet site tolerant

Shore Zone 3

Name	Type	Height	Traits
Hydrangea	shrub	8-10'	S-D
Leucothoe	shrub	4'	SH-E
Lilac	shrub	8-12'	S-D
Rhododendron	shrub	3-15'	S/SH-E
Rose of Sharon	shrub	8-10'	S-D
Scotch broom	shrub	5-6'	S-E
Arrowwood	native shrub	8'	S/SH-D-WS
Creeping willow	native shrub	3'	S
Groundsel bush	native shrub	8-10'	S-D-WS
Highbush blueberry	native shrub	6'	S-D
Marsh elder	native shrub	4'	S-D-WS
Mountain laurel	native shrub	8-10'	SH-E
New Jersey tea	native shrub	3'	S
Red Twig Dogwood	native shrub	7'	S-D
Scrub oak	native shrub	10-12'	S/SH-D
Sheep laurel	native shrub	3'	S-E
Staggerbush	native shrub	4-6'	S
Swamp azalea	native shrub	6-9'	S/SH-D-WS
Sweet bay magnolia	native shrub	15'	S-D-WS
Bittersweet	vine		S-D
Chinese wisteria	vine		S-D
Clematis hybrids	vine		S-D
Climbing hydrangea	vine		D
Japanese wisteria	vine		S-D
Black huckleberry	ground cover	18"	S/SH-D
Bracken fern	ground cover	18"	S-D
Lowbush blueberry	ground cover	18"	S/SH-D

Closing Thoughts

Things are forever changing, new research, better products, more understanding and desire to help our environment. While reading about, and working in our own landscapes, we learn how the planning, organization and maintenance of our own property truly does affect the overall environmental picture. Improving the soil, making compost, performing proper maintenance, using less chemicals, purchasing resistant shrubs, grass seed and trees and implementing Integrated Pest Management practices will all help the environment. Invite nature to your backyard - birds and butterflies and beneficial insects are all our friends. Turn your yard into an "Environmentally Friendly" yard. Is a perfectly "weed-free" lawn worth contaminating the groundwater? Is applying a broad spectrum, "kill all bugs good and bad" insecticide worth it when damage is being done by only one species.

We must design our landscape based on its natural form, the relationship of the plants that grow in it, and how they will affect us. Read about and use methods that save energy and resources. Plant the right plants in the right places to help cool your house in the summer and warm it in the winter. Stop wasting water. Plant flowers, trees and shrubs that require less water, species that will flourish under normal rainfall conditions. Let your yard go "natural." Don't leave the water running when you wash the car in the driveway. Gallons and gallons are being wasted. Don't overwater your plants, some of them you may be killing. Proper maintenance procedures should be implemented: sharp mower blades, pruning techniques, fertilizing times and amounts, soil tests, water conservation, IPM and low doses of pesticides as a last resort.

Ultimately, our landscape should be useful, pleasurable and ever changing, for this is how we learn. Ecology begins with "us".

Rutgers Cooperative Extension

Rutgers Cooperative Extension is a research-based educational program for New Jersey residents. It provides leadership development and offers practical information to help with decisions on problems facing the public relating to: Agriculture and the Environment, Management of Natural Resources, Improving Nutrition and Health, Family and Economic Well Being, and Youth Development.

Rutgers Cooperative Extension teaches the public through county extension faculty and program associates located in each of New Jersey's 21 counties. They are backed by extension subject matter specialists located on the Cook College campus of Rutgers University. Over 12,000 volunteers assist the faculty and staff in extending the information to the people. It is part of a nationwide network of the federal, state and county government to bring the research of the state land-grant universities to the people.

Programs are available to all persons without regard to race, color, national origin, sex, or handicap. Attend the classes and workshops, ask to be placed on the mailing list to receive information, watch your local newspaper about programs and activities, and listen to Cooperative Extension faculty on radio.

Rutgers Cooperative Extension Offices:

Atlantic County - (609) 625-0056
1200 W. Harding Highway
Mays Landing 08330

Bergen County - (201) 599-6162
327 Ridgewood Avenue
Paramus 07652

Burlington County - (609) 265-5051
122 High Street
Mount Holly 08060

Camden County - (609) 784-1001
152 Ohio Avenue
Clementon 08021

Cape May County - (609) 465-5115
Dennisville Road, Rt. 657
Cape May Court House 08210

Cumberland County - (609) 451-2800
RD 1, Morton Avenue
Millville 08332

Essex County - (201) 648-5525
15 South Munn Avenue
East Orange 07018

Gloucester County - (609) 881-1200
County Building
Delsea Drive
Clayton 08312

Hudson County - (201) 915-1399
114 Clifton Place, Murdoch Hall
Jersey City 07304

Hunterdon County - (201) 788-1338
Extension Center
4 Gauntt Place
Flemington 08822

Mercer County - (609) 989-6830
930 Spruce Street
Trenton 08648

Middlesex County - (201) 745-3445
7 Elm Row
New Brunswick 08901

Monmouth County - (201) 431-7260
20 Court Street
Freehold 07728

Morris County - (201) 285-8300
West Hanover Avenue
Morristown 07960

Ocean County - (908) 349-1227
1623 Whitesville Road
Toms River 08753

Passaic County - (201) 881-4537
1310 Route 23 North
Wayne 07470

Salem County - (609) 769-0090
Lakeview Complex, Rt. 45
Woodstown 08098

Somerset County - (201) 231-7000
308 Milltown Road
Bridgewater 08807

Sussex County - (201) 383-3800
330 Rt. 206 South
Newton 07860

Union County - (201) 654-9854
300 North Avenue E
Westfield 07090

Warren County - (201) 475-8000
Wayne Dumont Jr. Administration Bldg.
Rt. 519
Belvidere 07823

The Division Of Plant Industry

One of the New Jersey Department of Agriculture's (NJDA) primary goals is to protect our plant resources from injurious plant pests. Through its detection, inspection, eradication and control programs, the NJDA's Division of Plant Industry (DPI) helps to ensure that farmers and others buy and sell high quality, pest-free plants and plant products. The DPI's programs include the certification of nursery stock for intrastate, interstate, and international shipments; prevention of tree defoliation and loss due to gypsy moth in forested residential communities; inspection of honeybees for harmful bee diseases and other pests; regulation and promotion of the marketing of plant seeds; and production and release of beneficial insects to reduce crop damage and to decrease the amount of chemical pesticides used by farmers.

All nursery stock sold in New Jersey must be free of injurious plant pests. In addition to inspecting nurseries and plant dealers, DPI's inspection staff issues phytosanitary certificates needed to export plants and plant material to other states and countries. Plants, that have been imported, with injurious plant pests are rejected and destroyed. At the request of growers, DPI also conducts a voluntary certification program to encourage the commercial production of New Jersey-grown tomato and pepper transplants that are free of plant pests.

The gypsy moth is New Jersey's most destructive insect pest of shade and forest trees. Since 1970, in cooperation with municipalities and the US department of Agriculture's Forest Service, the DPI has supervised a voluntary aerial spray program to control gypsy moth in forested residential communities. The program includes locating gypsy moth-infested towns using aerial and ground survey techniques; preparing a federally-required environmental impact statement to enable towns to qualify for federal reimbursement of a portion of the spray costs; and supervising annual spring aerial treatments with the non-chemical insecticide Bacillus thuringiensis (B.t.).

Honeybees are used for crop pollination and honey production, two important aspects of New Jersey agriculture. To protect this valuable resource, the DPI maintains a program to monitor and control bee diseases and predators such as varroa and tracheal mites. Inspections and laboratory analyses are conducted routinely on New Jersey hives and those shipped into the state during the growing season in order to determine the areas affected by these mites and to minimize the risks associated with these and other bee pests.

New Jersey's seed law requires DPI's seed certification and control program to monitor the seed industry to ensure that only quality seed is sold in New Jersey. To accomplish this goal, DPI inspectors visit retail outlets regularly to check the labeling of seed offered for sale and collect samples for laboratory analysis. Agriculture seed is also sampled and tested to help farmers avoid planting seed that germinates poorly or is contaminated with weed seed. Inspectors also verify the quality of seed purchased by landscapers, parks, schools and government agencies through sampling and testing. Seed which doesn't meet the labeling requirements of the law is removed from sale. The seed certification program

is responsible for certifying superior varieties of high quality seed and propagating material to ensure genetic identity, genetic and mechanical purity, and a minimum of seed-borne diseases. Laboratory analysis is required for both programs and each lot of seed must meet established quality standards.

Under DPI's biological control program, exotic and native beneficial insects are raised in the laboratory for field release to control insect and weed pests of forest, vegetable, fruit, ornamental, field and forage crops. The use of beneficial insects reduces the amount of pesticides needed to control a variety of pests. For some of DPI's biological pest control projects, the beneficial insects cannot live through a New Jersey winter and must be raised in the laboratory for release during the growing season. Other beneficial insects have managed to establish themselves in the state and are closely monitored to evaluate the impact they are having on a variety of other insect and weed pests such as alfalfa weevil, gypsy moth and musk thistle.

Through this Division of Plant Industry, New Jersey is helping us create a better state to live in. We must do our part by becoming more educated and aware of environmental situations and read labels on landscape materials to make sure they are top quality and industry approved.

Plant Diagnostic Laboratory

The mission of the Plant Diagnostic Laboratory is to provide the citizens of New Jersey with accurate and timely diagnoses of plant problems. These goals are achieved in cooperation with New Jersey Experiment Station/Cook College Extension personnel and research faculty. It is a diagnostic service available to the residents of the State of New Jersey. The laboratory was established in 1991 on the Cook College campus of Rutgers University. The lab is fully operational, and there is a fee for its services.

The Plant Diagnostic Laboratory is staffed with two full-time diagnosticians who are trained in all aspects of plant health. Seasonal employees and students assist in the laboratory. The staff works in close cooperation with Rutgers Cooperative Extension specialists, county faculty, and other university personnel to provide accurate diagnoses and up-to-date control recommendations.

Sample submission forms may be obtained at your local county Rutgers Cooperative Extension office. Forms may also be requested by FAX (908-932-1270). There are four different forms. The green form is for plant identification. The yellow form is for golf course and landscape turf. The brown form is for home grounds and landscape samples, and the pink form is for commercial growers.

How To Submit A Sample

- Completely fill out the sample submission form.

- Collect the appropriate samples, carefully following all directions found on the back of the sample submission form.

- Properly package the sample, including the submission form and appropriate payment.

- Mail the sample to the appropriate address.

- The laboratory will respond with the diagnosis by mail in a timely manner.

Tips For Sample Submission

- Carefully follow all directions on the sample submission form.

- Send samples early in the week. Samples mailed on a Friday will sit in the post office over the weekend.

- Collect samples before applying pesticides.

- Avoid packaging samples in plastic unless they are to be shipped overnight. Keep the sample and all paperwork separate to keep the paperwork dry.

- Detailed information on the submission form is essential for an accurate diagnosis. Take the time to completely fill out the submission form.

The diagnostic services offered by the Plant Diagnostic Laboratory include:

- Disease and insect pest diagnoses.

- Plant and weed identification.

- Insect identification.

- Nematode detection.

- Screening for turfgrass endophytes.

- Screening for fungal resistance to benzimidazole fungicides.

- Other services available by contract.

The fees for the above services range anywhere from $20 to $75 or more depending on the service provided. The samples with the appropriate submission form and payment should be sent as follows:

Via U.S. Postal Service:

Plant Diagnostic Laboratory
Rutgers Cooperative Extension
P.O. Box 550
Milltown, NJ 08850

Via Other Delivery Services:

Plant Diagnostic Laboratory
Rutgers Cooperative Extension, Cook College
Building 6020, Dudley Road
New Brunswick, NJ 08903

Sources Of Seeds, Plants, Garden Supplies

Seeds and Plants

Breck's
6523 North Galena Road
Peoria, IL 61632

Netherland Bulb Co.
13 McFadden Road
Easton, PA 18045
1-800-78-Tulip

Shady Oaks Nursery
112 10th. Avenue S.E.
Waseca, MN 56093
1-800-504-8006

Burpee
010777 Burpee Building
Warminster, PA 18974

John Scheepers, Inc.
23 Tulip Drive
Bantam, CT 06750
1-860-567-0838

Van Engelen Inc.
23 Tulip Drive
Bantam, CT 06750
1-860-567-8734

The Daffodil Mart
7463 Heath Trail
Gloucester, VA 23061
1-800-255-2852

Shepherd's Garden Seeds
30 Irene Street
Torrington, CT 06790
1-860-482-3638

Wildflower Farm
PO Box 5, Route 7
Charlotte, VT 05445
1-802-425-3931

Michigan Bulb Co.
1950 Wailorf NW
Grand Rapids, MI 49550

Spring Hill Nurseries
6523 North Galena Rd.
Peoria, IL 61656
1-800-582-8527

Thompson & Morgan
P.O. Box 1308
Jackson, NJ 08527
1-800-274-7333

Garden Supplies

Alsto's Handy Helpers
P.O. Box 1267
Galesburg, IL 61402
1-800-447-0048

Gardeners Eden
P.O. Box 7307
San Francisco, CA 94120
1-800-822-9600

Mellinger's Inc.
2310 W. South Range Rd.
North Lima, OH 44452
1-800-321-7444

Ames
Box 1774
Parkersburg, WV 26102
1-800-624-2654

Gardener's Supply Co.
128 Intervale Rd.
Burlington, VT 05401
1-800-234-6630

Smith & Hawken
117 East Strawberry Drive
Mill Valley, CA 94941
1-415-389-8300

Frontgate
2800 Henkle Drive
Lebanon, OH 45036
1-800-626-6488

David Kay
One Jenni Lane
Peoria, IL 61614
1-800-535-9917

Forestry Suppliers
P.O. Box 8397
Jackson, MS 39284
1-800-647-5368

Gardens Alive
5100 Schenley Place
Lawrenceburg, IN 47025
1-812-537-8650

A.M. Leonard, Inc.
241 Fox Drive   PO Box 816
Piqua, OH 45356
1-800-543-8955

Worm's Way
7850 North Highway 37
Bloomington, IN 47404
1-800-274-9676

Organic Products

Harmony
808 Live Oak Drive, Suite 126
Chesapeake, VA 23320
1-800-343-6343

PennTurf Products, Inc.
149 West Fairmount Ave.
State College, PA 16801
1-814-234-0391

Sustane Corporation
310 Holiday Ave.
Cannon Falls, MN 55009
1-800-3529245

BioLogic
P.O. Box 177
Willow Hill, PA 17271
1-717-349-2789

Growth Products
P.O. Box 1259
White Plains, NY 10602
1-800-648-7626

Lights

Intermatic
Intermatic Plaza
Spring Grove, IL 60081

Fabrics

The DeWitt Company
Highway 61 South
Sikeston, MO 63801
1-800-888-9669

Reemay
70 Old Hickory Blvd.
Old Hickory, TN 37138
1-800-321-6271

Drip Watering

RAINDRIP
2250 Agate Court
Simi Valley, CA 93065
1-800-222-DRIP

Gardening Glossary

A

Acid Soil - A soil condition with a pH below 7.0.

Accumulative Pesticides - Those chemicals which tend to build up in animals or the environment.

Aerification (Aerate) - The process of opening up a compacted soil or thatch ridden lawn by slicing, spiking or removing plugs of soil, improving the movement of nutrients, water and air.

Alkali - The opposite of an acid and is usually dangerous in concentrated form. A soil condition with a pH above 7.0.

Annual - A plant that grows from seed, produces seed the same year and then dies. Completes its life cycle in one year.

B

Bed - A place where plants, flowers, shrubs are grown.

Barrier - The chemical boundary below the soil surface which prevents the germination of undesirable plants.

Biennial - A plant that has leafy growth the first year, flowers the second and sets seed, and then dies. Completes its life cycle in two years.

Blend - The combining of two or more varieties of a grass species. Park, Merion and Newport are all Kentucky bluegrasses, can be mixed together and planted as a blend.

Broadleaf Plants - Plants with wide, flat leaves and netted veins. Examples: Weed - dandelion, flower - rose.

Broad Spectrum Pesticides - General purpose or wide range of uses. They are effective when several different pests are a problem.

C

Castings - Digested plant remains excreted by earthworms that act as a soil conditioner. They can appear as small mounds at the soil surface.

Certified Seed - A seed that is grown under the inspection of a certified agency, and when it matures, approved as to its identity, purity and high quality standards. It guarantees freedom from most weeds and unwanted fillers.

Chlorosis - A result of poor chlorophyll production in green plants that causes a yellowish color.

Compost - Organic material resulting from the decomposition of animal or plant matter, such as vegetables and grass clippings, that can be returned to soil for enrichment.

Cultivar - A specific variety of plants that retain their own distinguishable characteristics or features when reproduced.

Cutting - A piece of plant taken, at the correct time of year and prepared correctly, to propagate more plants of the same species.

D

Deciduous - Plants that loose their leaves every year in autumn and winter.

Defoliant - A type of pesticide which causes the leaves of a plant to drop off.

Desiccation - When the turf dries out, usually referring to winter, due to a lack of snow to protect it from drying cold winds.

Dethatch - The removal of thatch in the turf either by hand raking or using a mechanical machine.

Dieback - When the tips of plant shoots die, usually caused by disease or damage.

Disease Tolerance - A plants ability to resist disease.

Division - The act of separating one plant into several to increase the plant population.

Dormant - A temporary reduction of plant growth usually due to stress or extreme changes such as drought, cold or heat.

Dry Wilt - A plant condition caused by the lack of moisture in soil.

E

Ecology - Study of the relationship between a plant or animal and its surroundings.

Environment - External conditions which affect an organism's growth, usually water, air, soil, plants and wildlife.

Enzymes - Complex organic substances or proteins that accelerate chemical reactions. They help release soil and plant nutrients and speed up microbial activity and help open up soil for water and air.

Endophytes - These are fungi that grow in the tissues of certain grasses. Benefits are a certain amount of resistance to insects, draught, heat and injury.

Erosion - Wearing away of soil by water or wind.

Evaporation - When liquid is changed to vapor or gas and disappears into the air. Evaporation occurs when the heat of the summer sun removes the moisture from the soil by drying.

F

Fertilizer Burn - A grass injury caused by a high concentrate of chemical salts that suck the water out of the plant. Usually caused by a fertilizer spill or overapplication.

Foliage - The leaf covering of any type of plant.

Formative Pruning - A particular method of pruning a shrub or tree at an early age, so that it develops a desired shape or branch formation.

Frass - Pelleted excrement.

Fungi - These are actual plants that lack chlorophyll and the ability to produce their own food. The parasitic forms are the ones that cause rot, mold and plant or turf diseases.

G

Germination - A process when a seed becomes a seedling, the start of visible growth as a plant emerges from seed.

Growth Regulator - A pesticide chemical which increases, decreases or changes the normal growth or reproduction of a plant.

H

Harden Off - To adapt a young plant, that was raised in a protected environment, to cooler conditions.

Hardiness - Usually referring to the degree to which plants tolerate adverse conditions such as cold. The ability to grow outside all year long.

Heel In - A term used to plant shrubs or trees temporarily before putting them in a permanent location.

Host - A plant or animal in or on which a parasite feeds.

Humus - Decomposed organic matter. It is the dark material left over after decay and is rich in nutrients and a good soil conditioner.

Hybrid - A plant that is created by crossing two species that have different characteristics.

I

Inorganic - Synthetic material that is non-living.

Interplanting - When you grow two or more different plants together in the same area or garden.

L

Larva - The wormlike development stage of insects before they metamorphosize into adults. A grub is a larva of a beetle.

Leaching - Removal of materials in a solution by the passage of water through the soil. Example - The passage of nitrogen in a fertilizer through the soil down into the groundwater.

Leader - The main stem of any plant.

Leaf - Lateral outgrowth of a stem. A grass plant has two parts: the sheath at the base is wrapped around the stem and the blade is the flat part of the leaf extending up and out from the sheath.

Lesion - A mark or scar on a plant caused by injury or disease.

Lime - Usually refers to calcium oxide (CaO). The most common form is ground limestone used to sweeten soil.

Loam - A fertile, balanced soil composed of silt, sand and clay.

N

Nematode - A tiny, hair-like worm that causes damage by feeding on roots or other plant parts.

Node - A joint where a leaf is attached to the stem of a plant.

Non-Persistent - Only lasts a short time after being applied and breaks down rapidly in the environment.

Non-Target - Any plant, animal or other organism that a pesticide application is not aimed at, but may accidentally be injured by the chemical.

O

Organic - Anything that is formed from decayed living matter.

Ornamentals - Plants used to add beauty to homes, lawns and gardens. They include trees, shrubs and small colorful plants.

Overseed - To seed into an existing lawn to help thicken the turf.

P

Parasite - A plant or animal that harms another living plant or animal (host) by living or feeding on or in it. Sometimes parasites are helpful to man by attacking or controlling pests which could injure crops or animals. These parasites are forms of biological control.

Peat - Partially decomposed organic matter used around landscapes as a mulch or amendment.

Percolation - Water movement through soil.

Perennial - A plant that normally lives for more than two years. Trees, shrubs, grasses and many types of flowers are perennials.

pH - This means "potential Hydrogen" and is a numeric measure used to determine the acidity or alkalinity of soil. 7 is neutral, below 7 is acid and above 7 is alkaline.

Phytotoxicity - Injury to plant life caused by a chemical or other agent.

Plug - A small core or mass of grass and roots (sod) that is planted, at intervals, to develop a turf in a given area.

R

Reentry Interval - The period of time between a pesticide application and when people can safely go back into an area without protective clothing.

Residual Pesticide - A pesticide that can destroy pests or keep them from causing damage for long periods of time after it is applied (days, weeks, months).

Rhizome - The underground shoot that roots, grows horizontally and forms a new plant, at a distance from the main plant.

S

Salt Tolerance - A plants ability to resist salty water or soil.

Saturation - When soil is at the peak of holding its total capacity of water.

Soil Amendments - Any material that is added to and worked into soil, to improve its condition.

Soil Sterilant - A chemical that destroys all vegetation in soil.

Species - A group of living organisms which are very nearly alike, are called by the same common name and can interbreed successfully.

Stolon - The aboveground shoot that grows along the surface of the soil, capable of rooting and forming a new plant at each node.

Stress - A turf condition under which the plant suffers because of excessive heat, cold or lack of nutrients or moisture.

T

Taproot - A long, single thick root, usually growing downwards.

Texture - When referring to grass, the width of grass leaf blades and the appearance of the overall lawn. A fine (thin) textured lawn is considered to be more attractive than a coarse (wider) textured lawn.

Tiller - A sprout that emanates from a parent plant, and forms it's own leaves.

Translocation - An internal process where nutrients or pesticides move about in a plant, from one part of the plant to another.

Transpiration - Loss of water through plant surfaces, accounting for the major portion of water loss.

Turf - The upper layer of soil that is bound together by grass and roots to form a thick mat.

V

Variegated - Leaves marked with one or more colors.

Variety - A specific type of plant that is distinguished in minor characteristics from other varieties of the same species.

Vermiculite - A mineral salt that expands and has absorption characteristics.

Vertical Mower - A machine with vertical blades that slices through the top layer of turf and thatch. It is mainly used for thatch removal, lawn renovation and reseeding.

Viable - When referring to plants, a seed capable of germination.

W

Weed - Any unwanted plant in a landscape.

Winterkill - A turf injury resulting from stress during excessive cold periods.

Acknowledgments and Credits (resources)

I would like to thank the following for providing me with the latest research and technical information available, along with illustrations, drawings and descriptions that were all used in the production of this book.

University of Vermont Extension System, Burlington, VT, BR-1214, BR-146.

Ohio State University Extension, Columbus, OH, FS-HYG-4002-93, FS-HYG-4008-93.

Iowa State University Cooperative Extension, Ames, IA, PM-1591, PM-491, PM-683, PM-1446, PM-930.

Michigan State University Extension, E. Lansing, MI, FS-WQ-35, FS-WQ-34, E-2453, HYG-001, SR-60, SR-63, SR-70, E-1936, E-2024, FS-556, FS-399, E-1566.

Rutgers Cooperative Extension, Rutgers University, New Brunswick, NJ, FS-595, FS-596, FS-597, FS-598, FS-433, FS-97-B, FS-E080, FS-402, FS-316, FS-122, OR560-92, FS-388, 4-H-Unit4, FS-426, FS-117, FS-074, FS-191, FS-399, FS-395, FS-389, FS-797, FS-618.

University of Connecticut Cooperative Extension, Storrs, CT, FS-73-31, FS-81-6.

United States Department of Agriculture, FS-2-3-5, SCS, FS-223, PA-1154, SCS-Enviro, YS-78-5, Pest Appl Train Man VT002-510.

State of New Jersey, Department of Environmental Protection, Department of Agriculture.

Mellinger's Inc., 2310 W. South Range Road, North Lima, Ohio 44452

Spring Hill Nurseries, 6523 North Galena Rd., Peoria, IL 61656

A.M. Leonard, Inc., 241 Fox Drive, Piqua, OH 45356

RAINDRIP, 2250 Agate Court, Simi Valley, CA 93065

Shepherd's Garden Seeds, 30 Irene Street, Torrington, CT 06790

Shady Oaks Nursery, 112, 10th Avenue S E, Waseca, MN 56093

Harmony, 808 Live Oak Drive, Chesapeake, VA 23320

Index

Monthly Garden Calendar

January

- Order seed and flower catalogs. Review last year's plantings and make any changes.
- Plan your landscape on paper before ordering any seeds or plants.
- After a severe storm, check all plants for damage. Do not walk on frozen grass.
- Start cleaning all plant containers that will be used in the spring.
- Sharpen mower blades and do any necessary repairs on lawn and garden equipment. Disinfect pruners, oil tools and repair or replace those that are broken.

February

- Check and repair all outdoor furniture, planters, gas grills etc.
- Organize your tools and hang them on pegboards with nails or hooks. Paint the handles of smaller tools with a bright color so they won't get lost around the yard.
- Add indoor color by forcing perennial bulbs (tulips, hyacinths, crocus, daffodils).
- Order seeds, flowers, roses and other nursery stock for early spring planting.
- When the seeds arrive, start them indoors, towards the end of the month, so they'll be ready for spring transplanting.
- If weather permits, remove any damaged or dead branches.
- Check all climbers to make sure they are still attached to their supports.
- Check stored bulbs, corms, and rhizomes for signs of excessive drying or rot.

March

- Read about soil and possible amendments. Soil is your landscape's **lifeblood**. If you have good, rich soil, you will have healthy plants.
- Read articles about the environment and different ways in which you can help.
- Towards the end of the month, start pruning trees and shrubs. Remove any damaged branches. Check for any insect activity.
- Weather permitting, start your spring cleanup. Rake the lawn, clean out beds and remove any leaves, branches and trash.
- Take a soil test and adjust the pH if necessary. Lime can be applied at this time.
- Weather permitting, towards the end of the month, cut the grass at a 2" height and bag it the first time. This helps the lawn get a spring cleaning too.
- If you have purchased seeds for ground covers and ornamental grasses, start the seeds indoors early in the month.
- To control scale insects on fruit trees, apply a dormant oil spray when temperatures are above 40° F.
- Prune roses while they are still dormant.
- Cut back any ground covers that have overgrown borders.

April

- Dethatch, aerate and fertilize the lawn.
- Sow grass seed or lay sod using disease resistant cultivars. Water as needed to establish growth.
- Check the entire landscape for insect infestation and disease problems. If there is damage, apply natural controls at first and observe the results. If pesticides are necessary, apply at low dosages.
- If crabgrass has been a severe problem in the past, apply a crabgrass pre-emergent on the lawn before soil temperature reaches 65° F.
- Plant most annuals, perennials, shrubs and flowering fruit trees.
- After a couple of cuttings, raise the mower height to 2 1/2".

May

- Keep cutting the grass at 2 1/2" with sharp blades.
- Try to put up with weeds in the lawn. New grass seedlings are maturing and may help eliminate weeds by drowning them out. If your lawn is becoming weed infested however, its time to apply a herbicide (weed killer).
- Do not remove bulb foliage until it yellows and begins to die back.
- Prune all spring flowering shrubs and trees after the flowers fade.
- Keep newly planted shrubs and trees well watered.
- Begin various controls of aphids and other unfriendly insects.
- Apply mulch where needed but I recommend no more than 2 to 3 inches in depth.
- Water the entire landscape once a week deeply, unless it rains.
- Stop feeding the birds. One feeding every 10 days should be enough to keep them in your area. We want the birds to eat insects.
- Watch for insects and diseases on roses. Water them once a week if the soil becomes dry.
- Deadhead any faded flowers to promote more blooms.
- Water container plants as needed and feed with a liquid fertilizer.
- Spot seed those areas in the lawn that are still bare. Add a little top soil if needed.

June

- Continue mowing at 2 1/2".
- Water landscape only when needed, but water deeply. Water and high humidity encourage disease.
- Spot kill weeds. Try to avoid applying weed control over the entire lawn.
- Deadhead old blossoms from spring-flowering perennials and flowering annuals.
- Remove weeds from shrub and flower beds and replace mulch where needed.
- Prune back overgrown ground covers and ornamental grasses to encourage new growth.
- Deadhead faded flowers from roses and water deeply during dry conditions.
- Water container plants as often as needed.
- Apply low dose of pesticides only if absolutely necessary to avoid infestation. Try natural methods.

July

- Mow grass between 2 1/2 to 3". High grass helps eliminate weeds and keeps the soil cool.
- Water deeply only when needed. Avoid watering at night. This encourages disease.
- Spot kill weeds, but do not fertilize lawns.
- Fill birdbaths with clean, fresh water. Attracting them to your yard will help control bugs.
- Keep checking for insect and disease problems.
- Spot treat small amounts of crabgrass with postemergence herbicide.
- Dig up any spring bulbs you may wish to divide.
- Fertilize roses towards the end of the month. Water only in the morning to help prevent leaf spot.
- Deadhead old blossoms on flowering plants to encourage new ones.

August

- Set mower height to 3". Cut grass only if it is growing.
- Take a soil test to determine requirements.
- Maintain flower and shrub beds.
- Water entire landscape deeply, only if needed.
- Water container plants as needed.
- Do not fertilize the lawn. Avoid spraying weeds until next month.
- Do not fertilize shrubs and trees.

September

- Lower mowing height to 2 1/2", unless weather is hot.
- Dethatch and aerate the lawn if not done in spring. Seed and fertilize immediately after. Purchase fertilizer made for fall use, promoting root growth.
- Continue watering only when needed. Usually one inch per week is enough.
- Plant bulbs towards the end of the month.
- Remove any dead or diseased wood from shrubs and trees.
- Sod may be laid until the ground freezes.
- Continue to maintain beds.
- Divide and plant peonies and lilies.
- Keep a check on insects and diseases.
- Cuttings can be taken from many perennials, annuals, and shrubs.
- Plant any new trees or shrubs and keep watered.
- Cut back perennial flowers, that are not blooming, to four inches above ground and water.
- Plant certain hardy annuals for some fall to winter color (pansies).

October

- Lower mowing height to 2" and continue cutting at this height until the grass stops growing.
- If you didn't fertilize in September, do so now for the last feeding of the year.
- Start your winter cleanup (leaves, twigs, weeds etc.).
- Plant any remaining spring-flowering bulbs for next season's flowers.
- Finish seeding any bare spots in lawns.
- Water evergreens again if fall is exceptionally dry.
- Prune and discard any diseased or dead branches.
- Lime can be applied at this time of year.

November

- Cut grass at 2" until it stops growing.
- Complete fall cleanup of entire landscape, remove leaves and other debris.
- Prepare shrubs for winter. Wrap any delicate shrubs exposed to winter winds with burlap (windbreaks). Allow space for plants to breathe. Stake small or young trees to prevent wind damage. If you have rabbit or mouse guards, install them around young trees.
- Cut back any late blooming perennials.
- Mulch does decompose. Check all areas and, if needed, add some now.
- Winterize roses by mounding and mulching.
- If weather has been dry, water evergreens and new plantings before ground freezes.
- Remove any remaining leaves and debris. Clean out all house gutters and drains.
- If you have an antidesiccant, spray all evergreen ground covers for winter protection.
- Empty gas from the lawnmower and other machinery. Clean all tools.

December

- Prepare any equipment used for snow removal.
- Start reading all those gardening articles you cut out during the year.
- Keep all bird feeders and birdbaths filled with clean, fresh water.
- Give your entire landscape one final inspection. Make sure all debris has been removed and all plants are prepared for and protected from a long cold winter.
- Check your gardening journal. Make sure any last minute notes have been entered.

This calendar is based on average previous weather conditions in New Jersey. As all things change, so does the weather and climate. The above are only suggestions to be performed during those particular months if Mother Nature permits. Opinions concerning timing, procedures and methods differ between gardeners all over the world.

Notes

Notes

Notes

Notes

THE ULTIMATE
ENCYCLOPEDIA OF

~

CHOCOLATE

THE ULTIMATE
ENCYCLOPEDIA OF

❦

CHOCOLATE

WITH OVER 200 RECIPES

—

CHRISTINE McFADDEN & CHRISTINE FRANCE

LORENZ BOOKS
LONDON • NEW YORK • SYDNEY • BATH

Three sets of equivalent measurements have been provided in the recipes here,
in the following order: Metric, Imperial and American. It is essential that units of
measurement are not mixed within each recipe. Where conversions
result in awkward numbers, these have been rounded for convenience
but are accurate enough to produce successful results.

This edition published in 1997 by Lorenz Books

Lorenz Books is an imprint of
Anness Publishing Limited
Hermes House
88-89 Blackfriars Road
London SE1 8HA

Distributed in Canada by Book Express,
an imprint of Raincoast Books Distribution Limited.

ISBN 1 85967 359 7

A CIP catalogue record for this book is available from the British Library.

Publisher: Joanna Lorenz
Text by: Christine McFadden
Recipes by: Christine France
Project Editor: Joanne Rippin
Assistant Editor: Emma Gray
Designer: Nigel Partridge
Special Photography: Don Last
Picture Researcher: Vanessa Miles
Handcrafted dishes on pp: 58, 206, 231, 237
by Sue Shaw 01252 726684

Printed and bound in Spain
by Artes Gráficas Toledo, S.A.
D.L. TO: 241-1997

1 3 5 7 9 10 8 6 4 2

The authors and publishers would like to thank the following people for supplying additional recipes in the book: Catherine Atkinson, Alex Barker, Carla Capalbo, Maxine Clark, Frances Cleary, Carole Clements, Roz Denny, Nicola Diggins, Joanne Farrow, Silvana Franco, Sarah Gates, Shirley Gill, Patricia Lousada, Norma MacMillan, Sue Maggs, Sarah Maxwell, Janice Murfitt, Annie Nichols, Angela Nilsen, Louise Pickford, Katherine Richmond, Hilaire Walden, Laura Washburn, Steven Wheeler, Judy Williams, Elizabeth Wolf-Cohen.
Additional recipe photographs supplied by: Karl Adamson, Edward Allwright, David Armstrong, Steve Baxter, James Duncan, Michelle Garrett, Amanda Heywood, Tim Hill, David Jordan.

CONTENTS

THE RECIPES 65

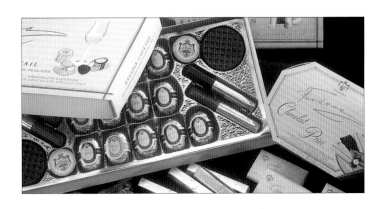

INTRODUCTION

One of the greatest treasures ever discovered was the bean from the tree *Theobroma cacao,* the original source of chocolate. Smooth in texture, intense in taste, subtly perfumed and elegant to behold, chocolate is a rich source of sensory pleasure, adored by almost everyone.

The Ultimate Encyclopedia of Chocolate is a celebration of this divine food, and divine it really is – translated from the Greek, *theobroma* literally means "food of the gods". In the first chapter chocolate's journey is traced from the land of the Maya in Central America to Spain and the rest of Europe, and then back across the Atlantic to the United States. Through doing so, it is evident that since the earliest days of its discovery chocolate has woven intricate links among people on every imaginable level – national, cultural, social, economic and spiritual. Chocolate has never failed to make an impact, initiating comment from the church, the medical profession, scientists, social reformers and royalty. Over the centuries it has been eagerly consumed in one form or another by all levels of society.

The chapter on Cultivation and Processing outlines where and how cacao is grown and harvested, and describes the different types of bean. The book follows the American, and less confusing, convention of using the term "cacao" for the plant and all

its products before processing; and the term "chocolate" for the processed beans, regardless of whether they are ground, liquid or in solid form. The word "cocoa" refers only to the concentrated cocoa powder invented by the Dutch.

The chapter goes on to trace the transformation from bean to beverage and from beverage to confectionery, and describes how this was made possible on a commercial scale. The industry's founding fathers, from the Quaker families in Britain – the Frys, the Terrys, the Cadburys and the Rowntrees – to the colourful Domingo Ghirardelli in San Francisco, and the persistent Dutch chemist Coenraad Van Houten, were all acutely aware of chocolate's popular appeal and commercial potential and went on to establish businesses that in most cases are still providing the world with chocolate today.

The taste and quality of chocolate is examined as we look at the specialist world of quality chocolate, demystifying terms such as couverture and cacao solids, praline and ganache. There is also a guide on how to taste chocolate properly – in the same way that wine-tasters evaluate a fine wine – for it is only by doing so that we learn to appreciate the alchemy that takes place during manufacture.

The international world of chocolate, including the characteristics of each country's chocolate, is also investigated. Flavourings and sweetness may vary, but what unites them is that smooth, sensuous, melt-in-the-mouth quality that is so hard and so pointless to resist. The book then delves into the physiology and psychology of chocolate, covering nutritional aspects, craving and addiction, passion and pleasure.

With this wealth of background knowledge, chocolate is then taken into the kitchen. The book's recipe section covers essential techniques to help you make the most of the two hundred tempting recipes that follow. You will find mouthwatering ideas for every kind of chocolate cake imaginable, from homely Chocolate Chip Walnut Loaf to the decadent White Chocolate Cappuccino Gâteau. A chapter on hot desserts will devastate you with Hot Chocolate Zabaglione, Hot Mocha Rum Soufflés and Chocolate Pecan Pie. Recipes for chocolate tarts and chilled desserts include classics such as luscious Mississippi Mud Pie and Tiramisu; and there are plenty of recipes for biscuits and little cakes. You will also see how to make your own chocolates and truffles, and the most deeply indulgent chocolate drinks. The recipes finish with a section on sauces, frostings and icings.

The *Ultimate Encyclopedia of Chocolate* is not only a celebration of a wonderful food, it will also fascinate, inform and instruct you in the history and production of this unique gastronomic treasure. Indulge yourself in a visual chocolate feast and accept the fact that if chocolate is not already an intrinsic part of your life, this book will make sure that it becomes so.

THE HISTORY OF CHOCOLATE

DRINK OF THE GODS

The origins of the solid, sensuous and, to some, addictive substance we know as chocolate are rooted in New World prehistory in the mysterious realm of the Olmec and the Maya. It was these ancient Mesoamerican civilizations living in the heart of equatorial Central America who were responsible for cultivating the tree from which chocolate is derived.

THE OLMEC

Three thousand years ago the Olmec people, one of the earliest Mesoamerican civilizations, occupied an area of tropical forests south of Veracruz on the Gulf of Mexico. Modern linguists have managed to reconstruct the ancient Olmec vocabulary and have found that it includes the word "cacao". Given the cacao tree's requirement for hot, humid and shady conditions, such as the land of the Olmecs, many historians are certain that the first civilization to cultivate the tree was the Olmec, and not the Aztecs, as is commonly believed.

THE MAYA

Around the fourth century AD, several centuries after the demise of the Olmec, the Maya had established themselves in a large region just south of present-day Mexico, stretching from the Yucatán peninsula in Central America across to the Chiapas and the Pacific coast of Guatemala. The humid climate there was perfect for the cacao tree, and it flourished happily in the shade of the tropical forest.

The Maya called the tree *cacahuaquchtl* – "tree" – as far as they were concerned, there was no other tree worth naming. They believed that the tree belonged to the gods and that the pods growing from its trunk were an offering from the gods to man.

LEFT: The Maya wrote their books on folding screens of bark paper. These two pages show a black-faced merchant god with cacao growers.

BELOW: Fifteenth-century Aztec stone figure holding a cacao pod.

ABOVE: This pre-Columbian codex shows Theobroma cacao, *with its pods, growing in a soil-filled sink-hole.*

The period around AD 300, known as the Classic Mayan civilization, was a time of great artistic, intellectual and spiritual development. The Maya built magnificent stone palaces and temples, carving into the sacred walls images of cacao pods – for them the symbol of life and fertility.

Known as "the people of the book", the Maya also devised a system of hieroglyphics, which were written down on fragile sheets of bark paper. Today only four of the Maya's books

---

— *THEOBROMA CACAO* —

The eighteenth-century Swedish botanist Linnaeus, who invented the binomial system of classification for all living things, later named the tree *Theobroma cacao,* meaning "drink of the gods", from the Greek *theos* (god) and *broma* (beverage). He felt it deserved a name that reflected the Mayan belief that the tree belonged to the gods, rather than the New World name of cacao or chocolate tree.

---

survive, and these are all from the post-Classic period. The books are full of drawings of gods who are depicted performing various religious rituals in which cacao pods frequently appear, and the text often refers to cacao as the god's food.

The Maya were the originators of a bitter brew made from cacao beans. This was a luxury drink enjoyed by kings and noblemen, and also used to solemnize sacred rituals. In their books the Maya describe several ways of making and flavouring the brew. It could be anything from porridge thickened with ground maize meal, to a thinner concoction for drinking. An early picture shows the dark brown liquid being poured from one vessel to another to produce an all-important froth. Various spices were used as flavourings, the favourite being hot chilli.

More evidence of Maya use of cacao survives on the many painted vessels that have been unearthed from their burial grounds. A tomb excavated in Guatemala in 1984 contained several vessels obviously used for chocolate drinking. One exotic and beautiful specimen bears the Mayan symbol for chocolate on its lid and was found still to contain residues of the drink.

THE TOLTECS AND AZTECS

After the mysterious fall of the Mayan empire around AD 900, the gifted and supremely civilized Toltecs, later followed by the Aztecs from Mexico, settled in former Mayan territory. Quetzalcoatl, the Toltec king, was also believed to be the god of air, whose mission was to bring the seeds of the cacao tree from Eden to man and to teach mortals how to cultivate various crops.

Because of political uprisings, Quetzalcoatl and his followers left the capital and fled south to the Yucatan. During a period of ill health he was persuaded to drink a mysterious cure, which, in fact, drove him insane. Convinced he must leave his kingdom, Quetzalcoatl sailed away on a small raft, promising to return in a preordained year to reclaim his kingdom. The legend of his exile became part of Aztec mythology, and astrologers predicted that in 1519 a white-faced king would return to release his people. This belief was to influence the whole future of the New World.

RIGHT: Aztecs greeting the white-skinned explorers landing on the coast of Tabasco. The Aztecs believed they were gods returning to recover their kingdom.

THE SPANISH ADVENTURERS

Although the Spanish explorer Hernán Cortés is generally considered to be the first European to recognize the potential of Aztec chocolate, the initial discovery must be attributed to Christopher Columbus. In 1502, on his fourth and final voyage to the Caribbean, Columbus reached the island of Guanaja off the Honduran coast. The story goes that he was greeted by Aztecs who offered him a sackful of what looked like large almonds in exchange for some of his own merchandise. Noticing his puzzlement, the Aztecs explained that a very special drink, *tchocolatl* (or *xocolatl*), could be made with these beans. Their chief demonstrated by having his servants prepare some on the spot. Columbus and his crew found the resulting dark and bitter concoction repellent but nevertheless took some cacao beans back to Spain for curiosity value, little realizing their future economic worth.

ABOVE: Hernán Cortés, the Conquistador.

CACAO AS CURRENCY

When Hernán Cortés arrived in the New World seventeen years later, Montezuma II, the then Aztec Emperor, believed Cortés to be a reincarnation of Quetzalcoatl, the exiled Toltec god-king whose return had been predicted to take place in the same year. The confusion made it easy for Cortés to gain access to Tenochtitlán, the Aztec capital, where Montezuma received him and his men with a royal welcome. The emperor offered them numerous gifts, including a cacao plantation, and an extravagant banquet was prepared in their honour.

Despite the overwhelming welcome, Montezuma eventually realized that he had made a mistake and had wrongly identified the Spaniard. Immediately recognizing the insecurity of his position, Cortés enlisted the help of sympathetic natives and managed to take Montezuma prisoner. Within the space of two or three years he brought about the downfall of the Aztec kingdom. Unlike Columbus, Cortés quickly realized the enormous economic value of the cacao bean, both as food and a form of currency. A contemporary of Cortés reported that a slave could be bought for one hundred cacao beans, the services of a prostitute for ten, and a rabbit for four. The Jesuit, Pedro Martyre de Angleria, called the beans "pecuniary almonds" and described them as "blessed money, which exempts its

ABOVE: A painting showing Montezuma giving a royal welcome to Cortés.

RIGHT: Aztecs greeting Columbus and his fleet with welcoming gifts as he lands on Guanaja.

possessors from avarice, since it cannot be hoarded or hidden underground". It is presumed that he was referring to the fact that the beans could not be stored for long without rotting.

The writings of Thomas Gage, a seventeenth-century English Dominican friar, are a rich source of information on chocolate. Visiting the City of Mexico, Gage describes how the cacao bean is used as "both meat and current money". Basing the exchange rate on the Spanish real, which at that time (1625) was worth sixpence (2½p), he explained that two hundred small cacao beans were worth one Spanish real, and "with these the Indians buy what they list, for five, nay for two cacaos, which is a very small part of a real, they do buy fruits and the like".

THE CACAO PLANTATIONS

When Cortés set out on his voyage to the New World, his primary goal was to find El Dorado – Aztec gold. When he failed to unearth the dreamed-of riches, his attention turned to cacao beans. Having seen them used as currency, and noticing the importance attached to them, Cortés soon realized that money could literally be made to grow on trees. He devoted the next few years to exploiting the commercial potential of this "liquid gold" by setting up cacao plantations around the Caribbean.

Cacao was cheap to cultivate and reasonably profitable, and the prospect of easy riches attracted plenty of Spanish colonists. Before long, the Spanish had established plantations in Mexico, Ecuador, Venezuela, Peru, and the islands of Jamaica and Hispaniola (now called Haiti and the Dominican Republic). Cacao production has since spread all over the world, but the plantations in these original regions still produce the most highly prized varieties of bean.

THE SPANISH SECRET

The Spanish colonists had tried to keep the secret of cultivating and preparing cacao to themselves, and with good reason – they were making fat profits out of processing the beans in Latin America before shipping them to Europe. However, the colonists did not remain in sole possession of their secret forever. In 1580, the first ever chocolate-processing plant was set up in Spain. From then on the popularity of chocolate gradually spread to other European countries.

LEFT: An early illustration showing cacao pods drying and a cacao tree growing under a shade-creating "mother" tree.

ABOVE: This lithograph, produced by the Empire Marketing Board, shows cacao pods being gathered.

These, in turn, established their own plantations, trade routes and processing facilities.

The Dutch transplanted the tree to their East Indian states of Java and Sumatra in the early seventeenth century, and from there it spread to the Philippines, New Guinea, Samoa and Indonesia with a degree of financial success made possible by the exploitation of hundreds of thousands of African slaves. The French settled in Martinique in 1660, and in Brazil in 1677, along with the Portuguese. Trinidad was fought over by the Dutch, the French and the British for years; it eventually went to the British in 1802. In the early nineteenth century, the Portuguese successfully transplanted Brazilian cacao saplings to the island of São Tomé off the African coast, and later to the island of Fernando Póo (now called Bioko) and West Africa. By the end of the nineteenth century, the Germans had settled in the Cameroons and the British in Sri Lanka. Plantations have since spread to South-East Asia, and Malaysia is now one of the world's leading producers.

— CACAO FEVER —

It was no easy job for the early planters to clear the jungle, but their fierce determination spurred them on. A Brazilian writer, Jorge Amado, described the vision of those early planters gripped by "cacao fever": "He does not see the forest … choked with dense creepers and century-old trees, inhabited by wild animals and apparitions. He sees fields planted with cacao trees, straight rows of trees bearing golden fruit, ripe and yellow. He sees plantations pushing the forest back and stretching as far as the horizon."

THE POWER OF CHOCOLATE

To the Aztecs, chocolate was a source of spiritual wisdom, tremendous energy and enhanced sexual powers. The drink was highly prized as a nuptial aid, and, predictably, was the favourite beverage at wedding ceremonies. The Emperor Montezuma was reputed to get through fifty flagons of chocolate a day, always fortifying himself with a cup before entering his harem.

Although drunk on a daily basis, chocolate was still considered an exotic luxury and consumed primarily by kings, noblemen and the upper ranks of the priesthood. (Some historians say that priests would not have drunk chocolate, arguing that it would have been the equivalent of a priest quaffing champagne every day.)

Because of its renowned energy-boosting properties, chocolate was also given to Aztec warriors to fortify them on military campaigns. The chocolate was compressed into conveniently travel-sized tablets and wafers. Perhaps as a kind of incentive scheme a special law was instated declaring that unless a warrior went to war, he was forbidden to drink chocolate or eat luxury meats, or wear cotton, flowers or feathers – even if he was a royal prince or nobleman.

The Spanish colonists, too, became infatuated by the chocolate mystique. Once they had become accustomed to the strangeness of the drink, they took to it with enthusiasm. The Jesuit, José de Acosta, wrote "The Spaniards, both men and women, that are accustomed to the country, are very greedy of this chocolaté. They say they make diverse sortes of it, some hote, some colde, and put therein much of that chili."

Increasingly aware of its restorative values, Cortés convinced Carlos I of Spain of the enormous potential of this New World health food: "… the divine drink which builds up resistance and

Chocolate has always been associated with gold, possibly originating from Montezuma's ritual of drinking chocolate from a golden goblet, which, immediately after use, was thrown into the lake beside his palace. The lake turned out to be quite literally a gold mine for the Spanish after the conquest. Evidence of the association with gold can still be seen today with chocolate manufacturers, especially the Swiss, selling fake gold bars and chocolate coins encased in gold wrapping.

fights fatigue. A cup of this precious drink enables a man to walk for a whole day without food".

Thomas Gage was heavily reliant on it too. He wrote: "Two or three hours after a good meal of three or four dishes of mutton, veal or beef, kid, turkeys or other fowles, our stomackes would bee ready to faint, and so wee were fain to support them with a cup of chocolatte".

RIGHTS, RITUALS AND CEREMONIES

The writings of New World travellers give us fascinating insights into the strange and sometimes barbaric rites, rituals and ceremonies attached to the cacao bean and the drinking of chocolate.

Religious rituals took place at different stages during cultivation. The Maya always held a planting festival in honour of the gods during which they sacrificed a dog with a cacao-coloured spot in its hair. Another practice, calling for a certain amount of commitment, required the planters to remain celibate for thirteen nights. They were allowed to return to their wives on the fourteenth night, and then the beans were sown. Another somewhat gory planting ceremony involved placing the seeds in small

LEFT: Chocolate was drunk by Aztec warriors in military campaigns, but it didn't win them victory over the Spanish.

RIGHT: An Aztec with his chocolate pot and molinillo. The molinillo has shaped paddles for making the drink frothy.

— *CHOCOLATE AND CUISINE* —

Contrary to what some cookery writers would have us believe, the Aztecs did not use chocolate as an ingredient in cooking. To do so would have been considered sacrilegious – rather like devout Christians using communion wine to make gravy. What possibly causes confusion is a classic Mexican recipe called *Mole Poblano*, turkey or chicken in a chilli sauce flavoured with chocolate. The recipe is often assumed to have Aztec origins, but the ingredients include several items – onions, tomatoes and garlic, for instance – that would not have been available then. This is a recipe for Mole Poblano:

8 dried mulato chillies; 4 dried ancho chillies; 4 dried pasilla chillies; 2 dried chipotle chillies; 1 small turkey; 50g/2oz/4 tbsp lard (or vegetable oil); 60ml/4 tbsp sesame seeds; 115g/4oz/1 cup blanched almonds; 1 corn tortilla; 2 crushed garlic cloves; 1 chopped onion; ¼ tsp each of ground cloves; cinnamon and anise; 6 black peppercorns; 50g/2oz/⅓ cup raisins; 3 peeled tomatoes; 5ml/1 tsp salt; 50g/2oz/2 squares unsweetened chocolate; chicken or turkey stock

Arrange the dried chillies in a single layer in a roasting tin and soften in a hot oven for 2–3 minutes, taking care not to let them burn. Discard the stems and seeds and put the chillies in a bowl. Cover with barely boiling water. Leave to soak for 20–30 minutes.

Divide the turkey into portions. Heat the lard or oil in a heavy-based flameproof casserole and fry the turkey until golden brown. Using a slotted spoon, remove the turkey portions from the casserole and set aside.

Roast the sesame seeds and almonds in a dry frying pan over a medium heat until golden. Remove from the pan. Cut the tortilla into strips and heat in the pan until brittle.

Put the almonds, tortilla and all but 5ml/1 tsp sesame seeds into a food processor. Add the garlic, onion, spices, raisins, tomatoes and salt. Drain the chillies, reserving the soaking water, add them to the processor and purée until smooth, adding some of the chilli soaking water if necessary. Add this purée to the fat remaining in the casserole. Fry gently for about 5 minutes, stirring constantly.

Return the turkey to the casserole, with the chocolate and enough stock to just cover. Bring to the boil, then lower the heat, cover and simmer gently for 45–60 minutes until the turkey is tender and cooked through and the sauce has thickened. Garnish with the reserved sesame seeds and serve with rice and tortillas.

NOTE: If you have difficulty in finding Mexican dried chillies, use 115g/4oz fresh green chillies and 2 small dried red chillies, and do not preheat them in the oven. Simply remove the seeds, tear the chillies into shreds and soak as above.

LEFT: A Mexican metate *was used for grinding cacao beans to a paste.*

LEFT: A mosaic of Quetzalcoatl, the Toltec king and god who, according to legend, brought the cacao bean as a gift to human kind.

bowls before performing secret rites in the presence of an idol. Blood was then drawn from different parts of the human body and used to anoint the idol. Other practices include sprinkling "the blood of slain fowls" over the land to be sown. There were also tales of frenzied dancing, orgiastic rituals and bloody sacrifices. The sixteenth-century Italian historian and traveller, Girolamo Benzoni, recorded that during festivals "they used to spend all the day and half the night in dancing with only cacao for nourishment". Another legend tells of how, as a prize, the winner of a type of ball game would be offered as a sacrifice. The unfortunate man was first fed vast quantities of chocolate in order "to colour his blood" before his heart was cut out and presented to the gods, who, it was believed, would be honoured by the chocolate-rich blood.

Another use of chocolate was as a face paint with which the Aztecs adorned themselves in religious ceremonies. Even the early Spanish planters believed that secret rites were necessary for a successful crop and performed planting ceremonies. From its earliest days, then, chocolate was regarded as a substance of power, a gift from the gods, a source of vitality and life.

BELOW: Cacao beans laid out to dry on plantain leaves.

FROM BEAN TO BEVERAGE

ABOVE: A seventeenth-century lithograph showing an imaginary scene on a plantation, with Aztecs harvesting, preparing and cooking chocolate.

The Aztec drink bore little resemblance to the deliciously smooth, rich and creamy beverage we know today; it was bitter, greasy and served cold. Early travellers give differing accounts of how it was made. Giramolo Benzoni, a sixteenth-century Italian botanist, described the method used in rural areas: "They take as many fruits as they need and put them in an earthenware pot and dry them over the fire. Then they break them between two stones and reduce them to flour just as they do when they make bread. They then transfer this flour into vessels made of gourd halves …, moisten the flour gradually with water, often adding their 'long pepper' [chilli]."

Still on the subject of ingredients, Thomas Gage described additions other than chilli: "But the meaner set of people, as Blackamoors and Indians, commonly put nothing in it, but Cacao, Achiotte, Maize, and a few Chillies with a little Aniseed". Maize was used to blot up the cacao butter which floated to the top, and also to bind and thicken the drink.

It seems that the grinding stone, or *metate,* was an important part of the production process. One writer describes the process in some detail: "For this purpose they have a broad, smooth stone, well polished and glazed very hard, and being made fit in all respects for their use, they grind the cacaos thereon very small, and when they have so done, they have another broad stone ready, under which they keep a gentle fire". Because of the crude manual processing, all sorts of undesirable bits and pieces – shells, husks and pith – were allowed to remain in the resulting

RIGHT: Aztec chocolate-making equipment: chocolate pot, drinking goblet, whisk and rolling pin.

liquor. In Benzoni's opinion: "This mixture looks more fit for the pigs than like a beverage for human beings".

A FROTHY BREW

The Jesuit José de Acosta wrote: "The chief use of this cacao is in a drincke which they call chocolaté, whereof they make great account, foolishly and without reason: for it is loathsome to such as are not acquainted with it, having a skumme or frothe that is very unpleasant to taste, if they be not well conceited thereof."

For the Maya and Aztecs the froth was an all-important and most delicious part of the drink. One historian pointed out the importance "of opening the mouth wide, in order to facilitate deglutition, that the foam may dissolve gradually and descend imperceptibly, as it were, into the stomach". The Maya made the drink frothy by pouring it from one bowl to another from a height. Later, the Aztecs invented a device that the Spanish called a *molinillo* – a wooden swizzle stick with specially shaped paddles at one end, which fitted into the hole in the lid of the chocolate pot.

The eighteenth-century missionary, Father Jean-Baptiste Labat, described this indispensable item in one of his books: "A stick is about ten inches longer than the chocolate pot, thus enabling it to be freely twirled between the palms of the hand." The *molinillo* is still in use today and can be found in Latin American shops and markets. The design of the basic wooden stick remains unchanged, but there are also beautiful antique pots and swizzle sticks in silver and other decorative materials, which have become collectors' items.

There is evidence of yet more ingredients than those

— *CHAMPURRADO (CHOCOLATE ATOLE)* —

The addition of maize would have turned the Aztec drink into a thin gruel or porridge known as *atole.* This is a type of fortified drink, not necessarily flavoured with chocolate, still served at meals or used as a pick-me-up by workers in the fields in Latin America today. The chocolate-flavoured version is always referred to as *champurrado,* from *champurrar,* meaning to mix one drink with another:

Put 65g / 2½oz / ½ cup masa harina (treated maize flour) or finely ground tortillas in a large pan with 750ml / 1¼ pints / 3 cups water. Stir over low heat until thickened. Remove from the heat and stir in 175g / 6oz / 1 cup soft light brown sugar (or to taste), and 750ml / 1¼ pints / 3 cups milk. Grate three 25g / 1oz squares unsweetened chocolate and add to the pan. Beat well with a molinillo *and serve steaming hot.*

> ### *A MEXICAN RECIPE FOR HAND-MADE CHOCOLATE*
> *Take 6 pounds [2.75kg] of good quality cacao beans, at least three different types, in equal quantities. Roast in a metal pan studded with holes just until they begin to give off their oil. Take care not to remove the beans from the heat too soon, or the resulting chocolate will be discoloured and indigestible. If the beans are allowed to burn, the chocolate will be bitter and acrid.*
> *Rub the roasted beans through a fine hair sieve to remove the husks. Next, place your metate (grinding stone) on a flat pan containing hot coals. Once the stone is warm begin to grind the chocolate. Grind the chocolate with 4 to 6 pounds [1.75–2.75kg] of sugar, depending on desired sweetness, pounding it with a large mallet.*
> *Shape the resulting paste into tablets as preferred – round, hexagonal or oblong – and place on a rack to air. If you wish, make dividing lines on the surface of the chocolate with the tip of a sharp knife.*

ABOVE: Aztecs poured chocolate from a height to make it frothy.

mentioned by Thomas Gage. The Spanish historian, Sahagún, describing a menu of chocolate drinks to be served to lords, tells us that there were "ruddy cacao; brilliant red cacao; orange cacao; black cacao; and white cacao". Many of the very early recipes for chocolate share common ingredients, and from these we can tell that the likely flavourings for the lords' impressive choice of cacao were chilli, allspice, cloves, vanilla, a type of black pepper, various flower petals, nuts and annatto.

BELOW: A modern chocolate pot, whisk and chocolate from Colombia. The design of the whisk has not changed since the days of the Aztecs.

Sugar was not added until much later. There is a story that the nuns of Oaxaca, an Aztec town occupied by the Spanish until 1522, developed new recipes in deference to the Spanish sweet tooth. They added sugar and sweet spices such as cinnamon and aniseed, and so the bitter beverage of the Aztecs began its transformation to the delicious drink that we know today.

THE SPANISH VERSION

In 1701 an Englishman travelling in Spain gave a detailed and lengthy account of the manufacturing process developed by the Spanish. After the preliminary roasting, dehusking and grinding, the cacao mass was ground again to a fine paste with plenty of sugar, cinnamon, vanilla, musk and annatto. The chocolate was formed into blocks, along the lines of modern block chocolate, but even so, these were still used only for making the beverage, rather than as confectionery.

As far as we know, this is the recipe that was used throughout Spain and the rest of Europe until the process was revolutionized in the nineteenth century by the technological achievements of the Dutchman Van Houten.

FROM BEVERAGE TO CONFECTIONERY

ABOVE: A 1893 poster with a background of cacao pods and leaves.

VAN HOUTEN'S PRESS

In its early days chocolate was an extremely rich beverage. It contained a fatty substance known as cacao butter, which tended to rise to the top, where it would float in unappetizing greasy pools. Manufacturers overcame this to some extent by adding starchy substances to absorb the fat – a process similar to the Aztec tradition of adding ground maize.

Manufacturers had also tried unsuccessfully for years to devise a way of separating out the greasy cacao butter. Breakthrough came in 1828 when, after years of trial and error, a Dutch chemist named Coenraad Van Houten patented a new and extremely efficient hydraulic press. His machine was able to extract about fifty per cent of the cacao butter present in the "liquor" (the paste produced after grinding the beans), leaving behind a refined, brittle, cake-like residue that could then be pulverized to a fine powder.

Not satisfied, Van Houten went one step further. He treated the powder with alkaline salts in order to improve the ease with which it could be mixed with water. The process, which came to be known as "Dutching", also darkened the colour of the chocolate and lightened the flavour – a curious anomaly since plain chocolate is usually assumed to have a stronger flavour. Today many people believe they prefer Dutch chocolate because of its strong flavour, but it may simply be the colour that attracts them.

Van Houten's inexhaustible patience revolutionized the chocolate industry. It led to the manufacture of what we now know as cocoa powder, which in Van Houten's time was called "cocoa essence". It also led to an all-round improvement within the industry. Van Houten sold his rights ten years after he took out the patent, and the machine came into general use. Among the first customers were the Frys and the Cadburys, ever eager to outdo

RIGHT: Modern packaging based on the art nouveau style.

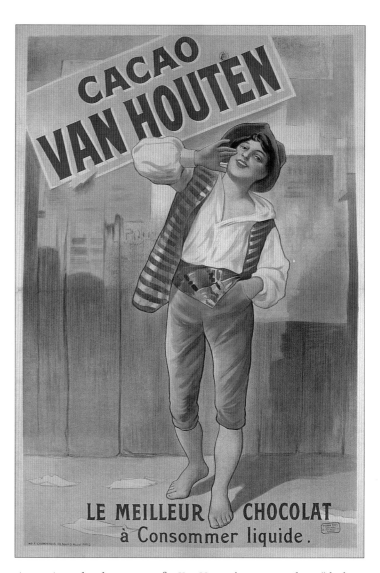

ABOVE: An early advertisement for Van Houten's cocoa powder – "the best liquid drinking chocolate".

each other. Both firms were quick to enter the cocoa essence market, actively promoting the product's purity and ease of preparation. The old-style starch-based products were classified as adulterated, resulting in several fierce legal battles between rival firms. Van Houten's press also initiated the industry's next step in gearing up – the large-scale production of chocolate as confectionery.

EATING CHOCOLATE

Having separated out the butter from the bean, the industry was left with the question of what to do with it – it was certainly too good to waste. What happened was that somehow one of the cocoa manufacturers – and there are conflicting claims as to who was the first – hit upon the idea of melting the cacao butter and combining it with a blend of ground cacao beans and sugar. The resulting mixture was a smooth and malleable paste

ABOVE: A charming poster for Bovril's nourishing new chocolate bars, or cakes. The lettering on the box refers to them as "the perfect food".

that tolerated the added sugar without becoming gritty; the fat helped to dissolve it. The paste was also thin enough to be poured into a mould and cast, and it is from this concept that "eating chocolate" was developed.

The Fry family claim to have been the first to market the new product. Reflecting the current popularity of French-style products, they named the bars "Chocolat Délicieux à Manger" and exhibited them at a trade fair in Birmingham in 1849. The bars were an immediate success, and eating chocolate

RIGHT: Hershey's famous little Kisses were introduced in 1907.

caught on in a big way. Not to be outdone Cadburys introduced the first box of small individual chocolates, followed by a Valentine's Day presentation box. Other companies, such as Bovril, began producing eating chocolate, and the new confectionery was firmly established.

As a result of the new craze the price of cacao butter rocketed and, predictably, eating chocolate became an expensive sought-after product popular with society's élite. Meanwhile, cocoa was relegated to the masses.

The United States developed their version of chocolate bars a little later on. After experimenting with cream and chocolate – time and time again, the mixture scorched or failed to set – Milton Hershey's milk chocolate bars finally appeared on the market in 1900. His world-famous Kisses followed in 1907. Over on the west coast, Ghirardelli was making use of new chocolate-moulding technology, and soon added chocolate bars to their

ABOVE: Modern packaging with old-fashioned appeal.

lines too. Specialist chocolate shops began to spring up all over the country and most towns had at least one well-respected establishment producing hand-made chocolates. The early chocolatiers were too small to import cacao beans or invest in expensive processing machinery. Instead, they bought industrial-sized blocks of coating chocolate from large companies such as Guittard and melted them down to use as "couverture" for their own hand-dipped fillings. Alice Bradley's 1917 *Candy Cook Book*, published in America, devoted a whole chapter to "Assorted Chocolates" with over sixty recipes for fillings. Bradley stated: "More than one

ABOVE: Ghirardelli's first chocolate bars were "full of toasted almonds".

hundred different chocolates may be found in the price lists of some manufacturers." The American chocolate industry got its biggest boost during the Second World War, when millions of chocolate bars were issued to the American armed forces in Europe. By this time both Ghirardelli and Hershey were well-equipped for the challenge of supplying them.

CHOCOLATE TRAVELS THE WORLD

During the sixteenth century chocolate began its journey into the countries of Europe as colonialists exploited their new world discoveries. Reaching Spain first, then following trade routes to Northern Europe and Great Britain, chocolate eventually made its way back across the Atlantic to North America.

SPAIN

It was probably through merchants and also through contact between New World convents and monasteries and their Spanish counterparts, that chocolate found its way to Spain.

Once the first commercial cargo of beans from Veracruz had been unloaded in 1585 and the official trade routes established, chocolate quickly became part of the Spanish way of life, especially among society's élite. However, a French noblewoman visiting Spain was unimpressed. She says of the drink: "They take it with so much pepper and so many spices, that it is impossible they don't burn themselves up." Nor was she impressed by their dental care and personal habits: "Their teeth are good, and would be white if they took care of them, but they neglect them. Besides the sugar and the chocolate which spoil them, they have the bad habit, men and women alike, of cleaning them with a toothpick, in whatever company they are."

Chocolaterías, chocolate houses, sprang up in cities all over the country, and it became the fashion to visit them in the afternoons to drink a cup of the foaming fragrant brew, accompanied by *picatoste*, fried bread, to dip in it. Today, the chocolate drinking habit remains strong in Spain, and there are still many *chocolaterías*. A traditional time to take the beverage is in the

RIGHT: The chambermaid model for "The Beautiful Chocolate Girl" married a wealthy aristocrat and so got to drink chocolate herself.

BELOW: This early eighteenth-century Spanish tiled panel shows gentlemen serving chocolate to their ladies.

The Spanish like their chocolate thick – so thick that a spoon will stand up in it, and it can almost be classified as a food rather than a drink. Cornflour is used as a thickener, or sometimes eggs, which practically turn the drink into chocolate mousse.

— SPANISH EGG CHOCOLATE —

In a double boiler, melt 50g/2oz/2 squares unsweetened chocolate in 475ml/16fl oz/2 cups milk until thick and smooth. Keep stirring and add 115g/4oz/½ cup sugar, pinch of salt, 10ml/2 tsp ground cinnamon and 5ml/1 tsp vanilla essence. Beat 1 egg in the bottom of a jug with a molinillo, pour over the hot chocolate mixture, whisk until frothy and serve immediately.

ABOVE: The pleasures of taking chocolate are captured in this seventeenth-century still life by Philippe Rousseau.

morning with freshly cooked *churros* (piped strips of deep-fried choux pastry), which replaced the *picatoste*.

In Spain, as in the rest of Europe, chocolate was always associated with stimulating foods such as spices, coffee and tea; it was a long while before chocolate was used as an ingredient for confectionery and desserts. Although its first use was as a beverage, chocolate was also a flavouring ingredient in savoury dishes. Both the Spanish and the Mexicans traditionally add chocolate to sauces for meat and game, and even fish.

THE NETHERLANDS

The Netherlands became part of the Spanish territories in the fourteenth century. Because of this, the Dutch were familiar with chocolate from an early stage.

The Dutch West India Company eventually defied the Spanish ban on foreign traders and started shipping cacao beans in bulk to Amsterdam during the seventeenth century. They then re-exported the beans in small lots to foreign buyers, as well as setting up their own processing plants in the Netherlands. Until the end of the eighteenth century, production was limited and chocolate was only seen in the homes of a few wealthy merchants and financiers.

ITALY

There are conflicting theories as to how and when chocolate reached Italy. Some historians believe it was around the middle of the sixteenth century when the exiled duke Emmanuel-Philibert returned to power, having experienced the delights of chocolate in Spain. The popular theory is that chocolate was imported by a Florentine merchant, Antonio Carletti, who discovered it while travelling the world in search of new products to sell. The most likely theory is that chocolate was brought in as a medicine through the convents and monasteries.

By the seventeenth century a growing number of chocolate companies had become established in northern Italy, particularly around the towns of Perugia and Turin. These companies in turn began to export their newly developed products to other European countries.

A collection of recipes by an eighteenth-century Italian priest shows the imagination of the Italians in their use of chocolate compared with other countries. Recipes included such dishes as: Liver dipped in chocolate and fried, Chocolate soup, Chocolate pudding with veal, marrow and candied fruit, and Chocolate polenta.

FRANCE

France was also quick to fall under chocolate's spell. As with Spain and Italy, there are conflicting theories about the circumstances surrounding its first appearance. Some say it was a result of networking between Spanish and French monasteries. Another theory states that chocolate entered France as a medicine. There is certainly some evidence from the French historian Bonaventure d'Argonne that the Cardinal of Lyons drank chocolate "to calm his spleen and appease his rage and foul temper", and that he may have "had the secret from some Spanish monks who brought it to France". However, there is also no doubt that the trend was largely set by nobility and the royal court as it was in other European countries.

ABOVE: Cardinal Mazarin travelled with a chocolate-maker.

The most popular theory is that the drink made its first appearance in 1615 when Louis XIII married Anne of Austria, the young daughter of Philip II of Spain. The new queen loved her chocolate with a passion and introduced it to members of the court. There were plenty of devotees: the king's personal adviser, the formidable Cardinal Mazarin, absolutely refused to travel anywhere without his personal chocolate-maker; and later

BELOW: A tapestry depicting the marriage of María Teresa, the Spanish princess, to Louis XIV. Chocolate and the king were her only passions.

Marie Antoinette, also very fond of chocolate, created the prestigious "Charge of chocolate-maker of the Queen". Chocolate parties held by royalty, *chocolat du roi,* became a fashionable social ritual to which it was the ultimate in chic to be invited.

The many anecdotes include the story of the Spanish princess María Theresa, who married Louis XIV in 1660. She is said to have declared: "Chocolate and the King are my only passions." (Note the order.) The princess brought with her a Spanish maid, who prepared chocolate each morning for her queen. The ladies of the French court were intrigued by this new drink, especially as word had got round that it was an aphrodisiac. Chocolate sales in France apparently sky-rocketed around that time. Another often-repeated story about the princess is that her passion for chocolate was so excessive that she developed a horrendous complexion, and that her teeth were black and riddled with cavities.

Throughout France, chocolate never failed to evoke strong feelings. In 1664 learned academics praised its food value, presumably because of the fat content, but at the same time it was violently attacked by other writers, who accused those who drank it of moral depravity. Even Madame de Sévigné, a French courtesan and a great devotee of chocolate, turned against it for a while. In one of her letters to her daughter she wrote: "Chocolate is no longer for me what it was, fashion has led me astray, as it always does … it is the source of vapors and palpitations; it flatters you for a while, and then suddenly lights a continuous fever in you that leads to death … In the name of God, don't keep it up …" In another letter she told a horrendous tale of the Marquise de

ABOVE: Chocolate consumption was often depicted as being risqué.

Coëtlogon who "took so much chocolate during her pregnancy last year that she produced a small boy as black as the devil, who died". Eventually Madame de Sévigné regained her enthusiasm, and in a wonderful letter she neatly got round the issue of fasting and chocolate: "I took some chocolate night before last to digest my dinner, in order to have a good supper. I had some yesterday for sustenance so that I could fast until the evening. What I find most pleasant about chocolate is that it acts according to one's wishes."

SWITZERLAND

After the mid-seventeenth century, chocolate was making an appearance in all the principal cities of Europe. Although

ABOVE: The elegant refreshment room where chocolate was served at Confiserie Sprüngli in Zurich.

Switzerland was later to become a major producer of chocolate as confectionery, chocolate as a beverage was relatively late in arriving. It was first noticed in Zurich in 1697 after the Mayor had enjoyed drinking chocolate on a trip to Brussels. By the mid-eighteenth century, chocolate was more widely available and was often brought into the country by travelling Italian merchants, known as *cioccolatieri,* who sold it at fairs and markets.

GERMANY AND AUSTRIA

Like Switzerland, Germany was also relatively late to take up chocolate. For years the Germans regarded it as medicine, and it was sold only by apothecaries. But by the middle of the seventeenth century, chocolate had become accepted among fashionable society, although enthusiasm varied from city to city. Berliners still looked on it as an unpleasant tonic, but the drink was a hit in Dresden and in Leipzig, where the city's *glitterati*

took to drinking it at the fashionable Felsche café, one of the earliest German *schokoladestuben* (chocolate houses).

Among Germany's confirmed chocoholics were the famous poets Goethe (1749–1832) and Schiller (1759–1805). Goethe was reputed to have found the beverage a deep source of inspiration and drank it well into ripe old age. During his travels he often wrote to his wife asking her to send supplies from his favourite chocolate-maker, Riquet, in Leipzig.

Germany started producing its own chocolate on a large scale in 1756 when Prince Wilhelm von der Lippe erected a factory at Steinhude and brought over Portuguese workers especially skilled in the art of chocolate-making.

In Austria, Viennese aristocracy were quick to take up the new drink, especially after the Emperor Charles VI had moved his court and his chocolate from Madrid to Vienna in 1711. Since Austria did not impose such punishing taxes on chocolate as Germany, it was drunk not just by the aristocracy but also by lesser mortals who could afford it. There is a story of a German traveller in Vienna who was horrified to see someone as common as a tailor drinking a cup of best quality chocolate.

Both the Germans and the Austrians were accomplished pastry-cooks. Indeed, in the Austrian imperial court it seemed that the head pâtisserie chef was on a par with the most senior general. Like the Italians, the German and Austrian pastry-cooks took a while to start using chocolate as an ingredient in their baking rather than just as a beverage. It was worth the wait — their most wickedly delicious creations, the rich Black Forest Cake from Germany and the Viennese Sachertorte, are now celebrated forms of indulgence the world over.

BELOW: "Goethe in the Campagna" (1787) by German painter Johann Tischbein. Goethe was a lifelong drinker of chocolate.

The popularity of chocolate spawned a whole new industry for the famous china factories in both Austria and Germany, and in France too. At the beginning of the eighteenth century, European factories from Vienna to Berlin to Sèvres started producing the most exquisite chocolate services in porcelain; before that earthenware or metal, including gold and silver, were the materials used. As well as the traditionally shaped serving pots, the new range included elegant cups known as *trembleuse.* These new porcelain wares were specially designed to protect the aristocracy from the embarrassment of accidental spills. They featured double-handled cups which fitted into a holder or a very deep saucer.

ABOVE: The interior of a typical seventeenth-century London chocolate house – hotbeds of gossip, frequented by politicians and the literary set.

GREAT BRITAIN

In the sixteenth century, when the Spanish were shifting cacao as if there were no tomorrow, the British couldn't have cared less about it. Even the pirates who plagued the Spanish ports and shipping routes seemed unaware of its economic and cultural importance, for they showed no interest in the valuable cargo. Like their Dutch counterparts, they are reputed to have thrown boatloads of it overboard in disgust.

When chocolate finally arrived in Britain, it did so more or less simultaneously with two other stimulants, tea from Asia and coffee from Africa. Coffee was the first to catch on in British society – it was relatively cheaper – but chocolate soon followed.

Documentary evidence of the first chocolate house in London appeared in *The Public Advertiser* in 1657, followed two years later by a paragraph in *Needham's Mercurius Politicus* that drew attention to "an excellent West India drink, sold in Queen's-Head alley, in Bishopsgate-street, by a Frenchman".

The most famous establishment was White's Chocolate House, near St James's Palace, opened by an Italian immigrant. A rival establishment was The Cocoa Tree in St James's Street.

LEFT: Sacks of cacao beans from the tropics arriving at an English warehouse.

RIGHT: "A Cup of Chocolate" by Sir John Lavery. Drinking chocolate in the new chocolate houses was a fashionable pastime for ladies of society.

By chance rather than design the two establishments catered to different political loyalties – The Cocoa Tree was the favourite haunt of members of the Tory party, while the Whig aristocrats and the literary set frequented White's. White's was the inspiration for some of the scenes from William Hogarth's famous series of paintings *The Rake's Progress*.

For the wealthy upper classes, both the coffee and chocolate houses were *the* place to be seen. They were hotbeds of vicious gossip and political intrigue, as well as popular gambling venues where vast fortunes were won and lost. In 1675, Charles II tried in vain to have both types of establishment closed down on the grounds that politicians and businessmen were frequenting them too often and were in danger of neglecting their families. It is also possible that he was trying to suppress the kind of talk that could potentially lead to a rebellion similar to the one that caused his father's execution in 1649.

The diarist Samuel Pepys (1633–1703) was an ardent fan of chocolate, or "jocolatte", and a regular frequenter of the chocolate houses. One entry in his diary records a horrendous hangover the morning after the king's coronation: "Waked in the morning with my head in a sad taking through last night's drink, which I am very sorry for; so rose, and went with Mr Creed to drink our morning draught, which he did give me in Chocolate to settle my stomach."

In England, as in other countries, the government seized on chocolate as a potential source of revenue. Importers were

LEFT: Examples of early packaging for Domingo Ghirardelli's revolutionary instant cocoa powder.

obliged to pay a hefty duty on every sack of cacao beans brought into the country, and in 1660 a tax of 8d (about 3p) a gallon was imposed on all chocolate made and sold in England.

These penalties led to an inevitable increase in smuggling cacao beans, as well as adulteration of the chocolate, for which anything from brick dust to red lead was used. Brandon Head in *The Food of the Gods* refers to "the reprehensible practice (strongly condemned)" of padding out chocolate with husks and shells. He goes on: "To prevent this practice it was enacted in 1770 that the shells or husks should be seized or destroyed." Some of these husks did not go to waste, however. Head tells us: "From these a light, but not unpalatable, table decoction is still prepared in Ireland and elsewhere, under the designation of 'miserables'."

By the mid-1800s, the high levels of taxation had come down, thanks to the vast volume of imports, as well as the influence of respected Quaker industrialists who had convinced the government of chocolate's nourishing virtues. Chocolate was now affordable by all and had become big business.

UNITED STATES OF AMERICA

The first chocolate found its way back across the Atlantic to North America around 1765, probably in the pockets of high-ranking English officials going to their posts in the east coast colonies. We also know that Domingo Ghirardelli, an Italian confectioner then trading in Lima in Peru, exported cacao beans and other essential commodities from South America to San Francisco to supply the needs of the gold rush hordes. Another possible route for cacao beans was directly from Jamaica after the Spanish had given up control there.

Thomas Jefferson (1743–1826), third president of the United States, is quoted as saying: "The superiority of chocolate, both for health and nourishment, will soon give it the preference over tea and coffee in America which it has in Spain." Because of the pioneering nature of North American society, chocolate was given a somewhat different reception to the one it had received in Europe. Although the wealthy east coast society enjoyed chocolate, they drank it at home – chocolate houses did not exist. Another difference was that chocolate was generally marketed to the masses rather than the elite (as in Europe), with the emphasis on wholesomeness rather than sophistication, so it consequently reached a far broader segment of society than it had in Spain, France and England.

The first chocolate factory was set up in 1765 in Massachusetts by Dr James Baker and John Hannon. The Walter Baker Company was established in 1780 by Baker's grandson and is still synonymous with quality chocolate. By 1884, Milton Hershey, of the Hershey Chocolate Company, was producing baking chocolate, cocoa and sweet chocolate coatings for his famous caramels; and by 1885, Domingo Ghirardelli had set up his California Chocolate Manufactory in San Francisco. Right from the start, chocolate was big business in North America.

BELOW: Nineteenth-century advertising poster for curious chocolate products from the Walter Baker Company.

CHOCOLATE AND THE CHURCH

The Church played an important role, directly and indirectly, in the early history of chocolate. The bitter and bloody religious wars raging between Catholics and Protestants in the sixteenth and seventeenth centuries, were, in a way, the cause of chocolate's appearance and gradual dispersal through Europe. The Jesuits, actively involved in the religious wars and fiercely committed to empowering the Catholic Church, were a driving political force both in Europe and Latin America. It was almost certainly the Jesuit missionaries, rather than New World explorers, who were responsible for bringing the first chocolate into Spain, Italy and France; it would have passed through an international network of monasteries and convents. It was also thanks to the pressure of Jesuit missionaries that raw, rather than processed, cacao beans were eventually shipped to Europe. Before this, the Spanish colonists had had a monopoly on processing the beans in Latin America, making fat profits by doing so.

In Italy, the religious wars resulted in a great many high-level marriages between aristocratic families and the ruling powers.

ABOVE: Friar Drinking Chocolate *by Jose M. Oropeza.*

Until its unification in 1879, Italy was a collection of self-governing states, and it was felt that marriages of this kind were the best way of cementing diplomatic relationships and consolidating the states' collective power. The aristocratic brides liked to take their maids, cooks and favourite foods with them when they moved from one Italian state or foreign country to another, and so through them chocolate began to appear in all sorts of places.

Until the eighteenth century, chocolate was made by monks and nuns, both in Europe and Latin America, using the methods handed down from the Aztecs. Thomas Gage, in his book *The English-American, His Travail by Sea and Land, or a New Survey of the West Indies* (published 1648), wrote of "cloister churches" run by nuns and friars. He said these were "talked off far and near, not for their religious practices, but for their skill in making drinkes which are used in those parts, the one called

BELOW: Part of Columbus's mission was to conquer new lands in the name of the Catholic Church. This picture illustrates that religious fervour.

ABOVE: This seventeenth-century Spanish still-life shows tablets of chocolate, which were often made by monks and nuns.

chocolatte, another atolle. Chocolatte is (also) made up in boxes, and sent not only to Mexico, but much of it yearly transported into Spain".

In the New World, the Church generally took a pragmatic view of chocolate. It was popular with nuns and monks because it sustained them through the lengthy fasts they had to endure, and they were convinced of its health-promoting properties. There was an occasional difference of opinion in the Old World, however. A Spanish monk was said to have declared the drink diabolical, claiming its invigorating properties were the work of evil spirits, but his views went unheard. In 1650 the Society of Jesus (the Jesuit school) issued an act outlawing the drink to Jesuits, but this was impossible to enforce, especially when students started to abandon the school because of it.

THE CHOCOLATE OF CHIAPA

One major objection to chocolate appears to have been raised by the Bishop of Chiapa whose Mass was continually disturbed by its use. A famous and rather lengthy story told by Thomas Gage is worth repeating. The upper-class white ladies of Chiapa Real claimed "much weakness and squeamishness of stomacke, which they say is so great that they are not able to continue in church … unless they drinke a cup of hot chocolatte …. For this purpose it was much used by them to make their maids bring them to church … a cup of chocolatte, which could not be done to all without a great confusion and interrupting both mass and sermon".

Driven to distraction by the endless disturbances, the Bishop posted a notice stating that anyone who ate or drank in church would be excommunicated. The scornful women carried on their chocolate drinking regardless, and eventually the situation exploded into an uproar in which swords were drawn against the priests as they tried to remove the cups of chocolate from the women's maids.

The women retaliated by refusing to attend the Bishop's services, and attending Mass at the convents instead. The local priest warned the Bishop that if the women "cannot have their wills, they will surely work revenge either by chocolate or conserves, or some fair present, which shall surely carry death along with it!" Lo and behold, the Bishop fell ill and died a most unpleasant death eight days later. Gage wrote: "His head and face, did so swell that the least touch upon any part of him caused the skin to break and cast out white matter, which had corrupted and overflown all his body." Rumour had it that a gentlewoman "noted to be somewhat too familiar with one of the Bishop's pages" had persuaded the innocent young man to administer a cup of poisoned chocolate to "him who so rigorously had forbidden chocolate to be drunk in Church". A popular proverb in the region thereafter was "Beware of the chocolate of Chiapa".

DANGEROUS STIMULANTS

At the time that chocolate was becoming all the rage in Europe, there was a similar rise in the consumption of other tropical commodities such as coffee, tea, tobacco, rum and sugar; it seems that the Europeans were developing a taste for stimulants. The Church took a strong position and, with the exception of sugar, denounced the new foods as potentially dangerous. Even so, there was a certain amount of rule-bending when it came to chocolate.

RIGHT: Detail from a diorama based on a seventeenth-century engraving of monks drinking chocolate.

CHOCOLATE AS MEDICINE

Chocolate was used therapeutically as long ago as the fourth century, when the Maya first started cultivating the cacao tree. Sorcerers, the predecessors of priests and doctors, prescribed cacao both as a stimulant and as a soothing balm. Warriors took it as an energy-boosting drink, and cacao butter was used as a dressing for wounds.

ABOVE: Utensils needed "to make cocoa to perfection".

Later on, the Aztecs prescribed a potion of cacao mixed with the ground exhumed bones of their ancestors as a cure for diarrhoea. The Spanish colonists, too, were aware of cacao's healing properties. A traveller reported of his countrymen: "They make paste thereof, the which they say is good for the stomacke, and against the catarre."

However, chocolate was given a mixed reception by the scientific and medical community, who were just as vociferous as the Church when it came to debating the rights and wrongs of this mysterious new substance. In the sixteenth century, when medicine was in its infancy, many of the theories were based on the principle of "hot" and "cold" humours, or body energies, which, if not kept in balance, would cause illness. The Spanish classified chocolate as "cold" and tried to neutralize its effect by

BELOW: French doctors believed chocolate was beneficial for chronic illnesses and broken hearts.

drinking it hot, flavoured with "hot" spices. They found it hard to understand why the Aztecs drank unheated chocolate when it was already a "cold" food.

By the seventeenth century, chocolate had been given the seal of approval by several botanists and medical men, who discovered that it contained all kinds of beneficial substances. Henry Stubbe (1632–72), the English court physician, visited the West Indies to investigate the physical effects of chocolate. On his return, he published *The Indian Nectar,* in which he had nothing but praise for the beverage, with the proviso that adding too much sugar or spice was unwise.

Among the many others who sang the praises of chocolate was Stephani Blancardi (1650–1702), an Italian physician. He commented: "Chocolate is not only pleasant of taste, but it is also a veritable balm of the mouth, for the maintaining of all glands and humours in a good state of health. Thus it is, that all who drink it, possess a sweet breath."

The French faculty of medicine officially approved its use in 1661. The magistrate and gastronome, Brillat-Savarin (1755–1826), summed up in *Physiologie du Gout:* "Chocolate, when carefully prepared, is a wholesome and agreeable form of food … is very suitable for persons of great mental exertion, preachers, lawyers, and above all travellers … it agrees with the feeblest stomachs, has proved beneficial in cases of chronic illness and remains the last resource in the diseases of the pylorus." Some of his contemporaries claimed that chocolate cured tuberculosis. A French doctor, probably sensing chocolate's ability to lift the spirits, was convinced of its merits as an antidote to a broken heart. He wrote "Those who love, and are unfortunate enough to suffer from the most universal of all gallant illnesses, will find [in chocolate] the most enlightening consolation."

Praise was by no means universal. An eighteenth-century physician to the Tuscan court threw a spanner in the works by declaring that chocolate was "hot" and that it was madness to add "hot drugs" to it. He obviously noticed the effects of caffeine for he lists as ill effects incessant chatter, insomnia, irritability and hyperactivity in children. The French, too, became disenamoured for a short period, blaming chocolate for "vapours", palpitations, wind and constipation.

In general, however, the medicinal and nutritional benefits

— *A MEXICAN RECIPE FOR LIP SALVE* —
Take half a teaspoon [2.5ml] of cocoa butter from freshly roasted beans and mix to an ointment with sweet almond oil.

RIGHT: *This eighteenth-century painting shows how chocolate was adopted by well-to-do households as a nutritious breakfast drink.*

BELOW: *This engraving from "Physiologie du Gout ou Méditations de Gastronomie Transcendante" (1848) depicts chocolate being served to uplift the spirits.*

BELOW: *This nineteenth-century advertisement shows British children enjoying cocoa. Medical experts in Britain proclaimed cocoa as "the drink par excellence for children, with whom it is a universal favourite".*

of chocolate were well accepted. An early English writer described it as "incomparable as a family drink for breakfast or supper, when both tea and coffee are really out of place unless the latter is nearly all milk". Brillat-Savarin commented on digestion: "When you have breakfasted well and copiously, if you swallow a generous cup of good chocolate at the end of the meal, you will have digested everything perfectly three hours later."

By the 1800s charlatans were beginning to cash in on chocolate's seal of approval by the medical profession. Various forms of "medicinal" chocolate started to appear including sinister-sounding products such as "pectoral chocolate" made with Indian tapioca, recommended for people suffering from consumption, and "analeptic" chocolate made with a mysterious "Persian tonic".

By the end of the century, the genuine article was approved of by hospitals and sanatoria, as well as by the navy, the army and various public institutions.

THE FOUNDING FATHERS

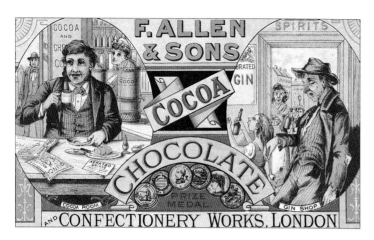

ABOVE: Nineteenth-century British cocoa manufacturers were keen to wean the poor off their favourite tipple of gin.

GREAT BRITAIN

The manufacture of drinking chocolate in Britain was transformed by the Industrial Revolution and the cultural, social and economic changes that followed in its wake. During the eighteenth century the pioneering chocolate manufacturers were still using primitive manufacturing methods, similar to those used by the Aztecs. Technology gradually entered the scene with two key developments: a hydraulic grinding press, invented in 1728 by Walter Churchman, and, in 1765, James Watt's steam engine, which changed the food industry overnight. Another crucial development in chocolate manufacture was a revolutionary type of chocolate press invented in 1828 by a Dutch chemist, Coenraad Van Houten.

In 1853 the taxes on drinking chocolate were reduced because the volume of imports had grown enormously. By then the new railways had made transport easier, and power-driven machinery had largely replaced the old slow method of making chocolate by hand. These changes radically brought down the price, meaning that drinking chocolate could potentially be enjoyed by all.

It was during this era that several

RIGHT: Cadburys printed endorsements from the medical press on their packaging.

eminent Quaker families – the Frys, the Cadburys, the Rowntrees and the Terrys – became involved in chocolate manufacturing. These families established themselves as the main producers in Britain and succeeded in transforming chocolate from the drink of the aristocracy to the drink of the people.

It was undoubtedly the Quakers' evangelical outlook which was behind their decision to choose chocolate as a commercial venture. Because the beverage was so wholesome, the Quakers hoped it would provide a means of weaning the poor off beer and gin, their favourite tipples, and improving the quality of their lives in general. The Quakers were also concerned for their employees' welfare. They created exemplary working conditions and built model villages where education, healthcare and community services were provided for the workers, both active and retired, without charge. Cadbury's Bournville village near Birmingham and Rowntree in York are famous examples.

The Frys were the sole suppliers of chocolate to the navy, making them the largest chocolate manufacturer in the world. Not to be outdone, the rival Cadbury family gained the privileged title of purveyors of chocolate to Queen Victoria.

ITALY

The Italians have always been accomplished sweet-makers. They started using chocolate as an ingredient very early on and thus established themselves as leading experts in the art of making fine chocolates. In 1884, when the Russian Czar commissioned from the jeweller Fabergé his first golden egg with its surprise filling of precious stones, Italian producers introduced what may have been the first chocolate Easter eggs containing a surprise gift.

ABOVE: Military-style packaging.

The Italian chocolate industry is centred around Turin in Piedmont and Perugia in Umbria. Production on a commercial level developed in the early nineteenth century when Bozelli, an engineer from Genoa, designed a machine capable of producing over 300kg/660lb of chocolate per day. By the end of the century the industry was booming.

There are several long-established firms in northern Italy. These include Caffarel, from whom the Italians learned to make chocolate, and Baratti & Milano, from the Turin area; Perugina (now owned by Nestlé) from Perugia, makers of the famous "Baci" (kisses) chocolates with the memorable pack; and Majani in Bologna, who now produce the ultimate in designer chocolates.

SWITZERLAND

Unsurprisingly, Switzerland boasts an incredible list of founding fathers. The first, an enterprising young man named François Cailler, travelled to Turin in 1815, learned the tricks of the trade from Caffarel, then opened the first Swiss chocolate factory four years later. Next to set up was Philippe Suchard, inventor of the world's first chocolate mixing machine. In 1845 Richard Sprüngli opened his world-famous shop in Zurich, followed by a factory in 1900. Henri Nestlé, a chemist, invented a type of evaporated milk powder, which was used by Daniel Peter, a chocolate-maker, to produce the first milk chocolate bars in 1879. In the same year Rodolphe Lindt invented the "conching" process, which revolutionized forever the texture and flavour of solid chocolate bars. Richard Sprüngli's grandson, David, bought out Lindt in 1899; five generations later, Lindt-Sprüngli is Switzerland's largest independent chocolate manufacturer. Finally, in 1908 Jean Tobler produced the famous "Toblerone" bar, now marketed by Suchard. Its distinctive triangular shape was designed to represent the Swiss Alps.

FRANCE

The first chocolate factories appeared in the mid-seventeenth century, and, as in England, production was a slow and primitive process. Life became easier in 1732, when a Frenchman named Dubuisson invented a grinding table. This allowed the workers to grind the beans standing up, instead of kneeling in front of a floor-level stone, which they had done until then.

France's most famous mass producers were Auguste Poulain and Jean-Antoine Menier. Poulain set up shop in Blois in 1848, making chocolate in a back room. By 1878 he was producing chocolate by the ton from five different factories. In 1884 his son Albert developed a chocolate breakfast drink, now known as Grand Arôme and still loved by French children. Meanwhile, Menier, a pharmacist famous for his "medicinal powders", bought a small chocolate factory near the River Marne, intending simply to produce chocolate to coat his pills. When he died in 1853, his son Émile-Justin stepped in, concentrating on full-scale chocolate manufacture. A man of capitalist vision, Émile built a new factory in France, opened a factory in

LEFT: Menier cooking chocolate is widely used today.

RIGHT: As this 1893 poster shows, Menier chocolate has always been popular with French children.

LEFT: Established for over a hundred years, Weiss still produces quality drinking chocolate.

London, a warehouse in New York, bought cacao plantations in Nicaragua, and built a Bournville-like model village for his workers. When he died Émile's son, Henri, continued in the same expansionary spirit. In 1889 he arranged for electricity lines and telephones to be installed in the workers' homes, and, many years before the rest of the French working population, gave them the right to retire at sixty.

France's chocolatiers also include a strong contingent of smaller specialist firms that played an important role in forming the character of France's present-day chocolate industry. Debauve & Gallais was established in Paris in 1800 and are the oldest producers of hand-made chocolates in the city today. Another prestigious company is Weiss, based in Saint-Étienne for over a hundred years, and famous for its delicious drinking chocolate and hefty foil-wrapped chocolate drops.

ABOVE: The electronic automobile bought by Hershey in 1900.

UNITED STATES OF AMERICA
Chocolate arrived relatively late in North America, around the middle of the eighteenth century. The first industrial producers were Dr James Baker and his partner John Hannon, who built a chocolate factory in 1765 on the banks of the River Neponset in Massachusetts. In 1780 the company was renamed the Walter Baker Company, after John Hannon's grandson, and is still a household name today, producing baker's (a confusing generic term) chocolate as well as better quality varieties under their own name of Baker's.

Over a century later Milton Hershey, a successful caramel manufacturer from Pennsylvania, visited the 1893 Chicago World's Fair and was overwhelmingly impressed by German chocolate production machinery on display. With a shrewd sense of timing, he decided that chocolate was going to be a runaway success; and his company has never looked back. Milton sold his first milk chocolate bar in 1895, and since then Hershey Bars and Hershey Kisses have become part of the American way of life – just as he predicted.

Like his Quaker counterparts in Britain, Milton had a social conscience. He enlisted nutritionists to vouch for the sanctity of his product, set up a squeaky-clean working environment, and built the factory town of Hershey in Pennsylvania. The main thoroughfares are East Chocolate Avenue and Cocoa Avenue, while the tree-lined side streets are named after places where cacao is grown, or by types of bean – Java, Caracas, Arriba and so on. Milton went one better than the Quaker factory villages in England and provided very generous out-of-town facilities for his employees such as an amusement park, a zoo, sporting facilities and a theatre. Milton also made it clear that no "taverns, piggeries, glue, soap, candle, lamp-black factories" were allowed, making sure that his model working communities stayed as wholesome as possible.

It is interesting that the early North American and British manufacturers of a product that was, and still is, associated with sensory enjoyment and indulgence, should have had quite a puritanical outlook. A cynical view might be that their social philanthropy was a clever marketing ploy, but these businessmen did have a genuine social conscience, and it is perhaps another illustration that chocolate is all things to all people – both a luxurious treat and a wholesome daily food.

Milton Hershey was not the only American producer

pushing the wholesomeness of chocolate. Like-minded but rather more extreme companies included the Taylor brothers, who entered the market with their Natural Hygienist Practitioners, and Dr William Hay, of the still-popular Hay System of food-combining. Taylor's selling point was the curative, homeopathic nature of chocolate. This shows a continuity with the earliest European marketeers, who sold their chocolate

ABOVE: Street signs to the main thoroughfares in Hershey.

through the apothecaries, monasteries and convents of the sixteenth and seventeenth centuries, and had much to say on the beneficial properties of the cacao bean and its products.

A much more colourful American chocolate producer was

BELOW: Early publicity for Taylor Brothers demonstrating their social conscience, while promoting the nourishing powers of chocolate.

ABOVE: A picture of the original Guittard building surrounded by scenes showing early chocolate manufacture.

Domingo Ghirardelli, an Italian confectioner with South American links who was originally in business in Lima, Peru. Ghirardelli befriended an American cabinetmaker named James Lick, who, in 1847 just before the discovery of gold at Sutter's Mill, moved from Lima to San Francisco, taking with him a large quantity of Ghirardelli's chocolate. Lured by reports of a lucrative market, Ghirardelli followed Lick to California. As astute and entrepreneurial as his fellow chocolate producers, both in

BELOW: The Ghirardelli company was the first in America to make easily dissolvable powdered cocoa.

the United States and worldwide, Ghirardelli foresaw the potential in satisfying the day-to-day needs of the goldrush pioneers, who by then were arriving in hordes. He set up a business in San Francisco importing and selling commodities such as sugar, coffee and, of course, chocolate.

There were various disasters over the years, including devastating bankruptcy and a serious fire, but business continued despite the inevitable setbacks in a volatile period of American history. By 1856 the company was known as Ghirardelli's California Chocolate Manufactory. The company was to make its mark on the chocolate industry in the 1860s when, by sheer accident, a way of making a low-fat powdered cocoa was discovered. The new product was known as Sweet Ground Chocolate and Cocoa and is still sold today.

The original factory buildings have become a well-known San Francisco landmark in Ghirardelli Square, and the company continues to flourish. It was bought by the Golden Grain Macaroni Company in 1963, which in turn was acquired as a subsidiary of the Quaker Oats Company in 1983.

Another chocolate maker, Etienne Guittard from France, set off for the gold fields of San Francisco in 1860. After three years, he hadn't found any gold, but the supply of fine chocolate he had brought with him to barter for prospecting gear had been enthusiastically received. The shopkeepers he traded with assured him that there was a future for him and his wonderful chocolate in San Francisco. Guittard went back to France, where he worked and saved to buy the equipment he would need. In 1868 he returned to San Francisco and opened the business that developed into one of the important American manufacturers of top-grade chocolate for wholesale customers. Some of the country's best confectioners, bakers and ice-cream makers (Baskin-Robbins, for one) use Guittard.

--- *GHIRARDELLI'S ACCIDENT* ---

Cacao beans have a high fat content and because of this do not combine easily with liquids when ground to a powder. Ghirardelli's most important contribution to the chocolate industry was the accidental discovery of a way of making a virtually fat-free powder.

A worker left some ground cacao beans hanging from a hook in a cloth bag overnight. By the morning, the floor was covered in cacao butter that had dripped from the bag. The ground chocolate left behind was almost fat-free and was found to combine with liquids much more smoothly. Ghirardelli's ever-popular Sweet Ground Chocolate and Cocoa was developed from this.

CULTIVATION AND PROCESSING

GROWING AND HARVESTING

ABOVE: Cacao tree and seedling.

There are many stages in the processing of chocolate, and there has been a corresponding amount of development in its history as it has grown from a cold drink to the complex and adaptable substance it is today. This chapter traces the most important steps in the production of chocolate.

GROWING

The cacao bean grows in large pods on the cacao tree, *Theobroma cacao*, an evergreen which thrives in tropical areas lying between 20° north and 20° south of the equator. The tree is an exacting specimen, for it refuses to grow where it is too high, too cold or too dry, and it demands shelter from wind and sun. It also needs protection from wild animals which delight in picking its pods, and it easily succumbs to various rots, wilts and fungal diseases.

It is traditional for the cacao tree to be grown under the protection of taller shade-creating trees, the conditions resembling its natural jungle habitat. In areas such as Grenada and parts of Jamaica, cacao trees grow successfully without additional shade, as long as there are sufficient moisture and nutrients in the soil. The cacao tree grows to about the size of an apple tree and starts

BELOW: A shady cacao plantation in the garden island of Grenada, where cacao production is a staple industry.

CACAO is essentially the botanical name and refers to the tree, the pods and, at one time, the unfermented beans from the pods. The term is now also used for beans that have been fermented.

COCOA refers to the manufactured powder sold for drinking or food manufacturing purposes.

bearing fruit in its third year. With luck, it will continue to do so until at least its twentieth year, and it is not unknown for a tree to live to be a hundred years old. The glossy dark green leaves, similar to those of the laurel, grow to nearly 30 cm/ 12 in long. The small pale pink flowers grow in dense clusters straight out of the trunk and main branches on little raised cushions, a feature technically known as "cauliflory".

After pollination, the flowers take about five months to develop into cacao pods. It's a colourful crop – the pods range from bright red, green, purple or yellow, changing hue as they ripen. Ripe pods are about 20 cm/8 in long, oval and pointed, each containing 20 to 40 beans, embedded in a soft white pulp.

HARVESTING

It is by assessing the colour of the pod and the sound it makes when tapped that the picker can be sure it is ready for picking. To be absolutely certain that the pod is ripe requires years of practice, and experienced pickers are highly valued.

The pods are removed from the tree by cutting through their stalks, those within reach with a cutlass, and those on higher branches with a curved knife fixed to a long pole. Cutting must be done with extreme care so as not to damage the "cauliflory", as this continually produces the flowers and therefore the fruit.

In some countries, harvesting takes place all year round, although most heavily from May to December. In other parts of the world, West Africa for instance, the main crop is harvested from September to February.

FERMENTING

The next stage is to split the pods with a cutlass, taking care not to damage the precious beans. These are scooped out, together with their surrounding pulp, and formed into a conical heap on a carefully arranged mat of banana leaves. When the heap is complete the leaves are folded over, and yet more of these giant

ABOVE: Early lithograph issued by the Empire Marketing Board in Britain showing cacao beans being scooped from the pods.

TYPES OF CACAO BEAN

There are two distinct species of cacao bean used in the manufacture of chocolate: the criollo (meaning "native") and the forastero (meaning "foreign").

The criollo, the Rolls Royce of beans and the most delicate, is in a way a "limited edition", representing only 10 to 15 per cent of the world's production. It is cultivated mainly in the countries where cacao originated, namely Nicaragua, Guatemala, Mexico, Venezuela and Colombia, as well as Trinidad, Jamaica and Grenada. The criollo's exceptional flavour and aroma are prized by chocolate manufacturers the world over. Not surprisingly, the bean is always used in combination with other varieties.

The much hardier and higher-yielding forastero bean is grown mainly in Brazil and Africa, and it accounts for about 80 per cent of the world's production. It has a stronger, more bitter flavour than the criollo and is mainly used for blending.

The one exception is the amenolado variety, known as the "Arriba" bean, grown in Ecuador. Its delicate flavour and fine aroma are considered equal to the world's best beans.

Finally, there are also several hybrid beans, of which the trinitario is the best known. As the name suggests, it began life in Trinidad where, following a hurricane in 1727 that all but destroyed the plantations, it was a result of cross-breeding. It has inherited the robustness of the forastero and the delicate flavour of the criollo, and it is used mainly for blending.

leaves are added to enclose the heap completely. This is the start of the fermentation process, which lasts for up to six days.

The chemical processes involved are complicated, but, basically, bacteria and yeasts present in the air multiply on the sugary pulp surrounding the beans, causing it to decompose to an acidic juice. The process raises the temperature of the heap and under these conditions magical changes take place within the bean itself. The colour changes from purple to chocolate brown and the familiar cacao smell begins to emerge – the first crucial stage in developing beans of superior quality. That said, the fermentation process is sometimes omitted, with planters and manufacturers arguing both for and against.

DRYING

After fermentation, the beans are spread out on bamboo mats or wooden drying floors. During the ten to twenty days needed for drying, the beans are regularly turned to keep them well aired and to prevent moulds forming. In some places, where rainfall and humidity are high, the beans are dried in commercial drying plants. However, the best quality cacao comes from beans that have been dried naturally in the warm tropical sun.

BELOW: The large and beautiful cacao pods grow directly from the tree branches and change colour as they ripen.

MODERN MANUFACTURING

ABOVE: A chocolate manufacturer inspects a shipment of beans.

CLEANING AND GRADING

Cacao beans arrive at a chocolate factory in the condition in which they leave the plantations in cacao-growing countries. They have been fermented and dried but are still a raw material with the edible part enclosed inside the hard skin, which is dusty with the remains of the dried pulp.

The beans are given a preliminary cleaning, during which any stones or other objects that may have arrived in the sacks are removed by sieving. The beans pass on a moving belt to storage hoppers, and from there they travel on another conveyor belt to the cleaning and grading machines. The beans are carefully inspected, and any shrivelled or double beans are discarded, as is any undesirable material still clinging to the beans. Next, the cleaned and graded beans are collected either in containers or passed on another continuous conveyor belt to the roasting machines.

ROASTING FOR FLAVOUR

Roasting is a crucial part of the process and serves several functions. First, it develops the flavour and aroma, and it enriches the colour. Roasting also dries the husk surrounding the "nib", or edible inner part of the bean, making its removal easier, and dries the nib itself so that it is ready for grinding.

The degree of roasting is extremely important. Overdoing

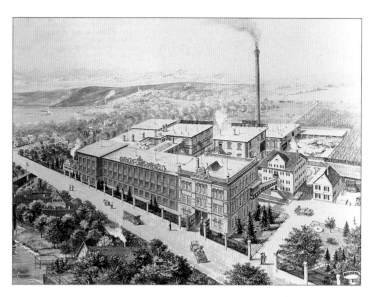

ABOVE: A contemporaneous picture of Richard Sprüngli's famous factory, which opened in Switzerland in 1900.

it destroys the natural flavour of the bean and produces a bitter product, while under-roasting makes the removal of the husk more difficult and also fails to eradicate the natural bitterness of the raw bean. Some manufacturers who want their chocolate to have a strong flavour, but who are not prepared to increase the cacao content, attempt to achieve the required intensity by roasting the beans longer.

Different types of bean need different roasting temperatures, depending on their texture and flavour; the mild varieties are usually roasted at lower temperatures than the stronger types.

After roasting, the beans are cooled as quickly as possible to prevent further internal roasting.

BELOW: The beans are cleaned and sifted through a mesh to get rid of small or shrivelled beans and foreign bodies.

BELOW: The beans are gently roasted to develop the aroma, enrich the colour and to dehydrate them prior to grinding.

WINNOWING

During the next stage the beans are passed through the husking and winnowing machine, which cracks open the roasted beans, and blows the lighter husks away from the heavier pieces of nib.

Manufacturers send the husks off for recycling as garden mulch, or use them to make low-quality soft "shell" butter.

THE CRUCIAL BLEND

During the blending process, specified quantities of different varieties of cacao nibs are weighed and transferred to a cylindrical blender before they are fed into the grinding machines.

The blending of beans for cocoa powder is generally less exacting than for eating chocolate. The latter requires the utmost skill from the chocolatier since knowledge of the characteristic flavours imparted by different beans is only acquired by years of experience. There are subtle differences of flavour in each type of bean, and the final flavour is obtained by blending two, three or more types of bean after roasting. In the same way that the winemaker blends his grapes, the chocolatier needs to determine the proportion of strong and mild cacao beans necessary

ABOVE: A picture of the grinding hall in the Sprüngli factory. The rollers can be seen on the left.

to produce a blend that will result in a satisfying chocolate, and the formulae are jealously guarded secrets.

GRINDING

Once in the grinding mill, the nibs pass through a series of rollers, resulting in coarse particles that eventually turn into a warm paste because of the frictional heat of the grinding action. Then follows a second grinding to bring the particles down to the required size, usually between 25 and 50 microns (about 0.001in). Large particles result in coarse grainy chocolate, while very finely ground particles will produce a pasty and slightly sticky chocolate. After grinding, the cacao mass or "liquor" flows out of the machine into shallow metal containers.

THE PARTING OF THE WAYS

At this stage, further treatment of the liquor depends on whether it is to be made into cocoa powder or eating chocolate. For cocoa powder the next step is the extraction of a large proportion of the cacao butter. This is pressed out of the liquor, and the residue is formed into cakes, which go through one more grinding. Some cocoa is "dutched", which helps to make cocoa powder easier to mix with water. It also improves the colour and lightens the flavour. Sometimes a wetting agent is added, especially to the "instant" varieties of cocoa intended for use as a cold drink; it makes the powder easier to mix with cold water or milk. The wetting agent is usually lecithin, a vegetable fat found in egg yolks and soy beans. Chocolate destined for eating is treated very differently from cocoa powder.

RIGHT: Two types of instant drinking chocolate.

— BEAN BLENDS —

The final flavour of chocolate depends largely on the chocolatier's skill and experience in selecting and blending various types of beans. Availability of supplies and cost also have to be taken into account.

Types of cacao beans may be divided into strong and mild varieties:

STRONG VARIETIES	MILD VARIETIES
St Lucia	Sri Lanka
Accra	Mauritius
Para	Caracas
Trinidad	Arriba
Grenada	Java
Surinam	Madras
Cuba	Jamaica
Dominica	Seychelles

Chocolate is made with either Bahia or Accra beans. If made only with Accra beans, the chocolate will have a very strong, harsh flavour, whereas Caracas beans make mild but excellently flavoured chocolate. Superb chocolate can be made with a blend of 42 per cent Trinidad beans (strong), 21 per cent Para or Accra beans (strong) and 37 per cent Caracas (mild).

THE MANUFACTURE OF EATING CHOCOLATE

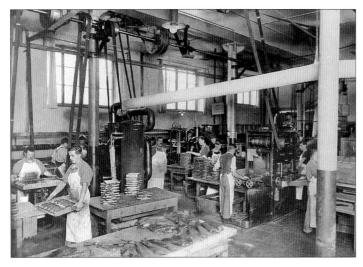

ABOVE: Rolls of ground chocolate paste (foreground) are moulded into bars and various shapes in the moulding hall.

ABOVE: Prolonged conching transforms the chocolate paste into velvety smoothness.

MIXING

Cacao beans used for manufacturing eating chocolate are processed in a different way from beans used in cocoa manufacture. First, a carefully selected blend of roasted and ground nibs, the edible centre of the bean, is mixed with pulverized sugar and enriched with cacao butter, not necessarily extracted from the same batch of nibs. The mass producers in the chocolate industry are very keen on adding lecithin, a vegetable fat, to replace some or all of the cacao butter. This means they can sell the valuable butter at a profit.

The mixture then goes to the *mélangeur*, a round machine with a horizontal rotating base on which run heavy rollers. After mixing, the chocolate paste that is discharged from the *mélangeur* resembles well-kneaded dough.

When manufacturing milk chocolate, powdered milk or evaporated sweetened milk is added to the rest of the ingredients in the mixer.

REFINING

Next, the chocolate paste is ground between a series of five rollers, each succeeding roller rotating faster than the previous one. The paste enters the first pair of rollers as a thin film, which is then taken up by the next pair, through a carefully adjusted gap – rather like making pasta with a machine. By the time the paste emerges from the fifth roller it is wafer-thin.

As far as some mass-producers are concerned this is the end of the process, but the finest quality chocolate needs further treatment known as "conching".

CONCHING

The conching machine was invented in 1880 by the Swiss chocolatier, Rodolfe Lindt. The name comes from the French (*conche*, meaning "shell") and is derived from the shape of the machine, a large shell-shaped container.

The function of the machine is to agitate the liquid chocolate gently over a period that may be as long as seven days. It is a vital process in which the flavour of the chocolate is developed and mellowed, any residual bitterness is removed, and the texture reaches that essential stage of velvety smoothness.

Manufacturers of cheaper chocolate give as little as twelve hours to the process. Quality producers will continue conching for up to a week, sometimes adding extra cacao butter to make the chocolate smoother still.

During conching, various flavours are added, such as vanilla, cloves or cinnamon.

LEFT: Luscious slices of crystallized fruit are enrobed with smooth, dark chocolate.

Vanilla is almost always used and dates back to the days of the Aztecs. Our palates have become so accustomed to its flavour in chocolate that leaving it out would be like making bread without salt. Pure vanilla extract is used for the best quality chocolate, but cheaper varieties are likely to contain vanillin, a synthetic substitute.

TEMPERING

Once the conching stage is complete, the chocolate is fed into tempering kettles, where it is stirred and carefully cooled but still remains liquid. This is a tricky process since cacao butter contains various types of fat, all with different melting and setting points. If the chocolate mass is cooled too slowly, some fats will remain liquid and separate from the mass, creating a bloom on the surface when the chocolate finally solidifies. Tempering causes rapid cooling resulting in a more even distribution of the various fats.

After tempering, chocolate to be made into bars is pumped into moulding machines, while chocolate to be used as coating is pumped into enrobing machines.

BELOW: Hollow Easter eggs, filled with small chocolates, are a classic example of chocolate moulding.

Mr R. Whymper in *Cocoa and Chocolate* (1921) told an interesting story of how, in the early 1900s, the popularity of milk chocolate "raised hopes in the breasts of manufacturers that a similar demand might be created among the masses for such articles as Date Chocolate, Egg Chocolate, Malt Chocolate". A number of patents were taken out, one of which was for mixing cacao beans and dates to a pulp, and covered the use of apples, pears and apricots for the same purpose. There was apparently a shortage of cane sugar at the time, and the fruit pulp was intended to be a sweetener.

Another patent was for "dietetic and laxative" chocolate. As Mr Whymper pointed out: "Such preparations must have only a very limited sale, so long as the chocolate-consuming public does not seek to find cures in its confections."

MOULDING

Liquid chocolate is also moulded into hollowed-out shapes which are sometimes filled with small chocolates. These products are often marketed as gifts for children, and specialist chocolate-makers give full rein to their creativity here, producing not simply exquisite Easter eggs, bunnies and hearts, but also pigs, fish, lions, hippos, crocodiles and

ABOVE: 1930's metal moulds for producing novelty chocolates.

cars. Because of the contact with the smooth tinned surfaces of the mould, good quality hollow chocolate has a high degree of gloss, which adds to its attraction.

ENROBING

Enrobing is the tricky process of coating confectionery centres. Liquid chocolate of a slightly "thin" consistency is pumped into the enrobing machine, where it is agitated once more and maintained at a temperature just high enough to keep it liquid. The centres themselves have to be warm when they enter the coating chamber, but not so warm that they lose their shape. The danger of a cold centre is that it is likely to expand when it comes in contact with the warm coating, resulting in burst chocolates. Enrobing is the process used not only for top quality chocolates in their luxury packaging, but also for the mass-produced candy bars that are bought as snacks around the world.

TASTE, QUALITY AND PRESENTATION

TYPES OF EATING CHOCOLATE

There is a wealth of wonderful chocolate products available, with an often confusing array of types, qualities, fillings and flavourings. Here is a brief guide on what you should look for and how to enjoy chocolate at its best.

PLAIN CHOCOLATE (ALSO KNOWN AS BITTERSWEET)

Plain or bittersweet chocolate must contain a minimum of 34 per cent cacao solids, but generally speaking, the higher the proportion the better the chocolate. Not so long ago, plain chocolate containing just 30 per cent cacao solids was considered high quality. Nowadays, as our taste and awareness of chocolate grows, 60 per cent is the preferred minimum, while for chocoholics 70-80 per cent is even more desirable. High quality dark chocolate contains a correspondingly small proportion of sugar. Adding sugar to chocolate has been compared with adding salt to food. You need just enough to enhance the flavour but not so much that the flavour is destroyed. Quality chocolate contains pure vanilla, an expensive flavouring sometimes called Bourbon Vanilla, extracted from a type of orchid grown in Madagascar. It also contains the minutest amount of lecithin, a harmless vegetable stabilizer. In unsweetened chocolate, which is found only in specialist shops, cacao solids are as high as 98 per cent.

ABOVE: Quality white, milk and dark chocolate.

COUVERTURE

This is high-quality chocolate in the professional league, used mainly for coating and in baking. Couverture usually has a minimum of 32 per cent cacao butter, which enables it to form a much thinner shell than ordinary chocolate.

LEFT: Couverture chocolate, which has a very high proportion of cacao solids.

RIGHT: Best quality couverture with a good sheen. Blocks of this size are supplied to chocolatiers.

— *FORMULA FOR QUALITY CHOCOLATE* —
56-70% cacao solids, to include 31% cacao butter
29-43% finely ground sugar
1% lecithin and pure vanilla extract

— *FORMULA FOR MASS-PRODUCED MILK CHOCOLATE* —
11% cacao solids
3% vegetable fat
20% milk solids
65% sugar
1% lecithin and synthetic vanillin

MILK CHOCOLATE

To some *aficionados,* milk chocolate is not really chocolate, but, increasingly, there are good brands around even though they may be difficult to find. A good brand will have a cacao solid content of around 40 per cent, but most mass-produced milk chocolate contains only 20 per cent. Mass-produced milk chocolate has a high sugar content, often up to 50 per cent. It can also contain up to 5 per cent vegetable fat, used as a substitute for expensive cacao butter, and artificial flavouring.

WHITE CHOCOLATE

This is basically cacao butter without any cacao solids, with some added sugar, flavouring and milk. White chocolate does not have the same depth of flavour as plain chocolate. It is mainly sold for its novelty value or to provide an attractive colour contrast

LEFT: A layered bar of plain, white and milk chocolate.

in chocolates and chocolate desserts. The best quality brands tend to be French and Swiss. British brands usually contain vegetable oil instead of cacao butter, as well as synthetic flavourings.

ASSESSING QUALITY

All our senses – sight, smell, sound, touch and taste – come into play when assessing the quality of plain chocolate. There are several points to watch out for:

APPEARANCE: The chocolate should be smooth, brilliantly shiny and pure mahogany-black in colour.

SMELL: The chocolate should not smell excessively sweet.

SOUND: The chocolate should be crisp and make a distinct "snap" when broken in two. If the chocolate splinters, it is too dry; if it resists breaking, it is too waxy.

TOUCH: Chocolate with a high cacao butter content should quickly start to melt when held in the hand – this is a good sign. In the mouth, it should feel ultra-smooth with no hint of graininess, and it should melt instantly.

TASTE: Chocolate contains a kaleidoscope of flavours and aromas which continue to develop in the mouth. The basic flavours are bitterness with a hint of acidity, sweetness with a suggestion of sourness, and just a touch of saltiness which helps release the aromas of cocoa, pineapple, banana, vanilla and cinnamon.

STORAGE

Humidity and heat are chocolate's greatest enemies; both can cause a "bloom" to appear on the surface. Heat-induced bloom

---

— TASTING TECHNIQUES —

It is best to taste chocolate on an empty stomach. If your chocolate is correctly stored, you will need to allow an hour or so for it to reach the recommended temperature of 19–25°C/66–77°F.

PLAIN CHOCOLATE: Allow the chocolate to sit in your mouth for a few moments to release its primary flavours and aromas. Then chew it five to ten times to release the secondary aromas. Let it rest lightly against the roof of your mouth so that you experience the full range of flavours. Finally, enjoy the lingering tastes in your mouth.

FILLED CHOCOLATE: Allow the chocolate to sit in your mouth for a few moments to release its primary flavours and aromas. Then chew it three to five times to mix the chocolate and the filling. Let the mixture melt slowly in your mouth so that you experience a new range of flavours. Enjoy the lingering tastes.

LEFT: The perfect bar of chocolate has a glossy sheen and a rich dark colour.

is the result of cacao butter crystals rising to the surface and recrystallizing. The flavour is unaffected but the appearance is spoiled.

Humidity-induced bloom is more damaging. It is a result of sugar crystals being drawn to the surface, where they dissolve in the moist atmosphere and eventually recrystallize to form an unpleasant grey coating. As the texture and taste of the chocolate deteriorate, too, the dustbin is the best place for chocolate that has suffered in this way. The ideal temperature for storage is 10–15°C (50–60°F), slightly warmer than the refrigerator, and the humidity should be 60–70 per cent. Chocolate also absorbs surrounding odours easily and should be kept in an airtight container.

— WHAT TO DRINK WITH CHOCOLATE —

Generally speaking, chocolate and wine do not mix. The lingering intensity of the chocolate competes with the aroma of the wine, and chocolate's bitterness can mask the tannins essential to the wine's flavour. White wine or champagne drunk with chocolate is a particularly uneasy combination. At the end of a meal, coffee, perhaps accompanied by a fine cognac, whisky or bourbon, is the best choice. Professional chocolate tasters swear by a glass of cold, fresh water; as it not only quenches the thirst but also cleanses the palate.

BELOW: A bloom has formed on the surface of the chocolate on the right. An unaffected piece on the left shows the difference in appearance.

Flavourings and Fillings

Every chocolate manufacturer has a secret condiment or blend of flavourings that he or she claims gives their product a unique character. Fillings and flavourings from the same tropical latitude as the cacao bean itself – vanilla, cinnamon, cardamom, coffee, rum, ginger, even pepper and chilli – are the ones most commonly used. Even in this age of "culinary fusion", when we happily mix and match cuisines in our never-ending quest for novelty, flavouring chocolate with spices from a more northerly latitude simply seems wrong – it is hard to imagine fennel or caraway-flavoured chocolate, for instance – but perhaps it is merely a matter of time before it happens.

Secret flavours

Every chocolate-consuming country has its favourite flavourings. Italy prefers its chocolate mixed with hazelnuts, almonds or chestnuts. France likes a nutty flavour too, but strongly flavoured dark bitter chocolate is also popular there. Spain likes spiced chocolate, and fillings such as almonds and dried fruits, America consumes mostly milk chocolate, often with whole peanuts or almonds embedded in it, while Britain

Above: Handmade "tartufini" from southern Italy – whole almonds coated in praline and dusted with dark cocoa and powdered sugar.

likes vanilla. Not only that, every country uses different blends of beans, and, as already mentioned, the subtle variations in the flavour of different bean varieties play their part in determining the final flavour of the chocolate. If we also take into account different processing methods used by individual factories, the number of flavour combinations is almost endless.

Within the scientific community, the complexity of chocolate's flavour is a source of enormous fascination to the flavour scientists who are regularly producing learned papers on the subject. Daniel Querici, speaking at the 1992 Oxford Symposium on Food & Cookery, summed up the subject of chocolate's flavour in a delightful way: "Its complex flavour profile looks like a royal peacock tail, although not fully deployed, as food scientists keep discovering new components."

Below: Plump and glistening, these unusual, luscious chocolate-covered figs come from Italy.

Left: Spanish chocolate packed with plump almonds.

— Fillings —

Boiled: based on sugar and glucose and including caramels, butterscotch and fudge.

Creams and fondants: a mixture of sugar crystals in a sugar syrup, with fruit or other flavourings, coated with tempered chocolate.

Croquet (or brittle): molten sugar with crushed nuts.

Ganache: a mixture of chocolate, cream and butter, either rolled in cocoa powder to make a truffle or enrobed in tempered chocolate.

Gianduja: finely ground nuts and sugar mixed with plain or milk chocolate.

Marzipan: molten sugar mixed with ground almonds, coated with plain or milk chocolate.

Nougat: a mixture of beaten egg white, boiled sugar, nuts and/or candied fruit. Known as *Montélimar* in France (after the town where it is made), *torrone* in Italy, and *turrón* in Spain.

Praline: similar to *gianduja* but with a coarser texture and usually coated with plain or milk chocolate.

ABOVE: Italian chocolates with succulent fillings of walnuts, dried fruit and pistachio marzipan.

FANTASTIC FILLINGS

Chocolate has been used as a coating for anything from almonds and dried fruit to bizarre ingredients such as ants, and a look at the contents of a global box of chocolates will reveal many more.

In the United States, chillies and chocolate come together once more in the whacky confectionery range created by two chocolatiers from Oregon. Their products, which won an award at the Fiery Foods Show at Albuquerque, New Mexico, include Mexican Zingers, a creamy, green jalapeño salsa encased in a white chocolate shell, and Southwest Coyote Kickers, a red jalapeño salsa cream covered in light milk chocolate.

Although chilli-filled chocolates are legal in the United States, alcoholic fillings are not universally acceptable. As recently as 1986, only one American state permitted the manufacture of alcoholic chocolates, only eleven states permitted their sale, and

BELOW: Handmade British chocolates with melt-in-the-mouth fondant fillings, delicately flavoured with violet and rose.

— A FILLING STORY —

In 1987, Ethel M Chocolates owned by 82-year-old Forrest Mars and named after his mother, attempted to introduce liqueur-filled chocolates to Las Vegas, Nevada. The chocolates were spiked with crème de menthe, brandy, Scotch and bourbon.

Mr Mars found that the sale and/or manufacture of alcoholic chocolates was illegal in most American states. Things were not looking good, especially as an appeal to legalize alcoholic chocolates had recently been rejected in Pennsylvania, home of Hersheyville. As was to be expected, the squeaky-clean Hershey Company added their support to the rejection on the grounds that "liquor-laced chocolates are inconsistent with values emphasized by religious and medical communities".

Not one to give up easily, the determined Mr Mars successfully petitioned the sale and manufacture of alcoholic chocolates in his home state of Nevada. This meant he could sell his chocolates there but not across the border, and so he had to content himself with selling to the twenty million tourists who visit Las Vegas each year. Ethel M Chocolates are still to be found at Las Vegas airport and in many of the city's luxury hotels.

even then the permitted alcohol levels were severely restricted.

Move on to Europe, however, and it is a different story. In Italy smooth dark chocolates are filled with decadent liqueur-soaked fruits – cherries, kumquats, slices of dried peach, pear, apricots and oranges. There are also plump prunes, dates and walnuts filled with marzipan and covered with dark chocolate.

In Britain, chocolate lovers can enjoy delicate fondant fillings such as violet and rose creams or marzipan; truffle fillings laced with champagne, Cointreau or Drambuie; or chunks of stem ginger, and whole Brazil nuts. France is the birthplace of the dusky chocolate truffle created in the late nineteenth century by the Duc de Praslin, one of Louis XIV's ministers. At that time it was considered amusing to create a food resembling something totally unrelated. *Truffes au chocolat* were deeply rich, buttery chocolate balls that were then rolled in dark cocoa powder to resemble the savoury black fungi from Périgord.

The dragée is a French confectionery classic that in its original form, almonds coated with sugar and honey, dates back to the thirteenth century. The dragée adapted well to the introduction of chocolate and now consists of praline or nuts covered in chocolate and a hard sugar coating.

CHOCOLATE WRAPPERS AND BOXES

Wrapping and packaging tell a great deal about what kind of chocolate is inside. Much can be learnt from the nutritional information on a bar, while the style of its presentation says much about who is expected to buy it.

LEFT: As well as listing the ingredients, some wrappers are packed with other interesting information.

WORDING ON WRAPPERS

As with the label on a bottle of fine wine or virgin olive oil, the wording on a chocolate wrapper can provide significant clues as to the quality of the product, so for a chocolate lover it is worth becoming familiar with the terminology.

An area of confusion arises over the terms "cacao liquor" and "cacao solids". Liquor is the term used in the United States, while Europe favours solids, but both refer to the same thing – the entire cacao content including the butter. This is usually expressed as a percentage of the net weight of the end product. Cacao content ranges from 15 per cent, which hardly comes into the category of chocolate, to an incredible 99 per cent, which is an almost inedible but interesting experience.

ABOVE: A wrapper that makes a feature of the high cacao content.

Since the setting up of the European Union, legislation on the labelling of food has become much more regulated, and the classification of chocolate has become an issue. Some chocolate-producing countries feel that Britain's product should be classified as "vegolate" because of its use of vegetable fat and low cacao content. Happily for British chocolate producers this has as yet remained a discussion point only.

WHAT TO LOOK FOR

The key indicator of quality is the cacao content – the combined total of cacao solids (liquor) and cacao butter. In some cases, couverture for instance, the cacao

butter content is itemized separately. In the case of plain chocolate, a minimum of 50 per cent total cacao is an indicator of quality. Quality milk chocolate should have a minimum of 30 per cent. Since sugar makes up the balance of the ingredients, a high sugar content is a warning of a correspondingly low cacao content.

Unlike wine labels, which mention the grape variety, chocolate wrappers rarely divulge the type of cacao bean used and are not obliged to do so. An exception is in France, where the words *fine cocoa* mean that the superior varieties of bean, such as the criollo, have been used.

Vegetable or animal fats are used as a cheap substitute for some or all of the cacao butter, so if either is listed as an ingredient, the chocolate is not going to come up to scratch. The fact that they are not listed, however, does not always necessarily mean they are not present. In Britain, for example, up to 5 per cent cacao butter substitutes can be included without mentioning them on the wrapper.

Lecithin, an emulsifier derived from egg yolk and soya beans, is used in all types of chocolate, and at 1 per cent or less is not an indicator of inferior quality. Its function is to stabilize the chocolate and to absorb any moisture.

As far as flavourings are concerned, look for the words "pure vanilla extract". If "vanillin", a synthetic substitute, or simply the word "flavouring" is listed, the chocolate is likely to be of inferior quality.

The Americans outdo any other nation in the world when it comes to providing information on the ingredients that go into their chocolate; the wrappers and packaging often read like a book. There are very precise

LEFT AND BELOW: Early chocolate boxes often featured inlaid metal decorations and intricate decorative painting.

Left: The ultimate in kitsch packaging, this opulent white plastic "grand piano" chocolate box comes from Germany.

— *National Preferences* —
According to the American writer, Nika Standen Hazelton, "Chocolate in a blue wrapper won't sell in Shanghai or Hong Kong because the Chinese associate blue with death. Neither Swiss nor Germans like girl pictures on their chocolate packages, but want a realistic reproduction of the contents."

specifications for the quantity of cacao solids in different types of chocolate; all flavouring ingredients must be fully declared; there are additional lists of sugars, such as dextrose and glucose, which all have maximum permitted levels; and there is always a detailed panel of nutritional information.

Chocolate Boxes

Chocolate-makers have been strongly aware of the value of shelf-appeal since the industry's early days. In France the most exquisitely designed chocolate boxes came into vogue as early as 1780, featuring beautiful paintings, intricately embossed plaques and inlaid semi-precious stones. Britain's chocolate boxes were not so ostentatious; they featured sentimental images that were very much the fashion when boxed chocolates came on the market. The first was produced in 1868 by Cadbury and featured a painting of a young girl cuddling a kitten; the model was Richard Cadbury's daughter Jessica.

Also part of the appeal are the beautiful papers used to line boxes and separate layers of chocolate. Although grease-resistant, the types of paper used have always had a special quality. They may be elaborately padded or embossed with gold or silver, or mysteriously translucent, like crisp tracing paper, with a swirly hammered finish. Another type of paper is known as glasine. It has a waxy feel and comes in wonderfully glossy, dark colours, almost smelling of chocolate in its own right.

Nowadays, packaging design veers from one extreme of style to another. Reminiscent of the glamourous thirties, there are amazingly lavish fabric-covered boxes trimmed with satiny ribbons and roses. In the kitsch category there is a large, white grand-piano-shaped box from Germany with chocolates hidden beneath the lid, and at the other end of the spectrum there is the ultimate in modern minimalist designer chocolates and packaging with slim chocolates wrapped in gold leaf.

Below: The packaging room at Cadbury's factory in 1932. Cadbury were the first manufacturer in Britain to produce boxed chocolates.

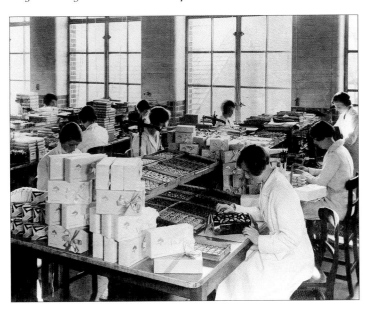

Below: Espresso-infused dark chocolate truffle fingers from the United States, end-wrapped with delicate gold foil.

A WORLD OF CHOCOLATE

In the next few pages of the book we survey some of the world's highest quality chocolate products. This is not a comprehensive selection, and it includes some of the most familiar quality brands as well as the more exclusive. Some products, such as the famous Toblerone bars, are internationally popular and universally available, and others, such as the exquisite chocolates made by the small specialist companies in America, are known to a much smaller market, but their first-class products are available by mail order and their market will increase as our appreciation of chocolate becomes more discerning.

BELGIUM

Belgium is renowned for its *ballotins,* chocolate-covered pralines, invented by Jean Neuhaus who, in 1912, developed coating chocolate capable of containing liquid fillings. Today NEUHAUS is well known for its flavoured Côte d'Or bars.

Of all Belgian chocolate companies, GODIVA must be the most recognized internationally. Established in 1929 by the Drap family, the company has 14-year old Joseph Drap to thank for its success. Realising people needed a little luxury in the austere post-war years Joseph created the chocolate truffle. They were marketed under the name of Godiva and were an instant success. Belgium also boasts many smaller specialists producing their own excellent chocolates.

CHARLEMAGNE produces superior quality thin squares of plain and white chocolate with exotic flavours such as spiced ginger,

ABOVE: A selection of Kim's Cachet chocolates, exported worldwide.

cardamom and coffee, and spiced Earl Grey tea.

KIM'S, established in 1987 and manufacturer of the widely available luxury Cachet brand, specializes in handmade fillings. Kim's range includes white, milk and plain chocolate bars with luscious cream fillings such as hazelnut, coconut truffle, mocha and vanilla.

PIERRE COLAS specializes in unusual bars of plain and milk chocolate that are set in antique moulds and flavoured with esoteric combinations of cardamom, juniper, pink peppercorns and lavender. The company supplies specialist retailers in Belgium, Spain, France and the London chocolate shop Rococo.

WITTAMER probably ranks highest with connoisseurs. The range includes unusual seasonal specialities and Wittamer's famous Samba cake made with two contrasting chocolate mousses.

THE NETHERLANDS

The Netherlands is the birthplace of Coenraad Van Houten who revolutionized the chocolate industry with his cocoa press. With this background, it is not surprising that the Dutch chocolate industry today concentrates largely on cocoa rather than eating chocolate. The four biggest companies, VAN HOUTEN, BENSDORP, DE ZAAN and GERKENS, were all set up in the nineteenth century and continue to supply the world with fine-quality unsweetened cocoa powder. Van Houten is now based in Germany, having undergone several takeovers

and mergers, and trades in Europe, the United States, Hong Kong and Singapore.

The Netherlands do produce a certain amount of eating chocolate, however, and enthusiasts enjoy Dutch chocolate for its dark colour and distinctive flavour. DROSTE, of the distinctive "Droste man" logotype, makes delicious chocolate discs, or pastilles, from which the logotype is derived. Bensdorp and Van Houten also make quality chocolate.

LEFT: Droste are famous for their chocolate pastilles.

GERMANY

The Germans are one of the largest consumers of chocolate in Europe. Faced with this demanding clientele, German chocolate manufacturers pride themselves on producing fresh, quality chocolates made with the very best ingredients.

CONFISERIE HEINEMANN, based in München-Gladbach and run by master chocolatier Heinz Heinemann, makes over sixty varieties of freshly made chocolates every day, including exceptional champagne truffles. Heinemann also offers an interesting range of moulded chocolate-filled seasonal specialities.

DREIMEISTER is a long-established family enterprise set up by the father of Hans Wilhelm Schröder, the present owner, and originally known as Café Schröder. Although the company has a large turnover and supplies to hotels, restaurants and airlines, Dreimeister produces the freshest of chocolates and truffles, made only with top-quality ingredients.

FEODORA is probably Germany's best-known brand

BELOW: Feodora's elegant range produced for the international market.

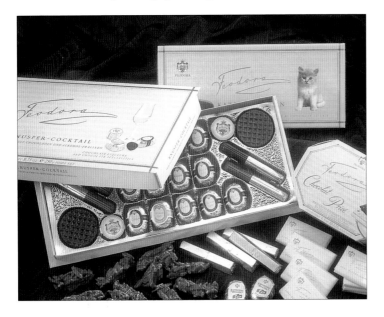

RIGHT: Leysieffer's freshly made seasonal chocolate.

internationally. Their chocolate is wonderfully smooth due to lengthy conching. The elegantly packaged quality chocolates include champagne truffles, bitter milk chocolate wafers, espresso Brazil chocolates and luxury pralines.

HACHEZ, based in Bremen since 1890, makes chocolates exclusively with rare cacao beans from Venezuela and Ecuador. Loved by generations of chocolate connoisseurs, the range includes melt-in-the-mouth cat's tongues, gold-covered nut sticks, ginger sticks, chocolate leaves and fruit cream-filled chocolate pastilles.

LEYSIEFFER has produced handmade chocolates in its Osnabrück bakery since 1909. In order to guarantee absolute freshness, the company starts manufacture only on receipt of an order. Its products include good quality white and milk chocolate, flavoured with a tempting range of ingredients – cinnamon, ginger, orange, pistachio and a mouthwatering combination of mocca and Jamaica rum.

STOLLWERCK in Cologne began as a bakery in 1839 and is now an international group with impressive headquarters on the banks of the River Elbe. The Imhoff-Stollwerck Museum boasts a fascinating collection of chocolate-related exhibits, including a collection of vending machines resembling grandfather clocks, porcelain chocolate services and printed ephemera, as well as a tropical greenhouse planted with young cacao trees. The company produces a wide range of chocolates for all levels of the market.

AUSTRIA

Austria's chocolate delicacies include both pâtisserie and confectionery. World-famous pâtisserie establishments are the palatial HOTEL IMPERIAL, Vienna's grandest, and home of Imperial Torte, an unbelievably rich layered square chocolate cake; and the HOTEL SACHER, famous for its delectable Sachertorte, a moist apricot-glazed rich chocolate cake; and DEMEL, the celebrated Viennese pâtisserie, which produces a rival version of Sachertorte based on a recipe said to have been given to Anna Demel by Franz Sacher's son. Demel also

produces whole roasted cacao beans coated with fine chocolate.

ALTMANN & KÜHNE, established in Vienna for more than eighty years, produce exquisite hand-dipped miniature chocolates, appropriately called Liliputconfekte, in the most unusual shapes. The chocolates are beautifully packaged in miniature chests of drawers and treasure chests.

MIRABELL in Salzburg produces traditional Mozartkugeln, an Austrian speciality consisting of creamy marzipan and hazelnut-nougat balls with a delicate chocolate coating.

ITALY

ABOVE: Gianduja *are Italy's favourite chocolate.*
RIGHT: *Italians prefer chocolate in bite-size pieces.*

Hazelnuts, chestnuts, almonds and honey have always been an integral part of Italian cuisine. It comes as no surprise therefore, that Italians like their chocolate nutty and sweet. They also like their chocolate small, so bars are often sold in single serving sizes – handy for a quick fix, should the need arise. Neapolitans, which look exactly like miniature chocolate bars, complete with individual wrappers, are well-known throughout Europe.

The Italians are creative chocolate-makers, and they excel at presentation too; Italian packaging is stunning, whether the design is traditionally ornate or 1990s minimalist.

CAFFAREL in Turin is one of Italy's oldest chocolate-makers. Established in 1826, the company purchased a chocolate-making machine designed by Bozelli, a Genoese engineer, and so became the pioneers in setting out on the route to industrialization. In 1865 Caffarel developed Italy's favourite confection, *gianduja*, a rectangle of luscious chocolate and hazelnut paste, instantly recognizable by its triangular profile and rounded ends. Nowadays most Italian chocolate-makers produce their own special version of *gianduja* using jealously guarded recipes. There is a glorious giant-sized version, *grangianduja*, as well as miniature *gianduiotti*.

An ancient culture of confectionery lives on in Italy's far south, and it was here in Salantino, in Italy's heel, that MAGLIO opened their factory in 1875. The business has passed from father to son and is now run by brothers Massimo and Maurizio. The Maglio range is based on plump, dark chocolates with inspirational fillings, including liqueur-infused dried kumquats, peaches, pears and oranges, marzipan-stuffed dates and prunes, and lemon-zest-coated figs stuffed with a whole almond.

Founded in 1796, MAJANI in Bologna is one of Italy's most creative chocolate-makers. Their specialities are *scorze*, deliciously bittersweet chocolate sticks still made to the same ancient recipe, and *"Fiat" Cremino*, launched in 1911 as a publicity stunt to celebrate the Fiat Tipo 4 car. The car has since gone out of production but *"Fiat" Cremino* live on. These stunning miniature squares are made with four types of layered chocolate, something like a brown striped liquorice allsort.

PERUGINA, based in the medieval city of Perugia, Umbria, was set up in 1907 by Francesco Buitoni, a descendant of the well-known pasta-making family. From humble beginnings making sugared almonds, Perugina is now one of Italy's largest chocolate manufacturers. The most popular brand in their extensive range is *Baci* (kisses), introduced in 1922 and still going strong. Lovers still like to discover the romantic messages hidden under the wrapper.

PEYRANO, an exclusive chocolatier in Turin, is almost unique in grinding their own cacao beans – very, very few chocolatiers do so. The chocolates are superb, especially their *gianduja*. Peyrano also sell *bicerin*, a very rare paste of bitter chocolate, cocoa, hazelnuts and honey used for sweetening coffee.

BELOW: *Romantically packaged Baci conceal a lover's message.*

SWITZERLAND

ABOVE: The Confiserie Sprüngli in Zurich, around 1895.

Three key developments undoubtedly contribute to Switzerland's national preference for its very delicate, melt-in-the-mouth milk chocolate. Switzerland is the birthplace of Rodolphe Lindt, inventor of the conching machine which transforms chocolate from a rough gritty paste to a state of silky-smooth perfection. Lindt also created soft, creamy fondant chocolate by adding cacao butter to the paste before conching. We have the Swiss to thank, too, for the invention of milk chocolate.

SPRÜNGLI in Zurich is one of the most famous chocolate establishments in the world. The shop in Bahnhofstrasse is renowned for its freshest of fresh *Truffes du Jour,* a heart-stopping mixture of finest chocolate, cream and butter, made to the highest possible standards. The company operates a worldwide delivery service which guarantees that the longed-for parcel will arrive within 24 hours of despatch.

Set up by master confectioner Rudolf Sprüngli in 1845, the company has been handed down through six generations of Sprünglis. When Rudolf retired, he divided his empire between his two sons. The younger, David, received the confectionery shops. The elder brother, Johann, became the owner of the

ABOVE: A 1935 street poster.

chocolate factory. In the same year he retired, Rudolf Sprüngli also decided to purchase Rodolphe Lindt's chocolate factory in Berne. Overnight, the company acquired all Lindt's manufacturing secrets, and it was this transaction that was the foundation for the success of the now world-famous Lindt & Sprüngli company.

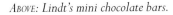

ABOVE: Lindt's mini chocolate bars.

LINDT & SPRÜNGLI operates entirely independently from Sprüngli. The company produces an enormous range of excellent quality chocolates sold in supermarkets and specialist shops world-wide. One of their best products is the tastefully thin Excellence bar, a sublime blend of finest cacao beans with a hint of pure

vanilla, and a cacao solid content of 70 per cent. This is closely followed in quality by Excellence Milk, possibly one of the best milk chocolate bars available. Another Lindt bar, called Swiss Bittersweet Chocolate, which is easily recognized by its traditional wrapper design, is also good.

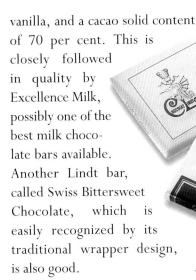

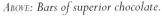

ABOVE: Bars of superior chocolate.

SUCHARD in Berne is another long-established and respected company, now owned by the American multinational Philip Morris. Suchard was a gold medallist several times over at the 1855 Exposition Universelle in Paris, and their milk chocolate bar, Milka, produced in 1901, is well-known all over Europe. Since 1970, Suchard have been the manufacturer of the famous Toblerone bars, although these were originally produced by their inventor Jean Tobler. The bars were designed with a triangular profile representing the Swiss Alps. The name is derived from merging that of the inventor, Tobler, together with the word *torrone,* the Italian word for nougat. Toblerone is made with a blend of chocolate, nougat, almonds and egg white, and the bar is one of Switzerland's most popular products – outside the country at least. Enthusiasts can enjoy giant bars weighing more than 4kg/8.8lb, miniature bars and a whole range in between.

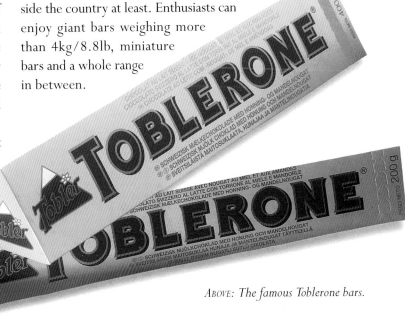

ABOVE: The famous Toblerone bars.

FRANCE

ABOVE: Early poster for the French Chocolate and Tea Company.

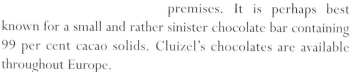

Quakers, the company provides daily lunch for the workers and, until recently, housed them in dormitories above the workshop. The Bernachons travel the world in search of the rarest cacao beans and the best nuts and fruit. Their chocolates are the very best. The range includes unusually flavoured chocolate bars, truffles, pralines, *giandujas* and marzipans.

BONNAT in Voiron near Grenoble is one of the few companies that roasts its own beans. A purist at heart, master chocolatier Raymond Bonnat uses a single *grand cru* bean, rather than a blend, for each of the chocolates in his range. Bonnat's choice of seven *crus,* which consist of Côte d'Ivoire, Madagascar, Ceylon, Trinité, Chuao, Maragnan and Puerto Cabellois, is selected from the world's finest cacao plantations. Bonnat chocolates are available from specialist outlets in France, and from Mortimer and Bennett's shop in London, which is the sole British importer.

ABOVE: Chocolate almonds.

CLUIZEL, in Paris, is a family-run business set up in 1947, producing excellent chocolate with rare South American and African beans ground and roasted on the premises. It is perhaps best known for a small and rather sinister chocolate bar containing 99 per cent cacao solids. Cluizel's chocolates are available throughout Europe.

CHRISTIAN CONSTANT, set up in 1970 in Paris, produces matchless ganache-filled chocolates. The flavourings read like an exotic travel brochure: Malabar cardamom, Yemeni jasmine, Chinese ginger and Tahitian vanilla.

The famous FAUCHON shop in Paris was established in 1925 by August Fauchon, whose passion was for collecting unusual merchandise. The company was taken over after his death by Joseph Pilosoff, whose granddaughter runs the business today. Fauchon specialities are the very best quality chocolate *marrons glacés,* truffles, pralines and ganaches, all exquisitely packaged.

LA MAISON DU CHOCOLAT in Paris was opened in 1977 by Robert Linxe, master chocolate-maker *extraordinaire*. Linxe's rigorous training and deep understanding of chocolate's complexities have played a major part in furthering the reputation

A large part of the French chocolate industry is made up of small, independent firms making ever more innovative *grand cru* chocolates to jealously guarded recipes. The French, who prefer dark, intensely flavoured chocolate, have a wide choice at their disposal.

BERNACHON, a greatly respected family of artisan chocolatiers, set up in 1955 in Lyon. Sharing the caring attitude of the

ABOVE: One of Bonnat's superb grand cru *bars.*

of France's chocolate-makers. It was Linxe's collaboration with Valrhona which set the quality of their *grand cru* couvertures, which they in turn supply to smaller chocolate-makers. Linxe's specialities are exquisitely shaped squares, pyramids and lozenges of the very best plain and milk chocolate, filled with praline, buttery caramel or the lightest and creamiest ganache. The chocolates are sold in Paris and by leading specialist outlets in New York, Houston and Dallas.

LE ROUX, founded in 1977 in Quiberon, Brittany, is renowned for *Caramel au Beurre Salé* (salted butter caramel), and for rare chocolate truffles containing fragments of Périgord truffle.

MICHEL CHAUDUN set up shop in Paris in 1986. His award-winning work includes not only the highest quality chocolates but ambitious chocolate sculptures. Only the rarest cacao beans are used together with top quality fruit and nuts. His chocolates are available in Paris and Tokyo.

RICHART DESIGN ET CHOCOLAT started life in 1925 in the laboratory of Lyon-based master chocolatier Joseph Richart. Using

BELOW: A Chocolat Carpentier poster from 1895.

ABOVE: Elegant chocolates and packaging from Richart Design et Chocolat.

only the finest cacao beans, Richart produces exquisite, smoother than smooth, miniature chocolate squares silk-screened with designs in cacao butter. Fillings and flavourings are equally inspired. The choice includes pure malt Scotch, green tea, blackcurrants, pineapple, clementines, the very best Andalucian almonds, chestnuts from the Ardèche, and pralines and ganaches flavoured with thyme, curry, bergamot, anise or nutmeg. Beautifully packaged in slim trays, Richart's chocolates are sold in boutiques in Paris, Lyon and New York.

VALRHONA, set up in 1922 and based in the Rhône valley, is the leading supplier of couverture chocolate for smaller chocolate-makers. The beans are all of superior quality and include guanaja, pur caraibe, manjari and jivara. Each shipment is tested by a panel of experts. Its products include *Carré,* small chocolate squares made from individual bean varieties, packed in beautiful tins; *BonBons de Chocolat,* individual chocolates packed in gift boxes with a guide recommending the order in which they should be eaten; and the well-known Valrhona bars in their distinctive black wrappers. The cacao content of the bars ranges from 71 per cent for *Noir Amer* (bitter) to a relatively high 40 per cent for *Le Lacté* (milk).

RIGHT: Valrhona Lacté has a high cacao content.

SPAIN

As recently as 1920, chocolate-makers in Spain were still using the curved granite metate for grinding cacao beans. The *chocolateros* would travel around with the *metate* strapped to their backs and bags of cacao beans under their arms. They would kneel on a little cushion in front of the stone and grind the beans in full public view so that the buyer could be sure he was getting unadulterated stone-ground chocolate. Nowadays chocolate-making in Spain is a fully industrialized process, but, even so, the tradition of quality craftsmanship is very much alive and well.

In some ways Spanish chocolate is indistinguishable from quality chocolate made in the rest of Europe. What sets it apart is the creativity and imagination of the chocolate-makers, and their use of the very best quality Mediterranean fruits and nuts. Spain grows some of the best nuts in the world, so there is no shortage of supply. Plump almonds, hazelnuts, pine kernels and mouth-puckeringly bitter Seville oranges are all used by the chocolate-makers with excellent results.

BLANXART, set up in 1954 in Barcelona, is one of Spain's smaller specialist firms, producing handmade high-quality chocolates from the very best cacao beans. The company prides itself on roasting and grinding the beans itself to achieve the desired perfection of flavour and aroma. The mouthwatering range includes a delicate curl of candied Seville orange dipped in bitter chocolate, clusters of chocolate-covered pine nuts, as well as liqueur-filled chocolates and several types of praline.

LUDOMAR, in Barcelona, specializes in superior, made-to-order chocolates, which they sell to pâtisserie shops in Spain, France, Germany and Britain. Specialities are plump, chocolate-smothered cherries; *postre de músico,* a chocolate-covered cluster of fresh almonds, hazelnuts and raisins; and *grageas,* almonds or hazelnuts drenched in dark chocolate, white chocolate or toffee.

RAMÓN ROCA is a large company set up in Gerona in 1928 by the Roca family. Roca chocolates are said to be a favourite of former US Secretary of State Henry Kissinger, and they certainly grace the tables of Spain's society élite, as well as finding their way on to first class intercontinental flights and the pillows of Spain's grandest hotels. Roca has always been imaginative in a showy type of way, producing masterpieces such as a 500g/1¼lb chocolate sculpture of the Statue of Liberty, and a hand-painted chocolate reproduction of the twelfth-century tapestry that hangs in Gerona cathedral. The company also

ABOVE: The Spanish love chocolate "a la taza" (in the cup).

produces a unique range of edible board games, particularly popular with the Japanese, which includes a draughts set in luxury dark and white chocolate. Their Victoria Bonbons (named after Ramón Roca's mother) — an elegant wafer of dark chocolate decorated with a perfectly positioned almond, a hazelnut, a walnut and four raisins — won first prize at the 1988 Chicago Fancy Food Fair.

RIGHT: The Valor range of chocolates.
LEFT: Chocolate croquettes from Roca.

VALOR in Villajoyosa, Alicante, was founded in 1881 by López Lloret, one of Spain's itinerant *chocolateros*. The fledgling enterprise has been handed down through three generations and is now one of Spain's largest and most technologically advanced chocolate companies with a gleaming stainless-steel fully computerized factory. Even though Valor has an enormous turnover and a vast range of products, the company prides itself on maintaining traditional quality, creativity and attention to detail.

Drinking chocolate is still widely enjoyed

RIGHT: Chunks of chocolate in tablet form, used in Spain for making thick, dark drinking chocolate.

in Spain, and Valor is the country's leading producer. It is sold both in powdered form and, more commonly, as a solid bar to be broken off as required and dissolved in foaming hot milk.

On the confectionery side, Valor's specialities are Chocolate Pearls – chocolate-covered almonds gathered from local almond groves; *doblones* – individually wrapped chocolate wafers; foil-wrapped hazelnut pralines; exquisite miniature four-piece gift boxes of chocolates; and luxury chocolate bars filled with toffee, cream caramel or *tiramisu*. Eye-catching and attractive packaging is a crucial part of the presentation, particularly as Valor's luxury chocolates are exported to speciality shops all over the world.

MEXICO

Chocolate as confectionery never really caught on in Mexico. The most important use of chocolate is still as a beverage, and as a flavouring in some of the special *moles* – rich, savoury sauces thickened with ground nuts and seeds. Chocolate is sold in rough, grainy tablets made with cacao, sugar, ground almonds and cinnamon – not so very different from the tablets made by the Spanish in the days of the conquistadors.

The most widely available brand outside Mexico is Ibarra, manufactured by CHOCOLATERA DE JALISCO in Guadalajara, and packaged in a striking red and yellow striped hexagonal box. The individually wrapped tablets are delicious whipped to a froth in hot milk and served with freshly baked *churros* (fried pastries).

RIGHT: Coarse, grainy tablets of Ibarra chocolate in traditional wrappers.
BELOW: The melted tablets make a delicious sauce for vanilla ice-cream.

They can be used in baking to give a unique spicy flavour to chocolate cake. The tablets can also be melted to make a wonderfully fudgey chocolate sauce that goes particularly well with good quality vanilla ice-cream.

GREAT BRITAIN

ABOVE: Ackermans chocolates, a favourite of the Royal family.

During the last few years British taste in chocolate has been undergoing a quiet revolution. Following the establishment of The Chocolate Society, a sort of sub-culture of chocolytes has emerged. Perhaps as a result of this new-found fervour, superior varieties of chocolate are increasingly finding their way into supermarkets, where they provide much-needed competition for the old-style sweet British milk chocolate.

ACKERMANS, a small family firm founded fifty years ago by German-born Werner Ackerman and his wife, is one of the major producers of handmade chocolates in Britain. Ackermans has a shop in north London, and also supplies leading supermarkets and specialist outlets in Britain, mainland Europe and the United States. Its chocolates are a favourite with Queen Elizabeth The Queen Mother, who awarded the firm her Royal Warrant in 1969. Ackermans offers a range of fresh cream truffles, chocolate-coated whole nuts, ginger wafers, hand-dipped crystallized fruits, and rose and violet fondant creams. It also produces a wonderful chocolate menagerie of hollow moulded hippos, crocodiles, bears and bunnies.

BENDICKS OF MAYFAIR, founded in the late 1920s by Colonel Benson and Mr Dickson, was granted a Royal Warrant by Elizabeth II in 1962. Bendicks are famous for their excellent peppermint chocolates – an essentially British taste not shared by other European countries. Best-loved by connoisseurs are Bendicks Bittermints, a powerful mint fondant disc drenched with smooth, dark unsweetened chocolate – a devastating combination. As well as the mint collection, Bendicks produces delicious truffles, chocolate-coated stem ginger, and the delightfully named Sporting & Military Chocolate.

CHARBONNEL ET WALKER, founded in 1825, is one of Britain's earliest producers of chocolates. With the encouragement of

BELOW: Bendicks are the premier supplier of superior mint chocolates.

BELOW: Exquisite chocolates from the Charbonnel et Walker range.

LEFT: *Organic chocolate made with Maya beans.*

Edward VII, the company began life as a partnership between Mrs Walker and Madame Charbonnel from the Maison Boissier chocolate house in Paris. Tempting items from the magnificent range include truffles flavoured with chartreuse, muscat or port and cranberry; chocolate-covered espresso beans; and cointreau-flavoured marzipan. The packaging is superb and caters for styles ranging from elegant navy-trimmed white boxes, nostalgic boxes with a faded pink floral pattern, and outrageously lavish, ruched red satin boxes.

GERARD RONAY is one of Britain's most highly respected private chocolatiers. A former psychiatric nurse, Ronay set up in 1989 having trained with the very best teachers – Linxe, Constant and Bernachon in France, Wittamer in Belgium and Charbonnel et Walker in Britain. His highly secretive recipes include geranium chocolate and superb hand-painted eggs.

GREEN AND BLACK'S, set up in the 1980s by Josephine Fairly, sells organic chocolate endorsed by The Soil Association. The company launched with its Organic Dark Chocolate, soon followed by its latest brain child, the "ethically correct" Maya Gold Organic Dark Chocolate, made with beans grown by the Kechi Maya in Belize. This product was the first in Britain to be awarded the Fairtrade mark which guarantees that small farmers are not exploited. Maya Gold contains 70 per cent cacao solids, but no cacao butter, and is described on the wrapper as having "the authentic Maya taste of rain forest spices and

BELOW: *Rococo's* grand cru *single bean bars with distinctive wrappers.*

ABOVE: *A tempting and imaginative range from The Chocolate Society.*

orange". Even though oranges were unknown to the Maya in pre-Conquest days, the chocolate still tastes pretty good.

ROCOCO, in London's King's Road, is an Aladdin's cave of a shop founded in 1983 by chocolate enthusiast Chantal Coady. Using cacao from the world's finest plantations, Rococo specialize in *grand cru* single bean bars; artisan bars with exotic flavourings such as pink pepper and juniper, lavender, petitgrain and cardamom; stunning chocolate dragées – try the dark green *Olives de Nyons;* and handmade boxed chocolates moulded into the most beautiful shapes.

SARA JAYNE, a London-based private chocolate-maker, is also public relations manager of the Académie Culinaire de France. She learnt her chocolate-making skills first hand from leading experts, including the Roux brothers. Blackberry and calvados, ginger and spice, and champagne are among the tempting flavourings used in her celebrated handmade truffles.

TERRYS OF YORK, founded in 1797, is perhaps alone among the mass-producers in manufacturing plain chocolate with a reasonable flavour. Their famous chocolate orange has been tucked in the toe of British children's Christmas stockings for generations, while their individually wrapped miniature Neapolitans have always been a welcome gift.

THE CHOCOLATE SOCIETY was formed in 1990 to promote the consumption of the finest chocolate. The society manufactures a range of products under its own label, as well as selling quality brands made by other companies. Its own range includes the most delicious chocolate-dipped candied citrus fruits; imaginative moulded items such as pigs, egg-filled nests, fish, hens and hearts; fresh handmade truffles with luscious flavourings such as raspberry, whisky or champagne; and elegant tins of drinking-chocolate flakes, cocoa powder and cooking chocolate.

THE UNITED STATES OF AMERICA

Chocolate consumers in the United States share the British liking for sweet milk chocolate, and the American chocolate industry is therefore dominated by a small number of very large mass-producers who satisfy this national need. However, in the same way that British consumers have become aware of and learned to appreciate quality handmade plain chocolate, American taste has been changing too. A number of small but sophisticated chocolate-makers have appeared on the scene and are taking advantage of the increasing popularity of European-style chocolate.

ABOVE: Glossy sugar-coated dragées from Dilettante.

DILETTANTE, in Seattle, was established in 1976 by Dana Davenport, a third-generation chocolatier and descendant of Hungarian master chocolatier Julius Franzen. Franzen emigrated to the USA in 1910, after studying in Paris, and won prestigious appointments in Vienna as Master Pâtissier to Emperor Franz Joseph, and later in St Petersburg as Master Chocolatier to Czar Nicholas II. Franzen passed on his skills to his brother-in-law Earl Remington Davenport, whose grandson Dana carries on the business today. Dilettante's signature product is its Aristocrat range of chocolate truffles, flavoured with ginger, raspberries, hazelnuts, pecans or coffee. Dilettante also makes intensely rich buttercream fondant, beautiful chocolate dragées with various coatings, and slim bars of good quality milk or dark chocolate.

ABOVE AND RIGHT: Ghirardelli, new and old.

FRAN'S, set up in Seattle by ex-accountant Fran Bigelow, is at the forefront of America's new generation of chocolatiers. She trained in cookery under Josephine Araldo, a 1921 graduate of the Cordon Bleu school in Paris, and later enrolled at the California Culinary Academy, where desserts became her passion. Bigelow opened a tiny dessert shop in 1982, supplying local restaurants with speciality cakes. Her reputation went from strength to strength, and, soon after, she started making the European-style chocolates on which her business is now founded. An award-winning speciality are Fran's baton-shaped Fixations – individual sticks of Belgian chocolate with soft, creamy centres, flavoured with espresso, peanut butter, orange or mint. Her range also includes rich dark truffles, hand-dipped fruit and nuts covered in smooth dark Belgian chocolate, GoldBars studded with macadamia nuts, and the smaller GoldBites with almonds, as well as chocolate and caramel sauces, and various seasonal items.

GHIRARDELLI, founded in 1856 in San Francisco and one of

ABOVE: Irresistible luxury from Fran's.

RIGHT: *Joseph Schmidt's stunning truffles.*

America's pioneering chocolate-makers, produces quality eating chocolate, chocolate products for use in baking, and powdered drinking chocolate. Ghirardelli's Sweet Ground Chocolate with Cocoa has been a signature product for over a century. Although a mass producer, Ghirardelli uses methods based on European traditions, producing bittersweet eating chocolate as well as the popular sweet milk varieties. Ghirardelli still grinds and roasts its own cacao beans shipped from quality plantations in Central and South America, and West Africa. Its range includes milk, white and plain chocolate squares and attractively wrapped bars with tempting flavours such as raspberry, white mocha and biscotti, and double chocolate mocha.

JOSEPH SCHMIDT CONFECTIONS was opened in San Francisco in 1983 by master chocolatier Joseph Schmidt and partner Audrey Ryan. Born in 1939 and raised in what was formerly known as Palestine, Schmidt looks to his Austrian roots for his skills. He was trained as a baker, but his supremely imaginative and sometimes outrageous creations show no evidence of this conventional background. Unusual in the chocolate world for his bold use of colour, and the large size of the individual chocolates, Schmidt's truffles gleam with perfect hand-painted spots of bright red or green, and his Slicks, thin chocolate discs, are beautifully painted in various colours. Special commissions include amazingly opulent sculpted creations for visiting dignitaries from abroad – including a giant panda for Prince Philip and a white dove for Nelson Mandela. Schmidt's chocolates are available from department stores in the United States and Harrods in London.

RICHARD DONNELLY, in Santa Cruz, California, is another of America's new breed of young, inspired artisan chocolate-makers.

Donnelly trained with several renowned chocolatiers both in Europe and the United States before setting up on his own in 1988. Donnelly uses French couverture chocolate to which he adds flavourings and fillings geared to the American market – coffee buttercream, and roasted salted macadamia nuts, for instance. His speciality is very slim, smooth chocolate bars which, in terms of quality, are among the very best chocolate in the world. The bars are beautifully wrapped in handmade Japanese papers.

MOONSTRUCK CHOCOLATIER in Portland, Oregon, is a young company set up by an impressive consortium of live-wire marketing experts. With more then a hundred outlets in the United States and a thriving mail order business they look set to make their name in the world of chocolate.

Moonstruck's chocolates are inspired creations from master chocolatier Robert Hammond, who served his apprenticeship in America and France, and who is now thought to be one of the leading experts in modern chocolate-making. Moonstruck's signature product is a moon-shaped, metallic blue box containing a stunning selection of beautifully designed chocolates. Flavourings include wine, brandy, coffee, *sake* and various fruits, often using award-winning local products. Favourites are wild huckleberry truffles made with white chocolate ganache and Clear Creek apple brandy truffles. There is also an impressive *gianduja* almond praline tower of crisp buttery toffee and toasted almonds.

RIGHT: *Elegance from Richard Donnelly.*

PHYSIOLOGY AND PSYCHOLOGY

CHOCOLATE'S THERAPEUTIC POWERS

The therapeutic properties of chocolate were much written about in the seventeenth and eighteenth centuries. The Aztec beliefs in the power of chocolate travelled with it, and great claims were made by manufacturers and converts alike for its powers as an antidote to exhaustion and weakness. Soldiers, scholars and clerics used it to keep them going during prolonged periods of physical, intellectual or spiritual endurance.

We now know that it is the fat and carbohydrate in chocolate which provide fuel for the body, and the fat content means that chocolate is digested slowly, thus maintaining a feeling of fullness and satiety. Even the iron content, which helps transport oxygen to the brain, may result in greater mental alertness, although this has yet to be proven.

(PER 100G)	PLAIN CHOCOLATE	MILK CHOCOLATE	WHITE CHOCOLATE
Protein (g)	4.7	8.4	8.0
Fat (g)	29.2	30.3	30.9
Calories	525	529	529
Carbohydrate (g)	64.8	59.4	58.3
Calcium (mg)	38	220	270
Magnesium (mg)	100	55	26
Iron (mg)	2.4	1.6	0.2
Zinc (mg)	0.2	0.2	0.9
Carotene (vitamin A) (mcg)	40	40	75
Vitamin E (mg)	0.85	0.74	1.14
Thiamin (vitamin B1) (mg)	0.07	0.10	0.08
Riboflavin (vitamin B2) (mg)	0.08	0.23	0.49
Niacin (vitamin B3) (mg)	0.4	0.2	0.2
Vitamin B6 (mg)	0.07	0.07	0.07
Vitamin B12 (mcg)	—	trace	trace
Folate (mcg)	10	10	10
Vitamin C	0	0	0

Source: McCance and Widdowson's The Composition of Foods, fifth edition.

NUTRITIONAL ANALYSIS

Although the relevance of nutritional analysis is questionable if the level of cacao solids or brand of chocolate used is not known, we can see from the comparative table above that plain chocolate, considered by the chocolate fraternity as infinitely superior, does not fare as well as might be expected.

Containing no milk, plain chocolate provides roughly half the protein of white and milk chocolate, and much less calcium. Protein is vital for the growth, repair and maintenance of the body; calcium is essential for muscle contraction, including the muscles which make the heart beat, and for healthy nerve function, enzyme activity and clotting of blood. Plain

LEFT: Early publicity material depicted cocoa as wholesome.
RIGHT: Chocolate fortified the army in the First World War.

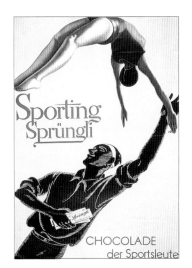

ABOVE: Carbohydrate in chocolate provides fuel for vigorous activity.

Plain chocolate contains slightly less fat, something we are advised to cut down on, and comes out on top in terms of carbohydrate, magnesium (an essential constituent of our body cells and involved with releasing energy from the food we eat), iron (essential for the production of red blood cells, and for transporting oxygen around the body) and niacin (also involved in energy release from food). Plain chocolate also contains slightly fewer calories.

White chocolate, sometimes dismissed by chocolate experts, contains more calcium, zinc, carotene and riboflavin (vitamin B2) than plain chocolate.

A NATURAL STIMULANT

As well as the more well-known nutrients, chocolate contains certain alkaloids – organic substances found in plants – which have a potent effect on the body. The most important is theobromine, which stimulates the kidneys as a mild diuretic. Chocolate is also a stimulant of the central nervous system, with an effect similar to caffeine, which is also present in chocolate. Theobromine makes up about 2 per cent of the cacao bean and about 200 mg finds its way into an average-sized bar. The caffeine content is much smaller – about 25 mg per bar, roughly one quarter the amount found in a fresh cup of coffee.

BELOW RIGHT: Many manufacturers depicted chocolate as providing growing children with plenty of energy for healthy activity.

— HOMEOPATHIC "PROVING" OF CHOCOLATE —
Experimental "provings" of chocolate by homeopaths clearly indicate its stimulating effect. One experiment conducted with a decoction of roasted ground cacao beans in boiling water produced "an excitement of the nervous system similar to that caused by a strong infusion of black coffee" and "an excited state of the circulation, shown by an accelerated pulse". Interestingly, when the same decoction was made with unroasted beans neither effect was noticeable, leading the provers to conclude that the physiological changes were caused by aromatic substances released during roasting.

— MYTHS AND PREJUDICES —
Claims that chocolate is bad for you are almost certainly based on the excess sugar and added vegetable fat in poor grade, mass-produced chocolate. Quality chocolate contains pure cacao butter with no added fat, as well as a high percentage of cacao solids and correspondingly less sugar – in some cases hardly any. Specific claims that chocolate causes migraine, obesity, acne, tooth decay and allergies have also been refuted by several medical experts:

MIGRAINE Cheese and chocolate have been cited as the cause of migraine, which can be set off by large doses of tyramine. Chocolate, however, contains only a very small quantity of tyramine, far less than cheese.

OBESITY Good quality plain chocolate is unlikely to be the cause of obesity because it contains far less sugar than junk chocolate and, because it is more expensive, is less likely to be eaten to excess.

ACNE American surveys show no correlation between chocolate consumption and acne in teenagers. Likely culprits are hormonal imbalances and a lack of fresh fruit and vegetables in the diet.

TOOTH DECAY Chocolate melts in the mouth and is therefore in contact with the teeth for a relatively short time. While the sugar content will contribute to tooth decay, the risk is far less than that associated with sticky sweets or toffee, which remain in the mouth for longer.

ALLERGY Less than 2 per cent of the population have a genuine food allergy, and an allergy to chocolate is extremely rare. It is more likely to be the nuts and milk in chocolate that are the cause, so check the ingredients.

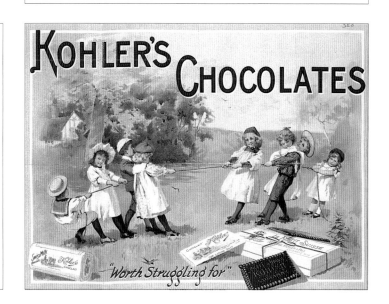

CHOCOLATE AND THE MIND

The question of whether or not chocolate is an addictive substance always raises spirited discussion. Some social historians have even reported tales of chocolate addiction and associated crimes committed in order to satisfy an ever-increasing need. And as recently as 1991, the French dietary expert Michel Montignac advised in his book *Dine Out and Lose Weight:* "Be sure to limit yourself, since chocolate is of an addictive nature. To control your 'chocoholism', drink a tall glass of water."

LEFT: A deeply indulgent chocolate experience.

Linda Henly, a contemporary American writer, positively recommends that addictive personalities should use chocolate to satisfy their needs, stating that its advantages vastly outweigh those of other substances: "Chocolate doesn't make you stupid and clumsy. It doesn't render you incapable of operating heavy machinery… You don't have to smuggle chocolate across the border…Possession, even possession with intent to sell, is perfectly legal."

Some medical experts believe that the theobromine and caffeine in chocolate are the cause of its so-called addictive properties, but it may well be the presence of another substance called phenylethylamine. This is one of a group of chemicals known as endorphins, which have an effect similar to amphetamine, to which phenylethylamine is related. When released into the bloodstream, endorphins lift the mood, creating positive energy and feelings ranging from happiness to euphoria, as experienced in the runner's "high" or the aerobic exerciser's "burn". Phenylethylamine is also naturally present in the human body. Levels in the brain have even been found to increase when we experience the state we refer to as "falling in love", which is no doubt why we experience that heady feeling when we eat good chocolate.

CRAVING AND ADDICTION

Chocolate lovers would do well to be aware of the wealth of difference there is between craving and addiction. Craving is an unmet desire for a pleasurable substance, whether it be chocolate, hot buttered toast, or a cup of coffee. The craving is usually brought on by stress, and the desired substance usually diffuses the stress more effectively than any other means, and may actually, as a result, enhance a person's performance by increasing concentration and reducing fatigue.

Addiction, on the other hand, is defined as the habitual use of a substance, such as alcohol or drugs, which becomes less and less effective at satisfying the need and results in unpleasant withdrawal symptoms should any attempt be made to give up the substance in question.

Chocolate hardly comes into the addictive category, although it has been said that the glucose in chocolate triggers a release in the production of endorphins – the body's natural opiates – which in turn can lead to a cycle of craving.

LEFT: A silver platter of gorgeous, high quality, hand-made chocolates is every chocolate lover's fantasy.

BELOW: An advertisement showing two French ladies sharing a bottle of chocolate as if it were wine. The initial effect can be very similar.

RIGHT: Dark, rich and irresistible, a slice of moist chocolate cake is both pleasure and temptation.

BELOW: French courtesan and famous chocolyte, Madame Du Barry, was well aware of the stimulating effect chocolate had on her lovers.

WOMEN'S CRAVING AND CHOCOLATE

Women are the greatest consumers of chocolate, and several studies have sought to explain why. Although some women may enjoy chocolate as a guilt-free treat or as an energy-boost, others seem almost obsessed by it. While researching her 1995 book *Why Women Need Chocolate*, Debra Waterhouse conducted a survey which revealed that of the women surveyed:

- 97 per cent reported cravings, 68 per cent of which are for chocolate
- 50 per cent would choose chocolate in preference to sex
- 22 per cent were more likely than men to choose chocolate as a mood elevator

Psychiatrists have suggested that the mechanism that regulates body levels of phenylethylamine may be faulty in some women. This may explain a tendency to binge on chocolate after an emotional upset – it is an instinctive form of self-medication to treat the imbalance of mood-controlling chemicals.

Waterhouse states that the foods we crave are defined by a multitude of factors that may include cultural influences, emotional attachments, taste and habit as well as biological, chemical and physiological factors. In the case of chocolate, the "prozac of plants", Waterhouse adds to its mood-changing components a substance called seratonin, known for its calming properties.

It must be said, however, that although statistically it may be the case that more women buy chocolate than men, it is also true that for both sexes, and for people of all ages, chocolate can be many things. There are probably many women who could instantly name a man whose chocolate consumption is more regular and compulsive than hers, and it is perhaps one of the many cultural myths that women are more addicted to it than men. What we can say is that the seduction of chocolate, and its comforting allure, is as strong in the present as it was for the Maya warrior princes and princesses of the fourth century.

CHOCOLATE AND LOVE

Chocolate has long been associated with passion and its reputation as an aphrodisiac can be traced back to the days of the Aztecs and the Spanish conquistadors. Conclusions were obviously drawn from the Emperor Montezuma's liking for copious flagons of chocolate before retiring to his harem. However, as observer Bernal Díaz del Castillo was careful to point out in his memoirs: "It [chocolate] was said to have aphrodisiac properties, but we did not pay any attention to this detail."

In *The True History of Chocolate* authors Sophie and Michael Coe state that the idea that Montezuma needed sexual stimulants was a Spanish obsession for which there was no factual basis. The conquistadors apparently suffered from constipation and "searched for native Mexican laxatives as avidly as they did for aphrodisiacs". However, once the rumour that chocolate was an aphrodisiac had taken root, there was no stopping it. When chocolate eventually appeared in Europe, eighteenth-century society took to it with suspicious enthusiasm.

Historical sources abound with tales of chocolate being used as an aphrodisiac. Casanova thought that hot chocolate was "the elixir of love", and drank it instead of champagne! It may well be that the unshakeable belief of the Spanish had something to do with chocolate being an ingredient in that notorious aphrodisiac "Spanish Fly". In the following tale, the Marquis de Sade uses both chocolate and Spanish fly to amuse his guests at a ball: "Into the dessert he slipped chocolate pastilles so good that a number of people devoured them … but he had mixed in some Spanish fly … those who ate the pastilles began to burn with unchaste ardor … Even the most respectable of women were unable to resist the uterine rage that stirred within them. And so it was that M. de Sade enjoyed the favors of his sister-in-law."

LEFT AND RIGHT: The images may not be as explicit as today, but advertising has always used chocolate's link with sensuality to sell its products.

RIGHT: An early Cadbury chocolate tin uses sensual imagery.

THE GREAT INFLAMER

Brandon Head, in *The Food of the Gods*, reported that even after chocolate had become widely accepted as a nourishing beverage, it was still regarded by some "as a violent inflamer of passions, which should be prohibited to the monks". In 1905 a journalist writing in the British Spectator magazine issued dire warnings: 'I shall also advise my fair readers to be in a particular manner careful how they meddle with romances, chocolates, novels, and the like inflamers, which I look upon as very dangerous to be made use of…"

SENSUAL ASSOCIATIONS

Although contemporary scientific research suggests that chocolate does not contain substances of a directly aphrodisiac nature, modern advertising clearly links chocolate with sensuality and sexuality. With the exception of chunky "macho" chocolate products, or situations in which the product is being used as a healthy, energy-boosting snack, chocolate is invariably depicted as a "naughty" indulgence, appearing in scenes heavy with sexual innuendo.

Advertising also demonstrates a definite gender bias by specifically targeting women as the primary users. Most advertisements show chocolate being enjoyed by beautiful

ABOVE: A poster illustrating the link between lovers and chocolate.

advertising made much of the wholesomeness of chocolate with posters of healthy, lively children enjoying cups of chocolate in the fresh air. The first chocolate boxes showed sentimental images of pretty young girls, flowers and kittens. Chocolate plays a large part in childhood the world over. Christmas treats, Easter eggs, birthday presents, party gifts, rewards or bribes from parents coaxing their offspring to behave well. Encouraged as most of us are to be passionate about chocolate from an early age, it is no wonder we carry that ardour with us through childhood and beyond.

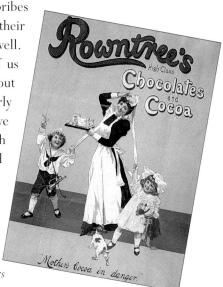

RIGHT: The famous Rowntree advertisement.

BELOW: A loving mother offers chocolate to her daughter.

women, or gifts of chocolate being offered to them by a man.

The association between women, sensuality and chocolate was reinforced by the cinema, too. A common image in the 1930s was the glamorous *femme fatale*, usually blonde and usually draped on satin sheets, languorously working her way through a lavish box of chocolates.

This association between chocolate and women perpetuated the association between chocolate and romantic love, as shown on Perugina's classic Baci box. *Baci* means "kisses" in Italian, and since the chocolates first appeared in 1922 they have been exchanged as gifts between lovers who look for the romantic message hidden beneath the foil wrapper of each chocolate.

CHOCOLATE AND CHILDHOOD

This association with love and nurture, but not necessarily passion, was also exploited by manufacturers. Chocolate cake mix packets carry homely scenes of mother in the kitchen; the earliest cocoa tins portrayed nursemaids or even parents serving nourishing mugs of chocolate to young children, and

THE PLEASURE OF CHOCOLATE

Research carried out by ARISE (Associates for Research Into the Science of Enjoyment) suggests that pleasure, far from being an emotion of indeterminate nature, is a distinct neuro-chemical process with its own pathway through the nervous system. Laboratory tests have shown that when we are experiencing pleasure, the body's defence system is more effective; and when we are unhappy, depressed or stressed, the system becomes less efficient, leaving us less resistant to infection.

So it seems that pleasure is good for us even if it means we indulge in "forbidden fruits" such as chocolate. The secret, it would seem, is to indulge in our "naughty" craving without feeling guilty or anxious. That said, ARISE make it clear that they are not advocating orgies of over-indulgence; the secret is to eat better chocolate, not more chocolate.

SENSORY PLEASURE

One of the reasons we love chocolate so much is the pure unmatched physical pleasure we get not just from eating it, but also from unwrapping it, smelling it, looking at it and feeling it. When we slip the wrapper off a slim bar of dark chocolate or open up the softly padded papers of a luxury box, our sense of anticipation is already at work. The pure chocolatey smell is like perfume and the chocolate looks so smooth and glossy we want to stroke it. Breaking off a piece, it snaps cleanly with a pleasing crack. When it finally passes the lips, chocolate melts instantly in the mouth – an exquisitely pleasurable sensation. Then the flavours come flooding through – overwhelming our taste buds with over five hundred of them, two-and-a-half times more than any other food. With such a wealth of sensory pleasure in store, no wonder chocolate should be eaten slowly.

Whether or not we choose to share our pleasure with others by attempting to describe the complex flavours is another matter. The current passion for chocolate indicates that perhaps a tasting language will evolve along the same lines as that used for wine and, more recently, olive oil. At the moment, fellow chocolate lovers get by without a specialized vocabulary – they just know when it is good and a roll of the eyes or a deep sigh is enough to communicate this.

Elaine Sherman, a twentieth-century American writer, more than adequately sums up: "Chocolate is heavenly, mellow, sensual, deep, dark, sumptuous, gratifying, potent, dense, creamy,

BELOW: Chocolate provides unmatched sensory pleasure – a delight to look at, a pleasure to touch, wonderful to smell and pleasurable to eat.

ABOVE: Chocolate has been used as a gift since the days of the Aztecs. It speaks a thousand words and feelings.

seductive, suggestive, rich, excessive, silky, smooth, luxurious, celestial. Chocolate is downfall, happiness, pleasure, love, ecstasy, fantasy … chocolate makes us wicked, guilty, sinful, healthy, chic, happy."

A CULTURAL AND SOCIAL LUBRICANT
Chocolate has always been used as a gift. As Michel Richart, an inspired chocolate-maker in Lyon, rightly states, when we share good quality chocolate it weaves links between people on many, many levels. Chocolate also creates valuable cultural, social and even spiritual awareness.

A small box of luxury chocolates says a thousand "thank-you's" to a hostess, a mother or a lover. Chocolate also says "good luck", "congratulations", "bon voyage" and "sorry". Queen Victoria symbolically sent 5,000 lbs/2,268 kg chocolate to her loyal troops at Christmas. Sales of chocolate rocket on Mother's Day and Valentine's Day. We use it in one form or another to celebrate Easter, Christmas and weddings.

There is hardly a country in the western world that does not have chocolate as part of its culinary culture, whether it be a moist chocolate brownie from America, a chocolate-covered pancake from Hungary, a velvety square of Swiss milk fondant chocolate, or a foaming cup of thick Spanish drinking chocolate. It is these chocolate "experiences" that unite chocolate lovers throughout the world in celebration of the food of the gods.

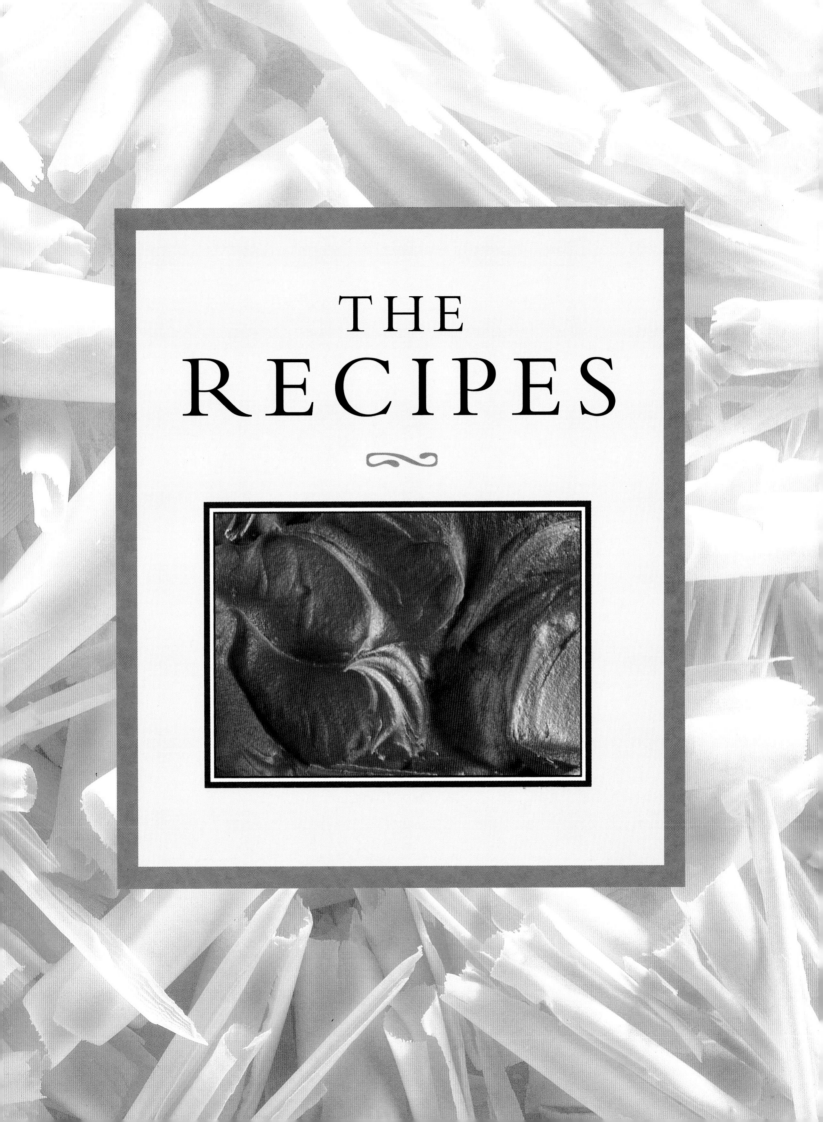

THE RECIPES

Types of Chocolate

COUVERTURE (LEFT)
The professionals' choice, this is a fine-quality pure chocolate with a high percentage of cocoa butter, which gives it a high gloss. It is suitable for decorative use and for making handmade chocolates. It must generally be tempered.

PLAIN DARK CHOCOLATE (BELOW)
Often called "luxury", "bitter" or "continental" chocolate, this has a high percentage of cocoa solids – around 75 per cent – with little or no added sugar. Its rich, intense flavour and good dark colour make it an ideal ingredient in desserts and cakes.

MILK CHOCOLATE (RIGHT)
This contains powdered or condensed milk and generally around 20 per cent cocoa solids. The flavour is mild and sweet. Although this is the most popular eating chocolate, it is not as suitable as plain chocolate for melting and cooking.

PLAIN CHOCOLATE (ABOVE)
Ordinary plain chocolate is the most widely available chocolate to use in cooking. It contains anywhere between 30 per cent and 70 per cent cocoa solids, so check the label before you buy. The higher the cocoa solids, the better the chocolate flavour will be.

COCOA (LEFT)
This is made from the pure cocoa mass after most of the cocoa butter has been extracted. The mass is roasted, then ground to make a powder. It is probably the most economical way of giving puddings and baked goods a chocolate flavour.

ORGANIC CHOCOLATE (ABOVE)
This is slightly more expensive than other types of chocolate but is a quality product, high in cocoa solids, produced without pesticides and with consideration for the environment.

CHOCOLATE CHIPS (ABOVE)
These are small pieces of chocolate of uniform size. They contain fewer cocoa solids than ordinary chocolate and are available in plain dark, milk and white flavours.

CHOCOLATE-FLAVOURED CAKE COVERING (LEFT)
This is a blend of sugar, vegetable oil, cocoa and flavourings. The flavour is poor, but the high fat content makes it suitable for chocolate curls – to improve the flavour, add some plain chocolate.

CHOCOLATE POWDER (BELOW)
Chocolate powder is used in baking and for making drinks. It has lower cocoa solids than pure cocoa and has a much milder, sweeter taste.

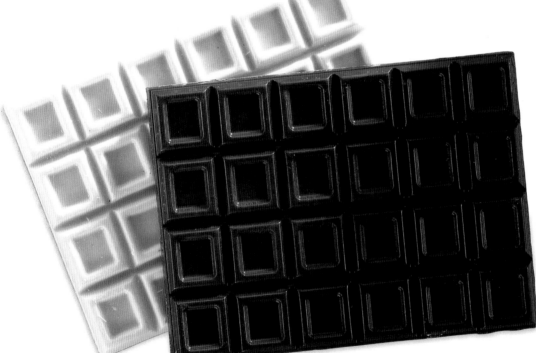

WHITE CHOCOLATE (BELOW LEFT)
This does not contain any cocoa solids but gets its flavour from cocoa buttter. It is sweet, and the better quality white chocolate is quite rich and smooth. White chocolate must be melted with care, as it does not withstand heat as well as plain chocolate.

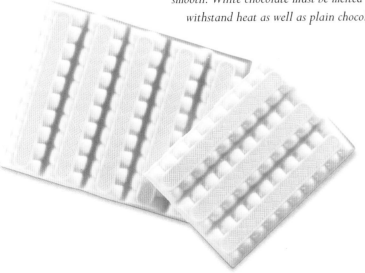

TECHNIQUES

MELTING CHOCOLATE

If chocolate is being melted on its own, all the equipment must be completely dry, as water may cause the chocolate to thicken and become a stiff paste. For this reason, do not cover chocolate during or after melting it, as condensation could form. If chocolate does thicken, add a little pure white vegetable fat (not butter or margarine) and mix well. If this does not work, start again. Do not discard the thickened chocolate; melt it with cream to make a sauce.

With or without liquid, chocolate should be melted very slowly. It is easily burned or scorched, and then develops a bad flavour. If any steam gets into the chocolate, it can turn into a solid mass. If this happens, stir in a little pure white vegetable fat. Dark chocolate should not be heated above 50°C/120°F. Milk and white chocolate should not be heated above 45°C/110°F. Take particular care when melting white chocolate, which clogs very easily when subjected to heat.

MELTING CHOCOLATE OVER SIMMERING WATER

1 Chop or cut the chocolate into small pieces with a sharp knife to enable it to melt quickly and evenly.

2 Put the chocolate in the top of a double boiler or in a heatproof bowl over a saucepan of barely simmering water. The bowl should not touch the water.

3 Heat gently until the chocolate is melted and smooth, stirring occasionally. Remove from the heat and stir.

MELTING CHOCOLATE OVER DIRECT HEAT

When a recipe recommends melting chocolate with a liquid such as milk, cream or even butter, this can be done over direct heat in a saucepan.

1 Choose a heavy-based saucepan. Add the chocolate and liquid and melt over a low heat, stirring frequently, until the chocolate is melted and the mixture is smooth. Remove from heat immediately. This method is also used for making sauces, icings and some sweets.

2 Chocolate can also be melted in a very low oven. Preheat oven to 110°C/ 225°F/Gas ¼. Put the chocolate in an ovenproof bowl and place in the oven for a few minutes. Remove the chocolate before it is completely melted and stir until smooth.

MELTING CHOCOLATE IN THE MICROWAVE

Check the chocolate at frequent intervals during the cooking time. These times are for a 650–700 W oven and are approximate, as microwave ovens vary.

1 Place 115g/4oz chopped or broken dark, bittersweet or semi-sweet chocolate in a microwave-safe bowl and microwave on Medium for about 2 minutes. The same quantity of milk or white chocolate should be melted on Low for about 2 minutes.

2 Check the chocolate frequently during the cooking time. The chocolate will not change shape, but will start to look shiny. It must then be removed from the microwave and stirred until completely melted and smooth.

TEMPERING CHOCOLATE

TEMPERING CHOCOLATE

Tempering is the process of gently heating and cooling chocolate to stabilize the emulsification of cocoa solids and butterfat. This technique is generally used by professionals handling couverture chocolate. It allows the chocolate to shrink quickly (to allow easy release from a mould, for example with Easter eggs) or to be kept at room temperature for several weeks or months without losing its crispness and shiny surface. All solid chocolate is tempered in production, but once melted loses its "temper" and must be tempered again unless it is to be used immediately. Untempered chocolate tends to "bloom" or becomes dull and streaky or takes on a cloudy appearance. This can be avoided if the melted chocolate is put in the fridge immediately: chilling the chocolate solidifies the cocoa butter and prevents it from rising to the surface and "blooming". General baking and dessert-making do not require tempering, which is a fussy procedure and takes practice. However, it is useful to be aware of the technique when preparing sophisticated decorations, moulded chocolates or coatings. Most shapes can be made without tempering if they are chilled immediately.

EQUIPMENT

To temper chocolate successfully, you will need a marble slab or similar cool, smooth surface, such as an upturned baking sheet. A flexible plastic scraper is ideal for spreading the chocolate, but you can use a palette knife. As the temperature is crucial, you will need a chocolate thermometer. Look for this at a specialist kitchen supply shop, where you may also find blocks of tempered chocolate, ready for immediate use.

1 Break up the chocolate into small pieces and place it in the top of a double boiler or a heatproof bowl over a saucepan of hot water. Heat gently until just melted.

2 Remove from the heat. Spoon about three-quarters of the melted chocolate on to a marble slab or other cool, smooth, non-porous work surface.

3 With a flexible plastic scraper or palette knife, spread the chocolate thinly, then scoop it up before spreading it again. Repeat the sequence, keeping the chocolate constantly on the move, for about 5 minutes.

4 Using a chocolate thermometer, check the temperature of the chocolate as you work it. As soon as the temperature registers 28°C/82°F, tip the chocolate back into the bowl and stir into the remaining chocolate.

5 With the addition of the hot chocolate, the temperature should now be 32°C/90°F, making the chocolate ready for use. To test, drop a little of the chocolate from a spoon on to the marble; it should set very quickly.

STORING CHOCOLATE

Chocolate can be stored successfully for up to a year if the conditions are favourable. This means a dry place with a temperature of around 20°C/68°F. At higher temperatures, the chocolate may develop white streaks as the fat comes to the surface. Although this will not spoil the flavour, it will mar the appearance of the chocolate, making it unsuitable for use as a decoration. When storing chocolate, keep it cool and dry. Place inside an airtight container, away from strong smelling foods. Check the "best before" dates on the pack.

PIPING WITH CHOCOLATE

Pipe chocolate directly on to a cake, or on to non-stick baking paper to make run-outs, small outlined shapes or irregular designs. After melting the chocolate, allow it to cool slightly so it just coats the back of a spoon. If it still flows freely it will be too runny to hold its shape when piped. When it is the right consistency, you then need to work fast as the chocolate will set quickly. Use a paper piping bag and keep the pressure very tight, as the chocolate will flow readily without encouragement.

MAKING A PAPER PIPING BAG

A non-stick paper cone is ideal for piping small amounts of messy liquids like chocolate as it is small, easy to handle and disposable, unlike a conventional piping bag, which will need cleaning.

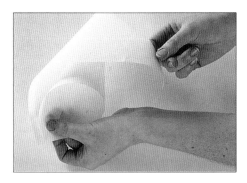

1 Fold a square of non-stick baking paper in half to form a triangle. With the triangle point facing you, fold the left corner down to the centre.

2 Fold the right corner down and wrap it around the folded left corner to form a cone. Fold the ends into the cone.

3 Spoon the melted chocolate into the cone and fold the top edges over. When ready to pipe, snip off the end of the point neatly to make a tiny hole, about 3 mm/⅛ in in diameter.

4 Another method is to use a small heavy-duty freezer or plastic bag. Place a piping nozzle in one corner of the bag, so that it is in the correct position for piping. Fill as above, squeezing the filling into one corner and twisting the top to seal. Snip off the corner of the bag, if necessary, so that the tip of the nozzle emerges, and squeeze gently to pipe the design.

CHOCOLATE DRIZZLES

You can have great fun making random shapes or, with a steady hand, special designs that will look great on cakes or biscuits.

1 Melt the chocolate and pour it into a paper cone or small piping bag fitted with a very small plain nozzle. Drizzle the chocolate on to a baking sheet lined with non-stick baking paper to make small, self-contained lattice shapes, such as circles or squares. Allow to set for 30 minutes then peel off the paper.

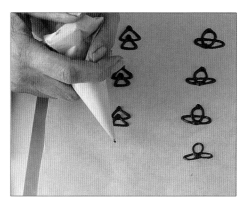

2 Chocolate can be used in many designs, such as flowers or butterflies. Use non-stick baking paper as tracing paper and pipe the chocolate over the chosen design or decorative shape.

3 For butterflies, pipe chocolate on to individually cut squares and leave until just beginning to set. Use a long, thin box (such as an egg carton) and place the butterfly shape in the box or between the cups so it is bent in the centre, creating the butterfly shape. Chill until needed.

PIPING ON TO CAKES

This looks effective on top of a cake iced with coffee glacé icing.

1 Melt 50g/2oz each of white and plain dark chocolate in separate bowls, and allow to cool slightly. Place the chocolates in separate paper piping bags. Cut a small piece off the pointed end of each bag in a straight line.

2 Hold each piping bag in turn above the surface of the cake and pipe the chocolates all over as shown in the picture. Alternatively, pipe a freehand design in one continuous curvy line, first with one bag of chocolate, then the other.

PIPING CURLS

Make lots of these curly shapes and store them in a cool place ready for using as cake decorations. Try piping the lines in contrasting colours of chocolate to vary the effect.

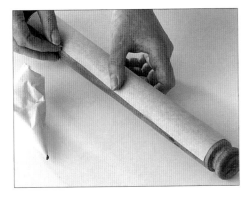

1 Melt 115g/4oz chocolate and allow to cool slightly. Cover a rolling pin with baking parchment and attach it with tape. Fill a paper piping bag with the chocolate and cut a small piece off the pointed end in a straight line.

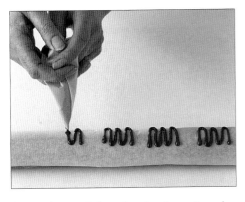

2 Pipe lines of chocolate backwards and forwards over the baking parchment.

3 Leave the piped curls to set in a cool place, then carefully peel off the baking parchment. Use a palette knife to lift the curls on to the cake.

FEATHERING OR MARBLING CHOCOLATE

These two related techniques provide some of the easiest and most effective ways of decorating the top of a cake, and they are also used when making a swirled mixture for cut-outs. Chocolate sauce and double cream can also be feathered or marbled to decorate a dessert.

1 Melt two contrasting colours of chocolate and spread one over the cake or surface to be decorated.

2 Spoon the contrasting chocolate into a piping bag and pipe lines or swirls over the chocolate base.

3 Working quickly before the chocolate sets, draw a skewer or cocktail stick through the swirls to create a feathered or marbled effect.

CHOCOLATE RUN-OUTS

Try piping the outline in one colour of chocolate and filling in the middle with another. The effect can be dramatic.

1 Tape a piece of greaseproof paper to a baking sheet or flat board. Draw around a shaped biscuit cutter on to the paper several times. Secure a piece of non-stick baking paper over the top.

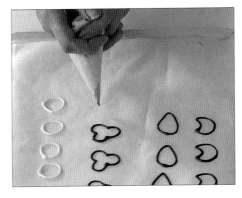

2 Pipe over the outline of your design in a continuous thread.

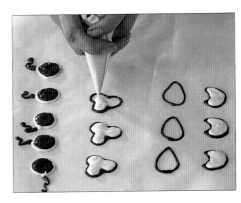

3 Cut the end off the other bag, making the hole slightly wider than before, and pipe the chocolate to fill in the outline so it looks slightly rounded. Leave the shapes to set in a cool place, then carefully lift them off the non-stick baking paper with a palette knife.

CHOCOLATE DECORATIONS

GRATED CHOCOLATE

Chocolate can be grated by hand or in a food processor. Make sure you grate it at the correct temperature.

__1__ Chill the chocolate and hold it with a piece of folded foil or paper towel to prevent the heat of your hand melting it. Hold a hand- or box-grater over a large plate and grate with an even pressure.

__2__ A food processor fitted with the metal blade can also be used to grate chocolate, but be sure the chocolate is soft enough to be pierced with a sharp knife. Cut the chocolate into small pieces and, with the machine running, drop the chocolate pieces through the feeder tube until very fine shavings are produced. Use the grater attachment and pusher to feed the chocolate through the processor for larger shavings.

COOK'S TIPS

The chocolate you use for decorating should not be too cold or it will splinter; warm chocolate will give a softer, looser curl, but do not allow it to become too soft or warm or it will be difficult to handle and may bloom. Use tempered chocolate for the best results.

COOK'S TIPS

If using a metal grater for grating chocolate, chill it in the freezer before use and the chocolate will be less likely to melt.
Experiment with different utensils when making chocolate curls. Metal palette knives, paint scrapers, tablespoons and even wide, straight pastry scrapers can be used.

MINI CHOCOLATE CURLS

Chocolate curls make an ideal decoration for many desserts and cakes, whether these are made from plain, bittersweet or white chocolate. These curls can be made very quickly using a vegetable peeler, and can be stored for several weeks in an airtight container in a cool, dry place.

__1__ Bring a thick piece or bar of chocolate to room temperature. (Chocolate that is too cold will "grate", or if too warm will slice.) With a swivel-bladed peeler held over a plate or baking sheet, pull the blade firmly along the edge of the chocolate and allow curls to fall on to the plate or baking sheet in a single layer.

__2__ Use a skewer or cocktail stick to transfer curls to the dessert or cake.

CHUNKY CHOCOLATE CURLS

These curls are best made with dark chocolate that has been melted with pure white vegetable fat (about 5ml/1tsp per 25g/1oz of chocolate), which keeps the chocolate from hardening completely.

__1__ Melt 175g/6oz plain or bittersweet chocolate with 30ml/2tbsp pure white vegetable fat, stirring until smooth. Pour into a small rectangular or square tin lined with foil or non-stick baking paper to produce a block about 2.5cm/1in thick. Chill until set.

__2__ Allow the block to come to room temperature, remove it from the tin, then hold it with a piece of folded foil or paper towel (to stop it melting) and use a swivel-bladed peeler to produce short chunky curls. The block of chocolate can also be grated.

COOK'S TIPS

The decorations on this page are useful for all kinds of cakes and desserts. When you have mastered the techniques, try marbling dark and white chocolate together for a special effect.

CHOCOLATE SCROLLS OR SHORT ROUND CURLS

Temper dark or white chocolate, or use chocolate prepared for Chunky Chocolate Curls to produce these scrolls.

1 Pour the prepared chocolate evenly on to a marble slab or the back of a baking sheet. Using a metal palette knife, spread to about 3mm/⅛in thick and allow to set for about 30 minutes until just firm.

2 To make long scrolls, use the blade of a long, sharp knife on the surface of the chocolate, and, with both hands, push away from your body at a 25–45° angle to scrape off a thin layer of chocolate. Twist the handle of the knife about a quarter of a circle to make a slightly wider scroll. Use a teaspoon to make cup-shaped curls.

3 A variety of shapes and sizes can be produced, depending on the temperature of the chocolate and the tool used.

CHOCOLATE SQUIGGLES

Melt a quantity of chocolate and spread fairly thinly over a cool, smooth surface, leave until just set, then draw a citrus zester firmly across the surface to remove curls or "squiggles" of the chocolate.

CHOCOLATE CUT-OUTS

You can make abstract shapes, or circles, squares and diamonds, by cutting them out free-hand with a sharp knife.

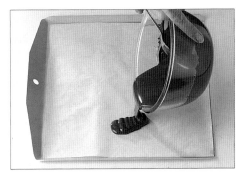

1 Cover a baking sheet with baking parchment and tape down at each corner. Melt 115g/4 oz dark, milk or white chocolate. Pour the chocolate on to the baking parchment.

2 Spread the chocolate evenly with a palette knife. Allow to stand until the surface is firm enough to cut, but not so hard that it will break. It should no longer feel sticky when touched lightly with your finger.

3 Press the cutter firmly through the chocolate and lift off the paper with a palette knife. Try not to touch the surface of the chocolate or you will leave marks on it and spoil its appearance.

4 The finished shapes can be left plain or piped with a contrasting chocolate for a decorative effect.

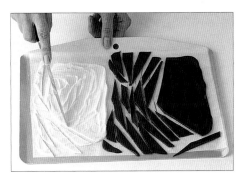

5 Abstract shapes can be cut with a knife free-hand. They look particularly effective pressed on to the sides of a cake iced with plain or chocolate buttercream.

COOK'S TIPS

If you do not feel confident about cutting chocolate cut-outs freehand, use biscuit or aspic cutters. Cut-outs look good around the sides of cakes or gâteaux. Space them at regular intervals or allow them to overlap.

CHOCOLATE LEAVES

You can use any fresh, non-toxic leaf with distinct veins, to make these decorations. Rose, bay or lemon leaves work well. If small leaves are required, for decorating petits fours, for instance, use mint or lemon balm leaves.

1 Wash and dry the leaves thoroughly. Melt plain or white chocolate and use a pastry brush or spoon to coat the veined side of each leaf completely.

2 Place the coated leaves chocolate-side up on a baking sheet lined with non-stick baking paper to set.

3 Starting at the stem end, gently peel away each leaf in turn. Store the chocolate leaves in a cool place until needed.

CHOCOLATE BASKETS

These impressive baskets make pretty, edible containers for mousse, or ice cream.

MAKES 6
175g/6oz plain, milk or white chocolate
25g/1oz/2 tbsp butter

1 Cut out six 15cm/6in rounds from non-stick baking paper.

2 Melt the chocolate with the butter in a heatproof bowl over barely simmering water. Stir until smooth. Spoon one-sixth of the chocolate over each round, using a teaspoon to spread it to within 2cm/¾in of the edge.

BELOW: Chocolate baskets can be used to hold many kinds of delicious desserts, such as mousse, ice cream and tiramisu.

3 Carefully lift each covered paper round and drape it over an upturned cup or ramekin, curving the edges to create a frilled effect.

4 Leave until completely set, then carefully lift off the chocolate shape and peel away the paper.

5 For a different effect, brush the chocolate over, leaving the edges jagged. Invert chocolate baskets on individual dessert plates and gently peel off the paper. Add your chosen filling, taking care not to break the chocolate.
6 For a simple filling, whip cream with a little orange-flavoured liqueur, pipe the mixture in swirls in the chocolate cups and top with mandarin segments, half-dipped in chocolate.

CHOCOLATE CUPS

Large or small cupcake papers or sweet cases can be used to make chocolate cups to fill with ice cream, mousse or liqueur. Use double liners inside each other for extra support.

1 Melt the chocolate. Using a paintbrush or pastry brush, completely coat the bottom and sides of the paper cases. Allow to set, then repeat once or twice to build up the layers. Allow to set for several hours or overnight.

2 Carefully peel off the paper case, set the chocolate cups on a baking sheet and fill as desired.

CHOCOLATE SHORTCRUST PASTRY (1)

Suitable for sweet flans and tarts, this quantity will line a 23cm/9in flan tin.

115g/4oz plain chocolate, broken into squares
225g/8oz/2 cups plain flour
115g/4oz/½ cup unsalted butter
15–30ml/1–2 tbsp cold water

1 Melt the chocolate in a heatproof bowl over hot water. Remove from the heat and allow to cool, but not set.

2 Place the flour in a mixing bowl. Rub in the butter until the mixture resembles fine breadcrumbs.

3 Make a well in the centre of the rubbed-in mixture. Add the cooled chocolate and mix in together with just enough cold water to mix to a firm dough. Knead lightly, then wrap in clear film and chill before rolling out. Once you have chilled the flan tin, chill again before baking.

LEFT: These tiny chocolate cups are ideal as a container for sweets. You can also fill them with nuts and fruit for petits fours. Look out for different sizes of cases for these little cups.

CHOCOLATE SHORTCRUST PASTRY (2)

An alternative sweet chocolate pastry, this time made with cocoa. Use a 23cm/9in flan tin.

175g/6oz/1½ cups plain flour
30ml/2 tbsp cocoa powder
30ml/2 tbsp icing sugar
115g/4oz/½ cup butter
15–30ml/1–2 tbsp cold water

1 Sift the flour, cocoa powder and icing sugar into a mixing bowl.
2 Place the butter in a pan with the water and heat gently until just melted. Cool.
3 Stir into the flour to make a smooth dough. Chill until firm, then roll out and use as required.

TIPS FOR COOKING WITH CHOCOLATE

Melt chocolate slowly, as overheating will spoil both the flavour and texture.

Avoid overheating – dark chocolate should not be heated above 49°C/120°F; milk and white chocolate should not be heated above 43°C/110°F.

Never allow water or steam to come into contact with melting chocolate, as this may cause it to stiffen. If the chocolate comes into contact with steam, and forms a solid mass, add a small amount of pure vegetable oil and mix in. If this does not work you will have to start again. Don't discard spoiled chocolate, it will probably melt when added to another ingredient such as milk, butter or cream.

Remember to use high quality chocolate for the best results.
Look for the cocoa solid content on the back of the wrapper.
Do not cover chocolate after melting, as condensation could cause it to stiffen.

TEA-TIME CHOCOLATE TREATS

SIMPLE CHOCOLATE CAKE

2 Cream the butter or margarine with the sugar in a mixing bowl until pale and fluffy. Add the eggs one at a time, beating well after each addition. Stir in the chocolate mixture until well combined.

3 Sift the flour and cocoa over the mixture and fold in with a metal spoon until evenly mixed. Scrape into the prepared tins, smooth level and bake for 35–40 minutes or until well risen and firm. Turn out on to wire racks to cool.

4 Sandwich the cake layers together with a thick, even layer of chocolate buttercream. Dust with a mixture of icing sugar and cocoa just before serving.

SERVES 6–8

115g/4oz plain chocolate, chopped into small pieces
45ml/3 tbsp milk
150g/5oz/⅔ cup unsalted butter or margarine, softened
150g/5oz/scant 1 cup light muscovado sugar
3 eggs
200g/7oz/1¾ cups self-raising flour
15ml/1 tbsp cocoa powder
1 quantity Chocolate Buttercream, for the filling
icing sugar and cocoa powder, for dusting

1 Preheat oven to 180°C/350°F/Gas 4. Grease two 18 cm/7 in round sandwich cake tins and line the base of each with non-stick baking paper. Select a small saucepan and a heatproof bowl that will fit over it. Place the chocolate and the milk in the bowl. Bring a small saucepan of water to just below simmering point. Place the bowl containing the chocolate mixture on top. Leave for about 5 minutes, until the chocolate softens, then stir until smooth. Leave the bowl over the saucepan, but remove from the heat.

ONE-MIX CHOCOLATE SPONGE

SERVES 8–10

*175g/6oz/³⁄₄ cup soft margarine, at room
temperature
115g/4oz/¹⁄₂ cup caster sugar
60ml/4 tbsp golden syrup
175g/6oz/1¹⁄₂ cups self-raising flour, sifted
30ml/2 tbsp cocoa powder, sifted
2.5ml/¹⁄₂ tsp salt
3 eggs, beaten
little milk (optional)
150ml/¹⁄₄ pint/²⁄₃ cup whipping cream
15–30ml/1–2 tbsp finely shredded marmalade
sifted icing sugar, to decorate*

1 Preheat the oven to 180°C/350°F/Gas 4. Grease two 18 mm/7 in sandwich cake tins. Cream the margarine, sugar, syrup, flour, cocoa, salt and eggs in a bowl.

2 If the mixture seems a little thick, stir in enough milk to give a soft dropping consistency. Spoon the mixture into the prepared tins, and bake for about 30 minutes, changing shelves if necessary after 15 minutes, until just firm and springy to the touch.

3 Leave the cakes to cool for 5 minutes, then remove from the tins and leave to cool completely on a wire rack.

4 Whip the cream and fold in the marmalade. Use the mixture to sandwich the two cakes together. Sprinkle the top with sifted icing sugar.

Chocolate and Beetroot Layer Cake

Serves 10–12

cocoa powder, for dusting
225g/8oz can cooked whole beetroot, drained
and juice reserved
115g/4oz/½ cup unsalted butter, softened
425g/15oz/2½ cups soft light brown sugar
3 eggs
15ml/1 tbsp vanilla essence
75g/3oz bittersweet chocolate, melted
225g/8oz/2 cups plain flour
10ml/2 tsp baking powder
2.5ml/½ tsp salt
120ml/4fl oz/½ cup buttermilk
chocolate curls (optional)

Chocolate Ganache Frosting

475ml/16fl oz/2 cups whipping cream or
double cream
500g/1¼lb fine quality, bittersweet or plain
chocolate, chopped into
small pieces
15ml/1 tbsp vanilla essence

1 Preheat the oven to 180°C/350°F/ Gas 4. Grease two 23 cm/9 in cake tins and dust the base and sides with cocoa. Grate the beetroot and add to the juice. Set aside. With a hand-held electric mixer, beat the butter, brown sugar, eggs and vanilla essence in a mixing bowl until pale. Reduce the speed and beat in the melted chocolate. Sift the flour, baking powder and salt into a bowl.

2 With the mixer on low speed gradually beat the flour mixture into the butter mixture, alternately with the buttermilk. Add the beetroot and juice and beat for 1 minute. Divide between the tins and bake for 30–35 minutes or until a cake tester inserted in the centre of each cake comes out clean. Cool for 10 minutes, then turn the cakes out on a wire rack and cool completely.

3 To make the ganache frosting, heat the cream in a heavy-based saucepan over medium heat, until it just begins to boil, stirring occasionally to prevent it from scorching. Remove from the heat and stir in the chocolate, stirring constantly until melted and smooth. Stir in the vanilla essence. Strain into a bowl. Cool, then chill, stirring every 10 minutes for about 1 hour, until spreadable.

4 Assemble the cake. Place one layer on a serving plate and spread with one-third of the ganache frosting. Place the second layer on top and spread the remaining ganache over the cake, taking it down the sides. Decorate with the chocolate curls, if using. Allow the ganache frosting to set for 20–30 minutes, then chill the cake before serving.

FRENCH CHOCOLATE CAKE

SERVES 10

*250g/9oz bittersweet chocolate, chopped into
small pieces
225g/8oz/1 cup unsalted butter, cut into
small pieces
90g/3½oz/scant ½ cup granulated sugar
30ml/2 tbsp brandy or orange-flavoured
liqueur
5 eggs
15ml/1tbsp plain flour
icing sugar, for dusting
whipped or soured cream, for serving*

1 Preheat oven to 180°C/350°F/Gas 4.
Generously grease a 23 x 5 cm/9 x 2 in
springform tin. Line the base with non-
stick baking paper and grease. Wrap the
bottom and sides of the tin in foil to
prevent water from seeping through into
the cake.

2 In a saucepan, over a low heat, melt the
chocolate, butter and sugar, stirring
frequently until smooth. Remove from
the heat, cool slightly and stir in the
brandy or liqueur.

3 In a large bowl beat the eggs lightly for
1 minute. Beat in the flour, then slowly
beat in the chocolate mixture until well
blended. Pour into the tin.

4 Place the springform tin in a large
roasting tin. Add enough boiling water to
come 2 cm/¾ in up the side of the
springform tin. Bake for 25–30 minutes,
until the edge of the cake is set but the
centre is still soft. Remove the
springform tin from the roasting tin and
remove the foil. Cool on a wire rack. The
cake will sink in the centre and become
its classic slim shape as it cools. Don't
worry if the surface cracks slightly.

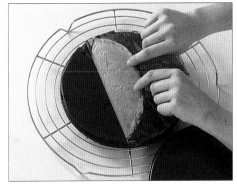

5 Remove the side of the springform tin
and turn the cake on to a wire rack. Lift
off the springform tin base and then
carefully peel back the paper, so the base
of the cake is now the top. Leave the cake
on the rack until it is quite cold.

6 Cut 6–8 strips of non-stick baking
paper 2.5 cm/1 in wide and place
randomly over the cake. Dust the cake
with icing sugar, then carefully remove
the paper. Slide the cake on to a plate and
serve with whipped or soured cream.

Hazelnut and Chocolate Cake

Serves 10

115g/4oz/¹⁄₂ cup unsalted butter, softened
150g/5oz plain chocolate
115g/4oz/¹⁄₂ cup caster sugar
4 eggs, separated
115g/4oz/1 cup ground lightly toasted
hazelnuts
50g/2oz/1 cup fresh breadcrumbs
grated rind of 1¹⁄₂ oranges
30ml/2 tbsp sieved marmalade, warmed
60ml/4 tbsp chopped hazelnuts, to decorate

For the Icing

150g/5oz plain chocolate, chopped into
small pieces
50g/2oz/¹⁄₄ cup butter, diced

1 Preheat oven to 180°C/350°F/Gas 4. Butter a 23 cm/9 in round cake tin and line the base with greaseproof paper.

2 Melt the chocolate and set aside. Beat the butter and sugar together, then gradually add the egg yolks, beating well. The mixture may curdle slightly. Beat in the melted chocolate, then the hazelnuts, breadcrumbs and orange rind. Whisk the egg whites until stiff, then fold into the chocolate mixture. Transfer to the cake tin. Bake for 40–45 minutes, until set.

3 Remove from the oven, cover with a damp dish towel for 5 minutes, then transfer to a wire rack until cold.

4 Make the icing. Place the chocolate and butter in a heatproof bowl over a pan of simmering water and stir until smooth. Leave until cool and thick. Spread the cake with the marmalade, then the icing. Scatter over the nuts, then leave to set.

CHOCOLATE AND ORANGE ANGEL CAKE

SERVES 10

25g / 1oz / ¼ cup plain flour
30ml / 2 tbsp cocoa powder
30ml / 2 tbsp cornflour
pinch of salt
5 egg whites
2.5ml / ½ tsp cream of tartar
115g / 4oz / ½ cup caster sugar
blanched and shredded rind of 1 orange,
to decorate

FOR THE ICING

200g / 7oz / scant 1 cup caster sugar
75ml / 5 tbsp cold water
1 egg white

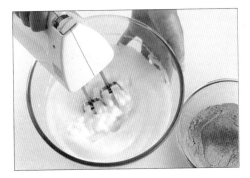

1 Preheat oven to 180°C / 350°F / Gas 4. Sift the flour, cocoa, cornflour and salt together three times. Beat the egg whites in a large bowl until foamy. Add the cream of tartar to the egg whites and whisk until soft peaks form.

2 Add the caster sugar to the egg whites a spoonful at a time, whisking after each addition. Add, by sifting, a third of the flour and cocoa mixture, and gently fold in. Repeat, sifting and folding in the flour and cocoa two more times. Spoon the mixture into a 20 cm / 8 in non-stick ring tin and level the top. Bake for 35 minutes or until springy when lightly pressed. When cooled, turn upside-down on to a wire rack and leave to cool in the tin.

3 Make the icing. Put the sugar in a pan with the water. Stir over a low heat until dissolved. Boil until the syrup reaches a temperature of 120°C / 250°F on a sugar thermometer, or when a drop of the syrup makes a soft ball when dropped into a cup of cold water. Remove the pan from the heat. Ease the cake out of the tin.

4 Whisk the egg white until stiff. Add the syrup in a thin stream, whisking all the time. Continue to whisk until the mixture is very thick and fluffy. Spread the icing over the top and sides of the cooled cake. Sprinkle the orange rind over the top of the cake and transfer it to a platter. Serve.

CHOCOLATE AND CHERRY POLENTA CAKE

SERVES 8

50g / 2oz / ⅓ cup quick-cook polenta
200g / 7oz plain chocolate, chopped into
small pieces
5 eggs, separated
175g / 6oz / ¾ cup caster sugar
115g / 4oz / 1 cup ground almonds
75ml / 5 tbsp plain flour
finely grated rind of 1 orange
115g / 4oz / 1 cup glacé cherries, halved
icing sugar, for dusting

1 Place the polenta in a heatproof bowl and pour over just enough boiling water to cover (about 120ml/4 fl oz/½ cup). Stir well, then cover the bowl and leave to stand for about 30 minutes, until the quick-cook polenta has absorbed all the excess moisture.

2 Preheat oven to 190°C/375°F/Gas 5. Grease a deep 22 cm/8½ in round cake tin and line the base with non-stick baking paper. Melt the chocolate.

3 Whisk the egg yolks with the sugar in a bowl until thick and pale. Beat in the chocolate, then fold in the polenta, ground almonds, flour and orange rind.

4 Whisk the egg whites in a grease-free bowl until stiff. Stir about 15ml/1 tbsp of the whites into the chocolate mixture to lighten it, then fold in the rest. Finally, fold in the cherries. Scrape the mixture into the prepared tin and bake for 45–55 minutes or until well risen and firm. Turn out and cool on a wire rack, then dust with icing sugar to serve.

MARBLED CHOCOLATE-PEANUT BUTTER CAKE

SERVES 12–14

*115g/4oz bittersweet chocolate, chopped into
small pieces
225g/8oz/1 cup unsalted butter, softened
225g/8oz/⅔ cup smooth or chunky
peanut butter
200g/7oz/scant 1 cup granulated sugar
225g/8 oz/1¼ cups soft light brown sugar
5 eggs
225g/8 oz/2 cups plain flour
10ml/2 tsp baking powder
2.5ml/½ tsp salt
120ml/4fl oz/½ cup milk
50g/2oz/⅓ cup chocolate chips*

CHOCOLATE PEANUT BUTTER GLAZE
*25g/1oz/2 tbsp butter, cut up
30ml/2 tbsp smooth peanut butter
45ml/3 tbsp golden syrup
5ml/1 tsp vanilla essence
175g/6oz plain chocolate, chopped into
small pieces
15ml/1 tbsp water*

<u>1</u> Preheat oven to 180°C/350°F/Gas 4.
Generously grease and flour a 3 litre/
5 pint/12 cup tube or ring tin. Melt
the chocolate. In a large mixing bowl beat
the butter, peanut butter and sugars until
light and creamy. Add the eggs one at a
time, beating well after each addition.
<u>2</u> In a medium bowl, sift together the
flour, baking powder and salt. Add to the
butter mixture alternately with the milk
until just blended. Pour half the mixture
into another bowl. Stir the melted
chocolate into one bowl of batter until
well blended. Stir the chocolate chips
into the other bowl of batter.

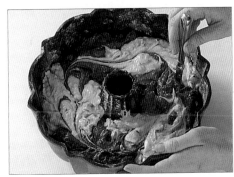

<u>3</u> Using a large spoon, drop alternate
spoonfuls of chocolate mixture and
peanut butter mixture into the prepared
tin. Using a knife, pull through the
batters to create a swirled marbled effect.
Bake for 50–60 minutes, until the top
springs back when touched. Cool the
cake in the tin for 10 minutes. Turn out
on to a rack to cool completely.

<u>4</u> Make the glaze. Combine all the
ingredients in a small saucepan. Melt over
a low heat, stirring until well blended and
smooth. Cool slightly. When slightly
thickened, drizzle the glaze over the cake,
allowing it to run down the sides.

CHOCOLATE-ORANGE BATTENBURG

3 Fold the rest of the flour and the cocoa into the remaining bowl of mixture, with sufficient milk to give a soft dropping consistency. Fill one half of the tin with the orange mixture and the second half with the chocolate. Flatten the top with a wetted spoon. Bake for 15 minutes, then reduce the heat to 160°C/325°F/Gas 3, and bake the cake for a further 20–30 minutes or until the top is just firm. Leave to cool in the tin for a few minutes. Turn out the cakes on to a board and cut each one into two identical strips. Trim so that they are even, then leave to cool.

4 Using the chocolate and nut spread, sandwich the cakes together, chocolate and orange side by side, then orange and chocolate on top. Spread the sides with more of the chocolate and nut spread. On a board lightly dusted with cornflour, roll out the white almond paste to a rectangle 18 cm/7 in wide and long enough to wrap all around the cake. Wrap the almond paste carefully around the cake, making the join underneath. Press to seal. Mark a criss-cross pattern on the almond paste with a knife, then pinch together the corners if desired. Store in a cool place. Cut with a sharp knife into chequered slices to serve.

SERVES 8

115g/4oz/½ cup soft margarine
115g/4oz/½ cup caster sugar
2 eggs, beaten
few drops of vanilla essence
115g/4oz/1 cup ground almonds
115g/4oz/1 cup self-raising flour, sifted
grated rind and juice of ½ orange
30ml/2 tbsp cocoa powder, sifted
30–45ml/2–3 tbsp milk
1 jar chocolate and nut spread
cornflour, to dust
225g/8oz white almond paste

1 Preheat oven to 180°C/350°F/Gas 4. Grease and line an 18 cm/7 in square cake tin. Arrange a double piece of foil across the middle of the tin, to divide it into two equal rectangles.

2 Cream the margarine and sugar in a mixing bowl, then beat in the eggs, vanilla essence and ground almonds. Divide the mixture evenly between two bowls. Fold half the flour into one bowl, then stir in the orange rind and sufficient juice to give a soft dropping consistency. Set the orange-flavoured mixture aside.

CHOCOLATE CHIP WALNUT LOAF

MAKES 1 LOAF

115g/4oz/½ cup caster sugar
115g/4oz/1 cup plain flour
5ml/1 tsp baking powder
60ml/4 tbsp cornflour
115g/4oz/½ cup butter, softened
2 eggs, beaten
5ml/1 tsp vanilla essence
30ml/2 tbsp currants or raisins
25g/1oz/¼ cup walnuts, finely chopped
grated rind of ½ lemon
45ml/3 tbsp plain chocolate chips
icing sugar, for dusting

1 Preheat oven to 180°C/350°F/Gas 4. Grease and line a 22 x 12 cm/8½ x 4½ in loaf tin. Sprinkle 25ml/1½ tbsp of the caster sugar into the pan and tilt to distribute the sugar in an even layer over the bottom and sides. Shake out any excess sugar.

2 Sift the flour, baking powder and cornflour into a mixing bowl. Repeat this twice more. Set aside.

3 With an electric mixer, cream the butter until soft. Add the remaining sugar and continue beating until light and fluffy. Add the eggs, one at a time, beating after each addition.

4 Gently fold the dry ingredients into the butter mixture, in three batches; do not overmix.

5 Fold in the vanilla essence, currants or raisins, walnuts, lemon rind and chocolate chips until just blended.

6 Pour the mixture into the prepared tin and bake for 45–50 minutes. Cool in the tin for 5 minutes before transferring to a rack to cool completely. Place on a serving plate and dust over an even layer of icing sugar before serving. Alternatively, top with glacé icing and decorate with walnut halves.

BITTER MARMALADE CHOCOLATE LOAF

SERVES 8

*115g/4oz plain chocolate, chopped into
small pieces*
3 eggs
200g/7oz/scant 1 cup caster sugar
175ml/6fl oz/¾ cup soured cream
200g/7oz/1¾ cups self-raising flour
FOR THE FILLING AND GLAZE
175g/6oz/⅔ cup bitter orange marmalade
*115g/4oz plain chocolate, chopped into
small pieces*
60ml/4 tbsp soured cream
shredded orange rind, to decorate

1 Preheat oven to 180°C/350°F/Gas 4.
Grease a 900g/2lb loaf tin lightly, then
line it with non-stick baking paper. Melt
the chocolate.

2 Combine the eggs and sugar in a mixing
bowl. Using a hand-held electric mixer,
whisk the mixture until it is thick and
creamy, then stir in the soured cream and
chocolate. Fold in the self-raising flour
evenly, using a metal spoon and a figure-
of-eight action.

3 Scrape the mixture into the prepared
tin and bake for about 1 hour or until
well risen and firm to the touch. Cool for
a few minutes in the tin, then turn out on
to a wire rack and leave the loaf to cool
completely.
4 Make the filling. Spoon two-thirds of
the marmalade into a small saucepan and
melt over a gentle heat. Melt the
chocolate and stir it into the marmalade
with the soured cream.
5 Slice the cake across into three layers
and sandwich back together with about
half the marmalade filling. Spread the rest
over the top of the cake and leave to set.
Spoon the remaining marmalade over the
cake and scatter with shredded orange
rind, to decorate.

CHOCOLATE CHIP MARZIPAN LOAF

MAKES 1 LOAF

115g/4oz/½ cup unsalted butter, softened
150g/5oz/scant 1 cup light muscovado sugar
2 eggs, beaten
45ml/3 tbsp cocoa powder
150g/5oz/1¼ cups self-raising flour
130g/3½ oz marzipan
60ml/4 tbsp plain chocolate chips

<u>**1**</u> Preheat oven to 180°C/350°F/Gas 4. Grease a 900g/2lb loaf tin and line the base with non-stick baking paper. Cream the butter and sugar in a mixing bowl until light and fluffy.

<u>**2**</u> Add the eggs to the creamed mixture one at a time, beating well after each addition to combine.

<u>**3**</u> Sift the cocoa and flour over the mixture and fold in evenly.

<u>**4**</u> Chop the marzipan into small pieces with a sharp knife. Tip into a bowl and mix with the chocolate chips. Set aside about 60ml/4 tbsp and fold the rest evenly into the cake mixture.

<u>**5**</u> Scrape the mixture into the prepared tin, level the top and scatter with the reserved marzipan and chocolate chips.

<u>**6**</u> Bake for 45–50 minutes or until the loaf is risen and firm. Cool for a few minutes in the tin, then turn out on to a wire rack to cool completely.

CHOCOLATE COCONUT ROULADE

4 Scrape the mixture into the prepared tin, taking it right into the corners. Smooth the surface with a palette knife, then bake for 20–25 minutes or until well risen and springy to the touch.

5 Turn the cooked roulade out on to the sugar-dusted greaseproof paper and carefully peel off the lining paper. Cover with a damp, clean dish towel and leave to cool completely.

6 Make the filling. Whisk the cream with the whisky in a bowl until the mixture just holds it shape, grate the creamed coconut and stir in with the sugar.

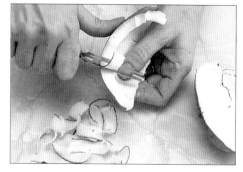

7 Uncover the sponge and spread about three-quarters of the cream mixture to the edges. Roll up carefully from a long side. Transfer to a plate, pipe or spoon the remaining cream mixture on top. Use a vegetable peeler to make coconut and chocolate curls and pile on the cake.

SERVES 8

115g / 4oz / ½ cup caster sugar
5 eggs, separated
50g / 2oz / ½ cup cocoa powder
FOR THE FILLING
300ml / ½ pint / 1¼ cups double cream
45ml / 3 tbsp whisky
or brandy
50g / 2oz piece solid creamed
coconut
30ml / 2 tbsp caster sugar
FOR THE TOPPING
a piece of fresh coconut
dark chocolate for curls

1 Preheat oven to 180°C / 350°F / Gas 4. Grease a 33 x 23 cm / 13 x 9 in Swiss roll tin. Lay a large sheet of greaseproof paper or non-stick baking paper on the work surface and dust it evenly with 30ml / 2 tbsp of the caster sugar.

2 Place the egg yolks in a heatproof bowl. Add the remaining caster sugar and whisk with a hand-held electric mixer until the mixture is thick enough to leave a trail. Sift the cocoa over, then fold in carefully and evenly with a metal spoon.

3 Whisk the egg whites in a clean, grease-free bowl until they form soft peaks. Fold about 15ml / 1 tbsp of the whites into the chocolate mixture to lighten it, then fold in the rest evenly.

CHOCOLATE CHESTNUT ROULADE

SERVES 10–12

*175g/6oz bittersweet chocolate, chopped into
small pieces
30ml/2 tbsp cocoa powder, sifted
60ml/4 tbsp hot strong coffee or espresso
6 eggs, separated
75g/3oz/6 tbsp caster sugar
pinch of cream of tartar
5ml/1 tsp pure vanilla essence
cocoa powder, for dusting
glacé chestnuts, to decorate*

CHESTNUT CREAM FILLING

*475ml/16fl oz/2 cups double cream
30ml/2 tbsp rum or coffee-flavoured liqueur
350g/12oz/1½ cups canned sweetened
chestnut purée
115g/4oz bittersweet chocolate, grated*

1 Preheat oven to 180°C/350°F/Gas 4.
Lightly grease the base and sides of a
39 x 27 x 2.5 cm/15½ x 10½ x 1 in Swiss
roll tin. Line with non-stick baking paper,
allowing a 2.5 cm/1 in overhang. Melt
the chocolate. Dissolve the cocoa in the
hot coffee to make a paste. Set aside.
2 Using a hand-held mixer, beat the egg
yolks with half the sugar in a mixing bowl
until pale and thick. Slowly beat in the
melted chocolate and cocoa-coffee paste
until just blended. In a separate bowl,
beat the egg whites and cream of tartar
until stiff peaks form. Sprinkle the
remaining sugar over the whites in two
batches and beat until the whites are
stiff and glossy, then beat in the
vanilla essence.
3 Stir a spoonful of the whites into the
chocolate mixture to lighten it, then
fold in the rest. Spoon into the tin.
Bake for 20–25 minutes or until the
cake springs back when touched with
a fingertip.

4 Dust a dish towel with cocoa. Turn the
cake out on to the towel immediately and
remove the paper. Trim off any crisp
edges. Starting at a narrow end, roll the
cake and towel together Swiss roll
fashion. Cool completely.

5 Make the filling. Whip the cream and
rum or liqueur until soft peaks form.
Beat a spoonful of cream into the
chestnut purée to lighten it, then fold in
the remaining cream and grated
chocolate. Set aside a quarter of this
mixture for the decoration. Unroll the
cake and spread chestnut cream to within
2.5 cm/1 in of the edge.
6 Using a dish towel to lift the cake,
carefully roll it up again. Place seam-
side down on a serving plate. Spread
some of the reserved chestnut cream
over the top and use the rest for
piped rosettes. Decorate with the
glacé chestnuts.

MARBLED SWISS ROLL

SERVES 6–8

90g / 3½oz / scant 1 cup plain flour
15ml / 1 tbsp cocoa powder
25g / 1oz plain chocolate, grated
25g / 1oz white chocolate, grated
3 eggs
115g / 4oz / ½ cup caster sugar
30ml / 2 tbsp boiling water
FOR THE FILLING
1 quantity Chocolate Buttercream
45ml / 3 tbsp chopped walnuts

1 Preheat oven to 200°C/400°F/Gas 6. Grease a 30 x 20 cm/12 x 8 in Swiss roll tin and line with non-stick baking paper. Sift half the flour with the cocoa into a bowl. Stir in the grated plain chocolate. Sift the remaining flour into another bowl. Stir in the grated white chocolate.

2 Whisk the eggs and sugar in a heatproof bowl set over a saucepan of hot water until it holds its shape when the whisk is lifted and a ribbon trail remains.
3 Remove the bowl from the heat and tip half the mixture into a separate bowl. Fold the plain chocolate mixture into one portion, then fold the white chocolate mixture into the other. Stir 15ml/1 tbsp boiling water into each half to soften.

BAKED ALASKA

For a delicious dessert that takes only minutes to prepare, make individual Baked Alaskas by topping slices of the roll with chocolate ice cream, covering both cake and ice cream thickly with meringue mixture and baking at 230°C/450°F/Gas 8 for 2–3 minutes, watching carefully, until the meringue is tinged with brown.

4 Place alternate spoonfuls of mixture in the prepared tin and swirl lightly together with a knife or slim metal skewer for a marbled effect. Bake for about 12–15 minutes or until the cake is firm and the surface springs back when touched with a fingertip. Turn the cake out on to a sheet of non-stick baking paper placed flat on the work surface.

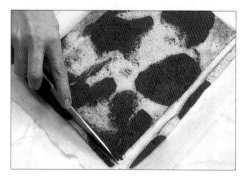

5 Trim the edges to neaten and cover with a damp, clean dish towel. Cool.
6 For the filling, mix the chocolate buttercream and walnuts in a bowl. Uncover the sponge, lift off the lining paper and spread the surface with the buttercream. Roll up carefully from a long side and place on a serving plate. Slice to serve, and store in an airtight container.

CHOCOLATE CHRISTMAS LOG

SERVES 12-14

*1 chocolate Swiss roll, see Chocolate
Chestnut Roulade
1 quantity of Chocolate Ganache or
Buttercream*

**FOR THE WHITE CHOCOLATE
CREAM FILLING**

*200g / 7oz fine quality white chocolate,
chopped into small pieces
475ml / 16fl oz / 2 cups double cream
30ml / 2 tbsp brandy or chocolate-flavoured
liqueur (optional)*

FOR THE CRANBERRY SAUCE

*450g / 1lb fresh or frozen cranberries, rinsed
and picked over
275g / 10oz / 1 cup seedless raspberry
preserve, melted
115g / 4oz / ½ cup granulated sugar, or
to taste*

1 Make the cranberry sauce. Process the
cranberries in a food processor fitted with
a metal blade, until liquid. Press through
a sieve into a small bowl, and discard
pulp. Stir in the melted raspberry
preserve and the sugar to taste. If the
sauce is too thick, add a little water to
thin. Cover and place in the fridge.

2 Make the filling. In a small pan, heat the
chocolate with 120ml / 4 fl oz / ½ cup of
the cream until melted, stirring. Strain
into a bowl and cool to room
temperature. In a separate bowl, beat the
remaining cream with the brandy or
liqueur until soft peaks form; fold into
the chocolate mixture.

3 Unroll the Swiss roll, spread with the
mixture and roll up again from a long
end. Cut off a quarter of the roll at an
angle and arrange both pieces on a cake
board to resemble a log.

4 If using chocolate ganache for the
topping, allow it to soften to room
temperature, then beat to a soft,
spreading consistency. Cover the log with
ganache or buttercream and mark it with
a fork to resemble bark. Dust lightly with
icing sugar and top with a sprig of holly
or similar Christmas decoration. Serve
with the cranberry sauce.

MERINGUE MUSHROOMS

Small, decorative mushrooms are
traditionally used to decorate the
yule log. Using meringue mix, pipe
the "caps" and "stems" separately, dry
out in a low oven, then sandwich
together with ganache or chocolate
buttercream. Dust with cocoa, if you
like. Alternatively, shape mushrooms
from marzipan.

RICH CAKES AND GATEAUX

CHOCOLATE DATE TORTE

SERVES 8

4 egg whites
115g/4oz/½ cup caster sugar
200g/7oz plain chocolate
*175g/6oz/scant 1 cup Medjool dates, pitted
and finely chopped*
*175g/6oz/1½ cups walnuts or pecan
nuts, chopped*
5ml/1 tsp vanilla essence

FOR THE FROSTING

200g/7oz/scant 1 cup fromage frais
*200g/7oz/scant 1 cup mascarpone
few drops of vanilla essence
icing sugar, to taste*

1 Preheat oven to 180°C/350°F/Gas 4. Grease a round 20 cm/8 in springform cake tin. Line the base of the tin with non-stick baking paper.

2 Make the frosting. Mix together the fromage frais and mascarpone, add a few drops of vanilla essence and icing sugar to taste, then set aside.

3 Whisk the egg whites in a bowl until they form stiff peaks. Whisk in 30ml/ 2 tbsp of the caster sugar until the meringue is thick and glossy, then fold in the remainder.

4 Chop 175g/6 oz of the chocolate, then carefully fold into the meringue with the dates, nuts and vanilla essence. Pour into the prepared tin, spread level and bake for about 45 minutes, until risen around the edges.

5 Allow the cake to cool in the tin for 10 minutes, then invert on a wire rack. Peel off the lining paper and leave until completely cold.

6 Swirl the frosting over the top of the torte. Melt the remaining chocolate. Use a small paper piping bag to drizzle the chocolate over the torte. Work quickly and keep up an even pressure on the piping bag. Chill the torte before serving, then cut into wedges. This torte is best eaten on the day it is made.

CHOCOLATE REDCURRANT TORTE

SERVES 8–10

115g/4oz/½ cup unsalted butter, softened
115g/4oz/⅔ cup dark muscovado sugar
2 eggs
150ml/¼ pint/⅔ cup soured cream
150g/5oz/1¼ cups self-raising flour
5ml/1 tsp baking powder
50g/2oz/½ cup cocoa powder
75g/3oz/¾ cup stemmed redcurrants, plus
115g/4oz/1 cup redcurrant sprigs, to decorate

FOR THE ICING

150g/5oz plain chocolate, chopped into small pieces
45ml/3 tbsp redcurrant jelly
30ml/2 tbsp dark rum
120ml/4fl oz/½ cup double cream

1 Preheat oven to 180°C/350°F/Gas 4. Grease a 1.2 litre/2 pint/5 cup ring tin and dust lightly with flour. Cream the butter with the sugar in a mixing bowl until pale and fluffy. Beat in the eggs and soured cream until thoroughly mixed.

2 Sift the flour, baking powder and cocoa over the mixture, then fold in lightly and evenly. Fold in the stemmed redcurrants. Spoon the mixture into the prepared tin and smooth the surface level. Bake for 40–50 minutes or until well risen and firm. Turn out on to a wire rack and leave to cool completely.

3 Make the icing. Mix the chocolate, redcurrant jelly and rum in a heatproof bowl. Set the bowl over simmering water and heat gently, stirring occasionally, until melted. Remove from the heat and cool to room temperature, then add the double cream, a little at a time. Mix well.

4 Transfer the cooked cake to a serving plate. Spoon the icing evenly over the cake, allowing it to drizzle down the sides. Decorate with redcurrant sprigs just before serving.

COOK'S TIP

Use a decorative gugelhupf tin or mould, if you have one. When preparing it, add a little cocoa powder to the flour used for dusting the greased tin, as this will prevent the cooked chocolate cake from being streaked with white.

Sachertorte

Serves 10–12

*225g/8oz plain dark chocolate, chopped into
small pieces*
150g/5oz/⅔ cup butter, softened
115g/4oz/½ cup caster sugar
8 eggs, separated
115g/4oz/1 cup plain flour
For the Glaze
225g/8oz/scant 1 cup apricot jam
15ml/1 tbsp lemon juice
For the Icing
*225g/8oz plain dark chocolate, cut into
small pieces*
200g/7oz/scant 1 cup caster sugar
15ml/1 tbsp golden syrup
250ml/8fl oz/1 cup double cream
5ml/1 tsp vanilla essence
plain chocolate leaves, to decorate

1 Preheat oven to 180°C/350°F/Gas 4.
Grease a 23 cm/9 in round springform
cake tin and line with non-stick baking
paper. Melt the chocolate in a heatproof
bowl over barely simmering water, then
set the bowl aside.

2 Cream the butter with the sugar in a
mixing bowl until pale and fluffy, then
add the egg yolks, one at a time, beating
after each addition. Beat in the melted
chocolate, then sift the flour over the
mixture and fold it in evenly.

3 Whisk the egg whites in a clean, grease-
free bowl until stiff, then stir about a
quarter of the whites into the chocolate
mixture to lighten it. Fold in the
remaining whites.

4 Tip the chocolate mixture into the
prepared cake tin and smooth level. Bake
for about 50–55 minutes or until firm.
Cool in the tin for 5 minutes, then turn
out carefully on to a wire rack and leave
to cool completely.

5 Make the glaze. Heat the apricot jam
with the lemon juice in a small saucepan
until melted, then strain through a sieve
into a bowl. Once the cake is cold, slice
in half across the middle to make two
even-size layers.

6 Brush the top and sides of each layer
with the apricot glaze, then sandwich
them together. Place on a wire rack.

7 Make the icing. Mix the chocolate,
sugar, golden syrup, cream and vanilla
essence in a heavy saucepan. Heat gently,
stirring constantly, until the mixture is
thick and smooth. Simmer gently for 3–5
minutes, without stirring, until the
mixture registers 95°C/200°F on a sugar
thermometer. Pour the icing quickly over
the cake, spreading to cover the top and
sides completely. Leave to set, decorate
with chocolate leaves, then serve with
whipped cream, if wished.

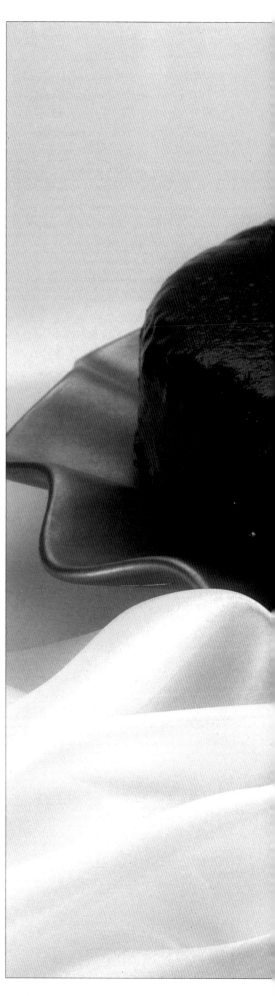

Queen of Sheba Cake

Serves 8–10

*100g / 3½oz / scant 1 cup whole blanched
almonds, lightly toasted*
115g / 4oz / ½ cup caster sugar
40g / 1½oz / ⅓ cup plain flour
115g / 4oz / ½ cup unsalted butter, softened
150g / 5oz plain chocolate, melted
3 eggs, separated
30ml / 2 tbsp almond liqueur (optional)
chopped toasted almonds, to decorate

For the Chocolate Glaze

175ml / 6fl oz / ¾ cup whipping cream
225g / 8oz plain chocolate, chopped
25g / 1oz / 2 tbsp unsalted butter
30ml / 2 tbsp almond liqueur (optional)

1 Preheat oven to 180°C / 350°F / Gas 4. Grease and base-line a 20–23 cm / 8–9 in springform cake tin. Dust the tin lightly with flour.

2 In the bowl of a food processor fitted with a metal blade, process the almonds and 30ml / 2 tbsp of the sugar until very fine. Transfer to a bowl and sift over the flour. Stir to mix, then set aside.

3 Beat the butter until creamy, then add half of the remaining sugar and beat for about 1–2 minutes until very light. Gradually beat in the melted chocolate, then add the egg yolks one at a time, beating well after each addition. Beat in the liqueur, if using.

4 In another bowl, beat the egg whites until soft peaks form. Add the remaining sugar and beat until the whites are stiff and glossy, but not dry. Fold a quarter of the whites into the chocolate mixture to lighten it, then alternately fold in the almond mixture and the remaining whites in three batches. Spoon the mixture into the prepared tin and spread evenly.

5 Bake for 30–35 minutes, until the edges are puffed but the centre is still soft. Cool in the tin for 15 minutes, then remove the sides and invert the cake on a wire rack. When quite cold, lift off the base of the tin and the paper.

6 To make the chocolate glaze, bring the cream to the boil in a saucepan. Remove from the heat and add the chocolate, stirring gently until it has melted and the mixture is smooth. Beat in the butter and almond liqueur, if using. Cool for about 20–30 minutes, until slightly thickened, stirring occasionally.

7 Place the cake on the wire rack over a baking sheet and pour over most of the warm glaze to cover completely. Cool slightly, then press the nuts on to the sides of the cake. Use the remaining glaze for a piped decoration. Transfer to a plate and chill until ready to serve.

STICKY CHOCOLATE, MAPLE AND WALNUT SWIRLS

SERVES 12

450g / 1lb / 4 cups strong white flour
2.5ml / ½ tsp ground cinnamon
50g / 2oz / ¼ cup unsalted butter, cut into small pieces
50g / 2oz / ¼ cup caster sugar
1 sachet easy-blend dried yeast
1 egg yolk
120ml / 4fl oz / ½ cup water
60ml / 4 tbsp milk
45ml / 3 tbsp maple syrup, to finish

FOR THE FILLING

40g / 1½oz / 3 tbsp unsalted butter, melted
50g / 2oz / ⅓ cup light muscovado sugar
175g / 6oz / 1 cup plain chocolate chips
75g / 3oz / ¾ cup chopped walnuts

1 Grease a deep 23 cm/9 in springform cake tin. Sift the flour and cinnamon into a bowl, then rub in the butter until the mixture resembles coarse breadcrumbs.

2 Stir in the sugar and yeast. In a jug or bowl, beat the egg yolk with the water and milk, then stir into the dry ingredients to make a soft dough.
3 Knead the dough on a lightly floured surface until smooth, then roll out to a rectangle measuring about 40 x 30 cm/ 16 x 12 in.

4 For the filling, brush the dough with the melted butter and sprinkle with the sugar, chocolate chips and nuts.

5 Roll up the dough from one long side like a Swiss roll, then cut into 12 thick even-size slices. Pack close together in the tin, cut sides up. Cover and leave in a warm place for about 1½ hours, until well risen and springy. Meanwhile, preheat oven to 220°C/425°F/Gas 7.
6 Bake for 30–35 minutes, until golden brown. Remove from the tin and cool on a wire rack. Brush with maple syrup while still warm. Pull swirls apart to serve.

WHITE CHOCOLATE MOUSSE AND STRAWBERRY LAYER CAKE

4 Make the mousse filling. In a medium saucepan over a low heat, melt the chocolate and cream until smooth, stirring frequently. Stir in the rum or strawberry-flavoured liqueur and pour into a bowl. Chill until just set. With a wire whisk, whip lightly.

SERVES 10

115g/4oz fine white chocolate, chopped into small pieces
120ml/4fl oz/½ cup double cream
120ml/4fl oz/½ cup milk
15ml/1 tbsp rum or vanilla essence
115g/4oz/½ cup unsalted butter, softened
175g/6oz/¾ cup granulated sugar
3 eggs
225g/8oz/2 cups plain flour
10ml/2 tsp baking powder
pinch of salt
675g/1½lb fresh strawberries, sliced, plus extra for decoration
750ml/1¼ pints/3 cups whipping cream
30ml/2 tbsp rum or strawberry-flavoured liqueur

WHITE CHOCOLATE MOUSSE FILLING

250g/9oz white chocolate, chopped into small pieces
350ml/12fl oz/1½ cups double cream
30ml/2 tbsp rum or strawberry-flavoured liqueur

1 Preheat oven to 180°C/350°F/Gas 4. Grease and flour two 23 x 5 cm/9 x 2 in cake tins. Line the base of the tins with non-stick baking paper. Melt the chocolate and cream in a double boiler over a low heat, stirring until smooth. Stir in the milk and rum or vanilla essence, and set aside to cool.

2 In a large mixing bowl, beat the butter and sugar with a hand-held electric mixer for 3–5 minutes, until light and creamy, scraping the sides of the bowl occasionally. Add the eggs one at a time, beating well after each addition. In a small bowl, stir together the flour, baking powder and salt. Alternately add flour and melted chocolate to the egg mixture in batches, until just blended. Pour the mixture into the tins and spread evenly.

3 Bake for 20–25 minutes, until a skewer inserted in the cake comes out clean. Cool in the tin for 10 minutes, then turn cakes out on to a wire rack, peel off the paper and cool completely.

5 Assemble the cake. With a serrated knife, slice both cake layers in half, making four layers. Place one layer on the plate and spread one third of the mousse on top. Arrange one third of the sliced strawberries over the mousse. Place the second layer on top and spread with another third of the mousse. Arrange another third of the sliced strawberries over the mousse. Place the third layer on top and spread with the remaining mousse. Cover with the remaining sliced strawberries. Top with the last cake layer.

6 Whip the cream with the rum or liqueur until firm peaks form. Spread about half the whipped cream over the top and the sides of the cake. Spoon the remaining cream into a decorating bag fitted with a medium star tip and pipe scrolls on top of the cake. Decorate with the remaining sliced strawberries, pressing half of them into the cream on the side of the cake and arranging the rest on top.

CHOCOLATE GINGER CRUNCH CAKE

SERVES 6

150g/5oz plain chocolate, chopped into small pieces
50g/2oz/¼ cup unsalted butter
115g/4oz ginger nut biscuits
4 pieces of preserved stem ginger
30ml/2 tbsp stem ginger syrup
45ml/3 tbsp desiccated coconut

TO DECORATE

25g/1oz milk chocolate, chopped into small pieces
pieces of crystallized ginger

1 Grease a 15 cm/6 in flan ring and place it on a sheet of non-stick baking paper. Melt the plain chocolate with the butter in a heatproof bowl over barely simmering water. Remove from the heat and set aside.

2 Crush the biscuits into small pieces. Tip them into a bowl.

3 Chop the stem ginger fairly finely and mix with the crushed ginger nut biscuits.

4 Stir the biscuit mixture, ginger syrup and coconut into the melted chocolate and butter, mixing well until evenly combined.

5 Tip the mixture into the prepared flan ring and press down firmly and evenly. Chill in the fridge until set.

6 Remove the flan ring and slide the cake on to a plate. Melt the milk chocolate, drizzle it over the top and decorate with the pieces of crystallized ginger.

FROSTED CHOCOLATE FUDGE CAKE

SERVES 6–8

115g/4oz plain chocolate, chopped into small pieces
175g/6oz/¾ cup unsalted butter or margarine, softened
200g/7oz/generous 1 cup light muscovado sugar
5ml/1 tsp vanilla essence
3 eggs, beaten
150ml/¼ pint/⅔ cup Greek-style yogurt
150g/5oz/1¼ cups self-raising flour
icing sugar and chocolate curls, to decorate

FOR THE FROSTING

115g/4 oz plain dark chocolate, chopped into small pieces
50g/2oz/¼ cup unsalted butter
350g/12oz/2¼ cups icing sugar
90ml/6 tbsp Greek-style yogurt

1 Preheat oven to 190°C/375°F/Gas 5. Lightly grease two 20 cm/8 in round sandwich cake tins and line the base of each with non-stick baking paper. Melt the chocolate.

2 In a mixing bowl, cream the butter or margarine with the sugar until light and fluffy. Beat in the vanilla essence, then gradually add the beaten eggs, beating well after each addition.

3 Stir in the melted plain chocolate and yogurt evenly. Fold in the flour with a metal spoon.

4 Divide the mixture between the prepared tins. Bake for 25–30 minutes or until the cakes are firm to the touch. Turn out and cool on a wire rack.

5 Make the frosting. Melt the chocolate and butter in a saucepan over a low heat. Remove from the heat and stir in the icing sugar and yogurt. Mix with a rubber spatula until smooth, then beat until the frosting begins to cool and thicken slightly. Use about a third of the mixture to sandwich the cakes together.

6 Working quickly, spread the remainder over the top and sides. Sprinkle with icing sugar and decorate with chocolate curls.

RICH CHOCOLATE LEAF GATEAU

SERVES 8

*75g/3oz plain dark chocolate, broken
into squares
150ml/¼ pint/⅔ cup milk
175g/6oz/¾ cup unsalted butter, softened
250g/9oz/1⅓ cups light muscovado sugar
3 eggs
250g/9oz/2¼ cups plain flour
10ml/2 tsp baking powder
75ml/5 tbsp single cream*

FOR THE FILLING AND TOPPING

*60ml/4 tbsp raspberry conserve
1 quantity Chocolate Ganache
dark and white chocolate leaves*

1 Preheat oven to 190°C/375°F/Gas 5. Grease and base-line two 22 cm/8½ in sandwich cake tins. Melt the chocolate with the milk over a low heat and allow to cool slightly.

2 Cream the butter with the light muscovado sugar in a mixing bowl until light and fluffy. Add the eggs, one at a time, beating well after each addition.

3 Sift the flour and baking powder over the mixture and fold in gently but thoroughly. Stir in the chocolate mixture and the cream, mixing until smooth. Divide between the prepared tins and level the tops.

4 Bake the cakes for 30–35 minutes or until they are well risen and firm to the touch. Cool in the tins for a few minutes, then turn out on to wire racks.

5 Sandwich the cake layers together with the raspberry conserve. Spread the chocolate ganache over the cake and swirl with a knife. Place the cake on a serving plate, then decorate with the chocolate leaves.

CHOCOLATE ALMOND MOUSSE CAKE

SERVES 8

*50g / 2oz plain dark chocolate, broken
into squares*
200g / 7oz marzipan, grated or chopped
200ml / 7fl oz / scant 1 cup milk
115g / 4oz / 1 cup self-raising flour
2 eggs, separated
*75g / 3oz / ½ cup light muscovado
sugar*

FOR THE MOUSSE FILLING

*115g / 4oz plain chocolate, chopped into
small pieces*
50g / 2oz / ¼ cup unsalted butter
2 eggs, separated
*30ml / 2 tbsp Amaretto di Saronno
liqueur*

FOR THE TOPPING

*1 quantity Chocolate Ganache
toasted flaked almonds, to decorate*

1 Preheat oven to 190°C / 375°F / Gas 5. Grease a deep 17 cm / 6½ in square cake tin and line with non-stick baking paper. Combine the chocolate, marzipan and milk in a saucepan and heat gently without boiling, stirring until smooth.
2 Sift the flour into a bowl and add the chocolate mixture and egg yolks, beating until evenly mixed.

3 Whisk the egg whites in a clean, grease-free bowl until stiff enough to hold firm peaks. Whisk in the sugar gradually. Stir about 15ml / 1 tbsp of the whites into the chocolate mixture to lighten it, then fold in the rest.
4 Spoon the mixture into the tin, spreading it evenly. Bake for 45–50 minutes, until well risen, firm and springy to the touch. Leave to cool on a wire rack.
5 Make the mousse filling. Melt the chocolate with the butter in a small saucepan over a low heat, then remove from the heat and beat in the egg yolks and Amaretto. Whisk the egg whites in a clean, grease-free bowl until stiff, then fold into the chocolate mixture.

6 Slice the cold cake in half across the middle to make two even layers. Return one half to the clean cake tin and pour over the chocolate mousse. Top with the second layer of cake and press down lightly. Chill until set.

7 Turn the cake out on to a serving plate. Allow the chocolate ganache to soften to room temperature, then beat it to a soft, spreading consistency. Spread the chocolate ganache over the top and sides of the cake, then press toasted flaked almonds over the sides. Serve chilled.

DEATH BY CHOCOLATE

SERVES 16–20

*225g/8oz plain dark chocolate, chopped into
small pieces*
115g/4 oz/½ cup unsalted butter
150ml/¼ pint/⅔ cup milk
225g/8oz/1¼ cups light muscovado sugar
10ml/2 tsp vanilla essence
2 eggs, separated
150ml/¼ pint/⅔ cup soured cream
225g/8oz/2 cups self-raising flour
5ml/1 tsp baking powder

FOR THE FILLING AND TOPPING

60ml/4 tbsp seedless raspberry jam
60ml/4 tbsp brandy
*400g/14oz plain dark chocolate, chopped
into small pieces*
200g/7oz/scant 1 cup unsalted butter
1 quantity Chocolate Ganache
plain chocolate curls, to decorate

1 Preheat oven to 180°C/350°F/Gas 4.
Grease and base-line a deep 23 cm/9 in
springform cake tin. Place the chocolate,
butter and milk in a saucepan. Stir over a
low heat until smooth. Remove from the
heat, beat in the sugar and vanilla essence,
then leave to cool slightly.
2 Beat the egg yolks and cream in a bowl,
then beat into the chocolate mixture. Sift
the flour and baking powder over the
surface and fold in.
3 Whisk the egg whites in a grease-free
bowl until stiff. Stir about 30ml/2 tbsp of
the whites into the chocolate cake
mixture, to lighten it. Fold in the
remaining whites, using a metal spoon.
4 Scrape the mixture into the prepared
tin and bake for about 45–55 minutes or
until firm to the touch. Cool in the tin for
15 minutes, then invert the cake on to a
wire rack, remove the tin and set aside
until completely cold.

5 Slice the cold cake across the middle to
make three even layers. Make the filling.
In a small saucepan, warm the raspberry
jam with 15ml/1 tbsp of the brandy, then
brush over two of the layers. Leave to set.
6 Place the remaining brandy in a
saucepan with the chocolate and butter.
Heat gently, stirring, until the mixture is
smooth. Pour into a bowl and cool until it
begins to thicken.

7 Spread the bottom layer of the cake
with half the chocolate filling, taking care
not to disturb the jam. Top with a second
layer, jam side up, and spread with the
remaining filling. Top with the final layer
and press lightly.

8 Leave to set, then spread the top and
sides of the cake with the chocolate
ganache. Decorate with chocolate curls
and then dust the top of the cake with
cocoa powder.

VEGAN CHOCOLATE GATEAU

SERVES 8–10

275g / 10oz / 2½ cups self-raising wholemeal flour
50g / 2oz / ½ cup cocoa powder
45ml / 3 tbsp baking powder
225g / 8oz / 1¼ cups caster sugar
few drops of vanilla essence
135ml / 9 tbsp sunflower oil
350ml / 12fl oz / 1½ cups water
sifted cocoa powder, for sprinkling
25g / 1oz / ¼ cup chopped nuts, to decorate

FOR THE CHOCOLATE FUDGE
50g / 2oz / ¼ cup vegan (soya) margarine
45ml / 3 tbsp water
250g / 9oz / 2 cups icing sugar
30ml / 2 tbsp cocoa powder
15–30ml / 1–2 tbsp hot water

1 Preheat oven to 160°C/325°F/Gas 3. Grease a deep 20 cm/8 in round cake tin, line with non-stick baking paper and grease the paper lightly with a little sunflower oil.

2 Sift the flour, cocoa and baking powder into a large mixing bowl. Add the caster sugar and vanilla essence, then gradually beat in the sunflower oil. Add the water in the same way, beating constantly to produce a smooth mixture with the consistency of a thick batter.

3 Pour the cake mixture into the prepared tin and smooth the surface with the back of a spoon.

4 Bake the cake for about 45 minutes or until a cake tester or fine metal skewer inserted in the centre comes out clean. Remove from the oven but leave in the tin for about 5 minutes, before turning out on to a wire rack. Peel off the lining paper and leave to cool. Cut the cake in half to make two equal layers.

5 Make the chocolate fudge. Place the margarine and water in a pan and heat gently until the margarine has melted. Remove from the heat and add the sifted icing sugar and cocoa powder, beating until shiny, adding more hot water if needed. Pour into a bowl and cool until firm enough to spread and pipe.

6 Place the bottom layer of the cake on a serving plate and spread over two-thirds of the chocolate fudge mixture. Top with the other layer. Fit a piping bag with a star nozzle, fill with the remaining chocolate fudge and pipe stars over the cake. Sprinkle with cocoa powder and decorate with the chopped nuts.

BLACK FOREST GATEAU

4 Prick each layer all over with a skewer or fork, then sprinkle with Kirsch. Using a hand-held electric mixer, whip the cream in a bowl until it starts to thicken, then gradually beat in the icing sugar and vanilla essence until the mixture begins to hold its shape.

5 To assemble, spread one cake layer with a thick layer of flavoured cream and top with about half the cherries. Spread a second cake layer with cream, top with the remaining cherries, then place it on top of the first layer. Top with the final cake layer.

6 Spread the remaining cream all over the cake. Dust a plate with icing sugar, and position the cake carefully in the centre. Press grated chocolate over the sides and decorate the cake with the chocolate curls and fresh or drained cherries.

SERVES 8–10

6 eggs
200g/7oz/scant 1 cup caster sugar
5ml/1 tsp vanilla essence
50g/2oz/½ cup plain flour
50g/2oz/½ cup cocoa powder
115g/4oz/½ cup unsalted butter, melted

FOR THE FILLING AND TOPPING
60ml/4 tbsp Kirsch
600ml/1 pint/2½ cups double cream
30ml/2 tbsp icing sugar
2.5ml/½ tsp vanilla essence
675g/1½lb jar stoned morello cherries,
well drained

TO DECORATE
icing sugar, for dusting
grated chocolate
Chocolate Curls
fresh or drained canned morello cherries

1 Preheat oven to 180°C/350°F/Gas 4. Grease three 19 cm/7½ in sandwich cake tins. Line the bottom of each with non-stick baking paper. Combine the eggs with the sugar and vanilla essence in a bowl and beat with a hand-held electric mixer until pale and very thick.

2 Sift the flour and cocoa powder over the mixture and fold in lightly and evenly with a metal spoon. Gently stir in the melted butter.

3 Divide the mixture among the prepared cake tins, smoothing them level. Bake for 15–18 minutes, until the cakes have risen and are springy to the touch. Leave them to cool in the tins for about 5 minutes, then turn out on to wire racks and leave to cool completely. Remove the lining paper from each cake layer.

WHITE CHOCOLATE CAPPUCCINO GATEAU

SERVES 8

4 eggs
115g/4oz/½ cup caster sugar
15ml/1 tbsp strong black coffee
2.5ml/½ tsp vanilla essence
115g/4oz/1 cup plain flour
75g/3oz white chocolate, coarsely grated

FOR THE FILLING
120ml/4fl oz/½ cup double cream or
whipping cream
15ml/1 tbsp coffee liqueur

FOR THE FROSTING AND TOPPING
15ml/1 tbsp coffee liqueur
1 quantity White Chocolate Frosting
white chocolate curls
cocoa powder or ground cinnamon,
for dusting

1 Preheat oven to 180°C/350°F/Gas 4. Grease two 18 cm/7 in round sandwich cake tins and line the base of each with non-stick baking paper.

2 Combine the eggs, caster sugar, coffee and vanilla essence in a large heatproof bowl. Place over a saucepan of hot water and whisk until pale and thick.

3 Sift half the flour over the mixture; fold in gently and evenly. Fold in the remaining flour with the grated white chocolate.

4 Divide the mixture between the prepared tins and smooth level. Bake for 20–25 minutes, until firm and golden brown, then turn out on wire racks and leave to cool completely.

5 Make the filling. Whip the cream with the coffee liqueur in a bowl until it holds its shape. Spread over one of the cakes, then place the second layer on top.

6 Stir the coffee liqueur into the frosting. Spread over the top and sides of the cake, swirling with a palette knife. Top with curls of white chocolate and dust with cocoa or cinnamon. Transfer the cake to a serving plate and set aside until the frosting has set. Serve the gâteau on the day it was made, if possible.

CHOCOLATE BRANDY SNAP GATEAU

SERVES 8

225g/8oz plain dark chocolate, chopped
225g/8oz/1 cup unsalted butter, softened
200g/7oz/generous 1 cup dark
muscovado sugar
6 eggs, separated
5ml/1 tsp vanilla essence
150g/5oz/1¼ cups ground hazelnuts
60ml/4 tbsp fresh white breadcrumbs
finely grated rind of 1 large orange
1 quantity Chocolate Ganache, for filling
and frosting
icing sugar, for dusting
FOR THE BRANDY SNAPS
50g/2oz/¼ cup unsalted butter
50g/2oz/¼ cup caster sugar
75g/3oz/⅓ cup golden syrup
50g/2oz/½ cup plain flour
5ml/1 tsp brandy

1 Preheat oven to 180°C/350°F/Gas 4.
Grease two 20 cm/8 in sandwich cake
tins and line the base of each with non-
stick baking paper. Melt the chocolate
and set aside to cool slightly.
2 Cream the butter with the sugar in a
mixing bowl until pale and fluffy. Beat in
the egg yolks and vanilla essence. Add the
chocolate and mix thoroughly.
3 In a clean, grease-free bowl, whisk the
egg whites to soft peaks, then fold them
into the chocolate mixture with the
ground hazelnuts, breadcrumbs and
orange rind.
4 Divide the cake mixture between the
prepared tins and smooth the tops. Bake
for 25–30 minutes or until well risen and
firm. Turn out on to wire racks. Leave
the oven on.
5 Make the brandy snaps. Line two baking
sheets with non-stick baking paper. Melt
the butter, sugar and syrup together.
6 Stir the butter mixture until smooth.
Remove from the heat and stir in the
flour and brandy.

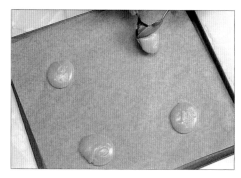

7 Place small spoonfuls of the mixture
well apart on the baking sheets and bake
for 8–10 minutes, until golden. Cool for
a few seconds until firm enough to lift on
to a wire rack.

8 Immediately pinch the edges of each
brandy snap to create a frilled effect. If
the biscuits become too firm, soften them
briefly in the oven.
9 Sandwich the cake layers together with
half the chocolate ganache, transfer to a
plate and spread the remaining ganache
on the top. Arrange the brandy snaps over
the gâteau and dust with icing sugar.

COOK'S TIP
To save time, you could use ready-
made brandy snaps. Simply warm
them for a few minutes in the oven
until they are pliable enough to
shape. Or use as they are, filling
them with cream, and arranging
them so that they fan out from the
centre of the gâteau.

Meringue Gateau with Chocolate Mascarpone

Serves about 10

4 egg whites
pinch of salt
175g/6oz/¾ cup caster sugar
5ml/1 tsp ground cinnamon
75g/3oz plain dark chocolate, grated
icing sugar and rose petals, to decorate

For the Filling

115g/4oz plain chocolate, chopped into
small pieces
5ml/1 tsp vanilla essence or rosewater
115g/4oz/½ cup mascarpone cheese

1 Preheat oven to 150°C/300°F/Gas 2. Line two large baking sheets with non-stick baking paper. Whisk the egg whites with the salt in a clean, grease-free bowl until they form stiff peaks.

2 Gradually whisk in half the sugar, then add the rest and whisk until the meringue is very stiff and glossy. Add the cinnamon and chocolate and whisk lightly to mix.

3 Draw a 20 cm/8 in circle on the lining paper on one of the baking sheets, replace it upside down and spread the marked circle evenly with about half the meringue. Spoon the remaining meringue in 28–30 small neat heaps on both baking sheets. Bake for 1½ hours, until crisp.

4 Make the filling. Melt the chocolate in a heatproof bowl over hot water. Cool slightly, then add the vanilla essence or rosewater and cheese. Cool the mixture until it holds it shape.

5 Spoon the chocolate mixture into a large piping bag and sandwich the meringues together in pairs, reserving a small amount of filling for assembling the gâteau.

6 Arrange the filled meringues on a serving platter, piling them up in a pyramid. Keep them in position with a few well-placed dabs of the reserved filling. Dust the pyramid with icing sugar, sprinkle with the rose petals and serve at once, while the meringues are crisp.

CARIBBEAN CHOCOLATE RING WITH RUM SYRUP

SERVES 8–10

115g/4oz/½ cup unsalted butter

115g/4oz/¾ cup light muscovado sugar

2 eggs, beaten

2 ripe bananas, mashed

30ml/2 tbsp desiccated coconut

30ml/2 tbsp soured cream

115g/4oz/1 cup self-raising flour

45ml/3 tbsp cocoa powder

2.5ml/½ tsp bicarbonate of soda

FOR THE SYRUP

115g/4oz/½ cup caster sugar

30ml/2 tbsp dark rum

50g/2oz plain dark chocolate, chopped

TO DECORATE

mixture of tropical fruits, such as mango, pawpaw, starfruit and cape gooseberries

chocolate shapes or curls

1 Preheat oven to 180°C/350°F/Gas 4. Grease a 1.5 litre/2½ pint/6¼ cup ring tin with butter.

2 Cream the butter and sugar in a bowl until light and fluffy. Add the eggs gradually, beating well, then mix in the bananas, coconut and soured cream.

3 Sift the flour, cocoa and bicarbonate of soda over the mixture and fold in thoroughly and evenly.

4 Tip into the prepared tin and spread evenly. Bake for 45–50 minutes, until firm to the touch. Cool for 10 minutes in the tin, then turn out to finish cooling on a wire rack.

5 For the syrup, place the sugar in a small pan. Add 60ml/4 tbsp water and heat gently, stirring occasionally until dissolved. Bring to the boil and boil rapidly, without stirring, for 2 minutes. Remove from the heat.

6 Add the rum and chocolate to the syrup and stir until the mixture is melted and smooth, then spoon evenly over the top and sides of the cake.

7 Decorate the ring with tropical fruits and chocolate shapes or curls.

SPECIAL OCCASION AND NOVELTY CAKES

STRAWBERRY CHOCOLATE VALENTINE GATEAU

SERVES 8

175g/6oz/1½ cups self-raising flour
10ml/2 tsp baking powder
75ml/5 tbsp cocoa powder
115g/4oz/½ cup caster sugar
2 eggs, beaten
15ml/1 tbsp black treacle
150ml/¼ pint/⅔ cup sunflower oil
150ml/¼ pint/⅔ cup milk

FOR THE FILLING

45ml/3 tbsp strawberry jam
150ml/¼ pint/⅔ cup double cream or
whipping cream
115g/4oz strawberries, sliced

TO DECORATE

1 quantity Chocolate Fondant
chocolate hearts
icing sugar, for dusting

1 Preheat oven to 160°C/325°F/Gas 3. Grease a deep 20 cm/8 in heart-shaped cake tin and line the base with non-stick baking paper. Sift the self-raising flour, baking powder and cocoa powder into a large mixing bowl. Stir in the sugar, then make a well in the centre of the dry ingredients.

2 Add the eggs, treacle, oil and milk to the well. Mix with a spoon to incorporate the dry ingredients, then beat with a hand-held electric mixer until the mixture is smooth and creamy.

3 Spoon the mixture into the prepared cake tin and spread evenly. Bake for about 45 minutes, until well risen and firm to the touch. Cool in the tin for a few minutes, then turn out on to a wire rack to cool completely.

4 Using a sharp knife, slice the cake neatly into two layers. Place the bottom layer on a board or plate. Spread with the strawberry jam.

5 Whip the cream in a bowl. Stir in the strawberries, then spread over the jam. Top with the remaining cake layer.
6 Roll out the chocolate fondant and cover the cake. Decorate with chocolate hearts and dust with icing sugar.

COOK'S TIP

If you do not have a heart-shaped cake tin, consider hiring one from a kitchen shop. All sorts of sizes are available, often for a modest fee.

DOUBLE HEART ENGAGEMENT CAKE

SERVES 20

*double quantity One-Mix Chocolate
Sponge mixture
double quantity Chocolate Buttercream
icing sugar, for sifting
chocolate curls and fresh raspberries,
to decorate*

VARIATIONS

Use plain buttercream, tinted to a
delicate shade of rose. Decorate with
strawberries, half-dipped in melted
chocolate.

Cover the cakes with Chocolate
Ganache and drizzle melted
chocolate over the top. Arrange
chocolate-dipped fruit on top.

Cover both the cakes with Chocolate
Fondant and top with pale apricot or
cream sugar roses and chocolate
leaves. Trim each cake with a narrow
apricot or cream ribbon.

1 Preheat oven to 160°C/325°F/Gas 3.
Grease and base-line with greaseproof
paper two 20 cm/8 in heart-shaped cake
tins. Divide the one-mix chocolate
sponge cake mixture evenly between the
tins and smooth the surfaces. Bake for 30
minutes. Turn on to a wire rack, peel off
the lining paper and leave to cool.

2 Cut each cake in half horizontally. Use
about one-third of the buttercream to fill
both cakes, then sandwich them together
to make two. Cover the tops of the cakes
with buttercream.

3 Arrange on a cake board. Use the
remaining icing to coat the sides of the
cakes. Make sure it is thickly covered.

4 Generously cover the tops and sides
of both the cakes with the chocolate
curls, beginning from the top of the heart
and arranging them as shown, and
pressing them gently into the
buttercream as you go.

5 Dust a little icing sugar over the top of
each cake and decorate with raspberries.
Chill until ready to serve.

WHITE CHOCOLATE CELEBRATION CAKE

SERVES 40–50

900g / 2lb / 8 cups plain flour
2.5ml / ½ tsp salt
20ml / 4 tsp bicarbonate of soda
450g / 1lb white chocolate, chopped
475ml / 16fl oz / 2 cups whipping cream
450g / 1lb / 2 cups unsalted butter, softened
900g / 2lb / 4 cups caster sugar
12 eggs
20ml / 4 tsp lemon essence
grated rind of 2 lemons
335ml / 11fl oz / 1⅓ cups buttermilk
lemon curd, for filling
chocolate leaves, to decorate

FOR THE LEMON SYRUP
200g / 7oz / scant 1 cup granulated sugar
250ml / 8fl oz / 1 cup water
60ml / 4 tbsp lemon juice

FOR THE BUTTERCREAM
675g / 1½lb white chocolate chopped
1kg / 2¼lb cream cheese, softened
500g / 1¼lb / 2½ cups unsalted butter, at room temperature
60ml / 4 tbsp lemon juice
5ml / 1 tsp lemon essence

1 Divide all the ingredients into two equal batches, so that the quantities are more manageable. Use each batch to make one cake. Preheat oven to 180°C/350°F/Gas 4. Grease a 30 cm/ 12 in round cake tin. Base-line with non-stick baking paper. Sift the flour, salt and bicarbonate of soda into a bowl and set aside. Melt the chocolate and cream in a saucepan over a medium heat, stirring until smooth. Set aside to cool to room temperature.

VARIATION

For a summer celebration, decorate the cake with raspberries and white chocolate petals. To make the petals, you will need about 20 x 7.5 cm/3 in foil squares. Spread melted white chocolate thinly over each piece of foil, so that it resembles a rose petal. Before the chocolate sets, bend the foil up to emphasize the petal shape. When set, peel away the foil.

2 Beat the butter until creamy, then add the sugar and beat for 2–3 minutes. Beat in the eggs, then slowly beat in the melted chocolate, lemon essence and rind. Gradually add the flour mixture, alternately with the buttermilk, to make a smooth pouring mixture. Pour into the tin and bake for 1 hour or until a skewer inserted in the cake comes out clean.

3 Cool in the tin for 10 minutes, then invert the cake on a wire rack and cool completely. Wrap in clear film until ready to assemble. Using the second batch of ingredients, make another cake in the same way.

4 Make the lemon syrup. In a small saucepan, combine the sugar and water. Over a medium heat, bring to the boil, stirring until the sugar dissolves. Remove from the heat, stir in the lemon juice and cool completely. Store in an airtight container until required.

5 Make the buttercream. Melt the chocolate. Cool slightly. Beat the cream cheese in a bowl until smooth. Gradually beat in the cooled white chocolate, then the butter, lemon juice and essence. Chill.

6 Split each cake in half. Spoon syrup over each layer, let it soak in, then repeat. Spread the bottom half of each cake with lemon curd and replace the tops.

7 Gently beat the buttercream in a bowl until creamy. Spread a quarter over the top of one of the filled cakes. Place the second filled cake on top. Spread a small amount of softened butter over the top and sides of the cake to create a smooth, crumb-free surface. Chill for 15 minutes, so that the buttercream sets a little.

8 Place the cake on a serving plate. Set aside a quarter of the remaining buttercream for piping, then spread the rest evenly over the top and sides of the filled cake.

9 Spoon the reserved buttercream into a large icing bag fitted with a small star tip. Pipe a shell pattern around the rim of the cake. Decorate with chocolate leaves, made with dark or white chocolate (or a mixture) and fresh flowers.

Chocolate Box with Caramel Mousse and Berries

Serves 8–10

275g/10oz plain chocolate, chopped into small pieces

For the Caramel Mousse

4 x 50g/2oz chocolate-coated caramel bars, coarsely chopped
25ml/1½ tbsp milk or water
350ml/12fl oz/1½ cups double cream
1 egg white

For the Caramel Shards

115g/4oz/½ cup granulated sugar
60ml/4 tbsp water

For the Topping

115g/4oz fine quality white chocolate, chopped into small pieces
350ml/12fl oz/1½ cups double cream
450g/1lb mixed berries or cut up fruits such as raspberries, strawberries, blackberries or sliced nectarine and orange segments

<u>1</u> Prepare the chocolate box. Turn a 23 cm/9 in square baking tin bottom-side up. Mould a piece of foil around the tin, then turn it right side up and line it with the foil, pressing against the edges to make the foil as smooth as possible.

<u>2</u> Place the plain chocolate in a heatproof bowl over a saucepan of simmering water. Stir until the chocolate has melted and is smooth. Immediately pour the melted chocolate into the lined tin. Tilt to coat the bottom and sides evenly, keeping the top edges of the sides as straight as possible. As the chocolate coats the sides, tilt the pan again to coat the corners and sides once more. Chill until firm.

<u>3</u> Place the caramel bars and milk or water in a heatproof bowl. Place over a pan of simmering water and stir until melted. Remove the bowl from the heat and cool for 10 minutes, stirring occasionally.

<u>4</u> Using a hand-held electric mixer, whip the cream in a bowl until soft peaks form. Stir a spoonful of the whipped cream into the caramel mixture to lighten it, then fold in the remaining cream. In another bowl beat the egg white until just stiff. Fold the egg white into the mousse mixture. Pour into the box. Chill for several hours or overnight, until set.

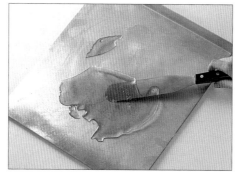

<u>5</u> Meanwhile, make the caramel shards. Lightly oil a baking sheet. In a small pan over a low heat, dissolve the sugar in the water, swirling the pan gently. Increase the heat and boil the mixture for 4–5 minutes, until the sugar begins to turn a pale golden colour. Protecting your hand with an oven glove, immediately pour the mixture on to the oiled sheet. Tilt the sheet to distribute the caramel in an even layer. (*Do not touch – caramel is dangerously hot.*) Cool completely, then using a metal palette knife, lift the caramel off the baking sheet and break into pieces.

<u>6</u> Make the topping. Combine the white chocolate and 120ml/4fl oz/½ cup of the cream in a small pan and melt over a low heat until smooth, stirring frequently. Strain into a medium bowl and cool to room temperature, stirring occasionally. In another bowl, beat the remaining cream with a hand-held electric mixer, until firm peaks form. Stir a spoonful of cream into the white chocolate mixture, then gently fold in the remaining whipped cream.

<u>7</u> Using the foil as a guide, remove the mousse-filled box from the tin and peel the foil carefully from the sides, then the bottom. Slide the box gently on to a serving plate.

<u>8</u> Spoon the chocolate-cream mixture into a piping bag fitted with a medium star tip. Pipe a decorative design of rosettes or shells over the surface of the set mousse. Decorate the cream-topped box with the mixed berries or cut up fruits and the caramel shards.

PUPPIES IN LOVE

SERVES 8–10

1 chocolate Swiss roll
115g/4oz yellow marzipan
60ml/4 tbsp Chocolate Buttercream
115g/4oz/1⅓ cups desiccated coconut
green, brown, pink and red food colourings
450g/1lb bought sugarpaste
icing sugar, for dusting
60ml/4 tbsp apricot jam, warmed and sieved

1 Cut the Swiss roll in half. Each half will form the body of one of the puppies. To make the faces, cut the marzipan in half and roll each portion into a ball, then into a squat cone shape. Use the buttercream to stick the faces on to the bodies.

2 Place the desiccated coconut in a bowl. Add a few drops of green food colouring and a few drops of water and stir until the coconut is flecked with green and white. Scatter it over a cake board, then position the two puppy shapes on the board.

3 Cut off about 25g/1oz of the sugarpaste and set aside, wrapped in clear film. Colour half the remaining icing brown and half pink. Cut off about 50g/2oz from each colour, wrap in clear film and set aside.

4 Lightly dust the work surface with icing sugar and roll out the larger portions of brown and pink paste into rectangles large enough to wrap each piece of Swiss roll. Cut each portion of paste in half widthways and trim the edges. Cover all four sections with clear film and set aside.

5 Roll out the reserved pieces of brown and white paste, then use a small round cutter to stamp out several circles. Gather up the paste trimmings and set aside, wrapped in clear film. Stick the white circles on to one of the brown rectangles, then the brown circles on to one of the pink rectangles, using a little water. Use a rolling pin to press them in slightly.

6 Use a sharp knife to slash all four paste rectangles along the two short edges. Brush each half of Swiss roll with jam, then lay the brown paste without spots over one body, and the pink paste without spots over the other. Place a little water on the back of each, then put the brown spotty paste over the brown dog and the pink spotty paste over the pink dog.

7 Roll half of the reserved trimmings, pink and brown, in your hands to make the tails. Stick them in place with a little jam. Make a fringe from the brown icing for the brown puppy, and tie a few strands of pink icing together with ribbon to make a fringe for the pink puppy. Stick them in place with a dab of water.

8 Use the remaining pieces of sugarpaste to shape eyes, a nose and a mouth for each puppy. Stick them on to the faces.

PORCUPINE

SERVES 15

1 quantity One-mix Chocolate Sponge Cake
1½ quantity Chocolate Buttercream
5–6 chocolate flake bars
60g/2oz white marzipan
cream, black, green, red, brown food
colourings
9 cocktail sticks

1 Preheat the oven to 180°C/350°F/ Gas 4. Grease and line the bottoms of a 900ml/1½ pint/3¾ cup and a 600ml/ 1 pint/2½ cup pudding basin (deep bowl). Spoon the cake mixture into both basins (bowls) to two-thirds full. Bake in a preheated oven allowing 55 mins–1 hour for the larger basin (bowl) and 35–40 mins for the smaller basin (bowl). Turn out and allow to cool on a wire rack.

2 When they are completely cool, place both cakes on a surface so the widest ends are underneath. Take the smaller cake and, holding a sharp knife at an angle, slice off a piece from one side, cutting down towards the middle of the cake. Then make a corresponding cut on the other side to make a pointed nose shape at one end.

3 Place the larger cake on the cake board behind the smaller one. Cut one of the cut-off slices in half and position either side, between the larger and smaller cake, to fill in the side gaps. Place the other cut-off piece on top to fill in the top gap, securing all with a little buttercream.

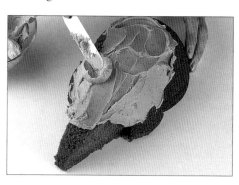

4 Spread the remaining buttercream over the cake. On the pointed face part, make markings with a cocktail stick.

5 Break or cut the flake bars into thin strips and stick at an angle into the buttercream over the body of the porcupine to represent spikes.

6 Reserve a small portion of marzipan. Divide the remainder into three and colour one portion black, one green and one cream. Colour a tiny portion of the reserved, white marzipan brown for the apple stems.

7 With the cream coloured marzipan, shape the ears and feet, using black and white make the eyes, and with the rest of the black shape the nose and the claws for the feet. With the green marzipan make the apples, painting on red markings with a fine paintbrush. Position the stems. Place everything except the apples in its proper place on the porcupine cake. Finally, place the apples on the board by the front of the porcupine.

APPLE TREE

SERVES 10–12

1 chocolate Swiss Roll
225g/8oz/1 cup Buttercream, tinted with
pale green food colouring
½ quantity Chocolate Buttercream
One-mix Chocolate Sponge Cake, baked in a
450g/1lb fluted round cake tin
225g/8oz marzipan
red and green food colouring
florist's tape and florist's wire, for the apples
green-coloured desiccated coconut (see Puppies
in Love, step 2)
tiny fresh flowers, to decorate (optional)

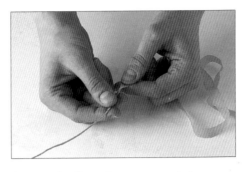

3 Twist the florist's tape around the florist's wire, then cut it into 7.5 cm/3 in lengths. Press the lengths of wire through most of the apples, bending the ends so the apples cannot fall off when hanging. Press the hanging apples into the tree, reserving the remaining apples.

4 Fill a piping bag with the remaining green buttercream. Pipe leaves all over the tree top. Scatter the green coconut around the base of the tree and pipe a few extra leaves. Add a few tiny fresh flowers for effect, if liked. Remove the wires from the cake before serving.

1 Stand the Swiss roll upright on a cake board, trimming it, if necessary. Anchor it on the board with a dab of the buttercream. Spread with chocolate buttercream, swirling the icing. Using about three-quarters of the green buttercream, thickly cover the round sponge cake. Draw the icing into peaks and swirls. Position the cake on top of the trunk to make the top of the tree.

2 Colour about 25g/1oz of the marzipan green. Colour the remainder red, then roll it into cherry-size apples. Roll the green marzipan into tiny sausage shapes and shape the stalks and leaves. Use a cocktail stick to make tiny holes in the tops of the apples, then insert a stalk and leaf into each.

HOT DESSERTS

CHOCOLATE CINNAMON CAKE WITH BANANA SAUCE

6 Fold a dollop of whites into the chocolate mixture to lighten it. Fold in the remaining whites in three batches, alternating with the sifted flour mixture.

7 Pour the mixture into the prepared tin. Bake for 40-50 minutes or until a skewer inserted in the centre comes out clean. Turn the cake out on to a wire rack. Preheat the grill.

8 Make the sauce. Slice the bananas into a shallow, flameproof dish. Stir in the brown sugar and lemon juice. Place under the grill for 8 minutes, stirring occasionally, until caramelized.

9 Mash the banana mixture until almost smooth. Tip into a bowl and stir in the cream and rum, if using. Slice the cake and serve with the sauce.

SERVES 6

25g/1oz plain chocolate, chopped into small pieces
115g/4oz/½ cup unsalted butter, at room temperature
15ml/1 tbsp instant coffee powder
5 eggs, separated
225g/8oz/1 cup granulated sugar
115g/4oz/1 cup plain flour
10ml/2 tsp ground cinnamon

FOR THE SAUCE

4 ripe bananas
45ml/3 tbsp soft light brown sugar
15ml/8oz/1 tbsp fresh lemon juice
175ml/6fl oz/¾ cup whipping cream
15ml/1 tbsp rum (optional)

1 Preheat oven to 180°C/350°F/Gas 4. Grease a 20 cm/8 in round cake tin.

2 Combine the chocolate and butter in the top of a double boiler or in a heatproof bowl set over a saucepan of simmering water. Stir until melted. Remove from the heat and stir in the coffee. Set aside.

3 Beat the egg yolks with the granulated sugar until thick and lemon-coloured. Add the chocolate mixture and beat on low speed until just blended.

4 Stir the flour and cinnamon together in a bowl.

5 In another bowl, beat the egg whites until they hold stiff peaks.

RICH CHOCOLATE AND COFFEE PUDDING

SERVES 6

75g/3oz/¾ cup plain flour
10ml/2 tsp baking powder
pinch of salt
50g/2oz/¼ cup butter or margarine
25g/1oz plain chocolate, chopped into
small pieces
115g/4oz/½ cup caster sugar
75ml/3fl oz/5 tbsp milk
1.5ml/¼ tsp vanilla essence
whipped cream, for serving

FOR THE TOPPING

30ml/2 tbsp instant coffee powder
325ml/11fl oz/generous ½ pint hot water
90g/3½oz/7 tbsp soft dark brown sugar
65g/2½oz/5 tbsp caster sugar
30ml/2 tbsp unsweetened cocoa powder

1 Preheat oven to 180°C/350°F/Gas 4. Grease a 23 cm/9 in square non-stick baking tin.

2 Sift the flour, baking powder and salt into a small bowl. Set aside.

3 Melt the butter or margarine, chocolate and caster sugar in a heatproof bowl set over a saucepan of simmering water, or in a double boiler, stirring occasionally. Remove the bowl from the heat.

4 Add the flour mixture and stir well. Stir in the milk and vanilla essence. Mix with a wooden spoon, then pour the mixture into the prepared baking tin.

5 Make the topping. Dissolve the coffee in the water in a bowl. Allow to cool.

6 Mix the brown sugar, caster sugar and cocoa powder in a bowl. Sprinkle the mixture over the pudding mixture.

7 Pour the coffee evenly over the surface. Bake for 40 minutes or until the pudding is risen and set on top. The coffee mixture will have formed a delicious creamy sauce underneath. Serve immediately with whipped cream.

Hot Chocolate Cake

Makes 10–12 slices

*200g/7oz/1¾ cups self-raising wholemeal
flour
25g/1oz/¼ cup cocoa powder
pinch of salt
175g/6oz/¾ cup soft margarine
175g/6oz/1 cup soft light brown sugar
few drops of vanilla essence
4 eggs
75g/3oz white chocolate, roughly chopped
chocolate leaves and curls, to decorate*

For the White Chocolate Sauce

*75g/3oz white chocolate chopped into
small pieces
150ml/¼ pint/⅔ cup single cream
30–45ml/2–3 tbsp milk*

1 Preheat oven to 160°C/325°F/Gas 3. Sift the flour, cocoa and salt into a bowl, then tip in the bran remaining in the sieve. Cream the margarine, sugar and vanilla essence until fluffy, then gently beat in 1 egg.

2 Gradually stir in the remaining eggs, one at a time, alternately with the flour mixture, to make a smooth mixture.

3 Stir in the white chocolate and spoon into a 675–900g/1½–2lb loaf tin or a 18 cm/7 in greased cake tin. Bake for 30–40 minutes or until just firm to the touch and shrinking away from the sides of the tin.

4 To make the sauce, heat the chocolate and cream very gently in a pan until the chocolate is melted. Add the milk and stir until cool. Spoon a little sauce on to each plate and add a slice of cake. Decorate with chocolate leaves and curls. Do this just before you are ready to serve.

STEAMED CHOCOLATE AND FRUIT PUDDINGS WITH CHOCOLATE SYRUP

SERVES 4

115g/4oz/⅔ cup dark muscovado sugar
1 eating apple
75g/3oz/¾ cup cranberries, thawed if frozen
115g/4oz/½ cup soft margarine
2 eggs
115g/4oz/½ cup self-raising flour
45ml/3 tbsp cocoa powder

FOR THE CHOCOLATE SYRUP

115g/4oz plain chocolate, chopped
30ml/2 tbsp clear honey
15ml/½oz/1 tbsp unsalted butter
2.5ml/½ tsp vanilla essence

1 Prepare a steamer or half fill a saucepan with water and bring it to the boil. Grease four individual pudding basins and sprinkle each one with a little of the muscovado sugar to coat well all over.

2 Peel and core the apple. Dice it into a bowl, add the cranberries and mix well. Divide the fruit among the prepared pudding basins.

3 Place the remaining muscovado sugar in a mixing bowl. Add the margarine, eggs, flour and cocoa. Beat until combined and smooth.

4 Spoon the mixture into the basins and cover each with a double thickness of foil. Steam for about 45 minutes, topping up the boiling water as required, until the puddings are well risen and firm.

5 Make the syrup. Mix the chocolate, honey, butter and vanilla essence in a small saucepan. Heat gently, stirring until melted and smooth.

6 Run a knife around the edge of each pudding to loosen it, then turn out on to individual plates. Serve at once, with the chocolate syrup.

CHOCOLATE, DATE AND WALNUT PUDDING

SERVES 4

25g / 1oz / ¼ cup chopped walnuts
25g / 1oz / 2 tbsp chopped dates
2 eggs
5ml / 1 tsp vanilla essence
30ml / 2 tbsp golden caster sugar
45ml / 3 tbsp plain wholemeal flour
15ml / 1 tbsp cocoa powder
30ml / 2 tbsp skimmed milk

1 Preheat oven to 180°C/350°F/Gas 4. Grease and base-line with greaseproof paper a 1.2 litre/2 pint/5 cup pudding basin. Spoon in the walnuts and dates.
2 Combine the egg yolks, vanilla essence and sugar in a heatproof bowl. Place over a pan of hot water.

3 Whisk the egg whites to soft peaks. Whisk the egg yolk mixture until it is thick and pale, then remove the bowl from the heat. Sift the flour and cocoa over the mixture and fold them in with a metal spoon. Stir in the milk, to soften the mixture, then fold in the egg whites.

4 Spoon the mixture over the walnuts and dates in the basin and bake for 40–45 minutes or until the pudding is well risen and firm to the touch. Run a knife around the pudding to loosen it from the basin, and then turn it out on to a plate and serve immediately.

MAGIC CHOCOLATE MUD PUDDING

SERVES 4

50g/2oz/4 tbsp butter, plus extra for greasing
90g/3½oz/scant 1 cup self-raising flour
5ml/1 tsp ground cinnamon
75ml/5 tbsp cocoa powder
200g/7oz/generous 1 cup light muscovado or
demerara sugar
475ml/16fl oz/2 cups milk
crème fraîche, Greek-style yogurt or vanilla
ice cream, to serve

1 Preheat oven to 180°C/350°F/Gas 4. Prepare the dish: use the extra butter to grease a 1.5 litre/2½ pint/6¼ cup ovenproof dish. Place the dish on a baking sheet and set aside.

2 Sift the flour and ground cinnamon into a bowl. Sift in 15ml/1 tbsp of the cocoa and mix well.

3 Place the butter in a saucepan. Add 115g/4oz/½ cup of the sugar and 150ml/¼ pint/⅔ cup of the milk. Heat gently without boiling, stirring from time to time, until the butter has melted and all the sugar has dissolved. Remove the pan from the heat.

4 Stir in the flour mixture, mixing evenly. Pour the mixture into the prepared dish and level the surface.

5 Mix the remaining sugar and cocoa in a bowl, then sprinkle over the pudding mixture.

6 Pour the remaining milk evenly over the pudding.

7 Bake for 45–50 minutes or until the sponge has risen to the top and is firm to the touch. Serve hot, with the crème fraîche, yogurt or ice cream.

Chocolate Chip and Banana Pudding

Serves 4

200g / 7oz / 1¾ cups self-raising flour
75g / 3oz / 6 tbsp unsalted butter or margarine
2 ripe bananas
75g / 3oz / 6 tbsp caster sugar
60ml / 4 tbsp milk
1 egg, beaten
60ml / 4 tbsp plain chocolate chips or chopped chocolate
Glossy Chocolate Sauce, to serve

1 Prepare a steamer or half fill a saucepan with water and bring it to the boil. Grease a 1 litre / 1¾ pint / 4 cup pudding basin. Sift the flour into a bowl and rub in the unsalted butter or margarine until the mixture resembles coarse breadcrumbs.

2 Mash the bananas in a bowl. Stir them into the flour and butter mixture, then add the caster sugar and mix well.
3 Whisk the milk with the egg in a jug or small bowl, then beat into the pudding mixture. Stir in the chocolate chips or chopped chocolate.

4 Spoon the mixture into the prepared basin, cover closely with a double thickness of foil, and steam for 2 hours, topping up the water as required.
5 Run a knife around the top of the pudding to loosen it, then turn it out on to a serving dish. Serve hot, with the sauce.

DARK CHOCOLATE RAVIOLI WITH WHITE CHOCOLATE AND CREAM CHEESE FILLING

SERVES 4

175g/6oz/1½ cups plain flour
25g/1oz/¼ cup cocoa powder
salt
30ml/2 tbsp icing sugar
2 large eggs, beaten
15ml/1tbsp olive oil
single cream and grated chocolate, to serve

FOR THE FILLING
175g/6oz white chocolate, chopped
350g/12oz/3 cups cream cheese
1 egg, plus 1 beaten egg to seal

1 Make the pasta. Sift the flour with the cocoa, salt and icing sugar on to a work surface. Make a well in the centre and pour the eggs and oil in. Mix together with your fingers. Knead until smooth. Alternatively, make the dough in a food processor, then knead by hand. Cover and rest for at least 30 minutes.

2 To make the filling, melt the white chocolate in a heatproof bowl placed over a pan of simmering water. Cool slightly. Beat the cream cheese in a bowl, then beat in the chocolate and eggs. Spoon into a piping bag fitted with a plain nozzle.

3 Cut the dough in half and wrap one portion in clear film. Roll the pasta out thinly to a rectangle on a lightly floured surface, or use a pasta machine. Cover with a clean damp dish towel and repeat with the remaining pasta.

4 Pipe small mounds (about 5ml/1 tsp) of filling in even rows, spacing them at 4 cm/1½ in intervals across one piece of the dough. Using a pastry brush, brush the spaces of dough between the mounds with beaten egg.

5 Using a rolling pin, lift the remaining sheet of pasta over the dough with the filling. Press down firmly between the pockets of filling, pushing out any trapped air. Cut the filled chocolate pasta into rounds with a serrated ravioli cutter or sharp knife. Transfer to a floured dish towel. Leave for 1 hour to dry out, ready for cooking.

6 Bring a frying pan of water to the boil and add the ravioli a few at a time, stirring to prevent them sticking together. (Adding a few drops of a bland oil to the water will help, too.) Simmer gently for 3–5 minutes, remove with a perforated spoon and serve with a generous splash of single cream and grated chocolate.

Hot Mocha Rum Souffles

Serves 6

25g/1oz/2 tbsp unsalted butter, melted
65g/2½ oz/generous ½ cup cocoa powder
75g/3oz/6 tbsp caster sugar
60ml/4 tbsp strong black coffee
30ml/2 tbsp dark rum
6 egg whites
icing sugar, for dusting

1 Preheat oven to 190°C/375°F/Gas 5. Grease six 250ml/ 8fl oz/1 cup soufflé dishes with melted butter.

2 Mix 15ml/1 tbsp of the cocoa powder with 15ml/1 tbsp of the caster sugar in a bowl. Tip the mixture into each of the dishes in turn, rotating them so that they are evenly coated.

3 Mix the remaining cocoa powder with the coffee and rum in a medium bowl.

4 Whisk the egg whites in a clean, grease-free bowl until they form firm peaks. Whisk in the remaining caster sugar. Stir a generous spoonful of the whites into the cocoa mixture to lighten it, then fold in the remaining whites.

5 Spoon the mixture into the prepared dishes, smoothing the tops. Place on the hot baking sheet, and bake for 12–15 minutes or until well risen. Serve immediately, dusted with icing sugar.

Easy Chocolate and Orange Souffles

Serves 4

600ml/1 pint/2½ cups milk
50g/2oz/generous ¼ cup semolina
50g/2oz/⅓ cup soft light brown sugar
grated rind of 1 orange
90ml/6 tbsp fresh orange juice
3 eggs, separated
65g/2½ oz plain chocolate, grated
icing sugar, for sprinkling
single cream, to serve

1 Preheat oven to 200°C/400°F/Gas 6. Butter a shallow 1.75 litre/3 pint/7½ cup ovenproof dish. Place a baking sheet in the oven to heat up.

2 Pour the milk into a heavy-based saucepan, sprinkle over the semolina and brown sugar, then heat, stirring the mixture all the time, until boiling and thickened. Remove the pan from the heat. Cool slightly, then beat in the orange rind and juice, egg yolks and all but 15ml/1 tbsp of the grated chocolate.

3 In a clean, grease-free bowl, whisk the egg whites until stiff but not dry, then lightly fold into the semolina mixture in three batches. Spoon the mixture into the dish. Place the dish on the baking sheet and bake for about 30 minutes, until just set in the centre and risen. Sprinkle the top with the reserved chocolate and dust with the icing sugar. Serve with cream.

CHOCOLATE AMARETTI PEACHES

SERVES 4

115g/4oz amaretti biscuits, crushed
50g/2oz plain chocolate, chopped
grated rind of ½ orange
15ml/1 tbsp clear honey
1.5ml/¼ tsp ground cinnamon
1 egg white, lightly beaten
4 firm ripe peaches
150ml/¼ pint/⅔ cup white wine
15ml/1 tbsp caster sugar
whipped cream, to serve

1 Preheat oven to 190°C/375°F/Gas 5. Mix together the crushed amaretti biscuits, chocolate, orange rind, honey and cinnamon in a bowl. Add the beaten egg white and mix to bind the mixture.

2 Halve and stone the peaches and fill the cavities with the chocolate mixture, mounding it up slightly.

3 Arrange the stuffed peaches in a lightly buttered, shallow ovenproof dish, which will just hold the peaches comfortably. Mix the wine and sugar in a jug.

4 Pour the wine mixture around the peaches. Bake for 30–40 minutes, until the peaches are tender when tested with a slim metal skewer and the filling is golden. Serve at once with a little of the cooking juices spooned over. Offer the whipped cream separately.

PEACHY CHOCOLATE BAKE

SERVES 6

*200g/7oz plain dark chocolate, chopped into
small pieces
115g/4oz/½ cup unsalted butter
4 eggs, separated
115g/4oz/½ cup caster sugar
425g/15oz can peach slices, drained
whipped cream or Greek-style yogurt,
to serve*

1 Preheat oven to 160°C/325°F/Gas 3.
Butter a wide ovenproof dish. Melt the
chocolate with the butter in a heatproof
bowl over barely simmering water.
Remove from the heat.

2 Whisk the egg yolks with the sugar
until thick and pale. In a clean, grease-
free bowl, whisk the whites until stiff.

3 Beat the chocolate into the egg yolk
mixture. Fold in the whites lightly.

4 Fold the peach slices into the mixture,
then tip into the prepared dish. Bake for
35–40 minutes or until risen and just
firm. Serve hot, with cream or Greek-
style yogurt if liked.

PUFFY PEARS

SERVES 4

225g/8oz puff pastry, thawed if frozen
2 pears, peeled
2 squares plain chocolate, roughly chopped
15ml/1 tbsp lemon juice
1 egg, beaten
15ml/1 tbsp caster sugar

1 Roll the pastry into a 25 cm/10 in square on a lightly floured surface. Trim the edges, then cut it into four equal smaller squares. Cover with clear film and set aside.
2 Remove the core from each pear half and pack the gap with the chopped chocolate. Place a pear half, cut-side down, on each piece of pastry and brush them with the lemon juice, to prevent them from going brown.
3 Preheat oven to 190°C/375°F/Gas 5. Cut the pastry into a pear shape, by following the lines of the fruit, leaving a 2.5 cm/1 in border. Use the trimmings to make leaves and brush the pastry border with the beaten egg.
4 Arrange the pastry and pears on a baking sheet. Make deep cuts in the pears, taking care not to cut right through the fruit, and sprinkle them with the sugar. Cook for 20–25 minutes, until lightly browned. Serve hot or cold.

VARIATION

Use apples instead of pears, if preferred. Cut the pastry into 10 cm/4 in rounds. Slice 2 peeled and cored eating apples. Toss with a little lemon juice, drain and arrange on the pastry. Dot with 25g/1oz/2 tbsp butter and chopped milk chocolate. Bake as for Puffy Pears. While still hot, brush the apple slices with warmed redcurrant jelly.

PEARS IN CHOCOLATE FUDGE BLANKETS

SERVES 6

6 ripe eating pears
30ml/2 tbsp lemon juice
75g/3oz/6 tbsp caster sugar
300ml/½ pint/1¼ cups water
1 cinnamon stick
FOR THE SAUCE
200ml/7fl oz/scant 1 cup double cream
150g/5oz/scant 1 cup light muscovado sugar
25g/1oz/2tbsp unsalted butter
25g/1oz/2 tbsp golden syrup
120ml/4fl oz/½ cup milk
200g/7oz plain dark chocolate, broken into squares

1 Peel the pears thinly, leaving the stalks on. Scoop out the cores from the base. Brush the cut surfaces with lemon juice to prevent them from browning.
2 Place the sugar and water in a large saucepan. Heat gently until the sugar dissolves. Add the pears and cinnamon stick with any remaining lemon juice, and, if necessary, a little more water, so that the pears are almost covered.
3 Bring to the boil, then lower the heat, cover the pan and simmer the pears gently for 15–20 minutes or until they are just tender when pierced with a slim skewer.
4 Meanwhile, make the sauce. Place the cream, sugar, butter, golden syrup and milk in a heavy-based saucepan. Heat gently until the sugar has dissolved and the butter and syrup have melted, then bring to the boil. Boil, stirring constantly, for about 5 minutes or until the sauce is thick. Remove from the heat and stir in the chocolate, a few squares at a time, until melted.
5 Using a slotted spoon, transfer the poached pears to a dish. Keep hot. Boil the syrup rapidly to reduce to about 45–60ml/3–4 tbsp. Remove the cinnamon stick and stir the syrup into the chocolate sauce. Serve poured over the pears in individual bowls.

PRUNE BEIGNETS IN CHOCOLATE ARMAGNAC SAUCE

SERVES 4

75g/3oz/¾ cup plain flour
45ml/3 tbsp ground almonds
45ml/3 tbsp oil or melted butter
1 egg white
60ml/4 tbsp water
oil, for deep frying
175g/6oz/1 cup ready-to-eat
stoned prunes
45ml/3 tbsp vanilla sugar
15ml/1 tbsp cocoa powder

FOR THE SAUCE

200g/7oz milk chocolate, chopped into
small pieces
120ml/4fl oz/½ cup crème fraîche
30ml/2 tbsp Armagnac or brandy

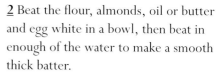

1 Start by making the sauce. Melt the chocolate, remove from the heat, stir in the crème fraîche until smooth, then add the Armagnac or brandy. Replace the bowl over the water, off the heat, so that the sauce stays warm.

2 Beat the flour, almonds, oil or butter and egg white in a bowl, then beat in enough of the water to make a smooth thick batter.

3 Heat the oil for deep frying to 180°C/350°F or until a cube of dried bread browns in 30–45 seconds. Dip the prunes into the batter and fry a few at a time until the beignets rise to the surface of the oil and are golden brown and crisp.

4 Remove each successive batch of beignets with a slotted spoon, drain on kitchen paper and keep hot. Mix the vanilla sugar and cocoa in a bowl or stout paper bag, add the drained beignets and toss well to coat.

5 Serve in individual bowls, with the chocolate sauce poured over the top of each serving.

COOK'S TIPS

Vanilla sugar is sold commercially in many European countries but is very easy to make. Simply store a vanilla pod in a jar of granulated or caster sugar for a few weeks, until the sugar has taken on the vanilla flavour. Shake the jar occasionally. Used in cakes, biscuits and puddings, vanilla sugar imparts a delicate flavour. If you do not have any vanilla sugar for tossing the beignets, use plain granulated or caster sugar and add a pinch of ground cinnamon, if you like.
Serve the beignets as soon as possible after cooking, as they do not keep well. Use stoned dates or dried apricots as a substitute for the prunes if you prefer.

CHOCOLATE, DATE AND ALMOND FILO COIL

SERVES 6

275g/10oz pack filo pastry, thawed if frozen
50g/2oz/4 tbsp unsalted butter, melted
icing sugar, cocoa powder and ground
cinnamon, for dusting

FOR THE FILLING

75g/3oz/6 tbsp unsalted butter
115g/4oz plain dark chocolate, chopped into
small pieces
115g/4oz/1 cup ground almonds
115g/4oz/⅔ cup chopped dates
75g/3oz/½ cup icing sugar
10ml/2 tsp rosewater
2.5ml/½ tsp ground cinnamon

1 Preheat oven to 180°C/350°F/Gas 4. Grease a 22 cm/8½ in round cake tin. Make the filling. Melt the butter with the chocolate, then stir in the other ingredients to make a paste. Leave to cool.

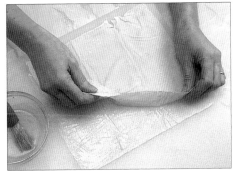

2 Lay one sheet of filo on a clean work surface. Brush it lightly with melted butter, then lay a second sheet on top and brush that with melted butter too.

3 Roll a handful of the chocolate almond mixture into a long sausage shape and place along one long edge of the layered filo. Roll the pastry tightly around the filling to make a roll. Keep the roll even, shaping it with your hands.

4 Place the roll in the tin, coiling it around against the sides. Make enough rolls to fill the tin and fit them in place.

5 Brush the coil with the remaining melted butter. Bake in the oven for 30–35 minutes, until the pastry is golden brown and crisp.

6 Remove the coil from the tin, and place it on a plate. Serve warm, dusted with icing sugar, cocoa and cinnamon.

Chocolate Almond Meringue Pie

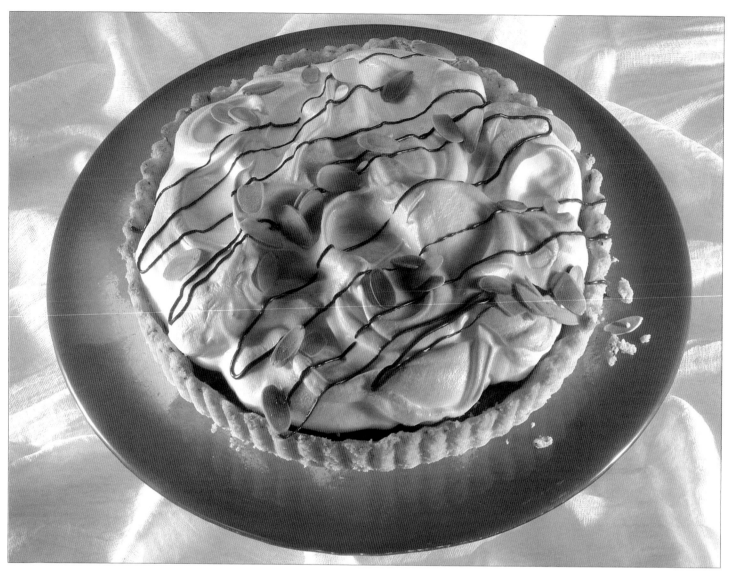

Serves 6

175g / 6oz / 1½ cups plain flour
50g / 2oz / ½ cup ground rice
150g / 5oz / ⅔ cup unsalted butter
finely grated rind of 1 orange
1 egg yolk
flaked almonds and melted plain dark
chocolate, to decorate

For the Filling

150g / 5oz plain dark chocolate, chopped into
small pieces
50g / 2oz / 4 tbsp unsalted butter, softened
75g / 3oz / 6 tbsp caster sugar
10ml / 2 tsp cornflour
4 egg yolks
75g / 3oz / ¾ cup ground almonds

For the Meringue

3 egg whites
150g / 5oz / ⅔ cup caster sugar

1 Sift the flour and ground rice into a bowl. Rub in the butter until the mixture resembles breadcrumbs. Stir in the orange rind. Add the egg yolks; bring the dough together. Roll out and use to line a 23 cm / 9 in round flan tin. Chill.

2 Preheat oven to 190°C / 375°F / Gas 5. Prick the pastry base, cover with grease-proof paper weighed down with baking beans and bake blind for 10 minutes.

3 Make the filling. Melt the chocolate, then cream the butter with the sugar in a bowl, and beat in the cornflour and egg yolks. Fold in the almonds, then the melted chocolate. Remove the paper and beans from the pastry case and add the filling. Bake for a further 10 minutes.

4 Make the meringue. Whisk the egg whites in a clean, grease-free bowl until stiff, then gradually whisk in about half the caster sugar. Fold in the remaining sugar with a metal spoon.

5 Spoon the meringue over the chocolate filling, lifting it up with the back of the spoon to form peaks. Reduce the oven temperature to 180°C / 350°F / Gas 4 and bake the pie for 15–20 minutes or until the topping is pale gold. Serve warm, scattered with the almonds and drizzled with the melted chocolate.

CHOCOLATE PECAN PIE

SERVES 6

200g / 7oz / 1¾ cups plain flour

75ml / 5 tbsp caster sugar

90g / 3½oz / scant ½ cup unsalted butter,
softened

1 egg, beaten

finely grated rind of 1 orange

FOR THE FILLING

200g / 7oz / ¾ cup golden syrup

45ml / 3 tbsp soft light muscovado sugar

150g / 5oz plain chocolate, chopped into
small pieces

50g / 2oz / ¼ cup butter

3 eggs, beaten

5ml / 1 tsp vanilla essence

175g / 6oz / 1½ cups pecan nuts

1 Sift the flour into a bowl and stir in the sugar. Work in the butter evenly with your fingertips until combined.

2 Beat the egg and orange rind in a bowl, then stir into the mixture to make a firm dough. Add a little water if the mixture is too dry, and knead briefly.

3 Roll out the pastry on a lightly floured surface and use to line a deep, 20 cm/8 in loose-based flan tin. Chill for 30 minutes.

4 Preheat oven to 180°C / 350°F / Gas 4. Make the filling. Melt the syrup, sugar, chocolate and butter in a small saucepan.

5 Remove the saucepan from the heat and beat in the eggs and vanilla essence. Sprinkle the pecan nuts into the pastry case and carefully pour over the chocolate mixture.

6 Place the tin on a baking sheet and bake the pie for 50–60 minutes or until the filling is set. Leave in the tin for 10 minutes, then remove the sides to serve. Serve plain, or with a little single cream.

BAKED CHOCOLATE AND RAISIN CHEESECAKE

SERVES 8–10

75g/3oz/¾ cup plain flour
45ml/3 tbsp cocoa powder
75g/3oz/½ cup semolina
50g/2oz/¼ cup caster sugar
115g/4oz/½ cup unsalted butter, softened

FOR THE FILLING

225g/8oz/1 cup cream cheese
120ml/4fl oz/½ cup natural yogurt
2 eggs, beaten
75g/3oz/6 tbsp caster sugar
finely grated rind of 1 lemon
75g/3oz/½ cup raisins
45ml/3 tbsp plain chocolate chips

FOR THE TOPPING

75g/3oz plain chocolate, chopped into
small pieces
30ml/2 tbsp golden syrup
40g/1½oz/3 tbsp butter

1 Preheat oven to 150°C/300°F/Gas 2. Sift the flour and cocoa into a mixing bowl and stir in the semolina and sugar. Using your fingertips, work the butter into the flour mixture until it makes a firm dough.

2 Press the dough into the base of a 22 cm/8½ in springform tin. Prick all over with a fork and bake in the oven for 15 minutes. Remove the tin but leave the oven on.

RUM AND RICOTTA CHEESECAKE

Use ricotta instead of cream cheese in the filling. Omit the lemon rind. Soak the raisins in 30ml/2 tbsp rum before stirring them in with the chocolate chips. Add 5ml/1 tsp rum to the topping.

3 Make the filling. In a large bowl, beat the cream cheese with the yogurt, eggs and sugar until evenly mixed. Stir in the lemon rind, raisins and chocolate chips.

4 Smooth the cream cheese mixture over the chocolate shortbread base and bake for a further 35–45 minutes or until the filling is pale gold and just set. Cool in the tin on a wire rack.

5 To make the topping, combine the chocolate, syrup and butter in a heatproof bowl. Set over a saucepan of simmering water and heat gently, stirring occasionally, until melted. Pour the topping over the cheesecake and leave until set. Remove the sides of the tin and carefully slide the chocolate and raisin cheesecake on to a serving plate. Serve sliced, with single cream, if you like.

CHOCOLATE AND ORANGE SCOTCH PANCAKES

SERVES 4

115g/4oz/1 cup self-raising flour
30ml/2 tbsp cocoa powder
2 eggs
50g/2oz plain chocolate, chopped into
small pieces
200ml/7fl oz/scant 1 cup milk
finely grated rind of 1 orange
30ml/2 tbsp orange juice
butter or oil, for frying
chocolate curls, to decorate

FOR THE SAUCE

2 large oranges
25g/1oz/2 tbsp unsalted butter
45ml/3 tbsp light muscovado sugar
250ml/8fl oz/1 cup crème fraîche
30ml/2 tbsp Grand Marnier or
Cointreau

1 Sift the flour and cocoa into a bowl and make a well in the centre. Add the eggs and beat well, gradually incorporating the surrounding dry ingredients to make a smooth mixture.

2 Mix the chocolate and milk in a saucepan. Heat gently until the chocolate has melted, then beat into the mixture until smooth and bubbly. Stir in the orange rind and juice to make a batter.

3 Heat a large heavy-based frying pan or griddle. Grease with a little butter or oil. Drop large spoonfuls of batter on to the hot surface, leaving room for spreading. Cook over a moderate heat. When the pancakes are lightly browned underneath and bubbly on top, flip over to cook the other side. Slide on to a plate and keep hot, then make more in the same way.

4 Make the sauce. Grate the rind of 1 orange into a bowl and set aside. Peel both oranges, taking care to remove all the pith, then slice the flesh fairly thinly.

5 Heat the butter and sugar in a wide, shallow pan over a low heat, stirring until the sugar dissolves. Stir in the crème fraîche and heat gently.

6 Add the pancakes and orange slices to the sauce, heat gently for 1–2 minutes, then spoon over the liqueur. Sprinkle with the reserved orange rind. Scatter over the chocolate curls and serve the pancakes at once.

CHOCOLATE CHIP BANANA PANCAKES

MAKES 16

2 ripe bananas
2 eggs
200ml / 7fl oz / scant 1 cup milk
150g / 5oz / 1¼ cups self-raising flour, sifted
25g / 1oz / ⅓ cup ground almonds
15ml / 1tbsp caster sugar
pinch of salt
15ml / 1tbsp plain chocolate chips
butter, for frying
50g / 2oz / ½ cup toasted flaked almonds

FOR THE TOPPING

150ml / ¼ pint / ⅔ cup double cream
15ml / 1 tbsp icing sugar

1 Mash the bananas in a bowl. Beat in the eggs and half the milk. Mix in the flour, ground almonds, sugar and salt. Add the remaining milk and the chocolate chips.

2 Stir the mixture well until it makes a thick batter. Heat a knob of butter in a non-stick frying pan. Spoon the pancake mixture into heaps, allowing room for them to spread. When the pancakes are lightly browned underneath, flip them over to cook the other side. Slide on to a plate and keep hot, then make more pancakes in the same way.

3 Make the topping. Pour the cream into a bowl. Add the icing sugar, to sweeten it slightly, and whip to soft peaks. Spoon the cream on to the pancakes and decorate with flaked almonds. Serve at once.

Chocolate Crepes with Plums and Port

Serves 6

50g / 2oz plain chocolate, chopped into
small pieces
200ml / 7fl oz / scant 1 cup milk
120ml / 4fl oz / ½ cup single cream
30ml / 2 tbsp cocoa powder
115g / 4oz / 1 cup plain flour
2 eggs
oil, for frying

For the Filling

500g / 1¼lb red or golden plums
50g / 2oz / ¼ cup caster sugar
30ml / 2 tbsp water
30ml / 2 tbsp port
150g / 5oz / ¾ cup crème fraîche or
Greek-style yogurt

For the Sauce

150g / 5oz plain chocolate, chopped into
small pieces
175ml / 6fl oz / ¾ cup double cream
15ml / 1 tbsp port

1 Make the crêpe batter. Place the chocolate in a saucepan with the milk. Heat gently, stirring occasionally, until the chocolate has dissolved. Pour the chocolate and milk mixture into a blender or food processor and add the cream, cocoa, flour and eggs. (If the blender or food processor is a small one, it may be necessary to do this in batches.) Process until smooth, then tip into a jug and chill for 30 minutes.

2 Meanwhile, make the filling. Halve and stone the plums. Place them in a saucepan and add the sugar and water. Bring to the boil, then lower the heat, cover, and simmer for about 10 minutes or until the plums are tender. Stir in the port, taking care not to break up the plums, then simmer for a further 30 seconds. Remove from the heat and keep warm.

3 Have ready a sheet of non-stick baking paper. Heat a crêpe pan, grease it lightly with a little oil, then pour in just enough batter to cover the base of the pan, swirling to coat evenly. Cook until the crêpe has set, then flip it over to cook the other side. Slide the crêpe out on to the sheet of paper, then cook 9–11 more crêpes in the same way. It should not be necessary to add more oil to the pan, but if the crêpes start to stick, add a very light coating.

4 Make the sauce. Combine the chocolate and cream in a saucepan. Heat gently, stirring until smooth. Add the port and heat gently, stirring, for 1 minute.

5 Divide the plum filling among the crêpes, add a dollop of crème fraîche or Greek-style yogurt to each and roll them up carefully. Serve in individual bowls, with the chocolate sauce spooned over the top of each portion.

RICH CHOCOLATE BRIOCHE BAKE

SERVES 4

40g / 1½oz / 3 tbsp unsalted butter, plus extra for greasing
200g / 7oz plain chocolate, chopped into small pieces
60ml / 4 tbsp bitter marmalade
4 individual brioches, cut into halves, or 1 large brioche loaf, cut into thick slices
3 eggs
300ml / ½ pint / 1¼ cups milk
300ml / ½ pint / 1¼ cups single cream
30ml / 2 tbsp demerara sugar

1 Preheat oven to 180°C / 350°F / Gas 4. Using the extra butter, lightly grease a shallow ovenproof dish.

2 Melt the chocolate with the marmalade and butter in a heatproof bowl over just simmering water, stirring the mixture occasionally, until smooth.

3 Spread the melted chocolate mixture over the brioche slices. Arrange them in the dish so that the slices overlap.

4 Beat the eggs in a large bowl, then add the milk and cream and mix well. Transfer to a jug and pour evenly over the slices. Sprinkle with the demerara sugar and bake for 40–50 minutes, until the custard has set lightly and the brioche slices are golden brown. Serve hot.

CHOCOLATE SOUFFLE CREPES

MAKES 12 CREPES

75g/3oz/¾ cup plain flour
15ml/1 tbsp cocoa powder
5ml/1 tsp caster sugar
pinch of salt
5ml/1 tsp ground cinnamon
2 eggs
175ml/6fl oz/¾ cup milk
5ml/1 tsp vanilla essence
50g/2oz/4 tbsp unsalted butter,
melted
raspberries, pineapple and mint sprigs,
to decorate

FOR THE PINEAPPLE SYRUP

½ medium pineapple, peeled, cored and
finely chopped
120ml/4fl oz/½ cup water
30ml/2 tbsp natural maple syrup
5ml/1 tsp cornflour
½ cinnamon stick
30ml/2 tbsp rum

FOR THE SOUFFLE FILLING

250g/9oz bittersweet chocolate, chopped into
small pieces
75ml/3fl oz/⅓ cup double cream
3 eggs, separated
25g/1oz/2 tbsp caster sugar

1 Prepare the syrup. In a saucepan over a medium heat, bring the pineapple, water, maple syrup, cornflour and cinnamon stick to the boil. Simmer for 2–3 minutes, until the sauce thickens, whisking frequently. Remove from the heat and discard the cinnamon. Pour into a bowl, and stir in the rum. Cool, then chill.

COOK'S TIP
You might be able to find ready-made crêpes in the shops, which will save time.

2 Prepare the crêpes. Sift the flour, cocoa, sugar, salt and cinnamon into a bowl. Stir, then make a well in the centre. In a bowl, beat the eggs, milk and vanilla. Gradually add to the well in the flour mixture, whisking in flour from the side of the bowl to form a smooth batter. Stir in half the melted butter and pour into a jug. Allow to stand for 1 hour.

3 Heat an 18–20 cm/7–8 in crêpe pan. Brush with butter. Stir the batter. Pour 45ml/3 tbsp batter into the pan; swirl the pan to cover the bottom. Cook over a medium-high heat for 1–2 minutes until the bottom is golden. Turn over and cook for 30–45 seconds, then turn on to a plate. Stack between sheets of non-stick baking paper and set aside.

4 Prepare the filling. In a saucepan over a medium heat, melt the chocolate and cream until smooth, stirring frequently.

5 In a bowl, with a hand-held electric mixer, beat the yolks with half the sugar for 3–5 minutes, until light and creamy. Gradually beat in the chocolate mixture. Allow to cool. In a separate bowl with cleaned beaters, beat the egg whites until soft peaks form. Gradually beat in the remaining sugar until stiff peaks form. Beat a large spoonful of whites in to the chocolate mixture to lighten it, then fold in the remaining whites.

6 Preheat oven to 200°C/400°F/Gas 6. Lay a crêpe on a plate, bottom side up. Spoon a little soufflé mixture on to the crêpe, spreading it to the edge. Fold the bottom half over the soufflé mixture, then fold in half again to form a filled triangle. Place on a buttered baking sheet. Repeat with the remaining crêpes. Brush the tops with melted butter and bake for 15–20 minutes, until the filling has souffléd. Decorate with raspberries, pineapple pieces and mint and serve with the syrup.

VARIATION
For a simpler version of the crêpes, just serve with a spoonful of maple syrup rather than making the pineapple syrup.

CHOCOLATE ORANGE MARQUISE

SERVES 6–8

200g/7oz/scant 1 cup caster sugar
60ml/4 tbsp freshly squeezed orange juice
350g/12oz plain dark chocolate, chopped
into small pieces
225g/8oz/1 cup unsalted butter, cubed
5 eggs
finely grated rind of 1 orange
45ml/3 tbsp plain flour
icing sugar and finely pared strips of orange
rind, to decorate

1 Preheat oven to 180°C/350°F/Gas 4. Grease a 23 cm/9 in round cake tin with a depth of 6 cm/2½ in. Line the base with non-stick baking paper.
2 Place 115g/4oz/½ cup of the sugar in a saucepan. Add the orange juice and stir over a gentle heat until the sugar has dissolved completely.

3 Remove from the heat and stir in the chocolate until melted, then add the butter, cube by cube, until thoroughly melted and evenly mixed.
4 Whisk the eggs with the remaining sugar in a large bowl until pale and very thick. Add the orange rind. Then, using a metal spoon, fold the chocolate mixture lightly and evenly into the egg mixture. Sift the flour over the top and fold in.

5 Scrape the mixture into the prepared tin. Place in a roasting pan, transfer to the oven, then carefully pour hot water into the roasting pan to come about halfway up the sides of the cake tin.
6 Bake for about 1 hour or until the cake is firm to the touch. Remove the cake tin from the water bath and place on a wire rack to cool for 15–20 minutes. To turn out, invert the cake on a baking sheet, place a serving plate upside down on top, then turn plate and baking sheet over together so that the cake is transferred to the plate.
7 Dust with icing sugar, decorate with strips of pared orange rind and serve still warm. This cake is wonderfully rich and moist and really doesn't need an accompaniment, but you could offer single cream, if you wish.

HOT CHOCOLATE ZABAGLIONE

SERVES 6

6 egg yolks
150g / 5oz / ⅔ cup caster sugar
45ml / 3 tbsp cocoa powder
200ml / 7fl oz / scant 1 cup Marsala
cocoa powder or icing sugar, for dusting

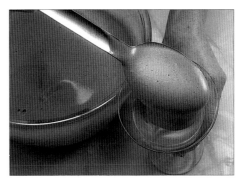

2 Add the cocoa and Marsala, then place the bowl over the simmering water. Whisk with a hand-held electric mixer until the mixture is thick and foamy.

3 Pour quickly into tall heatproof glasses, dust lightly with cocoa or icing sugar and serve immediately with chocolate cinnamon tuiles or amaretti biscuits.

1 Half fill a medium saucepan with water and bring to simmering point. Select a heatproof bowl that will fit over the pan, place the egg yolks and sugar in it, and whisk until the mixture is pale and all the sugar has dissolved.

CHOCOLATE FONDUE
SERVES 4-6

225g / 8oz plain chocolate, chopped into small pieces
300ml / ½ pint / 1¼ cups double cream
30ml / 2 tbsp Grand Marnier (optional)
25g / 1oz / 2 tbsp butter, diced
cherries, strawberries, sliced bananas, mandarin segments and cubes of sponge cake, for dipping

1 Combine the chocolate, cream and Grand Marnier (if using) in a fondue pan or small heavy-based saucepan. Heat gently until melted, stirring frequently.
2 Arrange the fruit and cake for dipping on a large platter. Stir the butter into the fondue until melted. Place the fondue pot or pan over a lighted spirit burner.
3 Guests spear the items of their choice on fondue forks and swirl them in the dip until coated. Anyone who loses his or her dipper pays a forfeit.

CHOCOLATE TARTS, PIES AND CHEESECAKES

GREEK CHOCOLATE MOUSSE TARTLETS

SERVES 6

1 quantity Chocolate Shortcrust Pastry
chocolate shapes, to decorate

FOR THE FILLING

200g/7oz white chocolate, chopped into
small pieces
120ml/4fl oz/½ cup milk
10ml/2 tsp powdered gelatine
30ml/2 tbsp caster sugar
5ml/1 tsp vanilla essence
2 eggs, separated
250ml/8fl oz/1 cup Greek-style yogurt

1 Preheat oven to 190°C/375°F/Gas 5.
Roll out the pastry and line six deep
10 cm/4 in loose-based flan tins.

2 Prick the pastry with a fork, cover with
greaseproof paper weighed down with
baking beans and bake blind for 10
minutes. Remove the baking beans and
paper, return to the oven and bake a
further 15 minutes. Cool in the tins.

3 Make the filling. Melt the chocolate.
Pour the milk into a saucepan, sprinkle
over the powdered gelatine and heat
gently, stirring until the gelatine has
dissolved completely. Remove from the
heat and stir in the chocolate.

4 Whisk the sugar, vanilla essence and egg
yolks in a large bowl, then beat in the
chocolate mixture. Beat in the yogurt
until evenly mixed.

5 Whisk the egg whites in a clean, grease-
free bowl until stiff, then fold into the
mixture. Divide among the pastry cases
and chill for 2–3 hours, until set.
Decorate with chocolate shapes, and dust
with icing sugar if wished.

CHOCOLATE AND PINE NUT TART

SERVES 8

200g/7oz/1¾ cups plain flour
50g/2oz/¼ cup caster sugar
pinch of salt
grated rind of ½ orange
115g/4oz/½ cup unsalted butter, cut into
small pieces
3 egg yolks, lightly beaten
15–30 ml/1–2 tbsp iced water

FOR THE FILLING

2 eggs
45ml/3 tbsp caster sugar
grated rind of 1 orange
15ml/1 tbsp orange-flavoured liqueur
250ml/8fl oz/1 cup whipping cream
115g/4oz plain chocolate, chopped into
small pieces
75g/3oz/1 cup pine nuts, toasted

FOR THE DECORATION

1 orange
50g/2oz/¼ cup granulated sugar
120ml/4fl oz/½ cup water

1 In a food processor fitted with a metal blade, process the flour, sugar, salt and orange rind. Add the butter and process for 20–30 seconds, until the mixture looks like coarse crumbs. Add the yolks and pulse until the dough begins to stick together. If the dough appears dry, add the iced water, little by little, until the mixture just holds together. Knead the dough gently, then wrap in clear film. Chill for 2–3 hours or overnight.

2 Lightly grease a 23 cm/9 in tart tin with a removable base. Let the dough soften briefly, then roll out on a well-floured surface into a 28 cm/11 in round. Ease the dough into the tin and press the overhang down slightly with floured fingers, to make the top edge thicker.

3 Roll a rolling pin over the top edge to cut off excess dough. Press the thicker top edge against the sides of the tin to form a raised rim. Prick the base with a fork. Chill for 1 hour. Preheat oven to 200°C/400°F/Gas 6. Line the tart shell with greaseproof paper; fill with baking beans and bake blind for 5 minutes. Lift out the foil and beans, then return the tart shell to the oven and bake for 5 minutes more, until set. Cool in the tin on a wire rack. Lower the oven temperature to 180°C/350°F/Gas 4.

4 Prepare the filling. Beat the eggs, sugar, orange rind and liqueur in a bowl. Stir in the cream. Sprinkle the chocolate evenly over the base of the tart shell, then sprinkle with the pine nuts.

5 Gently pour the filling into the tart shell. Bake for 20–30 minutes, until the pastry is golden and the custard is set. Cool slightly in the tin on a wire rack.

6 Prepare the decoration. Peel the orange thinly, avoiding the pith, then cut the rind into thin strips. Dissolve the sugar in the water in a pan over a medium heat, then add the orange rind strips. Boil for about 5 minutes, until the syrup is thick and has begun to caramelize. Off the heat, stir in about 15ml/1 tbsp cold water to prevent the mixture from darkening further.

7 Brush the orange syrup over the tart and decorate with the caramelized strips. Remove the side of the tin and slide the tart on to a plate. Serve warm.

CHOCOLATE TRUFFLE TART

SERVES 12

115g/4oz/1 cup plain flour
30g/1¼oz/⅓ cup cocoa powder
50g/2oz/¼ cup caster sugar
2.5ml/½ tsp salt
115g/4oz/½ cup unsalted butter, cut into pieces
1 egg yolk
15–30ml/1–2 tbsp iced water
25g/1oz fine quality white or milk chocolate, melted
whipped cream for serving (optional)
FOR THE TRUFFLE FILLING
350ml/12fl oz/1½ cups double cream
350g/12oz couverture or fine quality bittersweet chocolate, chopped
50g/2oz/4 tbsp unsalted butter, cut into small pieces
30ml/2 tbsp brandy or liqueur

1 Prepare the pastry. Sift the flour and cocoa into a bowl. In a food processor fitted with a metal blade, process the flour mixture with the sugar and salt. Add the butter and process for 15–20 seconds, until the mixture resembles coarse breadcrumbs.

2 In a bowl, lightly beat the yolk with the iced water. Add to the flour mixture and pulse until the dough begins to stick together. Turn out the dough on to a sheet of clear film. Use the film to help shape the dough into a flat disc. Wrap tightly. Chill for 1–2 hours, until firm.

3 Lightly grease a 23 cm/9 in tart tin with a removable base. Let the dough soften briefly, then roll it out between sheets of waxed paper or clear film to a 28 cm/11 in round, about 5 mm/¼ in thick. Peel off the top sheet and invert the dough into a tart tin. Remove the bottom sheet. Ease the dough into the tin. Prick with a fork. Chill for 1 hour.

4 Preheat oven to 180°C/350°F/Gas 4. Line the tart with foil or non-stick baking paper; fill with baking beans. Bake blind for 5–7 minutes. Lift out the foil with the beans, return the pastry case to the oven and bake for a further 5–7 minutes, until the pastry is just set. Cool completely in the tin on a rack.

5 Prepare the filling. In a medium pan over a medium heat, bring the cream to the boil. Remove the pan from the heat and stir in the chocolate until melted and smooth. Stir in the butter and brandy or liqueur. Strain into the prepared tart shell, tilting the tin slightly to level the surface. Do not touch the surface of the filling or it will spoil the glossy finish.

6 Spoon the melted chocolate into a paper piping bag and cut off the tip. Drop rounds of chocolate over the surface of the tart and use a skewer or toothpick to draw a point gently through the chocolate to produce a marbled effect. Chill for 2–3 hours, until set. To serve, allow the tart to soften slightly at room temperature.

CHOCOLATE TIRAMISU TART

SERVES 12–16

115g/4oz/½ cup unsalted butter
15ml/1 tbsp coffee-flavoured liqueur or water
175g/6oz/1½ cups plain flour
25g/1oz/¼ cup cocoa powder
25g/1oz/¼ cup icing sugar
pinch of salt
2.5ml/½ tsp vanilla essence
cocoa powder, for dusting

FOR THE CHOCOLATE LAYER

350ml/12fl oz/1½ cups double cream
15ml/1 tbsp golden syrup
115g/4oz bittersweet chocolate, chopped into small pieces
25g/1oz/2 tbsp unsalted butter, cut into small pieces
30ml/2 tbsp coffee-flavoured liqueur

FOR THE FILLING

250ml/8fl oz/1 cup whipping cream
350g/12oz/1½ cups mascarpone cheese, at room temperature
45ml/3 tbsp icing sugar
45ml/3 tbsp cold espresso or strong black coffee
45ml/3 tbsp coffee-flavoured liqueur
90g/3½oz plain chocolate, grated

1 Make the pastry. Lightly grease a 23 cm/9 in springform tin. In a saucepan, heat the butter and liqueur or water until the butter has melted. Sift the flour, cocoa, icing sugar and salt into a bowl. Remove the butter mixture from the heat, stir in the vanilla essence and gradually stir into the flour mixture until a soft dough forms.

2 Knead lightly until smooth. Press on to the base and up the sides of the tin to within 2 cm/¾ in of the top. Prick the dough. Chill for 40 minutes. Preheat oven to 190°C/375°F/Gas 5. Bake the pastry case for 8–10 minutes. If the pastry puffs up, prick it with a fork and bake for 2–3 minutes more until set. Cool in the tin on a rack.

3 Prepare the chocolate layer. Bring the cream and syrup to a boil in a pan over a medium heat. Off the heat, add the chocolate, stirring until melted. Beat in the butter and liqueur and pour into the pastry case. Cool completely, then chill.

4 Prepare the filling. Using a hand-held electric mixer, whip the cream in a bowl until soft peaks form. In another bowl, beat the cheese until soft, then beat in the icing sugar until smooth and creamy. Gradually beat in the cold coffee and liqueur; gently fold in the whipped cream and chocolate. Spoon the filling into the pastry case, on top of the chocolate layer. Level the surface. Chill until ready to serve.

5 To serve, run a sharp knife around the side of the tin to loosen the tart shell. Remove the side of the tin and slide the tart on to a plate. Sift a layer of cocoa powder over the tart to decorate, or pipe rosettes of whipped cream around the rim and top each with a chocolate-coated coffee bean. Chocolate Tiramisu Tart is very rich, so serve it in small wedges, with cups of espresso.

WHITE CHOCOLATE AND MANGO CREAM TART

SERVES 8

175g/6oz/1½ cups plain flour
75g/3oz/1 cup sweetened, desiccated coconut
115g/4oz/½ cup butter, softened
30ml/2 tbsp caster sugar
2 egg yolks
2.5ml/½ tsp almond essence
600ml/1 pint/2½ cups whipping cream
1 large ripe mango
50g/2oz/½ cup toasted flaked almonds,
to decorate

**FOR THE WHITE CHOCOLATE
CUSTARD FILLING**

150g/5oz fine quality white chocolate,
chopped into small pieces
120ml/4fl oz/½ cup whipping cream or
double cream
75ml/5 tbsp cornflour
15ml/1 tbsp plain flour
50g/2oz/¼ cup granulated sugar
350ml/12fl oz/1½ cups milk
5 egg yolks

1 Using a hand-held electric mixer at low speed, beat the flour, coconut, butter, sugar, egg yolks and almond essence in a deep bowl until the mixture forms a soft dough. Lightly grease a 23 cm/9 in tart tin with a removable base. Press the pastry on to the bottom and sides. Prick the pastry case with a fork. Chill the case for 30 minutes.

COOK'S TIP

Choose a mango that is a rich yellow in colour, with a pink or red blush. It should just yield to the touch, but should not be too soft. Peel it carefully, then cut it in half around the stone. Cut each piece in half again, then in neat slices.

2 Preheat oven to 180°C/350°F/Gas 4. Line the pastry case with non-stick baking paper; fill with baking beans and bake blind for 10 minutes. Remove the paper and beans and bake for a further 5–7 minutes, until golden. Cool the cooked pastry in the tin on a wire rack.

3 Prepare the custard filling. In a small saucepan over a low heat, melt the white chocolate with the cream, stirring until smooth. Set aside. Combine the cornflour, plain flour and sugar in a medium saucepan. Stir in the milk gradually. Place over a medium heat and cook, stirring constantly, until the mixture has thickened.

4 Beat the egg yolks in a small bowl. Slowly add about 250ml/8fl oz/1 cup of the hot milk mixture, stirring constantly. Return the yolk mixture to the rest of the sauce in the pan, stirring constantly.

5 Bring the custard filling to a gentle boil, stirring constantly until thickened. Stir in the melted white chocolate until well blended. Cool to room temperature, stirring frequently to prevent a skin from forming on the surface. Beat the whipping cream in a medium-sized bowl until soft peaks form. Fold approximately 120ml/4fl oz/½ cup of the whipped cream into the white chocolate custard and spoon half the custard into the base. Peel and slice the mango thinly.

6 With the aid of a slim metal spatula or palette knife, arrange the mango slices over the custard in concentric circles, starting at the rim and then filling in the centre. Try to avoid moving the mango slices once in position. Carefully pour the remaining custard over the mango slices, smoothing the surface evenly. Remove the side of the tin and slide the tart carefully on to a serving plate.

7 Spoon the remaining flavoured cream into a large piping bag fitted with a medium star tip. Pipe the cream in a scroll pattern in parallel rows on top of the tart, keeping the rows about 1 cm/½ in apart. Carefully sprinkle the toasted flaked almonds between the rows. Serve the tart chilled.

CHOCOLATE PECAN TORTE

SERVES 16

200g/7oz bittersweet or plain chocolate,
chopped into small pieces
150g/5oz/10 tbsp unsalted butter,
cut into pieces
4 eggs
90g/3½oz/scant ½ cup caster sugar
10ml/2 tsp vanilla essence
115g/4oz/1 cup ground pecan nuts
10ml/2 tsp ground cinnamon
24 toasted pecan halves, to decorate
FOR THE CHOCOLATE HONEY GLAZE
115g/4oz bittersweet or plain chocolate,
chopped into small pieces
50g/2oz/¼ cup unsalted butter,
cut into pieces
30ml/2 tbsp clear honey
pinch of ground cinnamon

1 Preheat oven to 180°C/350°F/Gas 4.
Grease a 20 x 5 cm/8 x 2 in springform
tin; line with non-stick baking paper.
Wrap the tin in foil to prevent water
from seeping in. Melt the chocolate and
butter, stirring until smooth. Beat the
eggs, sugar and vanilla essence in a
mixing bowl until the mixture is frothy.
Stir in the melted chocolate, ground nuts
and cinnamon. Pour into the tin.
2 Place the tin in a roasting pan. Pour in
boiling water to come 2 cm/¾ in up the
side of the springform tin. Bake for
25–30 minutes, until the edge of the cake
is set but the centre is still soft. Remove
the tin from the water bath and lift off
the foil. Cool the cake in the tin on a
wire rack.

3 Prepare the glaze. Heat all the
ingredients in a small pan until melted,
stirring until smooth. Off the heat, half-
dip the toasted pecan halves in the glaze
and place on a baking sheet lined with
non-stick baking paper until set.

4 Remove the cake from the tin, place it
on the rack and pour the remaining glaze
over. Decorate the outside of the torte
with the chocolate-dipped pecans and
leave to set. Transfer to a plate when
ready to serve, and slice in thin wedges.

CHOCOLATE LEMON TART

SERVES 8–10

175g / 6oz / 1½ cups plain flour
10ml / 2 tsp cocoa powder
25g / 1oz / ¼ cup icing sugar
2.5ml / ½ tsp salt
*115g / 4oz / ½ cup unsalted butter or
margarine*
15ml / 1 tbsp water

FOR THE FILLING

225g / 8oz / 1 cup caster sugar
6 eggs
grated rind of 2 lemons
175ml / 6fl oz / ¾ cup fresh lemon juice
*175ml / 6fl oz / ¾ cup double or
whipping cream*
chocolate curls, for decorating

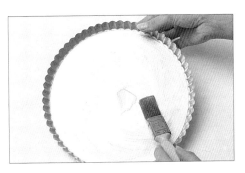

1 Grease a 25 cm / 10 in flan tin. Sift the flour, cocoa, icing sugar and salt into a bowl. Set aside. Melt the butter or margarine and water in a saucepan over a low heat. Pour over the flour mixture and stir until the flour has absorbed all the liquid and the dough is smooth.

2 Press the dough evenly over the base and side of the prepared tin. Chill the pastry case.

3 Preheat oven to 190°C / 375°F / Gas 5, and place a baking sheet inside to heat up. Prepare the filling. Whisk the sugar and eggs in a bowl until the sugar has dissolved. Add the lemon rind and juice and mix well. Stir in the cream. Taste and add more lemon juice or sugar if needed, for a sweet taste with a touch of tartness.

4 Pour the filling into the tart shell and place the tin on the hot baking sheet. Bake for 20–25 minutes or until the filling is set. Cool on a rack, then decorate with the chocolate curls.

CHOCOLATE APRICOT LINZER TART

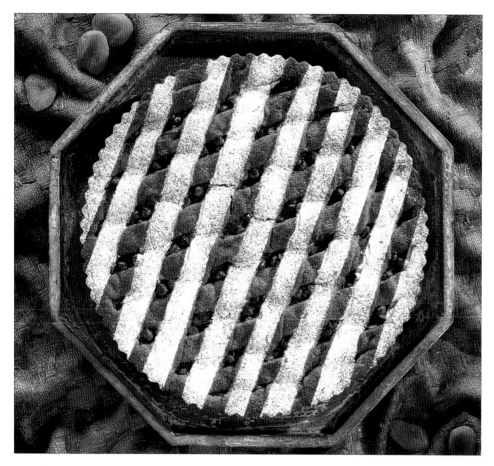

3 Turn the dough on to a flour-dusted work surface and knead lightly until just blended. Divide the dough in half. With floured fingers, press half the dough on to the bottom and sides of the tin. Prick the base of the dough with a fork. Chill for 20 minutes. Roll out the rest of the dough between two sheets of non-stick baking paper or clear film to a 28 cm/11 in round; slide on to a baking sheet and chill for 30 minutes.

4 Preheat oven to 180°C/350°F/Gas 4. Spread the filling on to the base of the pastry-lined tin. Sprinkle with chocolate chips. Set aside. Slide the dough round on to a lightly floured surface and cut into 1 cm/½ in strips; allow the strips to soften for 3–5 minutes so that they will be easier to work with.

SERVES 10–12

50g/2oz/½ cup whole blanched almonds
115g/4oz/½ cup caster sugar
175g/6oz/1½ cups plain flour
30ml/2 tbsp cocoa powder
5ml/1 tsp ground cinnamon
2.5ml/½ tsp salt
5ml/1 tsp grated orange rind
225g/8oz/1 cup unsalted butter, cut into small pieces
45–60ml/3–4 tbsp iced water
75g/3oz/½ cup plain mini chocolate chips
icing sugar, for dusting

FOR THE APRICOT FILLING

350g/12oz/1½ cups dried apricots
120ml/4fl oz/½ cup orange juice
175ml/6fl oz/¾ cup water
45ml/3 tbsp granulated sugar
50g/2oz/2 tbsp apricot jam
2.5ml/½ tsp almond essence

1 Prepare the filling. In a pan, simmer the apricots, orange juice and water until the liquid is absorbed, stirring often. Stir in the remaining ingredients. Strain into a bowl, cool, cover and chill.

2 Prepare the pastry. Lightly grease a 28 cm/11 in tart tin with removable base. In a food processor with a metal blade, process the almonds with half the sugar until finely ground. Into a bowl, sift the flour, cocoa, cinnamon and salt. Stir in the remaining caster sugar. Add to the food processor and process to blend. Add the rind and butter and process for 15–20 seconds until the mixture resembles coarse crumbs. Add about 30ml/2 tbsp iced water and pulse until the dough just begins to stick together. If the dough appears too dry, add 15–30ml/1–2 tbsp more iced water, little by little, until the dough just holds together.

5 Place half the dough strips over the filling, spacing them about 1 cm/½ in apart. Place the rest of the strips at an angle on top, as shown. With your fingertips, press down on both sides of each crossing to stress the lattice effect. Press the ends on to the side of the tart, cutting off any excess. Bake for 35–40 minutes, until the strips are golden and the filling bubbles. Cool on a rack. To serve, remove the side of the tin, then dust icing sugar over the top pastry strips.

RICH CHOCOLATE BERRY TART WITH BLACKBERRY SAUCE

SERVES 10

115g/4oz/½ cup unsalted butter, softened
115g/4oz/½ cup caster sugar
2.5ml/½ tsp salt
15ml/1 tbsp vanilla essence
50g/2oz/½ cup cocoa powder
175g/6oz/1½ cups plain flour
450g/1 lb fresh berries, for topping

FOR THE CHOCOLATE GANACHE FILLING

475ml/16fl oz/2 cups double cream
150g/5oz/½ cup blackberry or raspberry jelly
225g/8oz bittersweet chocolate, chopped into
small pieces
25g/1oz/2 tbsp unsalted butter, cut into
small pieces

FOR THE BLACKBERRY SAUCE

225g/8oz fresh or frozen blackberries or
raspberries
15ml/1 tbsp lemon juice
30ml/2 tbsp caster sugar
30ml/2 tbsp blackberry- or raspberry-
flavoured liqueur

1 In a food processor fitted with a metal blade, process the butter, sugar, salt and vanilla essence until creamy. Add the cocoa and process for 1 minute. Add the flour all at once, then pulse for 10–15 seconds. Place a piece of clear film on the work surface. Turn the dough out on to this, shape into a flat disc and wrap tightly. Chill for 1 hour.

2 Lightly grease a 23 cm/9 in flan tin with a removable base. Let the dough soften for 5–10 minutes, then roll out between two sheets of clear film to a 28 cm/11 in round, about 5 mm/¼ in thick. Peel off the top sheet of clear film and invert the dough into the prepared tin. Ease the dough into the tin, and when in position lift off the clear film.

3 With floured fingers, press the dough on to the base and sides of the tin, then roll the rolling pin over the edge to cut off any excess dough. Prick the base of the dough with a fork. Chill for 1 hour. Preheat oven to 180°C/350°F/Gas 4. Line the pastry case with non-stick baking paper; fill with baking beans and bake blind for 10 minutes. Remove the paper and beans and bake for 5 minutes more, until the pastry is just set. Cool in the tin on a wire rack.

4 Prepare the ganache filling. In a medium saucepan over a medium heat, bring the cream and berry jelly to the boil. Remove from the heat and add the chocolate all at once, stirring until melted and smooth. Stir in the butter until melted, then strain into the cooled tart shell, smoothing the top. Cool the tart completely.

5 Prepare the sauce. Process the berries, lemon juice and sugar in a food processor until smooth. Strain into a small bowl and add the liqueur.

6 To serve, remove the tart from the tin. Place on a serving plate and arrange the berries on top of the tart. With a pastry brush, brush the berries with a little of the blackberry sauce to glaze lightly. Serve the remaining sauce separately.

HAZELNUT CHOCOLATE MERINGUE TORTE WITH PEARS

SERVES 8–10

175g/6oz/¾ cup granulated sugar
1 vanilla pod, split
475ml/6fl oz/2 cups water
4 ripe pears, peeled, halved and cored
30ml/2 tbsp hazelnut- or pear-flavoured liqueur
150g/5oz/1¼ cups hazelnuts, toasted
6 egg whites
pinch of salt
350g/12oz/2¼ cups icing sugar
5ml/1 tsp vanilla essence
50g/2oz plain chocolate, melted
FOR THE CHOCOLATE CREAM
275g/10oz fine quality bittersweet or plain chocolate, chopped into small pieces
475ml/16fl oz/2 cups whipping cream
60ml/4 tbsp hazelnut- or pear-flavoured liqueur

1 In a saucepan large enough to hold the pears in a single layer combine the sugar, vanilla pod and water. Over a high heat, bring to the boil, stirring until the sugar dissolves. Lower the heat, add the pears to the syrup, cover and simmer gently for 12–15 minutes until tender. Remove the pan from the heat and allow the pears to cool in their poaching liquid. Carefully lift the pears out of the liquid and drain on kitchen paper. Transfer them to a plate, sprinkle with liqueur, cover and chill overnight.

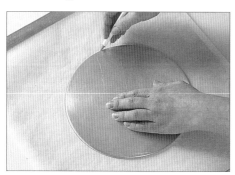

2 Preheat oven to 180°C/350°F/Gas 4. With a pencil draw a 23 cm/9 in circle on each of two sheets of non-stick baking paper. Turn the paper over on to two baking sheets (so that the pencil marks are underneath). Crumb the toasted hazelnuts in a food processor fitted with a metal blade.

3 In a large bowl, beat the whites with a hand-held electric mixer until frothy. Add the salt and beat on high speed until soft peaks form. Reduce the mixer speed and gradually add the icing sugar, beating well after each addition until all the sugar has been added and the whites are stiff and glossy; this will take 12–15 minutes. Gently fold in the nuts and vanilla essence and spoon the meringue on to the circles on the baking sheets, smoothing the top and sides.

4 Bake for 1 hour until the tops are dry and firm. Turn off the oven and allow to cool in the oven for 2–3 hours or overnight, until completely dry.

5 Prepare the chocolate cream. Melt the chocolate in a heatproof bowl set over a saucepan of simmering water. Stir the chocolate until melted and smooth. Cool to room temperature. Using a hand-held electric mixer beat the cream in a bowl to form soft peaks. Quickly fold the cream into the melted chocolate; fold in the liqueur. Spoon about one third of the chocolate cream into an icing bag fitted with a star tip. Set aside.

6 Thinly slice each pear half lengthwise with a sharp knife. Place one meringue layer on a serving plate. Spread with half the chocolate cream and arrange half the sliced pears evenly over the cream. Pipe a border of rosettes around the edge.

7 Top with the second meringue layer and spread with the remaining chocolate cream. Arrange the remaining pear slices in an attractive pattern over the chocolate cream. Pipe a border of rosettes around the edge. Spoon the melted chocolate into a small paper cone and drizzle the chocolate over the pears. Chill for at least 1 hour before serving.

CHILLED CHOCOLATE AND DATE SLICE

SERVES 6–8

115g/4oz/½ cup unsalted butter, melted
225g/8oz ginger biscuits, finely crushed
50g/2oz/⅔ cup stale sponge cake crumbs
75ml/5 tbsp orange juice
115g/4oz/⅔ cup stoned dates
25g/1oz/¼ cup finely chopped nuts
175g/6oz bittersweet chocolate
300ml/½ pint/1¼ cups whipping cream
grated chocolate and icing sugar, to decorate

1 Mix the butter and ginger biscuit crumbs in a bowl, then press the mixture on to the sides and base of an 18 cm/7 in loose-based flan tin. Chill the crust while making the filling.

2 Put the sponge cake crumbs into a bowl. Pour over 60ml/4 tbsp of the orange juice, stir well with a wooden spoon and leave to soak. Put the dates in a saucepan and add the remaining orange juice. Warm the mixture over a low heat. Mash the warm dates thoroughly and stir in the cake crumbs, with the finely chopped nuts.

3 Mix the chocolate with 60ml/4 tbsp of the cream in a heatproof bowl. Place the bowl over a saucepan of barely simmering water and stir occasionally until melted. In a separate bowl, whip the rest of the cream to soft peaks, then fold in the melted chocolate.

4 Add the cooled date, crumb and nut mixture to the cream and chocolate and mix lightly but thoroughly. Pour into the crumb crust. Using a spatula, level the mixture. Chill until just set, then mark the tart into portions, using a sharp knife dipped in hot water. Return the tart to the fridge and chill until firm. To decorate, scatter the grated chocolate over the surface and dust with icing sugar. Serve in wedges, with single cream, if desired. Fresh orange segments make an excellent accompaniment.

CHOCOLATE MARSHMALLOW PIE

Make the crumb crust as for the main recipe, but add a delicious marshmallow filling. Melt 275g/10oz/3 cups white marshmallows with 30ml/2 tbsp milk or single cream in the top of a double boiler over simmering water. Alternatively, use a deep bowl and microwave the mixture on High for about 4 minutes, stirring often. Off the heat, stir in 90g/3½oz grated chocolate until melted, then add 30ml/2 tbsp brandy. Tip the mixture into a clean bowl, cool, then chill until beginning to set. Fold in 250ml/8fl oz/1 cup whipped cream, pour into the crumb crust and return to the fridge until completely set. Decorate with chocolate curls.

BAKED CHOCOLATE CHEESECAKE

SERVES 10–12

275g/10oz plain chocolate, chopped into
small pieces
1.2kg/2½lb/5 cups cream cheese, at room
temperature
200g/7oz/scant 1 cup granulated sugar
10ml/2 tsp vanilla essence
4 eggs, at room temperature
175ml/6fl oz/¾ cup soured cream
15ml/1 tbsp cocoa powder

FOR THE BASE

200g/7oz chocolate biscuits, crushed
75g/3oz/6 tbsp butter, melted
2.5ml/½ tsp ground cinnamon

1 Preheat oven to 180°C/350°F/Gas 4.
Lightly grease the base and sides of a
23 x 7.5 cm/9 x 3 in springform tin.

2 To make the base, mix the crushed
biscuits with the butter and cinnamon.
Press the mixture evenly on to the base of
the tin to make a crust. Melt the
chocolate and set it aside.

3 Beat the cream cheese until smooth,
then beat in the sugar and vanilla essence.
Add the eggs, one at a time.

4 Stir the soured cream into the cocoa
powder to form a paste. Add to the
cream cheese mixture. Stir in the melted
chocolate and mix until smooth.

5 Pour the filling on to the base. Bake for
1 hour. Cool in the tin, then remove the
sides of the tin and slide the cheesecake
on to a plate. Serve chilled.

MARBLED CHOCOLATE CHEESECAKE

SERVES 6

50g/2oz/½ cup cocoa powder
75ml/5 tbsp hot water
900g/2lb cream cheese, at room temperature
200g/7oz/scant 1 cup caster sugar
4 eggs
5ml/1 tsp vanilla essence
75g/3oz digestive biscuits, crushed

1 Preheat oven to 180°C/350°F/Gas 4. Line a 20 x 8 cm/8 x 3 in cake tin with greaseproof paper. Grease the paper.
2 Sift the cocoa powder into a bowl. Pour over the hot water and stir to dissolve.
3 Beat the cheese until smooth, then beat in the sugar, followed by the eggs, one at a time. Do not overmix.
4 Divide the mixture evenly between two bowls. Stir the chocolate mixture into one bowl, then add the vanilla essence to the remaining mixture.

5 Pour a cup or ladleful of the plain mixture into the centre of the tin; it will spread out into an even layer. Slowly pour over a cupful of chocolate mixture in the centre. Continue to alternate the cake mixtures in this way until both are used up. Draw a thin metal skewer through the cake mixture for a marbled effect.
6 Set the tin in a roasting pan and pour in hot water to come 4 cm/1½ in up the sides of the cake tin.

7 Bake the cheesecake for about 1½ hours, until the top is golden. (The cake will rise during baking but will sink later.) Cool in the tin on a wire rack.
8 Run a knife around the inside edge of the cake. Invert a flat plate over the tin and turn out the cake.

9 Sprinkle the crushed biscuits evenly over the cake, gently invert another plate on top, and turn over again. Cover and chill for 3 hours, preferably overnight.

RASPBERRY, MASCARPONE AND WHITE CHOCOLATE CHEESECAKE

SERVES 8

50g / 2oz / ¼ cup unsalted butter
225g / 8oz ginger biscuits, crushed
50g / 2oz / ½ cup chopped pecan nuts
or walnuts
FOR THE FILLING
275g / 10oz / 1¼ cups mascarpone cheese
175g / 6oz / ¾ cup fromage frais
2 eggs, beaten
45ml / 3 tbsp caster sugar
250g / 9oz white chocolate, chopped into
small pieces
225g / 8oz / 1½ cups fresh or frozen raspberries
FOR THE TOPPING
115g / 4oz / ½ cup mascarpone cheese
75g / 3oz / ⅓ cup fromage frais
white chocolate curls and fresh raspberries,
to decorate

1 Preheat oven to 150°C / 300°F / Gas 2. Melt the butter in a saucepan, then stir in the crushed biscuits and nuts. Press into the base of a 23 cm / 9 in springform cake tin. Level the surface.

2 Make the filling. Using a wooden spoon, beat the mascarpone and fromage frais in a large mixing bowl, then beat in the eggs, a little at a time. Add the caster sugar. Beat until the sugar has dissolved, and the mixture is smooth and creamy.

3 Melt the white chocolate gently in a heatproof bowl over a saucepan of simmering water, then stir into the cheese mixture. Add the fresh or frozen raspberries and mix lightly.

4 Tip into the prepared tin and spread evenly, then bake for about 1 hour or until just set. Switch off the oven, but do not remove the cheesecake. Leave it until cold and completely set.

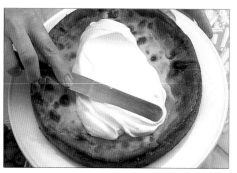

5 Remove the sides of the tin and carefully lift the cheesecake on to a serving plate. Make the topping by mixing the mascarpone and fromage frais in a bowl and spreading the mixture over the cheesecake. Decorate with chocolate curls and raspberries.

APRICOT AND WHITE CHOCOLATE CHEESECAKE

Use 225g / 8oz / 1 cup ready-to-eat dried apricots instead of the fresh or frozen raspberries in the cheesecake mixture. Slice the apricots thinly or dice them. Omit the mascarpone and fromage frais topping and serve the cheesecake with an apricot sauce, made by poaching 225g / 8oz stoned fresh apricots in 120ml / 4fl oz / ½ cup water until tender, then rubbing the fruit and liquid through a sieve placed over a bowl. Sweeten the apricot purée with caster sugar to taste, and add enough lemon juice to sharpen the flavour. Alternatively, purée drained canned apricots with a little of their syrup, then stir in lemon juice to taste.

LUXURY WHITE CHOCOLATE CHEESECAKE

SERVES 16–20

150g / 5oz (about 16–18) digestive biscuits
50g / 2oz / ½ cup blanched hazelnuts, toasted
50g / 2oz / ¼ cup unsalted butter, melted
2.5ml / ½ tsp ground cinnamon
white chocolate curls, to decorate
cocoa powder, for dusting (optional)

FOR THE FILLING

350g / 12oz fine quality white chocolate,
chopped into small pieces
120ml / 4fl oz / ½ cup whipping cream or
double cream
675g / 1½lb / 3 x 8oz packets cream
cheese, softened
50g / 2oz / ¼ cup granulated sugar
4 eggs
30ml / 2 tbsp hazelnut-flavoured liqueur or
15ml / 1 tbsp vanilla essence

FOR THE TOPPING

450ml / ¾ pint / 1¾ cups soured cream
50g / 2oz / ¼ cup granulated sugar
15ml / 1 tbsp hazelnut-flavoured liqueur or
5ml / 1 tsp vanilla essence

3 Using a hand-held electric mixer, beat the cream cheese and sugar in a large bowl until smooth. Add the eggs one at a time, beating well. Slowly beat in the white chocolate mixture and liqueur or vanilla essence. Pour the filling into the baked crust. Place the tin on the hot baking sheet. Bake for 45–55 minutes, and do not allow the top to brown. Transfer the cheesecake to a wire rack while preparing the topping. Increase the oven temperature to 200°C/400°F/Gas 6.

4 Prepare the topping. In a small bowl whisk the soured cream, sugar and liqueur or vanilla essence until thoroughly mixed. Pour the mixture over the cheesecake, spreading it evenly, and return to the oven. Bake for a further 5–7 minutes. Turn off the oven, but do not open the door for 1 hour. Serve the cheesecake at room temperature, decorated with the white chocolate curls. Dust the surface lightly with cocoa powder, if desired.

1 Preheat oven to 180°C/350°F/Gas 4. Grease a 23 x 7.5 cm/9 x 3 in springform tin. In a food processor, process the biscuits and hazelnuts until fine crumbs form. Pour in the butter and cinnamon. Process just until blended. Using the back of a spoon, press on to the base and to within 1 cm/½ in of the top of the sides of the cake tin. Bake the crumb crust for 5–7 minutes, until just set. Cool in the tin on a wire rack. Lower the oven temperature to 150°C/300°F/Gas 2 and place a baking sheet inside to heat up.

2 Prepare the filling. In a small saucepan over a low heat, melt the white chocolate and cream until smooth, stirring frequently. Set aside to cool slightly.

ITALIAN CHOCOLATE RICOTTA PIE

SERVES 6

225g / 8oz / 2 cups plain flour
30ml / 2 tbsp cocoa powder
60ml / 4 tbsp caster sugar
115g / 4oz / ½ cup unsalted butter
60ml / 4 tbsp dry sherry

FOR THE FILLING

2 egg yolks
115g / 4oz / ½ cup caster sugar
500g / 1¼lb / 2½ cups ricotta cheese
finely grated rind of 1 lemon
90ml / 6 tbsp dark chocolate chips
75ml / 5 tbsp chopped mixed peel
45ml / 3 tbsp chopped angelica

1 Sift the flour and cocoa into a bowl, then stir in the sugar. Rub in the butter using your fingertips, then work in the sherry to make a firm dough.

2 Preheat oven to 200°C / 400°F / Gas 6. Roll out three-quarters of the pastry on a lightly floured surface and line a 24 cm / 9½ in loose-based flan tin.

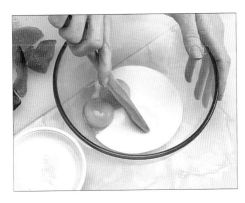

3 Make the filling. Beat the egg yolks and sugar in a bowl, then beat in the ricotta to mix thoroughly. Stir in the lemon rind, chocolate chips, mixed peel and angelica.

4 Scrape the ricotta mixture into the pastry case and level the surface. Roll out the remaining pastry and cut into strips. Arrange these in a lattice over the pie.

5 Bake for 15 minutes. Lower the oven temperature to 180°C / 350°F / Gas 4 and cook for a further 30–35 minutes, until golden brown and firm. Cool the pie in the tin. Serve at room temperature.

BLACK BOTTOM PIE

SERVES 6–8

250g/9oz/2¼ cups plain flour
150g/5oz/⅔ cup unsalted butter
2 egg yolks
15–30ml/1–2 tbsp iced water
FOR THE FILLING
3 eggs, separated
20ml/4 tsp cornflour
75g/3oz/6 tbsp golden caster sugar
400ml/14fl oz/1⅔ cups milk
*150g/5oz plain chocolate, chopped into
small pieces*
5ml/1 tsp vanilla essence
1 sachet powdered gelatine
45ml/3 tbsp water
30ml/2 tbsp dark rum
FOR THE TOPPING
*175ml/6 fl oz/¾ cup double cream or
whipping cream*
chocolate curls

1 Sift the flour into a bowl and rub in the butter until the mixture resembles coarse breadcrumbs. Stir in the egg yolks with just enough iced water to bind the mixture to a soft dough. Roll out on a lightly floured surface and line a deep 23 cm/9 in flan tin. Chill the pastry case for about 30 minutes.

2 Preheat oven to 190°C/375°F/Gas 5. Prick the pastry case all over with a fork, cover with greaseproof paper weighed down with baking beans and bake blind for 10 minutes. Remove the baking beans and paper, return the pastry case to the oven and bake for a further 10 minutes, until the pastry is crisp and golden. Cool in the tin.

POTS AU CHOCOLAT

The chocolate and chestnut mixture (minus the pastry) also makes delicious individual *pots au chocolat*. Make the fillings as described above, then simply pour the mixture into small ramekins that have been lightly greased with butter. Decorate with a blob of whipped cream and grated chocolate and serve with *langues de chat*.

CHOCOLATE AND CHESTNUT PIE

23 cm/9 in pastry case (see recipe above), cooked
FOR THE FILLING
115g/4oz/½ cup butter, softened
115g/4oz/¼ cup caster sugar
425g/15oz can unsweetened chestnut purée
225g/8oz plain chocolate, broken into small pieces
30ml/2 tbsp brandy

1 Make the filling. Cream the butter with the caster sugar in a mixing bowl until pale and fluffy. Add the unsweetened chestnut purée, about 30ml/2 tbsp at a time, beating well after each addition.

2 Put the chocolate in a heatproof bowl. Place over a saucepan of barely simmering water until the chocolate has melted, stirring occasionally until smooth. Stir the chocolate into the chestnut mixture until combined, then add the brandy.

3 Pour the filling into the cold pastry case. Using a spatula, level the surface. Chill until set. Decorate with whipped cream and chocolate leaves, if desired, or simply add a dusting of sifted cocoa.

3 Make the filling. Mix the egg yolks, cornflour and 30ml/2 tbsp of the sugar in a bowl. Heat the milk in a saucepan until almost boiling, then beat into the egg mixture. Return to the clean pan and stir over a low heat until the custard has thickened and is smooth. Pour half the custard into a bowl.

4 Put the chocolate in a heatproof bowl. Place over a saucepan of barely simmering water until the chocolate has melted, stirring occasionally until smooth. Stir the melted chocolate into the custard in the bowl, with the vanilla essence. Spread the filling in the pastry case and cover closely with dampened greaseproof paper or clear film to prevent the formation of a skin. Allow to cool, then chill until set.

5 Sprinkle the gelatine over the water in a bowl, leave until spongy, then place the bowl over a pan of simmering water until all the gelatine has dissolved. Stir into the remaining custard, then add the rum. Whisk the egg whites in a clean, grease-free bowl until peaks form. Whisk in the remaining sugar, a little at a time, until stiff, then fold the egg whites quickly but evenly into the rum-flavoured custard.

6 Spoon the rum-flavoured custard over the chocolate layer in the pastry case. Using a spatula, level the mixture, making sure that none of the chocolate custard is visible. Return the pie to the fridge until the top layer has set, then remove the pie from the tin and place it on a serving plate. Whip the cream, spread it over the pie and sprinkle with chocolate curls, to decorate.

MISSISSIPPI MUD PIE

SERVES 8

175g/6oz/1½ cups plain flour
2.5ml/½ tsp salt
115g/4oz/½ cup butter
30–45ml/2–3 tbsp iced water

FOR THE FILLING

75g/3oz plain chocolate, broken into small pieces
50g/2oz/¼ cup butter or margarine
45ml/3 tbsp golden syrup
3 eggs, beaten
150g/5oz/⅔ cup soft light brown sugar
5ml/1 tsp vanilla essence

TO DECORATE

115g/4oz chocolate bar
300ml/½ pint/1¼ cups whipping cream

1 Preheat oven to 220°C/425°F/Gas 7. Sift the flour and salt into a mixing bowl. Rub in the butter until the mixture resembles coarse breadcrumbs. Sprinkle in the water, about 15ml/1 tbsp at a time, and toss the mixture lightly with your fingers or a fork until the dough forms a ball.

2 On a lightly floured surface, roll out the pastry and line a 23 cm/9 in flan tin, easing in the pastry and being careful not to stretch it. With your thumbs, make a fluted edge.

3 Using a fork, prick the base and sides of the pastry case. Bake for 10–15 minutes, until lightly browned. Cool, in the pan.

4 Make the filling. In a heatproof bowl set over a pan of barely simmering water, melt the plain chocolate with the butter or margarine and the golden syrup. Remove the bowl from the heat and stir in the eggs, sugar and vanilla essence.

5 Lower the oven temperature to 180°C/350°F/Gas 4. Pour the chocolate mixture into the pastry case. Bake for 35–40 minutes, until the filling is set. Allow to cool completely in the flan tin, on a rack.

6 Make the decoration. Use the heat of your hands to soften the chocolate bar slightly. Working over a sheet of non-stick baking paper, draw the blade of a swivel-bladed vegetable peeler across the side of the chocolate bar to shave off short, wide curls. Chill the curls until required.

7 Before serving the pie, pour the cream into a bowl and whip to soft peaks. Spread over the top of the pie, hiding the chocolate filling completely. Decorate with the chocolate curls.

CHOCOLATE, BANANA AND TOFFEE PIE

SERVES 6

65g / 2½oz / 5 tbsp unsalted butter,
melted
250g / 9oz milk chocolate digestive biscuits,
crushed
chocolate curls, to decorate

FOR THE FILLING

397g / 13oz can condensed milk
150g / 5oz plain chocolate, chopped
120ml / 4fl oz / ½ cup crème fraîche
15ml / 1 tbsp golden syrup

FOR THE TOPPING

2 bananas
250ml / 8fl oz / 1 cup crème fraîche
10ml / 2 tsp strong black coffee

<u>1</u> Mix the butter with the biscuit crumbs. Press on to the base and sides of a 23cm / 9in loose-based flan tin. Chill.

<u>2</u> Make the filling. Place the unopened can of condensed milk in a deep saucepan of boiling water, making sure that it is completely covered. Lower the heat and simmer, covered for 2 hours, topping up the water as necessary. The can must remain covered at all times.

<u>3</u> Remove the pan from the heat and set aside, covered, until the can has cooled down completely in the water. Do not attempt to open the can until it is completely cold.

<u>4</u> Gently melt the chocolate with the crème fraîche and golden syrup in a heatproof bowl over a saucepan of simmering water. Stir in the caramelized condensed milk and beat until evenly mixed. Pour the filling into the biscuit crust and spread it evenly.

<u>5</u> Slice the bananas evenly and arrange them over the chocolate filling.

<u>6</u> Stir the crème fraîche and coffee together in a bowl, then spoon the mixture over the bananas. Sprinkle the chocolate curls on top. Alternatively, omit the crème fraîche topping and decorate with whipped cream and extra banana slices.

CHILLED CHOCOLATE DESSERTS

DOUBLE CHOCOLATE SNOWBALL

SERVES 12–14

350g / 12oz bittersweet or plain chocolate,
chopped into small pieces
350g / 12oz / 1¾ cups caster sugar
275g / 10oz / 1¼ cups unsalted butter, cut into
small pieces
8 eggs
60ml / 4 tbsp orange-flavoured liqueur or
brandy
cocoa powder, for dusting

FOR THE WHITE CHOCOLATE CREAM

200g / 7oz fine quality white chocolate,
chopped into small pieces
475ml / 16fl oz / 2 cups double or whipping
cream
15ml / 1 tbsp orange-flavoured liqueur
(optional)

1 Preheat oven to 180°C / 350°F / Gas 4. Carefully line a 1.75 litre / 3 pint / 7½ cup round ovenproof bowl with aluminium foil, smoothing the sides. Melt the bittersweet chocolate in a heatproof bowl over a pan of barely simmering water. Add the caster sugar and stir until the chocolate has melted and the sugar has dissolved. Strain the mixture into a medium bowl.

2 With a hand-held electric mixer at low speed, beat in the butter, then the eggs, one at a time, beating well after each addition. Stir in the liqueur or brandy and pour into the prepared bowl. Tap the sides of the bowl gently to release any large air bubbles.

3 Bake for 1¼–1½ hours until the surface is firm and slightly risen, but cracked. The centre will still be wobbly, but will set on cooling. Remove the bowl to a rack to cool to room temperature; the top will sink. Cover the surface of the cake with a dinner plate (to make an even surface for unmoulding); then wrap completely with clear film or foil and chill overnight.

4 To unmould, remove the film or foil, lift off the plate, and place an upturned serving plate over the top of the mould. Invert the mould on to the plate and shake firmly to release the cake. Carefully peel off the foil used for lining the bowl. Cover until ready to decorate.

5 In a food processor fitted with a metal blade, process the white chocolate until fine. Heat 120ml / 4fl oz / ½ cup of the cream in a small saucepan until just beginning to simmer. With the food processor running, pour the hot cream through the feeder tube and process until the chocolate has melted completely. Strain into a medium bowl and cool to room temperature, stirring occasionally.

6 In another bowl, beat the remaining cream with the electric mixer until soft peaks form. Add the liqueur and beat for 30 seconds or until the cream holds its shape, but is not yet stiff. Fold a spoonful of cream into the chocolate mixture to lighten it, then fold in the rest. Spoon into a piping bag fitted with a star tip and pipe rosettes over the surface of the cake. Dust lightly with cocoa powder to finish the decoration.

CHOCOLATE AMARETTO MARQUISE

SERVES 10–12

*15ml/1 tbsp flavourless vegetable oil, such as
groundnut or sunflower*

75g/3oz/7–8 amaretti biscuits, finely crushed

*25g/1oz/¼ cup unblanched almonds, toasted
and finely chopped*

*450g/1lb fine quality bittersweet or plain
chocolate, chopped into small pieces*

75ml/5 tbsp Amaretto liqueur

75ml/5 tbsp golden syrup

*475ml/16fl oz/2 cups double cream
cocoa powder, for dusting*

FOR THE AMARETTO CREAM

*350ml/12fl oz/1½ cups whipping cream or
double cream for serving*

*30–45ml/2–3 tbsp Amaretto di Soronno
liqueur*

1 Lightly oil a 23 cm/9 in heart-shaped or springform cake tin. Line the bottom with non-stick baking paper and oil the paper. In a small bowl, combine the crushed amaretti biscuits and the chopped almonds. Sprinkle evenly on to the base of the tin.

2 Place the chocolate, Amaretto liqueur and golden syrup in a medium saucepan over a very low heat. Stir frequently until the chocolate is melted and the mixture is smooth. Remove from the heat and allow it to cool for about 6–8 minutes, until the mixture feels just warm to the touch.

3 Pour the cream into a bowl. Whip with a hand-held electric mixer, until it just begins to hold its shape. Stir a large spoonful into the chocolate mixture, to lighten it, then quickly add the remaining cream and gently fold into the chocolate mixture. Pour into the prepared tin, on top of the amaretti and almond mixture. Level the surface. Cover the tin with clear film and chill overnight.

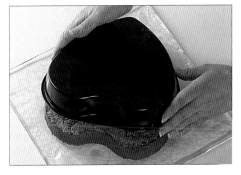

4 To unmould, run a thin-bladed sharp knife under hot water and dry carefully. Run the knife around the edge of the tin to loosen the dessert. Place a serving plate over the tin, then invert to unmould. Carefully peel off the paper, replacing any crust that sticks to it, and dust with cocoa powder. In a bowl, whip the cream and Amaretto liqueur to soft peaks. Serve separately.

Chocolate Puffs

Serves 4–6

65g/2½oz/generous ½ cup plain
flour
150ml/¼ pint/⅔ cup water
50g/2oz/¼ cup butter
2 eggs, beaten
For the Filling and Icing
150ml/¼ pint/⅔ cup double cream
225g/8oz/1½ cups icing sugar
15ml/1 tbsp cocoa powder
30–60ml/2–4 tbsp water

1 Preheat oven to 220°C/425°F/Gas 7. Sift the flour into a bowl. Put the water in a saucepan over a medium heat, add the butter and heat gently until it melts. Increase the heat and bring to the boil, then remove from the heat. Tip in all the flour at once and beat quickly until the mixture sticks together and becomes thick and glossy, leaving the side of the pan clean. Leave the mixture to cool slightly.

2 Add the eggs, a little at a time, to the mixture and beat by hand with a wooden spoon or with an electric whisk, until the mixture (choux pastry) is thick and glossy and drops reluctantly from a spoon. (You may not need to use all of the egg.) Spoon the choux pastry into a piping bag fitted with a 2 cm/¾ in nozzle. Dampen two baking sheets with cold water.

3 Pipe walnut-sized spoonfuls of the choux pastry on to the dampened baking sheets. Leave some space for them to rise. Cook for 25–30 minutes, until they are golden brown and well risen. Use a palette knife to lift the puffs on to a wire rack, and make a small hole in each one with the handle of a wooden spoon to allow the steam to escape. Leave to cool.

4 Make the filling and icing. Whip the cream until thick. Put it into a piping bag fitted with a plain or star nozzle. Push the nozzle into the hole in each puff and squirt a little cream inside. Put the icing sugar and cocoa in a small bowl and stir together. Add enough water to make a thick glossy icing. Spread a little icing on each puff and serve when set.

CHOCOLATE HAZELNUT GALETTES

SERVES 4

175g/6oz plain chocolate, chopped into small pieces
45ml/3 tbsp single cream
30ml/2 tbsp flaked hazelnuts
115g/4oz white chocolate, chopped into small pieces
175g/6oz/¾ cup fromage frais (8% fat)
15ml/1 tbsp dry sherry
60ml/4 tbsp finely chopped hazelnuts, toasted physalis (Cape gooseberries), dipped in white chocolate, to decorate

1 Melt the plain chocolate in a heatproof bowl over a saucepan of barely simmering water, then remove the pan from the heat and lift off the bowl. Stir the cream into the melted chocolate. Draw twelve 7.5 cm/3 in circles on sheets of non-stick baking paper.

2 Turn the baking paper over and spread the plain chocolate over each marked circle, covering in a thin, even layer. Scatter flaked hazelnuts over four of the circles, then leave until set.

3 Melt the white chocolate in a heatproof bowl over hot water, then stir in the fromage frais and dry sherry. Fold in the chopped, toasted hazelnuts. Leave to cool until the mixture holds its shape.

4 Remove the plain chocolate rounds carefully from the paper and sandwich them together in stacks of three, spooning the white chocolate hazelnut cream between the layers and using the hazelnut-covered rounds on top. Chill before serving.

5 To serve, place the galettes on individual plates and decorate with chocolate-dipped physalis.

CHOCOLATE PAVLOVA WITH PASSION FRUIT CREAM

SERVES 6

4 egg whites
200g/7oz/scant 1 cup caster sugar
20ml/4 tsp cornflour
45ml/3 tbsp cocoa powder
5ml/1 tsp vinegar
chocolate leaves, to decorate

FOR THE FILLING

150g/5oz plain chocolate, chopped into
small pieces
250ml/8fl oz/1 cup double cream
150g/5oz/²⁄₃ cup Greek-style yogurt
2.5ml/¹⁄₂ tsp vanilla essence
4 passion fruit

1 Preheat oven to 140°C/275°F/Gas 1. Cut a piece of non-stick baking paper to fit a baking sheet. Draw a 23 cm/9 in circle on the paper.

2 Whisk the egg whites in a clean, grease-free bowl until stiff. Gradually whisk in the sugar and continue to whisk until the mixture is stiff again. Whisk in the cornflour, cocoa and vinegar.

3 Place the baking paper upside down on the baking sheet. Spread the mixture over the marked circle, making a slight dip in the centre. Bake for 1¹⁄₂–2 hours.

4 Make the filling. Melt the chocolate in a heatproof bowl over barely simmering water, then remove from the heat and cool slightly. In a separate bowl, whip the cream with the yogurt and vanilla essence until thick. Fold 60ml/4 tbsp into the chocolate, then set both mixtures aside.

5 Halve all the passion fruit and scoop out the pulp. Stir half into the plain cream mixture. Carefully remove the meringue shell from the baking sheet and place it on a large serving plate. Fill with the passion fruit cream, then spoon over the chocolate mixture and the remaining passion fruit pulp.

6 Decorate with chocolate leaves and serve as soon as possible, while the meringue is still crisp on the outside and deliciously chewy within.

CHOCOLATE AND CHESTNUT POTS

SERVES 6

250g/9oz plain chocolate
60ml/4 tbsp Madeira
25g/1oz/2 tbsp butter, diced
2 eggs, separated
225g/8oz/1 cup unsweetened chestnut purée
crème fraîche and chocolate curls, to decorate

1 Make a few chocolate curls for decoration, then break the rest of the chocolate into squares and melt it with the Madeira in a heatproof bowl over a saucepan of barely simmering water. Remove from the heat and add the butter, a few pieces at a time, stirring until melted and smooth.

2 Beat the egg yolks quickly into the mixture, then beat in the chestnut purée, a little at a time, making sure that each addition is absorbed before you add the next, mixing until smooth.

3 Whisk the egg whites in a clean, grease-free bowl until stiff. Stir about 15ml/1 tbsp of the whites into the chestnut mixture to lighten it, then fold in the rest evenly.

4 Spoon the mixture into six small ramekin dishes or custard cups and chill until set. Serve the pots topped with a generous spoonful of crème fraîche or whipped double cream. Decorate with the chocolate curls.

MOCHA VELVET CREAM POTS

SERVES 8

15ml/1 tbsp instant coffee powder
475ml/16fl oz/2 cups milk
75g/3oz/6 tbsp caster sugar
225g/8oz plain chocolate, chopped into small pieces
10ml/2 tsp vanilla essence
30ml/2 tbsp coffee liqueur (optional)
7 egg yolks
whipped cream and crystallized mimosa balls, to decorate

1 Preheat oven to 160°C/325°F/Gas 3. Place eight 120ml/ 4fl oz/½ cup custard cups or ramekins in a roasting tin. Set the tin aside.

2 Put the instant coffee into a saucepan. Stir in the milk, then add the sugar and set the pan over a medium heat. Bring to the boil, stirring constantly, until both the coffee and the sugar have dissolved completely.

3 Remove the pan from the heat and add the chocolate. Stir until it has melted and the sauce is smooth. Stir in the vanilla essence and coffee liqueur, if using.

4 In a bowl, whisk the egg yolks to blend them lightly. Slowly whisk in the chocolate mixture until well mixed, then strain the mixture into a large jug and divide equally among the cups or ramekins. Pour enough boiling water into the roasting tin to come halfway up the sides of the cups or ramekins. Carefully place the roasting tin in the oven.

5 Bake for 30–35 minutes, until the custard is just set and a knife inserted into the custard comes out clean. Remove the cups or ramekins from the roasting tin and allow to cool. Place on a baking sheet, cover and chill completely. Decorate with whipped cream and crystallized mimosa balls, if desired.

CHOCOLATE VANILLA TIMBALES

SERVES 6

350ml / 12fl oz / 1½ cups semi-skimmed milk
30ml / 2 tbsp cocoa powder
2 eggs
10ml / 2 tsp vanilla essence
45ml / 3 tbsp granulated sweetener
15ml / 1 tbsp / 1 sachet powdered gelatine
45ml / 3 tbsp hot water
extra cocoa powder, to decorate

FOR THE SAUCE

115g / 4oz / ½ cup light Greek-style yogurt
25ml / 1½ tbsp vanilla essence

__1__ Place the milk and cocoa powder in a saucepan and stir until the milk is boiling. Separate the eggs and beat the egg yolks with the vanilla and sweetener in a bowl, until the mixture is pale and smooth. Gradually pour in the chocolate milk, beating well.

__2__ Return the mixture to the pan and stir constantly over a gentle heat, without boiling, until it is slightly thickened and smooth.

__3__ Remove the pan from the heat. Pour the gelatine into the hot water and stir until it is completely dissolved, then quickly stir it into the milk mixture. Put this mixture aside and allow it to cool until almost setting.

__4__ Whisk the egg whites until they hold soft peaks. Fold the egg whites quickly into the milk mixture. Spoon the timbale mixture into six individual moulds and chill them until set.

__5__ To serve, run a knife around the edge, dip the moulds quickly into hot water and turn out. Dust with cocoa. For the sauce, stir together the yogurt and vanilla and spoon on to the plates.

TIRAMISU IN CHOCOLATE CUPS

SERVES 6

1 egg yolk
30ml / 2 tbsp caster sugar
2.5ml / ½ tsp vanilla essence
250g / 9oz / generous 1 cup mascarpone cheese
120ml / 4fl oz / ½ cup strong black coffee
15ml / 1 tbsp cocoa powder
30ml / 2 tbsp coffee liqueur
16 amaretti biscuits
cocoa powder, for dusting

FOR THE CHOCOLATE CUPS

175g / 6oz plain chocolate, chopped
25g / 1oz / 2 tbsp unsalted butter

1 Make the chocolate cups. Cut out six 15 cm / 6 in rounds of non-stick baking paper. Melt the chocolate with the butter in a heatproof bowl over a saucepan of simmering water. Stir until smooth, then spread a spoonful of the chocolate mixture over each circle, to within 2 cm / ¾ in of the edge.

2 Carefully lift each paper round and drape it over an upturned teacup or ramekin so that the edges curve into frills. Leave until completely set, then carefully lift off and peel away the paper to reveal the chocolate cups.

3 Make the filling. Using a hand-held electric mixer, beat the egg yolk and sugar in a bowl until smooth, then stir in the vanilla essence. Soften the mascarpone if necessary, then stir it into the egg yolk mixture. Beat until smooth.

4 In a separate bowl, mix the coffee, cocoa and liqueur. Break up the biscuits roughly, then stir them into the mixture.

5 Place the chocolate cups on individual plates. Divide half the biscuit mixture among them, then spoon over half the mascarpone mixture.

6 Spoon over the remaining biscuit mixture (including any free liquid), top with the rest of the mascarpone mixture and dust lightly with cocoa powder. Chill for about 30 minutes before serving.

DEVILISH CHOCOLATE ROULADE

SERVES 6–8

175g/6oz plain dark chocolate, chopped into
small pieces
4 eggs, separated
115g/4oz/½ cup caster sugar
cocoa powder for dusting
chocolate-dipped strawberries, to decorate

FOR THE FILLING

225g/8oz plain chocolate, chopped into
small pieces
45ml/3 tbsp brandy
2 eggs, separated
250g/9oz/generous 1 cup mascarpone cheese

1 Preheat oven to 180°C/350°F/Gas 4.
Grease a 33 × 23 cm/13 × 9 in Swiss roll
tin and line with non-stick baking paper.
Melt the chocolate.

2 Whisk the egg yolks and sugar in a bowl
until pale and thick, then stir in the
melted chocolate. Place the egg whites in
a clean, grease-free bowl. Whisk them to
soft peaks, then fold lightly and evenly
into the egg and chocolate mixture.

3 Scrape into the tin and spread to the
corners. Bake for 15-20 minutes, until
well risen and firm to the touch. Dust a
sheet of non-stick baking paper with
cocoa powder. Turn the sponge out on
the paper, cover with a clean dish towel
and leave to cool.

4 Make the filling. Melt the chocolate
with the brandy in a heatproof bowl over
a saucepan of simmering water. Remove
from the heat. Beat the egg yolks
together, then beat into the chocolate
mixture. In a separate bowl whisk the
whites to soft peaks, then fold them
lightly and evenly into the filling.

5 Uncover the roulade, remove the lining
paper and spread with the mascarpone.
Spread the chocolate mixture over the
top, then roll up carefully from a long
side to enclose the filling. Transfer to a
serving plate with the join underneath,
top with fresh chocolate-dipped
strawberries and chill before serving.

COOK'S TIP

Chocolate-dipped strawberries make a
marvellous edible decoration for cakes
and desserts. Break plain, milk or
white chocolate into small pieces and
place in a small deep heatproof bowl
over a saucepan of barely simmering
water. While the chocolate melts, line
a baking sheet with non-stick baking
paper and set it aside.
Stir the melted chocolate until it is
completely smooth. Holding a
strawberry by its stalk or stalk end,
dip it partially or fully into the melted
chocolate, allowing any excess
chocolate to drip back into the bowl,
then place the fruit on the paper-lined
baking sheet. Repeat with the rest of
the fruit. Leave until the chocolate has
set. Use on the same day.
The same technique can be applied to
other relatively firm fruits, such as
cherries and orange segments.

CHOCOLATE CONES WITH APRICOT SAUCE

SERVES 6

*250g/9oz plain dark chocolate, chopped into
small pieces
350g/12oz/1½ cups ricotta cheese
45ml/3 tbsp double cream
30ml/2 tbsp brandy
30ml/2 tbsp icing sugar
finely grated rind of 1 lemon
pared strips of lemon rind, to decorate*

FOR THE SAUCE

*175g/6oz/⅔ cup apricot jam
45ml/3 tbsp lemon juice*

1 Cut twelve 10 cm/4 in double
thickness rounds from non-stick baking
paper and shape each into a cone. Secure
with masking tape.
2 Melt the chocolate over a saucepan of
simmering water. Cool slightly, then
spoon a little into each cone, swirling and
brushing it to coat the paper evenly.

3 Support each cone point downwards in
a cup or glass held on its side, to keep it
level. Leave in a cool place until the cones
are completely set. Unless it is a very hot
day, do not put the cones in the fridge, as
this may mar their appearance.
4 Make the sauce. Combine the apricot
jam and lemon juice in a small saucepan.
Melt over a gentle heat, stirring
occasionally, then press through a sieve
into a small bowl. Set aside to cool.

5 Beat the ricotta cheese in a bowl until
softened, then beat in the cream, brandy
and icing sugar. Stir in the lemon rind.
Spoon the mixture into a piping bag. Fill
the cones, then carefully peel off the non-
stick baking paper.
6 Spoon a pool of apricot sauce on to six
dessert plates. Arrange the cones in pairs
on the plates. Decorate with a scattering
of pared lemon rind strips and serve
immediately.

CHOCOLATE BLANCMANGE

SERVES 4

60ml/4 tbsp cornflour
600ml/1 pint/2½ cups milk
45ml/3 tbsp sugar
50–115g/2–4oz plain chocolate, chopped
few drops of vanilla essence
white and plain chocolate curls, to decorate

1 Rinse a 750ml/1¼ pint/3 cup fluted mould with cold water and leave it upside down to drain. Blend the cornflour to a smooth paste with a little of the milk in a medium-sized bowl.

2 Bring the remaining milk to the boil, preferably in a non-stick saucepan, then pour on to the blended mixture stirring constantly.

3 Pour all the milk back into the saucepan and bring slowly to the boil over a low heat, stirring constantly until the mixture boils and thickens. Remove the pan from the heat, then add the sugar, chocolate and vanilla essence and stir until the sauce is smooth, all the sugar has dissolved and the chocolate pieces have melted completely.

4 Pour the chocolate mixture into the mould, cover closely with dampened greaseproof paper (to prevent the formation of a skin) and leave in a cool place for several hours to set.

5 To unmould the blancmange, place a large serving plate upside down on top of the mould. Holding the plate and mould firmly together, turn them both over. Give both plate and mould a gentle but firm shake to loosen the blancmange, then lift off the mould. Scatter the chocolate curls over the top and serve.

CHOCOLATE MANDARIN TRIFLE

SERVES 6–8

4 trifle sponges

14 amaretti biscuits

60ml / 4 tbsp Amaretto di Saronno or sweet sherry

8 mandarin oranges

FOR THE CUSTARD

200g / 7oz plain chocolate, chopped into small pieces

30ml / 2 tbsp cornflour or custard powder

30ml / 2 tbsp caster sugar

2 egg yolks

200ml / 7fl oz / scant 1 cup milk

250g / 9oz / generous 1 cup mascarpone cheese

FOR THE TOPPING

250g / 9oz / generous 1 cup fromage frais

chocolate shapes

mandarin slices or segments

1 Break up the trifle sponges and place them in a large glass serving dish. Crumble the amaretti biscuits over and then sprinkle with Amaretto or sherry.

2 Squeeze the juice from 2 mandarins and sprinkle into the dish. Segment the rest and put in the dish.

3 Make the custard. Melt the chocolate. In a heatproof bowl, mix the cornflour or custard powder, caster sugar and egg yolks to a smooth paste.

4 Heat the milk in a small saucepan until almost boiling, then pour on to the egg yolk mixture, stirring constantly. Return to the clean pan and stir over a low heat until the custard has thickened slightly and is smooth.

5 Stir in the mascarpone until melted, then mix in the melted chocolate. Spread over the sponge and biscuit, cool, then chill.

6 To serve, spread the fromage frais over the custard, then decorate with chocolate shapes and mandarin slices or segments.

COOK'S TIP

You can use canned mandarin oranges, if you prefer. Spoon about 30ml / 2 tbsp of the juice over the sponge and biscuit mixture.

CHOCOLATE PROFITEROLES

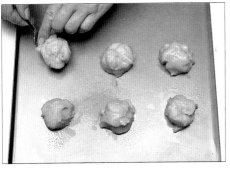

4 Beat 1 egg in a small bowl and set aside. Add the whole eggs, one at a time, to the flour mixture, beating well after each addition. Beat in just enough of the beaten egg to make a smooth, shiny dough. It should pull away and fall slowly when dropped from a spoon.

5 Using a tablespoon, ease the dough in 12 mounds on to the prepared baking sheet. Bake for 25–30 minutes, until the puffs are golden brown.

6 Remove the puffs from the oven and cut a small slit in the side of each of them to release the steam. Return the puffs to the oven, turn off the heat and leave them to dry out, with the oven door open.

7 Remove the ice cream from the freezer and allow it to soften for about 10 minutes. Split the profiteroles in half and put a small scoop of ice cream in each. Arrange on a serving platter or divide among individual plates. Pour the sauce over the profiteroles and serve at once.

SERVES 4-6

110g / 3¾oz / scant 1 cup plain flour
1.5ml / ¼ tsp salt
pinch of freshly grated nutmeg
175ml / 6fl oz / ¾ cup water
75g / 3oz / 6 tbsp unsalted butter, cut into 6 equal pieces
3 eggs
750ml / 1¼ pints / 3 cups vanilla ice cream

FOR THE CHOCOLATE SAUCE

275g / 10oz plain chocolate, chopped into small pieces
120ml / 4fl oz / ½ cup warm water

1 Preheat oven to 200°C/400°F/Gas 6. Grease a baking sheet. Sift the flour, salt and nutmeg on to a sheet of greaseproof paper or foil.

2 Make the sauce. Melt the chocolate with the water in a heatproof bowl placed over a saucepan of barely simmering water. Stir until smooth. Keep warm until ready to serve, or reheat when required.

3 In a medium saucepan, bring the water and butter to the boil. Remove from the heat and add the dry ingredients all at once, funnelling them in from the paper or foil. Beat with a wooden spoon for about 1 minute until well blended and the mixture starts to pull away from the pan, then set the pan over a low heat and cook the mixture for about 2 minutes, beating constantly. Remove from the heat.

VARIATION

Fill the profiteroles with whipped cream, if you prefer. Spoon the cream into a piping bag and fill the slit puffs, or sandwich the halved puffs with the cream.

BITTER CHOCOLATE MOUSSE

SERVES 8

225g/8oz plain chocolate, chopped into small pieces
60ml/4 tbsp water
30ml/2 tbsp orange flavoured liqueur or brandy
25g/1oz/2 tbsp unsalted butter, cut into small pieces
4 eggs, separated
90ml/6 tbsp whipping cream
1.5ml/¼ tsp cream of tartar
45ml/3 tbsp caster sugar
crème fraîche and chocolate curls, to decorate

1 Melt the chocolate with the water in a heatproof bowl over a pan of barely simmering water, stirring until smooth. Off the heat, whisk in the liqueur or brandy and butter.

2 With a hand-held electric mixer, beat the egg yolks for 2–3 minutes until thick and creamy, then slowly beat into the melted chocolate until well blended. Set aside.

3 Whip the cream until soft peaks form and stir a spoonful into the chocolate mixture to lighten it. Fold in the remaining cream.

4 In a grease free bowl, beat the egg whites slowly until frothy. Add the cream of tartar, increase the speed and continue beating until they form soft peaks. Gradually sprinkle over the sugar and continue beating until the whites are stiff and glossy.

5 Using a rubber spatula or large metal spoon, stir a quarter of the egg whites into the chocolate mixture, then gently fold in the remaining whites, cutting down to the bottom, along the sides and up to the top in a semicircular motion until they are just combined. Gently spoon into eight individual dishes. Chill for at least 2 hours or until set.

6 Spoon a little crème fraîche over each mousse and decorate with the chocolate curls.

WHITE CHOCOLATE VANILLA MOUSSE WITH DARK CHOCOLATE SAUCE

SERVES 6–8

200g/7 oz white chocolate, chopped into small pieces
2 eggs, separated
60ml/4 tbsp caster sugar
300ml/½ pint/1¼ cups double cream
1 sachet powdered gelatine
150ml/¼ pint/⅔ cup Greek-style yogurt
10ml/2 tsp vanilla essence

FOR THE SAUCE

50g/2oz plain chocolate, chopped into small pieces
30ml/2 tbsp dark rum
60ml/4 tbsp single cream

1 Line a 1 litre/1¾ pint/4 cup loaf tin with non-stick baking paper or clear film. Melt the chocolate. Whisk the egg yolks and sugar until pale and thick, then beat in the chocolate.

2 Heat the cream in a small saucepan until almost boiling, then remove from the heat. Sprinkle the powdered gelatine over, stirring until completely dissolved. Pour on to the chocolate mixture, whisking vigorously until smooth.

3 Whisk the yogurt and vanilla essence into the mixture. In a clean, grease-free bowl, whisk the egg whites until stiff, then fold them into the mixture. Tip into the prepared loaf tin, level the surface and chill until set.

4 Make the sauce. Melt the chocolate with the rum and cream in a heatproof bowl over a saucepan of simmering water, stirring occasionally, then leave to cool completely.

5 Serve the mousse in thick slices with the cooled chocolate sauce poured around.

MANGO AND CHOCOLATE CREME BRULEE

SERVES 6

2 ripe mangoes, peeled, stoned and chopped
300ml / ½ pint / 1¼ cups double cream
300ml / ½ pint / 1¼ cups crème fraîche
1 vanilla pod
115g / 4oz plain dark chocolate, chopped into
small pieces
4 egg yolks
15ml / 1 tbsp clear honey
90ml / 6 tbsp demerara sugar, for the topping

1 Divide the mangoes among six flameproof dishes set on a baking sheet.

2 Mix the cream, crème fraîche and vanilla pod in a large heatproof bowl. Place the bowl over a pan of barely simmering water.

3 Heat the cream mixture for 10 minutes. Do not let the bowl touch the water or the cream may overheat. Remove the vanilla pod and stir in the chocolate, a few pieces at a time, until melted. When smooth, remove the bowl, but leave the pan of water over the heat.

4 Whisk the egg yolks and clear honey in a second heatproof bowl, then gradually pour in the chocolate cream, whisking constantly. Place over the pan of simmering water and stir constantly until the chocolate custard thickens enough to coat the back of a wooden spoon.

5 Remove from the heat and spoon the custard over the mangoes. Cool, then chill in the fridge until set.

6 Preheat the grill to high. Sprinkle 15ml / 1 tbsp demerara sugar evenly over each dessert and spray lightly with a little water. Grill briefly, as close to the heat as possible, until the sugar melts and caramelizes. Chill again before serving the desserts.

WHITE CHOCOLATE PARFAIT

SERVES 10

225g/8oz white chocolate, chopped into
small pieces
600ml/1 pint/2½ cups whipping cream
120ml/4fl oz/½ cup milk
10 egg yolks
15ml/1 tbsp caster sugar
40g/1½oz/½ cup desiccated coconut
120ml/4fl oz/½ cup canned sweetened
coconut milk
150g/5oz/1¼ cups unsalted macadamia nuts
curls of fresh coconut, to decorate
FOR THE CHOCOLATE ICING
225g/8oz plain chocolate, chopped into
small pieces
75g/3oz/6 tbsp butter
20ml/generous 1 tbsp golden syrup
175ml/6fl oz/¾ cup whipping cream

1 Carefully line the base and sides of a 1.4 litre/2⅓ pint/6 cup terrine mould or loaf tin with clear film.

2 Melt the chopped white chocolate with 50ml/2fl oz/¼ cup of the cream in the top of a double boiler or a heatproof bowl set over a saucepan of simmering water. Stir continually until the mixture is smooth. Set aside.

3 Put the milk in a pan. Add 250ml/8fl oz/1 cup of the remaining cream and bring to boiling point over a medium heat stirring constantly.

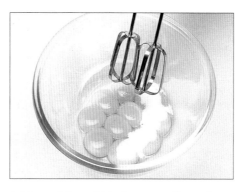

4 Meanwhile, whisk the egg yolks and caster sugar together in a large bowl, until thick and pale.

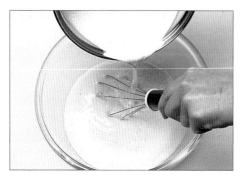

5 Add the hot cream mixture to the yolks, whisking constantly. Pour back into the saucepan and cook over a low heat for 2–3 minutes, until thickened. Stir constantly and do not boil. Remove the pan from the heat.

6 Add the melted chocolate, desiccated coconut and coconut milk, then stir well and leave to cool. Whip the remaining cream in a bowl until thick, then fold into the chocolate and coconut mixture.

7 Put 475ml/16fl oz/2 cups of the parfait mixture in the prepared mould or tin and spread evenly. Cover and freeze for about 2 hours, until just firm. Cover the remaining mixture and chill.

VARIATION

White Chocolate and Ginger Parfait: Use sliced stem ginger instead of macadamia nuts for the central layer of the parfait, and substitute syrup from the jar of ginger for the golden syrup in the icing. Leave out the coconut, if you prefer, and use sweetened condensed milk instead of the coconut milk.

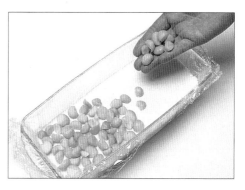

8 Scatter the macadamia nuts evenly over the frozen parfait. Spoon in the remaining parfait mixture and level the surface. Cover the terrine and freeze for 6–8 hours or overnight, until the parfait is firm.

9 To make the icing, melt the chocolate with the butter and syrup in the top of a double boiler set over hot water. Stir occasionally.

10 Heat the cream in a saucepan, until just simmering, then stir into the chocolate mixture. Remove the pan from the heat and leave the mixture to cool until lukewarm.

11 To turn out the parfait, wrap the terrine or tin in a hot towel and set it upside down on a plate. Lift off the terrine or tin, then peel off the clear film. Place the parfait on a rack over a baking sheet and pour the icing evenly over the top. Working quickly, smooth the icing down the sides with a palette knife. Leave to set slightly, then transfer to a freezer-proof plate and freeze for 3–4 hours more.

12 Remove from the freezer about 15 minutes before serving, to allow the ice cream to soften slightly. When ready to serve, cut into slices, using a knife dipped in hot water between each slice. Serve, decorated with coconut curls.

CHOCOLATE ICES AND SORBETS

WHITE CHOCOLATE RASPBERRY RIPPLE ICE CREAM

2 In a saucepan, combine the milk and 250ml/8fl oz/1 cup cream and bring to the boil. In a bowl beat the yolks and sugar with a hand-held mixer for 2–3 minutes until thick and creamy. Gradually pour the hot milk mixture over the yolks and return to the pan. Cook over a medium heat until the custard coats the back of a wooden spoon, stirring constantly.

3 Remove the pan from the heat and stir in the white chocolate until melted and smooth. Pour the remaining cream into a large bowl. Strain in the hot custard, mix well, then stir in the vanilla essence. Cool, then transfer the custard to an ice-cream maker and freeze it according to the manufacturer's instructions.

4 When the mixture is frozen, but still soft, transfer one third of the ice cream to a freezerproof bowl. Set half the raspberry sauce aside. Spoon a third of the remainder over the ice cream. Cover with another third of the ice cream and more sauce. Repeat. With a knife or spoon, lightly marble the mixture. Cover and freeze. Allow the ice cream to soften for 15 minutes before serving with the remaining raspberry sauce, and the mint.

MAKES 1 LITRE/1¾ PINTS/4 CUPS
250ml/8fl oz/1 cup milk
475ml/16fl oz/2 cups whipping cream
7 egg yolks
30ml/2 tbsp granulated sugar
225g/8oz fine quality white chocolate,
chopped into small pieces
5ml/1 tsp vanilla essence
mint sprigs to decorate
FOR THE RASPBERRY RIPPLE SAUCE
275g/10oz packet frozen raspberries in light
syrup or 275g/10oz jar reduced sugar
raspberry preserve
10ml/2 tsp golden syrup
15ml/1 tbsp lemon juice
15ml/1 tbsp cornflour mixed to a paste with
15ml/1 tbsp water

1 Prepare the sauce. Press the raspberries and their syrup through a sieve into a saucepan. Add the golden syrup, lemon juice and cornflour mixture. (If using preserve, omit cornflour, but add the water.) Bring to the boil, stirring often, then simmer for 1–2 minutes. Pour into a bowl and cool, then chill.

CHOCOLATE FUDGE SUNDAES

SERVES 4

4 scoops each vanilla and coffee ice cream
2 small ripe bananas
whipped cream
toasted flaked almonds

FOR THE SAUCE

50g / 2oz / ⅓ cup soft light brown sugar
120ml / 4fl oz / ½ cup golden syrup
45ml / 3 tbsp strong black coffee
5ml / 1 tsp ground cinnamon
150g / 5oz plain chocolate, chopped into
small pieces
75ml / 3fl oz / 5 tbsp whipping cream
45ml / 3 tbsp coffee-flavoured liqueur
(optional)

1 Make the sauce. Place the sugar, syrup, coffee and cinnamon in a heavy-based saucepan. Bring to the boil, then boil for about 5 minutes, stirring the mixture constantly.

2 Turn off the heat and stir in the chocolate. When the chocolate has melted and the mixture is smooth, stir in the cream and the liqueur, if using. Leave the sauce to cool slightly. If made ahead, reheat the sauce gently until just warm.

3 Fill four glasses with a scoop each of vanilla and coffee ice cream.

4 Peel the bananas and slice them thinly. Scatter the sliced bananas over the ice cream. Pour the warm fudge sauce over the bananas, then top each sundae with a generous swirl of whipped cream. Sprinkle the sundaes with toasted almonds and serve at once.

CHOCOLATE ICE CREAM

SERVES 4–6

750ml/1¼ pints/3 cups milk
10 cm/4 in piece of vanilla pod
4 egg yolks
115g/4oz/½ cup granulated sugar
225g/8oz plain chocolate, chopped into
small pieces

1 Heat the milk with the vanilla pod in a small saucepan. Remove from the heat as soon as small bubbles start to form on the surface. Do not let it boil. Strain the milk into a jug and set aside.

2 Using a wire whisk or hand-held electric mixer, beat the egg yolks in a bowl. Gradually whisk in the sugar and continue to whisk until the mixture is pale and thick. Slowly add the milk to the egg mixture, whisking after each addition. When all the milk has been added, pour the mixture into a heatproof bowl.

3 Place the heatproof bowl over a saucepan of simmering water and add the chocolate. Stir over a low heat until the chocolate melts, then raise the heat slightly and continue to stir the chocolate-flavoured custard until it thickens enough to coat the back of a wooden spoon lightly. Remove the custard from the heat, pour into a bowl and allow to cool, stirring occasionally to prevent skin forming on the surface.

4 Freeze the chocolate mixture in an ice-cream maker, following the manufacturer's instructions, or pour it into a suitable container for freezing. Freeze for about 3 hours, or until set. Remove from the container and chop roughly into 7.5 cm/3 in pieces. Place in a food processor and chop until smooth. Return to the freezer container and freeze again. Repeat two or three times, until the ice cream is smooth and creamy.

CHOCOLATE FLAKE ICE CREAM

SERVES 6
300ml / ½ pint / 1¼ cups whipping cream, chilled
90ml / 6 tbsp Greek-style yogurt
75–90ml / 5–6 tbsp caster sugar
few drops of vanilla essence
150g / 5oz / 10 tbsp flaked or roughly grated chocolate

COOK'S TIPS
Transfer the ice cream from the freezer to the fridge about 15 minutes before serving, so that it softens, and so that the full flavour can be appreciated.
Use a metal scoop to serve the ice cream, dipping the scoop briefly in warm water between servings. If the ice cream has been made in a loaf tin, simply slice it.

1 Have ready an ice-cream maker, or use a 600–900ml / 1–1½ pint / 2½–3¾ cup freezer-proof container, preferably with a lid. Prepare a place in the freezer so you can easily reach it. If necessary, turn the freezer to the coldest setting.

2 Softly whip the cream in a large bowl then fold in the yogurt, sugar, vanilla essence and chocolate. Stir gently to mix thoroughly, and then transfer to the ice-cream maker or freezer container.

3 Smooth the surface of the ice cream, then cover and freeze. Gently stir with a fork every 30 minutes for up to 4 hours until the ice cream is too hard to stir. If using an ice-cream maker, follow the manufacturer's instructions.

CHOCOLATE SORBET

SERVES 6

150g/5oz bittersweet chocolate, chopped
115g/4oz plain chocolate, grated
225g/8oz/1¼ cups caster sugar
475ml/16fl oz/2 cups water
chocolate curls, to decorate

1 Put all the chocolate in a food processor, fitted with the metal blade, and process for 20–30 seconds until finely chopped.
2 In a saucepan over a medium heat, bring the sugar and water to the boil, stirring until the sugar dissolves. Boil for about 2 minutes, then remove the pan from the heat.
3 With the machine running, pour the hot syrup over the chocolate in the food processor. Keep the machine running for 1–2 minutes until the chocolate is completely melted and the mixture is smooth, scraping down the bowl once.
4 Strain the chocolate mixture into a large measuring jug or bowl. Leave to cool, then chill, stirring occasionally. Freeze the mixture in an ice-cream maker. Alternatively, pour into a container suitable for use in the freezer, freeze until slushy, whisk until smooth, then freeze again. Whisk for a second time before the mixture hardens completely. Allow the sorbet to soften for 5–10 minutes at room temperature and serve in scoops, decorated with chocolate curls.

CHOCOLATE SORBET WITH RED FRUITS

SERVES 6

475ml/16fl oz/2 cups water
45ml/3 tbsp clear honey
115g/4oz/½ cup caster sugar
75g/3oz/¾ cup cocoa powder
50g/2oz plain dark or bittersweet chocolate, chopped into
small pieces
400g/14oz soft red fruits, such as raspberries, redcurrants
or strawberries

1 Place the water, honey, caster sugar and cocoa powder in a saucepan. Heat gently, stirring occasionally, until the sugar has completely dissolved.
2 Remove the pan from the heat, add the chocolate and stir until melted. Leave until cool.
3 Tip into an ice-cream maker and churn until frozen. Alternatively, pour into a container suitable for use in the freezer, freeze until slushy, whisk until smooth, then freeze again. Whisk for a second time before the mixture hardens completely, and cover the container.
4 Remove from the freezer 10–15 minutes before serving, so that the sorbet softens slightly. Serve in scoops in chilled dessert bowls, with the soft fruits.

ROCKY ROAD ICE CREAM

SERVES 6

*115g/4oz plain chocolate, chopped into
small pieces
150ml/¼ pint/⅔ cup milk
300ml/½ pint/1¼ cups double cream
115g/4oz/2 cups marshmallows, chopped
115g/4oz/½ cup glacé cherries, chopped
50g/2oz/½ cup crumbled shortbread biscuits
30ml/2 tbsp chopped walnuts*

1 Melt the chocolate in the milk in a saucepan over a gentle heat, stirring from time to time. Pour into a bowl and leave to cool completely.

2 Whip the cream in a separate bowl until it just holds its shape. Beat in the chocolate mixture, a little at a time, until the mixture is smooth and creamy.

3 Tip the mixture into an ice-cream maker and, following the manufacturer's instructions, churn until almost frozen. Alternatively, pour into a container suitable for use in the freezer, freeze until ice crystals form around the edges, then whisk with a strong hand whisk or hand-held electric mixer until smooth.

4 Stir the marshmallows, glacé cherries, crushed biscuits and nuts into the iced mixture, then return to the freezer container and freeze until firm.

5 Allow the ice cream to soften at room temperature for 15–20 minutes before serving in scoops. Add a wafer and chocolate sauce to each portion, if desired.

ICED CHOCOLATE NUT GATEAU

SERVES 6–8

75g/3oz/¾ cup shelled hazelnuts
about 32 sponge fingers
150ml/¼ pint/⅔ cup cold strong black coffee
30ml/2 tbsp brandy
475ml/16fl oz/2 cups double cream
75g/3oz/generous ½ cup icing sugar, sifted
150g/5oz plain chocolate, chopped into small pieces
icing sugar and cocoa powder, for dusting

1 Preheat oven to 200°C/400°F/Gas 6. Spread out the hazelnuts on a baking sheet and toast them in the oven for 5 minutes until golden. Tip the nuts on to a clean dish towel and rub off the skins while still warm. Cool, then chop finely.

2 Line a 1.2 litre/2 pint/5 cup loaf tin with clear film and cut the sponge fingers to fit the base and sides. Reserve the remaining biscuits. Mix the coffee with the brandy in a shallow dish. Dip the sponge fingers briefly into the coffee mixture and return to the tin, sugary side down to fit neatly.

3 Whip the cream with the icing sugar until it holds soft peaks. Fold half the chopped chocolate into the cream with the hazelnuts. Use a gentle figure-of-eight action to distribute the chocolate and nuts evenly.

4 Melt the remaining chocolate in a bowl set over a pan of barely simmering water. Cool, then fold into the cream mixture. Spoon into the tin.

5 Moisten the remaining biscuits in the coffee mixture, be careful not to soak the biscuits, as they will collapse. Lay the coffee-moistened biscuits over the filling. Wrap and freeze until firm.

6 To serve, remove from the freezer 30 minutes before serving to allow the ice cream to soften slightly. Turn out on to a serving plate and dust with icing sugar and cocoa.

ICED CHOCOLATE AND MANDARIN GATEAU

Dip the sponge fingers in a mixture of strong black coffee and mandarin or orange liqueur. Omit the hazelnuts from the cream filling. About 30 minutes before serving, remove the frozen gâteau from the tin and place it on a serving plate. Cover with whipped cream flavoured with mandarin or orange liqueur. Pipe more whipped cream around the base of the gâteau. Decorate with plain or chocolate-dipped mandarin or orange segments.

Ice Cream Bombes

Serves 6

1 litre / 1¾ pints / 4 cups soft-scoop chocolate
ice cream
475ml / 16fl oz / 2 cups soft-scoop vanilla
ice cream
50g / 2oz / ⅓ cup plain chocolate chips
115g / 4oz toffees
75ml / 5 tbsp double cream

<u>1</u> Divide the chocolate ice cream equally among six small cups. Push it roughly to the base and up the sides, leaving a small cup-shaped dip in the middle. Return to the freezer and leave for 45 minutes. Take the cups out again and smooth the ice cream in each into shape, keeping the centre hollow. Return to the freezer.

<u>2</u> Put the vanilla ice cream in a small bowl and break it up slightly with a spoon. Stir in the chocolate chips and use this mixture to fill the hollows in the cups of chocolate ice cream. Smooth the tops, then cover the cups with clear film, return to the freezer and leave overnight.

<u>3</u> Melt the toffees with the cream in a small pan over a very low heat, stirring constantly until smooth, warm and creamy.

<u>4</u> Turn out the bombes on to individual plates and pour the toffee sauce over the top. Serve immediately.

CHOCOLATE MINT ICE CREAM PIE

SERVES 8

75g / 3 oz plain chocolate chips
40g / 1½oz butter or margarine
50g / 2oz crisped rice cereal
1 litre / 1¾ pints / 4 cups mint-chocolate-chip
ice cream
chocolate curls, to decorate

1 Line a 23 cm/9 in pie tin with foil. Place a round of greaseproof paper over the foil in the bottom of the tin.

2 In a heatproof bowl set over a saucepan of simmering water melt the chocolate chips with the butter or margarine.

3 Remove the bowl from the heat and gently stir in the cereal, a little at a time.

4 Press the chocolate-cereal mixture evenly over the base and up the sides of the prepared tin, forming a 1 cm/½ in rim. Chill until completely hard.

5 Carefully remove the cereal base from the tin and peel off the foil and paper. Return the base to the pie tin.

6 Remove the ice cream from the freezer and allow it to soften for 10 minutes.

7 Spread the ice cream evenly in the biscuit case crust. Freeze until firm.

8 Scatter the chocolate curls over the ice cream just before serving.

CHOCOLATE BISCUITS AND COOKIES

CHOC-CHIP NUT BISCUITS

MAKES 36

115g/4oz/1 cup plain flour
5ml/1 tsp baking powder
5ml/1 tsp salt
75g/3oz/6 tbsp butter or margarine
115g/4oz/1 cup caster sugar
50g/2oz/⅓ cup soft light brown sugar
1 egg
5ml/1 tsp vanilla essence
115g/4oz/⅔ cup plain chocolate chips
50g/2oz/½ cup hazelnuts, chopped

1 Preheat oven to 180°C/350°F/Gas 4. Grease 2–3 baking sheets. Sift the flour, baking powder and salt into a small bowl. Set the bowl aside.
2 With a hand-held electric mixer, cream the butter or margarine and sugars together. Beat in the egg and vanilla essence. Add the flour mixture and beat well on low speed.
3 Stir in the chocolate chips and half of the hazelnuts. Drop teaspoonfuls of the mixture on to the prepared baking sheets, to form 2 cm/¾ in mounds. Space the biscuits about 5 cm/2 in apart to allow room for spreading.
4 Flatten each biscuit lightly with a wet fork. Sprinkle the remaining hazelnuts on top of the biscuits and press lightly into the surface. Bake for 10–12 minutes, until golden brown. Transfer the biscuits to a wire rack and allow to cool.

CHOC-CHIP OAT BISCUITS

MAKES 60

115g/4oz/1 cup plain flour
2.5ml/½ tsp bicarbonate of soda
1.5ml/¼ tsp baking powder
1.5ml/¼ tsp salt
115g/4oz/1 cup butter or margarine, softened
115g/4oz/1 cup caster sugar
75g/3oz/½ cup light brown sugar
1 egg
1.5ml/¼ tsp vanilla essence
75g/3oz/scant 1 cup rolled oats
175g/6oz/1 cup plain chocolate chips

1 Preheat oven to 180°C/350°F/Gas 4. Grease 3–4 baking sheets. Sift the flour, bicarbonate of soda, baking powder and salt into a mixing bowl. Set the bowl aside.
2 With a hand-held electric mixer, cream the butter or margarine and sugars together in a bowl. Add the egg and vanilla essence and beat until light and fluffy.
3 Add the flour mixture and beat on low speed until thoroughly blended. Stir in the rolled oats and chocolate chips, mixing well with a wooden spoon. The dough should be crumbly.
4 Drop heaped teaspoonfuls on to the prepared baking sheets, spacing the dough about 2.5 cm/1 in apart. Bake for about 15 minutes until just firm around the edge but still soft to the touch in the centre. With a slotted spatula, transfer the biscuits to a wire rack and allow them to cool.

CHOCOLATE-DIPPED HAZELNUT CRESCENTS

MAKES ABOUT 35

275g/10oz/2 cups plain flour
pinch of salt
225g/8oz/1 cup unsalted butter, softened
75g/3oz/6 tbsp caster sugar
15ml/1 tbsp hazelnut-flavoured liqueur
or water
5ml/1 tsp vanilla essence
75g/3oz plain chocolate, chopped into
small pieces
50g/2oz/1/2 cup hazelnuts, toasted and
finely chopped
icing sugar, for dusting
350g/12oz plain chocolate, melted, for
dipping

1 Preheat oven to 160°C/325°F/Gas 3. Grease two large baking sheets. Sift the flour and salt into a bowl. In a separate bowl, beat the butter until creamy. Add the sugar and beat until fluffy, then beat in the hazelnut liqueur or water and the vanilla essence. Gently stir in the flour mixture, then the chocolate and hazelnuts.

2 With floured hands, shape the dough into 5 x 1 cm/2 x 1/2 in crescent shapes. Place on the baking sheets, 5 cm/2 in apart. Bake for 20–25 minutes until the edges are set and the biscuits slightly golden. Remove the biscuits from the oven and cool on the baking sheets for 10 minutes, then transfer the biscuits to wire racks to cool completely.

3 Have the melted chocolate ready in a small bowl. Dust the biscuits lightly with icing sugar. Using a pair of kitchen tongs or your fingers, dip half of each crescent into the melted chocolate. Place the crescents on a non-stick baking sheet until the chocolate has set.

CHUNKY DOUBLE CHOCOLATE COOKIES

MAKES 18–20

115g/4oz/½ cup unsalted butter, softened
115g/4oz/⅔ cup light muscovado sugar
1 egg
5ml/1 tsp vanilla essence
150g/5oz/1¼ cups self-raising flour
75g/3oz/¾ cup porridge oats
115g/4oz plain chocolate, roughly chopped
115g/4oz white chocolate, roughly chopped

DOUBLE-CHOC ALMOND COOKIES:
Instead of the porridge oats, use 75g/3oz/¾ cup ground almonds. Omit the chopped chocolate and use 175g/6oz/1 cup chocolate chips instead. Top each heap of cake mixture with half a glacé cherry before baking.

1 Preheat oven to 190°C/375°F/Gas 5. Lightly grease two baking sheets. Cream the butter with the sugar in a bowl until pale and fluffy. Add the egg and vanilla essence and beat well.

2 Sift the flour over the mixture and fold in lightly with a metal spoon, then add the oats and chopped plain and white chocolate and stir until evenly mixed.

3 Place small spoonfuls of the mixture in 18–20 rocky heaps on the baking sheets, leaving space for spreading.

4 Bake for 12–15 minutes or until the biscuits are beginning to turn pale golden. Cool for 2–3 minutes on the baking sheets, then lift on to wire racks. The biscuits will be soft when freshly baked but will harden on cooling.

CHOCOLATE MARZIPAN COOKIES

MAKES ABOUT 36

200g/7oz/scant 1 cup unsalted butter,
softened
200g/7oz/generous 1 cup light muscovado
sugar
1 egg, beaten
300g/11oz/2¾ cups plain flour
60ml/4 tbsp cocoa powder
200g/7oz white almond paste
115g/4oz white chocolate, chopped into
small pieces

1 Preheat oven to 190°C/375°F/Gas 5. Lightly grease two large baking sheets. Using a hand-held electric mixer, cream the butter with the sugar in a mixing bowl until pale and fluffy. Add the egg and beat well.

2 Sift the flour and cocoa over the mixture. Stir in with a wooden spoon until all the flour mixture has been smoothly incorporated, then use clean hands to press the mixture together to make a fairly soft dough.

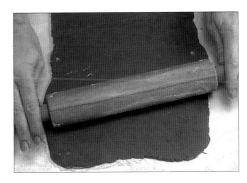

3 Using a rolling pin and keeping your touch light, roll out about half the dough on a lightly floured surface to a thickness of about 5 mm/¼ in. Using a 5 cm/2 in plain or fluted biscuit cutter, cut out 36 rounds, re-rolling the dough as required. Wrap the remaining dough in clear film and set it aside.

4 Cut the almond paste into 36 equal pieces. Roll into balls, flatten slightly and place one on each round of dough. Roll out the remaining dough, cut out more rounds, then place on top of the almond paste. Press the dough edges to seal.

5 Bake for 10–12 minutes, or until the cookies have risen well and are beginning to crack on the surface. Cool on the baking sheet for about 2–3 minutes, then finish cooling on a wire rack.

6 Melt the white chocolate, then either drizzle it over the biscuits to decorate, or spoon into a paper piping bag and quickly pipe a design on to the biscuits.

VARIATION

Use glacé icing instead of melted white chocolate to decorate the cookies, if you prefer.

BLACK AND WHITE GINGER FLORENTINES

MAKES ABOUT 30

120ml/4fl oz/½ cup double cream
50g/2oz/¼ cup butter
50g/2oz/¼ cup granulated sugar
30ml/2 tbsp honey
150g/5oz/1¼ cups flaked almonds
40g/1½oz/6 tbsp plain flour
2.5ml/½ tsp ground ginger
50g/2oz/⅓ cup diced candied orange peel
75g/3oz/½ cup diced stem ginger
50g/2oz plain chocolate, chopped into small pieces
150g/5oz bittersweet chocolate, chopped into small pieces
150g/5oz fine quality white chocolate, chopped into small pieces

1 Preheat oven to 180°C/350°F/Gas 4. Lightly grease two large baking sheets. In a saucepan over a medium heat, stir the cream, butter, sugar and honey until the sugar dissolves. Bring the mixture to the boil, stirring constantly. Remove from the heat and stir in the almonds, flour and ground ginger. Stir in the candied peel, ginger and plain chocolate.

2 Drop teaspoons of the mixture on to the baking sheets at least 7.5 cm/3 in apart. Spread each round as thinly as possible with the back of the spoon.

3 Bake for 8–10 minutes or until the edges are golden brown and the biscuits are bubbling. Do not under-bake or they will be sticky, but be careful not to over-bake as they burn easily. Continue baking in batches. If you wish, use a 7.5 cm/3 in biscuit cutter to neaten the edges of the florentines while they are still on the baking sheet.

4 Allow the biscuits to cool on the baking sheets for 10 minutes, until they are firm enough to move. Using a metal palette knife, carefully lift the biscuits on to a wire rack to cool completely.

5 Melt the bittersweet chocolate in a heatproof bowl over barely simmering water. Cool slightly. Put the white chocolate in a separate bowl and melt in the same way, stirring frequently. Remove and cool for about 5 minutes, stirring occasionally.

6 Using a small metal palette knife, spread half the florentines with the bittersweet chocolate and half with the melted white chocolate. Place on a wire rack, chocolate side up. Chill for 10–15 minutes to set completely.

CHEWY CHOCOLATE BISCUITS
MAKES 18

4 egg whites
350g/12oz/2½ cups icing sugar
115g/4oz/1 cup cocoa powder
30ml/2 tbsp plain flour
5ml/1 tsp instant coffee
15ml/1 tbsp water
115g/4oz/1 cup walnuts, finely chopped

1 Preheat oven to 180°C/350°F/Gas 4. Line two baking sheets with non-stick baking paper.
2 With a hand-held electric mixer, beat the egg whites in a bowl until frothy.
3 Sift the icing sugar, cocoa powder, flour and coffee into the whites. Add the water and continue beating on low speed to blend, then on high speed for a few minutes until the mixture thickens. With a rubber spatula, fold in the walnuts.
4 Place generous spoonfuls of the mixture 2.5 cm/1 in apart on the prepared baking sheets. Bake for 12–15 minutes, or until firm and cracked on top but soft on the inside. With a metal spatula, transfer the biscuits to a wire rack to cool.

CHOCOLATE CRACKLE-TOPS

MAKES ABOUT 38

200g/7oz bittersweet or plain chocolate,
chopped into small pieces
90g/3½oz/7 tbsp unsalted butter
115g/4oz/½ cup caster sugar
3 eggs
5ml/1 tsp vanilla essence
200g/7oz/1¾ cups plain flour
25g/1oz/¼ cup cocoa powder
2.5ml/½ tsp baking powder
pinch of salt
175g/6oz/1½ cups icing sugar, for coating

1 Grease two or more large baking sheets. In a heavy-based saucepan over a low heat, melt the chocolate and butter until smooth, stirring frequently. Remove from the heat. Stir in the sugar until dissolved. Add the eggs, one at a time, beating well after each addition. Stir in the vanilla essence.

2 Sift the flour, cocoa, baking powder and salt into a bowl. Gradually stir into the chocolate mixture in batches to make a soft dough. Cover in clear film and chill for at least 1 hour until the dough is firm enough to hold its shape.

3 Preheat oven to 160°C/325°F/Gas 3. Place the icing sugar in a small, deep bowl. Using a small ice cream scoop or round teaspoon, scoop the dough into small balls and roll between your palms.

4 Drop the balls, one at a time, into the icing sugar and roll until heavily coated. Remove each ball with a slotted spoon and tap the spoon against the bowl to remove excess sugar. Place the balls on the baking sheets, about 4 cm/1½ in apart.

5 Bake the biscuits for 10–15 minutes or until the top of each feels slightly firm when touched with a fingertip. Leave for 2–3 minutes, until just set. Transfer to wire racks and leave to cool completely.

CHUNKY CHOCOLATE DROPS

MAKES ABOUT 18

*175g/6oz bittersweet or plain chocolate,
chopped into small pieces
115g/4oz/½ cup unsalted butter, diced
2 eggs
115g/4oz/½ cup granulated sugar
50g/2oz/⅓ cup light brown sugar
40g/1½oz/6 tbsp plain flour
25g/1oz/¼ cup cocoa powder
5ml/1 tsp baking powder
10ml/2 tsp vanilla essence
pinch of salt
115g/4oz/1 cup pecan nuts, toasted and
coarsely chopped
175g/6oz/1 cup plain chocolate chips
115g/4oz fine quality white chocolate,
chopped into small pieces
115g/4oz fine quality milk chocolate,
chopped into small pieces*

1 Preheat oven to 160°C/325°F/Gas 3.
Grease two large baking sheets. In a
medium saucepan over a low heat, melt
the chocolate and butter until smooth,
stirring frequently. Remove from the heat
and leave to cool slightly.

2 In a large mixing bowl, beat the eggs
and sugars until pale and creamy.
Gradually pour in the melted chocolate
mixture, beating well. Beat in the flour,
cocoa, baking powder and vanilla
essence. Stir in the remaining ingredients.

3 Drop heaped tablespoons of the
mixture on to the baking sheets, 10 cm/
4 in apart. Flatten each to a 7.5 cm/ 3 in
round. (You will only get 4–6 biscuits on
each sheet.) Bake for 8–10 minutes until
the tops are shiny and cracked and the
edges look crisp. Do not over-bake or the
biscuits will break when they are
removed from the baking sheets.

4 Remove the baking sheets to wire racks
to cool for 2 minutes, until the biscuits
are just set, then carefully transfer them
to the wire racks to cool completely.
Bake the biscuits in batches, if necessary.
Store in airtight containers.

CHOCOLATE AMARETTI

MAKES ABOUT 24

115g/4oz/1 cup blanched whole almonds
115g/4oz/½ cup caster sugar
15ml/1 tbsp cocoa powder
30ml/2 tbsp icing sugar
2 egg whites
pinch of cream of tartar
5ml/1 tsp almond essence
flaked almonds, to decorate

1 Preheat oven to 180°C/350°F/Gas 4. Place the almonds on a small baking sheet and bake for 10–12 minutes, turning occasionally until golden brown. Cool to room temperature. Reduce the oven temperature to 160°C/325°F/Gas 3.

2 Line a large baking sheet with non-stick baking paper. In a food processor, process the toasted almonds with half the caster sugar until the almonds are finely ground but not oily. Transfer the ground almonds to a bowl and stir in the cocoa powder and icing sugar. Set aside.

3 In a medium mixing bowl, beat the egg whites and cream of tartar with a hand-held mixer, until stiff peaks form. Sprinkle in the remaining caster sugar about 15ml/1 tbsp at a time, beating well after each addition, and continue beating until the whites are glossy and stiff. Beat in the almond essence.

4 Sprinkle over the almond-sugar mixture and gently fold into the beaten egg whites until just blended. Spoon the mixture into a large piping bag fitted with a plain 1 cm/½ in nozzle. Pipe 4 cm/1½ in rounds about 2.5 cm/1 in apart on the prepared baking sheet. Press a flaked almond into the centre of each biscuit.

5 Bake the biscuits for 12–15 minutes or until they are crisp. Cool on the baking sheet for 10 minutes. With a metal palette knife, transfer the biscuits to wire racks to cool completely. When cool, store in an airtight jar or biscuit tin. Serve after a dinner party with coffee, or use in trifles.

CHOCOLATE KISSES

MAKES 24

75g/3oz dark plain chocolate, chopped into small pieces

75g/3oz white chocolate, chopped into small pieces

115g/4oz/½ cup butter, softened

115g/4oz/½ cup caster sugar

2 eggs

225g/8oz/2 cups plain flour

icing sugar, to decorate

1 Melt the plain and white chocolates in separate bowls and set both aside to cool.

2 Beat the butter and caster sugar together until pale and fluffy. Beat in the eggs, one at a time. Then sift in the flour and mix well.

3 Halve the creamed mixture and divide it between the two bowls of chocolate. Mix each chocolate in thoroughly so that each forms a dough. Knead the doughs until smooth, wrap them separately in clear film and chill for 1 hour. Preheat oven to 190°C/375°F/Gas 5.

4 Shape slightly rounded teaspoonfuls of both doughs roughly into balls. Roll the balls between your palms to neaten them. Arrange the balls on greased baking sheets and bake for 10–12 minutes. Dust liberally with sifted icing sugar and cool on a wire rack.

MOCHA VIENNESE SWIRLS

MAKES ABOUT 20

*115g/4oz plain chocolate, chopped into
small pieces*
*200g/7oz/scant 1 cup unsalted butter,
softened*
90ml/6 tbsp icing sugar
30ml/2 tbsp strong black coffee
200g/7oz/1¾ cups plain flour
50g/2oz/½ cup cornflour

TO DECORATE

about 20 blanched almonds
*150g/5oz plain chocolate, chopped into
small pieces*

1 Preheat oven to 190°C/375°F/Gas 5. Melt the chocolate in a bowl over barely simmering water. Cream the butter with the icing sugar in a bowl until smooth and pale. Beat in the melted chocolate, then the strong black coffee.

2 Sift the plain flour and cornflour over the mixture. Fold in lightly and evenly to make a soft biscuit dough.

3 Lightly grease two large baking sheets. Spoon the dough into a piping bag fitted with a large star nozzle. Pipe about 20 swirls on the baking sheets, allowing room for spreading. Keep the nozzle close to the sheet so that the swirls are flat.

4 Press an almond into the centre of each swirl. Bake for about 15 minutes or until the biscuits are firm and starting to brown. Cool for about 10 minutes on the baking sheets, then lift carefully on to a wire rack to cool completely.

5 When cool, melt the chocolate and dip the base of each swirl to coat. Place on a sheet of non-stick baking paper and leave to set completely.

CHOCOLATE MACAROONS

MAKES 24

50g/2oz plain chocolate, chopped into
small pieces
115g/4oz/1 cup blanched almonds
225g/8oz/1 cup granulated sugar
3 egg whites
2.5ml/½ tsp vanilla essence
1.5ml/¼ tsp almond essence
icing sugar, for dusting

1 Preheat oven to 160°C/325°F/Gas 3.
Line two baking sheets with non-stick
baking paper.

VARIATION

For Chocolate Pine Nut Macaroons,
spread 50g/2oz/⅔ cup toasted pine
nuts in a shallow dish. Press the balls of
chocolate macaroon dough into the nuts
to cover one side and bake as described,
nut-side up.

2 Melt the chocolate in the top of a
double boiler, or in a heatproof bowl
placed over a saucepan of barely
simmering water.

3 Grind the almonds finely in a food
processor, blender or nut grinder.
Transfer to a mixing bowl.

4 Add the sugar, egg whites, vanilla
essence and almond essence and stir to
blend. Stir in the chocolate. The mixture
should just hold its shape. If it is too soft,
chill it in the fridge for 15 minutes.

5 Use a teaspoon and your hands to shape
the dough into walnut-size balls. Place on
the baking sheets and flatten slightly.
Brush each ball with a little water and sift
over a thin layer of icing sugar. Bake for
10–12 minutes, until just firm. With a
metal spatula, transfer to a wire rack to
cool completely.

CHOCOLATE CINNAMON TUILES

3 In a separate bowl, mix together the cocoa and cinnamon. Stir into the larger quantity of mixture until well combined. Leaving room for spreading, drop spoonfuls of the chocolate-flavoured mixture on to the prepared baking sheets, then spread each gently with a palette knife to make a neat round.

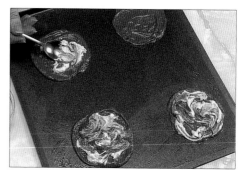

4 Using a small spoon, drizzle the reserved plain mixture over the rounds, swirling it lightly to give a marbled effect.

5 Bake for 4–6 minutes, until just set. Using a palette knife, lift each biscuit and drape it over a rolling pin, to give a curved shape as it hardens. Allow the tuiles to set, then remove them and finish cooling on a wire rack. Serve on the same day.

MAKES 12

1 egg white
50g/2oz/¼ cup caster sugar
30ml/2 tbsp plain flour
40g/1½oz/3 tbsp butter, melted
15ml/1 tbsp cocoa powder
2.5m/½ tsp ground cinnamon

1 Preheat oven to 200°C/400°F/Gas 6. Lightly grease two large baking sheets. Whisk the egg white in a clean, grease-free bowl until it forms soft peaks. Gradually whisk in the sugar to make a smooth, glossy mixture.

2 Sift the flour over the meringue mixture and fold in evenly; try not to deflate the mixture. Stir in the butter. Transfer about 45ml/3 tbsp of the mixture to a small bowl and set it aside.

CHOCOLATE CUPS

Cream 150g/5oz/⅔ cup butter with 115g/4oz/½ cup caster sugar. Stir in 75g/3oz/1 cup porridge oats, 15ml/1 tbsp cocoa powder and 5ml/1 tsp vanilla essence. Roll to the size of golf balls and space well on greased baking sheets. Bake at 180°C/350°F/Gas 4 for 12–15 minutes. Cool slightly then drape over greased upturned glasses until cool and firm. Makes 8–10.

CHOCOLATE PRETZELS

MAKES 28

150g / 5oz / 1¼ cups plain flour
pinch of salt
25g / 1oz / ¼ cup cocoa powder
115g / 4oz / ½ cup butter, softened
115g / 4oz / ½ cup caster sugar
1 egg
1 egg white, lightly beaten, for glazing
sugar crystals, for sprinkling

1 Sift the plain flour, salt and cocoa powder into a bowl. Set aside. Grease two baking sheets.

2 With a hand-held electric mixer, cream the butter. Add the caster sugar and beat until fluffy. Beat in the egg. Stir in the dry ingredients. Gather the dough into a ball and chill for 1 hour.

3 Roll the dough into 28 small balls. Preheat the oven to 190°C / 375°F / Gas 5. Roll each ball into a rope about 25 cm / 10 in long. With each rope, form a loop with the two ends facing you. Twist the ends and fold back on to the circle, pressing in to make a pretzel shape. Place on the greased baking sheets.

4 Brush the pretzels with the egg white. Sprinkle sugar crystals over the tops and bake for 10–12 minutes until firm. Transfer to a wire rack to cool.

LITTLE CAKES, SLICES AND BARS

CHOCOLATE FAIRY CAKES

MAKES 24

*115g/4oz plain chocolate, chopped into
small pieces*
15ml/1 tbsp water
275g/10oz/2½ cups plain flour
5ml/1 tsp baking powder
2.5ml/½ tsp bicarbonate of soda
pinch of salt
300g/11oz/scant 1½ cups caster sugar
*175g/6oz/¾ cup butter or margarine, at
room temperature*
150ml/¼ pint/⅔ cup milk
5ml/1 tsp vanilla essence
3 eggs
FOR THE ICING
40g/1½ oz/3 tbsp butter or margarine
115g/4oz/1 cup icing sugar
2.5ml/½ tsp vanilla essence
15–30ml/1–2 tbsp milk

1 Preheat oven to 180°C/350°F/Gas 4.
Grease 24 bun tins, about 6.5 cm/2¾ in
in diameter and line with paper cases.
2 Make the icing. Soften the butter or
margarine. Place it in a bowl and stir in
the icing sugar, a little at a time. Add the
vanilla essence, then, a drop at a time,
beat in just enough milk to make a
creamy, spreadable mixture. Cover the
surface closely with clear film and set the
bowl aside.

3 Melt the chocolate with the water in a
heatproof bowl over simmering water.
Remove from the heat. Sift the flour,
baking powder, bicarbonate of soda, salt
and sugar into a large bowl. Add the
chocolate mixture, butter or margarine,
milk and vanilla essence.

4 With a hand-held electric mixer on
medium speed, beat the mixture until
smooth. Increase the speed to high and
beat for 2 minutes. Add the eggs, one at a
time, and beat for 1 minute after each
addition. Divide the mixture evenly
among the prepared bun tins.

5 Bake for 20–25 minutes or until a
skewer inserted into the centre of a cake
comes out clean. Cool in the tins for
10 minutes, then turn out to cool
completely on a wire rack. Spread the top
of each cake with the icing, swirling it
into a peak in the centre.

CHOCOLATE MINT-FILLED CUPCAKES

MAKES 12

225g/8oz/2 cups plain flour
5ml/1 tsp bicarbonate of soda
pinch of salt
50g/2oz/½ cup cocoa powder
150g/5oz/10 tbsp unsalted butter, softened
350g/12oz/1⅔ cups caster sugar
3 eggs
5ml/1 tsp peppermint essence
250ml/8 fl oz/1 cup milk

FOR THE MINT CREAM FILLING

300ml/½ pint/1¼ cups double cream or whipping cream
5ml/1 tsp peppermint essence

FOR THE CHOCOLATE MINT GLAZE

175g/6oz plain chocolate, chopped into small pieces
115g/4oz/½ cup unsalted butter
5ml/1 tsp peppermint essence

1 Preheat oven to 180°C/350°F/Gas 4. Line a 12-hole bun tin with paper cases, using the cases double if they are thin. Sift the flour, bicarbonate of soda, salt and cocoa powder into a bowl. Set aside.

2 In a large mixing bowl, beat the butter and sugar with a hand-held electric mixer for about 3–5 minutes until light and creamy. Add the eggs, one at a time, beating well after each addition and adding a small amount of the flour mixture if the egg mixture shows signs of curdling. Beat in the peppermint essence until thoroughly mixed.

3 With the hand-held electric mixer on a low speed, beat in the flour-cocoa mixture alternately with the milk, until just blended. Spoon into the paper cases, filling them about three-quarters full.

4 Bake for 12–15 minutes, until a cake tester inserted in the centre of one of the cupcakes comes out clean.

5 Lift the cupcakes on to a wire rack to cool completely. When cool, carefully remove the paper cases.

6 Prepare the mint cream filling. In a small bowl, whip the cream and peppermint essence until stiff. Fit a small, plain nozzle into a piping bag and spoon in the flavoured cream. Gently press the nozzle into the bottom of one of the cupcakes. Squeeze gently, releasing about 15ml/1 tbsp of the flavoured cream into the centre of the cake. Repeat with the remaining cupcakes, returning each one to the wire rack as it is filled.

7 Prepare the glaze. In a saucepan over a low heat, melt the chocolate and butter, stirring until smooth. Remove from heat and stir in the peppermint essence. Cool then spread on the top of each cake.

CHOCOLATE LEMON TARTLETS

MAKES 12 TARTLETS

1 quantity Chocolate Shortcrust Pastry
lemon twists and melted chocolate to decorate

FOR THE LEMON CUSTARD SAUCE
grated rind and juice of 1 lemon
350ml/12fl oz/1½ cups milk
6 egg yolks
50g/2oz/½ cup caster sugar

FOR THE LEMON CURD FILLING
grated rind and juice of 2 lemons
175g/6oz/¾ cup unsalted butter, diced
450g/1lb/2 cups granulated sugar
3 eggs, lightly beaten

FOR THE CHOCOLATE LAYER
175ml/6fl oz/¾ cup double cream
175g/6oz bittersweet or plain chocolate,
chopped into small pieces
25g/1oz/2 tbsp unsalted butter, cut into
pieces

1 Prepare the custard sauce. Place the rind in a saucepan with the milk. Bring to the boil over a medium heat. Remove from the heat and allow to stand for 5 minutes to infuse. Strain the milk into a clean pan and reheat it gently.

2 In a bowl beat the yolks and sugar with a hand-held electric mixer for 2–3 minutes, until pale and thick. Pour over about 250ml/8fl oz/1 cup of the flavoured hot milk, beating vigorously.

3 Return the yolk mixture to the rest of the milk in the pan and cook gently, stirring constantly, over low heat until the mixture thickens and lightly coats the back of a spoon. (Do not allow sauce to boil or it will curdle.) Strain into a chilled bowl. Stir 30ml/2 tbsp lemon juice into the sauce. Cool, stirring occasionally, then chill until ready to use.

4 Prepare the lemon curd filling. Combine the lemon rind, juice, butter and sugar in the top of a double boiler. Set over simmering water and heat gently until the butter has melted and the sugar has completely dissolved. Reduce the heat to low.

5 Stir the lightly beaten eggs into the butter mixture. Cook over a low heat, for 15 minutes, stirring constantly, until the mixture coats the back of a spoon.

6 Strain the lemon curd into a bowl and cover closely with clear film. Allow to cool, stirring occasionally, then chill to thicken, stirring occasionally.

7 Lightly butter twelve 7.5 cm/3 in tartlet tins (if possible ones which have removable bases). On a lightly floured surface, roll out the pastry to a thickness of 3 mm/⅛ in. Using a 10 cm/4 in fluted cutter, cut out 12 rounds and press each one into a tartlet tin. Prick the bases with a fork. Place the tins on a baking sheet and chill for 30 minutes.

8 Preheat oven to 190°C/375°F/Gas 5. Cut out rounds of foil and line each pastry case; fill with baking beans or rice. Bake blind for 5–8 minutes. Remove the foil with the beans and bake for 5 more minutes, until the cases are golden. Remove to rack to cool.

9 Prepare the chocolate layer. In a saucepan over a medium heat, bring the cream to the boil. Remove from the heat and add the chocolate all at once; stir until melted. Beat in the butter and cool slightly. Pour the filling into each tartlet to make a layer 5 mm/¼ in thick. Chill for 10 minutes until set.

10 Remove the tartlets from the tins and spoon in a layer of lemon curd to come to the top of the pastry. Set aside, but do not chill. To serve, spoon a little lemon custard sauce on to a plate and place a tartlet in the centre. Decorate with a lemon twist. Dot the custard with melted chocolate. Draw a skewer through the chocolate to make heart motifs.

CHOCOLATE CREAM PUFFS

MAKES 12 LARGE CREAM PUFFS

115g/4oz/1 cup plain flour
30ml/2 tbsp cocoa powder
250ml/8fl oz/1 cup water
2.5ml/½ tsp salt
15ml/1 tbsp granulated sugar
115g/4oz/½ cup unsalted butter, diced
4 eggs

FOR THE CHOCOLATE PASTRY CREAM

450ml/¾ pint/2 cups milk
6 egg yolks
115g/4oz/½ cup granulated sugar
50g/2oz/½ cup plain flour
150g/5oz plain chocolate, chopped into small pieces
115ml/4fl oz/½ cup whipping cream

FOR THE CHOCOLATE GLAZE

300ml/½ pint/1¼ cups whipping cream
50g/2oz/¼ cup unsalted butter, diced
225g/8oz bittersweet or plain chocolate, chopped into small pieces
15ml/1 tbsp golden syrup
5ml/1 tsp vanilla essence

1 Preheat oven to 220°C/425°F/Gas 7. Lightly grease two large baking sheets. Sift the flour and cocoa powder into a bowl. In a saucepan over a medium heat, bring to the boil the water, salt, sugar and butter. Remove the pan from the heat and add the flour and cocoa mixture all at once, stirring vigorously until the mixture is smooth and leaves the sides of the pan clean.

2 Return the pan to the heat to cook the choux pastry for 1 minute, beating constantly. Remove from the heat.

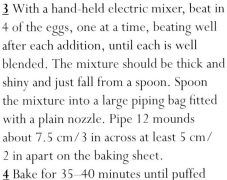

3 With a hand-held electric mixer, beat in 4 of the eggs, one at a time, beating well after each addition, until each is well blended. The mixture should be thick and shiny and just fall from a spoon. Spoon the mixture into a large piping bag fitted with a plain nozzle. Pipe 12 mounds about 7.5 cm/3 in across at least 5 cm/2 in apart on the baking sheet.

4 Bake for 35–40 minutes until puffed and firm. Remove the puffs. Using a serrated knife, slice off and reserve the top third of each puff; return the opened puffs to the oven for 5–10 minutes to dry out. Remove to a wire rack to cool.

5 Prepare the pastry cream. Bring the milk to the boil in a small pan. In a bowl, heat the yolks and sugar until pale and thick. Stir in the flour. Slowly pour about 250ml/8fl oz/1 cup of the hot milk into the yolks, stirring constantly. Return the yolk mixture to the remaining milk in the pan and cook, stirring until the sauce boils for 1 minute. Remove from the heat and stir in the chocolate until smooth.

6 Strain into a bowl and cover closely with clear film. Cool to room temperature. In a bowl, whip the cream until stiff. Fold into the pastry cream.

7 Using a large piping bag, fill each puff bottom with pastry cream, then cover each puff with its top. Arrange the cream puffs on a large serving plate in a single layer or as a pile.

8 Make the glaze by heating the cream, butter, chocolate, syrup and vanilla essence in a medium saucepan over low heat until melted and smooth, stirring frequently. Cool for 20–30 minutes until slightly thickened. Pour a little glaze over each of the cream puffs to serve.

CHOCOLATE RASPBERRY MACAROON BARS

2 In a medium bowl beat the butter, sugar, cocoa powder and salt with a hand-held electric mixer for about 1 minute, until well blended and creamy. Beat in the almond essence and the flour until the mixture forms a crumbly dough.

3 Turn the dough into the prepared tin and pat firmly over the base to make an even layer. Prick the dough with a fork. Bake for 20 minutes until the pastry has just set. Remove from the oven and increase the temperature to 190°C/375°F/Gas 5.

4 Make the topping. In a small bowl, combine the raspberry jam and the liqueur. Spread the mixture evenly over the chocolate crust, then sprinkle evenly with the chocolate chips.

5 In a food processor fitted with a metal blade, process the almonds, egg whites, salt, sugar and almond essence until well blended and foamy. Gently pour over the jam layer, spreading evenly to the edges of the tin. Sprinkle with the almonds.

6 Bake for 20–25 minutes more, until the top is golden and puffed. Cool in the tin on a wire rack for 20 minutes or until firm. Using the edges of the foil, carefully remove the bake from the tin and cool completely. Peel off the foil, and, using a sharp knife, cut into bars.

MAKES 16–18 BARS

115g/4oz/½ cup unsalted butter, softened
50g/2oz/⅓ cup icing sugar
25g/1oz/¼ cup cocoa powder
pinch of salt
5ml/1 tsp almond essence
115g/4oz/1 cup plain flour
FOR THE TOPPING
150g/5oz/½ cup seedless raspberry jam
15ml/1 tbsp raspberry-flavoured liqueur
175g/6oz/1 cup mini chocolate chips
175g/6oz/1½ cups ground almonds
4 egg whites
pinch of salt
225g/8oz/1¼ cups caster sugar
2.5ml/½ tsp almond essence
50g/2oz/¼ cup flaked almonds

1 Preheat oven to 160°C/325°F/Gas 3. Invert a 33 x 23 cm/13 x 9 in baking tin. Mould a sheet of foil over the tin and smooth the foil evenly around the corners. Lift off the foil and turn the tin right side up; line with the moulded foil. Grease the foil.

CHOCOLATE BUTTERSCOTCH BARS

MAKES 24

225g / 8oz / 2 cups plain flour
2.5ml / ½ tsp baking powder
150g / 5oz plain chocolate, chopped
115g / 4oz / ½ cup unsalted butter, diced
50g / 2oz / ⅓ cup light muscovado sugar
30ml / 2 tbsp ground almonds

FOR THE TOPPING

175g / 6oz / ¾ cup unsalted butter, diced
115g / 4oz / ½ cup caster sugar
30ml / 2 tbsp golden syrup
175ml / 6fl oz / ¾ cup condensed milk
150g / 5oz / 1¼ cups whole toasted hazelnuts
225g / 8oz plain chocolate, chopped into
small pieces

1 Preheat oven to 160°C / 325°F / Gas 3. Grease a shallow 30 x 20 cm / 12 x 8 in tin. Sift the flour and baking powder into a large bowl. Melt the chocolate in a bowl over a saucepan of simmering water.

2 Rub the butter into the flour until the mixture resembles coarse breadcrumbs, then stir in the sugar. Work in the melted chocolate and ground almonds to make a light biscuit dough.

3 Spread the dough roughly in the tin, then use a rubber spatula to press it down evenly into the sides and the corners. Prick the surface with a fork and bake for 25–30 minutes until firm. Leave to cool in the tin.

4 Make the topping. Heat the butter, sugar, golden syrup and condensed milk in a pan, stirring until the butter and sugar have melted. Simmer until golden, then stir in the hazelnuts.

5 Pour over the cooked base. Leave to set.

6 Melt the chocolate for the topping in a heatproof bowl over barely simmering water. Spread evenly over the butterscotch layer, then leave to set again before cutting into bars to serve.

Chocolate Walnut Bars

Makes 24

50g/2oz/½ cup walnuts
50g/2oz/¼ cup caster sugar
115g/4oz/1 cup plain flour, sifted
75g/3oz unsalted butter, cut into pieces

For the Topping

25g/1oz/2 tbsp unsalted butter
75ml/3fl oz/5 tbsp water
25g/1oz/¼ cup cocoa powder
115g/4oz/½ cup caster sugar
5ml/1 tsp vanilla essence
pinch of salt
2 eggs
icing sugar, for dusting

1 Preheat oven to 180°C/350°F/Gas 4. Grease the base and sides of a 20 cm/8 in square baking tin.

2 Grind the walnuts with 15–30ml/ 1–2 tbsp of the sugar in a food processor, blender or coffee grinder.

3 In a bowl, combine the ground walnuts, remaining sugar and flour. With your fingertips, rub in the butter until the mixture resembles coarse breadcrumbs. Alternatively, process all the ingredients in a food processor until the mixture resembles coarse breadcrumbs.

4 Pat the walnut mixture on to the base of the prepared tin in an even layer. Bake for 25 minutes.

5 Meanwhile make the topping. Heat the butter with the water in a saucepan over a medium heat. When all the butter has melted, gradually whisk in the cocoa powder and caster sugar. Remove from the heat, stir in the vanilla essence and salt and set the mixture aside to cool for 5 minutes. Whisk in the eggs until blended.

6 Pour the topping over the baked crust, return the baking tin to the oven and bake for about 20 minutes or until set. Transfer the tin to a wire rack to cool.

7 When the bake has cooled for 5 minutes, mark it into 6 x 2.5 cm/2½ x 1 in bars. Leave until completely cold, then separate the bars and transfer them to a wire rack. Dust lightly with icing sugar. Place the bars on a plate and serve.

Cook's Tip

Look out for walnut pieces in the supermarket or health food store. They are cheaper than walnut halves and are perfect for this recipe. Ground almonds would also work well, but because they are so fine you need to take care not to over-process the mixture or they may become oily.

Chocolate, Date and Orange Bars

Make the base as in the main recipe, but substitute hazelnuts for the walnuts. Roast the hazelnuts briefly in a hot oven or under the grill, rub off the skins using a clean, dry napkin or tea towel, then grind them with the sugar in a food processor. Complete the base and bake it as described, then set it aside.

Make the topping. Mix 225g/8oz/2 cups of sugar-rolled dates, 75g/3oz/6 tbsp butter and 120ml/4fl oz/½ cup water in a saucepan. Simmer, stirring occasionally, until the butter has dissolved and the dates have broken down to form a pulp. Stir in 50g/2oz/⅓ cup soft light brown sugar until dissolved. Remove the pan from the heat and beat in the grated rind of 1 orange, with 30ml/2 tbsp orange juice. Allow to cool.

Beat 175g/6oz/1½ cups self-raising flour and 1 egg into the date mixture, then spread the topping evenly over the hazelnut base. Bake in a preheated oven at 180°C/ 350°F/Gas 4 for 30 minutes. Cool in the tin, loosen around the edges with a knife then turn out so that the hazelnut base is now uppermost. Glaze with 150g/5oz melted chocolate. Cut into bars when set.

CHOCOLATE AND TOFFEE BARS

MAKES 32

350g / 12oz / 2 cups soft light brown sugar
450g / 1lb / 2 cups butter or margarine, at room temperature
2 egg yolks
7.5ml / 1½ tsp vanilla essence
450g / 1lb / 4 cups plain or wholemeal flour
2.5ml / ½ tsp salt
175g / 6oz plain chocolate, broken into squares
115g / 4oz / 1 cup walnuts or pecan nuts, chopped

1 Preheat oven to 180°C / 350°F / Gas 4. Beat the sugar and butter or margarine in a mixing bowl until light and fluffy. Beat in the egg yolks and vanilla essence, then stir in the flour and salt to make a soft dough.
2 Spread the dough in a greased 33 x 23 x 5 cm / 13 x 9 x 2 in baking tin. Level the surface. Bake for 25–30 minutes, until lightly browned. The texture will be soft.
3 Remove the bake from the oven and immediately place the chocolate on top. Set aside until the chocolate is soft, then spread it out with a spatula. Sprinkle with the chopped nuts.
4 While the bake is still warm, cut it into 5 x 4 cm / 2 x 1½ in bars, remove from the tin and leave to cool on a wire rack.

CHOCOLATE PECAN SQUARES

MAKES 16

2 eggs
10ml / 2 tsp vanilla essence
pinch of salt
175g / 6oz / 1½ cups pecan nuts, roughly chopped
50g / 2oz / ½ cup plain flour
50g / 2oz / ¼ cup granulated sugar
120ml / 4fl oz / ½ cup golden syrup
75g / 3oz plain chocolate, chopped into small pieces
40g / 1½oz / 3 tbsp unsalted butter
16 pecan nut halves, to decorate

1 Preheat oven to 160°C / 325°F / Gas 3. Line a 20 cm / 8 in square baking tin with non-stick baking paper.
2 In a bowl, whisk the eggs with the vanilla essence and salt. In another bowl, mix together the pecan nuts and flour.
3 Put the sugar in a saucepan, add the golden syrup and bring to the boil. Remove from the heat and stir in the chocolate and butter with a wooden spoon until both have dissolved and the mixture is smooth. Stir in the beaten egg mixture, then fold in the pecan nuts and flour.
4 Pour the mixture into the prepared tin and bake for about 35 minutes or until firm to the touch. Cool in the tin for 10 minutes before turning out on a wire rack. Cut into 5 cm / 2 in squares and press pecan halves into the tops while still warm. Cool completely before serving.

CHUNKY CHOCOLATE BARS

MAKES 12

*350g/12oz plain chocolate, chopped into
small pieces*
115g/4oz/½ cup unsalted butter
400g/14oz can condensed milk
225g/8oz digestive biscuits, broken
50g/2oz/⅓ cup raisins
*115g/4oz ready-to-eat dried peaches,
roughly chopped*
*50g/2oz/½ cup hazelnuts or pecan nuts,
roughly chopped*

<u>1</u> Line a 28 x 18 cm/11 x 7 in cake tin
with clear film.

<u>2</u> Melt the chocolate and butter in a large
heatproof bowl over a pan of simmering
water. Stir until well mixed.

<u>3</u> Pour the condensed milk into the
chocolate and butter mixture. Beat with a
wooden spoon until creamy.

<u>4</u> Add the broken biscuits, raisins,
chopped peaches and hazelnuts or pecans.
Mix well until all the ingredients are
coated in the rich chocolate sauce.

<u>5</u> Tip the mixture into the prepared tin,
making sure it is pressed well into the
corners. Leave the top craggy. Cool, then
chill until set.

<u>6</u> Lift the cake out of the tin using the
clear film and then peel off the film. Cut
into 12 bars and serve at once.

CHOCOLATE AND COCONUT SLICES

MAKES 24

175g/6oz digestive biscuits
115g/4oz/1 cup walnuts
50g/2oz/¼ cup caster sugar
pinch of salt
115g/4oz/½ cup butter or margarine, melted
75g/3oz/1 cup desiccated coconut
250g/9oz/1½ cups plain chocolate chips
250ml/8fl oz/1 cup sweetened condensed milk

1 Place the digestive biscuits in a paper bag, fold the top over so that the bag is sealed and use a rolling pin to crush the biscuits into coarse crumbs. Chop the walnuts into small pieces, and set aside.

2 Preheat oven to 180°C/350°F/Gas 4. Put a baking sheet inside to heat up.

3 In a bowl, combine the crushed biscuits, sugar, salt and melted butter or margarine. Press the mixture evenly over the base of an ungreased 33 x 23 cm/13 x 9 in baking dish.

4 Sprinkle the coconut over the biscuit base, then scatter over the chocolate chips. Pour the condensed milk evenly over the chocolate. Sprinkle the walnuts on top. Place on the hot baking sheet and bake for 30 minutes. Turn out on a wire rack and allow to cool. When cold, cut into slices.

WHITE CHOCOLATE MACADAMIA SLICES

MAKES 16

*150g/5oz/1¼ cups macadamia nuts,
blanched almonds or hazelnuts
400g/14oz white chocolate, broken into
squares
115g/4oz/½ cup ready-to-eat dried apricots
75g/3oz/6 tbsp unsalted butter
5ml/1 tsp vanilla essence
3 eggs
150g/5oz/scant 1 cup light muscovado sugar
115g/4oz/1 cup self-raising flour*

1 Preheat oven to 190°C/375°F/Gas 5.
Lightly grease two 20 cm/8 in round
sandwich cake tins and line the base of
each with greaseproof paper or non-stick
baking paper.
2 Roughly chop the nuts and half the
white chocolate, making sure that the
pieces are more or less the same size,
then use scissors to cut the apricots to
similar size pieces.

3 In a heatproof bowl over a saucepan of
barely simmering water, melt the
remaining white chocolate with the
butter. Remove from the heat and stir in
the vanilla essence.

4 Whisk the eggs and sugar together in a
mixing bowl until thick and pale, then
pour in the melted chocolate mixture,
whisking constantly.

5 Sift the flour over the mixture and fold
it in evenly. Finally, stir in the nuts,
chopped white chocolate and chopped
dried apricots.

6 Spoon into the tins and level the tops.
Bake for 30–35 minutes or until the top
is firm and crusty. Cool in the tins before
cutting each cake into 8 slices.

CRANBERRY AND CHOCOLATE SQUARES

MAKES 12

150g/5oz/1¼ cups self-raising flour, plus
extra for dusting
115g/4oz/½ cup unsalted butter
60ml/4 tbsp cocoa powder
215g/7½oz/1¼ cups light muscovado sugar
2 eggs, beaten
115g/4oz/1⅓ cups fresh or thawed frozen
cranberries
75ml/5 tbsp coarsely grated plain chocolate,
for sprinkling

FOR THE TOPPING

150ml/¼ pint/⅔ cup soured cream
75g/3oz/6 tbsp caster sugar
30ml/2 tbsp self-raising flour
50g/2oz/4 tbsp soft margarine
1 egg, beaten
2.5ml/½ tsp vanilla essence

1 Preheat oven to 180°C/350°F/Gas 4.
Grease a 27 x 18 cm/10½ x 7 in cake tin
and dust lightly with flour. Combine the
butter, cocoa powder and sugar in a
saucepan and stir over a low heat until
melted and smooth.

2 Remove the melted mixture from the
heat and stir in the flour and eggs, beating
until thoroughly mixed.

3 Stir in the cranberries, then spread the
mixture in the tin. Make the topping by
mixing all the ingredients in a bowl. Beat
until smooth, then spread over the base.

4 Sprinkle with the grated chocolate and
bake for 40–45 minutes, or until risen
and firm. Cool in the tin for 10 minutes.
Then cut neatly into 12 squares. Remove
from the tin and cool on a wire rack,

NUT AND CHOCOLATE CHIP BROWNIES

MAKES 16

150g/5oz plain chocolate, chopped into small pieces
120ml/4fl oz/½ cup sunflower oil
215g/7½oz/1¼ cups light muscovado sugar
2 eggs
5ml/1 tsp vanilla essence
65g/2½oz/generous ½ cup self-raising flour
60ml/4 tbsp cocoa powder
75g/3oz/¾ cup walnuts or pecan nuts, chopped
60ml/4 tbsp milk chocolate chips

1 Preheat oven to 180°C/350°F/Gas 4. Lightly grease a shallow 19 cm/7½ in square cake tin. Melt the plain chocolate in a heatproof bowl over a saucepan of barely simmering water.
2 Beat the oil, sugar, eggs and vanilla essence together in a large bowl. Stir in the melted chocolate, then beat well until evenly mixed and smooth.
3 Sift the flour and cocoa powder into the bowl and fold in thoroughly. Stir in the chopped nuts and chocolate chips, tip into the prepared tin and spread evenly to the edges.
4 Bake for 30–35 minutes, or until the top is firm and crusty. Cool in the tin before cutting into squares.

LOW-FAT BROWNIES

MAKES 9

75ml/5 tbsp fat-reduced cocoa powder
15ml/1 tbsp caster sugar
75ml/5 tbsp skimmed milk
3 large bananas, mashed
175g/6oz/1 cup soft light brown sugar
5ml/1 tsp vanilla essence
5 egg whites
75g/3oz/¾ cup self-raising flour
75g/3oz/¾ cup oat bran
15ml/1 tbsp icing sugar, for dusting

1 Preheat oven to 180°C/350°F/Gas 4. Line a 20 cm/8 in square cake tin with non-stick baking paper. Blend the cocoa powder and caster sugar with the milk in a bowl. Add the bananas, soft brown sugar and vanilla essence.
2 In a mixing bowl, lightly beat the egg whites with a fork. Add the chocolate mixture and continue to beat well. Sift the flour over the mixture and fold in with the oat bran. Pour the mixture into the prepared cake tin.
3 Bake for 40 minutes or until the top is firm and crusty. Cool in the tin before cutting into squares. Lightly dust the brownies with icing sugar before serving.

MARBLED BROWNIES

MAKES 24

225g/8oz plain chocolate, chopped into
small pieces
75g/3oz/6 tbsp butter, diced
4 eggs
300g/11oz/scant 1½ cups granulated sugar
150g/5oz/1¼ cups plain flour
2.5ml/½ tsp salt
5ml/1 tsp baking powder
10ml/2 tsp vanilla essence
115g/4oz/1 cup walnuts, chopped

FOR THE PLAIN MIXTURE

50g/2oz/¼ cup butter, at room temperature
175g/6oz/¾ cup cream cheese
75g/3oz/6 tbsp granulated sugar
2 eggs
25g/1oz/¼ cup plain flour
5ml/1 tsp vanilla essence

1 Preheat oven to 180°C/350°F/Gas 4.
Line a 33 x 23 cm/13 x 9 in baking tin
with greaseproof paper or non-stick
baking paper. Grease the paper lightly.

2 Melt the chocolate with the butter in a
heatproof bowl over barely simmering
water, stirring constantly until smooth.
Set the mixture aside to cool.

3 Meanwhile, beat the eggs in a bowl
until light and fluffy. Gradually add the
sugar and continue beating until blended.
Sift over the flour, salt and baking powder
and fold in gently but thoroughly.

4 Stir in the cooled chocolate mixture.
Add the vanilla essence and walnuts.
Measure and set aside 475ml/16fl oz/
2 cups of the chocolate mixture.

5 For the plain mixture, cream the butter
and cream cheese in a bowl. Add the
sugar and beat well. Beat in the eggs,
flour and vanilla essence.

6 Spread the unmeasured chocolate
mixture in the tin. Pour over the plain
mixture. Drop spoonfuls of the reserved
chocolate mixture on top.

7 With a metal palette knife, swirl the
mixtures to marble them. Do not blend
completely. Bake for 35–45 minutes,
until just set. Turn out when cool and cut
into squares for serving.

WHITE CHOCOLATE BROWNIES WITH MILK CHOCOLATE MACADAMIA TOPPING

SERVES 12

115g/4oz/1 cup plain flour
2.5ml/½ tsp baking powder
pinch of salt
175g/6oz fine quality white chocolate, chopped into small pieces
115g/4oz/½ cup caster sugar
115g/4oz/½ cup unsalted butter, cut into small pieces
2 eggs, lightly beaten
5ml/1 tsp vanilla essence
175g/6oz plain chocolate chips or plain chocolate, chopped into small pieces

FOR THE TOPPING

200g/7oz milk chocolate, chopped into small pieces
175g/6oz/1½ cups unsalted macadamia nuts, chopped

1 Preheat oven to 180°C/350°F/Gas 4. Grease a 23 cm/9 in springform tin. Sift together the flour, baking powder and salt, set aside.

2 In a medium saucepan over a low heat, melt the white chocolate, sugar and butter until smooth, stirring frequently. Cool slightly, then beat in the eggs and vanilla essence. Stir in the flour mixture until well blended. Stir in the chocolate chips or chopped chocolate. Spread evenly in the prepared tin.

3 Bake for 20–25 minutes, until a cake tester inserted in the cake tin comes out clean; do not over-bake. Remove the cake from the oven and place the tin on a heatproof surface.

4 Sprinkle the chopped milk chocolate evenly over the cake and return it to the oven for 1 minute.

5 Remove the cake from the oven again and gently spread the softened chocolate evenly over the top. Sprinkle with the macadamia nuts and gently press them into the chocolate. Cool on a wire rack for 30 minutes, then chill, for about 1 hour, until set. Run a sharp knife around the side of the tin to loosen, then unclip the side of the springform tin and remove it carefully. Cut into thin wedges.

DOUBLE CHOCOLATE CHIP MUFFINS

MAKES 16

400g/14oz/3½ cups plain flour
15ml/1 tbsp baking powder
30ml/2 tbsp cocoa powder
115g/4oz/⅔ cup dark muscovado sugar
2 eggs
150ml/¼ pint/⅔ cup soured cream
150ml/¼ pint/⅔ cup milk
60ml/4 tbsp sunflower oil
175g/6oz white chocolate, chopped into
small pieces
175g/6oz plain chocolate, chopped into
small pieces
cocoa powder, for dusting

1 Preheat oven to 180°C/350°F/Gas 4.
Place 16 paper muffin cases in muffin tins
or deep patty tins. Sift the flour, baking
powder and cocoa into a bowl and stir in
the sugar. Make a well in the centre.

2 In a separate bowl, beat the eggs with
the soured cream, milk and oil, then stir
into the well in the dry ingredients. Beat
well, gradually incorporating all the
surrounding flour mixture to make a
thick and creamy batter.
3 Stir the white and plain chocolate
pieces into the batter mixture.
4 Spoon the chocolate mixture into the
muffin cases, filling them almost to the
top. Bake for 25–30 minutes, until well
risen and firm to the touch. Cool on a
wire rack, then dust the muffins lightly
with cocoa powder.

CHOCOLATE WALNUT MUFFINS

MAKES 12

175g/6oz/¾ cup unsalted butter
150g/5oz plain chocolate, chopped into small pieces
200g/7oz/scant 1 cup caster sugar
50g/2oz/⅓ cup soft dark brown sugar
4 eggs
5ml/1 tsp vanilla essence
1.5ml/¼ tsp almond essence
110g/3¾oz/scant 1 cup plain flour
15ml/1 tbsp cocoa powder
115g/4oz/1 cup walnuts or pecan nuts, chopped

<u>1</u> Preheat oven to 180°C/350°F/Gas 4. Grease a 12-cup muffin tin, or use paper cases supported in a bun tin.

<u>2</u> Melt the butter with the chocolate in the top of a double boiler or in a heatproof bowl set over a saucepan of simmering water. Transfer to a large mixing bowl.

<u>3</u> Stir both the sugars into the chocolate mixture. Mix in the eggs, one at a time, then add the vanilla and almond essences.

<u>4</u> Sift over the flour and cocoa, fold in, then stir in the walnuts or pecan nuts.

<u>5</u> Fill the muffin cups or cases almost to the top and bake for 30–35 minutes, until a skewer inserted in a muffin comes out clean but slightly sticky. Leave to stand for 5 minutes before cooling the muffins on a rack.

CHOCOLATE CINNAMON DOUGHNUTS

MAKES 16

500g / 1¼lb / 5 cups strong plain flour
30ml / 2 tbsp cocoa powder
2.5ml / ½ tsp salt
1 sachet easy-blend dried yeast
300ml / ½ pint / 1¼ cups hand-hot milk
40g / 1½oz / 3 tbsp butter, melted
1 egg, beaten
115g / 4oz plain chocolate, broken into
16 pieces
sunflower oil, for deep frying

FOR THE COATING

45ml / 3 tbsp caster sugar
15ml / 1 tbsp cocoa powder
5ml / 1 tsp ground cinnamon

1 Sift the flour, cocoa and salt into a large bowl. Stir in the yeast. Make a well in the centre and add the milk, melted butter and egg. Stir, gradually incorporating the surrounding dry ingredients, to make a soft and pliable dough.

2 Knead the dough on a lightly floured surface for about 5 minutes, until smooth and elastic. Return to the clean bowl, cover with clear film or a clean dry dish towel and leave in a warm place until the dough has doubled in bulk.

3 Knead the dough lightly again, then divide into 16 pieces. Shape each into a round, press a piece of plain chocolate into the centre, then fold the dough over to enclose the filling, pressing firmly to make sure the edges are sealed. Re-shape the doughnuts when sealed, if necessary.

4 Heat the oil for frying to 180°C / 350°F or until a cube of dried bread browns in 30–45 seconds. Deep fry the doughnuts in batches. As each doughnut rises and turns golden brown, turn it over to cook the other side. Drain the cooked doughnuts well on kitchen paper.

5 Mix the sugar, cocoa and cinnamon in a shallow bowl. Toss the doughnuts in the mixture to coat them evenly. Pile on a plate and serve warm.

VARIATION

Instead of using a square of plain chocolate to fill each doughnut, try chocolate spread instead. Use about 5ml / 1 tsp of the spread for each doughnut. Seal well before frying.

CHOCOLATE ORANGE SPONGE DROPS

MAKES ABOUT 14

2 eggs
50g / 2 oz / ¼ cup caster sugar
2.5ml / ½ tsp grated orange rind
50g / 2oz / ½ cup plain flour
60ml / 4 tbsp finely shredded orange marmalade
40g / 1½oz plain chocolate, chopped into small pieces

<u>**1**</u> Preheat oven to 200°C/400°F/Gas 6. Line three baking sheets with baking parchment. Put the eggs and sugar in a large heatproof bowl and whisk over a pan of simmering water until the mixture is thick and pale.

2 Remove the bowl from the pan of water and continue whisking until the mixture is cool. Whisk in the grated orange rind. Sift the flour over the whisked mixture and fold it in gently.

<u>**3**</u> Put spoonfuls of the mixture on the baking sheets, spacing them well apart to allow for spreading. The mixture will make 28–30 drops. Bake for about 8 minutes or until the biscuits are golden. Allow them to cool on the baking sheets for a few minutes, then use a spatula to transfer them to a wire rack to cool completely. Sandwich the biscuits together in pairs with the marmalade.

<u>**4**</u> Melt the chocolate in a heatproof bowl set over a pan of barely simmering water. Drizzle or pipe the chocolate over the tops of the sponge drops. Leave to set before serving.

BRIOCHES AU CHOCOLAT

MAKES 12

250g/9oz/2¼ cups strong white flour
pinch of salt
30ml/2 tbsp caster sugar
1 sachet easy-blend dried yeast
3 eggs, beaten, plus extra beaten egg,
for glazing
45ml/3 tbsp hand-hot milk
115g/4oz/½ cup unsalted butter, diced
175g/6oz plain chocolate, broken into
squares

1 Sift the flour and salt into a large mixing bowl and stir in the sugar and yeast. Make a well in the centre of the mixture and add the eggs and milk.

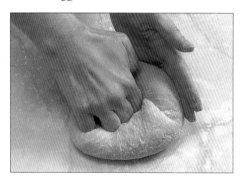

2 Beat the egg and milk mixture well, gradually incorporating the surrounding dry ingredients to make a fairly soft dough. Turn the dough on to a lightly floured surface and knead well for about 5 minutes, until smooth and elastic, adding a little more flour if necessary.
3 Add the butter to the dough, a few pieces at a time, kneading until each addition is absorbed before adding the next. When all the butter has been incorporated and small bubbles appear in the dough, wrap it in clear film and chill for at least 1 hour. If you intend serving the brioches for breakfast, the dough can be left overnight.

4 Lightly grease 12 individual brioche tins set on a baking sheet or a 12-hole brioche or patty tin. Divide the brioche dough into 12 pieces and shape each into a smooth round. Place a chocolate square in the centre of each round. Bring up the sides of the dough and press the edges firmly together to seal, use a little beaten egg if necessary.
5 Place the brioches, join side down, in the prepared tins. Cover and leave them in a warm place for about 30 minutes or until doubled in size. Preheat oven to 200°C/400°F/Gas 6.

6 Brush the brioches with beaten egg. Bake for 12–15 minutes, until well risen and golden brown. Place on wire racks and leave until they have cooled slightly. They should be served warm and can be made in advance and reheated if necessary. Do not serve straight from the oven, as the chocolate will be very hot.

COOK'S TIP

Brioches freeze well for up to 1 month. Thaw at room temperature, then reheat on baking sheets in a low oven and serve warm, but not hot. For a richer variation serve with melted chocolate drizzled over the top of the brioches.

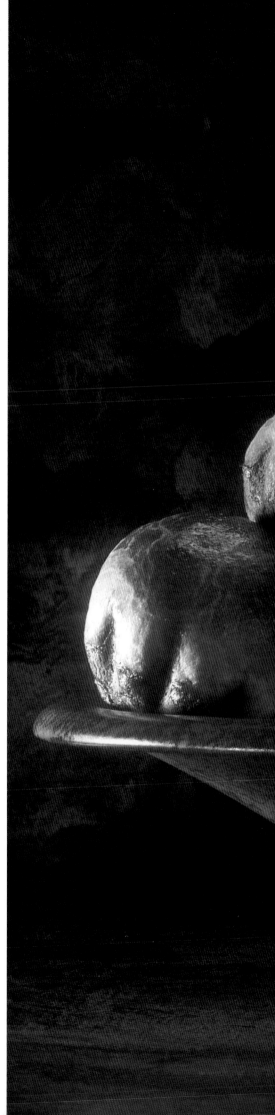

SWEETS, TRUFFLES AND DRINKS

CHOCOLATE AND CHERRY COLETTES

MAKES 18–20

115g/4oz plain dark chocolate, chopped into
small pieces
75g/3oz white or milk chocolate, chopped
into small pieces
25g/1oz/2 tbsp unsalted butter, melted
15ml/1 tbsp Kirsch or brandy
60ml/4 tbsp double cream
18–20 maraschino cherries or liqueur-soaked
cherries
milk chocolate curls, to decorate

1 Melt the dark chocolate, then remove it
from the heat. Spoon into 18–20 foil
sweet cases, spread evenly up the sides
with a small brush, then leave the cases in
a cool place until the chocolate has set.

2 Melt the white or milk chocolate with
the butter. Remove from the heat and stir
in the Kirsch or brandy, then the cream.
Cool until the mixture is thick enough to
hold its shape.

3 Carefully peel away the paper from the
chocolate cases. Place one cherry in each
chocolate case. Spoon the white or milk
chocolate cream mixture into a piping
bag fitted with a small star nozzle and
pipe over the cherries until the cases are
full. Top each colette with a generous
swirl, and decorate with milk chocolate
curls. Leave to set before serving.

COGNAC AND GINGER CREAMS

MAKES 18–20

*300g/11oz plain dark chocolate, chopped
into small pieces
45ml/3 tbsp double cream
30ml/2 tbsp cognac
4 pieces of stem ginger, finely chopped, plus
15ml/1 tbsp syrup from the jar
crystallized ginger, to decorate*

1 Polish the insides of 18–20 chocolate moulds carefully with cotton wool. Melt about two-thirds of the chocolate in a heatproof bowl over a saucepan of barely simmering water, then spoon a little into each mould. Reserve a little of the melted chocolate, for sealing the creams.

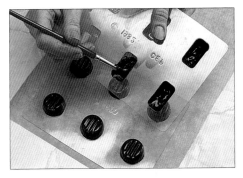

2 Using a small brush, sweep the chocolate up the sides of the moulds to coat them evenly, then invert them on to a sheet of greaseproof paper and set aside until the chocolate has set.

CHOCOLATE MARSHMALLOW DIPS

Have ready a large baking sheet lined with non-stick baking paper. Melt 175g/6oz plain or bittersweet chocolate in a heatproof bowl over barely simmering water. Stir until smooth. Remove the pan from the heat, but leave the bowl in place, so that the chocolate does not solidify too soon. You will need 15–20 large or 30–35 small marshmallows. Using cocktail sticks, spear each marshmallow and coat in the chocolate. Roll in ground hazelnuts. Place on the lined baking sheet and chill until set before removing the skewers. Place each marshmallow dip in a foil sweet case.

3 Melt the remaining chopped chocolate over simmering water, then stir in the cream, cognac, stem ginger and ginger syrup, mixing well. Spoon into the chocolate-lined moulds. If the reserved chocolate has solidified, melt, then spoon a little into each mould to seal.

4 Leave the chocolates in a cool place (not the fridge) until set. To remove them from the moulds, gently press them out on to a cool surface, such as a marble slab. Decorate with small pieces of crystallized ginger. Keep the chocolates cool if not serving them immediately.

CHOCOLATE TRUFFLES

MAKES 20 LARGE OR 30 MEDIUM TRUFFLES

250ml/8fl oz/1 cup double cream
275g/10oz fine quality bittersweet or plain chocolate, chopped into small pieces
40g/1½oz/3 tbsp unsalted butter, cut into small pieces
45ml/3 tbsp brandy, whisky or liqueur of own choice
cocoa powder, for dusting (optional)
finely chopped pistachio nuts, to decorate (optional)
400g/14oz bittersweet chocolate, to decorate (optional)

1 Pour the cream into a saucepan. Bring to the boil over a medium heat. Remove from the heat and add the chocolate, all at once. Stir gently until melted. Stir in the butter until melted, then stir in the brandy, whisky or liqueur. Strain into a bowl and cool to room temperature. Cover the mixture with clear film and chill for 4 hours or overnight.

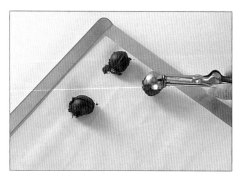

2 Line a large baking sheet with non-stick baking paper. Using a small ice cream scoop, melon baller or tablespoon, scrape up the mixture into 20 large balls or 30 medium balls and place on the lined baking sheet. Dip the scoop or spoon in cold water from time to time, to prevent the mixture from sticking.

3 If dusting with cocoa powder, sift a thick layer of cocoa on to a dish or pie plate. Roll the truffles in the cocoa, rounding them between the palms of your hands. (Dust your hands with cocoa to prevent the truffles from sticking.) Do not worry if the truffles are not perfectly round as an irregular shape looks more authentic. Alternatively, roll the truffles in very finely chopped pistachios. Chill on the paper-lined baking sheet until firm. Keep in the fridge for up to 10 days or freeze for up to 2 months.

4 If coating with chocolate, do not roll the truffles in cocoa, but freeze them for 1 hour. For perfect results, temper the chocolate. Alternatively, simply melt it in a heatproof bowl over a saucepan of barely simmering water. Using a fork, dip the truffles, one at a time, into the melted chocolate, tapping the fork on the edge of the bowl to shake off excess. Place on a baking sheet, lined with non-stick baking paper. If the chocolate begins to thicken, reheat it gently until smooth. Chill the truffles until set.

MALT WHISKY TRUFFLES

MAKES 25–30

200g/7oz plain dark chocolate, chopped into small pieces
150ml/¼ pint/⅔ cup double cream
45ml/3 tbsp malt whisky
115g/4oz/¾ cup icing sugar
cocoa powder, for coating

1 Melt the chocolate in a heatproof bowl over a saucepan of simmering water, stir until smooth, then cool slightly.

2 Using a wire whisk, whip the cream with the whisky in a bowl until thick enough to hold its shape.

3 Stir in the melted chocolate and icing sugar, mixing evenly, then leave until firm enough to handle.

4 Dust your hands with cocoa powder and shape the mixture into bite-size balls. Coat in cocoa powder and pack into pretty cases or boxes. Store in the fridge for up to 3–4 days if necessary.

TRUFFLE-FILLED EASTER EGG

MAKES 1 LARGE, HOLLOW EASTER EGG

350g/12oz plain couverture chocolate, tempered, or plain, milk or white chocolate, melted
Chocolate Truffles

1 Line a small baking sheet with non-stick baking paper. Using a small ladle or spoon, pour in enough melted chocolate to coat both halves of an Easter egg mould. Tilt the half-moulds slowly to coat the sides completely; pour any excess chocolate back into the bowl. Set the half-moulds, open side down, on the prepared baking sheet and leave for 1–2 minutes until just set.

2 Apply a second coat of chocolate and chill for 1–3 minutes more, until set. Repeat a third time, then replace the moulds on the baking sheet and chill for at least 1 hour or until the chocolate has set completely. (Work quickly to avoid having to temper the chocolate again; untempered chocolate can be reheated if it hardens.)

3 To remove the set chocolate, place a half-mould, open side up, on a board. Carefully trim any drops of chocolate from the edge of the mould. Gently insert the point of a small knife between the chocolate and the mould to break the air lock. Repeat with the second mould.

4 Holding the mould open side down, squeeze firmly to release the egg half. Repeat with the other half and chill, loosely covered. (Do not touch the chocolate surface with your fingers, as they will leave prints.) Reserve any melted chocolate to reheat for "glue".

5 To assemble the egg, hold one half of the egg with a piece of folded kitchen paper or foil and fill with small truffles. If necessary, use the remaining melted chocolate as "glue". Spread a small amount on to the rim of the egg half and, holding the empty egg half with a piece of kitchen paper or foil, press it on to the filled half, making sure the rims are aligned and carefully joined.

6 Hold for several seconds, then prop up the egg with the folded paper or foil and chill to set. If you like, decorate the egg with ribbons or Easter decorations.

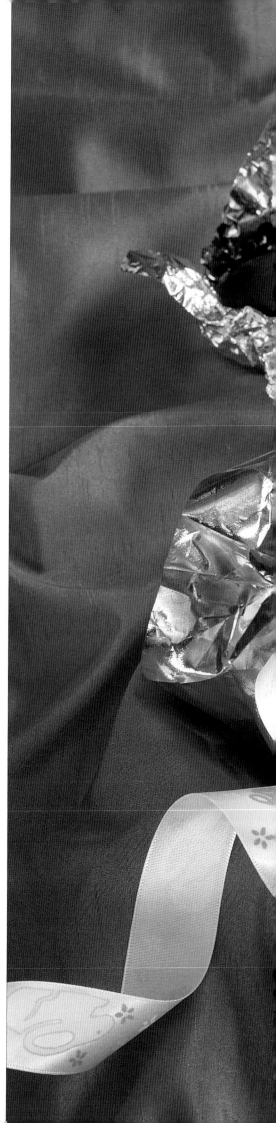

CHOCOLATE CHRISTMAS CUPS

MAKES ABOUT 35 CUPS

*275g/10oz plain chocolate, chopped into
small pieces
175g/6oz cold cooked Christmas pudding
75ml/2½fl oz/5 tbsp brandy or whisky
chocolate leaves and crystallized cranberries
to decorate*

1 Melt the chocolate and use to coat the
bottom and sides of about 35 sweet cases.
Allow to set, then repeat, reheating the
melted chocolate if necessary. Leave the
chocolate cups to cool and set. Reserve
the remaining chocolate. Crumble the
Christmas pudding into a small bowl,
sprinkle with brandy or whisky and allow
to stand for 30–40 minutes, until the
liquor is absorbed.
2 Spoon a little of the pudding mixture
into each cup, smoothing the top. Reheat
the remaining chocolate and spoon over
the top of each cup to cover the surface.
Leave to set, then peel off the cases and
place in clean foil cases. Decorate with
chocolate leaves and crystallized berries.

MARZIPAN LOGS

MAKES ABOUT 12

*225g/8oz marzipan, at room temperature
115g/4oz/⅔ cup candied orange peel,
chopped
30ml/2 tbsp orange-flavoured liqueur
15ml/1 tbsp soft light brown sugar
edible gold powder
75g/3oz plain chocolate, melted
gold-coated sweets*

1 Knead the marzipan well, then mix in
the chopped peel and liqueur. Set aside
for about 1 hour, to dry.
2 Break off small pieces of the mixture
and roll them into log shapes.
3 Dip the tops of half of the marzipan logs
in the sugar and brush them lightly with
edible gold powder.
4 Dip the remaining logs in the melted
chocolate. Place on non-stick baking
paper and press a gold-coated sweet in
the centre of each. When set, arrange all
the logs on a plate.

PEPPERMINT CHOCOLATE STICKS

MAKES ABOUT 80

115g/4oz/½ cup granulated sugar
150ml/¼ pint/⅔ cup water
2.5ml/½ tsp peppermint essence
200g/7oz plain dark chocolate, chopped into
small pieces
60ml/4 tbsp toasted desiccated coconut

1 Lightly oil a large baking sheet. Place the sugar and water in a small, heavy-based saucepan and heat gently, stirring until the sugar has dissolved.
2 Bring to the boil and boil rapidly without stirring until the syrup registers 138°C/280°F on a sugar thermometer. Remove the pan from the heat and stir in the peppermint essence.

3 Pour the mixture on to the greased baking sheet and leave until set.

4 Break up the peppermint mixture into a small bowl and use the end of a rolling pin to crush it into small pieces.
5 Melt the chocolate. Remove from the heat and stir in the mint pieces and desiccated coconut.

6 Lay a 30 x 25cm/12 x 10in sheet of non-stick baking paper on a flat surface. Spread the chocolate mixture over the paper, leaving a narrow border all around, to make a rectangle measuring about 25 x 20cm/10 x 8in. Leave to set. When firm, use a sharp knife to cut into thin sticks, each about 6cm/2½in long.

Chocolate Almond Torronne

Makes about 20 slices

*115g/4oz plain dark chocolate, chopped into
small pieces*
50g/2oz/¼ cup unsalted butter
1 egg white
115g/4oz/½ cup caster sugar
75g/3oz/¾ cup chopped toasted almonds
50g/2oz/½ cup ground almonds
75ml/5 tbsp chopped candied peel

For the coating

*175g/6oz white chocolate, chopped into small
pieces*
25g/1oz/2 tbsp unsalted butter
115g/4oz/1 cup flaked almonds, toasted

1 Melt the chocolate with the butter in a
heatproof bowl over a saucepan of barely
simmering water until smooth.

2 In a clean, grease-free bowl, whisk the
egg white with the sugar until stiff.
Gradually beat in the melted chocolate
mixture, then stir in the toasted almonds,
ground almonds and peel.
3 Tip the mixture on to a large sheet of
non-stick baking paper and shape into a
thick roll.

4 As the mixture cools, use the paper to
press the roll firmly into a triangular
shape. When you are satisfied with the
shape, twist the paper over the triangular
roll and chill until completely set.
5 Make the coating. Melt the white
chocolate with the butter in a heatproof
bowl over a saucepan of simmering water.
Unwrap the chocolate roll and with a
clean knife spread the white chocolate
quickly over the surface. Press the flaked
almonds in a thin even coating over the
chocolate, working quickly before the
chocolate sets.
6 Chill the coated chocolate roll again
until firm, then cut the torronne into
fairly thin slices to serve. Torronne is
ideal to finish a dinner party.

DOUBLE CHOCOLATE-DIPPED FRUIT

MAKES 24 COATED PIECES

fruits – about 24 pieces (strawberries, cherries, orange segments, large seedless grapes, physalis (Cape gooseberries), kumquats, stoned prunes, stoned dates, dried apricots, dried peaches or dried pears)
115g/4oz white chocolate, chopped into small pieces
115g/4oz bittersweet or plain chocolate, chopped into small pieces

1 Clean and prepare fruits; wipe strawberries with a soft cloth or brush gently with pastry brush. Wash firm-skinned fruits such as cherries and grapes and dry well. Peel and leave whole or cut up any other fruits being used.

CHOCOLATE PEPPERMINT CREAMS

1 egg white
90ml/6 tbsp double cream
5ml/1 tsp peppermint essence
675g/1½lb/5½ cups icing sugar, plus extra for dusting
few drops of green food colouring
175g/6oz plain chocolate, chopped into small pieces

1 Beat the egg white lightly in a bowl. Mix in the cream and peppermint essence, then gradually add the icing sugar to make a firm, pliable dough. Work in 1–2 drops of green food colouring (apply it from a cocktail stick if you are anxious about adding too much colour) until the dough is an even, pale green.
2 On a surface dusted with icing sugar, roll out the dough to a thickness of about 1cm/½in. Stamp out 4cm/1½in rounds of squares and place on a baking sheet lined with non-stick baking paper. Leave to dry for at least 8 hours, turning once.
3 Melt the chocolate in a bowl over barely simmering water. Allow to cool slightly. Spread chocolate over the top of each peppermint cream, and place them on fresh sheets of non-stick paper. Chill until set.

2 Melt the white chocolate. Remove from the heat and cool to tepid (about 29°C/84°F), stirring frequently. Line a baking sheet with non-stick baking paper. Holding each fruit by the stem or end and at an angle, dip about two-thirds of the fruit into the chocolate. Allow the excess to drip off and place on the baking sheet. Chill the fruits for about 20 minutes until the chocolate sets.

3 Melt the bittersweet or plain chocolate, stirring frequently until smooth.

4 Remove the chocolate from the heat and cool to just below body temperature, about 30°C/86°F. Take each white chocolate-coated fruit in turn from the baking sheet and, holding by the stem or end and at the opposite angle, dip the bottom third of each piece into the dark chocolate, creating a chevron effect. Set on the baking sheet. Chill for 15 minutes or until set. Before serving, allow the fruit to stand at room temperature 10–15 minutes before serving.

CHOCOLATE-COATED NUT BRITTLE

MAKES 20–24 PIECES

115g/4oz/1 cup mixed pecan nuts and whole almonds
115g/4oz/½ cup caster sugar
60ml/4 tbsp water
200g/7oz plain dark chocolate, chopped into small pieces

1 Lightly grease a baking sheet with butter or oil. Mix the nuts, sugar and water in a heavy-based saucepan. Place the pan over a gentle heat, stirring until all the sugar has dissolved.

2 Bring to the boil, then lower the heat to moderate and cook until the mixture turns a rich golden brown and registers 155°C/310°F on a sugar thermometer. If you do not have a sugar thermometer, test the syrup by adding a few drops to a cup of iced water. The mixture should solidify to a very brittle mass.

CHOCOLATE-COATED HAZELNUTS

Roast about 225g/8oz/2 cups hazelnuts in the oven or under the grill. Allow to cool. Melt the chocolate in a heatproof bowl over a pan of barely simmering water. Remove from the heat, but leave the bowl over the water so that the chocolate remains liquid. Have ready about 30 paper sweet cases, arranged on baking sheets. Add the roasted hazelnuts to the melted chocolate and stir to coat. Using two spoons, carefully scoop up a cluster of two or three chocolate-coated nuts. Carefully transfer the cluster to a paper sweet case. Leave the nut clusters in a cool place until set.

3 Quickly remove the pan from the heat and tip the mixture on to the prepared baking sheet, spreading it evenly. Leave until completely cold and hard.

4 Break the nut brittle into bite-size pieces. Melt the chocolate and dip the pieces to half-coat them. Leave on a sheet of non-stick baking paper to set.

CHOCOLATE NUT CLUSTERS

MAKES ABOUT 30

525ml/21fl oz/2½ cups double cream
25g/1oz/2 tbsp unsalted butter, cut into
small pieces
350ml/12fl oz/1½ cups golden syrup
200g/7oz/scant 1 cup granulated sugar
75g/3oz/½ cup light brown sugar
pinch of salt
15ml/1 tbsp vanilla essence
350g/12oz/3 cups combination of hazelnuts,
pecans, walnuts, brazil nuts and unsalted
peanuts
400g/14oz plain chocolate, chopped into
small pieces
15g/½oz/1 tbsp white vegetable fat

1 Lightly brush two baking sheets with vegetable oil. In a large heavy-based saucepan over a medium heat, cook the cream, butter, golden syrup, sugars and salt, stirring occasionally for about 3 minutes, until the sugars dissolve and the butter melts.

2 Bring to the boil and continue cooking, stirring frequently for about 1 hour, until the caramel reaches 119°C/238°F on a sugar thermometer, or until a small amount of caramel dropped into a cup of iced water forms a hard ball.

3 Plunge the bottom of the pan into cold water to stop cooking. Cool slightly, then stir in the vanilla essence.

4 Stir the nuts into the caramel until well coated. Using an oiled tablespoon, drop spoonfuls of nut mixture on to the prepared sheets, about 2.5cm/1in apart. If the mixture hardens, return to the heat to soften. Chill the clusters for 30 minutes until firm and cold, or leave in a cool place until hardened.

5 Using a metal palette knife, transfer the clusters to a wire rack placed over a baking sheet to catch drips. In a medium saucepan, over a low heat, melt the chocolate with the white vegetable fat, stirring until smooth. Set aside to cool slightly.

6 Spoon chocolate over each cluster, being sure to cover completely.

7 Place on a wire rack over a baking sheet. Allow to set for 2 hours until hardened. Store in an airtight container.

CHOCOLATE FUDGE TRIANGLES

MAKES ABOUT 48 TRIANGLES

*600g/1lb 5oz fine quality white chocolate,
chopped into small pieces*

375g/13oz can sweetened condensed milk

15ml/1 tbsp vanilla essence

7.5ml/1½ tsp lemon juice

pinch of salt

*175g/6oz/1½ cups hazelnuts or pecan nuts,
chopped (optional)*

*175g/6oz plain chocolate, chopped into
small pieces*

*40g/1½oz/3 tbsp unsalted butter, cut into
small pieces*

50g/2oz bittersweet chocolate, for drizzling

1 Line a 20cm/8in square baking tin with foil. Brush the foil lightly with oil. In a saucepan over low heat, melt the white chocolate and condensed milk until smooth, stirring frequently. Remove from the heat and stir in the vanilla essence, lemon juice and salt. Stir in the nuts if using. Spread half the mixture in the tin. Chill for 15 minutes.

2 In a saucepan over low heat, melt the plain chocolate and butter until smooth, stirring frequently. Remove from the heat, cool slightly, then pour over the chilled white layer and chill for 15 minutes until set.

3 Gently re-heat the remaining white chocolate mixture and pour over the set chocolate layer. Smooth the top, then chill for 2–4 hours until set.

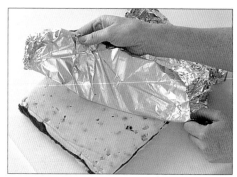

4 Using the foil as a guide, remove the fudge from the pan and turn it on to a cutting board. Lift off the foil and use a sharp knife to cut the fudge into 24 squares. Cut each square into a triangle. Melt the bittersweet chocolate in a heatproof bowl over a pan of barely simmering water. Cool slightly, then drizzle over the triangles.

EASY CHOCOLATE HAZELNUT FUDGE

MAKES 16 SQUARES

150ml / ¼ pint / ⅔ cup evaporated milk
350g / 12oz / 1½ cups sugar
large pinch of salt
50g / 2oz / ½ cup hazelnuts, halved
350g / 12oz / 2 cups plain chocolate chips

1 Generously grease a 20cm / 8in square cake tin.

2 Place the evaporated milk, sugar and salt in a heavy-based saucepan. Bring to the boil over a medium heat, stirring constantly. Lower the heat and simmer gently, stirring, for about 5 minutes.

3 Remove the pan from the heat and add the hazelnuts and chocolate chips. Stir gently with a metal spoon until the chocolate has completely melted.

4 Quickly pour the fudge mixture into the prepared tin and spread evenly. Leave to cool and set.

5 When the chocolate hazelnut fudge has set, cut it into 2.5cm / 1in squares. Store in an airtight container, separating the layers with greaseproof paper or non-stick baking paper.

TWO-TONE FUDGE

Make the Easy Chocolate Hazelnut Fudge and spread it in a 23cm / 9in square cake tin, to make a slightly thinner layer than for the main recipe. While it is cooling, make a batch of plain fudge, substituting white chocolate drops for the plain chocolate chips and leaving out the hazelnuts. Let the plain fudge cool slightly before pouring it carefully over the dark chocolate layer. Use a palette knife or slim metal spatula to spread the plain layer to the corners, then set aside to set as before. Cut into squares.

RICH CHOCOLATE PISTACHIO FUDGE

MAKES 36

250g/9oz/generous 1 cup granulated sugar
375g/13oz can sweetened condensed milk
50g/2oz/¼ cup unsalted butter
5ml/1 tsp vanilla essence
115g/4oz plain dark chocolate, grated
75g/3oz/¾ cup pistachio nuts, almonds
or hazelnuts

**CHOCOLATE AND
MARSHMALLOW FUDGE**

25g/1oz/2 tbsp butter
350g/12oz/1½ cups granulated sugar
175ml/6fl oz/¾ cup evaporated milk
pinch of salt
*115g/4oz/2 cups white mini
marshmallows*
225g/8oz /1¼ cups chocolate chips
5ml/1 tsp vanilla essence
*115g/4oz/½ cup chopped walnuts
(optional)*

1 Generously grease an 18cm/7 in cake tin. Mix the butter, sugar, evaporated milk and salt in a heavy-based saucepan. Stir over a medium heat until the sugar has dissolved, then bring to the boil and cook for 3–5 minutes or until thickened, stirring all the time.

2 Remove the pan from the heat and beat in the marshmallows and chocolate chips until dissolved. Beat in the vanilla essence. Scrape the mixture into the prepared cake tin and press it evenly into the corners, using a metal palette knife. Level the surface.

3 If using the walnuts, sprinkle them over the fudge and press them in to the surface. Set the fudge aside to cool. Before it has set completely, mark it into squares with a sharp knife. Chill until firm before cutting the fudge up and serving it.

1 Grease a 19cm/7½in square cake tin and line with non-stick baking paper. Mix the sugar, condensed milk and butter in a heavy-based pan. Heat gently, stirring occasionally, until the sugar has dissolved completely and the mixture is smooth.

2 Bring the mixture to the boil, stirring occasionally, and boil until it registers 116°C/240°F on a sugar thermometer or until a small amount of the mixture dropped into a cup of iced water forms a soft ball.

3 Remove the pan from the heat and beat in the vanilla essence, chocolate and nuts. Beat vigorously until the mixture is smooth and creamy.

4 Pour the mixture into the prepared cake tin and spread evenly. Leave until just set, then mark into squares. Leave to set completely before cutting into squares and removing from the tin. Store in an airtight container in a cool place.

TRUFFLE-FILLED FILO CUPS

MAKES ABOUT 24 CUPS

3–6 sheets fresh or thawed frozen filo pastry,
depending on size
40g / 1½ oz / 3 tbsp unsalted butter, melted
sugar, for sprinkling
pared strips of lemon zest, to decorate
FOR THE CHOCOLATE TRUFFLE
MIXTURE
250ml / 8fl oz / 1 cup double cream
225g / 8oz bittersweet or plain chocolate,
chopped into small pieces
50g / 2oz / ¼ cup unsalted butter, cut into
small pieces
30ml / 2 tbsp brandy or liqueur

1 Prepare the truffle mixture. In a
saucepan over a medium heat, bring the
cream to a boil. Remove from the heat
and add the pieces of chocolate, stirring
until melted. Beat in the butter and add
the brandy or liqueur. Strain into a bowl
and chill for 1 hour until thick.

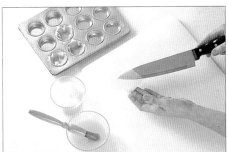

2 Preheat oven to 200°C/400°F/Gas 6.
Grease a 12-hole bun tray. Cut the filo
sheets into 6cm/2½ in squares. Cover
with a damp dish towel. Place one square
on a work surface. Brush lightly with
melted butter, turn over and brush the
other side. Sprinkle with a pinch of sugar.
Butter another square and place it over
the first at an angle; sprinkle with sugar.
Butter a third square and place over the
first two, unevenly, so the corners form
an uneven edge. Press the layered square
into one of the holes in the bun tray.

3 Continue to fill the tray, working
quickly so that the filo does not have time
to dry out. Bake the filo cups for 4–6
minutes, until golden. Cool for 10
minutes on the bun tray then carefully
transfer to a wire rack and cool
completely.
4 Stir the chocolate mixture; it should be
just thick enough to pipe. Spoon the
mixture into a piping bag fitted with a
medium star nozzle and pipe a swirl into
each filo cup. Decorate each with tiny
strips of lemon zest.

MEXICAN HOT CHOCOLATE

SERVES 4

1 litre/1¾ pints/4 cups milk
1 cinnamon stick
2 whole cloves
115g/4oz plain dark chocolate, chopped into
small pieces
2–3 drops of almond essence

1 Heat the milk gently with the spices in a saucepan until almost boiling, then stir in the plain chocolate over a moderate heat until melted.
2 Strain into a blender, add the almond essence and whizz on high speed for about 30 seconds until frothy. Alternatively, whisk the mixture with a hand-held electric mixer or wire whisk.
3 Pour into warmed heatproof glasses and serve immediately.

WHITE HOT CHOCOLATE

SERVES 4

1.75 litres/3 pints/7½ cups milk
175g/6oz white chocolate, chopped into
small pieces
10ml/2 tsp coffee powder
10ml/2 tsp orange-flavoured liqueur
(optional)
whipped cream and ground cinnamon, to serve

1 Pour the milk into a large heavy-based saucepan and heat until almost boiling. As soon as bubbles form around the edge of the pan remove the milk from the heat.
2 Add the white chocolate, coffee powder and orange-flavoured liqueur, if using. Stir until all the chocolate has melted and the mixture is smooth.
3 Pour the hot chocolate into four mugs. Top each with a swirl or spoonful of whipped cream and a sprinkling of ground cinnamon. Serve immediately.

ICED MINT AND CHOCOLATE COOLER

SERVES 4

60ml / 4 tbsp drinking chocolate
400ml / 14fl oz / 1⅔ cups chilled milk
150ml / ¼ pint / ⅔ cup natural yogurt
2.5ml / ½ tsp peppermint essence
4 scoops of chocolate ice cream
mint leaves and chocolate shapes, to decorate

1 Place the drinking chocolate in a small pan and stir in about 120ml/4fl oz/½ cup of the milk. Heat gently, stirring, until almost boiling, then remove the pan from the heat.
2 Pour the hot chocolate milk into a heatproof bowl or large jug and whisk in the remaining milk. Add the natural yogurt and peppermint essence and whisk again.
3 Pour the mixture into four tall glasses, filling them no more than three-quarters full. Top each drink with a scoop of ice cream. Decorate with mint leaves and chocolate shapes. Serve immediately.

CHOCOLATE VANILLA COOLER
Make the drink as in the main recipe, but use single cream instead of the natural yogurt and 5ml/1 tsp natural vanilla essence instead of the peppermint essence.

MOCHA COOLER
Make the drink as in the main recipe, but dissolve the chocolate in 120ml/4fl oz/½ cup strong black coffee, and reduce the milk to 300ml/½ pint/1¼ cups. Use cream instead of yogurt and leave the essence out.

IRISH CHOCOLATE VELVET

SERVES 4

250ml / 8fl oz / 1 cup double cream
400ml / 14fl oz / 1⅔ cups milk
115g / 4oz milk chocolate, chopped into small pieces
30ml / 2 tbsp cocoa powder
60ml / 4 tbsp Irish whiskey
whipped cream, for topping
chocolate curls, to decorate

1 Using a hand-held electric mixer, whip half the cream in a bowl until it is thick enough to hold its shape.
2 Place the milk and chocolate in a saucepan and heat gently, stirring, until the chocolate has melted.
3 Whisk in the cocoa, then bring to the boil. Remove from the heat and stir in the remaining cream and the Irish whiskey.
4 Pour quickly into four warmed heatproof mugs or glasses and top each serving with a generous spoonful of the whipped cream, then the chocolate curls. Serve with Peppermint Sticks for extra indulgence.

Hot Chocolate and Choc-tipped Biscuits

Serves 2

For the Choc-tipped Biscuits

115g/4oz/½ cup soft margarine

15ml/3 tbsp icing sugar, sifted

150g/5oz/1¼ cups plain flour

few drops of vanilla essence

75g/3oz plain chocolate, chopped into small pieces.

For the Hot Chocolate

90ml/6 tbsp drinking chocolate powder, plus a little extra for sprinkling

30ml/2 tbsp caster sugar, or more according to taste

600ml/1 pint/2½ cups milk

2 large squirts of cream (optional)

<u>1</u> Preheat oven to 180°C/350°F/Gas 4 and lightly grease two baking sheets. Make the choc-tipped biscuits. Put the margarine and icing sugar in a bowl and beat them together until very soft. Mix in the flour and vanilla essence.

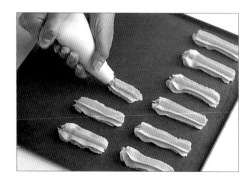

<u>2</u> Put the mixture in a large piping bag fitted with a large star nozzle. Pipe ten neat lines, each 13cm/5in long, on the baking sheets. Leave a little room between each biscuit. They will not spread much on cooking, but you need to be able to remove them easily. Cook for 15–20 minutes until the biscuits are pale golden brown. Allow to cool slightly before lifting on to a wire rack.

<u>3</u> Put the chocolate in a heatproof bowl over a saucepan of barely simmering water and leave to melt. Stir until creamy, then remove the bowl of melted chocolate from the heat. Dip both ends of each biscuit in the chocolate, put back on the rack and leave to cool and set.

<u>4</u> To make the drinking chocolate, put the drinking chocolate powder and the sugar in a saucepan. Add the milk and bring it to the boil, whisking all the time. Divide between two tall mugs. Add more sugar if needed. Top each drink with a squirt of cream, if you like.

SAUCES, FROSTINGS AND ICINGS

SIMPLE BUTTERCREAM

MAKES ABOUT 350G/12OZ

75g/3oz butter or soft margarine
225g/8oz/1½ cups icing sugar
5ml/1 tsp vanilla essence
10–15ml/2–3 tsp milk

1 If using butter, allow it to come to room temperature so that it can easily be creamed. Sift the icing sugar. Put the butter or margarine in a bowl. Add about a quarter of the icing sugar and beat with a hand-held electric mixer until fluffy.

2 Using a metal spoon, add the remaining sifted icing sugar, a little at a time, beating well with the electric mixer after each addition. Icing sugar is so fine that if you add too much of it at one time, it tends to fly out of the bowl.

3 Beat in 5ml/1 tsp of the milk. The mixture should be light and creamy, with a spreadable consistency. Add the vanilla essence, then more milk if necessary, but not too much, or it will be too sloppy to draw into peaks. Use as a filling and/or topping on layer cakes and cupcakes.

CHOCOLATE BUTTERCREAM

ENOUGH TO FILL A 20CM/8IN ROUND LAYER CAKE

75g/3oz/6 tbsp unsalted butter or margarine, softened
175g/6oz/1 cup icing sugar
15ml/1 tbsp cocoa powder
2.5ml/½ tsp vanilla essence

1 Place all the ingredients in a large bowl.

2 Beat well to a smooth spreadable consistency.

VARIATIONS

Coffee Buttercream: Stir 10ml/2 tsp instant coffee into 15ml/1 tbsp boiling water. Beat into the icing instead of the milk.
Mocha Buttercream: Stir 5ml/1 tsp cocoa powder into 10ml/2 tsp boiling water. Beat into the icing. Add a little coffee essence.
Orange Buttercream: Use orange juice instead of the milk and vanilla essence, and add 10ml/2 tsp finely grated orange rind. Omit the rind if using the icing for piping.

WHITE CHOCOLATE FROSTING

ENOUGH TO COVER A 20CM/8IN ROUND CAKE

175g/6oz white chocolate, chopped into small pieces
75g/3oz/6 tbsp unsalted butter
115g/4oz/¾ cup icing sugar
90ml/6 tbsp double cream

1 Melt the chocolate with the butter in a heatproof bowl over a saucepan of barely simmering water. Remove the bowl from the heat and beat in the icing sugar, a little at a time, using a wire whisk.

2 Whip the cream in a separate bowl until it just holds its shape, then beat into the chocolate mixture. Allow the mixture to cool, stirring occasionally, until it begins to hold its shape. Use immediately.

COOK'S TIP

White chocolate frosting is a rich frosting suitable for a dark chocolate sponge without a filling. Use a palette knife to form peaks for an attractive finish.

FUDGE FROSTING

MAKES 350g/12oz

50g/2oz plain chocolate, chopped into
small pieces
225g/8oz/2 cups icing sugar, sifted
50g/2oz/¼ cup butter or margarine
45ml/3 tbsp milk or single cream
15ml/1 tbsp vanilla essence

COOK'S TIP

When you have covered the cake
with the frosting, use the back of a
spoon or the tines of a fork to swirl
the fudge frosting and create an
attractive pattern on the cake, but do
this quickly, as it sets very fast.

1 Put the chocolate, icing sugar, butter or
margarine, milk or cream and vanilla
essence in a heavy-based saucepan.
2 Stir over a very low heat until the
chocolate and butter or margarine melt.
Turn off the heat, stir until smooth.

3 Beat the icing frequently as it cools until
it thickens sufficiently to use for
spreading or piping. Use immediately and
work quickly once it has reached the right
consistency. This is a popular frosting and
can be used for many kinds of cakes.

SATIN CHOCOLATE ICING

MAKES 225G/8OZ

*175g/6oz plain or bittersweet
chocolate, chopped into small pieces
150ml/¼ pint/⅔ cup double cream
2.5ml/½ tsp instant coffee powder*

COOK'S TIP
Do not touch the icing once it has
hardened or the attractive satin finish
will be spoilt. Cakes covered with
this icing need little by way of
decoration, but half-dipped cherries
look very effective.

1 Put the chocolate, cream and coffee in a
small heavy-based saucepan. Place the
cake to be iced on a wire rack over a
baking sheet or tray.

2 Place the saucepan over a very low heat
and stir the mixture with a wooden spoon
until all the pieces of plain or bittersweet
chocolate have melted and the mixture is
smooth and evenly blended.

3 Remove from the heat and immediately
pour the icing over the cake, letting it run
down the sides slowly to coat it
completely. Spread the icing with a
palette knife or slim spatula as necessary,
working quickly before the icing has time
to thicken.

CHOCOLATE FONDANT
**ENOUGH TO COVER AND DECORATE
A 23CM/9IN ROUND CAKE**

*350g/12oz plain chocolate, chopped into
small pieces
60ml/4 tbsp liquid glucose
2 egg whites
900g/2lb/7 cups icing sugar*

1 Put the chocolate and glucose in a
heatproof bowl. Place over a
saucepan of barely simmering water
and leave to melt, stirring the
mixture occasionally. When it is
smooth, remove the bowl from the
heat and cool slightly.
2 In a clean, grease-free bowl, whisk the
egg whites with a hand-held electric
mixer until soft peaks form, then stir
into the chocolate mixture with about
45ml/3 tbsp of the icing sugar.
3 Continue to beat the icing,
gradually adding enough of the
remaining icing sugar to make a stiff
paste. Wrap the fondant in clear film
if not using immediately.

BITTERSWEET CHOCOLATE SAUCE

QUICK CHOCOLATE SAUCE
MAKES 225ML/8FL OZ/1 CUP
150ml/¼ pint/⅔ cup double cream
15ml/1 tbsp caster sugar
150g/5oz plain chocolate, chopped into
small pieces
30ml/2 tbsp dark rum or whisky
(optional)

1 Bring the cream and sugar to the boil. Remove from the heat, add the chocolate and stir until melted. Stir in the rum or whisky.

2 Pour the chocolate sauce into a jar. When cool, cover and store for up to 10 days. Reheat by standing the jar in a saucepan of simmering water, or remove the lid and microwave on High power for 2 minutes. Stir before serving.

MAKES ABOUT 350ML/12FL OZ
45ml/3 tbsp granulated sugar
120ml/4fl oz/½ cup water
175g/6oz bittersweet chocolate, chopped into
small pieces
25g/1oz/2 tbsp unsalted butter, diced
60–90ml/4–6 tbsp single cream
2.5ml/½ tsp vanilla essence

1 Combine the sugar and water in a heavy-based saucepan. Bring to the boil over a medium heat, stirring constantly until all the sugar has dissolved.

2 Add the chocolate and butter to the syrup, stir with a wooden spoon, then remove the pan from the heat and continue to stir until smooth.

3 Stir in the single cream and vanilla essence. Serve the sauce warm, over vanilla ice cream, profiteroles, poached pears or crêpes.

GLOSSY CHOCOLATE SAUCE

SERVES 6
115g/4oz/½ cup caster sugar
60ml/4 tbsp water
175g/6oz plain chocolate, chopped into
small pieces
25g/1oz/2 tbsp unsalted butter
30ml/2 tbsp brandy or orange juice

COOK'S TIP
Any of these sauces would make a chocolate fondue, with fruit and dessert biscuits as dippers.

1 Place the caster sugar and water in a heavy-based saucepan and heat gently, stirring occasionally with a wooden spoon until all the sugar has dissolved.

2 Stir in the chocolate until melted, then add the butter in the same way. Do not allow the sauce to boil. Stir in the brandy or orange juice and serve warm.

CHOCOLATE FUDGE SAUCE

SERVES 6

150ml / ¼ pint / ⅔ cup double cream
50g / 2oz / ¼ cup butter
50g / 2oz / ¼ cup vanilla sugar
175g / 6oz plain chocolate, chopped into
small pieces
30ml / 2 tbsp brandy

1 Heat the cream with the butter and sugar in a bowl over a saucepan of barely simmering water. Stir until smooth, then leave to cool.

2 Add the chocolate to the cream mixture. Stir over simmering water until it is melted and thoroughly combined.

3 Stir in the brandy a little at a time, then cool to room temperature.

CHOCOLATE GANACHE
ENOUGH TO COVER A 23CM / 9IN ROUND CAKE

225g / 8oz plain chocolate, chopped into
small pieces
250ml / 8fl oz / 1 cup double cream

Melt the chocolate with the cream in a saucepan over a low heat. Pour into a bowl, leave to cool, then whisk until the mixture begins to hold its shape.

WHITE CHOCOLATE AND ORANGE SAUCE

SERVES 6

150ml / ¼ pint / ⅔ cup double cream
50g / 2oz / ¼ cup butter
45ml / 3 tbsp caster sugar
175g / 6oz white chocolate, chopped into
small pieces
30ml / 2 tbsp orange-flavoured liqueur
finely grated rind of 1 orange

COOK'S TIP
Serve with ice cream, or with hot waffles or fresh crêpes.

1 Pour the cream into a heavy-based saucepan. Cut the butter into cubes and add it to the pan, with the sugar. Heat gently, stirring the mixture occasionally until the butter has melted.

2 Add the chocolate to the cream. Stir over a very low heat until it is melted and thoroughly combined.

3 Stir in the orange rind, then add the liqueur a little at a time. Leave to cool.

CHOCOLATE SUPPLIERS AROUND THE WORLD

AUSTRALIA
Chocolatier Australia
224 Waterdale Road, Ivanhoe,
Victoria 3079 Tel: (3) 94 99 70 22

The Chocolate Box
761 Burke Road, Camberwell,
Victoria 3124 Tel: (3) 98 13 13 77

Darren Taylor's Handmade Chocolates
Seet Art, 96 Oxford Street, Paddington,
New South Wales 2021
Tel: (2) 93 61 66 17

Sweet William Chocolates
4 William Street, Paddington, New
South Wales 2021 Tel: (2) 93 31 54 68

Simon Johnson
181 Harris Street, Pyrmont, New South
Wales 2009 Tel: (2) 95 52 25 22

Haigh's Chocolates
Beehive Corner, 2 Rundle Mall,
Adelaide, South Australia
Tel: (8) 23 12 844

AUSTRIA
Altmann & Kühne
Graben 30, 1010 Wien
Tel: (1) 53 30 927

Demels
14 Kohlmarkt, 1010 Wien
Tel: (1) 53 51 717

Hotel Imperial
Kärtner Ring 16, A-1051 Wien
Tel: (1) 50 11 03 13
Fax: (1) 50 10 355

Mirabell Salzburger Confiserie
Hauptstrasse 14-16, A-5082 Grödig
Tel: (62) 46 20 110

BELGIUM
Charlemagne
Place Jacques Brel 8, 4040 Herstal
Tel: (41) 64 66 44

Godiva
Wapenstilstandstraat 5, 1081 Brussels
Tel: (2) 42 21 711

Kim's Chocolates
Nieuwlandlaan 12, Industriezone B-615,
B-3200 Aarschot
Tel: (16) 55 15 80

Neuhaus
Postbox 2, B - 1602 Vlenzenbeek
Tel: (2) 56 82 211

Pierre Colas
2 Rue Campagne, 4577 Modave
Tel: (2) 64 80 893

Wittamer
12 Place du Grand Sablon, Grote Zavel
12, 1000 Brussels Tel: (2) 51 28 451

FRANCE
Bonnat
8 Cours Senozan, 38500 Voiron
Tel: (76) 05 28 09

Christian Constant
26 Rue du Bac, 75007 Paris
Tel: (47) 03 30 00

Cluizel
La Fontaine au Chocolat
101 & 210 Rue Saint Honoré,
75001, Paris Tel: (1) 42 44 11 66

Fauchon
26-30 Place de la Madeleine,
75008 Paris Tel: (1) 47 42 60 11

Lalonde
59 Rue St Dizier, 54400 Nancy
Tel: 83 53 31 57

La Maison du Chocolat
225 Rue Faubourg St Honoré,
75008 Paris Tel: (1) 42 27 39 44

Le Roux
18 Rue du Port-Maria, 56170 Quiberon
Tel: 97 50 06 83

Richart Design et Chocolat
258 Bd. Saint-Germain, 75007 Paris
Tel: (1) 45 55 66 00

Chocolaterie Valrhona
BP 40, 26600 Tain L'Hermitage
Tel: 75 07 90 90

Weiss
18 Avenue Denfert-Rochereau,
42000 St Etienne
Tel: 77 49 41 41

GERMANY
Confiserie Heinemann
Krefelder Strasse 645
41066 München-Gladbach
Tel: (2161) 6930

Dreimeister
Weststrasse 47 - 49, Werl,
Westönnen Tel: 29 22 8 20 45

Feodora
Vertriebszentrale Bremen,
Postfach 105803, D28058 Bremen
Tel: (421) 59 90 61

Bremer Chocolade-Fabrik Hachez
Westerstrasse 32, D-28199 Bremen
Tel: (421) 59 50 64 62

Leysieffer
Benzstrasse 9, 49076 Osnabrück
Tel: (541) 91 420

Stollwerck
Stollwerckstrasse 27-31, 51149 Köln
Tel: (22) 03 430

Van Houten
Am Stamgleis, 22844 Norderstedt
Tel: (5) 26 020

GREAT BRITAIN
Ackermans
9 Goldhurst Terrace, Finchley Road,
London, NW6 3HX
Tel: (0171) 624 2742

Charbonnel et Walker
1 The Royal Arcade, 28 Old Bond
Street, London, W1X 4BT
Tel: (0171) 491 0939

Gerard Ronay
3 Warple Way, London, W3 0RF
Tel: (0181) 730 818

Godiva
247 Regent Street, London, W1
Tel: (0171) 409 0963

Grania & Sarnia
6 Sterne Street, London, W12 8AD
Tel: (0181) 749 8274

Green & Black
Whole Earth Food, 269 Portobello
Road, London, W1 1LR
Tel: (0171) 229 7545

JB Confectionery
Unit 3, The Palmerston Centre,
Oxford Road, Harrow, Middlesex
HA3 7RG Tel: (0181) 863 0011

Mortimer & Bennett
33 Turnham Green Terrace, London,
W4 1RG Tel: (0181) 995 4145

Rococo Chocolates
321 Kings Road, London, SW3 5EP
Tel: (0171) 352 5857
Fax: (0171) 352 7360

Sara Jayne
517 Old York Road, London, SW18 1TF
Tel: (0181) 874 8500

The Chocolate Society
Clay Pit Lane, Roecliffe, Near
Boroughbridge, N. Yorks, YO5 9LS
Tel: (01423) 322 230

The Cool Chile Company
P.O. Box 5702, London, W11 2GS
Tel: (0171) 229 9360

Town & Country Chocolates
52 Oxford Road, Denham, Uxbridge,
Middlesex, UB9 4DH
Tel: (01895) 256 166

ITALY
Caffarel/Peyrano
Via Gianevello 41 - 10062 Luserna,
S. Giovanni (TO), Piedmont
Tel: (121) 90 10 86

Maglio Arte Dolciaria
73024 Maglio, La Via Gioacchino
Toma 4 Tel: (836) 25 723

Majani
Via Lunga 19/C, Crespellano (BO)
Tel: 51 96 91 57

Perugina
Nestlé Italiana
Via Pievaiola, San Sisto, PGIT
Tel: (75) 52 761

MEXICO
Chocolatera de Jalisco
Av Narianotero 1420, Apartado Postal
33121, 44510 Guadalajara, Halisco

SPAIN
Blanxart
Tambor del Bruc, 13-08970 Sant Joan
Despi, Barcelona Tel: (3) 373 3761

Ludomar
Ciudad de la Asunción 58, 08030
Barcelona Tel: (72) 203 662

Ramón Roca
Mercaders, 6 17004, Gerona
Tel: (72) 203 662

Chocolates Valor
Pianista Gonzalo Soriano, 13 Villajoyosa
Tel: (6) 589 050

SWITZERLAND
Lindt & Sprüngli
Seestrasse 204, CH-8802 Kilchberg
Tel: (1) 71 62 233

Sprüngli
Bahnhofstrasse 21, 8022 Zurich
Tel: (1) 21 15 777

THE NETHERLANDS
Bensdorp
Heerenstraat 51, Postbus 4, 1400 AA
Bussum Tel: (35) 69 74 911

Gerkens Cacao
Veerdijk 82, Postbus 82, 1530 AB
Wormer Tel: (35) 69 74 911

Cacao De Zaan
Stationsstraat 76, Postbus 2, 1540 AA
Koog aan de Zaan
Tel: (75) 62 83 601

Droste
PO Box 5, 8170AA Vaassen
Tel: (578) 57 82 00

USA
Dilettante Chocolates
416 Broadway, Seattle, WA 98102
Tel: (206) 328 1530

Fran's
2805 East Madison, Seattle, Washington,
WA 98122-4020
Tel: (206) 322 0233

Ghirardelli
900 North Point Street, San Francisco,
CA 94109 Tel: (415) 474 1414

Joseph Schmidt Confections
3489 16th Street, San Francisco,
CA 9411 Tel: (415) 861 8682

Richard Donnelly Fine Chocolates
1509 Mission Street, Santa Cruz,
CA 95060 Tel: (408) 458 4214

Moonstruck Chocolatier
6663 SW BVTN Hillsdale Highway,
STE194, Portland, Oregon, OR9 7225
Tel: (503) 283 8843

ACKNOWLEDGEMENTS
Thanks to the following companies for
supplying chocolates for photography:

Ackermans, Alfred Ritter, Bendicks
(Mayfair) Ltd, Charbonnel et Walker,
The Cool Chile Company, The
Chocolate Society, Richard Donnelly,
Feodora Chocolate, Ghirardelli
Chocolate Company, Grania & Sarni,
Green and Black, The Jenks Group, JB
Confectionery, Leonidas, Lessiters,
Nestlé Rowntree Ltd, Parsons Trading
Ltd, Perugina, Richart Design et
Chocolat, Rococo, Ryne Quality
Confectionery, Joseph Schmidt, Town &
Country Chocolates, Trustin.

Thanks also to Stefano Raimondi of the
Italian Trade Centre, Patrizia De Vito of
the Associazione Industrie Dolciarie in
Rome, Elaine Ashton of Grania and
Sarnia, Dan Mortimer of Mortimer and
Bennet, David Lyle of Town and Country
Chocolates and John Bacon of JB
Confectionery.
    Christine McFadden is particularly
indebted to the late Sophie Coe, and her
husband Michael Coe, for their book *The
True History of Chocolate*, and to Chantal
Coady for the information in *The
Chocolate Companion*.

INDEX

PICTURE ACKNOWLEDGEMENTS

Thanks to the following picture libraries for supplying additional images in the book.
AKG, London: pp9(br) *Columbus discovers the New World*, Bernhard Rode; 10(br) *First landing on Guanaja*, wood engraving; 19(b) *Goethe in the Countryside*, Johann Tischbein; 24(b) *Healing plants, cacao*, from FE Bilz; 6 (bl) & 61(tr) Poster for chocolate, *Mother's Cocoa in Danger*.

Bridgeman Art Library: 6(r) *Cacao Van Houten*, Privit Livemont, Victoria and Albert, London; 18(r) *The chocolate girl*, Jean-Etienne Liotard, Dresden Gemäldegalerie; 19 *Still life*, Philippe Rousseau, Musée des Beaux Arts, Reims, Peter Willi; 20(t) *Cardinal Mazarin*, French School, Musée Condé, Chantilly; 20(bl) *Tapestry of Louis XIV's marriage*, Gobelins, Mobilier National, Paris; 22(br) *A cup of chocolate*, Sir John Lavery, Whitford and Hughes, London; 23(r) American poster for chocolate; 26(b) *Cocoa plantation in the Isle of Grenada*, O'Shea Gallery, London; 60(bl) *Cacao Van Houten*, Privet Livemont, Victoria and Albert, London; 60(br) Box of Cadbury's assorted chocolates, c1913.
    Mansell Collection: pp25(b).
    Public Records Office : pp6(l);

11(t); 27(t); 28(t); 30(br); p57(br).
    Visual Arts Library: pp8(l); 9(l); 10 *Montezuma offering chocolate to Herman Cortés*, PG Miguel, Artephot/Oronoz; 15(t) *Mexican making chocolate*, Codex Tuleda, Artephot/Oronoz; 20(r) *A horseman and a lady drinking chocolate*, Bonnart, Vision; 25(l) *Still Life: Chocolate set*, Luis Melendez, Museo del Prado, Madrid, Artephot/Oronoz; 26(b) *The morning cocoa*, Longhi; 25(tr) *The breakfast*, François Boucher, Musée du Louvre, Artephot/Oronoz; 25(tl) *Physiologie du Goût ou Méditations de Gastronomie Transcendante*, E Baneste; 29(br) *Advertisement, Chocolat Menier*, F Bouisset, Artephot/Perrin; 16(tl) *Cacao Van Houten*, Artephot/Perrin; 16(tr) Poster for Chocolate, H Gerbault; 48(tl) Poster for French Chocolate and Tea Company, Steilen, Artephot/Perrin; 49(l) Chocolat Capentier poster; 58(br) Chocolat Mondia, Artephot/Vision; 59(l) *Portrait of Madame Du Barry*, Greuze, Artephot/Varga; 61(br) *Chocolat Masson*, Grasset, Artephot/Perrin.
    Other pictures supplied courtesy of Bendick's (Mayfair) Ltd: 16(bl), Cadburys Ltd: 28(bl); 42(b); 43(bl); 60(tr). Fran's: 62. Godiva: 37(bl) 58(t). Nestlé Rowntree Ltd: 1; 27(b); 34(br) 36(tr&l), Rococo: 17(bl).

SELECTED BIBLIOGRAPHY

NATHALIE BAILLEUX, HERVÉ BIZEUL, JOHN FELTWELL, RÉGINE KOPP, CORBY KUMMER, PIERRE LABANNE, CRISTINA PAULY, ODILE PERRARD, MARIAROSA SCHIAFFINO, PREFACE JEANNE BOURIN 1995 *The Book of Chocolate*. Paris, New York: Flammarion.
BLYTHMAN, JOANNA 1996 *The Food We Eat*. London: Michael Joseph.
COADY, CHANTAL 1993 *Chocolate: The Food of the Gods*. London: Pavilion Books.
COADY, CHANTAL 1995 *The Chocolate Companion*. London: Quintet Publishing.
COE, SOPHIE D. AND MICHAEL D. 1996 *The True History of Chocolate*. London: Thames and Hudson.
COX, CAT 1993 *Chocolate Unwrapped: The Politics of Pleasure*. London: The Women's Environmental Network.
GAGE, THOMAS 1648 *The English-American His Travail by Land and Sea, or a New Survey of the West Indies*. London.
HEAD, BRANDON 1905 *The Food of the Gods*. London: George Routledge & Sons.

McGEE, HAROLD 1984 *On Food and Cooking: The Science and Lore of the Kitchen*. London, Australia: George Allen & Unwin.
MONTIGNAC, MICHEL 1991 *Dine Out and Lose Weight*. London: Artulen UK.
RICHART DESIGN ET CHOCOLAT *Le Petit Livre Blanc du Chocolat*.
SHERR, JEREMY *The Homoeopathic Proving of Chocolate*. Dynamis School.
Spicing up the Palate: Studies of Flavourings – Ancient and Modern. Proceedings of the Oxford Symposium on Food and Cookery 1992. Totnes, Devon: Prospect Books.
STOBART, TOM 1977 *Herbs, Spices and Flavourings*. Penguin Books.
TRAGER, JAMES 1995 *The Food Chronology*. Ontario: Fitzhenry & Whiteside.
WATERHOUSE, DEBRA 1995 *Why Women Need Chocolate*. London: Vermilion.
WHYMPER, R. 1921 *Cocoa and Chocolate: Their Chemistry and Manufacture*. London: J. & A. Churchill.
WILLIAMS, C. TREVOR 1953 *Chocolate and Confectionery*. London.